XML Programming Bible

Brian Benz
with John R. Durant

WILEY

Wiley Publishing, Inc.

XML Programming Bible

Published by
Wiley Publishing, Inc.
909 Third Avenue
New York, NY 10022
www.wiley.com

Copyright (c) 2003 by Wiley Publishing, Inc., Indianapolis, Indiana

Published by Wiley Publishing, Inc., Indianapolis, Indiana

Published simultaneously in Canada

Library of Congress Cataloging-in-Publication Data: 2003101925

ISBN: 0-7645-3829-2

Manufactured in the United States of America

10 9 8 7 6 5 4 3 2 1

1O/QT/QZ/QT/IN

XML Programming Bible

About the Authors

Brian Benz (bbenz@benztech.com) has more than 15 years experience designing and deploying systems infrastructures, designing and developing applications, migrating messaging systems and applications, and managing projects. He has established his expertise and reputation in the XML and Web service marketplace since 1998 through hands-on experience in various projects. Brian also makes frequent contributions as a writer for industry publications, including the IBM Redbook XML: Powered by Domino, The Notes and Domino 6 Programmer's Bible, Lotus Advisor magazine, e-Business Advisor magazine, WebSphere Advisor magazine, and e-Pro magazine. He is also a frequent presenter of highly rated technical seminars for IBM, Lotus Software, and Advisor Media at venues worldwide. Brian is CEO of Benz Technologies (http://www.benztech.com).

John R. Durant (jdurant@microsoft.com) is the site manager for Microsoft's Office Developer Center (http://msdn.microsoft.com/office). He is a noted author and speaker on Microsoft Office, Microsoft .NET, XML, Microsoft SharePoint, COM technologies, and enterprise development. He has authored magazine articles, courseware, and other materials on these same topics, and has traveled the world speaking to developers and other professionals about how these technologies work. Before joining Microsoft, he was employed independently, delivering customer solutions. He lives in the Seattle area with his beautiful wife and four boys.

Contributor **Tod Golding** has been a professional programmer since 1986 working in a variety of roles ranging from Software Engineer to Lead Architect for organizations of all shapes and sizes, including Microsoft and Borland. His programming skills span the spectrum of technologies and programming languages and include designing and constructing large-scale systems using both the Microsoft and Java (J2EE) platforms. His language experience has focused primarily on C++, Java, and C#. His chapters in this book cover Java Web Services, the details of Apache's Axis, JAX-RPC, and JAXM. He started his writing career as a journalist, writing sports for 2 years at the *Sacramento Bee* daily newspaper, and he has authored a number of white papers assessing the relative strengths of competing technologies.

Credits

Executive Editor
Chris Webb

Senior Acquisitions Editor
Sharon Cox

Acquisitions Editor
Jim Minatel

Project Editor
Kenyon Brown

Technical Editor
Sundar Rajan

Copy Editor
Anne L. Owen

Editorial Manager
Mary Beth Wakefield

Vice President & Executive Group Publisher
Richard Swadley

Vice President and Executive Publisher
Bob Ipsen

Executive Editorial Director
Mary Bednarek

Project Coordinator
Kristie Rees

Graphics and Production Specialists
Amanda Carter
Jennifer Click
Sean Decker
Michael Kruzil
Lynsey Osborn

Quality Control Technicians
JohnTyler Connoley
John Greenough
Carl William Pierce
Kathy Simpson
Brian H. Walls

Proofreading and Indexing
TECHBOOKS Production Services

Preface

The *XML Programming Bible* provides a single source for developers who need to implement XML and Web service solutions on an MS or J2EE platform, or both.

A recent Amazon.com search returned 393 book titles that contain the keyword "XML." However, most of them are introductory books that are heavy on XML theory and light on practical examples. After reading them, you could explain to your boss and colleagues what XML is, but you would be hard-pressed to be able to develop a practical XML solution. In addition, very few books provide practical examples of both XML and Web service solutions on both the J2EE and MS platforms. Programmers would most likely have to buy a minimum of four other books to match the same content that is found in the *XML Programming Bible*.

The *XML Programming Bible* is a comprehensive guide to architectural concepts and programming techniques for XML. We cover the mainstream industry XML and Web service technologies as well as tools and techniques for developing real-world XML solutions. The examples and techniques are designed to be useful for all skill levels of XML programmers, from beginner to advanced. We have endeavored to make the material understandable for beginners at the same time that specific topics are "shedding new light" on XML for experienced professionals. The intention is that a developer could use the information in the book to go from zero knowledge of XML and related technologies to designing and developing industrial-strength XML and Web service applications.

Being programmers, we know that theory can be tedious, and you probably want to get straight to work developing XML and Web service solutions. You are in luck, because this book is full of working examples, tips, and techniques to enable you to do that. We have distilled the theory down to the essentials and scattered it through the book, between the practical examples. The examples are constructed incrementally when possible. By following the examples, programmers will actually follow several applications that are developed from scratch using several different XML technologies.

Part I: Introducing XML

This section starts with an XML concepts chapter that gives an overview and history of XML, its purposes, and comparisons against previous and alternative data integration technologies. We then proceed to describe XML basic formats, XML well-formedness, and XML validation against DTDs and schemas. The chapters on XSL transformations and XSL formatting objects illustrate the transformation and formatting of XML data using XML via working examples. Part I ends with examples of parsing XML documents, including examples of XML parsing using SAX and DOM.

Chapter 1: XML Concepts provides readers who are new to XML with an overview and history of XML, its purposes, and comparisons against previous and alternative integration technologies. We end the chapter with an introduction to the next XML version, XML 1.1.

Chapter 2: XML Documents applies the theory from Chapter 1 to real-world, practical examples. This chapter expands on the theory and concepts introduced in the previous chapter. We introduce you to two example documents that contain many of the issues that confront an XML programmer. The first document is a compilation of XML from three sources. The second document separates and identifies the three parts of the document using XML namespaces. Along the way, we introduce you to some predefined XML attributes. We show you how to specify languages using the xml:lang attribute, and how to preserve space and linefeed settings in text data using the xml:space attribute.

Chapter 3: XML Data Format and Validation builds on the example XML documents introduced in Chapter 2. Chapter 3 explains ways to make sure that XML documents are not just well-formed, but also contain data in a predefined format as well as follow the rules that make up the predefined format. XML is an excellent transport medium for sharing data across systems and platforms. However, well-formed XML documents that adhere only to the basic XML syntax rules are very easy to generate at the source, but usually very hard to read at their destination without some kind of a description of the structure represented in the XML document. In addition to basic XML syntax rules, XML document formatting rules are described and enforced through a process called XML validation.

Chapter 4: XML Parsing Concepts covers techniques for integrating XML data with existing applications. XML document parsing identifies and converts XML elements contained in an XML document into either nested nodes in a tree structure or document events, depending on the type of XML parser that is being used. This chapter will focus on the concepts and theory behind XML document parsing and manipulation using node tree-based parsers and event-based parsers. After an introduction to the concepts, Chapters 5 and 6 provide practical examples of parsing an XML document using DOM and SAX.

Chapter 5: Parsing XML with DOM extends Chapter 4's basic concepts and provides a deep dive into XML Document Object Model (DOM) parsing. DOM parsing can initially appear to be a larger topic than it really is, because of the sheer volume of sources for DOM information. The number of DOM versions, the volume of related W3C Recommendation documents, and the addition of Microsoft's MSXML classes and methods that are not part of the W3C DOM Recommendation all complicate the DOM picture. In this chapter, we pull everything together into a single reference with a focus on what is important to XML programmers. For the most part, the DOM interfaces and nodes in MXSML and the W3C DOM are the same, except for the way that they are named. The real differences begin when you get into the properties and methods of nodes. For each interface, node, property, and method, we list the supporting DOM versions (W3C 1.0, 2.0, 3.0, and MSXML).

Chapter 6: Parsing XML with SAX extends Chapter 4's basic concepts and provides a deep dive into the Simple API for XML (SAX) parsing. SAX parsing takes a little more of a learning curve to master when compared to DOM parsing. While DOM nodes can be directly mapped to corresponding XML source document objects, SAX events do not provide the same level of direct comparison. Once you get around the theory of the event model concepts, SAX parsing solutions can actually be much easier to implement than DOM solutions. This is because there is only one official source for SAX event specifications and documentation: the SAX project. There is also an MSXML SAX implementation, which is based on SAX, but rewritten as Microsoft XML core nodes. These two sources are relatively simple to keep on top of when compared to the exponential growth of W3C DOM Working Drafts that appear with each new DOM version, and DOM node property and method variants that appear with every new version of the MXSML DOM parser. For each event in this chapter, we list the supporting SAX versions (SAX 1 and 2, and MSXML). We also point out the subtle differences in each event between the platforms.

Chapter 7: XSL Concepts discusses the syntax, structure, and theory of Extensible Stylesheet Language (XSL) and XSL Transformations (XSLT), with some basic examples for illustration.

Chapter 8: XSL Transformations applies the theory from Chapter 7 to real-world examples that use XSLT elements, functions, and XPath expressions to transform XML documents to other formats of XML, text documents, and HTML pages. All of the examples in this chapter use the same source XML file. We convert the source XML document into HTML, delimited text, and HTML to show advanced XSLT tips and tricks.

Chapter 9: XSL Formatting Objects provides the capability to format XML documents dynamically as "camera-ready" artwork or printable pages. With XSL:FO, an XML document can be the basis for a print version of XML data. This chapter extends the HTML example from Chapter 8 by using XSL:FO to gain more control over the output format. The example in this chapter produces a Portable Document format (PDF) file from a source XML document using the Apache FOP (Formatting Objects Processor) engine.

Part II: Microsoft Office and XML

This section provides examples of generating XML from MS access data as well as creating an Excel spreadsheet from an XML data source. These examples illustrate MS-specific techniques for parsing and generating MS-derived XML. We review the sample code in the chapters line-by line so that previous VBA/VB code knowledge is not necessary to understand and work with the examples.

Chapter 10: Microsoft XML Core Services covers the services Microsoft has provided for working with XML on Windows. The focus here is on Microsoft's pre-.NET software development environment, COM. The .NET XML toolset is extensive enough to require a separate discussion in later chapters of this book. In this chapter you will learn about how to install MSXML and get started using its core features. You will also learn about how MSXML is versioned and how to keep things straight when side-by-side versions are installed.

Chapter 11: Working with the MSXML DOM covers how to work with the DOM in applications. You will also learn the most commonly used methods and properties of the DOM.

Chapter 12: Generating XML from MS Access Data looks at the XML features in Access and shows you how they can be used to create more flexible and more full-featured applications. You will learn about how XML data can be imported and exported from access using the user interface as well as through code. You will learn how XML schemas can be used to ensure data integrity for imports and exports. You will also learn more about leveraging XSL to convert XML into a format that can be directly consumed by Access.

Chapter 13: Creating an Excel Spreadsheet from an XML Data Source covers the release of Excel 2002 with Office XP. This version of Excel has built-in native support for XML. Microsoft Excel 2002 now recognizes and opens XML documents including XSL processing instructions. In addition, Microsoft Excel spreadsheets can be converted to XML files while preserving the format, structure, and data through the XML spreadsheet file format. In this chapter, you will learn about how Excel can consume and produce XML. You will learn about the XML spreadsheet file format and the XML Spreadsheet Schema (XML-SS). You will see how to use Excel programmatically to export data to XML and how XML-SS can work with scripts or Web pages to produce alternate displays of Excel.

Part III: XML Web Applications Using J2EE

This section builds on the basic concepts that were introduced in Parts I and II, showing readers how to create XML Web Applications using J2EE. We review sample code line-by-line, so previous Java/J2EE knowledge is not necessary to understand and work with the examples. Open source libraries for working with Java tools are referenced and specific code examples are provided for working with Xalan and Xerces. We also provide examples for the XML APIs in the Sun Java Web services Developer Pack (WSDP), including the Java API for XML Processing (JAXP), Java Architecture for XML Binding (JAXB), and Java Server Pages Standard Tag Library (JSTL) APIs.

Chapter 14: XML Tools for J2EE: IBM, Apache, Sun, and Others covers J2EE API support for XML. There are several J2EE tools and code libraries that an XML developer can take advantage of to help develop and deploy J2EE XML applications in a timely and efficient manner. In this chapter, we review the most popular code libraries and introduce readers to the two most prominent J2EE developer tools: the IBM WebSphere Studio Application Developer and the Sun ONE Studio.

Chapter 15: Xerces introduces readers to Apache Xerces, what it is, where it came from, and how to integrate Xerces functionality into your applications. Xerces is a set of Java classes, properties, and methods that supports XML document parsing. Xerces is also an implementation and reference code library for the W3C XML DOM (Level 1 and 2) standards. It also provides classes, properties, and methods that keep up with the current Working Draft of the W3C DOM Level 3 standards, in preparation for the day that DOM Level 3 attains W3C Recommendation status. Xerces also supports SAX version 2.

Chapter 16: Xalan introduces readers to the Apache Xalan API, which facilitates XSL Transformations in J2EE applications. Xalan contains Apache's J2EE implementation classes for the W3C XSL Transformations (XSLT) Version 1.0 Recommendation and the XML Path Language (XPath) Version 1.0 Recommendation. Xalan accepts a stream of SAX or DOM input, and produces output formatted as a stream, SAX events, or a DOM node tree. Transformation output can be accepted from the results of a DOM or SAX parse and sent to another SAX or DOM parsing process. Output can also be sent to another transformation process that accepts stream, SAX, or DOM input.

Chapter 17: XML APIs from Sun provides examples for the Java API for XML Processing (JAXP), Java Architecture for XML Binding (JAXB), and the Java Server Pages Standard Tag Library (JSTL). We dive into the details of each API and provide Java code examples (and JSP page examples for the JSTL). In addition, we use these APIs in examples in the rest of the J2EE XML parts of this book. We also introduce you to the Web service APIs in the Java Web services Developer Pack. These are the Java API for XML Messaging (JAXM), the Java API for XML Registries (JAXR), Java WSDP Registry Server, Java API for XML-Based RPC (JAX-RPC), and the SOAP with Attachments API for Java (SAAJ). We cover the Web service APIs in more detail and provide Web service API code examples in Chapter 33.

Part IV: Relational Data and XML

Part IV provides examples of Web applications that use relational XML data. There are many relational XML formats, but most developers work with either SQL Server, DB2, or Oracle, each of which has its own XML output and interactive XML features. We provide an overview of each RDBMS XML access method, output options, associated unique features, and quirks. After we explain each format, we provide working examples for transforming data from one RDBMS XML format to another.

Chapter 18: Accessing and Formatting XML from SQL Server Data covers the FOR XML T-SQL extension, adding XML documents to a database, handling the data from the document as relational data set using OPENXML, and using XPath expressions to retrieve that data as XML documents.

Chapter 19: Accessing and Formatting XML from Oracle Data covers working with SQL/XML and Oracle XML functions using Oracle XML DB. We also introduce you to the XMLType data type and show you how to store data as XMLType and how to map relational data as XMLType data using W3C Schemas. We also show you how to store XML documents as relational data using W3C Schemas. PL/SQL developers will see how to use DBMS_XMLGEN() as part of a PL/SQL solution. We also show you how to use the XDK, XSQL, and the XML SQL Utility (XSU) in Java.

Chapter 20: Accessing and Formatting XML from DB2 Data shows you how to retrieve XML documents from DB2 as whole documents. We also show you techniques for extracting XML documents and document fragments from relational and CLOB data. We also show you how to use the DB2 XML Extender to store and retrieve XML documents in their original formats and as relational data.

Chapter 21: Building XML-Based Web Applications with JDBC applies many of the tools and techniques that have been reviewed so far in the book. First, we show you how to create a J2EE application that accesses relational data via JDBC. Next, we show you how to adapt the J2EE application into a multi-tier application. The multi-tier application uses servlets and JDBC to serve relational data via XML to Web browsers and/or J2EE applications, depending on parameters that are sent to the servlet. These examples are a great way to show you how to create applications that generate XML, parse XML, and transport XML between servers and client applications. Examples also include formatting considerations for displaying XML on the Web, how to call servlets from Web browsers and custom applications, and how to parse XML documents in a Web browser and client application.

Chapter 22: Transforming Relational XML Output into Other Formats reviews XSL transformation of XML relational data formats from MS SQL Server, Oracle, and DB2. We start with a comparison of each vendor's approach to transforming XML, then provide examples of transforming XML data from each RDBMS platform. We include examples of stylesheets for transforming XML output from MS SQL Server,

Oracle, and DB2. We also show you a way to transform a generalized XML format created by the JDBC-based J2EE application covered in Chapter 21. The result is a framework for transforming relational data formats, including tips for converting relational XML output to HTML. We finish up the chapter with an XML "data island" example that transforms relational data and manipulates the data in a Web browser client using Microsoft XML Core Services (MSXML).

Part V: Introduction to Web Services

This section introduces Web services that are based on XML formats and technologies. Web service concepts are introduced, and the three key components of Web services, SOAP, WSDL, and UDDI are discussed in detail, with illustrative examples of each technology. Part V ends with a comparison of J2EE and Microsoft Web services, which both use the same underlying technologies but implement them in subtly different ways.

Chapter 23: Web Service Concepts introduces readers to the concepts of Web services and how they relate to application development, whether the applications leverage XML or not. The chapter starts with the basic concepts of Web services architectures, SOAP, WSDL, and UDDI. These examples provide an introduction for the next chapters, which cover SOAP, WSDL, UDDI MS Web services, and J2EE Web services in deeper detail.

Chapter 24: SOAP introduces the protocol for packaging Web service requests and responses. SOAP makes it possible to communicate between applications running on different operating systems, with different technologies and programming languages all in play. This chapter covers the nuts and bolts of SOAP. The specific structure of SOAP messages, how to send and receive messages, and what is contained in the full payload of a SOAP message are described and examples are provided.

Chapter 25: WSDL covers the other moving part of a Web services architecture, which defines what SOAP calls and responses should look like, and helps Web service calling agents define what an interface should be to a specific Web service.

Chapter 26: UDDI introduces Universal Description, Discovery, and Integration (UDDI). UDDI is an industry effort started in September of 2000 by Ariba, IBM, Microsoft, and 33 other companies. Today, UDDI has over 200 community members. This chapter describes UDDI, the final piece of the Web service puzzle, in detail. It explains how UDDI links together consumers of Web services with providers and how it works.

Chapter 27: Microsoft Web Services introduces Microsoft's technology toolkit for creating and consuming Web services using its COM-based technologies. Without question, Microsoft's primary focus for Web services development is with .NET. However, Microsoft recognizes that not all companies can or will migrate to .NET at the drop of a hat. Adoption cycles for some organizations can take years. On the other hand, organizations that have a large body of COM-based applications do not want the Web services train to pass them by. Therefore, there must be a non-.NET way for Windows applications to take advantage of Web services technologies. The primary COM-based vehicle for Web services is contained in the MS SOAP Toolkit. This chapter describes how Microsoft has implemented its strategy in technologies that do not fall directly within the .NET initiative. This chapter covers version 3.0 of the MS SOAP Toolkit, a COM-based collection of code, and documentation for working with SOAP in COM-based applications. The Office XP Web services toolkit is also covered. It's a clever add-in that lets Office applications consume Web services, all using MS SOAP under the hood.

Chapter 28: J2EE Web Services introduces an example of a basic J2EE Web service architecture. We use the example to describe some of the advantages of working with Web services in J2EE. We also introduce readers to vendor platforms that support the architecture.

Part VI: Microsoft.NET and Web Services

This section covers the techniques and tools for building Web services for MS .NET. These include using ASP.NET for creating and deploying .NET Web services, accessing .NET Web services from Web applications, and building a Windows-based .NET Web services Client application using Visual Studio.Net and Visual Basic.NET.

Chapter 29: Creating and Deploying .NET Web Services introduces the .NET Framework. The .NET Framework comes with all of the building blocks for Web services built right in. Essentially, any server with the .NET Framework and IIS installed is ready to provide Web services. Furthermore, .NET carefully balances the need for making Web services easier to create, deploy, and maintain with the requirement that developers still be able to go under the hood and do more advanced techniques. This chapter shows readers how to build Web services using the .NET Framework and its associated APIs. The chapter also covers what is needed to deploy a Web service into a production scenario, and how Web services can be further customized. Most importantly, readers will see how XML is used throughout the .NET Framework support for Web services, which classes use XML, how the configuration files use XML, and how other Framework XML classes can be used when creating Web services.

Chapter 30: Accessing .NET Web Services takes a step back to look at some of the issues that encompass more than the simple client-server relationship. Security, performance, and deployment for .NET Web services, and upgrading MS applications to .NET Web services, are covered.

Chapter 31: Building a .NET Web Services Client provides examples of the many different forms of .NET Web service clients. They can be Windows Forms applications, Web applications, and custom components in a class library, a control, a Windows service, or even another Web service. The main difference between all of these approaches is that the Web service is simply being called from a different container, but the way it is called is largely the same. In this chapter, a couple of client applications are developed to call a Web service. Tips and techniques for getting a client application off the ground are explained in detail.

Part VII: Web Services and J2EE

This part of the book illustrates techniques and tools for building Web services using J2EE. Examples are illustrated using open-source Web service Tools for J2EE from IBM, Apache, Sun, and others. We specifically illustrate Web service development with the Sun Java Web services Developer Pack, which includes all of the tools in the Sun Java XML Pack, plus a Java Server Pages Standard Tag Library (JSTL), the Java WSDP Registry Server, a Web Application Deployment Tool, the Ant Build Tool, and the Apache Tomcat container. We also provide examples of working with the Apache SOAP toolkit and the IBM Web services Toolkit. We finish this part of the book with examples for deploying J2EE Web services and techniques for accessing J2EE Web services.

Chapter 32: Web Service Tools for J2EE: IBM, Apache, Sun, and Others shows readers some of the tools that can help build that architecture. Fortunately, for today's developers, Java development environments have evolved into rock-solid code tools that generate J2EE code, compile it, and let you test it on the J2EE application server of your choice. Tools for developing Web services have evolved as well. Today there are several excellent J2EE code libraries available for free that support Web service functions such as building SOAP envelopes and generating J2EE client proxy classes from WSDL files. You can also generate WSDL from Java classes, as we show you in Chapter 35. Most libraries even ship with the source code if you need to customize them for a particular application. In this chapter, we review developer tool offerings from IBM, Eclipse, Sun, and Apache. There are literally hundreds of other offerings that come and go over the years, but these providers offer consistency and reliability in their offerings, which are good things if you want to base your applications on them.

Chapter 33: Web Services with the Sun Java Web Services Developer Pack focuses on the APIs related to Web service development. This chapter explores the Java API for XML Messaging (JAXM), which provides developers with standard API for developing message-based solutions that use Web services and SOAP as their messaging infrastructure. The Soap with Attachments API for Java (SAAJ) presents developers and vendors with a standard API for assembling the SOAP messages that are at the heart of all Web service interactions. The chapter also covers the

Java API for XML-based RPC (JAX-RPC). This specification provides developers with a powerful, standard framework for consuming and developing Web services.

Chapter 34: Apache AXIS introduces readers to AXIS, the open-source tool that contains all the basic elements a developer needs to rapidly consume, build, deploy, and host a Web service. Axis strikes a nice balance between power and complexity, allowing developers to quickly build Web services with a relatively short learning curve while still allowing more advanced customization of message processing, type mapping, and so on. In this chapter, the fundamentals of the Axis architecture are covered, taking an in-depth look at how the Axis engine processes requests and responses. The chapter also examines some of the goals of the architecture and how these goals influenced the solution that was ultimately implemented. It also discusses each of the deployment models that are supported by Axis. Specifically, the chapter looks into how developers can customize their Web service configuration via deployment descriptors. Additionally, this chapter covers some of the tools that are provided with Axis. It provides an overview of how the Java2WSDL and WSDL2Java tools can be used to generate the client and Web service implementation files. Examples of the contents of these generated files are introduced and explained. Additionally, the chapter looks at the TCPMON utility and discuss how it can be used to monitor the flow of messages to and from your Web service.

Chapter 35: Accessing Web Services from Java Applications rewrites the servlet code that we developed for Chapter 21 for a Web service application. It's a common task for a developer these days to upgrade a servlet-based application to a Web service application. By showing you how to adapt the code from Chapter 21, you get to see how to set up a Web service, and also how to convert servlets to Web services. Instead of a servlet-to-J2EE client connection this time, we use Apache AXIS on the client side to create a SOAP envelope that is sent to the server. On the "server" (really just the local workstation), we show you how to use the Apache AXIS Simple Server, which is a very handy tool for developing and testing Web services.

Part VIII: Advanced Web Services

This final section covers RDBMS support for Web services. We also delve into the developing standards associated with Web service security. Standards-based options for Web service encryption, signatures, and authentication are discussed in detail in Chapter 37.

Chapter 36: Accessing Relational XML Data via Web Services covers the features that RDBMS vendors have added to their database products that handle WSDL and SOAP. In most cases, the Web service features are an extension of XML features in the same product. In this chapter, we cover the ways that MS SQL Server, IBM DB2, and Oracle databases support Web services. We outline each vendor's methods for

Web service support. We show examples of setting up a SQL Server Web service using IIS and SQLXML. We discuss implementation of Web services on Oracle9iAs Application Server. We also introduce you to DB2 Web service features, including the Web services Object Runtime Framework (WORF), and Document Access Definition Extension (DADX) files. We finish off the chapter by showing you an example that uses DB2 Web service functionality in a multi-tier J2EE Web service application.

Chapter 37: Authentication and Security for Web Services introduces readers to several projects that are under way to meet the needs of industry strength solutions. For Web services, this means security and authentication. There are several groups working alone and together to form standards around Web service security. Web services also need a way to interact with other Web services as a single, seamless process. Efforts are being made to develop standards that manage groupings of Web services as a single transaction, with commit and rollback functionality, among other features. The individuals and groups that are organizing these projects come from many different backgrounds. The W3C, the WS-I, and OASIS all have their hands in one or more of these projects. Some standards are competing, and some are complementary. In this chapter, we sort through the options and help you define the current projects, the problem that a project is trying to solve, and where overlap between projects occurs.

Companion Web Site

You can download the code examples that are listed in the *XML Programming Bible* from the book's companion Web site. Go to www.wiley.com/compbooks/benz to find the code examples that are used in the book, in addition to other valuable information.

Acknowledgments

While most technical books of this size are not a light undertaking, this particular book involved more than the usual difficulties. Most of these difficulties were, sadly, due to my own personal situation. During the writing of this book, my father was in the last stages of cancer, and passed away while I was working on the final few chapters. I'd like to thank the editors for their patience and professionalism during this difficult time. Especially I'd like to thank Senior Acquisitions Editor Jim Minatel for finding additional authors to keep us on (slipping) deadlines without sacrificing the quality of the content. I'd also like to thank my coauthor, John Durant, and contributor, Tod Golding, for providing excellent content that fits very well with the rest of the book. I'd also like to thank the project editor, Kenyon Brown, the copy editor, Anne Owen, and the technical editor, Sundar Rajan, for their flexibility. They all did a superb job.

—Brian Benz

A project like this is requires the genuine commitment of many people, and the forgiveness of still more. I must thank Brian for the main thought behind this work. He is a fine writer, and decent fellow. I must also thank Senior Acquisitions Editor Jim Minatel, the editors, Kenyon Brown, Anne Owen, and Sundar Rajan, as well as the rest of the production staff for limiting their complaints about my email habits. Moving from self-employment to working for Microsoft was not easy while engaged in this lengthy initiative. Primarily, I thank my sweet wife, Carolyn, and my boys, Andrew, James, John, and Paul, for being excited about the project and letting me work on it with impunity! I must also thank Lisa L. Graber for picking up all of the details of my life as I was obligated to let them fall. I thank Maikeli Wolfgramm for giving me the faith to improve, and I thank my dear parents for teaching me how to work, work, and work. It is a lesson best learned when young.

—John R. Durant

Contents at a Glance

Contents

Part VIII: Advanced Web Services   833

Chapter 36: Accessing Relational Data via Web Services 835

Introducing XML

Part I starts with an XML Concepts chapter that gives an overview and History of XML, its purposes, and comparisons against previous and alternative data integration technologies. We then proceed to describe XML basic formats, XML well-formedness and XML Validation against DTDs and Schemas. The chapters on XSL Transformations and XSL Formatting objects illustrate the transformation and formatting of XML data using XML via working examples. Part I ends with examples of parsing XML documents, including examples of XML parsing using SAX and DOM.

XML Concepts

This book is targeted at programmers who need to develop solutions using XML. Being a programmer myself, I know that theory without practical examples and applications can be tedious, and you probably want to get straight to real-world examples. You're in luck, because this book is full of working examples — but not in this chapter. Some theory is necessary so that you have a fundamental understanding of XML. I'll keep the theory of XML and related technologies to a minimum as I progress through the chapters, but we do need to cover some of the basics up front.

This chapter provides readers who are new to XML with an overview and history of XML, its purposes, and comparisons against previous and alternative integration technologies, and ends with an overview of the next XML version, XML 1.1. The rest of the chapters in this part of the book will use real-world examples to describe XML basic formats, the structure of well-formed XML documents, and XML validation against DTDs and Schemas. The chapters on XSL Transformations and XSL Formatting Objects will illustrate the transformation and formatting of XML data using XSLT via working examples. This part of the book will be finished with examples of parsing XML documents, as well as specific examples of XML parsing using Simple API for XML (SAX) and Document Object Model (DOM).

What Is XML?

XML stands for *Extensible Markup Language,* and it is used to describe documents and data in a standardized, text-based format that can be easily transported via standard Internet protocols. XML, like HTML, is based on the granddaddy of all markup languages, Standard Generalized Markup Language (SGML).

SGML is remarkable not just because it's the inspiration and basis for all modern markup languages, but also because of the fact that SGML was created in 1974 as part of an IBM document-sharing project, and officially became an

In This Chapter

What is XML?

What is XML not?

XML standards and the World Wide Web Consortium (W3C)

Elements and attributes

Document structure

Data source encoding

Document syntax

XML namespaces

XML data validation

Special characters and entity references

XML 1.1

International Organization for Standardization (ISO) standard in 1986, long before the Internet or anything like it was operational. The ISO standard documentation for SGML (ISO 8879:1986) can be purchased online at `http://www.iso.org`.

The first popular adaptation of SGML was HTML, which was developed as part of a project to provide a common language for sharing technical documents. The advent of the Internet facilitated the document exchange method, but not the display of the document. The markup language that was developed to standardize the display format of the documents was called *Hypertext Markup Language,* or *HTML*, which provides a standardized way of describing document layout and display, and is an integral part of every Web browser and Website.

Although SGML was a good format for document sharing, and HTML was a good language for describing the *layout* of the documents in a standardized way, there was no standardized way to describe and share *data* that was stored in the document. For example, an HTML page might have a body that contains a listing of today's closing prices of a share of every company in the Fortune 500. This data can be displayed using HTML in a myriad of ways. Prices can be bold if they have moved up or down by 10 percent, and prices that are up from yesterday's closing price can be displayed in green, with prices that are down displayed in red. The information can be formatted in a table, and alternating rows of the table can be in different colors.

However, once the data is taken from its original source and rendered as HTML in a browser, the values of the data only have value as part of the markup language on that page. They are no longer individual pieces of data, but are now simply pieces of "content" wedged between elements and attributes that specify how to display that content. For example, if a Web developer wanted to extract the top ten price movers from the daily closing prices displayed on the Web page, there was no standardized way to locate the top ten values and isolate them from the others, and relate the prices to the associated Fortune 500 Company.

Note that I say that there was no *standardized* way to do this; this did not stop developers from trying. Many a Web developer in the mid- to late-1990s, including myself, devised very elaborate and clever ways of scraping the data they needed from between HTML tags, mostly by eyeballing the page and the HTML source code, then coding routines in various languages to read, parse, and locate the required values in the page. For example, a developer may read the HTML source code of the stock price page and discover that the prices were located in the only table on the HTML page. With this knowledge, code could be developed in the developer's choice of language to locate the table in the page, extract the values nested in the table, calculate the top price movers for the day based on values in the third column in the table, and relate the company name in the first column of the table with the top ten values.

However, it's fair to say that this approach represented a maintenance nightmare for developers. For example, if the original Web page developers suddenly decided to add a table before the stock price table on the page, or add an additional column to the table, or nest one table in another, it was back to the drawing board for the developer who was scraping the data from the HTML page, starting over to find the values in the page, extract the values into meaningful data, and so on. Most developers who struggled with this inefficient method of data exchange on the Web were looking for better ways to share data while still using the Web as a data delivery mechanism.

But this is only one example of many to explain the need for a tag-based markup language that could describe data more effectively than HTML. With the explosion of the Web, the need for a universal format that could function as a lowest common denominator for data exchange while still using the very popular and standardized HTTP delivery methods of the Internet was growing.

In 1998 the World Wide Web Consortium (W3C) met this need by combining the basic features that separate data from format in SGML with extension of the HTML tag formats that were adapted for the Web and came up with the first Extensible Markup Language (XML) Recommendation. The three pillars of XML are Extensibility, Structure, and Validity.

Extensibility

XML does a great job of describing structured data as text, and the format is open to extension. This means that any data that can be described as text and that can be nested in XML tags will be generally accepted as XML. Extensions to the language need only follow the basic XML syntax and can otherwise take XML wherever the developer would like to go. The only limits are imposed on the data by the data itself, via syntax rules and self-imposed format directives via data validation, which I will get into in the next chapter.

Structure

The structure of XML is usually complex and hard for human eyes to follow, but it's important to remember that it's not designed for us to read. XML parsers and other types of tools that are designed to work with XML easily digest XML, even in its most complex forms. Also, XML was designed to be an open data exchange format, not a compact one—XML representations of data are usually much larger than their original formats. In other words, XML was not designed to solve disk space or bandwidth issues, even though text-based XML formats do compress very well using regular data compression and transport tools.

It's also important to remember that XML data syntax, while extensible, is rigidly enforced compared to HTML formats. I will get into the specifics of formatting rules a little later in this chapter, and will show examples in the next chapter.

Validity

Aside from the mandatory syntax requirements that make up an XML document, data represented by XML can optionally be validated for structure and content, based on two separate data validation standards. The original XML data validation standard is called Data Type Definition (DTD), and the more recent evolution of XML data validation is the XML Schema standard. I will be covering data validation using DTDs and Schemas a little later in this chapter, and showing working examples of data validation in the next chapter.

What Is XML Not?

With all the hype that continues to surround XML and derivative technologies such as XSL and Web Services, it's probably as important to review what XML is not as it is to review what XML is.

While XML facilitates data integration by providing a transport with which to send and receive data in a common format, XML is not data integration. It's simply the glue that holds data integration solutions together with a multi-platform "lowest common denominator" for data transportation. XML cannot make queries against a data source or read data into a repository by itself. Similarly, data cannot be formatted as XML without additional tools or programming languages that specifically generate XML data from other types of data. Also, data cannot be parsed into destination data formats without a parser or other type of application that converts data from XML to a compatible destination format.

It's also important to point out that XML is not HTML. XML may look like HTML, based on the similarities of the tags and the general format of the data, but that's where the similarity ends. While HTML is designed to describe display characteristics of data on a Web page to browsers, XML is designed to represent data structures. XML data can be transformed into HTML using Extensible Style Sheet Transformations (XSLT). XML can also be parsed and formatted as HTML in an application. XML can also be part of an XML page using XML data islands. I'll discuss XSLT transformations, XML parsing, and data islands in much more detail later in the book.

XML Standards and the World Wide Web Consortium

The World Wide Web Consortium (W3C) is where developers will find most of the specifications for standards that are used in the XML world. W3C specifications are referred to as "Recommendations" because the final stage in the W3C development process may not necessarily produce a specification, depending on the nature of the W3C Working Group that is producing the final product, but for all intents and purposes, most of the final products are specifications.

W3C specifications on the Recommendation track progress through five stages: Working Draft, Last Call Working Draft, Candidate Recommendation, Proposed Recommendation, and Recommendation, which is the final stop for a specific version of a specification such as XML.

W3C Working Groups produce Recommendations, and anyone can join the W3C and a Working Group. More information on joining the W3C can be found at `http://www.w3.org/Consortium/Prospectus/Joining`. Currently, W3C Working Groups are working hard at producing the latest recommendations for XML and related technologies such as XHTML, Xlink, XML Base, XML Encryption, XML Key Management, XML Query, XML Schema, XML Signature, Xpath, Xpointer, XSL, and XSLT.

XML Elements and Attributes

Because XML is designed to describe data and documents, the W3C XML Recommendation, which can be found buried in the links at `http://www.w3.org/XML`, is very strict about a small core of format requirements that make the difference between a text document containing a bunch of tags and an actual XML document. XML documents that meet W3C XML document formatting recommendations are described as being *well-formed* XML documents. Well-formed XML documents can contain elements, attributes, and text.

Elements

Elements look like this and always have an opening and closing tag:

```
<element></element>
```

There are a few basic rules for XML document elements. Element names can contain letters, numbers, hyphens, underscores, periods, and colons when namespaces are used (more on namespaces later). Element names cannot contain spaces;

underscores are usually used to replace spaces. Element names can start with a letter, underscore, or colon, but cannot start with other non-alphabetic characters or a number, or the letters *xml*.

Aside from the basic rules, it's important to think about using hyphens or periods in element names. They may be considered part of well-formed XML documents, but other systems that will use the data in the element name such as relational database systems often have trouble working with hyphens or periods in data identifiers, often mistaking them for something other than part of the name.

Attributes

Attributes contain values that are associated with an element and are always part of an element's opening tag:

```
<element attribute="value"></element>
```

The basic rules and guidelines for elements apply to attributes as well, with a few additions. The attribute name must follow an element name, then an equals sign (=), then the attribute value, in single or double quotes. The attribute value can contain quotes, and if it does, one type of quote must be used in the value, and another around the value.

Text

Text is located between the opening and closing tags of an element, and usually represents the actual data associated with the elements and attributes that surround the text:

```
<element attribute="value">text</element>
```

Text is not constrained by the same syntax rules of elements and attributes, so virtually any text can be stored between XML document elements. Note that while the value is limited to text, the format of the text can be specified as another type of data by the elements and attributes in the XML document.

Empty elements

Last but not least, elements with no attributes or text can also be represented in an XML document like this:

```
<element/>
```

This format is usually added to XML documents to accommodate a predefined data structure. I'll be covering ways to specify an XML data structure a little later in this chapter.

XML Document Structure

Although elements, attributes, and text are very important for XML documents, these design objects alone do not make up a well-formed XML document without being arranged under certain structural and syntax rules. Let's examine the structure of the very simple well-formed XML 1.0 document in Listing 1-1.

Listing 1-1: A Very Simple XML Document

```
<?xml version="1.0" encoding="UTF-8"?>
<rootelement>
    <firstelement position="1">
        <level1 children="0">This is level 1 of the nested
        elements</level1>
    </firstelement>
    <secondelement position="2">
        <level1 children="1">
            <level2>This is level 2 of the nested
            elements</level2>
        </level1>
    </secondelement>
</rootelement>
```

Most XML documents start with an `<?xml?>` element at the top of the page. This is called an XML document declaration. An XML document declaration is an optional element that is useful to determine the version of XML and the encoding type of the source data. It is not a required element for an XML document to be well formed in the W3C XML 1.0 specification. This is the most common XML document declaration:

```
<?xml version="1.0" encoding="UTF-8"?>
```

There are two attributes contained in this XML declaration that are commonly seen but not often explained. The XML version is used to determine what version of the W3C XML recommendation that the document adheres to. XML parsers use this information to apply version-specific syntax rules to the XML document.

Data Source Encoding

Data source encoding is one of the most important features for XML documents. Most developers based in the United States or other English-speaking countries are familiar with ASCII text only, and have not commonly tested the capacity of ASCII's 128-member character set. However, with the advent of the Internet, HTML and especially XML developers have been forced to examine the limitations of ASCII, and have worked with Unicode in HTML documents, even if they didn't know that they were (HTML code generators usually add the Unicode directives to HTML pages).

Because the XML Recommendation was developed by the W3C, an international organization which has offices at the Massachusetts Institute of Technology (MIT) in the United States, the European Research Consortium for Informatics and Mathematics (ERCIM) in France, and Keio University in Japan, Unicode was chosen as the standard text format to accommodate the world's languages, instead of just English. Most developers are used to seeing UTF-8 or sometimes UTF-16 in the encoding attribute of an XML document, but this is just the tip of the iceberg.

UTF stands for *Universal Character Set Transformation Format,* and the number 8 or 16 refers to the number of bits that the character is stored in. Each 8- or 16-bit container represents the value of the character in bits as well as the identity of each character and its numeric value. UTF-8 is the most common form of XML encoding; in fact, an XML document that does not specify an encoding type must adhere to either UTF-8 or UTF-16 to be considered a well-formed XML 1.0 document. Using UTF-8, UTF-16, and the newer UTF-32, XML editors, generators and parsers can identify and work with all major world languages and alphabets, including non-Latin alphabets such as Middle Eastern and Asian alphabets, scripts, and languages. This includes punctuation, non-Arabic numbers, math symbols, accents, and so on.

Unicode is managed and developed by a non-profit group called the Unicode Consortium. For more information on encoding and a listing of encoding types for XML, the Unicode consortium and the W3C has published a joint report, available at the Unicode Consortium site:
http://www.unicode.org/unicode/reports/tr20.

Aside from UTF declarations for XML document encoding, any ISO registered charset name that is registered by the Internet Assigned Numbers Authority (IANA) is an acceptable substitute. For example, an XML 1.0 document encoded in Macedonian would look like this in the XML declaration:

```
<?xml version="1.0" encoding="JUS_I.B1.003-mac"?>
```

A list of currently registered names can be found at
http://www.iana.org/assignments/character-sets.

Element and Attribute Structure

Under the optional XML declarations, every XML document contains a single-value root element, represented in this case by the rootelement element:

```
<rootelement>
```

Other elements and text values can be nested under the root element, but the root element must be first in the list and unique in the document. This can be compared to a computer hard drive, which contains one root directory, with files and/or sub-directories under the root directory.

Next in the sample XML document are the nested elements, attributes, and text, as illustrated by the nested `firstelement` under the root element in our example:

```
<firstelement position="1">
   <level1 children="0">This is level 1 of the nested
   elements</level1>
</firstelement>
```

The `firstelement` has an attribute called `position` with a value of 1. The `position` attribute provides additional data related to `firstelement`. In this case it indicates that the original sorting position of the first element in the XML document is 1. If the XML document data is altered and the order of the elements is rearranged as part of that alteration, the position element may be useful for reordering the element, or could be changed when the document is altered to reflect a new position of the element in the XML document, regardless of the element name. In general, attributes are great for adding more information and descriptions to the values of elements, and the text associated with elements, as shown in the previous example.

Nested under the `firstelement` element is the `level1` element, which contains an attribute, called `children`. The element name is used to describe the nesting level in the XML document, and the value of the `children` attribute is used to describe how many more levels of nesting are contained under the `level1` element, in this case, no more nested levels (0). The phrase `This is level 1 of the nested elements` represents a text data value that is part of the `level1` element. Text data contains values associated with a tag.

The second element under the root element is called `secondelement` and is a variation of the `firstelement` element. Let's compare the `firstelement` and `secondelement` elements to get a better sense of the structure of the document:

```
<secondelement position="2">
   <level1 children="1">
      <level2>This is level 2 of the nested
      elements</level2>
   </level1>
</secondelement>
```

Like the `firstelement`, the `secondelement` has an attribute called `position`, this time with a value of 2. Nested under the `secondelement` element is another `level1` element. The existence of this element illustrates the fact that well-formed XML documents can have more than one instance of the same element name. The only exception to this is the root element, which must be unique.

Also, like the `firstelement` element, the `level1` element also has an attribute called `children`. The `level1` element is again used to describe the nesting level in the XML document, and the attribute is used to describe how many more levels of nesting are contained under the `level1` element. In this case, the children attribute indicates that there is one more nesting level (1) inside the `level1` element. The phrase `This is level 2 of the nested elements` inside the `level2` element represents text data for the `level2` element.

Last but not least, to finish the XML document, the `rootelement` tag is closed:

```
</rootelement>
```

XML Document Syntax

Another important aspect of a well-formed XML document is the document syntax. XML represents data and not content or layout like other markup languages such as HTML. Data has very strict structure and format rules. XML also has very strict rules about the syntax used to represent that data. Developers who are used to coding with the somewhat forgiving syntax of HTML will have some adjustments to make when dealing with XML syntax.

For starters, XML element names must start and end with the same case. This is not well-formed XML:

```
<level2>This is level 2 of the nested elements</Level2>
```

The tag name started with `<level2>` must be closed with `</level2>`, not `</Level2>`, to be considered well-formed XML.

Quotes must be used on all attribute names. Something like this will not be considered well-formed XML:

```
<secondelement position=2>
```

Attributes must be formatted with single or double quotes to be considered well-formed XML:

```
<secondelement position="2">
```

Comments should always follow the SGML comment tag format:

```
<!--Comment tags should always follow this format when in XML
documents-->
```

Element tags must always be closed. HTML and other forms of markup are somewhat forgiving, and can often be left open or improperly nested without affecting the content or display of a page. XML parsers and other tools that read and manipulate XML documents are far less forgiving about structure and syntax than browsers.

XML Namespaces

Namespaces are a method for separating and identifying duplicate XML element names in an XML document. Namespaces can also be used as identifiers to describe data types and other information. Namespace declarations can be compared to defining a short variable name for a long variable (such as pi=3.14159....) in programming languages. In XML, the variable assignment is defined by an attribute declaration. The variable name is the attribute name, and the variable value is the attribute value. In order to identify namespace declarations versus other types of attribute declarations, a reserved xmlns: prefix is used when declaring a namespace name and value. The attribute name after the xmlns: prefix identifies the name for the defined namespace. The value of the attribute provides the unique identifier for the namespace. Once the namespace is declared, the namespace name can be used as a prefix in element names.

Listing 1-2 shows the very simple XML document I reviewed in Listing 1-1, this time with some namespaces to differentiate between nested elements.

Listing 1-2: **A Very Simple XML Document with Namespaces**

```
<?xml version="1.0" encoding="UTF-8"?>
<rootelement>
   <firstelement
    xmlns:fe="http://www.benztech.com/schemas/verybasic"
    position="1">
      <fe:level1 children="0">This is level 1 of the nested
       elements</fe:level1>
   </firstelement>
   <secondelement
    xmlns:se="http://www.benztech.com/schemas/verybasic"
    position="2">
      <se:level1 children="1">
         <se:level2>This is level 2 of the nested
          elements</se:level2>
      </se:level1>
   </secondelement>
</rootelement>
```

In this example, I am using two namespaces as identifiers to differentiate two level1 elements in the same document. The xmlns: attribute declares the namespace for an XML document or a portion of an XML document. The attribute can be placed in the root element of the document, or in any other nested element.

In our example, the namespace name for the firstelement element is fe, and the namespace name for the secondelement is se. Both use the same URL as the value for the namespace. Often the URL in the namespace resolves to a Web page that provides documentation about the namespace, such as information about the data encoding types identified in the namespace. However, in this case, we are just using the namespace to defined prefixed for unique identification of duplicate element names. The URL does resolve to an actual document, but is just used as a place-holder for the namespace name declarations.

Tip   Although the namespace declaration value does not need to be a URL or resolve to an actual URL destination, it is a good idea to use a URL anyway, and to choose a URL that could resolve to an actual destination, just in case developers want to add documentation for the namespace to the URL in the future.

When to use namespaces

Namespaces are optional components of basic XML documents. However, name-space declarations are recommended if your XML documents have any current or future potential of being shared with other XML documents that may share the same element names. Also, newer XML-based technologies such as XML Schemas, SOAP, and WSDL make heavy use of XML namespaces to identify data encoding types and important elements of their structure. I'll be showing many more exam-ples of namespaces being used in context to identify elements for XML document data encoding, identification, and description as the examples progress through the book.

XML Data Validation

As I've shown you so far in this chapter, there are very strict rules for the basic structure and syntax of well-formed XML documents. There are also several formats within the boundaries of well-formed XML syntax that provide standardized ways of representing specific types of data.

For example, NewsML offers a standard format for packaging news information in XML. NewsML defines what the element name should be that contains the title, publication date, headline, article text, and other parts of a news item. NewsML also defines how these elements should be arranged, and which elements are optional. NewsML documents are well-formed XML, and they also conform to NewsML specifications.

The validity of an XML document is determined by a Document Type Definition (DTD) or an XML Schema. There are several formats for data validation to choose from. A good listing for XML validation formats can be found at `http://www.oasis-open.org/cover/schemas.html`. However, the most common and offi-cially W3C sanctioned formats are the Document Type Definition (DTD) and the W3C Schema, which I will focus on in this chapter.

XML documents are compared to rules that are specified in a DTD or schema. A well-formed XML document that meets all of the requirements of one or more specifications is called a *valid* XML Document.

 Note   XML documents do not validate themselves. XML validation takes place when a document is parsed. Most of today's parsers have validation built-in to the core functionality, and usually support W3C Schema and DTD validation, and may support other types of validation, depending on the parser. In addition, defining a variable or calling a different class in the parser can often disable validation by ignoring DTD and/or Schema directives in the XML document. Parsers or parser classes that don't support validation are called *nonvalidating parsers,* and parsers or classes that support validation are called *validating parsers.*

For example, the NewsML specification is defined and managed by the International Press Telecommunications Council (IPTC). The IPTC has published a DTD that can be used by news providers to validate NewsML news items (Reuters and other news providers have NewsML-compatible news feeds). If a member of the press wants to produce NewsML formatted news items, they can download the DTD from the IPTC Website at `http://www.iptc.org`. Once the DTD is downloaded, XML developers can validate their NewsML output against the DTD using a validating parser.

Listing 1-3 shows the same simple XML document in Listing 1-1, but this time there is a DTD and a Schema reference in the document.

Listing 1-3: A Very Simple XML Document with a Schema and DTD Reference

```
<?xml version="1.0" encoding="UTF-8"?>
<!DOCTYPE rootelement SYSTEM "verysimplexml.dtd">
<rootelement xmlns:xsi="http://www.w3.org/2001/XMLSchema-
instance" xsi:noNamespaceSchemaLocation="verysimplexml.xsd">
   <firstelement position="1">
      <level1 children="0">This is level 1 of the nested
      elements</level1>
   </firstelement>
   <secondelement position="2">
      <level1 children="1">
         <level2>This is level 2 of the nested
         elements</level2>
      </level1>
   </secondelement>
</rootelement>
```

It is not common to see both DTD and Schema references in a single document that verify the same structural rules, but it's a good example of the fact that you can combine Schema and DTD references in a single document. References to a DTD and a schema can occur when an XML document is made up of two or more source documents. The DTD and schema references maintain all of the structure rules that were present in the original document. Dual references can also be used when illegal XML characters are represented in an XML document by entity references. I'll describe entity references in more detail later in this chapter.

Cross-Reference

The following section of this chapter is intended to give you an introductory overview of DTDs and W3C Schemas. For more detail on XML document validation with real-world examples, please see Chapter 3.

Validating XML documents with DTDs

Document Type Definition (DTD) is the original way to validate XML document structure and enforce specific formatting of select text, and probably still the most prevalent. Although the posting of the XML declaration at the top of the DTD would lead one to believe that this is an XML document, DTDs are in fact non-well-formed XML documents. This is because they follow DTD syntax rules rather than XML document syntax. In Listing 1-3, the reference is to the DTD located in the first element under the XML document declaration:

```
<!DOCTYPE rootelement SYSTEM "verysimplexml.dtd">
```

Listing 1-4 shows the `verysimplexml.dtd` file that is referred to in the XML document in Listing 1-3.

Listing 1-4: **Contents of the verysimplexml.dtd File**

```
<?xml version="1.0" encoding="UTF-8"?>
<!ELEMENT rootelement (firstelement, secondelement)>
<!ELEMENT firstelement (level1)>
<!ATTLIST firstelement
   position CDATA #REQUIRED
>
<!ELEMENT level1 (#PCDATA | level2)*>
<!ATTLIST level1
   children (0 | 1) #REQUIRED
>
<!ATTLIST secondelement
   position CDATA #REQUIRED
>
<!ELEMENT level2 (#PCDATA)>
<!ELEMENT secondelement (level1)>
```

Let's go through this DTD line by line to get to know DTD structure. The first line is an XML document declaration, which tells parsers the version of XML and the encoding type for the document. The next line specifies that valid XML documents must contain a firstelement and the secondelement, which have to be present under the rootelement, and have to be in the order listed:

```
<!ELEMENT rootelement (firstelement, secondelement)>
```

Next, the DTD describes the firstelement. The firstelement must have a level1 element nested directly under the firstelement.:

```
<!ELEMENT firstelement (level1)>
```

Next, the DTD specifies an attribute for the firstelement. The ATTLIST declaration tells us that valid XML documents need a position attribute for each instance of the firstelement (#REQUIRED), and that it is regular character data (CDATA):

```
<!ATTLIST firstelement
   position CDATA #REQUIRED
>
```

The next element declaration tells us that the level1 element can contain one of two things. The | is equivalent to an or in a DTD. The level1 element can contain another nested element called level2, or a value of parsed character data (PCDATA):

```
<!ELEMENT level1 (#PCDATA | level2)*>
```

The next ATTLIST declaration tells us that level1 can have one of two values, 0 or 1:

```
<!ATTLIST level1
   children (0 | 1) #REQUIRED
>
```

The ATTLIST declaration for secondelement tells us that valid XML documents need a position attribute for each instance of the secondelement (#REQUIRED), and that it is regular character data (CDATA):

```
<!ATTLIST secondelement
   position CDATA #REQUIRED
>
```

Following the nesting deeper into the document, a declaration for the level2 element is defined. The level2 element declaration simply states that the element must contain a value of parsed character data (PCDATA):

```
<!ELEMENT level2 (#PCDATA)>
```

Last but not least, the `secondelement` is defined, along with a mandatory `level1` element nested underneath it:

```
<!ELEMENT secondelement (level1)>
```

As you can see from the last few lines of this DTD, the element and attribute declarations do not have to be in the same order as the element and attributes that they represent. It is up to the parser to reassemble the DTD into something that defines the relationship of all the elements and enforces all the rules contained in each line of the DTD.

Validating XML documents with Schemas

The W3C Schema is the officially sanctioned Schema definition. Unlike DTDs, the format of W3C Schemas follows the rules of well-formed XML documents. The Schema also allows for much more granular control over the data that is being described. Because of the XML format and the detailed format controls, Schemas tend to be very complex and often much longer than the XML documents that they are describing. Paradoxically, Schemas are often much more easy for developers to read and follow, due to the less cryptic nature of the references in Schemas versus DTDs.

References to schemas are defined by creating an instance of the `XMLSchema-instance` namespace. Here is the Schema declaration in the XML document in Listing 1-3:

```
<rootelement xmlns:xsi="http://www.w3.org/2001/XMLSchema-
instance" xsi:noNamespaceSchemaLocation="verysimplexml.xsd">
```

In this case, the namespace declaration reference to `http://www.w3.org/2001/XMLSchema-instance` resolves to an actual document at that location, which is a brief description of the way that the W3C Schema should be referenced. The `noNamespaceSchemaLocation` value tells us that there is no predefined namespace for the Schema. This means that all of the elements in the XML document should be validated against the schema specified. The location of the Schema I am using is verysimplexml.xsd. Because there is no path defined, the file containing the schema should be located in the same directory as the XML file to be validated by the Schema.

You can also define the schema location, and map it to a specific namespace by using the `schemaLocation` attribute declaration instead of `noNamespaceSchemaLocation`. If you do so, you have to declare a namespace that matches the `schemaLocation` attribute value. The declaration must be made before you reference the schema in a `schemaLocation` attribute assignment. Here's an example of a `schemaLocation` assignment in a root element of an XML document:

```
<rootelement
xmlns:fe="http://www.benztech.com/schemas/verybasic"
xsi:schemaLocation="http://www.benztech.com/schemas/verybasic
">
```

Listing 1-5 shows the `verysimplexml.xsd` file that is referred to in the XML document in Listing 1-3.

Listing 1-5: Contents of the verysimplexml.xsd File

```xml
<?xml version="1.0" encoding="UTF-8"?>
<xs:schema xmlns:xs="http://www.w3.org/2001/XMLSchema"
elementFormDefault="qualified">
   <xs:element name="firstelement">
      <xs:complexType>
         <xs:sequence>
            <xs:element ref="level1"/>
         </xs:sequence>
         <xs:attribute name="position" type="xs:boolean"
          use="required"/>
      </xs:complexType>
   </xs:element>
   <xs:element name="level1">
      <xs:complexType mixed="true">
         <xs:choice minOccurs="0" maxOccurs="unbounded">
            <xs:element ref="level2"/>
         </xs:choice>
         <xs:attribute name="children" use="required">
            <xs:simpleType>
               <xs:restriction base="xs:NMTOKEN">
                  <xs:enumeration value="0"/>
                  <xs:enumeration value="1"/>
               </xs:restriction>
            </xs:simpleType>
         </xs:attribute>
      </xs:complexType>
   </xs:element>
   <xs:element name="level2" type="xs:string"/>
   <xs:element name="rootelement">
      <xs:complexType>
         <xs:sequence>
            <xs:element ref="firstelement"/>
            <xs:element ref="secondelement"/>
         </xs:sequence>
      </xs:complexType>
   </xs:element>
   <xs:element name="secondelement">
      <xs:complexType>
         <xs:sequence>
            <xs:element ref="level1"/>
         </xs:sequence>
         <xs:attribute name="position" type="xs:byte"
          use="required"/>
      </xs:complexType>
   </xs:element>
</xs:schema>
```

I'll go through this code line by line to introduce readers to the W3C Schema XSD format. After the declaration, the next line refers to the xs namespace for XML Schemas. The reference URL, http://www.w3.org/2001/XMLSchema, actually resolves to the W3C Website and provides documentation for Schemas, as well as reference materials for data types and Schema namespace formatting.

```
<?xml version="1.0" encoding="UTF-8"?>
<xs:schema xmlns:xs="http://www.w3.org/2001/XMLSchema"
elementFormDefault="qualified">
```

The first element definition describes the firstelement as a complex data type, that the element contains one nested element called level1, and an attribute called position, and that the attribute is required.

```
<xs:element name="firstelement">
    <xs:complexType>
        <xs:sequence>
            <xs:element ref="level1"/>
        </xs:sequence>
        <xs:attribute name="position" type="xs:boolean"
         use="required"/>
    </xs:complexType>
</xs:element>
```

The next element describes the level1 element, that it is an optional element (minOccurs="0"), and that the level1 element can occur an unlimited number of times in the document (maxOccurs="unbounded"). Nested in the level1 element is a reference to the level2 element, just as it is in the document. Next, the children attribute is specified as required, and defined as a simple Schema data type called NMTOKEN value for the base attribute, which is, for the purposes of this schema, a string. The children string must be one of two predefined values, "0" and "1", as defined by the enumeration values nested inside of the restriction element.

```
<xs:element name="level1">
    <xs:complexType mixed="true">
        <xs:choice minOccurs="0" maxOccurs="unbounded">
            <xs:element ref="level2"/>
        </xs:choice>
        <xs:attribute name="children" use="required">
            <xs:simpleType>
                <xs:restriction base="xs:NMTOKEN">
                    <xs:enumeration value="0"/>
                    <xs:enumeration value="1"/>
                </xs:restriction>
            </xs:simpleType>
        </xs:attribute>
    </xs:complexType>
</xs:element>
```

Because the `level2` element has no attributes or nested elements, it can be described in one line and referred to as a nested element in the `level1` element via the `ref=` reference:

```
    <xs:element name="level2" type="xs:string"/>
  <xs:element ref="level2"/>
```

As with the DTD example, the element and attribute declarations in a W3C Schema do not have to be in the same order as the element and attributes that they represent in an XML document. Like the DTD, it is up to the parser to reassemble the Schema into something that defines the relationship of all the elements and enforces all the rules contained in each line of the Schema, regardless of the order. The next element in this Schema example is the `rootelement`. The `rootelement` must have a `firstelement` and a `secondelement` nested under it to be considered a valid XML document when using this Schema. The previous definitions for the `firstelement`, `secondelement`, and all the nested elements underneath them are defined earlier in the Schema.

```
    <xs:element name="rootelement">
      <xs:complexType>
        <xs:sequence>
           <xs:element ref="firstelement"/>
           <xs:element ref="secondelement"/>
        </xs:sequence>
      </xs:complexType>
    </xs:element>
```

The schema defines the `secondelement`, which must contain a nested `level1` element, and have an attribute named `position`, this time a `byte` value.

```
    <xs:element name="secondelement">
      <xs:complexType>
        <xs:sequence>
           <xs:element ref="level1"/>
        </xs:sequence>
        <xs:attribute name="position" type="xs:byte"
         use="required"/>
      </xs:complexType>
    </xs:element>
```

Finally, the closing of the schema tag indicates the end of the schema.

```
    </xs:schema>
```

Special Characters and Entity References

The W3C XML Recommendation also supports supplements to the default encoding. Special characters in a well-formed XML document can be referenced via a declared entity, Unicode, or hex character reference. Entity references must start with an ampersand (&), Unicode character references start with an ampersand and a pound sign (&#), and hexadecimal character references start with an ampersand, pound sign, and an x (&#x). All entity, Unicode, and hexadecimal references end with a semicolon (;).

Listing 1-6 shows a simple XML document that uses Entity, Unicode, and Hex references to generate a copyright symbol ((c)) and a registered trademark symbol ((r)) in an XML document.

Listing 1-6: **Entity, Unicode, and Hex Character References in an XML Document**

```
<?xml version="1.0" encoding="UTF-8"?>
<!DOCTYPE rootelement SYSTEM "specialcharacters.dtd">
<rootelement>
    <entityreferences>&copy; &reg;</entityreferences>
    <unicodereferences>&#169; &#174;</unicodereferences>
    <hexreferences>&#xA9; &#xAE;</hexreferences>
</rootelement>
```

The values in the `unicodereferences` and `hexreferences` elements are the Unicode and hex values that represent the symbols. Both follow the character reference rules outlined earlier. The addition of a DTD is necessary for the entity references in the `entityreferences` element. The values for the entity references must be defined outside of the XML document. Listing 1-7 shows the specialcharacters.dtd file, including the entity definitions for &copy and &reg. This very basic DTD defines the structure of the document, and also defines two entity references and their values. I've created a Hex and a Unicode reference to illustrate that entity references in XML documents can refer to either format. The first ENTITY tag in the DTD defines the copy reference as the hex character reference %A9. The value follows XML rules for formatting a hex character reference, which makes the hex value "©". The second ENTITY tag refers to the Unicode character 174, formatted as "®" according to XML document Unicode character reference rules.

Listing 1-7: **The specialcharacters.dtd File with Entity Definitions for &copy and &reg**

```
<?xml version="1.0" encoding="UTF-8"?>
<!ENTITY copy "&#xA9;">
<!ENTITY reg "&#174;">
<!ELEMENT rootelement (entityreferences, unicodereferences,
hexreferences)>
<!ELEMENT entityreferences (#PCDATA)>
<!ELEMENT hexreferences (#PCDATA)>
<!ELEMENT unicoderefcrences (#PCDATA)>
```

Listing 1-8 shows the output from the XML document, with the resolved character references. This is what the document looks like when the character and entity references are rendered by a Microsoft Internet Explorer 6 browser.

Listing 1-8: **MSIE Rendered Character and Entity References Using the specialcharacters.dtd File**

```
<?xml version="1.0" encoding="UTF-8" ?>
<!DOCTYPE rootelement (View Source for full doctype...)>
<rootelement>
   <entityreferences>(c) (r)</entityreferences>
   <unicodereferences>(c) (r)</unicodereferences>
   <hexreferences>(c) (r)</hexreferences>
</rootelement>
```

Using entity references as variables

Entity references can also be used as variables and combined with other entity references in a DTD, which is a handy way of standardizing certain declarations and other unalterable components of an XML document. For example, an entity reference called `copyline` can be created in a DTD like this:

```
<!ENTITY copy "&#xA9;">
<!ENTITY copyline "&copy; Benz Technologies, Inc, all rights
reserved;">
```

When a reference to the &copyline; entity is made in an XML document, the output would look like this:

```
(c) Benz Technologies, Inc, all rights reserved
```

Using this technique ensures that XML document validation imposes a standard format for certain important pieces of text in an XML document, as well as the structure of the document.

Reserved character references

All of the character reference formats defined earlier include an ampersand. So how do you represent an ampersand in XML documents? To accommodate ampersands and four other special characters that are part of the XML core syntax special reserved character references are defined. Less than and greater than symbols (which are used to define XML elements), and quotes (which are used to define attribute values) are supported via special predefined character substitutions without any Entity, Unicode, or Hex references needed. An ampersand (&) is used at the beginning and a semicolon (;) is placed at the end of the reference. Table 1-1 shows the reserved character entity and its reference.

| Table 1-1 | |
| **Reserved Character Entities and References** | |
Entity Reference	*Special Character*
&amp;	ampersand (&)
&apos	apostrophe or single quote (')
&gt;	greater-than (>)
&lt;	less-than (<)
&quot;	double quote (")

XML 1.1

XML 1.1 represents an incremental development of the W3C XML recommendation. The new recommendation is actually split into two significant recommendations, XML 1.1 and XML Namespaces 1.1. Most of the new features are "behind the scenes" enhancements, which will have little or no effect on most XML applications. For example, the new way of handling line-endings in XML 1.1 documents will probably affect developers who are coding XML 1.1 parsers or XML 1.1 development tools. They will probably not, however, significantly affect developers who are using XML 1.1 parsers or development tools to develop XML applications.

XML 1.1 new features

New character sets accommodation for evolving Unicode specifications form the base of new features for XML 1.1. Since the first W3C XML document recommendation was released in 1998, Unicode has expanded to accommodate much more of the alphabets and characters of the world. This was addressed to some extent in the second edition of the XML Recommendation in 2000, but the newer recommendation goes beyond the second edition to redefine what a well-formed document is, based on new Unicode standards.

Defining XML 1.1 documents

The version number in the optional XML declaration defines XML 1.1 documents, like this:

```
<?xml version="1.1">
```

Any document that does not specifically state the XML document version as 1.1 is treated as an XML 1.0 document. XML 1.1 documents are backward compatible with XML 1.0 documents. There is an exception: Some new Unicode characters that XML 1.1 processors recognize as part of well-formed element, attribute, and namespace names are not accepted by XML 1.0 document syntax rules. These characters could already be used in XML 1.0 text and attribute values. XML 1.1 officially adds these characters and character sets into structural items of XML documents — element names, attribute names, and namespaces.

XML 1.1 character sets

A more inclusive philosophy is the basis of XML 1.1. This is a reaction to the evolution of Unicode specifications, which has outpaced XML recommendation updates. Instead of the XML 1.0 approach of defining which characters cannot be included within XML documents and considering markup with undefined characters as not well formed, XML 1.1 instead defines which characters can specifically not be included in well-formed XML documents and considers any undefined characters as part of well-formed XML. This makes it easier to accommodate developing Unicode specifications. This rule applies to all XML markup, including elements, attributes, and namespaces. XML 1.0 documents will be limited to the character set defined in Unicode 2.0, and XML 1.1 documents theoretically should handle any Unicode from 2.0 to the current 3.2 and beyond.

New characters and the new philosophy will be supported by the requirement of normalization in XML 1.1 document parsed entities. This means that XML 1.1 processors that generate data will have to conform to the W3C Character Model for the

World Wide Web 1.0 (CHARMOD), currently at the "Working Draft" stage of the W3C Recommendation process, and XML 1.1. Next, the character data should be resolved into one of five formats: Cdata, CharData, content, name, or nmtoken. Parsers will have to verify normalization based on the same character model.

XML 1.1 line-end characters

Another feature of XML 1.1 is the capability to handle line-end characters generated in IBM mainframe file formats, which has been a long-standing issue between XML documents generated and shared across ASCII and EBCDIC-based platforms. XML 1.1 parsers are required to recognize and accept EBCDIC line-end characters (#x85) and the Unicode line separator (#x2028). These values should be converted to one of the XML 1.0 ASCII line-end characters-—linefeed (decimal 10, #xA), or carriage return (decimal 13, #xD).

The place that most XML developers may see and/or use the XML 1.1 line-end and character set rules will be when including hard-coded values in character or entity references. For example, if you want to hard-code a carriage return in an XML 1.0 document, the following hex character reference can be used:

```
<?xml version="1.0" encoding="UTF-8"?>
<LineEndExample>An example of a hard coded&#xD;new
line</LineEndExample>
```

The results look like this when parsed:

```
<?xml version="1.0" encoding="UTF-8"?>
<LineEndExample>An example of a hard coded
new line</LineEndExample>
```

In XML 1.1, you could also hard-code an EBCDIC value to be used on IBM mainframe systems. When parsed on non-IBM mainframe systems, the line end should be replaced with an XML 1.0 ASCII value.

```
<?xml version="1.1" encoding="UTF-8"?>
<LineEndExample>An example of a hard coded&#x85;IBM new
line</LineEndExample>
```

These results look like this when parsed:

```
<?xml version="1.1" encoding="UTF-8"?>
<LineEndExample>An example of a hard coded
IBM new line</LineEndExample>
```

Namespaces for XML 1.1The essential difference between the XML Namespaces 1.0 and 1.1 recommendations is the ability to "undeclare" a previously defined namespace declaration and its associated prefix. As with XML 1.1 updates, this is a change that will mostly affect XML parser and development tool developers, rather than the average XML application developer.

Being able to "undeclare" a namespace provides a more flexible and efficient way of managing and reusing namespaces and their prefixes. Namespaces are applicable to any nested elements above the namespace declaration. Being able to remove a prefix and/or re-declare it in another part of a large XML document has benefits in parser performance. It also provides an out for a document that may have the same namespace prefix defined to different namespaces.

Namespaces for XML 1.1 is a separate document at the W3C but is closely linked to the XML 1.1 Recommendation. XML 1.0 documents use XML Namespace 1.0 rules, and XML 1.1 documents use XML Namespace 1.1 recommendation rules.

XML 1.1 references

More information on XML 1.1 can be found at `http://www.w3.org/TR/2002/CR-xml11-20021015/`, the namespaces for XML 1.1 working draft can be found at `http://www.w3.org/TR/2002/WD-xml-names11-20020905/`, and the CHARMOD working draft can be found at `http://www.w3.org/TR/charmod`. Also, all of the links are located on the W3C XML core Working Group page at `http://www.w3.org/XML/Activity#core-wg`.

Summary

In this chapter, I've kept the examples to a minimum to illustrate the basics of technologies that make up the XML world. The concepts introduced here will be extended with real-world examples throughout the rest of the book.

I've also introduced you to the real changes in the XML 1.1 Recommendation. These changes will affect parsers and generators and those who develop them the most. XML 1.1 parsers will probably contain normalizing and non-normalizing parser classes for conversions of line endings and character sets, just as most XML 1.0 parsers contain validating and non-validating parser classes.

- ✦ An introduction to XML
- ✦ XML structure
- ✦ Working with well-formed XML documents
- ✦ Validating XML documents
- ✦ Character and entity references
- ✦ Changes in XML 1.1 and XML Namespaces 1.1

In the next few chapters, I'll dive much deeper into XML documents, and the components that make up well-formed XML documents, by showing some real-world examples of documents, how they are generated, how they can be combined, and how namespaces can track element parts of combined documents.

✦   ✦   ✦

XML Documents

In This Chapter

An example XML
document

Elements and
attributes

XML document
structure and syntax

International XML
with xml:lang

Keeping your space
with xml:space

XML namespaces

Element name tips

In the last chapter, I provided those of you who are new to
XML with an overview and history of XML and what it can
be used for. I covered an overview XML document syntax and
structure rules. I also provided some information on the latest
XML version, XML 1.1. Most developers probably found the
last chapter a bit dry, but as I've said before, a good grasp of
the basic XML concepts and theory are a necessary part of
XML. Skipping over the basics means missing pieces of the
puzzle throughout the rest of the book.

Now that I've shown you the basics, you can start applying
some of this knowledge with real-world, practical examples.
This chapter expands on the theory and concepts introduced
in the previous chapter. I'll introduce you to two example documents that contain many of the issues that confront an XML
programmer. The first document is a compilation of XML from
three sources. The second document separates and identifies
the three parts of the document using XML namespaces.

Along the way I'll introduce you to some predefined XML
attributes. I'll show you how to specify languages using the
xml:lang attribute, and how to preserve space and linefeed
settings in text data using the xml:space attribute.

An Example XML Document

Let's get right into an example. Listing 2-1 shows an example
XML document that provides some very good examples of
real-life XM document development issues. The example document is an assembly of XML documents from three sources.
The first part of the document is a custom XML format that
describes quotations. The quotations are from Shakespeare's
Macbeth. After the list of selected quotes from William
Shakespeare, then goes on to list three books that contain the
quotes that are available for purchase from Amazon.com, and
a Spanish translation of Macbeth, Romeo and Juliet, Hamlet,
and other volumes that are available from http://www.
elcorteingles.es. It should be noted that Amazon.com
provides a service that returns XML documents based on a

URL query, and the format that Amazon returns is what the elements nested under the Amazon element is based on. The elcorteingles book listing format and the quote listing, as well as other parts of the document that I've added to illustrate several features of XML element and attributes, are all developed as part of the quote application that I will be developing as this book progresses.

Listing 2-1: **An Example XML Document**

```
<?xml version="1.0" encoding="ISO-8859-1"?>
<quotedoc>
  <quotelist author="Shakespeare, William" quotes="4">
    <quote source="Macbeth" author="Shakespeare,
    William">When the hurlyburly's done, / When the battle's
    lost and won.</quote>
    <quote source="Macbeth" author="Shakespeare,
    William">Out, damned spot! out, I say!-- One; two; why,
    then 'tis time to do't ;--Hell is murky!--Fie, my lord,
    fie! a soldier, and afeard? What need we fear who knows
    it, when none can call our power to account?--Yet who
    would have thought the old man to have had so much blood
    in him?</quote>
    <quote source="Macbeth"  author="Shakespeare, William">Is
    this a dagger which I see before me, the handle toward
    my hand? Come, let me clutch thee: I have thee not, and
    yet I see thee still. Art thou not, fatal vision,
    sensible to feeling as to sight? or art thou but a
    dagger of the mind, a false creation, proceeding from
    the heat-oppressed brain?</quote>
    <quote source="Macbeth" author="Shakespeare, William">To-
    morrow, and to-morrow, and to-morrow, creeps in this
    petty pace from day to day, to the last syllable of
    recorded time; and all our yesterdays have lighted fools
    the way to dusty death. Out, out, brief candle! Life's
    but a walking shadow; a poor player, that struts and
    frets his hour upon the stage, and then is heard no
    more: it is a tale told by an idiot, full of sound and
    fury, signifying nothing. </quote>
    <quote/>
  </quotelist>
  <catalog items="4">
    <Amazon items="3">
      <product>
        <ranking>1</ranking>
        <title>Hamlet/MacBeth</title>
        <asin>8432040231</asin>
        <author>Shakespeare, William</author>
        <image>http://images.Amazon.com/images/
        P/8432040231.01.MZZZZZZZ.jpg</image>
        <small_image>http://images.Amazon.com/images/
         P/8432040231.01.TZZZZZZZ.jpg</small_image>
        <list_price>$7.95</list_price>
```

```
        <release_date>19910600</release_date>
        <binding>Paperback</binding>
        <availability/>
        <tagged_url>http://www.Amazon.com:80/exec/obidos/
         redirect?tag=associateid&amp;
         benztechnologies=9441&amp;
         camp=1793&amp;link_code=xml&amp;path=ASIN/8432040231
        </tagged_url>
      </product>
      <product>
        <ranking>2</ranking>
        <title>MacBeth</title>
        <asin>1583488340</asin>
        <author>Shakespeare, William</author>
        <image>http://images.Amazon.com/images/P/
         1583488340.01.MZZZZZZZ.jpg</image>
        <small_image>http://images.Amazon.com/images/P/
         1583488340.01.TZZZZZZZ.jpg</small_image>
        <list_price>$8.95</list_price>
        <release_date>19991200</release_date>
        <binding>Paperback</binding>
        <availability/>
        <tagged_url>http://www.Amazon.com:80/exec/obidos/
         redirect?tag=associateid&amp;benztechnologies=9441
         &amp;camp=1793&amp;link_code=xml&amp;path=ASIN/
         1583488340</tagged_url>
      </product>
      <product>
        <ranking>3</ranking>
        <title>William Shakespeare: MacBeth</title>
        <asin>8420617954</asin>
        <author>Shakespeare, William</author>
        <image>http://images.Amazon.com/images/P/
         8420617954.01.MZZZZZZZ.jpg</image>
        <small_image>http://images.Amazon.com/images/P/
         8420617954.01.TZZZZZZZ.jpg</small_image>
        <list_price>$4.75</list_price>
        <release_date>19810600</release_date>
        <binding>Paperback</binding>
        <availability/>
        <tagged_url>http://www.Amazon.com:80/exec/obidos/
         redirect?tag=associateid&amp;benztechnologies=9441
         &amp;camp=1793&amp;link_code=xml&amp;path=ASIN/
         8420617954</tagged_url>
      </product>
    </Amazon>

    <elcorteingles items="1">
      <product xml:lang="es">
        <titulo>Romeo y Julieta/Macbeth/Hamlet/Otelo/La
         fierecilla domado/El sueño de una noche de verano/
         El mercader de Venecia</titulo>
```

Continued

Listing 2-1 *(continued)*

```
        <isbn>8484036324</isbn>
        <autor>Shakespeare, William</autor>
        <imagen>http://libros.elcorteingles.es/producto/
         verimagen_blob.asp?ISBN=8449503639</imagen>
        <precio>7,59 &#x20AC;</precio>
        <fecha_de_publicación>6/04/1999
        </fecha_de_publicación>
        <Encuadernación>Piel</Encuadernación>
        <librourl>http://libros.elcorteingles.es/producto/
         libro_descripcion.asp?CODIISBN=8449503639</librourl>
      </product>
    </elcorteingles>
  </catalog>
</quotedoc>
```

XML Document Structure and Syntax

Let's start at the top and review the structure of the document, the element and attributes, and the syntax, applying what you learned in Chapter 1 into a real-world XML document context:

```
<?xml version="1.0" encoding="ISO-8859-1"?>
```

The XML declaration at the top of the document is an example of one of the most common formats of an XML declaration, with an XML version of 1.0 and an encoding style of ISO-8859-1 (Latin-1). The most common encoding format is UTF-8, but documents that contain certain characters used in Western European languages, such as Spanish accented characters, won't show correctly in browsers that have Western European encoding as the default if the XML document is formatted as UTF-8. Some non-English author's names and book titles can't be written to HTML without character transformation because they may include those special characters, so it's better to use the more specific ISO-8859-1 encoding to handle display correctly in browsers.

Keep in mind that the XML declaration is optional and is an optional element in a well-formed XML document. If the XML declaration is not present, the default XML version is 1.0, and the default encoding is UTF-8.

```
<quotedoc>
```

The `quotedoc` element is the root element for this document. As mentioned in the previous chapter, there can only be one root element in a well-formed XML document.

```
<quotelist author="Shakespeare, William" quotes="4">
```

The `quotelist` element defines not only the list of quotes that are nested inside the quotelist, but the attributes tell us that the author of the quotes in the quotelist is William Shakespeare, and that there are four quotes in the list. Although attributes can be used for many purposes, using them to define and extend descriptions of data, as I have here, is the best use.

Some relational databases and other XML data sources have chosen to use attributes to contain actual data values instead of data descriptions, which can be a mistake. When choosing between using elements or attributes for data storage, keep in mind that attributes in their native format are only intended to contain a single value, while element structures can contain multiple values through nested elements. Also, elements can represent structures in documents through nesting, and can be extended, while attributes are limited to the element they are contained in.

```
<quote source="Macbeth" author="Shakespeare,
 William">When the hurlyburly's done, / When the battle's
 lost and won.</quote>
<quote source="Macbeth" author="Shakespeare,
 William">Out, damned spot! out, I say!-- One; two; why,
 then 'tis time to do't ;--Hell is murky!--Fie, my lord,
 fie! a soldier, and afeard? What need we fear who knows
 it, when none can call our power to account?--Yet who
 would have thought the old man to have had so much blood
 in him?</quote>
<quote source="Macbeth"  author="Shakespeare, William">Is
 this a dagger which I see before me, the handle toward
 my hand? Come, let me clutch thee: I have thee not, and
 yet I see thee still. Art thou not, fatal vision,
 sensible to feeling as to sight? or art thou but a
 dagger of the mind, a false creation, proceeding from
 the heat-oppressed brain?</quote>
<quote source="Macbeth" author="Shakespeare, William">To-
 morrow, and to-morrow, and to-morrow, creeps in this
 petty pace from day to day, to the last syllable of
 recorded time; and all our yesterdays have lighted fools
 the way to dusty death. Out, out, brief candle! Life's
 but a walking shadow; a poor player, that struts and
 frets his hour upon the stage, and then is heard no
 more: it is a tale told by an idiot, full of sound and
 fury, signifying nothing. </quote>
```

The rest of the quotelist contains the actual quotes. We've chosen to include more information in attributes for each quote in case the document is parsed or transformed and added to another document. This way, as long as the element structure stays intact, the quote will always have information on the author and the book associated with it, no matter where the element ends up.

The quotes in this document are also a great example of the syntax rules that apply to elements but don't apply to text in XML documents. Note that most of the quotes have characters in the text that would generate errors if the same characters were in the element names, but are permissible as part of well-formed XML in text values. The second quote can also be adapted to show a good example of what attributes can contain, in this modified element:

```
<author quote="Out, damned spot! out, I say!-- One; two; why,
then 'tis time to do't ;--Hell is murky!--Fie, my lord, fie! a
soldier, and afeard? What need we fear who knows it, when none
can call our power to account?--Yet who would have thought the
old man to have had so much blood in him?">Shakespeare,
William</author>
```

Believe it or not, despite all the characters which may look to the naked eye like nonstandard characters that a parser would choke on in the quote attribute of the author element in the preceding example, this attribute is well-formed XML. The semicolons by themselves, the question marks, the commas, the dashes, and the exclamation points do not cause a problem for the W3C XML 1.0 recommendation. The only character that could potentially cause a problem is the apostrophe, or single quote, but because they are contained inside two double quotes, they pass the test for well-formed XML as well. The same rule works in reverse for double quotes that are contained in single quotes.

However, despite the fact that the quote contained in an attribute is well-formed XML, this does not mean that it is a good idea. In general, although parsers are getting better at parsing attributes and schemas are good at enforcing attribute rules, both are better at handling elements than they are attributes, so key pieces of payload data in XML documents should always be contained in text values, and items that help define and describe the data should be associated to the text data via attributes.

```
</quotelist>
<catalog items="4">
```

Next, I complete the quotelist section of the document by closing the quote element, and start the catalog section of the document by opening the catalog tag. The items attribute tells us that there are four listings in the catalog related to the Macbeth quotes.

```
<Amazon items="3">
```

The items attribute in the nested Amazon element of the catalog tells us that there are three items in the catalog that are available though links at Amazon.com. Next, the products are listed in the order that they were returned from a query to the Amazon XML feed site URL:

```
<product>
  <ranking>1</ranking>
  <title>Hamlet/MacBeth</title>
  <asin>8432040231</asin>
  <author>Shakespeare, William</author>
  <image>http://images.Amazon.com/images/P/
    8432040231.01.MZZZZZZZ.jpg</image>
   <small_image>http://images.Amazon.com/images/P/
     8432040231.01.TZZZZZZZ.jpg</small_image>
  <list_price>$7.95</list_price>
  <release_date>19910600</release_date>
  <binding>Paperback</binding>
  <availability/>
  <tagged_url>http://www.Amazon.com:80/exec/obidos/
    redirect?tag=associateid&amp;benztechnologies=9441
    &amp;camp=1793&amp;link_code=xml&amp;path=ASIN/
    8432040231</tagged_url>
</product>

<product>
  <ranking>2</ranking>
  <title>MacBeth</title>
  <asin>1583488340</asin>
  <author>Shakespeare, William</author>
  <image>http://images.Amazon.com/images/P/
    1583488340.01.MZZZZZZZ.jpg</image>
  <small_image>http://images.Amazon.com/images/P/
    1583488340.01.TZZZZZZZ.jpg</small_image>
  <list_price>$8.95</list_price>
  <release_date>19991200</release_date>
  <binding>Paperback</binding>
  <availability/>
  <tagged_url>http://www.Amazon.com:80/exec/obidos/
    redirect?tag=associateid&amp;benztechnologies=9441
    &amp;camp=1793&amp;link_code=xml&amp;path=ASIN/
    1583488340</tagged_url>
</product>

<product>
  <ranking>3</ranking>
  <title>William Shakespeare: MacBeth</title>
  <asin>8420617954</asin>
  <author>Shakespeare, William</author>
  <image>http://images.Amazon.com/images/P/
    8420617954.01.MZZZZZZZ.jpg</image>
  <small_image>http://images.Amazon.com/images/P/
    8420617954.01.TZZZZZZZ.jpg</small_image>
```

```
          <list_price>$4.75</list_price>
          <release_date>19810600</release_date>
          <binding>Paperback</binding>
          <availability/>
          <tagged_url>http://www.Amazon.com:80/exec/obidos/
           redirect?tag=associateid&amp;benztechnologies=9441
           &amp;camp=1793&amp;link_code=xml&amp;path=ASIN/
           8420617954</tagged_url>
       </product>
```

Each product listing contains a reference to a single book at the Amazon.com Website, and is in the standard, unmodified format of all XML documents that are returned from the site. Amazon also publishes a DTD and Schema for the generated data, but I will use my own validation formats for the documents that I produce. I will cover data validation in much more detail in the next chapter.

The XML format closely mirrors the information for the books that are on display in HTML documents at Amazon.com. The ranking tells us the order in which the items were returned from the Amazon.com search. The title is the book title. The ASIN is Amazon's unique identifier for a product, in the case of books; the ASIN is equivalent to the book's International Standard Book Number (ISBN), the unique identifier for all books in print. Next is a listing for the author, a link to small and regular size book cover images on the Amazon.com Website, the list price, the release date, the type of binding for the book, an indicator for availability, and a link to the HTML page for the book on the Amazon.com Website.

There are three important things to note in the Amazon product elements: empty elements, SML housekeeping, and entity references and special characters.

Empty elements

Note that the availability element takes this format:

```
<availability/>
```

This format for empty elements is added to Amazon.com book listings, but a value is not provided. Logic would dictate that an unused element should not be included in the output, but in the case of XML documents, unused and empty elements are often kept in XML output to accommodate a predefined data structure that is specified for data validation in a DTD or Schema.

XML housekeeping

The layout of the XML for each product is an example of good XML design. The sequence of the elements and the element names are logical, and all of the items that are represented on the Amazon HTML page for a book are equally represented in XML. The lack of attributes in the elements is probably due to the very simple string data types represented in the document.

Entity references and special characters

It's important to note the ampersand entity references (&) in the `tagged_URL` elements:

```
<tagged_url>http://www.Amazon.com:80/exec/obidos/redirect?tag=
associateid&amp;benztechnologies=9441&amp;camp=1793&amp;link_
code=xml&amp;path=ASIN/8420617954</tagged_url>
```

The ampersands are an important part of the URL queries on the Amazon site and are used to separate parameters that are passed to Amazon.com as part of the query. Code on the Amazon.com site parses the URL that is passed and uses the parameters to execute the query and retrieve the data. However, the ampersands in the text value of the `target_url` elements also cause the XML document not to be well formed. To remedy this, the predefined XML `&amp;` entity reference that I discussed in the special characters section of the previous chapter is used to store the XML, and when the document is parsed the original ampersands are replaced to look like this:

```
http://www.Amazon.com:80/exec/obidos/redirect?tag=associateid&
benztechnologies=9441&camp=1793&link_code=xml&path=ASIN/
8420617954
```

Next, closing the Amazon tag completes the listing of books at the Amazon site:

```
</Amazon>
```

International XML with xml:lang

The next item in the list is the `elcorteingles` listing of one book, as indicated by the `items` attribute:

```
<elcorteingles items="1">
```

`http://www.elcorteingles.es` is a Spanish language Website, based in Spain, that sells a variety of items, including Spanish translations of popular books and classics. We've added the `elcorteingles` reference to show the multilingual features of XML and provide an example of handling special characters in an XML document.

The XML document format we've chosen for the Spanish translation of Shakespeare's most popular works is based on the Amazon format, but the element names have been translated to Spanish. The `elcorteingles` and the product reference remain in English, because that information is universal across any language that the book record could be in, and I'm a native English speaker, so the universal language I've chosen in my documents is English. However, the rest of the document is in Spanish, so it makes sense that the elements for the Spanish text data are in Spanish too, in case this document ends up being reused in a Spanish language application or Website.

The language of the product element for the `elcorteingles` listing is defined by using one of the predefined XML attributes, `xml:lang`:

```
<product xml:lang="es">
```

Unicode renders the text based on a certain predetermined byte format, and `xml:lang` tells parsers to handle the text defined in a specific `xml:lang` element as using a special set of instructions for a specific language. Parsers will continue to follow those specific language rules in nested elements and attributes until either the element tag is closed or another `xml:lang` attribute is encountered.

Language codes can be defined in a variety of ways, some completely standardized, as in the case of the International Organization of Standardization (ISO) 639 language codes (make sure you use the two character ISO 639 codes and not the three character ISO 639-2 codes) and the ISO 3166 country codes, of which any combination is a legal `xml:lang` language identifier, a registered IANA name tag (which can be linguistic or computer languages), or you can make one up, using an x- or an X- as a prefix, as long as the name hasn't already been registered as part of the ISO or IANA languages. A complete listing of ISO language codes and country codes can be found at `http://www.iso.org`, and the IANA registered language names can be found at `http://www.iana.org`.

```
<titulo>Romeo y Julieta/Macbeth/Hamlet/Otelo/La fierecilla
  domado/El sueño de una noche de verano/ El mercader de
  Venecia</titulo>
<isbn>8484036324</isbn>
<autor>Shakespeare, William</autor>
<imagen>http://libros.elcorteingles.es/producto/
  verimagen_blob.asp?ISBN=8449503639</imagen>
<precio>7,59 &#x20AC;</precio>
<fecha_de_publicación>6/04/1999</fecha_de_publicación>
<Encuadernación>Piel</Encuadernación>
<librourl>http://libros.elcorteingles.es/producto/
  libro_descripcion.asp?CODIISBN=8449503639</librourl>
```

The `titulo` element is the book title, and the `isbn` element is the book's International Standard Book Number (ISBN), the unique identifier for all books in print, regardless of language or country. Next is a listing for the author (`autor`), a link to a small book cover image (`imagen`) on the `elcorteingles.es` Website, the list price (precio), the publication date (fecha_de_publicación), the type of binding for the book, and a link to the HTML page for the book on the elcorteingles.es Website (librourl).

One item worthy of note in this book record is that all the accented characters in the Spanish book record were accepted as part of the default ISO-8859-1 (Latin-1) character encoding for this document. However, one character provides us with another review of the entity references in the "Special Characters and Entity References" section of Chapter 1. The price (precio) of the book has an entity reference to the euro symbol, which is part of the price listing for Europe, but is a character that is unsupported by the document's ISO-8859-1 (Latin-1) character encoding. The entity reference to the %20AC hex character is combined with the XML entity reference format for hex characters (&#x):

```
<precio>7,59 &#x20AC;</precio>
```

And when the precio element is parsed, it looks like this:

```
<precio>7,59 ¤</precio>
```

Next, the product element tag for the elcorteingles listing is closed. Because the product element defined the xml:lang as Spanish (es), when it is closed, the default language of the document is restored.

```
</product>
    </elcorteingles>
```

Last but not least, the catalog and the quotedoc element tags are closed, which completes the quotedoc document:

```
    </catalog>
</quotedoc>
```

Keeping Your Space with xml:space

Aside from xml:lang, there is one more important predefined attribute in XML documents that can help maintain layout of source data that is being transported by XML: xml:space. For example, the original format for the third quote in the quotelist in Listing 2-1 is:

```
Is this a dagger which I see before me,
The handle toward my hand? Come, let me clutch thee:--
I have thee not, and yet I see thee still.
Art thou not, fatal vision, sensible
To feeling as to sight? or art thou but
A dagger of the mind, a false creation,
Proceeding from the heat-oppressed brain?
```

However, the XML document that I am using has stripped away the line formatting, and looks like this:

```
Is this a dagger which I see before me, the handle toward my
hand? Come, let me clutch thee: I have thee not, and yet I see
thee still. Art thou not, fatal vision, sensible to feeling as
to sight? or art thou but a dagger of the mind, a false
creation, proceeding from the heat-oppressed brain?
```

Because Shakespeare text is often formatted in a very particular way, the loss of the original formatting, and the inability of XML to restore the formatting to its original condition, is a problem. To maintain the text spacing through XML document manipulation and future reformatting, the `xml:space="preserve"` attribute can be used to make sure that the spacing and the line formats stay intact:

```
<quote source="Macbeth" author="Shakespeare, William"
xml:space="preserve">
Is this a dagger which I see before me,
The handle toward my hand? Come, let me clutch thee:--
I have thee not, and yet I see thee still.
Art thou not, fatal vision, sensible
To feeling as to sight? or art thou but
A dagger of the mind, a false creation,
Proceeding from the heat-oppressed brain?
</quote>
```

The `xml:space="default"` attribute can also be defined, but just for fun because it doesn't tell the parser to do anything it wouldn't do anyway. Unfortunately, even when the space attribute is set to `"preserve"`, the retention of text formatting is up to the parser, as there is nothing in the W3C XML document recommendation that specifically requires the `xml:space` attributes to be respected. This means that some parsers may ignore the `xml:space`, but most are good XML citizens and respect the text formatting if the `"preserve"` attribute is set.

One more item of note: The space that is defined around text but part of the text formatting is referred to as "whitespace" in XSL and parsing lingo, which I will be covering later in this book.

XML Namespaces

As mentioned in Chapter 1, XML namespaces are a method for separating and identifying XML elements that may have the same element name on the same page. Namespaces can also be used as specifications to describe specific types of data and other atrributes that are contained inside elements that use that namespace. I've added namespaces to the example in Listing 2-2 to illustrate how you can identify different segments of an XML document as different grouped entities using namespaces.

Listing 2-2: **An Example XML Document with Namespaces**

```
<?xml version="1.0" encoding="ISO-8859-1"?>
<quotedoc xmlns:qtlist="http://www.benztech.com/xsd/quotelist"
xmlns:azlist="http://www.benztech.com/xsd/amazonlist"
xmlns:ellist="http://www.benztech.com/xsd/elcorteingleslist">
  <qtlist:quotelist author="Shakespeare, William" quotes="4">
    <qtlist:quote source="Macbeth" author="Shakespeare,
    William">When the hurlyburly's done, / When the battle's
    lost and won.</qtlist:quote>
    <qtlist:quote source="Macbeth" author="Shakespeare,
    William">Out, damned spot! out, I say!-- One; two; why,
    then 'tis time to do't ;--Hell is murky!--Fie, my lord,
    fie! a soldier, and afeard? What need we fear who knows
    it, when none can call our power to account?--Yet who
    would have thought the old man to have had so much blood
    in him?</qtlist:quote>
    <qtlist:quote source="Macbeth" author="Shakespeare,
    William">Is this a dagger which I see before me, the
    handle toward my hand? Come, let me clutch thee: I have
    thee not, and yet I see thee still. Art thou not, fatal
    vision, sensible to feeling as to sight? or art thou but
    a dagger of the mind, a false creation, proceeding from
    the heat-oppressed brain?</qtlist:quote>
    <qtlist:quote source="Macbeth" author="Shakespeare,
    William">To-morrow, and to-morrow, and to-morrow, creeps
    in this petty pace from day to day, to the last syllable
    of recorded time; and all our yesterdays have lighted
    fools the way to dusty death. Out, out, brief candle!
    Life's but a walking shadow; a poor player, that struts
    and frets his hour upon the stage, and then is heard no
    more: it is a tale told by an idiot, full of sound and
    fury, signifying nothing. </qtlist:quote>
    <qtlist:quote/>
  </qtlist:quotelist>
  <catalog items="4">
    <azlist:amazon items="3">
      <azlist:product>
        <azlist:ranking>1</azlist:ranking>
        <azlist:title>Hamlet/MacBeth</azlist:title>
        <azlist:asin>8432040231</azlist:asin>
        <azlist:author>Shakespeare, William</azlist:author>
        <azlist:image>http://images.amazon.com/images/
        P/8432040231.01.MZZZZZZZ.jpg</azlist:image>
        <azlist:small_image>http://images.amazon.com/images/P
        /8432040231.01.TZZZZZZZ.jpg</azlist:small_image>
        <azlist:list_price>$7.95</azlist:list_price>
        <azlist:release_date>19910600</azlist:release_date>
        <azlist:binding>Paperback</azlist:binding>
        <azlist:availability/>
```

Continued

Listing 2-2 *(continued)*

```
      <azlist:tagged_url>http://www.amazon.com:80/exec/
      obidos/redirect?tag=associateid&amp;
      benztechnologies=9441&amp;camp=1793&amp;
      link_code=xml&amp;path=ASIN/8432040231
    </azlist:tagged_url>
  </azlist:product>
  <azlist:product>
    <azlist:ranking>2</azlist:ranking>
    <azlist:title>MacBeth</azlist:title>
    <azlist:asin>1583488340</azlist:asin>
    <azlist:author>Shakespeare, William</azlist:author>
    <azlist:image>http://images.amazon.com/images/P/
    1583488340.01.MZZZZZZZ.jpg</azlist:image>
    <azlist:small_image>http://images.amazon.com/images
    /P/1583488340.01.TZZZZZZZ.jpg</azlist:small_image>
    <azlist:list_price>$8.95</azlist:list_price>
    <azlist:release_date>19991200</azlist:release_date>
    <azlist:binding>Paperback</azlist:binding>
    <azlist:availability/>
    <azlist:tagged_url>http://www.amazon.com:80/exec
    /obidos/redirect?tag=associateid&amp;
    benztechnologies=9441&amp;camp=1793&amp;
    link_code=xml&amp;path=ASIN/1583488340
    </azlist:tagged_url>
  </azlist:product>
  <azlist:product>
    <azlist:ranking>3</azlist:ranking>
    <azlist:title>William Shakespeare:
    MacBeth</azlist:title>
    <azlist:asin>8420617954</azlist:asin>
    <azlist:author>Shakespeare, William</azlist:author>
    <azlist:image>http://images.amazon.com/images/P/
    8420617954.01.MZZZZZZZ.jpg</azlist:image>
    <azlist:small_image>http://images.amazon.com/images
    /P/8420617954.01.TZZZZZZZ.jpg</azlist:small_image>
    <azlist:list_price>$4.75</azlist:list_price>
    <azlist:release_date>19810600</azlist:release_date>
    <azlist:binding>Paperback</azlist:binding>
    <azlist:availability/>
    <azlist:tagged_url>http://www.amazon.com:80/exec/
    obidos/redirect?tag=associateid&amp;
    benztechnologies=9441&amp;camp=1793&amp;
    link_code=xml&amp;path=ASIN/8420617954
    </azlist:tagged_url>
  </azlist:product>
</azlist:amazon>
<ellist:elcorteingles.es items="1">
  <ellist:product xml:lang="es">
    <ellist:titulo>Romeo y Julieta/Macbeth/Hamlet/Otelo/
    La fierecilla domado/El sueño de una noche de
    verano/ El mercader de Venecia</ellist:titulo>
```

```
        <ellist:isbn>8484036324</ellist:isbn>
        <ellist:autor>Shakespeare, William</ellist:autor>
        <ellist:imagen>http://libros.elcorteingles.es/
         producto/verimagen_blob.asp?ISBN=8449503639
        </ellist:imagen>
        <ellist:precio>7,59 &#x20AC;</ellist:precio>
        <ellist:fecha-de-publicación>6/04/1999</ellist:fecha-
         de-publicación>
        <ellist:Encuadernación>Piel</ellist:Encuadernación>
        <ellist:librourl>http://libros.elcorteingles.es/
         producto/libro_descripcion.asp?CODIISBN=8449503639
        </ellist:librourl>
      </ellist:product>
    </ellist:elcorteingles.es>
  </catalog>
</quotedoc>
```

In this example, the XML document uses three namespaces as identifiers to differentiate three separate sections of grouped data in the same document. The `xmlns:` attribute declares the namespace for an XML document or a portion of an XML document. The attributes that declare namespaces can be placed in the root element of the document, as in this case, or in any nested element:

```
xmlns:qtlist="http://www.benztech.com/xsd/quotelist"
xmlns:azlist="http://www.benztech.com/xsd/amazonlist"
xmlns:ellist="http://www.benztech.com/xsd/elcorteingleslist"
```

The document is divided into three separate sections: one for the quote listing, which will be identified by the `qtlist` Namespace, one for the Amazon list of books, which uses the `azlist` namespace prefix, and one for the elcorteingles list, which is identified by the `ellist` namespace prefix.

In the document itself, the segments of the document that correspond to the namespaces are identified by XML element prefixes. For example, the prefix for the quote list looks like this:

```
<qtlist:quotelist author="Shakespeare, William" quotes="4">
```

Closing tags must also contain a corresponding `Namespace` prefix for well-formed XML:

```
</qtlist:quotelist>
```

Often the URL in the namespace also resolves to a Website that provides documentation about the namespace, or information about the encoding types identified in the namespace, and so on. However, in this case, the URLs do not resolve to an actual document, but are used as a placeholder when declaring namespace names, which can be used at a future date for documentation if it is needed.

When to use namespaces

The namespaces in this example perform the basic function of namespaces to act as identifiers to group together logical segments of the XML document. Other XML-based technologies such as XML Schemas, SOAP, and WSDL make heavy use of XML namespaces to identify data encoding types and important elements of their structure. I'll be showing many more examples of namespaces being used in context to identify elements for data validation in the next chapter, and examples of namespaces used for encoding, and descriptions of SOAP and WSDL documents in the Web Services section of the book. For now, let's look at the namespaces and how namespaces affect XML document structure.

Namespaces are useful in identifying sections of documents that are being parsed, transformed, or manipulated in some other way. The parser or transformation engine can identify groups of elements and attributes by their namespace prefix instead of by their element values alone, and this helps to keep logical portions of an XML document together during manipulation.

URIs, URLs, and URNs

In order to understand namespaces, developers must first understand one of their basic components, URIs. HTTP URIs (Uniform Resource Identifiers) are a format specification for Uniform Resource Locators (URLs), which anyone who uses the Web is probably already familiar with, and Uniform Resource Names (URNs), which they may not be. The main difference is that URLs are used to specify a location-specific resource on the Web, such as `http://www.ibm.com`, while URNs are used to describe any value, such as a relative /servlet subdirectory or a variable name. URNs and URLs can be assigned to a URI. In the case of namespaces, URNs are usually used to mask a complicated `Namespace` or value for later reference, similar to the way DNS replaces an IP address with a URL.

For example, we could have used the following URNs for namespace references:

```
xmlns:qtlist="http://www.benztech.com/xsd/quotelist"
xmlns:azlist="fred"
xmlns:ellist="This is a urn, part of a uri"
```

The URIs in the declarations here are qtlist, azlist, and ellist. The first namespace declaration, assigned to the qtlist, is clearly a URL. The second assignment to the azlist is a URN. The last namespace declaration assigned to the ellist URI is a valid URN, but is formatted to make an important point. The URN value of the namespace can contain anything that the W3C namespace Recommendation allows, but because the URI will be used in element names, it has to adhere to the W3C XML document element name rules for characters. ellist is fine as a URI, but a URI formatted as ellist is not well-formed XML.

After defining URLs and URNs to the namespaces, the next task for developers it to assign the URIs to elements in the XML document. We've added the qtlist, azlist, and ellist URIs as prefixes to specific elements in the sample document in Listing 2-2.

It's worth noting that we specifically excluded the root quotedoc and the catalog elements in the document from `Namespaces`, because they are not part of any logical segment of the document, but just contain the logical segments. Therefore, anything that happens to them during XML document manipulation does not affect the other logical groupings that they contain.

More information on namespaces, including features in the new namespaces for XML 1.1, currently at the "Working Draft" stage of the XML Recommendation process, can be found at `http://www.w3.org/TR/2002/WD-xml-names11-20020905`.

Element Name Tips

A discussion of element and attribute names in the real world would not be complete without a mention of a couple of important element and attribute formatting issues. We've added a couple of XML booby traps into the ellist Namespace grouping:

```
<ellist:elcorteingles.es items="1">
      <ellist:product xml:lang="es">
      <ellist:titulo>Romeo y Julieta/Macbeth/Hamlet/Otelo/La
fierecilla domado/El sueño de una noche de verano/ El mercader
de Venecia</ellist:titulo>
      <ellist:isbn>8484036324</ellist:isbn>
      <ellist:autor>Shakespeare, William</ellist:autor>

<ellist:imagen>http://libros.elcorteingles.es/producto/verimage
n_blob.asp?ISBN=8449503639</ellist:imagen>
      <ellist:precio>7,59 &#x20AC;</ellist:precio>
      <ellist:fecha-de-publicación>6/04/1999</ellist:fecha-
de-publicación>
      <ellist:Encuadernación>Piel</ellist:Encuadernación>

<ellist:librourl>http://libros.elcorteingles.es/producto/libro_
descripcion.asp?CODIISBN=8449503639</ellist:librourl>
      </ellist:product>
 </ellist:elcorteingles.es>
```

The dangers lurking in this segment of the XML document look perfectly normal and are technically part of well-formed XML documents, but are accidents waiting to happen. The first one is hidden in this line:

```
<ellist:elcorteingles.es items="1">
```

Note that the element name contains a period, which resolves the element name to the `elcorteingles.es` Website. While this is acceptable as well-formed XML, it is a problem for some destination data formats, which may recognize this element name as the `es` method of the `elcorteingles` class, and try to resolve it as such.

Also, most relational databases will have formatting issues with this element name if it is intended to be added to a RDBMS system as a field or item name.

The second problem is here:

```
<ellist:fecha-de-publicación>6/04/1999</ellist:fecha-de-
publicación>
```

The dash that is substituting spaces in the fecha de publicación (publication date) element name has similar issues to the period in the previous example. In this case, the destination system accepting the value may try to subtract the values from each other, or if the element name is intended to become a field name in an RDBMS system, the dashes would probably cause errors.

In each case, it's best and safest to go with underscores to define the elements:

```
<ellist:elcorteingles_es items="1">
```

```
<ellist:fecha_de_publicación>6/04/1999</ellist:fecha-de-
publicación>
```

The preceding examples are also well-formed XML and will probably not have any issues when arriving at their intended destination.

Summary

In this chapter, I expanded on the theory in the previous chapter to show some real-world applications of XML via practical examples, but this is only half of the XML document story.

✦ An introduction to real-world XML document structure and syntax

✦ Specifying the language of XML data using xml:lang

✦ Formatting text data using xml:space

✦ Real-world XML namespace examples

✦ Entity references in test data—URLs

✦ Tips for naming elements and attributes

In the next chapter I'll show you how to validate XML documents using DTDs, and Schemas. I'll show you how to make sure that XML documents not only conform to XML document syntax and structure specifications, but also make sense from a data point of view.

✦   ✦   ✦

XML Data Format and Validation

In the last chapter, you were introduced to XML syntax and the requirements of well-formed XML using real-world example XML documents. This chapter will build on the example XML documents introduced in Chapter 2 to describe ways to make sure that XML documents are not just well formed, but also contain data in a predefined format, and how to enforce the rules that make up the predefined format.

XML is an excellent transport medium for sharing data across systems and platforms. However, well-formed XML documents that adhere only to the basic XML syntax rules are very easy to generate at the source, but usually very hard to read at their destination without some kind of a description of the structure represented in the XML document. This is where XML validation comes in.

XML document formatting rules that are in addition to the basic XML syntax rules are described and enforced through a process called XML validation. XML validation uses a separate document that is passed with the XML document, or published and stored separately at a URL. The validation document describes the data structure and format that is contained in the XML document.

XML validation documents are usually produced at the same time and from the same source as an XML document. XML documents can reference the validation document as part of the elements and/or attributes in that document, and are used by parsers to make sure that the XML document meets the criteria described in the validating document. If the XML document is well formed and the parser is able to determine that the XML document meets the structure and format requirements described in the validating document, the document is said to be valid XML.

The two most common types of data validation are Document Type Definitions (DTDs) and W3C XML Schemas. DTDs and Schemas are documents that describe the contents of XML documents and are used for XML validation. DTDs are text documents that describe data formats in other XML documents but are not formatted in XML. Schemas are the next generation of data validation formats, and like DTDs they describe data formats in other XML documents, but unlike DTDs, Schemas themselves are formatted in XML. Schemas can also go into much more detail in describing the structure and format of XML.

The concept of valid XML can extend from a single document format shared between two organizations with a common validation document, to a published validation format for specific types of data represented as XML.

For example, even though the W3C reviews and declares industry Schema standards as recommendations, there is no official central registry of XML validation documents. XML.org has published a DTD/Schema registry that comes close, at `http://www.xml.org/xml/registry.jsp`. A search of "News" at the XML.org DTD/Schema registry returns a link to XMLnews.org at `http://www.xmlnews.org`, the publishers of the NewsML format. NewsML is a standardized XML format for news content developed by the International Press Telecommunications Council (IPTC), a consortium of news providers, including Associated Press, Reuters, Dow Jones, the Newspaper Association of America, the *New York Times,* and many other household-name news providers. Part of NewsML is two DTDs. The XMLNews-Meta DTD describes requirements for valid metadata related to a news item, and the XMLNews-Story DTD describes the structure of a NewsML story. Third-party news content developers can use these DTDs to create and share NewsML formatted news stories between Websites and content syndicators, vastly improving compatibility for News content delivery on the Web.

The XML.org DTD/Schema registry also provides a great example of that old saying that "The great thing about standards is that there are so many of them." It doesn't take a lot of imagination to see that anyone who controls the most popular valid XML format for an industry can wield a lot of power over that industry as XML develops. Competing standards bodies as well as competing companies are pushing to make their own brand of valid XML the "standard" for an industry, and as a result there are several competing formats vying for first place in the valid XML popularity contest. This has resulted in several valid XML formats for many key industries to be listed side by side in the XML.org DTD/Schema registry. It's up to the developer to decide which one suits their needs, if any, based on industry support, ease of reference, and quality of documentation.

The proliferation of standards is complicated by the fact that version control of XML validation document references is difficult; once thousands of documents have been produced that conform to a certain DTD or Schema, it's very difficult to re-factor the old documents to conform to a new Schema. For this reason alone it's likely that DTDs will be around for many years to come, despite more data control, better readability, and more advanced features in Schemas.

XML Parsers for Data Validation

There is no valid XML without a parser, just a reference to a validation document in an XML document. XML parsers read an XML document and split apart the elements, attributes, and text data to create a representation of the document that can be used for integration into other data types. A parser's first task is to check an XML document's syntax and make sure the document is well formed. The second task for some parsers is to look for a validation document reference in the XML document and validate the XML document based on the document description in the validation document. Parsers that perform the validation step are called validating parsers, while parser that don't are called non-validating parsers.

Cross-Reference For a full description of parsers, including a listing of validating and non-validating parsers, please see to Chapter 7, "XML Parsing Concepts."

Document Type Definitions

DTDs (Document Type Definitions) were originally developed as part of SGML, and then extended to the W3C HTML recommendation to declare which specification an HTML document uses. Web browsers, HTML editors, and other programs that validate the syntax of HTML documents use an optional reference at the top of an HTML page to identify the HTML version for page rendering and validation purposes. DTDs were extended to function as XML validation documents as part of the W3C XML 1.0 recommendation in 1998.

Original DTD development was done by hand, and many DTDs are still edited this way. Hand-crafting DTDs using a text editor that doesn't check syntax and testing DTD development by running a validating parser against the XML document and watching for errors is, thankfully, becoming an anachronism. There are now many tools on the market that can help developers generate DTDs based on sample documents, and DTD editors that can check syntax while a document is being created. A good listing of DTD editors can be found on the XML.com Website at `http://www.xml.com/pub/pt/2`. Most of the DTD tools listed are free or have free trial downloads available. Most of the DTDs in this chapter were edited using Altova's xmlspy 5 Enterprise edition. A trial version xmlspy can be downloaded from `http://www.altova.com`.

Listing 3-1 shows the DTD that I will be using as an example for this chapter. The AmazonMacbethSpanish.dtd is referenced and validates the contents of the AmazonMacbethSpanishwithDTDref.xml document.

On The Web All of the DTDs and XML documents in this chapter can be downloaded from the xmlprogrammingbible.com Website.

Listing 3-1: **Contents of AmazonMacbethSpanish.dtd**

```
<?xml version="1.0" encoding="UTF-8"?>
<!-- edited with XMLSPY v5 rel. 2 U (http://www.xmlspy.com) by
Brian Benz (Wiley) -->
<!ELEMENT quotedoc (quotelist, catalog)>
<!ELEMENT quotelist (quote+)>
<!ATTLIST quotelist
  author CDATA #REQUIRED
  quotes CDATA #REQUIRED
>
<!ELEMENT quote (#PCDATA)>
<!ATTLIST quote
  source CDATA #IMPLIED
  author CDATA #IMPLIED
>
<!ELEMENT catalog (amazon, elcorteingles)>
<!ATTLIST catalog
  items CDATA #REQUIRED
>
<!ELEMENT amazon (product+)>
<!ATTLIST amazon
  items CDATA #REQUIRED
>
<!ELEMENT elcorteingles (product)>
<!ATTLIST elcorteingles
  items CDATA #REQUIRED
>
<!ELEMENT product (ranking?, (title | titulo)+, (asin | isbn)+,
(author | autor)+, (image | imagen)+, small_image?, (list_price
| precio)+, (release_date | fecha_de_publicación)+, (binding |
Encuadernación)+, availability?, (tagged_url | librourl)+)>
<!ATTLIST product
  xml:lang CDATA #IMPLIED
>
<!ELEMENT Encuadernación (#PCDATA)>
<!ELEMENT asin (#PCDATA)>
<!ELEMENT isbn (#PCDATA)>
<!ELEMENT author (#PCDATA)>
<!ELEMENT autor (#PCDATA)>
<!ELEMENT availability (#PCDATA)>
<!ELEMENT binding (#PCDATA)>
<!ELEMENT fecha_de_publicación (#PCDATA)>
<!ELEMENT image (#PCDATA)>
<!ELEMENT imagen (#PCDATA)>
<!ELEMENT librourl (#PCDATA)>
<!ELEMENT list_price (#PCDATA)>
<!ELEMENT precio (#PCDATA)>
<!ELEMENT ranking (#PCDATA)>
<!ELEMENT release_date (#PCDATA)>
```

```
<!ELEMENT small_image (#PCDATA)>
<!ELEMENT tagged_url (#PCDATA)>
<!ELEMENT title (#PCDATA)>
<!ELEMENT titulo (#PCDATA)>
```

Applying DTDs

The `AmazonMacbethSpanish.dtd` is referenced by adding a `DOCTYPE` declaration to the `AmazonMacbethSpanishwithDTDref.xml` document:

```
<!DOCTYPE quotedoc SYSTEM "AmazonMacbethSpanish.dtd">
```

The `!DOCTYPE` element is called a Document Type Declaration. This is not to be confused with the Document Type Definition that is contained in a DTD document, despite the same DTD acronym. There can be only one Document Type Declaration in an XML document, and the declaration must be placed below the XML declaration if there is one, and above all the other elements in the document. Validating parsers look for the declaration in that spot only, and validate the data based on the DTD reference.

The next item after `!DOCTYPE` is the element name for the Document Type Declaration. The element name is mandatory, and should always match the root element in the document. The element name specified in the Document Type Declaration becomes the starting point for a parser to validate the XML document using the DTD.

PUBLIC and SYSTEM source references

There are two possible sources for Document Type Declarations, `SYSTEM` and `PUBLIC`.

The most widely used Declaration source is `SYSTEM`. Then `SYSTEM` is used, the reference to the DTD can be a URL or a file system reference. For example, if the DTD is located in the c:\temp directory of the developer's workstation, the reference would look like this:

```
"C:/temp/AmazonMacbethSpanish.dtd"
```

Or if the workstation has access to the Web, the original DTD could be referenced at

```
"http://xmlprogrammersbible.com/DTDs/AmazonMacbethSpanish.dtd"
```

Either format is a valid DTD reference, as long as the file path resolves to well-formed DTD document.

The second type of Document Type Declaration source is PUBLIC and is rarely used. You probably just need to know about PUBLIC sources in case you see one in an older XML document or documentation. PUBLIC sources refer to relative or mapped directories where the DTD can be located, and are usually for use within an organization or as part of a VPN. PUBLIC sources must also have a backup SYSTEM source, and are therefore generally redundant. For example, a Document Type Declaration with a PUBLIC source would combine our two previous examples:

<!DOCTYPE quotedoc PUBLIC "C:/Program Files/Altova/XMLSPY/Examples/ XMLBible/AmazonMacbethSpanish.dtd" "http://xmlprogrammersbible.com/DTDs/ AmazonMacbethSpanish.dtd">

Note that the SYSTEM source is not specifically declared, but implied, based on the relative positioning in the declaration, just after the PUBLIC declaration.

Including DTDS in XML documents

The standalone attribute of the XML declaration has not been covered in the book so far, and for good reason. Like the PUBLIC source DTD declaration, it's another legacy DTD feature that can be used, but is not recommended. It is only mentioned here so you can recognize it if you see it in older XML documents or as part of an older validation system. To most novice XML developers, simple XML documents with a simple DTD embedded in them looks like a good idea, because the validation criteria can be transported with the XML data as a unit to the destination. But including DTDs in standalone XML documents makes the documents bloated and hard to read, and represent a maintenance nightmare if a centralized DTD is ever implemented or edited, and actually defeats the purpose of validating data in the first place. XML validation should be done against a standardized DTD that validates all documents. If each XML document has its own DTD based on the data in that document, it is always valid, even if it no longer suits the purpose of the destination application.

To include a DTD in an XML document, use the standalone attribute:

```
<?xml version="1.0" encoding="ISO-8859-1" standalone="yes"?>
```

The standalone attribute in the XML declaration tells parsers that everything needed for this document is contained in the document. The standalone attribute is optional, and rarely used. Not including the standalone attribute is the same as declaring standalone="no" in the XML declaration, meaning that if there is a reference to a validation document, it is outside of the current XML document.

XML documents with the standalone attribute do not specify a SYSTEM or PUBLIC source. Instead, the DTD is nested between square brackets in the Document Type Declaration:

```
<?xml version="1.0" encoding="ISO-8859-1" standalone="yes"?>
<!DOCTYPE quotedoc
[<!ELEMENT quotedoc (quotelist, catalog)>.......]
```

Note that the root element name for the XML document must still be declared, even in a standalone XML document. After the DTD, the root element starts the XML document:

```
<quotedoc>
  <quotelist author="Shakespeare, William" quotes="4">.....
```

The above example has been truncated for brevity. The full example document is a combination of the XML document from Chapter 2 and the DTD from Listing 3-1. The file name is AmazonMacbethSpanishwithinternalDTD.xml, and can be downloaded from the xmlprogrammersbible.com Website.

DTD structure

Now that you have an understanding of how to reference a DTD, the next step is to understand how DTDs describe XML documents. The first element in a DTD is usually an XML declaration, even though most of the other elements in a DTD do not look like well-formed XML. This is due to the special syntax rules for DTD documents. Each element in a DTD must have an exclamation mark as the first character in the element name. All other XML syntax rules apply to the element name.

DTD declarations

There are four declarations that can be used in DTDs: ELEMENT, ATTLIST, ENTITY, and NOTATION. Although the elements conform to the rules of well-formed XML, in a DTD elements that start with a ! are referred to as DTD declarations. This is to separate the description of XML documents from the documents themselves, and also because one of the four declaration types is called ELEMENT, and references to the ELEMENT element would make DTD documentation start to sound like Monty Python's "Department of redundancy department" sketch.

The ELEMENT declaration describes XML document elements and optional nested elements. The ATTLIST declaration describes XML document attributes and optional values. The ENTITY declaration describes special characters and references to variables, and is the same as the entity references in XML documents that I discussed in Chapter 2. The Notation declaration is used to contain references to external data such as URLs to an image in a DTD. In addition, comments can be contained in a DTD using the same format as XML document comments.

It's worth noting that the DTD I am using in this example is edited, but not generated by, xmlspy. While xmlspy has a very good facility for generating DTDs, probably the best on the market, in this case a DTD already existed that was much simpler than the one generated by xmlspy. Naturally, the simpler and more read-able DTD was chosen and cleaned up using xmlspy's editor. The moral of the story is that even though many tools can generate DTDs, developers still need to know something about DTD structure if they want to make sure that the DTD that was generated is doing the best job possible in validating XML document data, or to repurpose a generated DTD if there is a problem with it. In other words, you can't skip this chapter just because you know about tools that generate DTDs!

The example DTD in Listing 3-1 starts with an XML declaration then contains a comment that tells us that this DTD was edited using xmlspy. Note that the DTD comment format is the same as an XML document comment format:

```
<?xml version="1.0" encoding="UTF-8"?>
<!-- edited with XMLSPY v5 rel. 2 U (http://www.xmlspy.com) by
Brian Benz (Wiley) -->
```

Next is a declaration for the root quotedoc element. The quotedoc element speci-fies two nested elements in an element list. The quotelist and catalog elements have to be present, and have to be in the order specified in the list under the quotedoc element, as specified by the comma separator:

```
<!ELEMENT quotedoc (quotelist, catalog)>
```

There are five ways to represent element structures in DTD documents, as shown in Table 3-1.

Table 3-1
DTD Element Structures

Representation	Description
<!ELEMENT quotedoc ANY >	The quotedoc element is mandatory, but any type of well-formed XML can be nested under quotedoc element, in any order.
<!ELEMENT quotedoc EMPTY>	The quotedoc element is mandatory, but cannot have any other elements nested under it. Attributes can be defined for the quotedoc element.
<!ELEMENT quotedoc (#PCDATA)>	The quotedoc element is mandatory, and can contain only text data, not nested elements. PCDATA stands for Parsed Character Data. Attributes can be defined for the quotedoc element. This format is known as the text-only content model.

Representation	Description
<!ELEMENT quotedoc (quotelist, catalog)> <!ELEMENT quotedoc (quotelist | catalog)>	The quotedoc element is mandatory and can contain only the elements specified, not text values. Attributes can be defined for all elements and text can be contained in nested elements, if the declaration for that element permits it. This format is known as the element-only content model. Comma-separated element lists are called sequence lists, and the XML document element order must match the order of the elements listed. Lists separated by the vertical bar (|) are called choice lists and the vertical bar is equivalent to a logical "or" operator, meaning one of the elements in the list must be present under the quotedoc element.
<!ELEMENT quotedoc can (#PCDATA | quotelist, catalog)>	The quotedoc element is mandatory and can contain the elements specified and/or text values. Attributes can be defined for all elements and text can be contained in nested elements as well, if the declaration for that element permits it. This format is known as the mixed content model.

The next line in the DTD provides an example of the element cardinality, as specified by the "+" cardinality operator:

```
<!ELEMENT quotelist (quote+)>
```

There are four ways to specify how many times an element can appear under the current element, represented by three cardinality operators and a default rule, as shown in Table 3-2.

Table 3-2
DTD Cardinality Operators

Cardinality Rule	Description
`<!ELEMENT quotelist (quote+)>`	The `quote` element is a required child element of the `quotelist` element. There can be one or more `quote` child elements under the `quotelist` element.
`<!ELEMENT quotelist (quote?>`	The `quote` element is an optional child element of the `quotelist` element. If it is present, there can be only one `quote` child element under the `quotelist` element.
`<!ELEMENT quotelist (quote*)>`	The `quote` element is an optional child element of the `quotelist` element. If it is present, there can any number of `quote` child elements under the `quotelist` element.
`<!ELEMENT quotelist (quote)>`	(default) The `quote` element is a required child element of the `quotelist` element. There can be only one `quote` child element under the `quotelist` element.

Next in the example DTD is the attribute list for the `quotelist` element, which indicates that there are two required attributes containing character data:

```
<!ATTLIST quotelist
   author CDATA #REQUIRED
   quotes CDATA #REQUIRED
>
```

Table 3-3 shows the list of keywords that control attributes in DTDs, which are called attribute declaration keywords.

Table 3-3
DTD Attribute Declaration Keywords

Declaration Keyword	Description
No declaration Keyword (default) author CDATA quotes CDATA "0"	The `author` attribute is optional. If no `quotes` attribute value is specified when the document is parsed, a 0 value can be added to the XML document.
#IMPLIED author CDATA #IMPLIED	The `author` attribute is optional.

Declaration Keyword	Description
#FIXED author CDATA #FIXED "Shakespeare, William"	The `author` attribute is optional in the XML document but is specified in the DTD. When the XML document is parsed, the `author` attribute value is checked to make sure it matched the value specified in the DTD. If there is no attribute value in the XML document, the value is automatically supplied from the DTD instead of generating a parser error.
#REQUIRED author CDATA #REQUIRED	The `author` attribute is required and must be supplied in the XML document.

In addition to the attribute declaration keywords, there are several additional ways to control the type of data that are contained in the attribute value. CDATA is the most common data type for DTDs. IDs are used occasionally, and the rest of the data types are used and seen infrequently, but it's good to know about them, just in case you have a need for them or have to understand a DTD that uses them. Table 3-4 shows the available list of attribute data types in DTDs, and compatible attribute declaration keywords.

Table 3-4
DTD Attribute Data Types

Data Type	Description
CDATA author CDATA author CDATA "Shakespeare, William" author CDATA #IMPLIED author CDATA #FIXED "Shakespeare, William" author CDATA #REQUIRED	Character data. The most common attribute description. All types of attribute declaration keywords can be used with cdata.
NMTOKEN/NMTOKENS author NMTOKEN author NMTOKEN "William Shakespeare" author NMTOKEN #IMPLIED author NMTOKENS #IMPLIED author NMTOKEN #FIXED "William Shakespeare" author NMTOKEN #REQUIRED author NMTOKENS #REQUIRED	NMTOKEN is more restrictive than CDATA, which can contain any character data. NMTOKEN attribute values must conform to the rules of well-formed XML names. NMTOKENS can refer to a multiple value list of choices that are specified in the XML document attribute by a single space. All values must conform to the rules of well-formed XML names.

Continued

Table 3-4 *(continued)*

Data Type	Description
ENTITY/ENTITIES Entity References: <!ENTITY bookimage SYSTEM "http://images.amazon.com/images/P/8432040231.01.MZZZZZZZ.jpg"> <!ENTITY small_bookimage SYSTEM "http://images.amazon.com/images/P/8432040231.01.TZZZZZZZ.jpg"> Attribute references: <!ATTLIST quotelist bookimage ENTITY> <!ATTLIST quotelist bookimages ENTITIES>	DTD entity attribute data types are similar to XML document entity references in the sense that they let you link to data that is outside the scope of the current document. Attribute entity references are most commonly used to link to images that must be included in an XML document, but that you want to specify the location of in a centralized document. Entities are not parsed, but referenced. In the XML document, the attribute value of `bookimage` can be used to refer to the entity references show on the left, instead of the full URL. If the URL changes, the reference in the DTD can be updated centrally with the new URL. References to multiple images are formatted in an XML document attribute by using the `bookimages` attribute name and specifying entity names separated by a space.
NOTATION <!ENTITY w3cwebsite SYSTEM "http://www.w3c.org"> <!NOTATION text_html SYSTEM "http://www.iana.org/assignments/media-types/text/html"> <!ATTLIST quotelist w3cwebsite ENTITY text_html NOTATION >	DTD NOTATION attribute data types specify methods for handling non-parsed data, which is represented as Entitles in attributes. The example on the left shows an entity declaration that represents the URL for the W3C home page. Notation for the Internet Assigned Numbers Authority (IANA) mime type definition for HTML is shown in the notation element. The ATTLIST shows a reference to the w3cwebsite entity and a reference to notation for the handling of the entity reference. Parsers will not parse the entity, but will pass on the reference and the notation to the XML document destination.

Data Type	Description
ID quoteid ID #REQUIRED	A unique value of Character data. For example, to uniquely identity quotes in the document. In this example, a quoteid attribute is attached to each quote element that uniquely identifies that quote in the XML document. ID attributes should never use the #FIXED attribute declaration, and should not be #IMPLIED, or optional in any other way, to ensure each element contains an attribute with a unique identifier.
IDREF/IDREFS quotelist ID attribute: <!ATTLIST quotelist author ID #REQUIRED > quote IDREF: <!ATTLIST quote author IDREF #REQUIRED > -or- <!ATTLIST quote author IDREFS #REQUIRED >	IDREFS can refer to an ID data type in an XML document on a one-to-one or one-to-many basis, and are used to define relationships between elements that are not explicitly linked together in the document through attributes. For example, you may want to enforce that a quotelist contains quotes by a certain author or list of authors. The quotelist could have an ID attribute, as shown on the left. Next, the quote could refer to the quotelist ID for the author name, or in the second example, to one or more authors in the quotelist author ID attribute.

In addition to the data types here, a predefined choice list of attribute values can be manually specified. For example, an attribute that is restricted to be either William Shakespeare or Geoffrey Chaucer in lastname, firstname format could be explicitly defined like this:

```
<!ATTLIST quotelist
author (Shakespeare, William | Chaucer, Geoffrey)
>
```

Choices are separated by a vertical bar character (|). Note that unlike the ELEMENT declaration, the commas are not part of the order specification for the choices, they are treated as a part of a choice in a list.

While the first few elements provided opportunities to introduce you to the basic declarations and syntax of DTD documents, the rest of the DTD provides additional examples of DTD descriptions of XML documents. The next element that is defined in the DTD is the `quote` element, which is a child of the `quotelist` element. The `quote` element has two optional attributes, `source` and `author`.

```
<!ELEMENT quote (#PCDATA)>
<!ATTLIST quote
  source CDATA #IMPLIED
  author CDATA #IMPLIED
>
```

The `catalog` element must contain two elements in sequence, starting with `amazon` and ending with `elcorteingles`. The `catalog` element has one required attribute, called `items`, which contains a count of the items in the catalog:

```
<!ELEMENT catalog (amazon, elcorteingles)>
<!ATTLIST catalog
  items CDATA #REQUIRED
>
```

The `amazon` element contains one child element called `product`. The + cardinality operator indicates that there can be one or more `product` child elements under `amazon`:

```
<!ELEMENT amazon (product+)>
<!ATTLIST amazon
  items CDATA #REQUIRED
>
```

The `elcorteingles` element contains one child element called `product`. Because no cardinality operator is specified, there can be only one `product` child element under `elcorteingles`:

```
<!ELEMENT elcorteingles (product)>
<!ATTLIST elcorteingles
  items CDATA #REQUIRED
>
```

The next element declaration is a great example of the combination of the DTD element declaration, sequence and choice list operators, and cardinality operators working in concert to solve a tricky data validation problem. The XML document supports both English and Spanish translations in nested elements of the product element. Unfortunately, parsers have no way of automatically recognizing and translating the element names, so it's up to the DTD developer to make sure that all possibilities in both formats are covered as part of the validation process.

In this example, all elements that have English and Spanish translations are offered as choice lists components in a sequence list of nested elements under the `product` element. Each translation choice list is completed with the + cardinality operator outside of the braces that contain the list choices, which means that at least one instance of the element has to be present in one of the languages, and more instances are permissible. The Amazon.com `product` element also contains some nested elements that the elcorteingles `product` element does not. Those elements have been listed in sequence and end with a ? cardinality operator, indicating that the nested elements are optional, but if they are present they must be in the sequence specified in the listing. In summary, the product DTD element declaration enforces either an English product listing from Amazon.com, or a smaller Spanish listing from the elcorteingles.com Website.

```
<!ELEMENT product (ranking?, (title | titulo)+, (asin | isbn)+,
(author | autor)+, (image | imagen)+, small_image?, (list_price
| precio)+, (release_date | fecha_de_publicación)+, (binding |
Encuadernación)+, availability?, (tagged_url | librourl)+)>
```

There is one optional attribute for the product element, called `xml:lang`. The language of the `product` element for the elcorteingles listing is defined by using the predefined `xml:lang` attribute. In the DTD this is represented by an optional attribute for the product:

```
<!ATTLIST product
  xml:lang CDATA #IMPLIED
>
```

The rest of the elements have no children or attributes and are represented by PCDATA (Parsed Character Data) element declarations. Parent element declarations need these element declarations to be in the DTD. The PCDATA declaration indicates a text-only content model, which means that these elements can contain text and attributes but not nested elements.

```
<!ELEMENT Encuadernación (#PCDATA)>
<!ELEMENT asin (#PCDATA)>
<!ELEMENT isbn (#PCDATA)>
<!ELEMENT author (#PCDATA)>
<!ELEMENT autor (#PCDATA)>
<!ELEMENT availability (#PCDATA)>
<!ELEMENT binding (#PCDATA)>
<!ELEMENT fecha_de_publicación (#PCDATA)>
<!ELEMENT image (#PCDATA)>
<!ELEMENT imagen (#PCDATA)>
<!ELEMENT librourl (#PCDATA)>
<!ELEMENT list_price (#PCDATA)>
<!ELEMENT precio (#PCDATA)>
<!ELEMENT ranking (#PCDATA)>
<!ELEMENT release_date (#PCDATA)>
```

```
<!ELEMENT small_image (#PCDATA)>
<!ELEMENT tagged_url (#PCDATA)>
<!ELEMENT title (#PCDATA)>
<!ELEMENT titulo (#PCDATA)>
```

While DTDs are still in use and still often the data validation tool of choice for many XML developers, the W3C Schema promises, and in most cases, delivers, much more control over data validation than DTDs. In the next section of this chapter, I'll introduce you to Schemas and show how Schemas are structured and validate XML data.

W3C XML Schemas

Schemas are an updated document format for XML data validation. Schemas can be less cryptic than DTDs, but consequently are much more verbose, and are much easier to grasp for XML developers than DTD syntax because Schemas are more closely based on XML syntax. Nested elements are represented by nested elements, and attributes are assigned explicitly as part of the element. Cardinality operators, attribute data types, and choice lists are replaced by element representations and attribute keywords, and there is much more control over data types. The XML Schema 1.0 is an official W3C Recommendation as of May 2001, and XML 1.1 is in the works at the W3C. More information can be found at http://www.w3.org/TR/2001/REC-xmlschema-1-20010502.

A good listing of Schema editors can be found on the XML.com Website at http://www.xml.com/pub/pt/2. Most of the Schema tools listed are free or have free trial downloads available. As with the DTD example earlier in this chapter, this Schema example is edited using Altova's xmlspy (http://www.altova.com). I was also able to use xmlspy to translate the DTD used in the previous example to a Schema that almost worked. As with DTDs, xmlspy's W3C Schema generator is probably the best on the market, but there was one crucial item that xmlspy missed in the DTD to Schema translation that had to be added manually, which I will get into later in this chapter. The point is that as with DTDs, developers still need to know something about Schemas structure if they want to make sure that the Schema generated is the best format possible for validating XML document data, or to fix a generated Schema if there is a problem with it.

W3C Schema data types

DTDs were developed as part of the original SGML specifications, and extended to describe HTML markup as well. They are great as a legacy data validation tool, but have several drawbacks when applied to modern XML documents. DTDs require that elements be text, nested elements, or a combination of nested elements and text. DTDs also have limited support for predefined data types.

Schemas can support all of the DTD attribute data types (ID, IDREF, IDREFS, ENTITY, ENTITIES, NMTOKEN, NMTOKENS and NOTATION). CDATA, is replaced by the primitive string data type. Other data types can be used in a multitude of formats, as shown in Table 3-5

Table 3-5 Schema Data Types		
Name	**Base Type**	**Description**
String		
String	Primitive	Any well-formed XML string
normalizedString	string	Any well-formed XML string that also does not contain line feeds, carriage returns, or tabs.
Token	normalizedString	Any well-formed XML string that does not contain line feeds, carriage returns, tabs, leading or trailing spaces, or more than one space.
language	token	A valid language id, matching xml:lang format, which is usually International Organization of Standardization (ISO) 639 format.
QName	Primitive	XML namespace qualified name (Qname).
Name	token	A string based on well-formed element and tribute name rules.
NCName	name	The part of a namespace name to the right of the namespace prefix and colon.
Date		
date	Primitive	Date value in the format YYYY-MM-DD.
time	Primitive	Time value in the format HH:MM:SS.
dateTime	Primitive	Combined date and time value in the format YYYY-MM-DDT HH:MM:SS.
gDay	Primitive	The day part of a date in the format DD. Also the national greeting of Australia.
gMonth	Primitive	The month part of a date in the format MM.
gMonthDay	Primitive	The month and day part of a date in the format MM-DD.

Continued

Table 3-5 *(continued)*		
Name	**Base Type**	**Description**
gYear	Primitive	The month part of a date in the format YYYY.
gYearMonth	Primitive	The year and month part of a date in the format YYYY-MM.
duration	Primitive	Represents a time interval the ISO 8601 extended format P1Y1M1DT1H1M1S. This example represents one year, one month, one day, one hour, one minute, and one second.
Numeric		
number	Primitive	Any numeric value up to 18 decimal places.
decimal	Primitive	Any decimal value number.
float	Primitive	Any 32-bit floating-point type real number.
double	Primitive	Any 64-bit floating-point type real number.
integer	number	Any integer.
byte	short	Any signed 8-bit integer.
short	int	Any signed 16-bit integer.
int	integer	Any signed 32-bit integer.
long	integer	Any signed 64-bit integer.
unsignedByte	integer	Any unsigned 8-bit integer.
unsignedShort	unsignedInt	Any unsigned 16-bit integer.
unsignedInt	unsignedLong	Any unsigned 32-bit integer.
unsignedLong	nonNegativeInteger	Any unsigned 64-bit integer.
positiveInteger	nonNegativeInteger	Any integer with a value greater than 0.
nonPositiveInteger	integer	Any integer with a value less than or equal to 0.
negativeInteger	nonPositiveInteger	Any integer with a value less than 0.
nonNegativeInteger	integer	Any integer with a value greater than or equal to 0.

Name	Base Type	Description
Other		
anyURI	Primitive	Represents a URI, and can contain any URL or URN.
Boolean	Primitive	Standard binary logic, in the format of 1, 0, true, or false.
hexBinary	Primitive	Hex-encoded binary data
base64Binary	Primitive	Base64-encoded binary data.

Primitive and derived data types can be extended to create new data types. Data types that extend existing data types are called user-derived data types.

W3C Schema elements

Data types are formatted as attributes in element declarations of Schema documents, just as data types are usually defined by attributes in XML documents. Data types are contained in four types of elements:

✦ **Element declarations**: Describe an element in an XML document.

✦ **Simple type definitions:** Contain values in a single element, usually with attributes that define one of the primitive or derived W3C data types, but can contain user-derived data types as well.

✦ **Complex type definitions:** A series of nested elements with attributes that describe a complex XML document structure and primitive, derived, or user-derived data types.

✦ **Attribute declarations:** Elements that describe attributes and attributes that define a data type for the attribute.

Element declarations, simple type definitions, complex type definitions, and attribute declarations are all defined by declaring one or more of the Schema elements listed in Table 3-6 in a Schema document:

Table 3-6
Schema Elements

Element	Description
all	Nested elements can appear in any order. Each child element is optional, and can occur no more than one time.
annotation	Schema comments. Contains appInfo and documentation. appInfo: Information for parsing and destination applications - must be a child of annotation. documentation: Schema text comments; must be a child of annotation.
any	Any type of well-formed XML can be nested under the any element, in any order. Same as the DTD <!ELEMENT element_name ANY > declaration.
anyAttribute	Any attributes composed of well-formed XML can be nested under the anyAttribute element, in any order.
attribute	An attribute.
attributeGroup	Reusable attribute group for complex type definitions.
choice	A list of choices, one of which must be chosen. Same as using the vertical bar character (|) in a DTD choice list.
complexContent	Definition of mixed content or elements in a complex type.
complexType	Complex type element.
element	Element element.
extension	Extends a simpleType or complexType.
field	An element or attribute that is referenced for a constraint. Similar to the DTD IDREF attribute data type, but uses an XPATH expression for the reference.
group	A group of elements for complex type definitions.
import	Imports external Schemas with different Namespaces.
include	Includes external Schemas with the same Namespace.
key	Defines a nested attribute or element as a unique key. Same as the DTD ID attribute data type.
keyref	Refers to a key element. Same as the DTD IDREF attribute data type.
list	A list of values in a simple type element.
notation	Defines the format of non-parsed data within an XML document. Same as the DTD NOTATION attribute data type.

Element	Description
restriction	Imposes restrictions on a simpleType, simpleContent, or a complexContent element.
schema	The root element of every W3C Schema document.
selector	Groups a set of elements for identity constraints using an XPath expression.
sequence	Specifies a strict order on child elements. Same as using the comma to separate nested elements in a DTD sequence.
simpleContent	Definition of text-only content in a simple type.
simpleType	Declares a simple type definition.
union	Groups simple types into a single union of values.
unique	Defines an element or an attribute as unique at a specified nesting level in the document.

W3C Schema element and data type restrictions

Aside from the elements listed in Table 3-6, there are several other types of elements that define constraints on other elements in the Schema.

Data type properties, including constraints, on simple data types, are called facets. Simple data types can be constrained by fundamental facets, which specify fundamental constraints on the data type such as the order of display or the cardinality, much like using the DTD cardinality operators (+, ?, *), commas and vertical bar characters were used to predefine DTD element constraints. Constraining facets extend beyond predefined rules to control behavior based on Schema definitions. Table 3-7 shows a listing of W3C Schema fundamental facets that constrain simple data types.

Table 3-7
Schema Element Restrictions

Restriction	Description
choice	A list of choices predefined in the Schema document. Same as the DTD enumeration for attribute list data types.
fractionDigits	Maximum decimal placed for a value. Integers are 0.
length	Number of characters, or for lists, number of list choices.

Continued

	Table 3-7 *(continued)*
Restriction	**Description**
maxExclusive	Maximum up to, but not including the number specified.
maxInclusive	Maximum including the number specified.
maxLength	Maximum number of characters, or for lists, number of list choices.
minExclusive	Minimum down to, but not including the number specified.
minInclusive	Minimum including the number specified.
minLength	Minimum number of characters, or for lists, number of list choices.
pattern	Defines a pattern and sequence of acceptable characters.
totalDigits	Number of non-decimal, positive, non-zero digits.
whiteSpace	How line feeds, tabs, spaces, and carriage returns are treated when the document is parsed.

A listing of which constraints apply to which simple data types can be found as part of the W3C Schema Recommendation at `http://www.w3.org/TR/xmlschema-2`.

Namespaces and W3C Schemas

One of the additional features of Schemas is the ability to handle XML namespaces as part of the Schema. One of the best examples of this is the XML Schema Schema. Schema namespaces and data types are defined by a Schema that is referenced by the root element of every W3C Schema. The namespace declaration looks like this:

```
<xs:schema xmlns:xs="http://www.w3.org/2001/XMLSchema">
```

The URL, `http://www.w3.org/2001/XMLSchema`, actually resolves to document that links to the Schema Schema. The Schema specifies the elements and data types used in the Schema. It also is a very long Schema document that includes embedded DTDS, imported and included external Schemas, and just about every type of Schema situation imaginable. This makes it a great start for finding working examples of Schema structure and syntax.

An example W3C Schema document

Listing 3-2 shows the Schema that I will be using as an example for this chapter. The AmazonMacbethSpanish.xsd is referenced and validates the contents of the AmazonMacbethSpanishwithXSDref.xml document.

Listing 3-2: **Contents of AmazonMacbethSpanish.xsd**

```xml
<?xml version="1.0" encoding="UTF-8"?>
<!--W3C Schema generated by XMLSPY v5 rcl. 2 U
(http://www.xmlspy.com)-->
<xs:schema xmlns:xs="http://www.w3.org/2001/XMLSchema"
elementFormDefault="qualified">
  <xs:import namespace="http://www.w3.org/XML/1998/namespace"
   schemaLocation="http://www.w3.org/2000/10/xml.xsd"/>
  <xs:element name="Encuadernación" type="xs:string"/>
  <xs:complexType name="amazonType">
    <xs:sequence>
      <xs:element name="product" type="productType"
       maxOccurs="unbounded"/>
    </xs:sequence>
    <xs:attribute name="items" type="xs:string"
     use="required"/>
  </xs:complexType>
  <xs:element name="asin" type="xs:string"/>
  <xs:element name="author" type="xs:string"/>
  <xs:element name="autor" type="xs:string"/>
  <xs:element name="availability" type="xs:string"/>
  <xs:element name="binding" type="xs:string"/>
  <xs:complexType name="catalogType">
    <xs:sequence>
      <xs:element name="amazon" type="amazonType"/>
      <xs:element name="elcorteingles"
       type="elcorteinglesType"/>
    </xs:sequence>
    <xs:attribute name="items" type="xs:string"
     use="required"/>
  </xs:complexType>
  <xs:complexType name="elcorteinglesType">
    <xs:sequence>
      <xs:element name="product" type="productType"/>
    </xs:sequence>
    <xs:attribute name="items" type="xs:string"
     use="required"/>
  </xs:complexType>
  <xs:element name="fecha_de_publicación" type="xs:string"/>
  <xs:element name="image" type="xs:string"/>
  <xs:element name="imagen" type="xs:string"/>
  <xs:element name="isbn" type="xs:string"/>
  <xs:element name="librourl" type="xs:string"/>
  <xs:element name="list_price" type="xs:string"/>
  <xs:element name="precio" type="xs:string"/>
  <xs:complexType name="productType">
    <xs:sequence>
      <xs:element ref="ranking" minOccurs="0"/>
      <xs:choice maxOccurs="unbounded">
```

Continued

Listing 3-2 *(continued)*

```
            <xs:element ref="title"/>
            <xs:element ref="titulo"/>
        </xs:choice>
        <xs:choice maxOccurs="unbounded">
          <xs:element ref="asin"/>
          <xs:element ref="isbn"/>
        </xs:choice>
        <xs:choice maxOccurs="unbounded">
          <xs:element ref="author"/>
          <xs:element ref="autor"/>
        </xs:choice>
        <xs:choice maxOccurs="unbounded">
          <xs:element ref="image"/>
          <xs:element ref="imagen"/>
        </xs:choice>
        <xs:element ref="small_image" minOccurs="0"/>
        <xs:choice maxOccurs="unbounded">
          <xs:element ref="list_price"/>
          <xs:element ref="precio"/>
        </xs:choice>
        <xs:choice maxOccurs="unbounded">
          <xs:element ref="release_date"/>
          <xs:element ref="fecha_de_publicación"/>
        </xs:choice>
        <xs:choice maxOccurs="unbounded">
          <xs:element ref="binding"/>
          <xs:element ref="Encuadernación"/>
        </xs:choice>
        <xs:element ref="availability" minOccurs="0"/>
        <xs:choice maxOccurs="unbounded">
          <xs:element ref="tagged_url"/>
          <xs:element ref="librourl"/>
        </xs:choice>
      </xs:sequence>
      <xs:attribute ref="xml:lang" type="xs:string"/>
    </xs:complexType>
    <xs:complexType name="quoteType">
      <xs:simpleContent>
        <xs:extension base="xs:string">
          <xs:attribute name="source" type="xs:string"/>
          <xs:attribute name="author" type="xs:string"/>
        </xs:extension>
      </xs:simpleContent>
    </xs:complexType>
    <xs:element name="quotedoc">
      <xs:complexType>
        <xs:sequence>
```

```
            <xs:element name="quotelist" type="quotelistType"/>
            <xs:element name="catalog" type="catalogType"/>
        </xs:sequence>
      </xs:complexType>
  </xs:element>
  <xs:complexType name="quotelistType">
    <xs:sequence>
      <xs:element name="quote" type="quoteType"
       maxOccurs="unbounded"/>
    </xs:sequence>
    <xs:attribute name="author" type="xs:string"
     use="required"/>
    <xs:attribute name="quotes" type="xs:string"
     use="required"/>
  </xs:complexType>
  <xs:element name="ranking" type="xs:string"/>
  <xs:element name="release_date" type="xs:string"/>
  <xs:element name="small_image" type="xs:string"/>
  <xs:element name="tagged_url" type="xs:string"/>
  <xs:element name="title" type="xs:string"/>
  <xs:element name="titulo" type="xs:string"/>
</xs:schema>
```

Applying Schemas

Referencing Schemas in XML documents is done via namespace declarations in the root element of the document:

```
<quotedoc xmlns:xsi="http://www.w3.org/2001/XMLSchema-
instance"
xsi:noNamespaceSchemaLocation="AmazonMacbethSpanishwithXSDRef2.
xsd">
```

In this case, the namespace declaration reference to http://www.w3.org/2001/ XMLSchema-instance resolves to an actual document at that location, which is a brief description of the way that the W3C Schema should be referenced, and a link to the actual Schema that describes Schema data types, elements, and other Schema descriptions based on the current W3C Recommendation. The noNamespaceSchemaLocation value tells us that there is no predefined Namespace for the Schema, but that the location of the Schema is AmazonMacbethSpanishwithXSDRef2.xsd, which should be in the same directory as the XML file to be validated by the Schema.

Schema structure and syntax

The example Schema in Listing 3-2 starts with an XML declaration that contains a comment that tells you that this Schema was generated using xmlspy. Note that the Schema comment format is the same as the XML and DTD document comment formats:

```
<?xml version="1.0" encoding="UTF-8"?>
<!--W3C Schema generated by XMLSPY v5 rel. 2 U
(http://www.xmlspy.com)-->
```

Next, the W3C Schema namespace declaration is shown as part of the root element. Note that the root element already uses the xs: namespace prefix, which is the standard prefix for Schema declarations. The elementformdefault attribute tells the parser that every element in this document must be prefixed (qualified) with the xs namespace in order for the document to be valid:

```
<xs:schema xmlns:xs="http://www.w3.org/2001/XMLSchema"
elementFormDefault="qualified">
```

You may recall from the introduction to Schemas section in this chapter that a change to the Schema that was generated by xmlspy was required before the generated Schema was valid. The generated Schema was based on the DTD example from earlier in this chapter, and included the predefined xml:lang attribute. The generated XML Schema didn't recognize the xml:lang attribute until this line was added to the Schema:

```
 <xs:import namespace="http://www.w3.org/XML/1998/namespace"
schemaLocation="http://www.w3.org/2000/10/xml.xsd"/>
```

This imported the Schema from http://www.w3.org/2000/10/xml.xsd as part of the current Schema document. This Schema defines the xml:lang, xml:space, and xml:base elements and prefix names. For xml:lang, the declaration defines the lang attribute as the derived Schema data type language:

```
<attribute name="lang" type="language">
  <annotation>....truncated</annotation>
</attribute>
```

Once the connection was made between the xml:lang data attribute and the language derived data type, the xml:lang attribute was accepted as part of the Schema elements. Note that the xml: prefix did not have to be defined, xml: is the only predefined namespace in xml, according to the W3C Recommendation.

Next, the Encuadernación (Spanish for binding) element is defined, and assigned a primitive string data type, in a simple Schema data type:

```
<xs:element name="Encuadernación" type="xs:string"/>
```

Next, a complex data type is declared and named `amazonType`. It requires that at least one child `product` element be present (with another complex data type, `productType`), and that there is no limit on how many `product` child elements are present. Also, the `amazonType` has to have one attribute called items, and a value is required.

```
<xs:complexType name="amazonType">
  <xs:sequence>
    <xs:element name="product" type="productType"
     maxOccurs="unbounded"/>
  </xs:sequence>
  <xs:attribute name="items" type="xs:string"
   use="required"/>
</xs:complexType>
```

After that, several other simple data types are defined, bound to Schema data types. Note that the simple and complex data type declarations do not need to appear in the order that they are structured in an actual XML document, it's up to the parser to make all the necessary links and build a representation of the document, regardless of the order of declarations. This goes for DTDs as well.

```
<xs:element name="asin" type="xs:string"/>
<xs:element name="author" type="xs:string"/>
<xs:element name="autor" type="xs:string"/>
<xs:element name="availability" type="xs:string"/>
<xs:element name="binding" type="xs:string"/>
```

Next, another complex data type is defined for the `catalog` element, called `catalogType`. It specifies that each element that is assigned to the `catalogType` must meet the requirements of the `amazonType` and an `elcorteinglesType` complex data types, in that order, and must have an attribute called `items`, which must have a value. This is a great example of the advantages of using reusable complex data types in a Schema, rather than defining simple data types. Though the entire document could be defined in a single complex data type or a series of simple data types, it's best to use complex types and restrict each complex type to an element and its children only, and define another complex data type for further nesting. For example, if the amazon catalog format changes, only the `amazonType` complex data type in this Schema needs to be changed, and does not affect the definition of the other elements in the Schema:

```
<xs:complexType name="catalogType">
  <xs:sequence>
    <xs:element name="amazon" type="amazonType"/>
    <xs:element name="elcorteingles"
     type="elcorteinglesType"/>
  </xs:sequence>
  <xs:attribute name="items" type="xs:string"
   use="required"/>
</xs:complexType>
```

Next, the `elcorteinglesType` is defined that from the `catalogType` in the last code segment. Like the `amazonType`, it uses the `productType` to specify the structure of products.

```
<xs:complexType name="elcorteinglesType">
  <xs:sequence>
    <xs:element name="product" type="productType"/>
  </xs:sequence>
  <xs:attribute name="items" type="xs:string"
   use="required"/>
</xs:complexType>
```

Then a few more elements are declared as simple data types:

```
<xs:element name="fecha_de_publicación" type="xs:string"/>
<xs:element name="image" type="xs:string"/>
<xs:element name="imagen" type="xs:string"/>
<xs:element name="isbn" type="xs:string"/>
<xs:element name="librourl" type="xs:string"/>
<xs:element name="list_price" type="xs:string"/>
<xs:element name="precio" type="xs:string"/>
```

The next complex data type declaration is a good interpretation of the DTD requirements and was converted to the W3C Schema format by xmlspy. As with the DTD, this data type was a challenge that xmlspy handled very well. The XML document supports both English and Spanish translations in nested elements of the product element. Unfortunately, parsers have no way of automatically recognizing and translating the element names, so it's up to the Schema developer to make sure that all possibilities in both formats are covered as part of the validation process.

In this data type, all elements that have English and Spanish translations are offered as choice lists components in a sequence list of nested elements under the `product` element, as represented in the `productType` complex data type. Each translation choice list is completed with a `choice` element, which means that at least one instance of the element has to be present in one of the languages. The Amazon.com `product` element also contains some nested elements that the elcorteingles `product` element does not. Those elements have been listed in sequence and include a `minOccurs="0"` constraint attribute, indicating that the nested elements are optional, but if they are present they must be in the sequence specified in the listing.

```
<xs:complexType name="productType">
  <xs:sequence>
    <xs:element ref="ranking" minOccurs="0"/>
    <xs:choice maxOccurs="unbounded">
      <xs:element ref="title"/>
      <xs:element ref="titulo"/>
    </xs:choice>
```

```
        <xs:choice maxOccurs="unbounded">
          <xs:element ref="asin"/>
          <xs:element ref="isbn"/>
        </xs:choice>
        <xs:choice maxOccurs="unbounded">
          <xs:element ref="author"/>
          <xs:element ref="autor"/>
        </xs:choice>
        <xs:choice maxOccurs="unbounded">
          <xs:element ref="image"/>
          <xs:element ref="imagen"/>
        </xs:choice>
        <xs:element ref="small_image" minOccurs="0"/>
        <xs:choice maxOccurs="unbounded">
          <xs:element ref="list_price"/>
          <xs:element ref="precio"/>
        </xs:choice>
        <xs:choice maxOccurs="unbounded">
          <xs:element ref="release_date"/>
          <xs:element ref="fecha_de_publicación"/>
        </xs:choice>
        <xs:choice maxOccurs="unbounded">
          <xs:element ref="binding"/>
          <xs:element ref="Encuadernación"/>
        </xs:choice>
        <xs:element ref="availability" minOccurs="0"/>
        <xs:choice maxOccurs="unbounded">
          <xs:element ref="tagged_url"/>
          <xs:element ref="librourl"/>
        </xs:choice>
      </xs:sequence>
      <xs:attribute ref="xml:lang" type="xs:string"/>
    </xs:complexType>
```

Next is a definition for the quote segment of the XML document, which is represented by a complex data type of quoteType. Each quote must contain two attributes, a source and an author, for each quote. Note that this complex data type uses an extension element to define two simple data types inside of the complex data type:

```
    <xs:complexType name="quoteType">
      <xs:simpleContent>
        <xs:extension base="xs:string">
          <xs:attribute name="source" type="xs:string"/>
          <xs:attribute name="author" type="xs:string"/>
        </xs:extension>
      </xs:simpleContent>
    </xs:complexType>
```

The next element in the element nesting structure is the root `quotedoc` element description. This complex data type simply states that the `quotedoc` element must have two children, quotelist and catalog, each represented by their assigned complex data types:

```
<xs:element name="quotedoc">
  <xs:complexType>
    <xs:sequence>
      <xs:element name="quotelist" type="quotelistType"/>
      <xs:element name="catalog" type="catalogType"/>
    </xs:sequence>
  </xs:complexType>
</xs:element>
```

Next is a complex data type defined for the `quotelist`, which contains the quotes. Once again, each element is assigned a corresponding complex data type:

```
<xs:complexType name="quotelistType">
  <xs:sequence>
    <xs:element name="quote" type="quoteType"
    maxOccurs="unbounded"/>
  </xs:sequence>
  <xs:attribute name="author" type="xs:string"
   use="required"/>
  <xs:attribute name="quotes" type="xs:string"
   use="required"/>
</xs:complexType>
```

The Schema element declarations are finished with a final list of simple data types that are needed in the complex data types, and close the `root` Schema tag:

```
<xs:element name="ranking" type="xs:string"/>
<xs:element name="release_date" type="xs:string"/>
<xs:element name="small_image" type="xs:string"/>
<xs:element name="tagged_url" type="xs:string"/>
<xs:element name="title" type="xs:string"/>
<xs:element name="titulo" type="xs:string"/>
</xs:schema>
```

Summary

In this chapter, I introduced you to the concept of data validation and showed you detailed techniques with examples on developing DTDs and W3C Schemas for validating your XML documents.

✦ Validating XML data

✦ Applying DTDs to XML documents

✦ DTD structure and syntax

✦ Applying W3C Schemas to XML documents

✦ W3C Schema structure and syntax

✦ Real-world examples of DTD and Schemas

I discussed parsers a little in this chapter, and in the next two chapters you will become much more acquainted with them, what they do, and how they do it, including parsing XML documents using the Document Object Model (DOM) and the Simple API for XML (SAX).

✦   ✦   ✦

XML Parsing Concepts

One of the great advantages of using XML data is transportability. But up until this point in the book, the mechanics of how to deliver XML data to another system have not yet been covered. As explained in Chapter 1, XML alone is not data integration. Applications that send and receive XML data need interfaces to generate XML and to integrate XML data into applications. XML document parsing is used to integrate XML data with existing applications.

> **Note** The word *parse* comes from the Latin *pars orationis*, meaning "part of speech." In linguistics, parsing is the act of breaking down sentences and word structures to establish relationships and structures of language. These structures are most often represented in a tree structure. Computer-based parsing is similar, but is most commonly used to break down and interpret characters in a string. Since XML is by definition a set of characters in a string, breaking down and separating parts of XML documents is also referred to as *parsing*.

XML document parsing identifies and converts XML elements contained in an XML document into either nested nodes in a tree structure or document events, depending on the type of XML parser that is being used:

✦ **Document Object Model (DOM)** parsing breaks a document down into nested elements, referred to as *nodes* in a DOM document representation. DOM nodes refer to documents or fragments of documents, elements, attributes, text data, processing instructions, comments, and other types of data that I'll cover in more detail in Chapter 5.

✦ **Simple API for XML (SAX)** parsing breaks XML documents down into events in a SAX document representation. These nodes and events, once identified, can be used to convert the original XML document elements into other types of data, based on the data represented by the elements, attributes, and text values in the original XML document.

This chapter will focus on the concepts and theory behind XML document parsing and manipulation using node tree-based parsers and event-based parsers. After an introduction to the concepts, Chapters 5 and 6 provide practical examples of parsing an XML document using DOM and SAX.

 Cross-Reference   Chapters 4, 5, and 6 provide examples of how parsers work. For examples of how to enable XML through Java code, refer to Chapter 16.

Document Object Model (DOM)

The W3C Document Object Model Recommendation is the only XML Document parsing model that is officially recommended for XML document parsing by the W3C. The full recommendation can be found at `http://www.w3.org/TR/DOM-Level-2-HTML`. The W3C DOM can be used to create XML documents, navigate DOM structures, and add, modify, or delete DOM nodes. DOM parsing can be slower than SAX parsing because DOM creates a representation of the entire document as nodes, regardless of how large the document is. However, DOM can be handy for retrieving all the data from a document, or retrieving a piece of data several times. The DOM stays resident in memory as long as the code that created the DOM representation is running.

What is DOM?

The *Document Object Mode (DOM)* is a tree representation of XML data, with root and nested elements and attributes in an XML document represented by instances of nodes inside a single document node. Each node in the DOM tree represents a matching item in the original XML document. Element, attribute, and text nodes are nested at multiple levels matching the nested elements at the same level of the XML document. The DOM root node always matches the root element in an XML document, and other nodes in the tree are located by their relationship to the root node.

Listing 4-1 shows the very simple XML document from Chapter 1. In Chapter 1, I compared the structure of an XML document to the structure of a computer's hard drive, with a single root directory that contains subdirectories and files. This comparison is perhaps even more applicable to the structure of a DOM node tree. The DOM nodes map to the directories on a hard drive, with one or more files in some of the directories. The hard drive starts with a root directory and several subdirectories. Even if there are no files in a directory, the directory has a name and it can contain subdirectories that contain files. In the same way, element nodes have names but no associated value. Element nodes, however, may contain other nodes, such as attributes or text values. Attribute and text nodes can contain values associated with an element node, just like directories can contain files that contain data.

DOM nodes represent all types of data in XML documents. Nodes have `nodeType`, `nodeName`, and `nodeValue` properties. For example, the parsed DOM node for the root element has a `nodeName` of `rootelement` and is an element `nodeType`. The `firstelement` element is also an element `nodetype`. Both elements have a `nodeValue` of `null`, as all elements do. The `position` attribute becomes a node with an attribute `nodeType`, a `nodeName` of `position`, and a value of 1. The text value of the `level1` element has a `nodeName` of `#text`, a `nodeType` of `text`, and a `nodeValue` of `This is level 1 of the nested elements`.

Listing 4-1: **A Very Simple XML Document**

```
<?xml version="1.0" encoding="UTF-8"?>
<rootelement>
    <firstelement position="1">
        <level1 children="0">This is level 1 of the nested
elements</level1>
    </firstelement>
    <secondelement position="2">
        <level1 children="1">
            <level2>This is level 2 of the nested
elements</level2>
        </level1>
    </secondelement>
</rootelement>
```

You can easily visualize XML document structures and DOM structures by using free tools that are available for download on the Web. Most tools use DOM parsers to integrate XML document data with their own custom UI, and display XML documents using customized document node tree representations. I've included two good ones in the list below, but you can find more at `http://www.xmlsoftware.com/browsers.html`.

✦ **The Microsoft XML Notepad** is a small, simple XML document editor and reader for Windows. It's been a while since it was updated, but it's still a good, basic XML editor and viewer. You can download it by going to `http://www.microsoft.com/xmlnotepad`.

✦ **The IBM XML Viewer** is great for viewing XML documents on non-Windows machines that support Java. You can download it at `http://alphaworks.ibm.com/tech/xmlviewer`. It's a simple tool very similar to XML Notepad but is better at handling more advanced XML such as namespaces. The trade-off is that it lacks the basic editing capabilities of the Microsoft XML Notepad.

Figure 4-1 shows an example of the very simple XML document from Listing 4-1 displayed in the Microsoft XML Notepad. Note how the tree structure in the parsed XML document representation resembles the directory structures on a hard drive.

The `rootlement` and `firstelement` elements have a `nodeValue` of `null`. The `position` attribute is an attribute `nodeType` with and a value of `1`. In the XML Notepad, text values show up as values of their associated elements. The text value of the `level1` element, for example, is shown as a value of the `level1` element, even though in reality the text value is a separate DOM node with a `nodeType` of text.

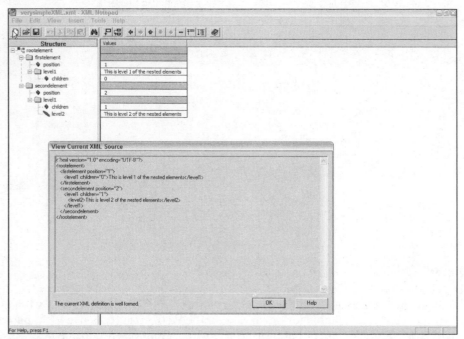

Figure 4-1: A very simple XML document displayed in the Microsoft XML Notepad

About DOM 1, DOM 2, and DOM 3

The DOM Level 1 and Level 2 specifications are both W3C Recommendations. Both specifications are final, and developers that build applications based on either specification can be assured that the standards are complete and will not be updated. However, it's worth noting that DOM Level 1 is not compatible with DOM Level 2, and there are no guarantees that DOM Level 1 or 2 will be compatible with DOM Level 3, which is currently winding its way through the recommendation process at the W3C. DOM 1 supports basic navigation and editing of DOM nodes in

HTML and XML documents. DOM 2 extends Level 1 with support for XML name-spaces, and a few new features that are similar to SAX functionality such as filtered views, ranges, and events.

Simple API for XML (SAX)

SAX parsing is faster than DOM parsing, but slightly more complicated to code. XML document representations in SAX don't follow the same type of directory and file structure that defines DOM documents. SAX parsing is more appropriately compared to getting information from this chapter of the book by going to the page where the chapter starts, reading the chapter, and stopping when the chapter ends. DOM parsers would extract the same information from this chapter by reformatting the entire book into a DOM format, then reading through the DOM representation of the book to find the beginning of the chapter, and reading the chapter. In other words, SAX provides a specific chunk of information that you need from an XML document, while DOM retrieves and reformats the whole document, and then extracts the same chunk of information from the reformatted document.

What is SAX?

Like DOM, SAX is used to describe, parse, and manipulate XML documents. Unlike DOM, SAX breaks a document down into a series of events that represent parts of an XML document, such as `StartDocument`, `StartElement`, `EndElement`, `ProcessingInstruction`, `SAXWarning`, `SAXError`, and `EndDocument`.

SAX is not developed or "recommended" by the W3C, though subsequent DOM implementations usually borrow useful new features from the more advanced SAX feature set. In general, SAX is usually ahead of DOM implementations, because the W3C recommendation process does not hinder SAX development. There is no official specification of SAX, just the implementation of the `XMLReader` class, which is only written in Java at this time. There are other implementations of SAX on other platforms, but these are either a result of bindings to code in the SAX Java archive file, sax.jar, or a complete rewrite of code that simply mimics the functionality of SAX Java classes, methods, and properties.

Updates to SAX can be downloaded at `http://www.saxproject.org`. The site also contains information about parser implementations and bindings, and the FAQ at that site is a fun read. Really.

SAX 1 and SAX 2

Most current parsers implement the SAX2 interfaces. Unlike DOM 1 and 2, SAX 2 parsers are usually backward compatible with SAX 1. SAX 1 supports Navigation around a document and manipulation of content via SAX 1 events via the SAX 1 `Parser` class. SAX 2 supports namespaces, filter chains, and querying and setting features and properties via SAX events via the SAX 2 XMLReader interface.

In the previous DOM section of this chapter, I showed you two free tools that parse an XML document into DOM nodes and display the nodes in a tree-based UI. At the time of writing, there are unfortunately no simple tools that break down an XML document into a visual display of SAX events. There is sample code written in Java and other languages that parse XML documents with SAX and return output of events to a screen, but no downloadable tools. The code ships with most SAX parsers. You can find a good list of SAX parsers at the SAX project Website, http://www.saxproject.org/?selected=links.

I'll cover sample SAX code in more detail in Chapters 14 and 16.

Listing 4-2 shows an example of the very simple XML document from Listing 4-1 with annotation that identifies each SAX event associated with the original XML document objects.

SAX parsers represent the `rootlement` element as the `startDocument` event, because it's the root element of the document.

Remember from Chapter 1 that the XML declaration is optional! This means that an XML document actually starts at the root element, which is the first element after the optional XML declaration.

The `rootlement` element is also represented by the `startElement` event, because every event in the document has an associated `startElement` and `endElement` event, including the `root` element.

The `firstelement`'s `startElement` event also contains an `attributes` object. The `attributes` object contains information about one or more attributes associated with an element. The `attributes` object contains a single object, with a name of `position` and a value of `1`. SAX attribute names and values can be retrieved by using several methods implemented in the SAX `attributes` interface, which I will cover in more detail in Chapter 6.

Text values in SAX show up as values of the `characters` event. The text value `This is level 1 of the nested elements`, for example, is a value of the `characters` event after the `level1` element `startElement` event and before the `level1` element `endElement` event.

There is no `startCharacters` or `endCharacters` event. SAX parsers see the `characters` event as one uninterrupted string between `startElement` and `endElement` events.

Listing 4-2: A Very Simple XML Document with SAX Event Listings

```
<?xml version="1.0" encoding="UTF-8"?>
<rootelement>
<!--SAX Events:startDocument, startElement-->

  <firstelement position="1">
  <!--SAX Events:startElement, Attributes=position value=1-->

    <level1 children="0">
    <!--SAX Events:startElement Attributes=children value=0-->

        This is level 1 of the nested elements
        <!--SAX Event:characters-->

    </level1>
    <!--SAX Event:endElement-->

  </firstelement>
  <!--SAX Event:endElement-->

  <secondelement position="2">
  <!--SAX Events:startElement, Attributes=position value=2-->

    <level1 children="1">
     <!--SAX Events:startElement, Attributes=children value=1-->

      <level2>
      <!--SAX Event:startElement-->

      This is level 2 of the nested elements
      <!--SAX Event:characters-->

      </level2>
      <!--SAX Event:endElement-->

    </level1>
    <!--SAX Event:endElement-->

  </secondelement>
  <!--SAX Event:endElement-->

</rootelement>
<!--SAX Events:endDocument, endElement-->
```

About XML Parsers

There are several XML parsers on the market, and a fairly complete listing of parsers can be found at `http://www.xmlsoftware.com/parsers.html`. Of all the parsers on the market, three parsers stand out from the pack in terms of standards support and general marketplace acceptance: Apache Xerces, IBM XML4J (XML for Java), and Microsoft's MSXML parser.

All of these parsers are available as free downloads. They include a parsing engine and source code samples. Apache Xerces even includes the source code for the parsing engine itself. Some of the downloads also include tools and functionality for other purposes, such as processing XSL transformations.

Cross-Reference   XSL transformations are covered in Chapters 7 and 8.

The Java API for XML (JAXP) "pluggable interface" from Sun for XML document parsing is also worthy of mention. The JAXP interface can be used as a front-end for other parsers. JAXP seeks to mitigate some of the issues surrounding incompatible and deprecated parser versions.

Parsers generally fall into two categories:

✦ **Non-validating parsers** check that an XML document adheres to basic XML structure and syntax rules (well-formed XML).

✦ **Validating parsers** have the option to verify that an XML document is valid according to the rules of a DTD or schema, as well as checking for a well-formed document structure and syntax.

The latest versions of Apache Xerces, IBM XML for Java (XML4J), Sun's JAXP, and Microsoft's MSXML parser are all validating parsers, and validation can be enabled or disabled as needed by developers. All of these downloads also support both the DOM and SAX interfaces for XML document parsing. Which parsing method is left up to the developer. I'll cover the pros and cons of each parsing method in the last section of this chapter.

Tip   While the MSXML parser stands alone in its implementation and reuse in browsers, on servers, and in .Net applications, the Java parsers tend to reuse parts of other Java parsers to implement their functionality. For example, the parser in XML4J is an implementation of the Xerces DOM parser, which IBM heavily contributes to, and has subsequently reused for the DOM parser in XML4J. Consequently, Java developers have to keep a close watch of the version of parser they are using to ensure compatibility with their current code implementations.

Apache's Xerces

The Xerces parser is a validating parser that is available in Java and C++. Apparently, the parser was named after the now extinct Xerces blue butterfly, a native of the San Francisco peninsula. The butterfly was named after Xerxes, emperor of Persia from 486 to 465 BC, the height of Persian power. Xerces the emperor is also assumed to be extinct.

The Persian empire under Xerces' rule stretched from India to parts of Turkey and Greece. This led to several language and infrastructure integration issues. The solution to these issues was one of the greatest features of the empire: a royal messaging infrastructure that was used to translate native languages and scripts from over 100 far-flung provinces. *Xerces* is subsequently the Persian word for *king* to this day.

Xerces the parser fully supports the W3C XML DOM (Levels 1 and 2) standards, the DOM3 standards when they finally become a W3C recommendation, and SAX version 2. Xerces is a validating parser, and provides support for XML document validation against W3C Schemas and DTDs. The C++ version of the Xerces parser also includes a Perl wrapper and a COM wrapper that works with the MSXML parser. Xerces can be downloaded at `http://xml.apache.org`.

For more details on Xerces and examples of using Xerces in J2EE applications, please refer to Chapter 16.

IBM's XML4J

The IBM XML for Java (XML4J) libraries, with some more recent help from the Apache Xerces project and Sun (via project Crimson), is the mother of all Java-based XML parsers, starting with version 1.0 in 1998. IBM and the Apache group work closely on XML document parsing technologies. Consequently the IBM XML4J libraries are based on Xerces. The latest version of the XML4J libraries support the W3C XML Schema Recommendation when implementing the validating parser interfaces. Parsers include SAX 1 and 2, DOM 1 and 2, and some basic features of the as-yet-unreleased DOM 3 standard, currently in the recommendation process. XML4J also adds support for Sun's JAXP, plus multi-lingual error messages. Recent updates to XML4J can be downloaded from http://www.alphaworks.ibm.com/tech/xml4j.

For more details on XML4J and examples of using XML4J in J2EE applications, please refer to Chapter 14.

Sun's JAXP

As readers may have already noticed, not only are there several types of XML parsers available from a single source, but also several versions of each Parser. The Java API for XML Processing (JAXP) is designed to smooth over the various versions of SAX and DOM parsers and their associated incompatibilities through a single "pluggable" interface. The pluggable interface consists of a set of Java classes that can be reused to access different back-end parser classes at different levels without having to change the Java code on the front end of the application.

A document could, for example, currently be parsed using DOM1 or DOM2. When the new DOM3 recommendation is graduated through the W3C recommendation process, DOM3 could be plugged into the same application, without having to change the underlying code when the new parser is added to an application or server, but still providing the newer performance and functionality.

JAXP can be downloaded from `http://java.sun.com/xml/jaxp/`.

Cross-Reference   For more details on JAXP and examples of using JAXP in J2EE applications, please refer to Chapter 15.

Microsoft's XML parser (MSXML)

Microsoft's XML parser is part of Internet Explorer 5.5 or later, and the latest version is separated from IE browser code, so that the parser does not have to wait for the next version of the browser, and vice versa. The MSXML parser was recently renamed the Microsoft XML Core Services, but is usually still referred to by the original MSXML acronym. MSXML supports most XML standards and works with JavaScript (and DHTML), Visual Basic, ASP, and C++, but not Java. MSXML4.x includes support for DOM, XML Schema definition language for validating parsers, the Schema Object Model (SOM, a Microsoft invention which parses XML Schemas into an object model), XSLT, XPath, and SAX. Recent MSXML updates can be downloaded from `http://www.microsoft.com/msxml`.

Cross-Reference   For more details on Microsoft XML Core Services and examples of using MSXML in Microsoft applications, please refer to Chapters 10 and 11.

DOM or SAX: Which Parser to Use?

I've provided an introduction to XML document parsing methods and some of the parsers that are available on the market today. Building on this knowledge, I'll review some of the more esoteric issues related to XML document parsing.

The top three questions for XML document parsing are:

✦ What is a validating parser?

✦ Why are there two ways to parse XML documents?

✦ Which parsing method should I use?

It's fairly easy to answer the first question by explaining validating parsers versus non-validating parsers. It's also fairly easy to explain the genesis of the DOM and SAX parsers for XML, and why there are two. The most difficult thing to explain about XML document parsing is the last question, "DOM or SAX: which one to use?"

I've already provided an explanation of validating parsers versus non-validating parsers in the section "About XML Parsers." I'll provide the easy answer first about the genesis of two parsers for XML document parsing first. The history leads in to the more difficult question of which parser to use.

Back in the early days of XML, before the standards had completely gelled and W3C recommendations were actually recommendations that could be followed or not, everyone wrote their own XML document parsers. However, as standards emerged, the W3C XML working group, who create the standards for most of the XML technologies in the marketplace today, standardized on a DOM parsing model, which was the most flexible and easiest to understand. This was accepted by the community at the time, because XML document structures were usually pretty simple and small back then, and DOM is very good at efficiently handling small, simple XML documents. IBM wrote the XML4J parser and handed it over to the Apache group, which renamed it Xerces. Everyone was happy, for a while.

As XML was rapidly adopted by the IT and business world, XML documents grew consistently larger and more complex. Xerces and other DOM parsers started to get bogged down when reading an entire large, complex XML document from start to finish and converting it to a node tree. Developers tried to make the code and the methods more efficient, but they consistently ran up against the limitations of the DOM architecture.

In the meantime, members of the XML-DEV mailing list got together and started developing a leaner and more efficient model of document parsing that could find and parse a segment of an XML document. This meant that developers and parsers could focus on just the necessary parts of an XML document while ignoring irrelevant data. This model proved to be very efficient. David Megginson coordinated the development of the original SAX parser and maintained earlier Java versions.

Because of the speed and efficiency of the SAX parser, it was rapidly adopted by Java application developers. Though SAX is not a W3C-sanctioned XML recommendation, most of the better features in the SAX parser usually find their way into subsequent versions of the W3C DOM recommendation, which can be found at http://www.w3.org/TR/DOM-Level-2-HTML. Current SAX parser code maintenance is being handled by David Brownell, and the current SAX project Website and parser code can be found at http://www.saxproject.org.

But just because SAX is faster and more efficient than DOM at handling large documents doesn't mean SAX is better for every application. SAX is better at parsing large documents. If your application is using smaller documents or needs to navigate an XML document more than once, DOM parsing is probably more applicable.

SAX is very good at parsing parts of a large document efficiently, but SAX passes through a document once to collect needed data, and has to start over as more document data is needed. DOM, on the other hand, holds a node tree in memory until your application is finished with it, so once a document is parsed, pieces of the document can be retrieved without having to re-parse the document.

As for which is better for a specific application, individual mileage may vary, depending on the data you are working with. But in general, there is no downside to using DOM to parse smaller XML documents that represent unstructured data, such as a single-item inventory record. If you are working with a large document of structured data, such as the XML output of an inventor listing with hundreds of thousands of records, SAX is probably the parser method to try first.

Summary

In this chapter I introduced readers to the theories behind parsing XML documents:

✦ An overview of XML document parsing

✦ Validating versus non-validating parsers

✦ Document Object Model (DOM) parsing

✦ Simple API for XML (SAX) parsing

✦ An introduction to popular XML parsers

✦ DOM versus SAX: when to use what

In the next chapter, I'll discuss the details of parsing XML documents using the W3C Document Object Model (DOM). Chapter 8 will cover the details of parsing XML documents using the Simple API for XML (SAX). Both chapters will provide practical examples using the XSL document examples from our book application.

✦   ✦   ✦

Parsing XML with DOM

Chapter 4 provided a theoretical overview of the concepts behind XML document parsing. This chapter extends Chapter 4's basic concepts and provides a deep dive into XML Document Object Model (DOM) parsing. Chapter 6 provides the same level of detail for SAX parsing.

DOM parsing can initially appear to be a larger topic than it really is, because of the sheer volume of sources for DOM information. The number of DOM versions, the volume of related W3C Recommendation documents, and the addition of Microsoft's MSXML classes and methods that are not part of the W3C DOM all complicate the DOM picture. In this chapter, I pull everything together into a single reference with a focus on what's important to XML programmers. For the most part, the DOM interfaces and nodes in MXSML and the W3C DOM are the same, except for the way that they are named. The real differences begin when you get into the properties and methods of nodes. For each interface, node, property, and method, I list the supporting DOM versions (W3C 1.0, 2.0, 3.0, and MSXML).

The original DOM working drafts provided bindings for Java and ECMAScript, a standardized version of JavaScript promoted by the European Computer Manufacturers Association. The Java interface caught on, but the ECMAScript version did not. Since then, the DOM implementations have been developed by specific vendors for C, C++, PL/SQL, Python, and Perl.

Currently W3C documents use the Interface Definition Language (IDL) to represent code examples using DOM node properties and methods. IDL is an abstract language from the Object Management Group (OMG) and is not portable to other languages, such as Java, VB, or JScript.

Cross-Reference Since the IDL is not particularly practical as a development environment, this chapter covers W3C DOM parsing in detail, but does not cover techniques for writing code for working with DOM objects. Typically, DOM parsing is enabled by using the Apache Xerces classes in Java, or using the Microsoft XML Core Services (MSXML) in applications developed with MS Visual Studio. Java manipulation of DOM objects, including plenty of Java code examples, can be found in Chapter 16. Using MSXML for DOM parsing is covered in Chapters 10 and 11.

The W3C defines the specifications for DOM parsing in the W3C DOM Recommendation. As I outlined in Chapter 4, the W3C DOM can be used to create XML documents, navigate DOM structures, and add, modify, or delete DOM nodes. DOM parsing can be slower than SAX parsing because DOM creates a representation of the entire document as nodes, regardless of how large the document is. However, DOM can be handy for retrieving all the data from a document, or retrieving a piece of data several times. The DOM stays resident in memory as long as the code that created the DOM representation is running.

Understanding the DOM

The first Document Object Model for HTML pages was created by the Netscape browser development team, as a standardized way to access HTML documents from JavaScript. The original DOM shipped in 1995 with JavaScript in the Netscape 2.0 browser. Microsoft subsequently created a similar DOM for JScript, which was included in the 1996 Internet Explorer 3.0 release.

DOM creates a representation of HTML and XML documents as a tree-like hierarchy of Node objects. There is always one root node in a document. Some Node objects can have child nodes, and are referred to as branch nodes. Other nodes are standalone nodes with no children, which are commonly referred to as leaf nodes. Some nodes are colorful with fragrant essences, and are only available in the spring. These nodes are referred to as blossom nodes. I'm just kidding about the blossom nodes, but hopefully by now you get the whole "node and tree" concept, including roots, branches, and leaves.

The W3C DOM 1 Recommendation

In 1997, a World Wide Web Consortium DOM working group was created to provide a standardized DOM interface for all browsers. The result of this was the first W3C DOM Recommendation, which can be viewed at `http://www.w3.org/TR/REC-DOM-Level-1/`.

The first DOM Recommendation was developed just as corporate IT shops were beginning to take notice of XML. Consequently, although most of the recommendation is applicable to XML objects because of similarities to HTML objects, the DOM 1 Recommendation focus is on HTML page objects. XML is only mentioned by name in the abstract of the DOM 1 Recommendation document. DOM 1 consists of a set of *core* nodes, which are applicable to HTML pages. Several *extended* nodes accommodate XML document objects. Both types of nodes are listed later in this chapter.

The W3C DOM 2 Recommendation

The 2000 DOM Level 2 Recommendation adds to the functionality defined in DOM Level 1 core. The following list describes the different Recommendations of DOM Level 2. At the time of this writing, the DOM Level 2 core specification is the current W3C DOM Recommendation. The DOM 2 Core Recommendation can be found at `http://www.w3.org/TR/DOM-Level-2-Core`.

Five more recommendations are currently associated with the DOM 2 Core Recommendation. All parsers must follow W3C DOM 2 Core Recommendations. The rest of the related recommendations are not compulsory for W3C-compliant parsers. Most parsers, however, do support most or all of the recommendations. I'll cover how to tell what version and feature sets are supported by a parser a little later in this chapter, for now you just need to know what each Recommendation is:

✦ The **DOM Level 2 Traversal-Range Recommendation** defines a set of interfaces for traversing node sets and working with ranges of an XML or HTML document.

✦ The **DOM Level 2 HTML Recommendation** defines HTML 4.01 and XHTML 1.0 document structures.

✦ The **DOM Level 2 Views Recommendation** defines functionality for defining and manipulating different representations, or views, of an XML or HTML document.

✦ The **DOM Level 2 Style Recommendation** defines interfaces for dynamically accessing and manipulating Cascading Style Sheets (CSS).

✦ The **DOM Level 2 Events Recommendation** defines a standardized set of interactive browser events for HTML pages and XML document node tree events.

The W3C DOM 3 Recommendation

DOM 3 is currently under development, and at the time of this writing, most of the core and related Recommendation documents are in the "Working Draft" stage. There are three more stages for DOM 3 to go through (Candidate Recommendation, Proposed Recommendation, and Recommendation) before the full and complete feature set is published as a W3C Recommendation. We list the features in the current DOM 3 Working Draft documents in this chapter, but keep in mind that although most of these features will be in DOM 3, there is no guarantee that they will all be present in their current form in the final Recommendation.

On The Web

I'll post any changes to the DOM 3 Recommendation and updates to this chapter as they evolve. The updated text can be downloaded from `http://www. XMLProgrammingBible.com`.

There are several DOM 3 Recommendation Working Drafts currently in progress, which represent DOM 3 modules. DOM modules usually end up as a class or set of classes in whatever programming language they are developed in. Features in the modules become subclasses, methods, and properties of the module base classes.

The **DOM 3 Core Recommendation Working Draft** extends namespace support methods in DOM 2.

The **DOM 3 Events Recommendation Working Draft** adds more events on top of the DOM 2 Events Recommendation. The specific objects and methods are listed later in this chapter.

DOM 3 also has a very critical new Recommendation for XML programmers: **The DOM 3 Load and Save Recommendation Working Draft** enables parsers to load XML documents using DOM objects exclusively. Currently, in DOM 2, there is no standardized way to feed a DOM parser an XML document directly from the file system. XML document parsing code currently uses whatever methods are available in the language used to call the parser to load XML documents from a file, and then feed the loaded document to a parser. Even more important, new DOM 3 objects can be saved to a file. Currently, in DOM 2, there is no way to extract a manipulated DOM object and save it to the file system using DOM objects. Nodes can be extracted and passed to another programming language, where they can be saved as text or converted to other types of data. DOM 3 provides a standardized way to save a Node tree directly from the DOM 3 object to a file system.

Another DOM 3 feature that will be very useful for developers is the support of XPath for navigating and manipulating DOM nodes, courtesy of the **DOM 3 XPath Recommendation Working Draft**. XPath provides a standard syntax for accessing and manipulating the parsed nodes of an XML document. XPath for DOM makes sense, as W3C XSLT Recommendations also support XPath. DOM support for XPath streamlines what a developer needs to learn to navigate XML documents when parsing and transforming XML documents, and will help standardize organizational code libraries that only have to support one method for navigating XML documents programmatically.

The **DOM 3 Validation Recommendation Working Draft** defines interfaces that enforce validation of new or manipulated documents based on a DTD or Schema.

The **DOM 3 Views and Formatting Working Draft** builds on the DOM 2 Views Recommendation. Views and Formatting Recommendation provide standard ways to update the content of a DOM 3 node tree and related formatting instructions.

Microsoft MSXML DOM enhancements

Microsoft's XML parser is part of Internet Explorer 5.5 or later. The MSXML parser is currently called the Microsoft XML Core Services, but is usually still referred to by the original MSXML acronym. The MSXML parser uses the same DOM interfaces as W3C parsers. In addition to the W3C objects, MSXML parser has added several additional methods and properties to the W3C DOM interface methods and properties. These methods and properties are commonly referred to as Microsoft DOM extensions or MSXML extensions. MSXML extensions can be used in IE browser applications and other types of Windows applications that use the MSXML parser as their DOM parser. They are not supported by other parsers, such as Xerces.

Because MSXML and the Internet Explorer are so widely used, most XML programmers need to know about Microsoft's additional properties and methods. The other practical reason for knowing which methods and properties are part of the W3C DOM and which are MXSML extensions is to know what properties and methods are available in a specific parser, and when you can use them.

The MSXML download includes a great help database will full documentation and examples for working with the MSXML DOM in JScript, Visual Basic, and C/C++. Recent MSXML updates can be downloaded from
`http://www.microsoft.com/msxml`.

 On The Web We're documenting the MSXML 4.01 parser in this chapter, which may be updated by the time this book is in print. We'll post any changes to the MSXML documentation and updates to this chapter as they evolve. The updated text can be downloaded from.

DOM Interfaces and Nodes

As mentioned in the introduction to this chapter, XML documents that are represented in DOM are parsed into a tree of root, branch, and leaf nodes. In addition to nodes, a few DOM interfaces are not extensions of a DOM node, and consequently are not considered part of the node "family." Also, unlike some DOM nodes, none of the DOM interfaces have children.

Note MSXML DOM node and interface names do not follow the W3C interface naming standards, even though the interfaces support most of the W3C properties and methods. For example, the W3C Document node is called `IXMLDOM DocumentNode` in the MXSML DOM, and `Document` in the W3C DOM. The other key difference between the MSXML DOM and the W3C DOM is error handling. W3C DOM error handling is implemented in the W3C `DOMException` interface. MSXML error handling is implemented through the `parseError` property of the `IXMLDOMDocumentNode`.

Table 5-1 shows the current listing of these DOM interfaces.

Table 5-1	
DOM Interfaces for HTML and XML Documents	
Interface Name	*Description*
DOMImplementation **Supported by:** W3C DOM 1 2, 3, and MSXML	The DOMImplementation interface defines the version of a DOM implementation that a parser supports, and DOM features that are supported by the parser. The hasFeature method of DOMImplementation returns true if the feature is supported, or false if it is not.
DOMException **Supported by:** W3C DOM 1, 2, 3	An exception is passed to the calling program by a parser when a parsing exception occurs, such as modification of a node that can't be modified, or adding a node in the wrong place, such as trying to add an Attr node to an Attr node (XML document attributes can't have attributes). **Note:** The MSXML DOM does not use the DOMException class for parsing error reporting. The MSXML ParseError property of the IXMLDOMDocumentNode object is used for the same purpose in MSXML implementations.
Node **Supported by:** W3C DOM 1, 2, 3, and MSXML	The Node object is the base of a Document Object Model, and represents a single node in the document tree. All DOM nodes inherit properties and methods from the node object. The node object is not part of a document node tree. It serves as a properties and methods container for other node types to inherit from. Table 5-2 lists and explains all of the types of DOM nodes.

Interface Name	*Description*
NodeList **Supported by:** W3C DOM 1, 2, 3, and MSXML	The NodeList object represents an editable in-memory representation of a collection of Node objects. The NodeList interface is used to contain child nodes of a W3C DOM node. For example, an XML document element that has an attribute and a text value is parsed into an Element node. The Attr node and Text node associated with the Element node are accessible via a NodeList from the element Node. Nodes in a NodeList are accessible by index number, starting with 0. NodeLists are useful if programmers know the position of a node in the structure of a Node tree.
NamedNodeMap **Supported by:** W3C DOM 1 2, 3 and MSXML	A NamedNodeMap object represents and editable in-memory representation of a collection of Node objects that can be accessed by name. The NamedNodeMap element is used to retrieve a list of attributes, entities, or any other node that has a name associated with it. This enables developers to retrieve a node by name, instead of having to know the position of the node in the node tree or a NodeList.
DOMSelection **Supported by:** MSXML	A DOMSelection object contains a list of nodes returned by an XML Path Language (XPath) expression.
DOMSchemaCollection **Supported by:** MSXML	A DOMSchemaCollection contains one or more Schema documents.
CharacterData **Supported by:** W3C DOM 1, 2, 3, and MSXML	The CharacterData object is a base object for manipulating text. The CDATASection, Comment, and Text nodes inherit properties and methods from CharacterData.

Understanding DOM nodes

Table 5-1 describes the DOM node object from which all DOM nodes are derived. DOM nodes that represent different types of XML document objects have different node data types, but all DOM nodes inherit the same properties and methods from the DOM node object. The only node that differs between the W3C DOM and the MSXML DOM is element attributes, which are represented by the `Attr` object in the W3C DOM and the `Attribute` object in the MXSML DOM. Table 5-2 shows the node data types that are part of the DOM Core Recommendation.

Table 5-2
Core DOM Nodes for HTML and XML Documents

Node Name	Description
DocumentType **Children:** None **Supported by:** W3C DOM 1, 2, 3, and MSXML	Represents a document's doctype property, which can reference a DTD that can contain entity references. The DocumentType object also provides an interface to any elements with a notation attribute.
ProcessingInstruction **Children:** None **Supported by:** W3C DOM 1, 2, 3, and MSXML	Represents document processing instructions, including, for example, XML document declarations and stylesheet references, without the element delimiters (<? and ?>).
Document **Children:** Element, ProcessingInstruction, Comment, DocumentType, DocumentFragment. **Supported by:** W3C DOM 1, 2, 3, and MSXML	Represents an XML document and serves as the root node for entry to the rest of the node tree.
DocumentFragment **Children:** Element, ProcessingInstruction, Comment, Text, CDATASection, EntityReference **Supported by:** W3C DOM 1, 2, 3, and MSXML	Represents part of a DOM Document node tree, or a new fragment that can then be inserted into a document. A DocumentFragment can represent a new node tree, starting with any child of a Document object.
Element **Children:** Element, ProcessingInstruction, Comment, Text, CDATASection, EntityReference **Supported by:** W3C DOM 1, 2, 3, and MSXML	Represents an XML document element. Attributes and text values associated with an element become child leaf nodes of the element in the node tree.

Node Name	Description
Text **Children:** None **Supported by:** W3C DOM 1, 2, 3, and MSXML	Represents the text of an Element object.
CDATASection **Children:** None **Supported by:** W3C DOM 1, 2, 3, and MSXML	Contains contents of an XML document CDATA element content in a single node, without trying to parse it into different types of nodes.
Attr **Children:** Text, EntityReference **Supported by:** W3C DOM 1, 2, 3 (MSXML as Attribute)	Represents an attribute of an Element object in the W3C DOM.
Comment **Children:** None **Supported by:** W3C DOM 1, 2, 3, and MSXML	Represents an XML document comments, without the element delimiters (<!-- and -->).
Notation **Children:** None **Supported by:** W3C DOM 1, 2, 3, and MSXML	Contains the read-only format for unparsed entities or notation attribute values, including application processing instructions.
Entity **Children:** Element, ProcessingInstruction, Comment, Text, CDATASection, EntityReference	Represents a parsed or unparsed entity. In non-validating parsers, the unparsed entity is contained in the entity node and there are no child nodes. In validating DOM parsers, the Entity node's child list represents the replaced node value.
EntityReference **Children:** Element, ProcessingInstruction, Comment, Text, CDATASection **Supported by:** W3C DOM 1, 2, 3, and MSXML	Represents a parsed or unparsed entity reference. In non-validating parsers, the reference is contained in the EntityReference node and there are no child nodes. In validating DOM parsers, the EntityReference node's child list represents the replaced node value.

Note

While NodeLists, NamedNodeMaps, DocumentFragments, DOMSelection, and DOMSchemaCollection all contain a collection of nodes, they all serve different purposes. The NodeList interface contains a list of child nodes at a single level in the DOM node tree. None of the nodes in a NodeLists have children. The NamedNodeMap interface contains a list of nodes accessible by name regardless of their position in a node tree. Node names are accessible by the nodeName property of a DOM node. A list of DOM nodes with names is shown in Table 5-6. A DocumentFragment can represent an entire node tree, starting with any child of a

Document object. DOMSelection and DOMSchemaCollection objects are used in MSXML only. DOMSelection returns a nodeList from an XPath Expression, while DOMSchemaCollection can represent one or more parsed XML Schemas.

W3C DOM nodeTypes, constants, nodeNames, and nodeValues

Each of the DOM nodes listed in Table 5-2 has a NodeType and a constant value assigned to it. Nodes can be referred to by number or constants. W3C DOM nodes can also be referenced by using the nodeType, nodeName, and nodeValue properties of the node interface. Table 5-3 lists all of the W3C DOM node types, with their nodeType, nodeName, and nodeValue property values.

Table 5-3
Node Constants for XML and HTML Documents

nodeType	Constant	nodeName	nodeValue
1	ELEMENT_NODE	element name	Null
2	ATTRIBUTE_NODE	attribute name	Attribute value
3	TEXT_NODE	#text	Text
4	CDATA_SECTION_NODE	#cdata-section	CDATA text
5	ENTITY_REFERENCE_NODE	entity reference name	Null
6	ENTITY_NODE	entity name	Null
7	PROCESSING_INSTRUCTION_NODE	target name	processing instruction text
8	COMMENT_NODE	#comment	Comment text
9	DOCUMENT_NODE	#document	Null
10	DOCUMENT_TYPE_NODE	document type name	Null
11	DOCUMENT_FRAGMENT_NODE	#document- fragment	Null
12	NOTATION_NODE	notation name	Null

The MSXML DOM nodeTypeString property

The functionality of the MSXML DOM parser and W3C DOM parsers are identical when dealing with W3C DOM nodes and interfaces, with one important exception. DOM nodes that are created with and inherit from the MSXML parser DOM Node object support the nodeTypeString property. In addition to the W3C nodeType and constant values, the nodeTypeString can be used to access all node data types. Table 5-4 shows the MSXML nodeType, Constant values, and nodeTypeString values for the corresponding W3C DOM node data types.

	Table 5-4	
	Node Constants for MSXML Node Trees	
nodeType	*Constant*	*nodeTypeString*
1	ELEMENT_NODE	element
2	ATTRIBUTE_NODE	attribute
3	TEXT_NODE	text
4	CDATA_SECTION_NODE	cdatasection
5	ENTITY_REFERENCE_NODE	entityreference
6	ENTITY_NODE	entity
7	PROCESSING_INSTRUCTION_NODE	processinginstruction
8	COMMENT_NODE	comment
9	DOCUMENT_NODE	document
10	DOCUMENT_TYPE_NODE	documenttype
11	DOCUMENT_FRAGMENT_NODE	documentfragment
12	NOTATION_NODE	notation

DOM node properties

As illustrated in Table 5-3 by the values for the nodeType, nodeName, and nodeValue properties, all of the nodes listed in Table 5-2 and many of the interfaces listed in Table 5-1 share properties and methods specified by the W3C DOM Recommendation. Most W3C DOM node properties and methods are also supported in the MSXML DOM parser, along with several MSXML DOM extensions.

For all properties and methods in this chapter, we're including annotations that specify if the property or method is supported in the W3C DOM and/or the MSXML DOM, and which version of W3C DOM is supports the property or method.

The common properties for all node data types are listed in Table 5-5.

Table 5-5
DOM Node Properties

Property	Property Value
Attributes **Supported by:** W3C DOM 1, 2, 3, and MSXML	A NamedNodeMap with an attribute list of attributes of the current node.
baseName **Supported by:** MSXML	Returns the Namespace prefix for a namespace. For example, the baseName of "xmlns:azlist="http://www.benztech.com/xsd/amazonlist" is aszlist.
childNodes **Supported by:** W3C DOM 1, 2, 3, and MSXML	A NodeList containing the child nodes of the current node.
dataType **Supported by:** MSXML	Text containing the data type for this node. Data types can be assigned using a dt: prefix on an attribute name, and an attribute value that maps to a standard or schema-defined data type.
Definition **Supported by:** MSXML	Text containing the entity reference definition from a DTD or Schema.
firstChild **Supported by:** W3C DOM 1, 2, 3, and MSXML	The first child node of the current node.
lastChild **Supported by:** W3C DOM 1, 2, 3, and MSXML	The last child node of the current node.
localName **Supported by:** W3C DOM 2 and 3	The local name of the node.
namespaceURI **Supported by:** W3C DOM 2, 3, and MSXML	Returns the URI for a namespace. For example, the namespaceURI of "xmlns:azlist="http://www.benztech.com/xsd/amazonlist" is http://www.benztech.com/xsd/amazonlist.
nextSibling **Supported by:** W3C DOM 1, 2, 3, and MSXML	The next sibling node of the current node. (Siblings are nodes that share a parent node.)
nodeName **Supported by:** W3C DOM 1, 2, 3, and MSXML	The node name of the current node.

Property	*Property Value*
nodeType **Supported by:** W3C DOM 1, 2, 3, and MSXML	The number of the of the current node type.
nodeTypedValue **Supported by:** MSXML	The specified node expressed in the named data type of that node. Data types can be assigned using a dt: prefix on an attribute name, and an attribute value that maps to a standard or schema-defined data type.
nodeTypeString **Supported by:** MSXML	A text value representing the node data type. Table 5-4 lists the nodeTypeString for all DOM node data types.
nodeValue **Supported by:** W3C DOM 1, 2, 3, and MSXML	The value of the current node. Can also be used to set attribute values.
ownerDocument **Supported by:** W3C DOM 1, 2, 3, and MSXML	The Document node of the node tree.
parentNode **Supported by:** W3C DOM 1, 2, 3, and MSXML	The parent node of the current node.
parsed **Supported by:** MSXML	The parsed status of a node and child nodes. Useful for checking to see if parsing is finished on an XML document before node tree reading and manipulation begins.
prefix **Supported by:** W3C DOM 2, 3, and MSXML	Returns the prefix for a namespace. For example, the namespaceURI of "xmlns:azlist= "http://www.benztech.com/xsd/ amazonlist" is xmlns.
previousSibling **Supported by:** W3C DOM 1, 2, 3, and MSXML	The previous sibling node of the current node. (Siblings are nodes that share a parent node.)
specified **Supported by:** MSXML	Boolean indicating that the node is a value in the XML document or the result of an entity reference.
text **Supported by:** MSXML	A concatenated text value of the current node and its descendants.
xml **Supported by:** MSXML	An XML representation of the node and its descendants.

W3C DOM node methods

DOM node properties can be manipulated using the DOM node methods in Table 5-6.

Table 5-6 **Core DOM Node Methods**	
Method	*Description*
appendChild (nodeName) **Supported by:** W3C DOM 1, 2, 3, and MSXML	Appends a new node to the current node. The example on the left appends the (nodename) node to the child nodes of the current node.
cloneNode (Boolean) **Supported by:** W3C DOM 1 2, 3 and MSXML	Copies the current node. If the Boolean value is true, the new node contains the current node and all the child nodes of the current node.
isSupported (feature, version) **Supported by:** W3C DOM 2 and 3	Returns true if a feature and version are supported. Functionally the same as the hasFeature in the DOMImplementation interface. The version of DOM that a parser supports is found by passing a number to the hasFeature method: 1.0 for DOM Level 1, 2.0 for Level 2, and 3.0 for Level 3. DOM feature constants for the hasFeature method are not version specific, but can be called using the following syntax: hasFeature(feature, version) DOM 2 Constants for features are: Core, XML, HTML, Views, StyleSheets, CSS, CSS2, Events, UIEvents, MouseEvents, MutationEvents, HTMLEvents, Range, and Traversal. Constants are not case sensitive.
hasAttributes () **Supported by:** W3C DOM 2 and 3	Returns true if the current node has associated attributes.
hasChildNodes () **Supported by:** W3C DOM 1, 2, 3, and MSXML	Returns true if the current node has child nodes.
insertBefore (nodeToInsert, nodeName) **Supported by:** W3C DOM 1, 2, 3, and MSXML	Inserts a new node before an existing node. The example on the left inserts the nodeToInsert node before the nodeName node in the node tree.

Method	Description
normalize() **Supported by:** W3C DOM 2 and 3	Creates a single concatenated text node out of any adjacent child text nodes. **Note:** This method is supported in the element interface in DOM 1 and in the node interface in DOM 2 and 3.
removeChild (childNodeName) **Supported by:** W3C DOM 1, 2, 3, and MSXML	Removes a child node of the current node from a node tree. In the example on the left, the childNodeName child node of the current node is removed from the node tree.
replaceChild (newChildNodeName, oldChildNodeName) **Supported by:** W3C DOM 1, 2, 3, and MSXML	Replaces a child node of the current node with a new node. In the example on the left, the newChildNodeName child node of the current node is replaced with the newChildNodeName node.
selectNodes () **Supported by:** MSXML	Returns a nodeList that is the result of an XPath expression.
selectSingleNode () **Supported by:** MSXML	Returns the first matching node that is the result of an XPath expression.
transformNode (stylesheet) **Supported by:** MSXML	Returns the result of an XSL Transformation on the selected node and its children using a specified XSLT stylesheet. Chapters 7, 8, and 9 provide more details on XSLT transformations.
transformNodeToObject (stylesheet,object) **Supported by:** MSXML	Passes the result of an XSL Transformation to a specified object. Commonly used to pass the results of an XSLT to a file on the file system. Chapters 7, 8, and 9 provide more details on XSLT transformations.

Other DOM node properties and methods

Each data type that inherits from the DOM node supports specific properties and methods that are unique to that data type. The following node data types can be assumed to also inherit and support all DOM node properties and methods in Tables 5-5 and 5-6, unless otherwise specified.

DOMImplementation

DOMImplementation is used in the W3C DOM 1 and MSXML parsers to check for DOM version and feature support via the `hasFeature` method. In DOM 2, the `createDocument` and `creatDocumentType` methods allow developers to create their own document node trees and DTDs in a DOM parser. Table 5-7 shows the methods for the DOMImplementation interface.

Table 5-7	
Methods for the DOMImplementation Interface	
Method	*Description*
hasFeature (feature, version) **Supported by:** W3C DOM 1, 2, 3, and MSXML	Returns the DOM version and feature sets. The version of DOM that a parser supports is found by passing a number to the hasFeature method: 1.0 for DOM Level 1, 2.0 for Level 2, and 3.0 for Level 3. DOM feature constants for the hasFeature method are not version specific, but can be called using the following syntax: hasFeature(feature, version) DOM 2 Constants for features are: Core, XML, HTML, Views, StyleSheets, CSS, CSS2, Events, UIEvents, MouseEvents, MutationEvents, HTMLEvents, Range, and Traversal. Constants are not case sensitive.
createDocument (namespaceURI, qualifiedName, doctype) **Supported by:** W3C DOM 2 and 3	Creates a new document node tree. This node tree can be created, but not saved directly from a parser. It needs to be passed to classes in a programming language that can save to the file system. A document type definition created with the DOMImplementation createDocumentType method can be associated with a document using the doctype parameter of the createDocument method.
createDocumentType (qualifiedName, publicID, systemID) **Supported by:** W3C DOM 2 and 3	Creates a new documentType node. The new documentType node can be use to provide a DTD for new node trees created with the DOMImplementation createDocument method.

ProcessingInstruction

Processing instructions are used to pass information and instructions to processors outside of the parser environment. In DOM 1, 2, 3, and the MSXML parser, the processing instruction target can be read and the instructions can be modified. Table 5-8 shows the properties for the ProcessingInstruction data type.

Table 5-8
Properties for the ProcessingInstruction Data Type

Property	Description
data **Supported by:** W3C DOM 1, 2, 3, and MSXML	Retrieves contents of the processing instruction and the target. Also used to update the processing instruction. The target cannot be edited, as it is read-only.
target **Supported by:** W3C DOM 1, 2, 3, and MSXML	The processing instruction target.

Document

The property listings of the DOM document class reflects the new direction in the DOM 3 Recommendations toward filtering data segments and producing smaller, faster, leaner DOM nodes of document portions, rather than entire XML documents. Table 5-9 shows the properties for the Document data type.

Table 5-9
Properties for the Document Data Type

Property	Description
async **Supported by:** MSXML	True if asynchronous download is permitted by this document.
doctype **Supported by:** W3C DOM 1, 2, 3, and MSXML	A documentType node that specifies the DTD for an XML document.
documentElement **Supported by:** W3C DOM 1, 2, 3, and MSXML	The root element of an XML document.

Continued

Table 5-9 *(continued)*	
Property	**Description**
implementation **Supported by:** W3C DOM 1, 2, 3, and MSXML	The DOM Implementation for the document.
ondataavailable **Supported by:** MSXML	The event handler for the ondataavailable event. When the async property is set to true, the ondataavailable property is used to begin parallel processing of a DOM document when a specific piece of data is available. The readyState property is used to check download and parsing status of an XML document.
onreadystatechange **Supported by:** MSXML	An event handler to be called when the readyState property changes.
ontransformnode **Supported by:** MSXML	An event handler for ontransformnode events in this document, which is triggered when an XSLT transformation occurs on a node using the transformNode or transformNodetoObject method.
parseError **Supported by:** MSXML	Returns an MSXML DOMParseError object that contains information about the last parsing error. Returns null if there are no parsing errors. MSXML DOM parsing code usually checks this property for parsing errors before proceeding.
preserveWhiteSpace **Supported by:** MSXML	If true, XML document whitespace (line feeds, tabs, spaces, and carriage returns) is preserved. If false, MSXML ignores any whitespace in the XML document. MSXML respects the xml:space attribute, so any space designated with the xml:space attribute is preserved regardless of the preserveWhiteSpace property value.
readyState **Supported by:** MSXML	The current state of the XML document. There are four states that the readyState property represents: 1 The load is in progress; parsing has not yet begun. 2 The document is loaded and parsing has begun, but the DOM is not yet at a stage that it can be used. 3 The document may or may not be loaded completely, but enough of the data is parsed, so processing can begin on what is parsed so far. 4 The document has been completely loaded and parsed, or the parsing was aborted due to an error.

Property	Description
resolveExternals **Supported by:** MSXML	If true, external definitions such as entity and namespace references are resolved when the document is parsed. If false, references are not resolved.
url **Supported by:** MSXML	The URL for the current XML document.
validateOnParse **Supported by:** MSXML	If true, the parser validates the XML document during parsing.

DOM document methods also reflect new directions for DOM Recommendations, this time into full support for namespaces. Table 5-10 shows the methods for the Document data type.

Table 5-10
Methods for the Document Data Type

Method	Description
abort () **Supported by:** MSXML	Aborts an asynchronous download.
createAttribute (attributeName) **Supported by:** W3C DOM 1, 2, 3, and MSXML	Creates a new attribute node with the specified name.
createAttributeNS (attributeName, qualifiedName) **Supported by:** W3C DOM 2 and 3	Creates a new attribute node with the specified name and a namespace prefix using the Namespace qualified name.
createCDATASection (textData) **Supported by:** W3C DOM 1, 2, 3, and MSXML	Creates a CDATAsection node that contains the supplied text data.
createComment (commentData) **Supported by:** W3C DOM 1, 2, 3, and MSXML	Creates a comment node that contains the supplied text data.
createDocumentFragment() **Supported by:** W3C DOM 1, 2, 3, and MSXML	Creates an empty DOM DocumentFragment object.

Continued

Table 5-10 *(continued)*

Method	Description
createElement (elementName) **Supported by:** W3C DOM 1, 2, 3, and MSXML	Creates an element node using the specified name.
createElementNS (elementName, qualifiedName) **Supported by:** W3C DOM 2 and 3	Creates an element node using the specified name and a namespace prefix using the Namespace qualified name.
createEntityReference (referenceName) **Supported by:** W3C DOM 1, 2, 3, and MSXML	Creates a new EntityReference object with the supplied name.
createNode (Type, name, namespaceURI) **Supported by:** MSXML	Creates a node using the supplied nodeType, node name, and namespace URI. Valid nodeTypes are listed in Table 5-3.
createProcessingInstruction (target, data) **Supported by:** W3C DOM 1, 2, 3, and MSXML	Creates a processing instruction node that contains the supplied target and data.
createTextNode (textData) **Supported by:** W3C DOM 1, 2, 3, and MSXML	Creates a text node that contains the supplied text data.
getElementByID (elementID) **Supported by:** W3C DOM 2 and 3	Returns an element that has a matching ID attribute value.
getElementsByTagName (elementName) **Supported by:** W3C DOM 1, 2, 3, and MSXML	Returns a collection of elements that match the specified name.
getElementsByTagNameNS (namespaceURI, localName) **Supported by:** W3C DOM 2 and 3	Returns a collection of elements that match the specified name and namespace URI.
importNode (nodetoImport, includeChildren) **Supported by:** W3C DOM 2 and 3	Import a node from another document. If the second parameter is true all child nodes of the named node are imported as well.
Load(url) **Supported by:** MSXML	Loads an XML document from the specified URL location.

Method	Description
loadXML **Supported by:** MSXML	Loads a passed XML document in string form.
nodeFromID **Supported by:** MSXML	Returns the node that matches the ID attribute. This is an MXSML-specific method that loads any node by ID, not just element nodes.
save **Supported by:** MSXML	Saves an XML document to the specified object. The object can be a file name (but not a URL), DOMDocument object, or any object that supports persistence.

documentType

documentType nodes contain DTDs that can either be used for data validation or to store values for entity references. Table 5-11 shows the properties for the documentType data type.

Table 5-11
Properties for the DocumentType Data Type

Property	Description
dataType **Supported by:** MSXML	Specifies the data type for a node. A full list of DOM dataTypes is available in Table 5-3.
entities **Supported by:** W3C DOM 1, 2, 3	Returns a namedNodeMap of entity nodes representing entities declared in a DTD.
Name **Supported by:** W3C DOM 1, 2, 3, and MSXML	Returns the name of the document type.
publicId **Supported by:** W3C DOM 2 and 3	Returns the public identifier associated with the entity.
systemId **Supported by:** W3C DOM 2 and 3	Returns the system identifier associated with the entity.
internalSubset **Supported by:** W3C DOM 2 and 3	Returns text containing internal subset declarations.

nodeList

`nodeList` does not inherit from the DOM Node interface, and therefore does not support DOM node properties and methods. All of the properties and methods that `nodeList` supports are listed in Tables 5-12 and 5-13, respectively.

Table 5-12 shows the properties for the `nodeList` data type.

<table>
<tr><td colspan="2" align="center">Table 5-12
Properties for the nodeList Data Type</td></tr>
<tr><td>*Property*</td><td>*Description*</td></tr>
<tr><td>**Length**
Supported by:
W3C DOM 1, 2, 3, and MSXML</td><td>Indicates the number of items in the collection. Read-only.</td></tr>
</table>

Table 5-13 shows the methods for the `nodeList` data type.

<table>
<tr><td colspan="2" align="center">Table 5-13
Methods for the nodeList Data Type</td></tr>
<tr><td>*Method*</td><td>*Description*</td></tr>
<tr><td>**Item**
Supported by:
W3C DOM 1, 2, 3, and MSXML</td><td>Facilitates access to individual nodes within the nodeList.</td></tr>
<tr><td>**nextNode**
Supported by:
MSXML</td><td>Returns the next node in the nodeList.</td></tr>
<tr><td>**reset**
Supported by:
MSXML</td><td>Resets the iterator to 1, moves the pointer to the first node (item) in the list.</td></tr>
</table>

namedNodeMap

`namedNodeMap` does not inherit from the DOM Node interface, and therefore does not support DOM node properties and methods. All of the properties and methods that `namedNodeMap` supports are listed in Tables 5-14 and 5-15, respectively.

Table 5-14 shows the property for the `namedNodeMap` data type.

Table 5-14
Properties for the namedNodeMap Data Type

Property	Description
length **Supported by:** W3C DOM 1, 2, 3, and MSXML	Indicates the number of items in the namedNodeMap

Table 5-15 shows the methods for the namedNodeMap data type. Note the divergence between the W3C DOM method names and the MSXML method names. For example, there are two namespace-aware methods for getNamedItem. The W3C DOM implementation calls theirs getNamedItemNS, while MSXML refers to the same thing as getQualifiedItem. Hopefully, this is a short-term situation. Personally, I'd like to see the getNamedItem method do the job with an optional second namespace parameter.

Table 5-15
Methods for the namedNodeMap Data Type

Method	Description
getNamedItem (nodeName) **Supported by:** W3C DOM 1, 2, 3, and MSXML	Returns a node with the specified name.
getNamedItemNS (nodeName, qualifiedName) **Supported by:** W3C DOM 2 and 3	Returns a node with the specified name and namespace.
getQualifiedItem (nodeName) **Supported by:** MSXML	Returns a node with the specified namespace and attribute name.
Item() **Supported by:** W3C DOM 1, 2, 3, and MSXML	Facilitates access to individual nodes within the namedNodeMap.
removeNamedItem (nodeName) **Supported by:** W3C DOM 1, 2, 3, and MSXML	Removes a named node from the namedNodeMap.
removeNamedItemNS (nodeName, qualifiedName) **Supported by:** W3C DOM 2 and 3	Removes an attribute specified by name and namespace from the collection.

Continued

Table 5-15 *(continued)*	
Method	**Description**
removeQualifiedItem (nodeName, qualifiedName) **Supported by:** MSXML	Removes the attribute with the specified namespace and attribute name.
reset() **Supported by:** MSXML	Resets the iterator to 1, moves the pointer to the first node (item) in the list.
setNamedItem (nodeName) **Supported by:** W3C DOM 1, 2, 3, and MSXML	Adds the supplied node to the collection.
setNamedItemNS (nodeName, qualifiedName) **Supported by:** W3C DOM 2 and 3	Adds the supplied node to the collection with a specific namespace prefix.

Element

Note that the MSXML DOM does not support the MXSML-specific `nodeTypedValue` property for element nodes that it does for all other nodes. Table 5-16 shows the property for the element data type.

Table 5-16 **Properties for the element Data Type**	
Property	**Description**
tagName **Supported by:** W3C DOM 1, 2, 3, and MSXML	Returns an element name.

Note that aside from the lack of `nodeTypedValue` support for element node properties, there are also a couple of anomalies in the DOM 2 element node methods. MSXML does not support the `hasAttribute` method, and DOM 2 does not have a namespace variant for the `removeAttributeNode` method. Table 5-17 shows the methods for the element data type.

Table 5-17
Methods for the element Data Type

Method	Description
getAttribute (attributeName) **Supported by:** W3C DOM 1, 2, 3, and MSXML	Returns an attribute value.
getAttributeNS (attributeName, qualifiedName) **Supported by:** W3C DOM 2 and 3	Returns an attribute value within a namespace.
getAttributeNode (attributeName) **Supported by:** W3C DOM 1, 2, 3, and MSXML	Gets an attribute node.
getAttributeNodeNS (attributeName, qualifiedName) **Supported by:** W3C DOM 2 and 3	Gets an attribute node within a namespace.
getElementsByTagName (elementName) **Supported by:** W3C DOM 1, 2, 3, and MSXML	Returns a list of all elements that match the supplied name.
getElementsByTagNameNS (elementName, qualifiedName) **Supported by:** W3C DOM 2 and 3	Returns a list of all elements that match the supplied name within a namespace.
hasAttribute (attributeName) **Supported by:** W3C DOM 2 and 3	Returns true if a node has an attribute.
hasAttributeNS (attributeName, qualifiedName) **Supported by:** W3C DOM 2 and 3	Returns true if a node has an attribute within a namespace.
normalize() **Supported by:** W3C DOM 1 and MSXML	Creates a single concatenated text node out of any adjacent child text nodes. Note: The W3C normalize method is part of the DOM 2 and DOM 3 node interface. MSXML and DOM 1 implementations still use normalize as part of the element interface.

Continued

Table 5-17 *(continued)*

Method	Description
removeAttribute (attributeName) **Supported by:** W3C DOM 1, 2, 3, and MSXML	Removes the named attribute. If the attribute that is being removed has a default value, the attribute is re-created with the default value.
removeAttributeNS (attributeName, namespaceURI) **Supported by:** W3C DOM 2 and 3	Removes the named attribute within a namespace. If the attribute that is being removed has a default value, the attribute is re-created with the default value.
removeAttributeNode (attributeName) **Supported by:** W3C DOM 1, 2, 3, and MSXML	Removes an attribute node from the current element.
setAttribute (attributeName) **Supported by:** W3C DOM 1, 2, 3, and MSXML	Sets the value of the named attribute.
setAttributeNS (attributeName, qualifiedName) **Supported by:** W3C DOM 2 and 3	Sets the value of the named attribute within a specific namespace.
setAttributeNode (attributeName) **Supported by:** W3C DOM 1, 2, 3, and MSXML	Sets or updates the named attribute node in the current element.
setAttributeNodeNS (attributeName, qualifiedName) **Supported by:** W3C DOM 2 and 3	Sets or updates the named attribute node in the current element within a specific namespace.

Attr

There are only a few properties for the DOM `Attr` interface and no `Attr` methods. Manipulation of DOM attributes is done through the element interface, because all attributes have to have an associated element. Table 5-18 shows the properties for the `Attr` data type.

Table 5-18
Properties for the Attr Data Type

Property	Description
name **Supported by:** W3C DOM 1, 2, 3, and MSXML	Returns an attribute name.
value **Supported by:** W3C DOM 1, 2, 3, and MSXML	Returns an attribute value.
ownerElement **Supported by:** W3C DOM 2 and 3	Returns the element that an attribute belongs to.

CharacterData and Comment

Comment inherits properties and methods from CharacterData and has no additional properties or methods, so we've listed them together. Table 5-19 shows the properties for the CharacterData and Comment data types.

Table 5-19
Properties for the CharacterData and Comment Data Types

Property	Description
data **Supported by:** W3C DOM 1, 2, 3, and MSXML	Returns node character data if there is a character value associated with the node type.
length **Supported by:** W3C DOM 1, 2, 3, and MSXML	Returns the number of characters in a string.

Table 5-20 shows the methods for the CharacterData and Comment data types.

Table 5-20
Methods for the CharacterData and Comment Data Types

Method	Description
appendData (string) **Supported by:** W3C DOM 1, 2, 3, and MSXML	Appends a string to the existing string data.
deleteData (start, **numberofCharacters)** **Supported by:** W3C DOM 1, 2, 3, and MSXML	Deletes a substring, string starting at a specific point in a string and continuing for a specific number of characters.
insertData (start, string) **Supported by:** W3C DOM 1, 2, 3, and MSXML	Inserts the specified string starting at a specific point in a string.
replaceData (start, **numberofCharacters, string)** **Supported by:** W3C DOM 1, 2, 3, and MSXML	Replaces a substring, string starting at a specific point in a string and continuing for a specific number of characters.
substringData (start, **numberofCharacters)** **Supported by:** W3C DOM 1, 2, 3, and MSXML	Returns a substring of a string using a specified range.

CDATASection and Text

CDATASection and Text nodes also inherit properties and methods from CharacterData, but both have one additional method — SplitText, so they can't be listed with the comment properties and methods without confusion. Because both the CDATASection and Text nodes have the same properties and methods, we've listed them together.

Table 5-21 shows the properties for the CDATASection and Text data types.

Table 5-21 Properties for the CDATASection and Text Data Types	
Property	**Description**
Data Supported by: W3C DOM 1, 2, 3, and MSXML	Returns node character data if there is a character value associated with the node type.
Length Supported by: W3C DOM 1, 2, 3, and MSXML	Returns the number of characters in a string.

Table 5-22 shows the methods for the data types.

Table 5-22 Methods for the CDATASection and Text Data Types	
Method	**Description**
appendData (string) Supported by: W3C DOM 1, 2, 3, and MSXML	Appends a string to the existing string data.
deleteData (start, numberofCharacters) Supported by: W3C DOM 1, 2, 3, and MSXML	Deletes a substring, string starting at a specific point in a string and continuing for a specific number of characters.
insertData (start, string) Supported by: W3C DOM 1, 2, 3, and MSXML	Inserts the specified string starting at a specific point in a string.
replaceData (start, numberofCharacters, string) Supported by: W3C DOM 1, 2, 3, and MSXML	Replaces a substring, string starting at a specific point in a string and continuing for a specific number of characters.
splitText Supported by: W3C DOM 1, 2, 3, and MSXML	Creates a new sibling text node that starts at specific point in a string and continues for a specific number of characters.
substringData (start, numberofCharacters) Supported by: W3C DOM 1, 2, 3, and MSXML	Returns a substring of a string using a specified range.

Entity

Entities can be parsed or unparsed in the DOM entity node. Table 5-23 shows the properties for the entity data type.

Table 5-23
Properties for the entity Data Type

Property	Description
notationName **Supported by:** W3C DOM 1, 2, 3, and MSXML	Contains the notation name of an unparsed entity. If the entity is parsed, the notationName is null.
publicId **Supported by:** W3C DOM 1, 2, 3, and MSXML	Returns the public identifier associated with the entity.
systemId **Supported by:** W3C DOM 1, 2, 3, and MSXML	Returns the system identifier associated with the entity.

Notation

Table 5-24 shows the properties for the Notation data type.

Table 5-24
Properties for the Notation Data Type

Property	Description
publicId **Supported by:** W3C DOM 1, 2, 3, and MSXML	Returns the public identifier associated with the entity.
systemId **Supported by:** W3C DOM 1, 2, 3, and MSXML	Returns the system identifier associated with the entity.

Summary

In this chapter, I've provided a deep dive into the details of the Document Object Model (DOM):

✦ A history of the DOM

✦ DOM versions and evolution

✦ Understanding differences in W3C and MSXML DOM parser implementations

✦ DOM interfaces and nodes

✦ DOM node values

✦ The node data types

✦ Properties and methods for W3C and MSXML DOM node data types

In the next chapter, I'll dive into the details at the other end of the parsing pool: the Simple API for XML (SAX). SAX is an event-driven interface, which contrasts sharply with DOM parsing concepts. It is, however, worth the learning curve because of superior performance over many DOM parsing solutions.

✦   ✦   ✦

Parsing XML with SAX

In This Chapter

Understanding
SAX versions

Understanding
differences in SAX
and MSXML
SAX parser
implementations

SAX interfaces
and events

SAX event values

Properties and
methods for SAX API
and MSXML SAX
events

Chapter 4 provided a theoretical overview of the concepts behind XML document parsing, and Chapter 5 provided a deep dive into what makes DOM parsing tick. This
chapter extends Chapter 4's basic concepts and provides a
deep dive into the Simple API for XML (SAX) parsing.

SAX parsing takes a little more of a learning curve to master
when compared to DOM parsing. While DOM nodes can be
directly mapped to corresponding XML source document
objects, SAX events do not provide the same level of direct
comparison.

Once you get around the theory of the event model concepts,
SAX parsing solutions can actually be much easier to implement than DOM solutions. This is because there is only one
official source for SAX event specifications and documentation: the SAX project. There is also an MSXML SAX implementation, which is based on SAX, but rewritten as Microsoft XML
core nodes. But these two sources are relatively simple to
keep on top of when compared to the exponential growth of
W3C DOM Working Drafts that appear with each new DOM
version, and DOM node property and method variants that
appear with every new version of the MXSML DOM parser. For
each event we discuss in this chapter, we list the supporting
SAX versions (SAX 1 and 2, and MSXML), and the differences
in each event between the platforms.

In addition, SAX parsers only have to handle XML documents,
while DOM interfaces must work for HTML and XML documents. This single-purpose approach greatly streamlines the
interfaces needed to implement a full SAX solution versus the
W3C DOM, which needs to consider HTML objects when
developing new interfaces, properties, and methods.

One other thing that makes SAX solutions simpler to implement is that they are less diplomatic about the language used
to describe objects and develop parser classes — Java. The
W3C uses the Interface Definition Language (IDL) to represent

DOM code examples. IDL is an abstract language from the Object Management Group (OMG) and is not portable to other languages, such as Java, VB, or Jscript. Because SAX uses Java as a base for examples and development, it's much easier to implement Java solutions using Java-based parsers such as the Apache Xerces parser. Microsoft has copied SAX objects and events, but they are not implements in Java.

The W3C defines the specifications for DOM parsing in the W3C DOM recommendation. As I showed you in Chapter 4 and 5, the W3C DOM can be used to create XML documents, navigate DOM structures, and add, modify, or delete DOM nodes. DOM parsing can be slower than SAX parsing because DOM creates a representation of the entire document as nodes, regardless of how large the document is. However, DOM can be handy for retrieving all the data from a document, or retrieving a piece of data several times. The DOM stays resident in memory as long as the code that created the DOM representation is running.

Understanding SAX

SAX parsing tends to be faster than DOM parsing in most situations, but can also be more complicated to code. SAX's event-based parsing model can be compared to getting information from this chapter of the book by going to the page where the chapter starts, reading the chapter, and stopping when the chapter ends. DOM would extract the same information from this book by creating a copy of the book as a collection of several chapter objects, then looking through the objects to find this chapter, then extracting information from the chapter. SAX parsers look for a particular object in an XML document and commit that object to memory as they pass though the document, using start and end events for that object. As a SAX parser passes through a document, it passes the objects it collects to the calling program for reading and manipulation.

Where SAX comes from

Like DOM, SAX is used to describe, parse, and manipulate XML Documents. Unlike DOM, SAX breaks a document down into a series of events, such as the start of a document (`StartDocument`), the start of an element (`StartElement`), the end of an element (`EndElement`), encountering a processing instruction (`Processing Instruction`), a condition that requires a warning message (`SAXWarning`), or the end of a document (`EndDocument`).

It's important to note that SAX is not developed or "recommended" by the W3C, though evolving DOM implementations often borrow features from more advanced SAX feature sets. In general, SAX is usually ahead of DOM implementations, because the W3C recommendation process does not hinder SAX development. There is no official specification of SAX, just the implementation of the `XMLReader` class, which is only written in Java at this time. There are other implementations of SAX on other platforms, but these are either a result of bindings to code in the SAX archive file, sax.jar, or a complete rewrite of code that simply mimics the functionality of SAX classes, as in the case of the MSXML SAX parser objects, properties, and methods.

Official updates to SAX are implemented in the latest version of the sax.jar file. This file and associated documentation can be downloaded at `http://www.saxproject.org/`. The site also contains information about parser implementations and bindings, and the FAQ at that site is not only helpful and informative, but probably the funniest parser API FAQ you'll ever read. Other implementations of SAX parsers can be found on the links page of `http://www.saxproject.org/`, and a more or less complete listing of available parsers of all kinds is available at `http://www.xmlsoftware.com/parsers.html`.

SAX 1 and SAX 2

Unlike DOM 1 and 2, SAX 2 is backward compatible with SAX 1. Though most current Parsers implement the SAX2 interface and its updated feature set, the SAX 1 interface will still work. A SAX 1 driver implements the Parser interface and a SAX 2 Driver implements the XMLReader interface, but SAX 2 parsers still support properties and methods of the parser interface. SAX 1 supports Navigation around a document and manipulation of content via SAX events. SAX 2 enhancements include support for Namespaces, filter chains, plus querying and setting features and properties via SAX Events.

Microsoft MSXML SAX extensions

Microsoft's XML parser is part of Internet Explorer 5.5 or later. The MSXML parser is currently called the Microsoft XML Core Services, but is usually still referred to by the original MSXML acronym. The MSXML parser uses the same SAX events as Java-based SAX parsers such as Xerces, but the MSXML SAX implementation is an unofficial copy of the SAX project events. The SAX project offers their materials with no copyright royalty restrictions, so there is no legal issue with the Microsoft copy, but there are inevitable compatibility issues between original events and copied events. We'll highlight the differences in the listing of properties and methods later in this chapter.

Tip

The biggest difference in the MSXML SAX implementation versus other SAX implementations is that the MSXML 4 SAX parser does not support XML document validation against DTDs, just Schemas. On the other hand, the SAX API does not explicitly support Schema validation, just DTD (though most SAX implementations including Xerces support Schema validation). If you are developing an XML application using MS Visual Studio.Net and your application requires a validating parser that supports DTDs, you can use a combination of a SAX and DOM parsing using the MSXML IMXWriter interface to pass a DOM object from SAX to DOM. We cover the IMXWriter interface later in this chapter. If this doesn't work for your solution, you'll have to use the MSXML DOM parser or develop/download a third-party SAX implementation that supports DTD validation and works with your programming language of choice.

Just as in the MXSMLDOM implementation, the MSXML SAX parser adds several additional methods and properties to the W3C DOM interface methods and properties. These methods and properties are commonly referred to as Microsoft SAX extensions or MSXML extensions. MSXML extensions can be used in IE browser applications and other types of Windows applications that use the MSXML parser as their SAX parser. Other parsers, such as Xerces, do not support these applications.

Because MSXML and the Internet Explorer are so widely used, most XML programmers need to know about Microsoft's additional properties and methods. The other practical reason for knowing which methods and properties are part of Java SAX implementations and which are MXSML extensions is to know what properties and methods are available in a specific parser, and when you can use them.

The MSXML download includes a great help database will full documentation and examples for working with the MSXML SAX events in JScript, Visual Basic, and C/C++. Recent MSXML updates can be downloaded from http://www.microsoft.com/msxml.

We're documenting the MSXML 4.01 parser in this chapter, which may be updated by the time this book is in print. We'll post any changes to the MSXML documentation and updates to this chapter as they evolve. The updated text can be downloaded from http://www.XMLProgrammingBible.com.

Interfaces for SAX and MSXML

As with W3C and MSXML DOM implementations, SAX uses a set of interfaces to provide access to XML document events. Each interface has a number of properties and methods that I will review later in this chapter. In addition, SAX has several helper classes for Java implementations, and MSXML has two extension interfaces for manipulating attributes and writing parsed output.

MSXML SAX interface names do not follow the official SAX interface naming standards, even though MSXML interfaces support most of the SAX interfaces, properties, and methods. For example, the SAX XMLReader interface is ISAXXMLReader in the MXSML SAX implementations.

SAX interfaces are the "official" interfaces that are listed in the SAX API documentation at http://www.saxproject.org/apidoc. They consist of core interfaces and extension interfaces.

SAX core interfaces

Complete XML documents are not usually represented in SAX. Individual objects in XML documents are identified and collected through a series of events. While SAX 1 and 2 are supported by standard SAX implementations such as Xerces, SAX 2 should be used for new development, unless there is a very good reason for using the older, slower, more limited SAX 1 classes. Also, note that SAX 1 classes are not supported by MSXML 4. Table 6-1 shows the current listing of SAX 1 and 2 core interfaces.

Table 6-1
SAX 1 and 2 Interfaces for XML Documents

Interface Name	Description
XMLReader **Supported by:** SAX 2, MSXML	The main interface for SAX 2 XML parsing functionality.
Parser **Supported by:** SAX 1	The main interface for SAX 1 XML parsing functionality. The Parser interface has been replaced by the SAX2 XMLReader interface, and should not be used for new development.
XMLFilter **Supported by:** SAX 2, MSXML	XMLFilters are similar to the XML Reader interface, except that an XMLFilter source is another XMLReader object, not an XML document from the file system. XMLFilters can be used to quickly and easily produce fragments of documents. For example, a XMLFIlter could be used to create a representation of an XML document without any comments, or a document representation that has all attributes removed.
ContentHandler **Supported by:** SAX 2, MSXML	The main interface for a SAX 2 document's content.
DocumentHandler **Supported by:** SAX 1	The main interface for a SAX 1 document's content. This interface has been replaced by the SAX2 ContentHandler interface, and should not be used for new development.
Locator **Supported by:** SAX 2, MSXML	Associates a SAX event with a document location. Locators provide the line and column in an XML document that a SAX event takes place. Information about public and/or system IDs associated with that location can also be provided, if there are any.

Continued

	Table 6-1 *(continued)*
Interface Name	**Description**
Attributes **Supported by:** SAX 2, MSXML	The SAX 2 interface for a list of XML attributes.
AttributeList **Supported by:** SAX 1	The SAX 1 interface for a list of XML attributes. This interface has been replaced by the SAX2 Attributes interface, and should not be used for new development.
DTDHandler **Supported by:** SAX 1 and 2, MSXML (MSXML SAX is non-validating)	The main interface for a DTD document's content. **Note:** The MSXML DOM parser and other SAX parsers, such as Xerces, provide support for validation and parsing for DTDs and Schemas. The MSXML 4 SAX parser can parse DTD documents, but does not provide support for validating documents using DTDs, just Schemas. DTD can still be used as containers for entity references when using the MSXML SAX parser.
EntityResolver **Supported by:** SAX 1 and 2, MSXML	The SAX 1 and 2 interface for creating custom methods for resolving entitles. SAX parsers resolve regular entity references with values in DTDs automatically. The EntityResolver interface allows developers to create a custom interface to external values that can be used during SAX parsing.
ErrorHandler **Supported by:** SAX 1 and 2, MSXML	The SAX 1 and 2 interface for handling errors while parsing an XML document.

SAX extension interfaces

Aside from the SAX core interfaces, there are several extension interfaces that are implemented using the SAX extension API, as described in Table 6-2. SAX extensions are optional interfaces for SAX parsers. For example, the MSXML parser supports the DeclHandler and LexicalHandler interfaces, while the Apache Xerces parser classes support all extension interfaces. They can also be implemented independently of the SAX core interfaces. All extensions have been developed using the SAX 2 extensions API, and are not available in SAX 1.

Note You may see SAX documentation that refers to "SAX Extensions 1.x." This refers to the SAX 2 Extensions 1.x API, not SAX 1. There is no SAX extension API for SAX 1.

Table 6-2 SAX Extension Interfaces	
Interface Name	*Description*
Attributes2 **Supported by:** SAX 2 (Optional)	Checks a DTD to see if an attribute in an XML document was declared in a DTD, and if the DTD specifies a default value.
DeclHandler **Supported by:** SAX 2 (Optional), MSXML	Returns declared values in a DTD for attributes, elements, and internal and external entities.
EntityResolver2 **Supported by:** SAX 2 (Optional)	Programmatically adds external entity reference subsets to an XML document that has no subset reference in the DOCTYPE declaration, or has no DOCTYPE declaration.
LexicalHandler **Supported by:** SAX 2 (Optional), MSXML	Returns information about lexical events in an XML document. Comments, the start and end of a CDATA section, the start and end of a DTD declaration, and the start and end of an entity can be tracked with LexicalHandler.
Locator2 **Supported by:** SAX 2 (Optional)	Extends the Locator interface to return the encoding and the XML version for an XML document.

SAX also provides a number of Java helper classes that are used to gain access to the XMLReader classes, identify input sources, access extension classes, and other tasks. I'll cover these in mode detail later in the chapter.

MSXML SAX extension interfaces

MSXML has implemented SAX extension classes that support additional functionality for MSXML SAX applications, as described in Table 6-3. SAX schemas gain access to information via the IMXSchemaDeclHandler interface. The IMXAttributes interface provides the ability to create and edit attribute collections. The IMXWriter Interface permits writing to the file system.

Table 6-3 MSXML SAX Extension Interfaces	
Interface Name	Description
IMXAttributes **Supported by:** MSXML	Provides access to edit, add, and delete attribute names and values.
IMXSchemaDeclHandler **Supported by:** MSXML	Provides schema information about an element being parsed, including attributes.
IMXWriter **Supported by:** MSXML	Writes parsed XML output to: An IStream object: A stream object representing a sequence of bytes that can be forwarded to another object such as a file or a screen. A string (remember, all XML documents are technically strings). A DOMDocument object, which can be passed to the MSXML DOM parser for further processing. For example, a new XML document could be parsed using SAX for speed, then sent to the DOM parser for DTD validation.

SAX Methods and Properties

Each of the interfaces listed previously in Tables 6-1, 6-2, and 6-3 contains methods and properties that are accessible through the SAX API. I've listed them in the same order that they are listed in Tables 6-1, 6-2, and 6-3. This is the same way that you would most likely encounter them in a SAX parsing application.

Note One of the key differences between the SAX API and the MSXML implementation is that the SAX API relies exclusively on methods for interface functionality. The MSXML SAX parser has implemented a few properties, but these are not part of the "official" API, and usually have a SAX method equivalent.

SAX interfaces

SAX interfaces are the "official" interfaces that are listed in the SAX API documentation at http://www.saxproject.org/apidoc. They consist of core interfaces and extension interfaces.

XMLReader

XMLReader is the main interface for SAX 2 XML parsing functionality. The methods are described in Table 6-4.

Note MSXML XMLReader Interface methods differ slightly. The SAX `setFeature` and `setProperty` methods are the same as the MSXML `putFeature` and `putProperty` methods. Also, the MSXML `parseURL` method is the same as using a SAX parse method with a `systemID` parameter.

Table 6-4	
XMLReader Interface Methods	
Method Name	**Description**
getContentHandler() **Supported by:** SAX 2, MSXML	Returns the current ContentHandler object, which contains the content of a source XML document.
getDTDHandler() **Supported by:** SAX 2, MSXML	Returns the current DTDHandler object, which contains the content of a source DTD.
getEntityResolver() **Supported by:** SAX 2, MSXML	Returns the current entityResolver object.
getErrorHandler() **Supported by:** SAX 2, MSXML	Returns the current errorHandler object.
getFeature(name) **Supported by:** SAX 2, MSXML	Look up the value of a feature flag. Feature flags tell you if your SAX parser supports a specific feature, such as namespaces or Schema validation, or the optional Attributes2 interface. The MSXML getFeature method also gets the XML document namespace support, schema validation support, and a few other features. SAX properties vary by parser. MSXML SAX parser properties are listed in the MSXML Core documentation, under the SAXXMLReader interface. SAX feature flags vary by parser. Official SAX feature flags are listed at `http://www.saxproject.org/apidoc/org/xml/sax/package-summary.html#package_description`.

Continued

Table 6-4 *(continued)*	
Method Name	**Description**
getProperty(name) **Supported by:** SAX 2, MSXML	Looks up the value of a property. SAX properties tell you a SAX object class supports the default class or a custom class for entity declarations, lexical handlers, and a few other items. The MSXML getProperty method also gets the XML document declaration encoding, version, and standalone attributes. Otherwise, it's the same as setProperty in the SAX API. SAX properties vary by parser. Official SAX properties are listed at `http://www.saxproject.org/apidoc/org/xml/sax/package-summary.html#package_description`.
Parse(InputSource input) **Supported by:** SAX 2 , MSXML	Parses the InputSource XML document.
parse(systemId) **Supported by:** SAX 2, MSXML	Parses the XML document specified by systemID.
parseURL(URL) **Supported by:** MSXML	Parses an XML document at the specified URL.
setContentHandler **(ContentHandler handler)** **Supported by:** SAX 2, MSXML	Sets the current ContentHandler object, which contains the content of a source XML document.
setDTDHandler(DTDHandler handler) **Supported by:** SAX 2, MSXML	Sets the current DTDHandler object, which contains the content of a source DTD.
setEntityResolver **(EntityResolver resolver)** **Supported by:** SAX 2, MSXML	Sets the current entityResolver object.
setErrorHandler **(ErrorHandler handler)** **Supported by:** SAX 2, MSXML	Sets the current errorHandler object.

Method Name	Description
setFeature(name, boolean value) **Supported by:** SAX 2 , MSXML	Sets the value of a feature flag. Feature flags tell you if your SAX parser supports a specific feature, such as namespaces or Schema validation, or the optional Attributes2 interface. Similar to putFeature in the MSXML SAX parser. SAX feature flags vary by parser. Official SAX feature flags are listed at `http://www.saxproject.org/apidoc/org/xml/sax/package-summary.html#package_description`.
putFeature **Supported by:** MSXML, MSXML	Sets the value of a feature flag. Feature flags tell you if your SAX parser supports a specific feature, such as namespaces or Schema validation, or the optional Attributes2 interface. MSXML also sets the XML document namespace support, schema validation support, and a few other features putFeature. Otherwise, it's the same as setFeature in the SAX API. SAX properties vary by parser. MSXML SAX parser properties are listed in the MSXML Core documentation, under the SAXXMLReader interface.
setProperty(name, dataType) **Supported by:** SAX 2 , MSXML	Sets the value of a property. SAX properties tell you a SAX object class supports the default class or a custom class for entity declarations, lexical handlers, and a few other items. Similar to putProperty in the MSXML SAX parser. SAX properties vary by parser. Official SAX properties are listed at `http://www.saxproject.org/apidoc/org/xml/sax/package-summary.html#package_description`.
putProperty(name, dataType) **Supported by:** MSXML	Sets the value of a property. SAX properties tell you a SAX object class supports the default class or a custom class for entity declarations, lexical handlers, and a few other items. MSXML also sets the XML document declaration encoding, version and standalone attributes from putProperty. Otherwise, it's the same as setProperty in the SAX API. SAX properties vary by parser. MSXML SAX parser properties are listed in the MSXML Core documentation, under the SAXXMLReader interface.

Parser

Parser is the main interface for SAX 1 XML parsing functionality, as described in Table 6-5. The Parser interface has been replaced by the SAX2 XMLReader interface and should not be used for new development. We've included it here so you can understand legacy applications when upgrading them to SAX 2 Interfaces.

Table 6-5
Parser Interface Methods

Method Name	Description
parse(InputSource source) or parse(systemId) Supported by: SAX 1	Parses the InputSource document or an XML document specified by a System ID.
setDocumentHandler (DocumentHandler handler) Supported by: SAX 1	Sets the documentHandler object.
setDTDHandler(DTDHandler handler) Supported by: SAX 1	Sets the DTDHandler object.
setEntityResolver (EntityResolver resolver) Supported by: SAX 1	Sets the entityResolver object.
setErrorHandler (ErrorHandler handler) Supported by: SAX 1	Sets an errorHandler for an application.
setLocale(locale) Supported by: SAX 1	Returns a locale for errors and warnings.

XMLFilter

XMLFilters are similar to the XML Reader interface, except that an XMLFilter source comes from an existing XMLReader object. XMLFilters can be used to quickly and easily produce fragments of documents. For example, an XMLFIlter could be used to create a representation of an XML document without any comments, or a document representation that has all attributes removed. Table 6-6 describes the properties, and Table 6-7 describes the methods.

Note The MSXML SAX implementation parent property supports the same functionality as the SAX `setParent` and `getParent` methods. Also, the MSXML parent property is the same as the SAX API `getParent()` method.

Table 6-6	
XMLFilter Interface Properties	
Property Name	**Description**
Parent **Supported by:** MSXML	Sets or gets the XMLReader parent of the XMLFilter.

Table 6-7	
XMLFilter Interface Methods	
Method Name	**Description**
getParent() **Supported by:** SAX 2, MSXML	Gets the XMLReader parent of the XMLFilter.
setParent(XMLReader parent) **Supported by:** SAX 2, MSXML	Sets the XMLReader parent of the XMLFilter.

ContentHandler

ContentHandler is the main interface for a SAX 2 document's content. XMLReader uses ContentHandler to track all of the SAX events for an XML document.

Note The SAX API ContentHandler interface uses the `setDocumentLocator` method to get a locator interface, while MSXML SAX uses the `ContentHandler` `documentLocator` property to do the same thing.

Handling attributes in SAX

Note that there are no `startAttribute` and `endAttribute` events in SAX. On first look at SAX, handling attribute events like other document content events may seem logical, but attributes are only associated with elements, and there are enough exceptions when working with groups of attributes to warrant that they have their own interface. Attributes in SAX are returned by the `startElement` event in their own `Attributes` object, which is manipulated using the attributes interface. Table 6-8 describes the properties, and Table 6-9 describes the methods.

Table 6-8
ContentHandler Interface Properties

Property Name	Description
documentLocator **Supported by:** MSXML	Returns a pointer to the Locator interface, which returns the column number, line number, public ID, or system ID for a SAX event.

Table 6-9
ContentHandler Interface Methods

Method Name	Description
startDocument() **Supported by:** SAX 2, MSXML	This event is triggered when the parser encounters the beginning of a document.
endDocument() **Supported by:** SAX 2, MSXML	This event is triggered when the parser encounters the end of a document.
startElement(uri, localName, **qName, Attributes atts)** **Supported by:** SAX 2, MSXML	This event is triggered when the parser encounters the beginning of an element.
endElement(uri, localName, qName) **Supported by:** SAX 2, MSXML	This event is triggered when the parser encounters the end of an element.
startPrefixMapping(prefix, uri) **Supported by:** SAX 2, MSXML	Explicitly map a prefix to a URI. This is used with the startElement and endElement events to map a prefix to a URI at time of parsing. The prefix and/or URI do not need to be in the original XML document.
endPrefixMapping(prefix) **Supported by:** SAX 2, MSXML	End the explicit mapping of a prefix to a URI.
characters(char[] ch, start, length) **Supported by:** SAX 2, MSXML	This event is triggered when the parser encounters character data.
ignorableWhitespace **(char[] ch, start, length)** **Supported by:** SAX 2, MSXML	This event is triggered when the parser encounters ignorable whitespace in element content.

Method Name	Description
processingInstruction(target, data) **Supported by:** SAX 2, MSXML	This event is triggered when the parser encounters a processing instruction.
setDocumentLocator(Locator locator) **Supported by:** SAX 2	Returns a pointer to the Locator interface, which returns the column number, line number, public ID, or system ID for a SAX event.
skippedEntity(name) **Supported by:** SAX 2, MSXML	This event is triggered when the parser encounters a skipped entity.

DocumentHandler

DocumentHandler is the main interface for a SAX 1 document's content, as described in Table 6-10. This interface has been replaced by the SAX2 ContentHandler interface, and should not be used for new development.

Note The documentHandler interface is associated with the deprecated `Parser` class. Neither should be used for new development. We've included the method listing to help developers debug and upgrade legacy code to the SAX 2 ContentHandler and XMLReader interfaces.

Table 6-10 **DocumentHandler Interface Methods**	
Method Name	Description
characters(char[] ch, start, length) **Supported by:** SAX 1	This event is triggered when the parser encounters character data.
endDocument() **Supported by:** SAX 1	This event is triggered when the parser encounters the end of a document.
endElement(name) **Supported by:** SAX 1	This event is triggered when the parser encounters the end of an element.
ignorableWhitespace (char[] ch, start, length) **Supported by:** SAX 1	This event is triggered when the parser encounters ignorable whitespace in element content.

Continued

Method Name	Description
Table 6-10 *(continued)*	

Method Name	Description
processingInstruction(target, data) **Supported by:** SAX 1	This event is triggered when the parser encounters a processing instruction.
setDocumentLocator(Locator locator) **Supported by:** SAX 1	Returns a pointer to the Locator interface, which returns the column number, line number, public ID, or system ID for a SAX event.
startDocument() **Supported by:** SAX 1	This event is triggered when the parser encounters the beginning of a document.
startElement **(name, AttributeList atts)** **Supported by:** SAX 1	This event is triggered when the parser encounters the beginning of an element.

Locator

Locator associates a SAX event with a document location. Locators provide the line and column in an XML document that a SAX event takes place. Information about public and/or system IDs associated with that location can also be provided, if there are any.

The Locator interface is accessible via the ContentHandler interface, as described in Table 6-11. Use the setDocumentLocator method for SAX API-compliant parsers such as Xerces, and the documentLocator property in MSXML.

Method Name	Description
Table 6-11 **Locator Interface Methods**	

Method Name	Description
getColumnNumber() **Supported by:** SAX 1, 2, and MSXML	Returns the ending column number of a SAX event. XML document columns start at the beginning of a new line. The first column (1) is the first character of a line in an XML document. The column counts increments by one for each character in the line, until a line end is encountered.
getLineNumber() **Supported by:** SAX 1, 2, and MSXML	Returns the ending line number of a SAX event. Lines in Locators start at 1.

Method Name	Description
getPublicId() **Supported by:** SAX 1, 2, and MSXML	Returns the public ID of a SAX event.
getSystemId() **Supported by:** SAX 1, 2, and MSXML	Returns the system ID of a SAX event.

Attributes

Attributes is the SAX 2 interface for a list of XML attributes. The properties and methods are described in Table 6-12 and Table 6-13, respectively. Attributes in SAX are returned by the ContentHandler interface startElement event. They are contained in their own Attributes object.

Note   Calling the MSXML getIndexFromName and getIndexFromQName return the same results as calling the SAX API getIndex with a namespace name or a Qname. The same goes for the SAX getType and getValue methods. Also, the MSXML length property returns the same result as the SAX getLength() method. The only difference is that if there are no attributes.

Table 6-12 Attributes Interface Properties	
Property Name	Description
Length **Supported by:** MSXML	Returns the count of element attributes, starting at 0.

Table 6-13 Attributes Interface Methods	
Method Name	Description
getIndex(qName) **or** **getIndex(uri, localName)** **Supported by:** SAX 2	Returns the index of an attribute by qualified name or namespace name. Attribute indexes start at 0.

Continued

	Table 6-13 *(continued)*	
Method Name	**Description**
getIndexFromName (uri, localName) **Supported by:** MSXML	Returns the index of an attribute by name. Attribute indexes start at 0.
getIndexFromQName (qName) **Supported by:** MSXML	Returns the index of an attribute by qualified name. Attribute indexes start at 0.
getLength() **Supported by:** SAX 2	Returns the count of element attributes, starting at 0.
getLocalName(index) **Supported by:** SAX 2 and MSXML	Returns an attribute name from an index. Attribute indexes start at 0.
getQName(index) **Supported by:** SAX 2 and MSXML	Returns an attribute qualified name from an index. Attribute indexes start at 0.
getType(index) **Supported by:** SAX 2 and MSXML	Returns an attribute type from an index. SAX API values are "CDATA", "ID", "IDREF", "IDREFS", "NMTOKEN", "NMTOKENS", "ENTITY", "ENTITIES", or "NOTATION" (all in uppercase).
getType(qName) or **getType(uri, localName)** **Supported by:** SAX 2	Returns an attribute type from an attribute qualified name or namespace name. SAX API values are "CDATA", "ID", "IDREF", "IDREFS", "NMTOKEN", "NMTOKENS", "ENTITY", "ENTITIES", or "NOTATION" (all in uppercase).
getTypeFromName (uri, localName) **Supported by:** MSXML	Returns an attribute type from a namespace name. SAX API values are "CDATA", "ID", "IDREF", "IDREFS", "NMTOKEN", "NMTOKENS", "ENTITY", "ENTITIES", or "NOTATION" (all in uppercase).
getTypeFromQName (qName) **Supported by:** MSXML	Returns an attribute type from a qualified name. SAX API values are "CDATA", "ID", "IDREF", "IDREFS", "NMTOKEN", "NMTOKENS", "ENTITY", "ENTITIES", or "NOTATION" (all in uppercase).
getURI(index) **Supported by:** SAX 2 and MSXML	Returns an attribute's namespace URI by index.
getValue(index) **Supported by:** SAX 2 and MSXML	Returns an attribute's value by index.

Method Name	Description
getValue(qName) or getValue(uri, localName) Supported by: SAX 2	Returns an attribute's value by qualified name or namespace name.
getValueFromName (qName) Supported by: MSXML	Returns an attribute's value by qualified name.
getValueFromQName (uri, localName) Supported by: MSXML	Returns an attribute's value by namespace name.

AttributeList

AttributeList is the SAX 1 interface for a list of XML attributes, as described in Table 6-14. As with the Parser and ContentHandler interfaces, AttributeList should not be used for new development. We've included it here to help debug and upgrade SAX 1 code to the SAX 2 XMLReader, ContentHandler, and Attributes interfaces.

Table 6-14
AttributeList Interface Methods

Method Name	Description
getLength() Supported by: SAX 1	Returns the count of element attributes, starting at 0.
getName(i) Supported by: SAX 1	Returns the name of an attribute by index. Attribute indexes start at 0.
getType(i) Supported by: SAX 1	Returns the type of an attribute by index. Attribute indexes start at 0.
getType(name) Supported by: SAX 1	Returns the type of an attribute by name.
getValue(i) Supported by: SAX 1	Returns the value of an attribute by index. Attribute indexes start at 0.
getValue(name) Supported by: SAX 1	Returns the value of an attribute by name.

DTDHandler

DTDHandler is the main interface for a DTD document's content. Table 6-15 describes the methods.

Note

> The SAX 2 API does not currently supply explicit support for Schema validation. However, SAX parser implementations, such as Xerces, provide support for validation and parsing for Schemas and DTDs.
>
> The MSXML 4 SAX parser can parse DTD documents, but does not provide support for validating documents using DTDs, just schemas. DTD can still be used as containers for entity references when using the MSXML SAX parser, but not for data validation. MSXML developers who want to validate against schemas can use the MSXML DOM parser, or download/develop a SAX parser that supports schema validation.

Table 6-15
DTDHandler Interface Methods

Method Name	Description
notationDecl(name, publicId, systemId) **Supported by:** SAX 1, 2, and MSXML	This event is triggered when the parser encounters a notation declaration event.
unparsedEntityDecl(name, publicId, systemId, notationName) **Supported by:** SAX 1, 2, and MSXML	This event is triggered when the parser encounters an unparsed entity declaration event.

EntityResolver

EntityResolver is the SAX 1 and 2 interface for creating custom methods for resolving entitles, as described in Table 6-16. SAX parsers resolve regular entity references with values in DTDs automatically. The EntityResolver interface allows developers to create a custom interface to external values that can be used during SAX parsing.

Table 6-16
EntityResolver Interface Methods

Method Name	Description
resolveEntity(publicId, systemId) **Supported by:** SAX 1, 2, and MSXML	Designate a public ID and/or System ID for resolving external entities. This reference will be called first when resolving external entities.

ErrorHandler

ErrorHandler is The SAX 1 and 2 interface for handling errors while parsing an XML document. Table 6-17 describes the methods.

Note   The SAX warning and the MSXML `ignorableWarning` are similar in functionality. The SAX API passes a `SAXParseException` object to the ErrorHandler interface, which contains an error message string, a Locator, and an error code. MSXML does not support the `SAXPArseException` class, so it passes the error message string, Locator, and error code directly to the ErrorHandler interface. We'll cover the `SAXParseException` class and several other SAX helper classes in the next part of this chapter.

Table 6-17	
ErrorHandler Interface Methods	

Method Name	*Description*
error **Supported by:** SAX 1, 2, and MSXML	This event is triggered when the parser encounters a recoverable error. Passed values are (SAXParseException exception) for SAX or (Locator, errorMessage, errorCode) for MSXML.
fatalError **Supported by:** SAX 1, 2, and MSXML	This event is triggered when the parser encounters a non-recoverable error. Passed values are (SAXParseException exception) for SAX or (Locator, errorMessage, errorCode) for MSXML.
warning(SAXParseException exception) **Supported by:** SAX 1 and 2	This SAX API event is triggered when the parser encounters a warning.
ignorableWarning (Locator, errorMessage, errorCode) **Supported by:** MSXML	This MSXML event is triggered when the parser encounters a warning.

SAX helper classes

So far in this chapter you've read all about SAX API interfaces. Interfaces are a great way to describe features for an application, but interfaces alone do not allow programmatic access to their properties and methods. To gain programmatic access to the SAX API interface properties and methods, object classes have to be implemented that support the interfaces. SAX Helper classes are optional classes that are included in most Java implementations of the SAX parser.

Note The SAX Helper classes are only for Java implementations. Currently, MSXML does not support helper classes, though they do support some of the functionality through additional methods in the core interfaces.

XMLReaderFactory

This class has one single purpose, to gain access to the XMLReader interface and its associated properties and methods. The createXMLReaderFactory method of the XMLReaderFactory is used by the calling program to create the XMLReader object. Table 6-18 describes the methods.

Table 6-18
XMLReaderFactory Class Methods

Method Name	Description
createXMLReader()	Create an XMLReader from system default reader. The system default reader is the value specified by the org.xml.sax.driver system property.
createXMLReader(className)	Create an XMLReader from a supplied class name.

XMLReaderAdapter

XMLReaderAdapter implements the SAX1 Parser interface for backward compatibility. To implement this helper class in your Java applications, just replace any instances of calls to the Parser interface with calls to the XMLReaderAdapter interface. This interface supports all of the methods of the SAX 2 ContentHandler and the SAX 1 DocumentHandler interfaces for inter-version compatibility. Table 6-19 describes the methods.

Note When using the XMLReaderAdapter class in Java applications, the http://xml.org/sax/features/namespace-prefixes property must be set to true.

Table 6-19
XMLReaderAdapter Class Methods

Method Name	Description
Parse(InputSource source) or parse(systemId) **Supported by:** SAX 1 and 2	Parses the InputSource document or an XML document specified by a System ID.

Method Name	Description
setDocumentHandler (DocumentHandler handler) **Supported by:** SAX 1	Sets the documentHandler object.
setDTDHandler(DTDHandler handler) **Supported by:** SAX 1	Sets the DTDHandler object.
setEntityResolver (EntityResolver resolver) **Supported by:** SAX 1	Sets the entityResolver object.
setErrorHandler (ErrorHandler handler) **Supported by:** SAX 1	Sets an errorHandler for an application.
setLocale(locale) **Supported by:** SAX 1	Returns a locale for errors and warnings.
startDocument() **Supported by:** SAX 2	This event is triggered when the parser encounters the beginning of a document.
endDocument() **Supported by:** SAX 2	This event is triggered when the parser encounters the end of a document.
startElement(uri, localName, qName, Attributes atts) **Supported by:** SAX 2	This event is triggered when the parser encounters the beginning of an element.
endElement(uri, localName, qName) **Supported by:** SAX 2	This event is triggered when the parser encounters the end of an element.
startPrefixMapping(prefix, uri) **Supported by:** SAX 2	Explicitly map a prefix to a URI. This is used with the startElement and endElement events to map a prefix to a URI at time of parsing. The prefix and/or URI do not need to be in the original XML document.
endPrefixMapping(prefix) **Supported by:** SAX 2	End the explicit mapping of a prefix to a URI.

Continued

Table 6-19 (continued)	
Method Name	**Description**
characters(char[ ] ch, start, length) **Supported by:** SAX 2	This event is triggered when the parser encounters character data.
ignorableWhitespace(char[ ] ch, **start, length)** **Supported by:** SAX 2	This event is triggered when the parser encounters ignorable whitespace in element content.
processingInstruction(target, data) **Supported by:** SAX 2	This event is triggered when the parser encounters a processing instruction.
setDocumentLocator **(Locator locator)** **Supported by:** SAX 2	Returns a pointer to the Locator interface, which returns the column number, line number, public ID, or system ID for a SAX event.
skippedEntity(name) **Supported by:** SAX 2	This event is triggered when the parser encounters a skipped entity.

AttributesImpl

AttributesImpl is the implementation class for the SAX 2 Attributes interface. It supports all the methods of the Attributes interface for retrieving information about attributes associated with an element. In addition, it has methods that can be used to add, edit, and remove attributes, as described in Table 6-20.

Note   MSXML implements much of the functionality of the Attributes interface through the IMXAttributes interface. The optional SAX 2 Attributes 2 extension interface supports additional functionality. Access to the Attributes 2 interface is through the Attributes2Impl class. We cover these topics later in this chapter.

Table 6-20
AttributesImpl Class Methods

Method Name	Description
getIndex(qName) or getIndex(uri, localName) Supported by: SAX 2	Returns the index of an attribute by qualified name or namespace name. Attribute indexes start at 0.
getLength() Supported by: SAX 2	Returns the count of element attributes, starting at 0.
getLocalName(index) Supported by: SAX 2 and MSXML	Returns an attribute name from an index. Attribute indexes start at 0.
getQName(index) Supported by: SAX 2	Return an attribute's qualified (prefixed) name.
getType(index) Supported by: SAX 2 and MSXML	Returns an attribute type from an index. SAX API values are "CDATA", "ID", "IDREF", "IDREFS", "NMTOKEN", "NMTOKENS", "ENTITY", "ENTITIES", or "NOTATION" (all in uppercase).
getType(qName) or getType(uri, localName) Supported by: SAX 2	Returns an attribute type from an attribute qualified name or namespace name. SAX API values are "CDATA", "ID", "IDREF", "IDREFS", "NMTOKEN", "NMTOKENS", "ENTITY", "ENTITIES", or "NOTATION" (all in uppercase).
getURI(index) Supported by: SAX 2 and MSXML	Returns an attribute's namespace URI by index.
getValue(index) Supported by: SAX 2 and MSXML	Returns an attribute's value by index.
getValue(qName) or getValue(uri, localName) Supported by: SAX 2	Returns an attribute's value by qualified name or namespace name.
addAttribute(uri, localName, qName, type, value) Supported by: SAX 2	Add an attribute to the end of the attribute list.

Continued

Table 6-20 (continued)

Method Name	Description
removeAttribute(index) **Supported by:** SAX 2	Remove an attribute from the attribute list.
clear() **Supported by:** SAX 2	Clear the attribute list.
setAttribute(index, uri, **localName, qName, type, value)** **Supported by:** SAX 2	Change the attribute at the specified index position in the list. Attribute indexes start at 0.
setAttributes(Attributes atts) **Supported by:** SAX 2	Copy the specified Attributes object to a new Attributes object. Attribute indexes start at 0.
setLocalName **(index, localName)** **Supported by:** SAX 2	Set the local name of the attribute at the specified index position in the list. Attribute indexes start at 0.
setQName(index, qName) **Supported by:** SAX 2	Set the qualified name of the attribute at the specified index position in the list. Attribute indexes start at 0.
setType(index, type) **Supported by:** SAX 2	Set the type of the attribute at the specified index position in the list. Attribute indexes start at 0.
setURI(index, uri) **Supported by:** SAX 2	Set the namespace of the attribute at the specified index position in the list. Attribute indexes start at 0.
setValue(index, value) **Supported by:** SAX 2	Set the value of the attribute at the specified index position in the list. Attribute indexes start at 0.

DefaultHandler

The DefaultHandler class is a grab bag of properties and methods in various SAX 2 interfaces with all have one thing in common—they are all callback methods. Callback methods in SAX applications are methods that return something when they are triggered by an event. The event actions are predefined in the application code using these methods. When a SAX parser encounters an event, the method is triggered, which invokes some kind of action in the application.

DefaultHandler is very useful for developers who are developing a bare-bones parsing application using SAX. DefaultHandler implements access to the key methods of ContentHandler, DTDHandler, EntityResolver, and ErrorHandler in one class. Table 6-21 describes the methods.

<table>
<tr><td colspan="2" align="center">Table 6-21
DefaultHandler Class Methods</td></tr>
<tr><td>*Method Name*</td><td>*Description*</td></tr>
<tr><td>**startDocument()**
Supported by:
SAX 2</td><td>This event is triggered when the parser encounters the beginning of a document. Source Interface is ContentHandler.</td></tr>
<tr><td>**endDocument()**
Supported by:
SAX 2</td><td>This event is triggered when the parser encounters the end of a document. Source Interface is ContentHandler.</td></tr>
<tr><td>**startElement(uri, localName, qName, Attributes atts)**
Supported by:
SAX 2</td><td>This event is triggered when the parser encounters the beginning of an element. Source Interface is ContentHandler.</td></tr>
<tr><td>**endElement(uri, localName, qName)**
Supported by:
SAX 2</td><td>This event is triggered when the parser encounters the end of an element. Source Interface is ContentHandler.</td></tr>
<tr><td>**startPrefixMapping(prefix, uri)**
Supported by:
SAX 2</td><td>Explicitly map a prefix to a URI. This is used with the startElement and endElement events to map a prefix to a URI at time of parsing. The prefix and/or URI do not need to be in the original XML document. Source Interface is ContentHandler.</td></tr>
<tr><td>**endPrefixMapping(prefix)**
Supported by:
SAX 2</td><td>End the explicit mapping of a prefix to a URI. Source Interface is ContentHandler.</td></tr>
<tr><td>**characters(char[] ch, start, length)**
Supported by:
SAX 2</td><td>This event is triggered when the parser encounters character data. Source Interface is ContentHandler.</td></tr>
<tr><td>**ignorableWhitespace(char[] ch, start, length)**
Supported by:
SAX 2</td><td>This event is triggered when the parser encounters ignorable whitespace in element content. Source Interface is ContentHandler.</td></tr>
<tr><td>**processingInstruction(target, data)**
Supported by:
SAX 2</td><td>This event is triggered when the parser encounters a processing instruction. Source Interface is ContentHandler.</td></tr>
</table>

Continued

Table 6-21 *(continued)*	
Method Name	**Description**
setDocumentLocator (Locator locator) Supported by: SAX 2	Returns a pointer to the Locator interface, which returns the column number, line number, public ID, or system ID for a SAX event. Source Interface is ContentHandler.
skippedEntity(name) Supported by: SAX 2	This event is triggered when the parser encounters a skipped entity. Source Interface is ContentHandler.
notationDecl(name, publicId, systemId) Supported by: SAX 1, 2	This event is triggered when the parser encounters a notation declaration event. Source Interface is DTDHandler.
unparsedEntityDecl(name, publicId, systemId, notationName) Supported by: SAX 1, 2	This event is triggered when the parser encounters an unparsed entity declaration event. Source Interface is DTDHandler.
resolveEntity(publicId, systemId) Supported by: SAX 1, 2	Designate a public ID and/or System ID for resolving external entities. This reference will be called first when resolving external entities. Source Interface is EntityResolver.
error Supported by: SAX 1, 2	This event is triggered when the parser encounters a recoverable error. Passed values are (SAXParseException exception) for SAX or (Locator, errorMessage, errorCode) for MSXML. Source Interface is ErrorHandler.
fatalError Supported by: SAX 1, 2	This event is triggered when the parser encounters a non-recoverable error. Passed values are (SAXParseException exception) for SAX or (Locator, errorMessage, errorCode) for MSXML. Source Interface is ErrorHandler.
warning(SAXParseException exception) Supported by: SAX 1, 2	This SAX API event is triggered when the parser encounters a warning. Source Interface is ErrorHandler.

LocatorImpl

`LocatorImpl` is the implementation class for locator, which associates a SAX event with a document location. Locators provide the line and column in an XML document that a SAX event takes place.

The Locator interface is accessible via the ContentHandler interface. Use the `setDocumentLocator` method for SAX API-compliant parsers such as Xerces, and the `documentLocator` property in MSXML. Table 6-22 describes the methods.

<table>
<tr><th colspan="2">Table 6-22
LocatorImpl Class Methods</th></tr>
<tr><th>Method Name</th><th>Description</th></tr>
<tr><td>**getColumnNumber()**
Supported by:
SAX 1, 2</td><td>Returns the ending column number of a SAX event. XML document columns start at the beginning of a new line. The first column (1) is the first character if a line in an XML document. The column count increments by one for each character in the line, until a line end is encountered.</td></tr>
<tr><td>**getLineNumber()**
Supported by:
SAX 1, 2</td><td>Returns the ending line number of a SAX event. Lines in Locators start at 1.</td></tr>
<tr><td>**getPublicId()**
Supported by:
SAX 1, 2</td><td>Returns the public ID of a SAX event.</td></tr>
<tr><td>**getSystemId()**
Supported by:
SAX 2</td><td>Returns the saved system identifier.</td></tr>
<tr><td>**setColumnNumber(columnNumber)**
Supported by:
SAX 2</td><td>Sets the column number of a Locator. XML document columns start at the beginning of a new line. The first column (1) is the first character of a line in an XML document. The column count increments by one for each character in the line, until a line end is encountered.</td></tr>
<tr><td>**setLineNumber(lineNumber)**
Supported by:
SAX 2</td><td>Sets the line number of a Locator. Lines in Locators start at 1.</td></tr>
<tr><td>**setPublicId(publicId)**
Supported by:
SAX 2</td><td>Sets the public ID of a Locator.</td></tr>
<tr><td>**setSystemId(systemId)**
Supported by:
SAX 2</td><td>Sets the system ID of a Locator.</td></tr>
</table>

NamespaceSupport

Individual namespaces associated with element events can be accessed by the startPrefixMapping() and endPrefixMapping() methods in the Content Handler interface. NameSPaceSupport provides features to globally declare and track namespaces in a Java application, as described in Table 6-23.

<table>
<tr><td colspan="2" align="center">Table 6-23
NameSpaceSupport Class Methods</td></tr>
<tr><td>*Method Name*</td><td>*Description*</td></tr>
<tr><td>**declarePrefix(prefix, uri)**
Supported by:
SAX 2</td><td>Declare a namespace prefix and associated uri.</td></tr>
<tr><td>**getDeclaredPrefixes()**
Supported by:
SAX 2</td><td>Return all prefixes declared in this context in enumeration format.</td></tr>
<tr><td>**getPrefix(uri)**
Supported by:
SAX 2</td><td>Return a prefix associated with a provided uri.</td></tr>
<tr><td>**getPrefixes()**
Supported by:
SAX 2</td><td>Return all prefixes active in this context in enumeration format.</td></tr>
<tr><td>**getPrefixes(uri)**
Supported by:
SAX 2</td><td>Return all prefixes declared for a provided uri in enumeration format.</td></tr>
<tr><td>**getURI(prefix)**
Supported by:
SAX 2</td><td>Return a uri associated with a provided prefix.</td></tr>
<tr><td>**processName(qName, [] parts, boolean isAttribute)**
Supported by:
SAX 2</td><td>Add a namespace to a name. The parts parameter is a string array that contains the namespace information.</td></tr>
<tr><td>**setNamespaceDeclUris (boolean value)**
Supported by:
SAX 2</td><td>Turns on and off the ability for processName to declare namespace attributes.</td></tr>
<tr><td>**isNamespaceDeclUris()**
Supported by:
SAX 2</td><td>Checks the current state of the ability for processName to declare namespace attributes.</td></tr>
</table>

Method Name	Description
pushContext() **Supported by:** SAX 2	Starts a new namespace context. Namespaces are in a stack model, which is usually "pushed" at the startElement event and "popped" at the endElement event.
popContext() **Supported by:** SAX 2	Reverts to the previous namespace context. Namespaces are in a stack model, which is usually "pushed" at the startElement event and "popped" at the endElement event.
reset() **Supported by:** SAX 2	Resets the NameSpaceSupport object.

XMLFilterImpl

`XMLFilterImpl` is an implementation class for the XMLFilter interface in Java applications. XMLFilters are similar to the XML Reader interface, except that an XMLFilter source comes from an existing `XMLReader` object. XMLFilters can be used to quickly and easily produce fragments of documents. Table 6-24 describes the methods.

Note   `XMLFilterImpl` implements all of the methods of the ContentHandler, XMLReader, XMLFilter, DTDHandler, EntityResolver, and ErrorHandler interfaces.

Table 6-24 **XMLFilterImpl Class Methods**	
Method Name	Description
startDocument() **Supported by:** SAX 2, MSXML	Filtering is triggered when the parser encounters the beginning of a document. Source interface is ContentHandler.
endDocument() **Supported by:** SAX 2, MSXML	Filtering is triggered when the parser encounters the end of a document. Source interface is ContentHandler.
startElement(uri, localName, qName, Attributes atts) **Supported by:** SAX 2, MSXML	Filtering is triggered when the parser encounters the beginning of an element. Source interface is ContentHandler.

Continued

Method Name	Description
endElement(uri, localName, qName) **Supported by:** SAX 2, MSXML	Filtering is triggered when the parser encounters the end of an element. Source interface is ContentHandler.
startPrefixMapping(prefix, uri) **Supported by:** SAX 2, MSXML	This is used with the startElement and endElement events to filter on a namespace prefix. Source interface is ContentHandler.
endPrefixMapping(prefix) **Supported by:** SAX 2, MSXML	End the filtering of a namespace prefix event. Source interface is ContentHandler.
characters(char[] ch, start, length) **Supported by:** SAX 2, MSXML	Filtering is triggered when the parser encounters character data. Source interface is ContentHandler.
ignorableWhitespace(char[] ch, start, length) **Supported by:** SAX 2, MSXML	Filtering is triggered when the parser encounters ignorable whitespace in element content. Source interface is ContentHandler.
processingInstruction(target, data) **Supported by:** SAX 2, MSXML	Filtering is triggered when the parser encounters a processing instruction. Source interface is ContentHandler.
setDocumentLocator(Locator locator) **Supported by:** SAX 2	Filtering is triggered when the parser encounters a new document locator event. Source interface is ContentHandler.
skippedEntity(name) **Supported by:** SAX 2, MSXML	Filtering is triggered when the parser encounters a skipped entity. Source interface is ContentHandler.
getContentHandler() **Supported by:** SAX 2	Returns the current ContentHandler object, which contains the content of a source XML document. Source interface is XMLReader.
getDTDHandler() **Supported by:** SAX 2	Returns the current DTDHandler object, which contains the content of a source DTD. Source interface is XMLReader.
getEntityResolver() **Supported by:** SAX 2	Returns the current entityResolver object. Source interface is XMLReader.
getErrorHandler() **Supported by:** SAX 2	Returns the current errorHandler object. Source interface is XMLReader.

Table 6-24 *(continued)*

Method Name	Description
getFeature(name) **Supported by:** SAX 2	Look up the value of a feature flag. Feature flags tell you if your SAX parser supports a specific feature, such as namespaces or Schema validation, or the optional Attributes2 interface. Source interface is XMLReader. SAX feature flags vary by parser. Official SAX feature flags are listed at `http://www.saxproject.org/apidoc/org/xml/sax/package-summary.html#package_description`.
getProperty(name) **Supported by:** SAX 2	Looks up the value of a property. SAX properties tell you a SAX object class supports the default class or a custom class for entity declarations, lexical handlers, and a few other items. Source interface is XMLReader. SAX properties vary by parser. Official SAX properties are listed at `http://www.saxproject.org/apidoc/org/xml/sax/package-summary.html#package_description`.
Parse(InputSource input) **Supported by:** SAX 1 and 2	Parses the InputSource XML document. Source interface is XMLReader.
Parse(systemId) **Supported by:** SAX 1 and 2	Parses the XML document specified by systemID. Source interface is XMLReader.
setContentHandler (ContentHandler handler) **Supported by:** SAX 2	Sets the current ContentHandler object, which contains the content of a source XML document. Source interface is XMLReader.
setDTDHandler(DTDHandler handler) **Supported by:** SAX 2	Sets the current DTDHandler object, which contains the content of a source DTD. Source interface is XMLReader.
setEntityResolver (EntityResolver resolver) **Supported by:** SAX 2	Sets the current entityResolver object. Source interface is XMLReader.
setErrorHandler (ErrorHandler handler) **Supported by:** SAX 2	Sets the current errorHandler object. Source interface is XMLReader.

Continued

Table 6-24 *(continued)*

Method Name	Description
setFeature(name, boolean value) **Supported by:** SAX 2	Sets the value of a feature flag. Feature flags tell you if your SAX parser supports a specific feature, such as namespaces or Schema validation, or the optional Attributes2 interface. Source interface is XMLReader. SAX feature flags vary by parser. Official SAX feature flags are listed at `http://www.saxproject.org/apidoc/org/xml/sax/package-summary.html#package_description`.
setProperty(name, java.lang.Object value) **Supported by:** SAX 2	Sets the value of a property. SAX properties tell you a SAX object class supports the default class or a custom class for entity declarations, lexical handlers, and a few other items. SAX properties vary by parser. Source interface is XMLReader. Official SAX properties are listed at `http://www.saxproject.org/apidoc/org/xml/sax/package-summary.html#package_description`.
getParent() **Supported by:** SAX 2	Gets the XMLReader parent of the XMLFilter. Source interface is XMLReader.
setParent(XMLReader parent) **Supported by:** SAX 2	Sets the XMLReader parent of the XMLFilter. Source interface is XMLReader.
resolveEntity(publicId, systemId) **Supported by:** SAX 2	Designate a public ID and/or System ID for resolving external entities. This reference will be called first when resolving external entities. Source interface is EntityResolver.
notationDecl(name, publicId, systemId) **Supported by:** SAX 2	Filtering is triggered when the parser encounters a notation declaration event. Source interface is DTDHandler.
unparsedEntityDecl(name, publicId, systemId, notationName) **Supported by:** SAX 2	Filtering is triggered when the parser encounters an unparsed entity declaration event. Source interface is DTDHandler.
error(SAXParseException e) **Supported by:** SAX 2	Filtering is triggered when the parser encounters a recoverable error. Passed values are (SAXParseException exception) for SAX or (Locator, errorMessage, errorCode) for MSXML. Source interface is ErrorHandler.

Method Name	Description
fatalError(SAXParseException e) **Supported by:** SAX 2	Filtering is triggered when the parser encounters a non-recoverable error. Passed values are (SAXParseException exception) for SAX or (Locator, errorMessage, errorCode) for MSXML. Source interface is ErrorHandler.
warning(SAXParseException e) **Supported by:** SAX 2	Filtering is triggered when the parser encounters a warning. Source interface is ErrorHandler.

ParserAdapter

`ParserAdapter` adds namespace support and other SAX 2 XMLReader interface features to a SAX 1 parser. To implement this helper class in your Java applications, call `ParserAdapter()` to create a new embedded SAX 2 parser object and `Parser Adapter(parserName)` to adapt an existing SAX 1 parser. Once the `ParserAdapter` is available, it can be used like an `XMLReader` object. Table 6-25 describes the methods.

Note   This interface supports all of the methods of the SAX 2 XMLReader and ContentHandler interfaces (except for startPrefixMapping, endPrefixMapping, and skippedEntity) for inter-version compatibility. However, most of the Content Handler methods are intended to be used exclusively by the `ParserAdapter` class to convert the Parser object to an XMLReader object, and should not be called from applications, even though they are exposed and documented. For this reason I've excluded all of the adapter implementation methods from the documentation. Also, `getFeature`, `setFeature`, `getProperty`, and `setProperty` are limited (see the notes in the table).

Table 6-25 **ParserAdapter Class Methods**	
Method Name	Description
getContentHandler() **Supported by:** SAX 2, MSXML	Returns the current ContentHandler object, which contains the content of a source XML document.
getDTDHandler() **Supported by:** SAX 2, MSXML	Returns the current DTDHandler object, which contains the content of a source DTD.

Continued

Method Name	Description
getEntityResolver() **Supported by:** SAX 2, MSXML	Returns the current entityResolver object.
getErrorHandler() **Supported by:** SAX 2, MSXML	Returns the current errorHandler object.
getFeature(name) **Supported by:** SAX 2, MSXML	Look up the value of a feature flag. SAX feature flags for ParserAdapter are limited to namespaces and namespace-prefixes.
Parse(InputSource input) **Supported by:** SAX 2 , MSXML	Parses the InputSource XML document.
parse(systemId) **Supported by:** SAX 2, MSXML	Parses the XML document specified by systemID.
setContentHandler (ContentHandler handler) **Supported by:** SAX 2, MSXML	Sets the current ContentHandler object, which contains the content of a source XML document.
setDTDHandler(DTDHandler handler) **Supported by:** SAX 2, MSXML	Sets the current DTDHandler object, which contains the content of a source DTD.
setEntityResolver (EntityResolver resolver) **Supported by:** SAX 2, MSXML	Sets the current entityResolver object.
setErrorHandler (ErrorHandler handler) **Supported by:** SAX 2, MSXML	Sets the current errorHandler object.
setFeature(name, boolean value) **Supported by:** SAX 2 , MSXML	Sets the value of a feature flag. SAX feature flags for ParserAdapter are limited to namespaces and namespace-prefixes.

Table 6-25 *(continued)*

ParserFactory

This helper class was implemented in SAX 1 for use with the Parser interface. It is no longer recommended for new development, but is included here to debug and upgrade SAX 1 code to SAX 2. Table 6-26 describes the methods.

Table 6-26
ParserFactory Class Methods

Method Name	Description
makeParser() **Supported by:** SAX 1	Create a new SAX parser using the 'org.xml.sax.parser' system property.
makeParser(className) **Supported by:** SAX 1	Create a new SAX parser object using the class name provided.

AttributeListImpl

`AttributeListImpl` is the SAX helper class of the SAX 1 interface for a list of XML attributes. As with the Parser and ContentHandler interfaces, AttributeList interface should not be used for new development. Consequently, the `AttributeListImpl` class should not be used either. We've included it here to help debug and upgrade SAX 1 code to the SAX 2 XMLReader, ContentHandler, and Attributes interfaces. Table 6-27 describes the methods.

Table 6-27
AttributeListImpl Class Methods

Method Name	Description
addAttribute(name, type, value) **Supported by:** SAX 1	Adds an attribute to an attribute list.
clear() **Supported by:** SAX 1	Clears the attribute list.
getLength() **Supported by:** SAX 1	Returns the count of element attributes, starting at 0.
getName(i) **Supported by:** SAX 1	Returns the name of an attribute by index. Attribute indexes start at 0.
getType(i) **Supported by:** SAX 1	Returns the type of an attribute by index. Attribute indexes start at 0.

Continued

Table 6-27 *(continued)*	
Method Name	*Description*
getType(name) **Supported by:** SAX 1	Returns the type of an attribute by name.
getValue(i) **Supported by:** SAX 1	Returns the value of an attribute by index. Attribute indexes start at 0.
getValue(name) **Supported by:** SAX 1	Returns the value of an attribute by name.
removeAttribute(name) **Supported by:** SAX 1	Removes an attribute from the attribute list.
setAttributeList(AttributeList atts) **Supported by:** SAX 1	Reset the contents of the attribute list.

SAX extension interfaces

Aside from the SAX core interfaces, there are several extension interfaces that are implemented using the SAX extension API. SAX extensions are optional interfaces for SAX parsers. For example, the MSXML parser supports the DeclHandler and LexicalHandler interfaces, while the Apache Xerces parser classes support all extension interfaces. They can also be implemented independently of the SAX core interfaces. All extensions have been developed using the SAX 2 extensions API, and are not available in SAX 1.

At the beginning of this chapter, you reviewed the SAX extensions at the interface level. Now let's review the methods that are contained in the extension interfaces.

 Note You may see SAX documentation that refers to "SAX Extensions 1.x." This refers to the SAX 2 Extensions 1.x API, not SAX 1. There is no SAX extension API for SAX 1.

Attributes2

The Attributes2 interface checks a DTD to see if an attribute in an XML document was declared in a DTD. It also checks to see if the DTD specifies a default value for the attribute. This interface is used mainly for data validation. Table 6-28 describes the methods.

Table 6-28
Attributes2 Interface Methods

Method Name	Description
isDeclared(index) or isDeclared(qName) or isDeclared(uri, localName) **Supported by:** SAX 2	Returns true if attribute was declared in the DTD. isDeclared accepts an index (starting with 0), a qualified name, or a local name.
isSpecified(index) or isSpecified(qName) or isSpecified(uri, localName) **Supported by:** SAX 2	Returns false if the default attribute value was specified in the DTD. isSpecified accepts an index (starting with 0), a qualified name, or a local name.

DeclHandler

The DeclHandler interface returns declaration values in a DTD for attributes, elements, and internal and external entities. Table 6-29 describes the methods.

Table 6-29
DeclHandler Interface Methods

Method Name	Description
attributeDecl(eName, aName, type, mode, value) **Supported by:** SAX 2 and MSXML	Returns a DTD attribute type declaration. Values returned include any valid DTD values, such as "CDATA", "ID", "IDREF", "IDREFS", "NMTOKEN", "NMTOKENS", "ENTITY", or "ENTITIES", a token group, or a NOTATION reference.
elementDecl(name, model) **Supported by:** SAX 2 and MSXML	Returns a DTD element type declaration. Values returned include any valid DTD values, such as "EMPTY", "ANY", order specification, and so on.
externalEntityDecl(name, publicId, systemId) **Supported by:** SAX 2 and MSXML	Returns a parsed external entity declaration.
internalEntityDecl(name, value) **Supported by:** SAX 2 and MSXML	Returns a parsed internal entity declaration.

EntityResolver2

EntityResolver2 extends the EntityResolver interface by programmatically adding external entity reference subsets. This can be useful for automatically adding pre-defined DTD references to an XML document for validation while parsing. Table 6-30 describes the methods.

Table 6-30
EntityResolver2 Interface Methods

Method Name	Description
getExternalSubset(name, baseURI) **Supported by:** SAX 2	Returns an external subset for documents without a valid DOCTYPE declaration.
resolveEntity(name, publicId, baseURI, systemId) **Supported by:** SAX 2	Allows applications to map external entities to XML document inputSources, or map an external entity by URI.

LexicalHandler

LexicalHandler returns information about lexical events in an XML document. Comments, the start and end of a CDATA section, the start and end of a DTD declaration, and the start and end of an entity can be tracked with LexicalHandler. Table 6-31 describes the methods.

Table 6-31
LexicalHandler Interface Methods

Method Name	Description
comment(char[] ch, start, length) **Supported by:** SAX 2 and MSXML	This event is triggered when the parser encounters a comment anywhere in the document.
endCDATA() **Supported by:** SAX 2 and MSXML	This event is triggered when the parser encounters the end of a CDATA section.
endDTD() **Supported by:** SAX 2 and MSXML	This event is triggered when the parser encounters the end of a DTD declaration.

Method Name	Description
endEntity(name) **Supported by:** SAX 2 and MSXML	This event is triggered when the parser encounters the end of an entity.
startCDATA() **Supported by:** SAX 2 and MSXML	This event is triggered when the parser encounters the start of a CDATA section.
startDTD(name, publicId, systemId) **Supported by:** SAX 2 and MSXML	This event is triggered when the parser encounters the start of DTD a declaration.
startEntity(name) **Supported by:** SAX 2 and MSXML	This event is triggered when the parser encounters the beginning of internal or external XML entities.

Locator2

Locator2 extends the Locator interface to return the encoding and the XML version for an XML document. Table 6-32 describes the methods.

Table 6-32
Locator2 Interface Methods

Method Name	Description
getXMLVersion() **Supported by:** SAX 2	Returns the entity XML version.
getEncoding() **Supported by:** SAX 2	Returns the type of character encoding for the entity.

SAX extension helper classes

The SAX extension helper classes provide the same programmatic access to the SAX Extension interfaces that the SAX helpers do to the SAX Core Interfaces. The optional SAX 2 Extension API interface properties, methods and object classes have to be implemented to support these classes.

> **Note**   The SAX Extension Helper classes are only for Java implementations. Currently, MSXML does not support helper classes, though they do support some of the functionality through additional methods in the core interfaces.

Attributes2Impl

The Attributes2Impl helper class is the implementation class of the Attributes2 interface. Attributes2 checks a DTD to see if an attribute in an XML document was declared in a DTD. It also checks to see if the DTD specifies a default value for the attribute. It's used mainly for data validation. Attributes2Impl extends the interface functionality by letting you add, edit, and delete attributes from lists, as described in Table 6-33.

Table 6-33
Attributes2Impl Interface Methods

Method Name	Description
addAttribute(uri, localName, qName, type, value) **Supported by:** SAX 2	Adds an attribute to the end of the attribute list, setting its "specified" flag to true.
isDeclared(index) or isDeclared(qName) or isDeclared(uri, localName) **Supported by:** SAX 2	Returns true if attribute was declared in the DTD. isDeclared accepts an index (starting with 0), a qualified name, or a local name.
isSpecified(index) or isSpecified(qName) or isSpecified(uri, localName) **Supported by:** SAX 2	Returns false if the default attribute value was specified in the DTD. isSpecified accepts an index (starting with 0), a qualified name, or a local name.
removeAttribute(index) **Supported by:** SAX 2	Removes an attribute from the attribute list. Attribute indexes start at 0.
setAttributes(Attributes atts) **Supported by:** SAX 2	Copy the specified Attributes object to a new Attributes object.
setDeclared(index, boolean value) **Supported by:** SAX 2	Set the "declared" flag of a specified attribute. Attribute indexes start at 0.

Method Name	Description
setSpecified(index, boolean value) **Supported by:** SAX 2	Set the "specified" flag of a specified attribute. Attribute indexes start at 0.

DefaultHandler2

The DefaultHandler2 class extends the SAX2 DefaultHandler class with properties and methods from the SAX2 LexicalHandler, DeclHandler, and EntityResolver2 extension interfaces. Table 6-34 describes the methods.

Table 6-34
DefaultHandler2 Interface Methods

Method Name	Description
attributeDecl(eName, aName, type, mode, value) **Supported by:** SAX 2	Returns a DTD attribute type declaration. Values returned include any valid DTD values, such as "CDATA", "ID", "IDREF", "IDREFS", "NMTOKEN", "NMTOKENS", "ENTITY", or "ENTITIES", a token group, or a NOTATION reference. Source interface is DeclHandler.
elementDecl(name, model) **Supported by:** SAX 2	Returns a DTD element type declaration. Values returned include any valid DTD values, such as "EMPTY", "ANY", order specification, etc. Source interface is DeclHandler.
externalEntityDecl(name, publicId, systemId) **Supported by:** SAX 2	Returns a parsed external entity declaration. Source interface is DeclHandler.
internalEntityDecl(name, value) **Supported by:** SAX 2	Returns a parsed internal entity declaration. Source interface is DeclHandler.
comment(char[] ch, start, length) **Supported by:** SAX 2	This event is triggered when the parser encounters a comment anywhere in the document. Source interface is LexicalHandler.
startDTD(name, publicId, systemId) **Supported by:** SAX 2	This event is triggered when the parser encounters the start of a DTD declaration. Source interface is LexicalHandler.

Continued

Table 6-34 *(continued)*

Method Name	Description
endDTD() **Supported by:** SAX 2	This event is triggered when the parser encounters the end of a DTD declaration Source interface is LexicalHandler.
startCDATA() **Supported by:** SAX 2	This event is triggered when the parser encounters the start of a CDATA section. Source interface is LexicalHandler.
endCDATA() **Supported by:** SAX 2	This event is triggered when the parser encounters the end of a CDATA section. Source interface is LexicalHandler.
startEntity(name) **Supported by:** SAX 2	This event is triggered when the parser encounters the beginning of internal or external XML entities. Source interface is LexicalHandler.
endEntity(name) **Supported by:** SAX 2	This event is triggered when the parser encounters the end of internal or external XML entities. Source interface is LexicalHandler.
getExternalSubset(name, baseURI) **Supported by:** SAX 2	Returns an external subset for documents without a valid DOCTYPE declaration. Source interface is EntityResolver2.
resolveEntity(publicId, systemId) **Supported by:** SAX 2	Allows applications to map an external entity by URI. Source interface is EntityResolver2.
resolveEntity(name, publicId, baseURI, systemId) **Supported by:** SAX 2	Allows applications to map external entities to XML document inputSources, or map an external entity by URI. Source interface is EntityResolver2.

Locator2Impl

Locator2Impl is the implementation class for the Locator2 SAX extension interface. Locator2 extends the Locator interface to return the encoding and the XML version for an XML document. Table 6-35 describes the methods.

Table 6-35
Locator2Impl Interface Methods

Method Name	Description
getEncoding() **Supported by:** SAX 2	Returns the type of character encoding for the entity.
getXMLVersion() **Supported by:** SAX 2	Returns the entity XML version.
setEncoding(encoding) **Supported by:** SAX 2	Sets the type of character encoding for the entity.
setXMLVersion(version) **Supported by:** SAX 2	Sets the entity XML version.

MSXML Extension Interfaces

This section explains the MSXML extension interfaces.

IMXAttributes

The IMXAttributes extension interface provides access to edit, add, and delete attribute names and values. Table 6-36 describes the methods.

Note Many of the methods in IMXAttributes are similar to the Attributes2 SAX API extension class methods.

Table 6-36
IMXAttributes Interface Methods

Method Name	Description
addAttribute (URI, LocalName, **QName, Type, Value)** **Supported by:** MSXML	Adds an attribute to the end of an attribute list.

Continued

Table 6-36 *(continued)*

Method Name	Description
addAttributeFromIndex (attributes, index) Supported by: MSXML	Adds the attribute specified by an index value to the end of an attribute list. Attribute indexes start with 0.
clear Supported by: MSXML	Clears the attribute list. Attribute indexes start with 0.
removeAttribute (index) Supported by: MSXML	Removes an attribute from the attribute list. Attribute indexes start with 0.
setAttribute (index, URI, localName, QName, type, value) Supported by: MSXML	Sets an attribute in the list. Attribute indexes start with 0.
setAttributes (attributes) Supported by: MSXML	Resets the contents of the attribute list.
setLocalName (index, localName) Supported by: MSXML	Sets the local name of a specified attribute. Attribute indexes start with 0.
setQName (index, QName) Supported by: MSXML	Sets the qualified name (QName) of a specified attribute. Attribute indexes start with 0.
setType (index, type) Supported by: MSXML	Sets the type of a specified attribute. Attribute indexes start with 0.
setURI (index, URI) Supported by: MSXML	Sets the namespace URI of a specified attribute. Attribute indexes start with 0.
setValue (index, value) Supported by: MSXML	Sets the value of a specified attribute. Attribute indexes start with 0.

IMXSchemaDeclHandler

The MSXML IMXSchemaDeclHandler extension interface provides schema information about an element being parsed, including attributes. Table 6-37 describes the methods.

Table 6-37
IMXSchemaDeclHandler Interface Methods

Method Name	Description
schemaElementDecl **Supported by:** MSXML	Declares a schema for validation of an element. Assists in MSXML SAX validation when parsing.

IMXWriter

IMXWriter writes parsed XML output to:

✦ An `IStream` object: A stream object representing a sequence of bytes that can be forwarded to another object such as a file or a screen.

✦ A string (remember, all XML documents are technically strings).

✦ A `DOMDocument` object: Can be passed to the MSXML DOM parser for further processing. For example, a new XML document could be parsed using SAX for speed, then sent to the DOM parser for DTD validation.

Note The encoding and version properties of IMXWriter are similar to the `getXMLVersion()` and `getEncoding()` methods of the SAX API Locator2 extension interface. Also, one piece of trivia: Note that this is the only SAX interface that has more properties than methods.

Table 6-38 describes the properties.

Table 6-38
IMXWriter Interface Properties

Property Name	Description
byteOrderMark (boolean) **Supported by:** MSXML	Controls the writing of the Byte Order Mark (BOM) for encoding, according to XML 1.0 specifications.
disableOutputEscaping (boolean) **Supported by:** MSXML	Sets the flag for the disable-output-escaping attribute of the <xsl:text> and <xsl:value-of> elements. If True, entity reference symbols and other non-XML data are passed without entity resolution.

Continued

Table 6-38 (continued)

Property Name	Description
encoding (string) **Supported by:** MSXML	Sets and gets XML document encoding for the written output.
Indent (boolean) **Supported by:** MSXML	Sets indentation in the output.
omitXMLDeclaration (boolean) **Supported by:** MSXML	If true, the output will not include the XML declaration.
output (variant) **Supported by:** MSXML	Sets the destination and the type of IMXWriter output.
standalone (boolean) **Supported by:** MSXML	Sets the XML declaration standalone attribute to "yes" or "no."
version (string) **Supported by:** MSXML	Specifies the XML declaration version.

Table 6-39 describes the methods.

Table 6-39
IMXWriter Interface Methods

Method Name	Description
flush()	Flushes the object's internal buffer to its destination (not for DOMDocument output).

Summary

In this chapter, I provided a deep dive into the details of the Simple API for XML (SAX):

✦ A history of SAX

✦ SAX versions and evolution

✦ Understanding differences in W3C and MSXML SAX parser implementations

✦ SAX interfaces, extension interfaces, and helper classes

✦ SAX interface event callback methods

✦ SAX helper classes for implementing SAX 1 to SAX 2 compatibility

✦ Properties and methods for W3C and MSXML SAX interfaces

In the next chapter, we move on to something completely different: Extensible Stylesheet transformations. The chapters will follow the same format as the parsing chapters. Chapter 7 is an introduction to XSL and XSLT, while Chapter 8 provides more information on implementing XSLT and includes working examples.

✦   ✦   ✦

XSLT Concepts

Chapters 1, 2, and 3 showed you what XML was all about, how to develop XML documents, and how to make sure that XML document structures are enforced using data validation. Chapters 4, 5, and 6 showed you some of the things you can do with XML documents, namely parsing them for conversion to other types of data.

This chapter will discuss the syntax, structure, and theory of Extensible Stylesheet Language (XSL) and XSL Transformations (XSLT), with some basic examples for illustration. Chapter 8 will show you XML and XSLT in real-world examples and tips for writing XSL stylesheets for XML documents. Chapter 9 will extend those examples to show you how to use XSL: Formatting Objects (XSL:FO) with XML documents.

All of the XML document and stylesheet examples contained in this chapter can be downloaded from the xmlprogrammersbible.com Website, in the Downloads section.

Introducing the XSL Transformation Recommendation

XSL stands for *Extensible Stylesheet Language*. The XSL stylesheet XSL Transformation Recommendation describes the process of applying an XSL stylesheet to an XML document using a transformation engine, and also specifies the XSL language covered in this chapter. XSLT is based on *DSSSL (Document Style Semantics and Specification Language)*, which was originally developed to define SGML document output formatting. XSLT 1.0 became a W3C Recommendation in 1999, and the full specification is available for review at `http:// www.w3.org/TR/xslt`.

The XSLT Recommendation should not be confused with the very confusingly named Extensible Stylesheet Language (XSL) Version 1.0 Recommendation, which achieved W3C

In This Chapter

Introduction to XSLT

How XSLT uses XPath

An introduction to XSL stylesheet elements

Useful XPath and XSLT functions for stylesheet developers

Extending XSLT with the help of EXSLT.org

Recommendation status on 15 October 2001. This recommendation has more to do with XSL: Formatting Objects (XSL:FO) than XSL Transformations (XSLT). You can view the Extensible Stylesheet Language (XSL) Version 1.0 Recommendation at `http://www.w3.org/TR/xsl/`. Chapter 9 covers XSL XSL: Formatting Objects, including most of the W3C Extensible Stylesheet Language 1.0 Recommendation.

Another W3C Recommendation that affects XSLT is the XML Path Language (XPath). XPath is a tree-based representation model of an XML document that is used in XSLT to describe elements, attributes, text data, and relative positions in an XML document. The full recommendation document can be seen at `http://www.w3.org/TR/xpath`.

Version 2.0 of XSLT and XPath are currently in the Recommendation process, and are expected to become W3C Recommendations sometime in late 2003. The current documents and their status can be reviewed at `http://www.w3.org/TR/xslt20req` and `http://www.w3.org/TR/xpath20req`.

Stylesheet structure and syntax is defined in the W3C XSLT Recommendation document, and Transformation engines are based on these definitions. Transformation engines support a variety of programming languages, usually based on the language that they are developed in. At time of writing, there is no comprehensive list of XSLT engines available, but the Open Directory Project provides a good overview at `http://dmoz.org/Computers/Data_Formats/Markup_Languages/XML/Style_Sheets/XSL/Implementations/`. Despite a multitude of XSLT engines supporting a multitude of languages, mainstream XSLT engines are split into two platform camps: Java and Microsoft.

One of the first Java transformation engines was the LotusXSL engine, which IBM donated to the Apache Software Group, where it became the Xalan Transformation engine. Since then, Apache has developed Xalan Version 2, which implements a pluggable interface into Xalan 1 and 2, as well as integrated SAX and DOM parsers. Both of the Java versions of XALAN implement the W3C Recommendations XSLT and XPath. You can find more information on Xalan at `http://xml.apache.org/xalan-j/index.html`.

Microsoft support for XML 1.0 and a reduced implementation of the W3C XSLT recommendation began with the MS Internet Explorer 5, which also supported the Document Object Model (DOM), XML `Namespaces`, and beta support for XML Schemas. XML and XSL functionality was extended in later browser versions and separated from the browser into the MSXML parser, more recently renamed the Microsoft XML Core Services. MSXML is for use in client applications, via Web browsers, Microsoft server products, and is a core component of the .NET platform.

How an XSL Transformation Works

Developers create code that identifies an XML source, an XSL stylesheet, and a transformation output method and destination to a transformation engine, which is usually described as an XSL processor. Instructions from source code to the XSL processor perform a transformation using the predefined components. The XSL processor reads the Source XML document and performs a transformation of the XML attributes, elements, and text values based on instructions in the XSL stylesheet.

XSLT stylesheets are well-formed XML documents that conform to W3C standards for syntax. Output format is specified in the XSL document as well, and can be HTML, text, or XML.

XSL stylesheets

XSL processors use XSL stylesheets to gather instructions for transforming source XML documents to output XML documents. Stylesheets describe XML documents as a series of templates, much like our W3C XML Schema example in Chapter 3 described XML document structures as a series of XML data types. Stylesheets can be used to change the structure of an XML document by moving, adding, or removing elements, attributes, and text data from a source XML document.

XSL for attributes and elements

XSL directives and functions combined with XPath functions make up the vocabulary for XSL stylesheet transformations. All of the directives and functions will be explained a little later in this chapter. Before I get into the full list of directives and functions, let's step through a very basic transformation using very basic source, output, and stylesheet formats. Listing 7-1 shows the very simple XML document that is based on the first XML document examined in Chapter 1. The document has a root element and a few nested elements, a few attributes, and a few text data values.

Listing 7-1: **A Very Simple XML Document**

```
<?xml version="1.0" encoding="UTF-8"?>
<?xml-stylesheet type="text/xsl" href=
"attributestoelements.xsl"?>
<rootelement>
  <firstelement position="1">
    <level1 children="0">This is level 1 of the nested
    elements</level1>
```

Continued

Listing 7-1 *(continued)*

```
    </firstelement>
    <secondelement position="2">
      <level1 children="1">
        <level2>This is level 2 of the nested elements</level2>
      </level1>
    </secondelement>
</rootelement>
```

The XML document starts with a standard declaration for an XML document, then contains a second XML declaration that explicitly links the XML document to the attributestoelements.xsl document. In this case, the XML document has to be in the same directory as the XSL document for the transformation to take place:

```
<?xml version="1.0" encoding="UTF-8"?>
<?xml-stylesheet type="text/xsl"
href="attributestoelements.xsl"?>
```

This is a minimal XML-stylesheet processing instruction, showing the mandatory type and the `href` attributes. Here's a full listing:

✦ **type:** Must contain a valid MIME type, and is almost always text/xsl, or sometimes text/xml.

✦ **href:** Must be a valid URI.

✦ **title:** Used for distinguishing between more than one XML-stylesheet processing instruction in the same XML document.

✦ **media:** A list of values as defined in the W3C HTML Recommendation Version 4.0 and higher. Used in addition to or instead of the title attribute.

✦ **charset:** Used to specify a separate encoding for a stylesheet. For example, the XML document may be UTF-8, and the XSL stylesheet could be ISO-8859-1. Theoretically, the XSLT processor should know how to handle the charset differences.

✦ **alternate:** For use when more than one XML-stylesheet processing instruction is in the same XML document. If the attribute value is `no`, the stylesheet should be used first. All other stylesheets should have an alternate attribute value of `yes`.

There are three ways that transformations happen:

✦ **Referencing the XSL explicitly:** As illustrated in the reference code earlier, and in Listing 7-1, a reference to a stylesheet can be explicitly declared using the XML-stylesheet processing instruction. This is useful when automatic client-side XSLT transformations are necessary and the client software, usually a Web browser, is W3C XSLT compliant. Explicit referencing is most commonly used for separation of data in XML documents from display characteristics in XSL stylesheets. The XML is usually transformed to HTML on a server or in a browser client before the HTML is displayed to a user.

✦ **Referencing the stylesheet programmatically:** Programs can declare the XML source, the XSL stylesheet, and the output destination, then invoke an XSLT processor to perform the transformation. This is the technique used on servers to separate XML document data from XSL stylesheet HTML display characteristics in XML-based Websites, where one stylesheet controls the display of many XML documents. It is also the way that most XML-to-XML and XML-to-text transformations occur in XML applications.

✦ **Embedding XML into an XSL stylesheet:** XML data can also be embedded into an XSL document. This is not recommended for the same reasons that embedded DTDs are not recommended. This is only mentioned here in case a developer comes across this technique in a legacy system. Embedded stylesheets represent a maintenance nightmare if the transformation or the source data should ever need to be altered, and defeat the purpose of transformations. In most cases, the transformed document can be substituted for the XML data and stylesheet combination document.

Next is the remainder of the XML document, which consists of a single-value rootelement element:

```
<rootelement>
```

Next are the nested elements, attributes, and text, as illustrated by the nested firstelement under the root element in our example:

```
<firstelement position="1">
   <level1 children="0">This is level 1 of the nested
    elements</level1>
</firstelement>
```

The firstelement has an attribute called position with a value of 1. The position attribute adds a little more information about the firstelement, in this case that the original sorting position of the first element in the XML document is 1. Nested under the "firstelement" element is the level1 element, which contains an attribute called children. The element name is used to describe the nesting level in the XML document, and the attribute is used to describe how many more levels of nesting are contained under the level1 element, in this case, no more nested levels (0). The phrase This is level 1 of the nested elements represents a textual data value for the level1 element that the text is nested in.

The secondelement element is a variation of the firstelement element. Let's compare the firstelement and secondelement elements to get a better sense of the structure of the document:

```
<secondelement position="2">
   <level1 children="1">
      <level2>This is level 2 of the nested
       elements</level2>
   </level1>
</secondelement>
```

Like the `firstelement`, the `secondelement` has an attribute called `position`, this time with a value of 2. Nested under the `secondelement` element is another `level1` element. The `level1` element in the `secondelement` also has an attribute called `children`. The `level1` element is again used to describe the nesting level in the XML document, and the attribute is used to describe how many more levels of nesting are contained under the `level1` element, in this case, one more nested level (1). The phrase `This is level 2 of the nested elements` inside the `level2` element represents a textual data value for the `level2` element.

Last but not least, to finish the XML document, the `rootelement` tag is closed:

```
</rootelement>
```

Listing 7-2 shows a stylesheet that transforms attributes in Listing 7-1 to elements by matching a pattern and applying a template to items in the source XML document that transforms them into a new format in the destination XML document.

Listing 7-2: A Very Simple XSL Stylesheet

```
<?xml version="1.0" encoding="UTF-8"?>
<xsl:stylesheet version="1.0"
xmlns:xsl="http://www.w3.org/1999/XSL/Transform">
  <xsl:output method="xml"/>
  <xsl:template match="@*">
    <xsl:element name="{name()}">
      <xsl:value-of select="."/>
    </xsl:element>
  </xsl:template>
  <xsl:template match="*">
    <xsl:copy>
      <xsl:apply-templates select="*|@*"/>
    </xsl:copy>
  </xsl:template>
</xsl:stylesheet>
```

The XSL stylesheet starts with an optional XML declaration and an attribute that sets the encoding style for the XSL stylesheet. Encoding style for the transformation output is handled separately:

```
<?xml version="1.0" encoding="UTF-8"?>
```

Next is the stylesheet `Namespace` declaration in the root element:

```
<xsl:stylesheet version="1.0"
xmlns:xsl="http://www.w3.org/1999/XSL/Transform">
```

The `xsl:` prefix is mandatory for well-formed stylesheets, but the `stylesheet` element name can be replaced with `transform`. However, `stylesheet` is the element name that is used most, and therefore `transform` is recommended only if there is a good reason for not using `stylesheet`. For XSLT 1.0, the `version` attribute is optional if `stylesheet` is used as the element name, but must be included if `transform` is used. When using `stylesheet` as the element name, the default version is 1.0 if the attribute is not included, which does not impact XSLT transformations until XSLT 2.0 becomes an official W3C Recommendation.

There is one other `Namespace` declaration that developers may see in legacy applications and older stylesheets:

```
<xsl:Stylesheet xmlns:xsl="http://www.w3.org/TR/WD-xsl">
```

This `Namespace` declaration was used in older stylesheets to maintain compatibility with Microsoft IE 5.0 browsers, which supported an older version of the W3C Recommendation. This `Namespace` should not be used unless compatibility with 5.0 browsers needs to be maintained.

XSLT Elements

The `stylesheet` element is used to specify the root element of W3C stylesheets. XSLT vocabularies are mostly made up of elements that describe template instructions or types of data that XSLT processors use during transformations. Table 7-1 describes the full listing of XSL elements available to stylesheet developers.

Table 7-1
W3C XSLT Elements

Element	Description
stylesheet	Defines a root element of a stylesheet. Can be used interchangeably with transform, but most stylesheets use stylesheet as a de facto standard.
transform	Defines a root element of a stylesheet. Should only be used to replace stylesheet as the root element of a stylesheet, but only if there is a good reason not to use stylesheet.
output	Defines the format of the output document. html, xml, and text output methods are predefined. If the output method is xml, output is well-formed xml, html formats the output as HTML, and text is any character data, including RTF and PDF files. If no output method is specified, the XSLT processor usually checks to see if the document is html-based on html output document tree node prefixes, and defaults to xml if no other determination can be made. Must be a child of the stylesheet element. Several optional attributes can also be used to define the output version, the encoding type, to include or not include an XML declaration declaration, define the standalone attribute, define a doctype, support output document indentation, and indicate a media type.
namespace-alias	Replaces a source document Namespace with a new Namespace in the output node tree. Must be a child of the stylesheet element.
preserve-space	Defines whitespace preservation for elements. Must be a child of the stylesheet element.
strip-space	Defines whitespace removal for elements. Must be a child of the stylesheet element.
key	Adds key values to each node in the result of an XPath expression. Must be defined as a child of the stylesheet element. For use with the key function in XPath expressions (functions are defined in Table 7-4).
import	Imports an external stylesheet into the current stylesheet. If there are conflicts between the current stylesheet and the imported stylesheet, the current stylesheet takes precedence. Must be defined as a child of the stylesheet element.
apply-imports	Follows the apply-template rules but overrides a stylesheet template with the template from an imported template. Normally, the current stylesheet takes precedence over the imported stylesheet.

Element	Description
Include	Includes an external stylesheet in the current stylesheet. If there are conflicts between the current stylesheet and the included stylesheet, it's up to the XSLT processor to decide precedence. Must be defined as a child of the `stylesheet` element.
template	Applies rules in a match or select action. Optional attributes can be used for specifying a node-set by match, template name, processing priority for this template in case of conflicts in the stylesheet, and an optional QName for a subset of nodes in a nodeset.
apply-templates	Applies templates to all children of the current node, or a specified node-set using the optional `select` attribute. Parameters can be passed using the `with-param` element.
call-template	Calls a template by name. Parameters can be passed using the `with-param` element. Results can be assigned to a variable.
param	Defines a parameter and a default value in a stylesheet template. A global parameter can be defined as a child of the `stylesheet` element.
with-param	Passes a parameter value to a template when call-template or apply-templates is used.
variable	Defines a variable in a template or a stylesheet. A global variable can be defined as a child of the `stylesheet` element.
copy	Copies the current node and any related `Namespace` only. Output matches the current node (element, attribute, text, processing instruction, comment, or `Namespace`).
copy-of	Copies the current node, `Namespaces`, descendant nodes, and attributes. Scope can be controlled with a select attribute.
If	Conditionally applies a template if the `test` attribute expression evaluates to `true`.
choose	Makes a choice based on multiple options. Used with `when` and `otherwise`.
when	An action for `choose` elements.
otherwise	A default action for `choose` elements. Must be the last child of a `choose` element
for-each	Iteratively processes each node in a node-set defined by an XPath expression.
sort	Defines a sort key used by apply-templates to a node-set and by for-each to specify the order of iterative processing of a node set.

Continued

Table 7-1 *(continued)*	
Element	*Description*
element	Adds an element to the output node tree. Names, Namespaces, and attributes can be added with the names, Namespaces, and use-attribute-sets attributes.
attribute	Adds an attribute to the output node tree. Must be a child of an element.
attribute-set	Adds a list of attributes to the output node tree. Must be a child of an element.
text	Adds text to the output node tree.
value-of	Retrieves a string value of a node and write it to the output node tree.
decimal-format	Specifies the format of numeric characters and symbols when converting to strings. Used with the format-number function only, not with the number element. (Functions are defined in Table 7-4.)
number	Adds a sequential number to the nodes of a node-set, based on the value attribute. Can also define the number format for the current node in the output node tree.
fallback	Defines alternatives for instructions that the current XSL processor does not support.
message	Adds a message to the output node tree. This element can also optionally stop processing on a stylesheet with the terminate attribute. Mostly used by developers for debugging stylesheets and XSLT processors.
processing-instruction	Adds a processing instruction to the output node tree.
comment	Adds a comment to the output node tree.

Note   All of the elements in Table 7-1 should be prefixed by xsl: and follow the format xsl:elementname.

Next, our sample stylesheet declares the output method for the transformation, which, in this case, is XML, using the XSLT output element:

```
<xsl:output method="xml"/>
```

The other XSLT 1.0 output options are text or HTML, or a valid prefixed QName that can be resolved into a URI. For more complete documentation on this element, please refer to the XSLT element listings in Table 7-1.

Next, the stylesheet goes hunting for all the attributes in the XML document using the `template` element and the `match` attribute:

```
<xsl:template match="@*">
```

The `match` attribute is available with the `template` and `key` elements, and is used to match the pattern specified by the `match` attribute value. When an XSLT processor is invoked, the source XML document is parsed into a set of nodes in a tree, starting with the root element in the document. XSLT uses pattern matching to look through the document node tree and retrieve nodes that match the patterns specified. The `@*` attribute value is an XPath expression and instructs the processor to look at all child nodes of the root node (`*`) and find all the attributes (`@`) in the source XML document.

XSL and XPath

The `match` attribute is one of several XSLT pattern-matching attributes that are used to find nodes in an XML source document. The `match` attribute is used to match a pattern in an XML document, for example, to detect the root element, or an attribute in the second element under the root element. Pattern matching is facilitated through XPath expressions, which express the parsed nodes of an XML document in tree hierarchy references. XPath follows a syntax that closely mirrors file system paths but in the context of an XML document. XPath tree representations break XML documents down into a series of connected root, element, text, attribute, `Namespace`, processing instruction, and comment nodes.

Imagine that the XSLT processor parses a document and places each of the elements in the document into a directory on a file system, and defining attributes, `Namespaces`, and text data in each directory with special identifiers. The new file system starts with the root directory (`/`), and each descendant element can be found in a subdirectory under the root. XPath doesn't work *exactly* like this, but on the surface it appears to, and the directory metaphor is a good point of reference for starting to understand how XPath really does work. Table 7-2 shows the basic location operators for XPath expressions.

Table 7-2
XPath Location Operators

Operator	Description
.	The current node
. .	The parent node
/	The root element
/ /	All descendants
@	Attribute identifier
*	All child nodes

The location operators are actually abbreviations of commonly used XPath node axes. Node axes are expressions that relate to the current node and radiate out from that node in different directions, to locate parents, ancestors, children, descendants, and siblings, in relation to the current node. Table 7-3 lists and describes the XPath node axes.

Table 7-3
XPath Node Axes

Axis	Description
self	The current node
ancestor	Ancestors, excluding the current node
ancestor-or-self	The current node and all ancestors
attribute	The attributes of the current node
child	Children of the current node
descendant	Descendants, excluding the current node
descendant-or-self	The current node and all descendants
following	The next node in the document order, including all descendants of the next node, and excluding the current node descendants and ancestors
following-sibling	The next sibling node in the document order, including all descendants of the sibling node, and excluding the current node descendants and ancestors
namespace	All Namespace nodes of the current node
parent	The parent of the current node

Axis	Description
preceding	The previous node in the document order, including all descendants of the previous node, and excluding the current node descendants and ancestors
preceding-sibling	The previous sibling node in the document order, including all descendants of the sibling node, and excluding the current node descendants and ancestors

XPath axes, attributes, and namespaces

XPath axis nodes treat attributes and Namespaces differently than they treat elements, text values, processing instructions, and comments, depending on the axis and the current node. This is because attributes and Namespaces in the document are not part of the hierarchy of elements, text values, processing instructions, and comments, but are located separately in the node tree.

✦ Attributes are only available from element nodes or the root node, not from other attribute and namespace nodes.

✦ The child, descendant, following, following-sibling, preceding, and preceding-sibling axes do not contain attributes or Namespaces, and are empty if the current node is an attribute or a Namespace node.

✦ Attributes of the current node can be accessed using the attribute axis or the attribute identifier (@), as long as the current node is an element node.

The next few lines in our example stylesheet create a new element based on the name of the current node in the XML document tree. The current node is set to an attribute in the XML document, based on the previous line in the XSL stylesheet (xsl:template match="@*"). However, XPath has limitations on what can be accessed if the current node is an attribute or Namespace. To get around this limitation, the XSLT name() function is used to pass the name of the current attribute node to the new element declaration. The XPath location operator representing the self node (.) is used to pass the value of the attribute into the value of the new element using the value-of select element, and then the new element is finished with a hard-coded closing tag, and the template is finished with the template closing tag:

```
    <xsl:element name="{name()}">
      <xsl:value-of select="."/>
    </xsl:element>
  </xsl:template>
```

The name() function is one of many functions that can be used in stylesheets. Unlike other types of XML, XPath supports five types of data, even though the data itself remains text.

✦ **boolean objects:** True or false values.

✦ **numbers:** Any numeric value.

✦ **string:** Any string.

✦ **node-set:** A set of nodes selected by an XPath expression or series of expressions.

✦ **external object:** A set of nodes returned by an XSLT extension function other than an XPath or XSLT expression. Support for external objects depends on the XSLT processor support for extensions.

There are also several functions related to each data type that can be used in XSL stylesheets. Table 7-4 describes the functions supported for each data type.

Table 7-4
Functions by Data Type

Function	Description
Boolean Functions	
boolean()	Converts an expression to the Boolean data type value and returns true or false.
true()	Binary true.
false()	Binary false.
not()	Reverse binary true or false: not(true expression)=false, not(false expression)=true
Number Functions	
number()	Converts an expression to a numeric data type value.
round()	Rounds a value up or down to the nearest integer: round(98.49) = 98, round(98.5) = 99
floor()	Rounds a value down to the nearest integer: floor(98.9) = 98.
ceiling()	Rounds a value up to the nearest integer: ceiling(98.4) = 99.
sum()	Sums the numeric values in a node-set.
count()	Counts the nodes in a node-set.

Function	Description
String Functions	
string()	Converts an expression to a string data type value.
format-number()	Converts a numeric expression to a string data type value, using the decimal-format element values as a guide if the decimal-format element is present in a stylesheet.
concat()	Converts two or more expressions to a concatenated string data type value.
string-length()	Counts the characters in a string data type value.
contains()	Checks for a substring in a string. Returns Boolean true or false.
starts-with()	Checks for a substring at the beginning of a string. Returns Boolean true or false.
translate()	Replaces an existing substring with a specified substring in a specified string data type value.
substring()	Retrieves a substring in a specified string data type value starting at a numeric character position and optionally ending at a specified numeric length after the starting point.
substring-after()	Retrieves a substring of all characters in a specified string data type that occurs after a numeric character position.
substring-before()	Retrieves a substring of all characters in a specified string data type that occurs before a numeric character position.
normalize-space()	Replaces any tab, newline, and carriage return characters in a string data type value with spaces, then removes any leading or trailing spaces from the new string.
Node Set Functions	
current()	The current node in a single-node node-set.
position()	The position of the current node in a node-set.
key()	A node-set defined by the key element.
name()	The name of the selected node
local-name()	The name of a node without a prefix, if a prefix exists.
namespace-uri()	The full URI of a node prefix, if a prefix exists.
unparsed-entity-uri()	The URI of an unparsed entity via a reference to the source document DTD, based on the entity name.
id()	A node-set with nodes that match the id value.

Continued

Table 7-4 *(continued)*

Function	Description
`generate-id()`	A unique string for a selected node in a node-set. The syntax follows well-formed XML rules.
`lang()`	A Boolean true or false depending on if the `xml:lang` attribute for the selected node matches the language identifier provided in an argument.
`last()`	The position of the last node in a node-set.
`document()`	Builds a node tree from an external XML document when provided with a valid document URI.
External Object Functions	(Note: These functions may also apply to other data types.)
`system-property()`	Returns information about the processing environment. Useful when building multi-version and multi-platform stylesheets in conjunction with the fallback element.
`element-available()`	A Boolean true or false based on if a processing instruction or extension element is supported by the XSLT processor.
`function-available()`	A Boolean true or false based on if a function is supported by the XSLT processor.

The next segment of the sample stylesheet uses the wildcard to create a template from all child nodes in the document. The copy element is used to copy the contents of the current XML document and apply the predefined templates related to the attribute match (`@*`) and the current template match (`*`) while copying by using the `select` attribute of the `apply-templates` element. After that, the XSL stylesheet is closed by the `stylesheet` closing tag.

```
    <xsl:template match="*">
    <xsl:copy>
      <xsl:apply-templates select="*|@*"/>
    </xsl:copy>
  </xsl:template>
</xsl:stylesheet>
```

Listing 7-3 shows the output from the transformation. Note that there are no longer any attributes or values in the new XML document, just elements and text data. The `attribute` template was applied when the copy took place, replacing attributes with child elements.

Listing 7-3: **The transformation output document**

```
<?xml version="1.0" encoding="UTF-8"?>
<rootelement>
  <firstelement>
    <position>1</position>
    <level1>
      <children>0</children>
    </level1>
  </firstelement>
  <secondelement>
    <position>2</position>
    <level1>
      <children>1</children>
      <level2/>
    </level1>
  </secondelement>
</rootelement>
```

XSLT Extensions with EXSLT.org

As mentioned earlier in this chapter, the W3C XSLT stylesheet Recommendation will probably be updated from Version 1.0 to Version 2.0 in late 2003. In the meantime, the 1999 1.0 Recommendation has been showing its age. The 1.0 specification does, however, leave room for extensions to existing stylesheet structure and syntax via the external-object data type and the extension-element-prefixes attribute in the stylesheet and transform elements, and the element-available and function-available functions. Many XSLT processors now support external extensions, and a good source of extensions can be found at EXSLT.org. Most extensions take the form of code that acts as add-in modules to existing XSLT processors and support functions that can be used as if they were part of the W3C Recommendation, once the modules are installed. EXSLT.org provides several free-distribution modules, plus setup instructions and function documentation. Developers are also welcomed to contribute to the group with their own extensions.

Summary

In this chapter, I provided an introduction to XSL and provided a theoretical overview of XSLT, XSL stylesheet elements, structure, and syntax, XPath axes, functions, and data types, and a few XSLT-specific functions.

✦ The history of XSLT

✦ How XSLT works

✦ An introduction to XPath

✦ XSL stylesheet elements

✦ XPath and XSLT tips and tricks for stylesheet developers

✦ Extending XSLT

✦ All about EXSLT.org

In the next chapter, you'll be putting all the lessons you have learned so far about XSLT Transformations to use by showing examples for transforming XML to text and HTML. We'll also cover changing the format of XML documents using transformation.

✦   ✦   ✦

XSL Transformations

In the last chapter, you were introduced to the theory of XSLT, XSL stylesheets, and XPath expressions. In this chapter, you'll apply that theory to real-world examples that will show you how to use XSLT elements, functions, and XPath expressions to transform XML documents to other formats of XML, text, and HTML. The next chapter will extend the HTML examples in this chapter even further by using XSL:FO in our transformations.

 All of the XML document and stylesheet examples contained in this chapter can be downloaded from the `xmlprogrammingbible.com` Website, in the Downloads section.

To Begin...

All of the examples in this chapter use the same source XML file, which is the sample XML document I have used in previous chapters. This example starts with a list of selected quotes from William Shakespeare, then goes on to list three books that contain the quotes that are available for purchase from Amazon.com, and a Spanish translation of Macbeth, Romeo and Juliet, Hamlet, and other volumes that are available from `http://www.elcorteingles.es`. Amazon.com provides a service that returns XML documents based on a URL query, and the `Amazon` element is based on this format. The `elcorteingles.com` book listing format and the quote listing, as well as other parts of the document are used to illustrate several features of XSLT stylesheet transformations. I convert the source document into HTML, delimited text, and HTML to show you some advanced XSLT tips and tricks.

Listing 8-1 shows the XML document, named AmazonMacbethSpanish.xml, which I will refer back to in the next few examples.

Listing 8-1: **The Contents of AmazonMacbethSpanish.xml**

```xml
<?xml version="1.0" encoding="ISO-8859-1"?>
<quotedoc>
  <quotelist author="Shakespeare, William" quotes="4">
    <quote source="Macbeth" author="Shakespeare,
    William">When the hurlyburly's done, / When the battle's
    lost and won.</quote>
    <quote source="Macbeth" author="Shakespeare,
    William">Out, damned spot! out, I say!-- One; two; why,
    then 'tis time to do't ;--Hell is murky!--Fie, my lord,
    fie! a soldier, and afeard? What need we fear who knows
    it, when none can call our power to account?--Yet who
    would have thought the old man to have had so much blood
    in him?</quote>
    <quote source="Macbeth" author="Shakespeare, William">Is
    this a dagger which I see before me, the handle toward
    my hand? Come, let me clutch thee: I have thee not, and
    yet I see thee still. Art thou not, fatal vision,
    sensible to feeling as to sight? or art thou but a
    dagger of the mind, a false creation, proceeding from
    the heat-oppressed brain?</quote>
    <quote source="Macbeth" author="Shakespeare, William">To-
    morrow, and to-morrow, and to-morrow,creeps in this
    petty pace from day to day, to the last syllable of
    recorded time; and all our yesterdays have lighted fools
    the way to dusty death. Out, out, brief candle! Life's
    but a walking shadow; a poor player, that struts and
    frets his hour upon the stage, and then is heard no
    more: it is a tale told by an idiot, full of sound and
    fury, signifying nothing. </quote>
    <quote/>
  </quotelist>
  <catalog items="4">
    <amazon items="3">
      <product>
        <ranking>1</ranking>
        <title>Hamlet/MacBeth</title>
        <asin>8432040231</asin>
        <author>Shakespeare, William</author>
        <image>http://images.amazon.com/images/P/
        8432040231.01.MZZZZZZZ.jpg</image>
        <small_image>http://images.amazon.com/images/P/
        8432040231.01.TZZZZZZZ.jpg</small_image>
        <list_price>$7.95</list_price>
        <release_date>19910600</release_date>
        <binding>Paperback</binding>
        <availability/>
```

```
    <tagged_url>http://www.amazon.com:80/exec/obidos
      /redirect?tag=associateid&amp;benztechnonogies=9441
      &amp;camp=1793&amp;link_code=xml&amp;path=ASIN/
      8432040231</tagged_url>
  </product>
  <product>
    <ranking>2</ranking>
    <title>MacBeth</title>
    <asin>1583488340</asin>
    <author>Shakespeare, William</author>
    <image>http://images.amazon.com/images/P/
      1583488340.01.MZZZZZZZ.jpg</image>
    <small_image>http://images.amazon.com/images/P/
      1583488340.01.TZZZZZZZ.jpg</small_image>
    <list_price>$8.95</list_price>
    <release_date>19991200</release_date>
    <binding>Paperback</binding>
    <availability/>
    <tagged_url>http://www.amazon.com:80/exec/obidos/
      redirect?tag=associateid&amp;benztechnonogies=9441
      &amp;camp=1793&amp;link_code=xml&amp;path=ASIN/
      1583488340</tagged_url>
  </product>
  <product>
    <ranking>3</ranking>
    <title>William Shakespeare: MacBeth</title>
    <asin>8420617954</asin>
    <author>Shakespeare, William</author>
    <image>http://images.amazon.com/images/P/
      8420617954.01.MZZZZZZZ.jpg</image>
    <small_image>http://images.amazon.com/images/P/
      8420617954.01.TZZZZZZZ.jpg</small_image>
    <list_price>$4.75</list_price>
    <release_date>19810600</release_date>
    <binding>Paperback</binding>
    <availability/>
    <tagged_url>http://www.amazon.com:80/exec/obidos/
      redirect?tag=associateid&amp;benztechnonogies=9441
      &amp;camp=1793&amp;link_code=xml&amp;path=ASIN/
      8420617954</tagged_url>
  </product>
</amazon>
<elcorteingles items="1">
  <product xml:lang="es">
    <titulo>Romeo y Julieta/Macbeth/Hamlet/Otelo/La
      fierecilla domado/El sueño de una noche de verano/
      El mercader de Venecia</titulo>
    <isbn>8484036324</isbn>
    <autor>Shakespeare, William</autor>
    <imagen>http://libros.elcorteingles.es/producto/
      verimagen_blob.asp?ISBN=8449503639</imagen>
```

Continued

Listing 8-1 *(continued)*

```
        <precio>7,59 &#x20AC;</precio>
        <fecha_de_publicación>6/04/1999
        </fecha_de_publicación>
        <Encuadernación>Piel</Encuadernación>
        <librourl>http://libros.elcorteingles.es/producto
        /libro_descripcion.asp?CODIISBN=8449503639</librourl>
      </product>
    </elcorteingles>
  </catalog>
</quotedoc>
```

XML to XML

Transforming XML to other forms of XML is probably the second most common type of transformation, after XML to HTML transformations. As you learned in Chapter 7, XSLT processors parse XML documents into document node trees before transforming them. In an XML to XML transformation, it's important to identify the source XML document nodes needed in the source and target of the transformation.

A simple technique using xsl:copy-of

One of the simplest ways to start using XSL is to use the `xsl:copy-of` element to create a new XML document using a subset of a larger XML document. Listing 8-2 shows the contents of the XMLtoQuotes.xsl stylesheet. This stylesheet creates a new XML document containing just the quotes from the sample XML document in Listing 8-1.

Listing 8-2: **The Code for the XMLtoQuotes.xsl Stylesheet**

```
<?xml version="1.0" encoding="UTF-8"?>
<xsl:stylesheet
xmlns:xsl="http://www.w3.org/1999/XSL/Transform" version="1.0">
  <xsl:output method="xml"/>
  <xsl:template match="/">
    <transformedquotes>
      <xsl:apply-templates select="/quotedoc/quotelist/*">
</xsl:apply-templates>
    </transformedquotes>
  </xsl:template>
  <xsl:template match="*">
    <xsl:copy-of select="."/>
  </xsl:template>
</xsl:stylesheet>
```

Walking through the transformation, I declare the XSL stylesheet as an XML document, and then declare an `xsl:` Namespace for the XSL elements in the stylesheet. Next, I specify the output method for the stylesheet as `xml`, and also specify the encoding for the output as `ISO-8859-1`, the same as the origin document. Note that the output encoding differs from the stylesheet encoding. This is a good illustration of the fact that the source XML document, the XSL stylesheet, and the transformation output can all be different encoding types if needed. However, it's worth pointing out that most XSLT processors support only UTF-8 and UTF-16 encoding. I also set the indent attribute to `"yes"`. The indent attribute is one of the optional and vague attributes that must be recognized but do not necessarily need to be supported in an XSLT processor. If the indent attribute is set to `"yes"`, the XSLT processor is supposed to perform rudimentary formatting on the XSLT output.

Stylesheet	Output XML Document Result

`<?xml version="1.0" encoding="UTF-8"?>`
 	
`<xsl:stylesheet xmlns:xsl="http://www.w3.org/1999/XSL/Transform" version="1.0">`
 	
`<xsl:output method="xml" encoding="ISO-8859-1" indent="yes"/>`
	`<?xml version="1.0" encoding="ISO-8859-1"?>`

Once this is done, I specify the output as XML and start XPath pattern matching at the root element (`/`). Next, a hard-coded element is added to the output to illustrate that the output was manipulated by the stylesheet. The original quotes element becomes a `transformedquotes` element in the XSLT output. At the root element I instruct the XSL processor to apply the template to all descendants of the `quotelist` element in the source document, which is a child of the `quotedoc` root element using the select attribute of the `apply-templates` element (`select="/quotedoc/quotelist/*">`):

Stylesheet	Output XML Document Result

`<xsl:template match="/">`
 	
`<transformedquotes>`
 	
`  <xsl:apply-templates select="/quotedoc/quotelist/*">`
	`<transformedquotes>`

The only template in the stylesheet is called as a result of the `apply-templates` element. The template is applied to all XML data in the node-set via the `match="*"` attribute of the template element. In this case, the node-set contains all the descendants of the `/quotedoc/quotelist` element. The `xsl:copy-of` element makes a copy of all the nodes in a node-set without exception, including namespaces, attributes, and so on. The select attribute could limit the `copy-of` element to a specific scope, for example all of the attributes in the node-set, but in this case the select just passes the whole node-set to the transformation output document by using the XPath current node operator (`.`):

Stylesheet	Output XML Document Result

`<xsl:template match="*">`
 	
  `<xsl:copy-of select="."/>`
 	
`</xsl:template>`
	`<quote source="Macbeth" author="Shakespeare, William">When the hurlyburly's done, / When the battle's lost and won.</quote>` `<quote source="Macbeth" author="Shakespeare, William">Out, damned spot! out, I say!-- One; two; why, then 'tis time to do't ;--Hell is murky!--Fie, my lord, fie! a soldier, and afeard? What need we fear who knows it, when none can call our power to account?--Yet who would have thought the old man to have had so much blood in him?</quote>` `<quote source="Macbeth" author="Shakespeare, William">Is this a dagger which I see before me, the handle toward my hand? Come, let me clutch thee: I have thee not, and yet I see thee still. Art thou not, fatal vision, sensible to feeling as to sight? or art thou but a dagger of the mind, a false creation, proceeding from the heat-oppressed brain?</quote>`

Stylesheet	Output XML Document Result
	```<quote source="Macbeth" author="Shakespeare, William">To-morrow, and to-morrow, and to-morrow,creeps in this petty pace from day to day, to the last syllable of recorded time; and all our yesterdays have lighted fools the way to dusty death. Out, out, brief candle! Life's but a walking shadow; a poor player, that struts and frets his hour upon the stage, and then is heard no more: it is a tale told by an idiot, full of sound and fury, signifying nothing.</quote>```

Once the template is finished, control is passed back to the template that called the copy-of template, and the hard-coded `transformedquotes` closing tag is added to the XSLT output. Next, the template and the stylesheet closing tags finish the XSLT process.

Stylesheet	Output XML Document Result

```</xsl:apply-templates>```
```</transformedquotes>```
```</xsl:template>......```
 	
```</xsl:stylesheet>```
	```</transformedquotes>```

Listing 8-3 shows the final XSLT transformation output in its entirety.

Listing 8-3: **The XSLT Output Document**

```
<?xml version="1.0" encoding="ISO-8859-1"?>
<transformedquotes>
  <quote source="Macbeth" author="Shakespeare, William">When
the hurlyburly's done, / When the battle's lost and
won.</quote>
```

Continued

Listing 8-3 *(continued)*

```
   <quote source="Macbeth" author="Shakespeare, William">Out,
damned spot! out, I say!-- One; two; why, then 'tis time to
do't ;--Hell is murky!--Fie, my lord, fie! a soldier, and
afeard? What need we fear who knows it, when none can call our
power to account?--Yet who would have thought the old man to
have had so much blood in him?</quote>
   <quote source="Macbeth" author="Shakespeare, William">Is this
a dagger which I see before me, the handle toward my hand?
Come, let me clutch thee: I have thee not, and yet I see thee
still. Art thou not, fatal vision, sensible to feeling as to
sight? or art thou but a dagger of the mind, a false creation,
proceeding from the heat-oppressed brain?</quote>
   <quote source="Macbeth" author="Shakespeare, William">To-
morrow, and to-morrow, and to-morrow,creeps in this petty pace
from day to day, to the last syllable of recorded time; and all
our yesterdays have lighted fools the way to dusty death. Out,
out, brief candle! Life's but a walking shadow; a poor player,
that struts and frets his hour upon the stage, and then is
heard no more: it is a tale told by an idiot, full of sound and
fury, signifying nothing. </quote>
   <quote/>
</transformedquotes>
```

Advanced techniques using iteration, sorting, and variables

The stylesheet in Listing 8-4 shows you many more advanced techniques to overcome several common XSLT challenges. This time the stylesheet is building a product catalog from the products in the stylesheet. This sounds simple enough, but there are actually several hurdles to overcome in making this work with the XML source document that I have to work with. For example, products are nested under the amazon and the elcorteingles elements, and they need to be grouped together and sorted as a single list without losing the original structure of the products. Instead of using the xsl:copy-of element to copy a hierarchy, this stylesheet builds a hierarchy using an iterative for-each element, replaces element names using variables, and sorts the output by ISBN number.

Listing 8-4: **The Code for the XMLtoCatalog.xsl Stylesheet**

```
<?xml version="1.0" encoding="UTF-8"?>
<xsl:stylesheet
xmlns:xsl="http://www.w3.org/1999/XSL/Transform" version="1.0">
   <xsl:output method="xml" encoding="ISO-8859-1" indent="yes"/>
```

```xml
    <xsl:template match="/">
      <catalogproducts>
        <xsl:apply-templates select="/quotedoc/catalog/*/*">
        <xsl:sort select="asin | isbn" data-type="number"
order="ascending"></xsl:sort>
        </xsl:apply-templates>
      </catalogproducts>
    </xsl:template>
    <xsl:template match="*">
      <catalogproduct>
        <xsl:for-each select="*">
                <xsl:variable name="isbnname">
            <xsl:choose>
              <xsl:when test="name()='asin'">isbn</xsl:when>
              <xsl:otherwise>
                <xsl:value-of select="name()"/>
              </xsl:otherwise>
            </xsl:choose>
          </xsl:variable>
          <xsl:element name="{$isbnname}">
            <xsl:value-of select="."/>
          </xsl:element>

        </xsl:for-each>
      </catalogproduct>
    </xsl:template>
</xsl:stylesheet>
```

As with the previous example, I'll break up the stylesheet code into pieces and show the effect that each piece of code has on the output. The initial template declarations are the same as the last example:

Stylesheet	Output XML Document Result

`<?xml version="1.0" encoding="UTF-8"?>`
 	
`<xsl:stylesheet xmlns:xsl="http://www.w3.org/1999/XSL/Transform" version="1.0">`
 	
`<xsl:output method="xml" encoding="ISO-8859-1" indent="yes"/>`
 	
`<xsl:template match="/">`
	`<?xml version="1.0" encoding="ISO-8859-1"?>`

After starting at the root element via the `xsl:template` element and the `match` attribute with a value of `/`, I hard-code a root element for the new XML document called `catalogproducts`. Next, the apply-templates element makes a selection of all products in the source XML document, which are identified as the grandchildren of the `catalog` element, using the abbreviated XPath operators (`/quotedoc/catalog/*/*`). The `xsl:sort` element is processed next. The data is not exactly sorted right away, but node-set templates are sorted and processed simultaneously, based on the sorting criteria. Note that the sorting takes place on the source data and the original element names, not on the output and any new element names.

Stylesheet	Output XML Document Result

`<catalogproducts>`
 	
`<xsl:apply-templates select=`
`"/quotedoc/catalog/*/*">`
 	
`<xsl:sort select="asin |`
`isbn" data-type="number" order=`
`"ascending"></xsl:sort>`
	`<catalogproducts>`

The `apply-templates` element calls the `template` element. The `template` element contains a wildcard operator (`*`) that processes all the elements and text in the node-set that it receives. The `for-each` select attribute contains the same value. In a select attribute, however, the same character (`*`) instructs an XSLT processor to transform the child elements of the current node-set only. By passing all the product elements and their children, but only processing the children, I am able to maintain the same structure for the product elements and children as they had in the original document.

The original product structure is maintained, but there are two changes to the products themselves for the new XML document. First, I rename the `product` element to `catalogproduct` by adding a hard-coded element to the selected child elements. The `for-each` statement will be called each time a new product and its child elements are called, which will create a new `catalogproduct` element for each original `product` element:

Stylesheet	Output XML Document Result

`<xsl:template match="*">`
 	
`<catalogproduct>`
 	
`<xsl:for-each select="*">`
	`<catalogproduct>`

Next, the ASIN in the Amazon book records needs to be changed to an ISBN to be consistent in all products. ASIN is Amazon's unique ID for all items on their Website, not just books. However, in this case, our listing only contains books, so we want to maintain the ISBN identifier on all book records. To change the ASIN element names to ISBN, I create a new variable called "isbnname" with the xsl:variable element, then conditionally assign a value to the variable using the xsl:choose element combined with the xsl:when and the xsl:otherwise elements. Multiple xsl:when elements and a single xsl:otherwise element can only be children of the xsl:choose element, and xsl:otherwise must be the last child element. The xsl:if element can be used for the same effect in a simple Boolean decision, but if there's a possibility of adding additional decision conditions in the future, xsl:choose is probably better to use from the start. This code checks the name of the node using the name() function, and if the name is asin, the xsl:when element renames it to isbn. The xsl:otherwise element catches all other conditions and saves the name of the source element to the isbnname variable. This variable is used to assign a name to an element for each element in the source XML document. If the source element was named asin, it's renamed to isbn, otherwise the original element name is passed to the new element name:

Stylesheet	Output XML Document Result
`<xsl:variable name="isbnname">`	`<isbn>1583488340</isbn>`
`<xsl:choose>`	
`<xsl:when test="name()=` `'asin'">isbn</xsl:when>`	
`<xsl:otherwise>`	
`<xsl:value-of select="name()"/>`	
`</xsl:otherwise>`	
`</xsl:choose>`	
`</xsl:variable>`	
`<xsl:element name="{$isbnname}">`	

Next, the value of the current element, if any, is passed to the element as a value, and then the element tag is closed. The process is repeated for each element that is a child of a product element in the source document. Each time a new product element child node-set is called, the for-each exits, and the catalogproduct element closing tag is added to the output document:

Stylesheet	Output XML Document Result
`<xsl:value-of select="."/>`	`<catalogproduct>`
`</xsl:element>`	`<ranking>2</ranking>`
`</xsl:for-each>`	`<title>MacBeth</title>`
`</catalogproduct>`	`<isbn>1583488340</isbn>`
`</xsl:template>`	`<author>Shakespeare, William</author>`
	`</catalogproduct>`

Once all of the product elements are processed, control is passed back to the original template that made the original `apply-templates` call. The hard-coded `catalogproducts` root element closing tag is added to the XML document, and processing is finished with the final `xsl:template` element closing tag:

Stylesheet	Output XML Document Result
`</xsl:apply-templates>`	`</catalogproducts>`
`</catalogproducts>`	
`</xsl:template>`	

Listing 8-5 shows the complete output for this stylesheet.

Listing 8-5: **The XSLT Output Document**

```
<?xml version="1.0" encoding="ISO-8859-1"?>
<catalogproducts>
  <catalogproduct>
    <ranking>2</ranking>
    <title>MacBeth</title>
    <isbn>1583488340</isbn>
    <author>Shakespeare, William</author>
    <image>http://images.amazon.com/images/P/
      1583488340.01.MZZZZZZZ.jpg</image>
    <small_image>http://images.amazon.com/images/P/
      1583488340.01.TZZZZZZZ.jpg</small_image>
```

```
        <list_price>$8.95</list_price>
        <release_date>19991200</release_date>
        <binding>Paperback</binding>
        <availability />
        <tagged_url>http://www.amazon.com:80/exec/obidos
          /redirect?tag=associateid&amp;benztechnonogies=9441
          &amp;camp=1793&amp;link_code=xml&amp;path=ASIN/
          1583488340</tagged_url>
    </catalogproduct>
    <catalogproduct>
        <ranking>3</ranking>
        <title>William Shakespeare: MacBeth</title>
        <isbn>8420617954</isbn>
        <author>Shakespeare, William</author>
        <image>http://images.amazon.com/images/P/
          8420617954.01.MZZZZZZZ.jpg</image>
        <small_image>http://images.amazon.com/images/P/
          8420617954.01.TZZZZZZZ.jpg</small_image>
        <list_price>$4.75</list_price>
        <release_date>19810600</release_date>
        <binding>Paperback</binding>
        <availability />
        <tagged_url>http://www.amazon.com:80/exec/obidos/
          redirect?tag=associateid&amp;benztechnonogies=9441&amp;
          camp=1793&amp;link_code=xml&amp;path=ASIN/8420617954
          </tagged_url>
    </catalogproduct>
    <catalogproduct>
        <ranking>1</ranking>
        <title>Hamlet/MacBeth</title>
        <isbn>8432040231</isbn>
        <author>Shakespeare, William</author>
        <image>http://images.amazon.com/images/P
          /8432040231.01.MZZZZZZZ.jpg</image>
        <small_image>http://images.amazon.com/images/P
          /8432040231.01.TZZZZZZZ.jpg</small_image>
        <list_price>$7.95</list_price>
        <release_date>19910600</release_date>
        <binding>Paperback</binding>
        <availability />
        <tagged_url>http://www.amazon.com:80/exec/obidos
          /redirect?tag=associateid&amp;benztechnonogies=9441
          &amp;camp=1793&amp;link_code=xml&amp;
          path=ASIN/8432040231</tagged_url>
    </catalogproduct>
    <catalogproduct>
        <titulo>Romeo y Julieta/Macbeth/Hamlet/Otelo/La
          fierecilla domado/El sueño de una noche de verano/ El
          mercader de Venecia</titulo>
        <isbn>8484036324</isbn>
        <autor>Shakespeare, William</autor>
```

Continued

Listing 8-5 *(continued)*

```
      <imagen>http://libros.elcorteingles.es/producto/
       verimagen_blob.asp?ISBN=8449503639</imagen>
      <precio>7,59 ¤</precio>
      <fecha_de_publicación>6/04/1999</fecha_de_publicación>
      <Encuadernación>Piel</Encuadernación>
      <librourl>http://libros.elcorteingles.es/producto/
       libro_descripcion.asp?CODIISBN=8449503639</librourl>
   </catalogproduct>
</catalogproducts>
```

More advanced techniques: namespaces, XSLT extensions, and fallbacks

The stylesheet in Listing 8-6 shows you a few more advanced techniques. This time the stylesheet creates two namespaces and assigns them to catalog data depending on the language of the source data, represented by the xml:lang predefined attribute.

This stylesheet also shows an example of implementing XSLT extensions. The XSLT document element is part of the XSLT 2.0 working draft. Currently, the result of XSL transformations has to be passed to an external processor or object to be written to a file. The document element adds the ability to produce transformation output directly to a file without the aid of external objects or processors. The document element will probably make it into the final XSLT 2.0 Recommendation, but some XSLT engine developers have already added the functionality into their products as an extension. EXSLT.org has implemented an extension interface that can be used to implement the document element into stylesheets. For now, XSLT processors that support EXSLT.org extensions can use the document element to produce an XML document, and if not, the fallback element in the stylesheet produces normal XSLT 1.0 transformation output.

Listing 8-6: **The XMLtoCatalogNamespaces.xsl Stylesheet**

```
<?xml version="1.0" encoding="UTF-8"?>
<xsl:stylesheet
xmlns:xsl="http://www.w3.org/1999/XSL/Transform" version="1.0"
xmlns:azlist="http://www.benztech.com/xsd/amazonlist"
xmlns:ellist="http://www.benztech.com/xsd/elcorteingleslist"
xmlns:exsl="http://exslt.org/common" extension-element-
prefixes="exsl">
  <xsl:import href="exsl/exsl.xsl"/>
```

```
<exsl:document href="exsloutput.xml" method="xml"
  indent="yes">
  <xsl:fallback>
    <xsl:output method="xml" indent="yes"/>
  </xsl:fallback>
</exsl:document>
<xsl:template match="/">
  <catalogproducts>
    <xsl:apply-templates select="/quotedoc/catalog/*/*[1]">
      <xsl:sort select="asin | isbn" data-type="number"
        order="ascending"/>
    </xsl:apply-templates>
  </catalogproducts>
</xsl:template>
<xsl:template match="*">
  <xsl:variable name="namespaceelementname">
    <xsl:choose>
      <xsl:when test="@xml:lang='es'">ellist</xsl:when>
      <xsl:otherwise>azlist</xsl:otherwise>
    </xsl:choose>
  </xsl:variable>
  <xsl:element
    name="{$namespaceelementname}:catalogproduct">
    <xsl:for-each select="*">
      <xsl:variable name="isbnname">
        <xsl:choose>
          <xsl:when test="name()='asin'">isbn</xsl:when>
          <xsl:otherwise>
            <xsl:value-of select="name()"/>
          </xsl:otherwise>
        </xsl:choose>
      </xsl:variable>
      <xsl:element
        name="{$namespaceelementname}:{$isbnname}">
        <xsl:value-of select="."/>
      </xsl:element>
    </xsl:for-each>
  </xsl:element>
</xsl:template>
</xsl:stylesheet>
```

In the interest of brevity, I'll omit most of what I have covered in previous examples. After the XML declaration, there are few additional namespaces in the `xsl:stylesheet` element, and an `extension-element-prefixes` element. The first two namespaces are used to differentiate between the data in the XML source document that comes from Amazon (`azlist`) and elcorteingles (`ellist`).

The exsl namespace is used to define extension elements in the stylesheet. The extension-element-prefixes attribute defines the exsl namespace prefix as an indicator of extension elements in the stylesheet. If more than one extension Namespace prefix is being used, the extension-element-prefixes attribute should contain a whitespace-delimited list of prefixes. The processor does not evaluate exsl elements and expressions as W3C stylesheet elements, but follows the rules specified in the EXSLT.org specifications and/or via imported stylesheets, which in this case are imported from the exsl/exsl.xsl stylesheet using the xsl:import element:

```
<xsl:stylesheet
xmlns:xsl="http://www.w3.org/1999/XSL/Transform" version="1.0"
xmlns:azlist="http://www.benztech.com/xsd/amazonlist"
xmlns:ellist="http://www.benztech.com/xsd/elcorteingleslist"
xmlns:exsl="http://exslt.org/common" extension-element-
prefixes="exsl">
<xsl:import href="exsl/exsl.xsl"/>
```

The imported stylesheet can be downloaded from http://EXSLT.org, in the downloads section, and implementation instructions for XSLT processor developers and stylesheet developers are located at the site as well.

Next, the exsl:document element instructs the XSLT processor to create a new output file in the same directory as the stylesheet, with the name exsloutput.xml. Note that the esxl:document element has the same attributes as the xsl:output element, which makes creating the subsequent fallback element very easy. The xsl:fallback element is used to provide an alternative for the extension element, in case the processor does not support the extended element, or there is something wrong with the extension implementation. The xsl:fallback element is part of the W3C XSLT 1.0 Recommendation and must be the child of an extension element.

In this case, the xsl:fallback element specifies that if the XSLT processor is unable to process the esxl:document element, the xsl:output element should be substituted, reverting the stylesheet to a basic XML-to-XML transformation:

```
<exsl:document href="exsloutput.xml" method="xml"
 indent="yes">
  <xsl:fallback>
    <xsl:output method="xml" indent="yes"/>
  </xsl:fallback>
</exsl:document>
```

Next, I create a new XML document for transformation output with a hard-coded root element called catalogproducts.

The xsl:apply-templates select attribute elects all of the grandchildren (/*/*) of the quotedoc/catalog element that appear in source document order. The [1] conditional XPath expression instructs the processor to just retrieve the first child that is encountered for each grandchild. Most developers would probably expect that this would retrieve only one set of data, but because there are two grand-children under the `quotedoc/catalog` element (amazon/product and elcorteingles/product), the first grandchild each is selected:

```
<xsl:template match="/">
  <catalogproducts>
    <xsl:apply-templates select="/quotedoc/catalog/*/*[1]">
      <xsl:sort select="asin | isbn" data-type="number"
       order="ascending"/>
    </xsl:apply-templates>
  </catalogproducts>
</xsl:template>
```

Now that the stylesheet has selected the two grandchildren to process, the name-spaces for each grandchild must be assigned. One of the main things that sets the elcorteingles elements apart from the amazon elements in the source document is the `xml:lang` attribute, which is set to `"es"` for the elcorteingles elements. Using this difference, an `xsl:choose` element can assign the correct Namespace to a local variable named `namespaceelementname`, which can be reused during the transformation. If the `xml:lang` attribute exists and is set to `"es"`, the `ellist` namespace prefix is assigned; otherwise, the variable defaults to the `azlist` Namespace prefix:

```
<xsl:template match="*">
  <xsl:variable name="namespaceelementname">
    <xsl:choose>
      <xsl:when test="@xml:lang='es'">ellist</xsl:when>
      <xsl:otherwise>azlist</xsl:otherwise>
    </xsl:choose>
  </xsl:variable>
```

Next, I select all the child elements of the product element and change the product element name by hard-coding the `catalogproduct` element name and attaching the Namespace prefix in the process. Then I select the children of each original product element with the `xsl:for-each` element, and change any `asin` elements in Amazon records to `isbn` elements using the `isbnname` variable, as I did in the last example. After defining all the variables needed to create a new element, the stylesheet creates the new element that combines the current Namespace prefix with the current variable value to create the new element value with a namespace prefix attached, and adds the text value associated with the element.

The `isbnname` variable is reassigned each time a new element is encountered in the source XML document, courtesy of the select attribute in the `xsl:for-each` element. The `namespaceelementname` is reassigned each time the template finds a match from the original select attribute at the top of the stylesheet.

```
<xsl:element
 name="{$namespaceelementname}:catalogproduct">
  <xsl:for-each select="*">
```

```
                    <xsl:variable name="isbnname">
                      <xsl:choose>
                        <xsl:when test="name()='asin'">isbn</xsl:when>
                        <xsl:otherwise>
                          <xsl:value-of select="name()"/>
                        </xsl:otherwise>
                      </xsl:choose>
                    </xsl:variable>
                    <xsl:element
                     name="{$namespaceelementname}:{$isbnname}">
                      <xsl:value-of select="."/>
                    </xsl:element>
                  </xsl:for-each>
                </xsl:element>
              </xsl:template>
            </xsl:stylesheet>
```

Listing 8-7 shows the transformation output, with namespaces attached to each individual book record, depending on the source.

Listing 8-7: **Output from the XMLtoCatalogNamespaces.xsl Transformation**

```
<?xml version="1.0" encoding="UTF-8"?>
<catalogproducts
xmlns:azlist="http://www.benztech.com/xsd/amazonlist"
xmlns:ellist="http://www.benztech.com/xsd/elcorteingleslist">
  <azlist:catalogproduct>
    <azlist:ranking>1</azlist:ranking>
    <azlist:title>Hamlet/MacBeth</azlist:title>
    <azlist:isbn>8432040231</azlist:isbn>
    <azlist:author>Shakespeare, William</azlist:author>
    <azlist:image>http://images.amazon.com/images/P/
     8432040231.01.MZZZZZZZ.jpg</azlist:image>
     <azlist:small_image>http://images.amazon.com/images/P/
      8432040231.01.TZZZZZZZ.jpg</azlist:small_image>
    <azlist:list_price>$7.95</azlist:list_price>
    <azlist:release_date>19910600</azlist:release_date>
    <azlist:binding>Paperback</azlist:binding>
    <azlist:availability />
    <azlist:tagged_url>http://www.amazon.com:80/exec/
    obidos/redirect?tag=associateid&amp;
    benztechnonogies=9441&amp;camp=1793&amp;
    link_code=xml&amp;path=ASIN/8432040231
    </azlist:tagged_url>
  </azlist:catalogproduct>
  <ellist:catalogproduct>
    <ellist:titulo>Romeo y Julieta/Macbeth/Hamlet/Otelo/La
     fierecilla domado/El sueño de una noche de verano/ El
     mercader de Venecia</ellist:titulo>
    <ellist:isbn>8484036324</ellist:isbn>
```

```
      <ellist:autor>Shakespeare, William</ellist:autor>
      <ellist:imagen>http://libros.elcorteingles.es/
       producto/verimagen_blob.asp?ISBN=8449503639
      </ellist:imagen>
      <ellist:precio>7,59 ¤</ellist:precio>
      <ellist:fecha_de_publicación>6/04/1999
      </ellist:fecha_de_publicación>
      <ellist:Encuadernación>Piel</ellist:Encuadernación>
      <ellist:librourl>http://libros.elcorteingles.es/producto
       /libro_descripcion.asp?CODIISBN=8449503639
      </ellist:librourl>
    </ellist:catalogproduct>
  </catalogproducts>
```

XML to text

XML to text transformations are paradoxically very simple when implemented for basic transformations and very complex for detailed requirements. This is usually due to how an XSLT processor handles whitespace (tabs, new lines, carriage returns, and spaces) in a document. W3C specifications are very explicit for some aspects of whitespace, and vague for many others, so it's usually up to the developer to be as explicit as possible about how whitespace should be preserved in transformation output. There are two ways to manipulate whitespace in transformation output.

You can use the xsl:preserve-space element to preserve the whitespace from the source XML document, and the xsl:strip-space to remove unwanted whitespace. For a single element, the normalize-space() function can be used to strip leading and trailing spaces, and replace any whitespace characters with a single space character.

For our fairly simple example, however, the stylesheet is leaving the whitespace as-is and showing one technique for maintaining other whitespace in the output XML. Listing 8-8 shows the entire XMLtoCatalogText.xsl stylesheet.

Listing 8-8: The XMLtoCatalogText.xsl Stylesheet

```
<?xml version="1.0" encoding="UTF-8"?>
<xsl:stylesheet
xmlns:xsl="http://www.w3.org/1999/XSL/Transform" version="1.0">
  <xsl:output method="text"/>
  <xsl:template match="/">
XML Bible Catalog Example:
<xsl:apply-templates select="/quotedoc/catalog/*/*">
```

Continued

Listing 8-8 *(continued)*

```
        <xsl:sort select="asin | isbn" data-type="number"
        order="ascending"/>
    </xsl:apply-templates>
-End of File-
  </xsl:template>
  <xsl:template match="*">
    <xsl:for-each select="*[text()]">"<xsl:value-of
    select="."/>"<xsl:if test="position()!=last()">,
    </xsl:if>
    </xsl:for-each>
    <xsl:text>&#xA;</xsl:text>
  </xsl:template>
</xsl:stylesheet>
```

For this example, I start by changing the output method to text and hard-code an example explanation as a heading in the text output:

```
<?xml version="1.0" encoding="UTF-8"?>
<xsl:stylesheet
xmlns:xsl="http://www.w3.org/1999/XSL/Transform" version="1.0">
  <xsl:output method="text"/>
  <xsl:template match="/">
XML Bible Catalog Example:
```

As in previous examples, the stylesheet sorts the data by the asin/isbn elements in the original source XML document as the results are processed, even though these elements will not be in the destination output. When the templates are finished building the output text, I add an -End of File- indicator to the text:

```
<xsl:apply-templates select="/quotedoc/catalog/*/*">
        <xsl:sort select="asin | isbn" data-type="number"
        order="ascending"/>
    </xsl:apply-templates>
-End of File-
  </xsl:template>
```

The next template of the stylesheet is usually where things get tricky. The xsl:preserve-space and the xsl:strip-space elements and the normalize-space() are used to handle whitespace from the source document elements, not add space in the output. Whitespace that is specified in an XSLT stylesheet has to be explicitly declared in most places, because XSLT processor engines may handle arbitrary hard-coding of spaces, carriage returns, tabs, and new lines differently. In the case of the following example, the xsl:for-each statement is explicitly located in one long line rather than in a nested structure to be sure that an XSLT processor that uses this stylesheet will not misinterpret a new line that formats an element as a new line that needs to be added to the output. Conversely, each representation of a book record in the source XML document should indicate an end-of record with a new line, so an xml:text element has been added to the stylesheet under the for-each element, with a hard-coded new line value as an entity reference (
).

Node selection is limited to text nodes only by using the conditional XPath expression as part of the select attribute (*[text()]). The rest of the output follows basic delimited text rules, with text values being wrapped with double quotes and separated by commas. The xsl:if element checks to see if the element is the last in the list and does not add the comma unless there are more elements for that book record:

```
<xsl:template match="*">
  <xsl:for-each select="*[text()]">"<xsl:value-of
  select="."/>"<xsl:if test="position()!=last()">,
  </xsl:if>
  </xsl:for-each>
  <xsl:text>&#xA;</xsl:text>
</xsl:template>
</xsl:stylesheet>
```

Listing 8-9 shows the text file that results from this transformation. Each element value is delimited with double quotes, and each set of elements is separated by a new line character.

Listing 8-9: Results of the XMLtoCatalogText.xsl Stylesheet Transformation

```
XML Bible Catalog Example:
"2", "MacBeth", "1583488340", "Shakespeare, William",
"http://images.amazon.com/images/P/1583488340.01.MZZZZZZ.jpg",
"http://images.amazon.com/images/P/1583488340.01.TZZZZZZ.jpg",
"$8.95", "19991200", "Paperback",
"http://www.amazon.com:80/exec/obidos/redirect?tag=associateid&
benztechnonogies=9441&camp=1793&link_code=xml&path=ASIN/1583488
340"
"3", "William Shakespeare: MacBeth", "8420617954",
"Shakespeare, William",
"http://images.amazon.com/images/P/8420617954.01.MZZZZZZ.jpg",
"http://images.amazon.com/images/P/8420617954.01.TZZZZZZ.jpg",
"$4.75", "19810600", "Paperback",
"http://www.amazon.com:80/exec/obidos/redirect?tag=associateid&
benztechnonogies=9441&camp=1793&link_code=xml&path=ASIN/8420617
954"
```

Continued

Listing 8-9 *(continued)*

```
"1", "Hamlet/MacBeth", "8432040231", "Shakespeare, William",
"http://images.amazon.com/images/P/8432040231.01.MZZZZZZZ.jpg",
"http://images.amazon.com/images/P/8432040231.01.TZZZZZZZ.jpg",
"$7.95", "19910600", "Paperback",
"http://www.amazon.com:80/exec/obidos/redirect?tag=associateid&
benztechnonogies=9441&camp=1793&link_code=xml&path=ASIN/8432040
231"
"Romeo y Julieta/Macbeth/Hamlet/Otelo/La fierecilla domado/El
sueÃ±o de una noche de verano/ El mercader de Venecia",
"8484036324", "Shakespeare, William",
"http://libros.elcorteingles.es/producto/verimagen_blob.asp?ISB
N=8449503639", "7,59 â,¬", "6/04/1999", "Piel",
"http://libros.elcorteingles.es/producto/libro_descripcion.asp?
CODIISBN=8449503639"
-End of File-
```

XML to HTML

Just a few years ago, most XML, XSL, and even some HTML development was done in simple text editors without the aid of customized tools for the job. Because of the complexity of modern HTML page formats, XML data issues, and XSL stylesheet development issues, XML to HTML conversions should not be attempted without the aid of one of the many easy-to-use tools out there for formatting and debugging XML, XSL, and HTML documents. The tool used to develop and debug the examples in this chapter is ALtova's XMLSPy 5 Enterprise Edition. A trial version can be downloaded from http://www.xmlspy.com.

For this example, Altova's XMLSpy stylesheet designer was used to develop the basic format of the stylesheet, and a few custom touches were added by hand. Altova's Stylesheet designer is a separate product from the XMLSpy UI and is a good environment for generating stylesheets by example. For the example in this chapter, a DTD was added to the stylesheet designer, and HTML tables were created from XML elements and attributes. The Altova stylesheet designer was very impressive, and most of the formatting I needed was facilitated by dragging and dropping element, attribute, and text nodes from the DTD to an example HTML page. Once the overall format of the HTML page was completed, the Generate XSLT Stylesheet option was used to generate a stylesheet called XMLtoCatalogHTML.xsl, which is based on the original DTD and the target HTML page. There were a few small things that could not be cleaned up in the stylesheet designer UI, which does not permit editing of the stylesheet directly. The stylesheet was saved and reopened in the XMLSpy's XML editor, and a few items were added, which are highlighted here.

The full XMLtoCatalogHTML.xsl stylesheet (the generated version is very repetitive and much too long to print in the book) can be downloaded from the XML Programmer's Bible Website. Figure 8-1 shows the HTML output that was generated by the transformation.

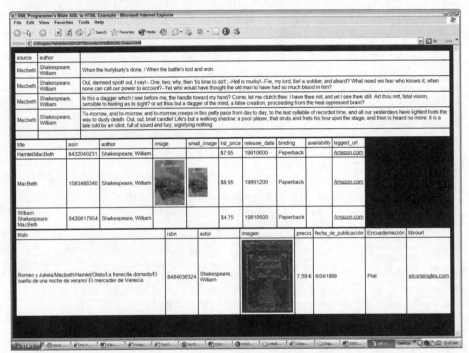

Figure 8-1: HTML output that was generated by the transformation using XMLtoCatalogHTML.xsl

Most of the code in the sample file will be very familiar to anyone who has worked with or viewed HTML. However, what happened to get there is probably somewhat new. For example, the following code segment contains the elements and attributes that define the stylesheet and start template processing at the root element, just as in the previous examples. Note that the generated stylesheet does not specify the output method as HTML, via the xsl:output element, but lets the processor figure it out via the HTML tag a few elements down in the stylesheet. This is acceptable but not recommended for most stylesheets; it's always best to define the output method explicitly if possible. Next, there are a few hard-coded HTML tags defining the HTML head and body. The TEXT and BGCOLOR attributes for the page were hand-coded after stylesheet generation. The text is set to white, and the page background is set to black.

The rest of this segment of the stylesheet takes the XSLT processor on a trip though the node tree to get to the `quotedoc/quotelist/quote` element, before defining a table heading (`thead`) for the table that will display the quotes from the XML document. Elements are added using a combination of the `xsl:text` element, the `disable-output-escaping` attribute, which suppresses an XSLT processor's normal conversion of illegal XML characters to their entity reference equivalent. In this case, the less than (<) and greater than (>) symbols need to be wrapped around the body tag to make it a well-formed HTML element. Once this is done, the table can be formatted.

```
<?xml version="1.0" encoding="UTF-8"?>
<xsl:stylesheet version="1.0"
xmlns:xsl="http://www.w3.org/1999/XSL/Transform">
  <xsl:template match="/">
    <html>
      <head>
        <title>XML Programmer&apos;s Bible XML to HTML
          Example</title>
      </head>
      <body title="XML Programmer&apos;s Bible XML to HTML
       Example" TEXT="000000" BGCOLOR="#000000">
        <xsl:for-each select="quotedoc">
          <xsl:for-each select="quotelist">
            <xsl:for-each select="quote">
              <xsl:if test="position()=1">
                <xsl:text disable-output-
                  escaping="yes">&lt;table
                  border="0"&gt;</xsl:text>
              </xsl:if>
              <xsl:if test="position()=1">
                <thead>
                  <tr>
                    <td style="background-color:white;
                      padding-bottom:5; padding-left:5;
                      padding-right:5; padding-top:5">
```

The next challenge was to get the URLs for images and links that are stored in the XML document formatted to be displayed and active on the HTML page. This was done by wrapping some hard-coded element and tribute values around existing templates. Here's what the generated stylesheet values for the images looked like before they were altered:

```
<td style="background-color:white;
  padding-bottom:5; padding-left:5;
  padding-right:5; padding-top:5">
<xsl:for-each select="small_image">
  <span style="background-color:white;
    font-family:Arial; font-size:small">
```

```
        <xsl:apply-templates/>
          </span>
      </xsl:for-each>
   </td>
```

In this case, the original elements were simply passed to the HTML page as table data using the xsl:apply-templates element. However, the small_image element contains a URL that could be used to display an image, so adding an HTML img element with an src attribute that links to the image for display on the page would probably be a better use for the data. To convert the URL to an image reference, the image element is wrapped around the value using the xsl:element element, and the src attribute becomes the new location for the source XML document URL:

```
<td style="background-color:white;
 padding-bottom:5; padding-left:5;
 padding-right:5; padding-top:5">
<xsl:for-each select="small_image">
  <span style="background-color:white;
   font-family:Arial; font-size:small">
    <xsl:element name="img">
      <xsl:attribute name="src">
       <xsl:apply-templates/>
      </xsl:attribute>
      </xsl:element>
    </span>
  </xsl:for-each>
</td>
```

The same technique was applied to link URLs as well. Instead of just passing URLs to the table as content, the URLs in the source XML document are converted to active links in the HTML page by adding an HTML element and a related href attribute, which is passed the value of the source document URL:

```
<td style="background-color:white;
 padding-bottom:5; padding-left:5;
 padding-right:5; padding-top:5">
<xsl:for-each select="tagged_url">
  <span style="background-color:white;
   font-family:Arial; font-size:small">
    <xsl:element name="a"> <xsl:attribute
     name="href"> <xsl:apply-templates/>
     </xsl:attribute>Amazon.com
     </xsl:element>
    </span>
  </xsl:for-each>
</td>
```

Summary

In this chapter, you built on your introduction to XSLT in Chapter 7 and illustrated several techniques for transforming various formats of XML to other formats of XML, text, and HTML. I also reviewed ways to generate and format stylesheets that convert XML to HTML using XMLSpy.

✦ XML to XML transformations

✦ XML to HTML transformations

✦ XML to text transformations

✦ Advanced XSLT topics: conditions, variables, iteration, and sorting

✦ XSLT extensions and fallbacks

In the next chapter, I'll expand on this knowledge to transform XML documents using XSL: Formatting Objects (XSL:FO) to convert XML documents to PDF files, PostScript, and other nonstandard document formats.

✦   ✦   ✦

XSL Formatting Objects

XSL Formatting Objects (XSL:FO) provides the capability to dynamically format XML documents as "camera-ready" artwork or printable pages. For example, let's say that a publishing house maintains content as standardized XML documents. The source XML document can be transformed into HTML and displayed on a Website, using techniques we showed you in Chapters 7 and 8. With XSL:FO, the same source XML document can also be the basis for a print version of the article.

In Chapter 7, we applied the XSL theory covered in Chapter 6 to transform a sample XML file to other formats of XML, text, and HTML. To do this, we used XSLT elements, functions, and XPath expressions to perform the transformations. This chapter will extend our HTML example from Chapter 8 further by using XSL:FO in an XSL transformation to gain more control over the output format. We're using the same source XML document, named AmazonMacbethSpanish.xml, for the example in this chapter. This time, however, we're transforming an XML document to a Portable Document format (PDF) file.

The XML document and XSL:FO Stylesheet examples contained in this chapter can be downloaded from the http://www.xmlprogrammingbible.com Website, in the Downloads section.

Understanding XSL Formatting Objects

The W3C stylesheet working group has actually produced two parts to the Extensible Stylesheet Language Recommendation. Chapter 7 introduced the *XSL Stylesheet Transformation (XSLT) 1.0* Recommendation, which describes the process of applying an XSL stylesheet to an XML document using a transformation engine. XSLT is based on DSSSL (Document Style Semantics and Specification Language), which was originally developed to define SGML document output formatting. XSLT 1.0 became a W3C Recommendation in 1999, and the full specification is available for review at `http://www.w3.org/TR/xslt`. The second part of the XSL 1.0 Recommendation is called *Extensible Stylesheet Language (XSL) 1.0*. XSL 1.0 achieved W3C Recommendation status on 15 October 2001. The 2001 XSL 1.0 Recommendation has more to do with XSL: Formatting Objects (XSL:FO) than XSL transformations (XSLT). The Extensible Stylesheet Language (XSL) Version 1.0 Recommendation can be viewed at `http://www.w3.org/TR/xsl/`.

XSL Formatting Objects (XSL:FO) is the biggest part of the 2001 XSL Recommendation, so most developers refer to the XSL 1.0 Recommendation as XSL:FO, which describes the page formatting part of the Recommendation document. XSL:FO is a page description language that converts an XML document into an electronic presentation format. To create a useful presentation, you need to be able to assign page events to the part of an application that will display content on a screen. That's relatively hard to do with a single, unframed XML or HTML document that flows from top to bottom without page start, end, and column markers.

XSL:FO addresses page structure issues by breaking down a page into headers, footers, left and right margins, columns, and lines. XSL:FO *Regions* contain text blocks, and text blocks can contain just about any type of content that can be displayed as text.

When the XSL:FO Recommendation was released in 2001, there were high hopes among XML developers that browsers would implement XSL:FO adapters. Such a feature would provide developers with much more control over page layouts than any competing formatting standards today. HTML, XHTML, and CSS, for example, are great for rapidly developing content and separating presentation from data, but none of them can provide developers with the same layout control of a Windows client application, or other type of application that supports rich text formats.

Alas, currently there are no XSL:FO adapters or plug-ins on the market for mainstream browsers, though some niche browsers do support XSL:FO page formatting. There has been, however, a great deal of interest in one aspect of XSL:FO: transforming XML data to PDF files. Most of the activity in XSL:FO revolves around producing PDFs from XML data, which is the example covered later in this chapter.

Adobe Portable Document Format (PDF) is a universal file format that preserves all the fonts, formatting, graphics, and color of any source document, regardless of the application and platform used to create it. Adobe PDF files are compact and can be shared, viewed, navigated, and printed—but by default, not edited—by anyone with free Adobe Acrobat Reader software or any other compatible reader (MS Word 2003 supports reading *and editing* of PDFs). When a solution requires a document that can be easily and efficiently transported and printed without loss of the original document format, PDF is the most common format chosen.

Understanding FOP Servers

XSL Transformations need an XSLT processor to make transformations happen. In the same way, XSL:FO processing requires a FOP (Formatting Objects Processor) engine to make XSL:FO processing happen. XML that is formatted with XSL:FO tags is fed into a FOP, which produces a print-ready document. XSL:FO theoretically supports the display output in a number of common output standards: Portable Document Format (PDF), Hewlett-Packard PCL Printer Format, PostScript, Rich Text Format (RTF), Standard Vector Graphics (SVG), Java AWT events (content is described and displayed as graphics), the Maker Interchange Format (MIF) for Adobe FrameMaker, and text.

The original and most popular FOP server is the Apache FOP server, which is distributed as open source software, and can be found at `http://xml.apache.org/fop`. The engine can be downloaded and run from a command prompt, or integrated with one of several XSL:FO editors on the market, a partial list of which can also be found at `http://www.xmlsoftware.com/xslfo.html`. A list of other XSL:FO tools, including several FOP servers for several platforms and languages, can be viewed at `http://www.xmlsoftware.com/xslfo.html`.

Converting XML to PDF

As we've indicated earlier in this chapter, currently the most popular task for XSL:FO is to transform and display XML data in PDF format. On top of that, the most popular FOP engine is the Apache FOP processor. With this in mind, we've put together an example that converts an XML document to a PDF using the Apache FOP server.

Although the Apache FOP server can be run from the command line, there are several editing tools that integrate the FOP server for syntax checking, previewing, and debugging. As we did in previous chapters, we're using XMLSpy to develop a stylesheet and preview it using Acrobat (a free trial version of XMLSpy can be found at `http://www.xmlspy.com`). The Apache FOP engine, or any other engine that can be run from the command line, can be easily integrated with XMLSpy.

When compared to XSL, XSL:FO stylesheets are even more verbose and complex, which is one of the factors that has hampered XSL:FO marketplace adoption so far. On top of this, there are numerous formatting options for XSL:FO output that you'll be tempted to fuss with. The simple example that later in this chapter results in a two-page PDF that shows a table with a few rows of data in it. The XSL:FO output for this document generates a 378-line stylesheet. We highly recommend using a FOP-compliant editor to create XSL:FO stylesheets, to save you time and sanity. Figure 9-1 shows the XMLSpy Stylesheet designer displaying the contents of the XSL:FO stylesheet. XMLSpy supports previewing an XML document in an IE browser and an Adobe PDF client directly in the UI, which is a great time saver for iterative development.

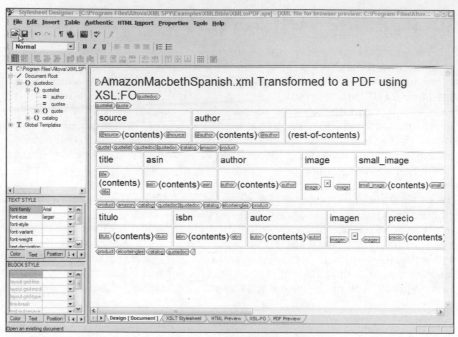

Figure 9-1: Working with the XMLSpy Stylesheet Designer

Figure 9-2 shows the final result of the transformation and FOP processing, saved on the file system as a PDF and opened in the Adobe Acrobat PDF reader.

Let's review the XSL:FO stylesheet, named XMLtoPDF.xsl, which we're using for this example. It transforms our sample AmazonMacbethSpanish.xml document into a PDF. We'll break it down by segment for you so you can get a better understanding of what is happening in each piece when it is passed to a FOP server.

We haven't included the entire stylesheet in the printed version of the book because at 378 lines, it's simply too long, and all three of the tables in the example output use the same functionality, so the final two-thirds of the stylesheet has no new information. As mentioned before, the XSL:FO stylesheet can be quite verbose, so if you have an XML editor available on a nearby computer that formats and color-codes XSL stylesheets and is XSL:FO compliant, you can download the full file at http://www.XMLProgrammingBible.com and follow along with the descriptions here.

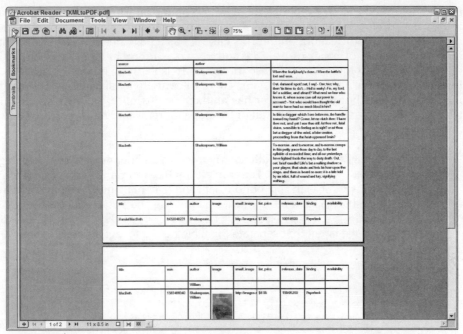

Figure 9-2: PDF output that was generated by the XSL:FO transformation using XMLtoCatalogHTML.xsl

The first part of the document is a straightforward XML declaration, followed by an xsl and fo namespace declaration. XSL-FO uses the xmlns:fo = "http:// www.w3.org/1999/XSL/Format namespace to identify Formatting Object elements. This can be confusing, because the part of the Recommendation that includes XSL:FO is the 2001 XSL Recommendation, the full text of which can be found at http://www.w3.org/TR/xsl.

```
<?xml version="1.0" encoding="UTF-8"?>
<xsl:stylesheet version="1.0" xmlns:xsl="http://www.w3.org/1999/XSL/Transform"
xmlns:fo="http://www.w3.org/1999/XSL/Format">
```

Next, an XSL variable declaration defines the layout of the page by using layout-master-set as a variable name. A layout-master-set is a container for one or more page masters. This example has one page master, with a name of default-page-master. default-page-master defines parameters for global page layout settings, such as page margins and page sizes. Note that in this example we use a landscape page format by simply reversing the default portrait page measurements (page-height="11in" page-width="8.5in") to landscape (page-height= "8.5in" page-width="11in").

Page masters contain regions of a page, which define information for the header, footer, and body of the page. The region-before and region-after regions contain header information, and in this case act as a page header and footer. The extent attribute of region-before and region-after indicate the actual size of the header and footer. In this case, the extent is set to 0, meaning that the header and footer on this page are just there to contain header and footer margins, not content. The body region never has an extent attribute, because its extent is whatever is left of the page when all of the page margins and header/ information are set within the page layout.

Note   The page-height and page-width specify the outside bounds of a printable page, and are offset by any margins. For example, an 8.5 inch page-width and an 11 inch page-height with top, bottom, left, and right margins of 1 inch results in a printable area of 7.5 inches X 10 inches on the page output. Additionally, margins in the region-before, region-after, and region-body specify other off-sets to the page layout that separate printable output in regions of the page.

```
<xsl:variable name="fo:layout-master-set">
   <fo:layout-master-set>
    <fo:simple-page-master master-name="default-page-master" page-
      height="8.5in" page-width="11in" margin-top="0.79in" margin-
      bottom="0.79in" margin-left="0.6in" margin-right="0.6in">
      <fo:region-before margin-right="0.6in" extent="0cm"/>
      <fo:region-body margin-top="0cm" margin-bottom="0cm" font-
        family="Helvetica,Times,Courier" font-size="14pt" line-
        height="16pt"/>
      <fo:region-after extent="0cm"/>
    </fo:simple-page-master>
   </fo:layout-master-set>
  </xsl:variable>
```

Next is a standard XSLT template element with a match attribute that we covered in Chapters 7 and 8. That's a good reminder that this is still an XSL stylesheet, despite all of the XSL:FO formatting taking place. The next line is the fo:root element, which is the root element of a XSL:FO output document format. Next, the layout-master-set variable that defined earlier in the stylesheet is passed to the output during transformation.

A couple of empty block, start-content, and flow elements are defined next. These are empty because their region-before and region-after containers are empty. flow represents text that will flow from one page to another, and static-content represents text that will be the same on every page.

```
    <xsl:template match="/">
    <fo:root>
      <xsl:copy-of select="$fo:layout-master-set"/>
      <fo:page-sequence master-reference="default-page-master">
        <fo:static-content flow-name="xsl-region-before">
          <fo:block/>
```

```
</fo:static-content>
<fo:static-content flow-name="xsl-region-after">
  <fo:block/>
</fo:static-content>
```

The next line is a result of typing text values into the XMLSpy stylesheet designer. Based on the placement of the text, the stylesheet designer decided that the text was part of the output body, which places it at the top of the first page of the PDF output. The output displays a title that says "AmazonMacbethSpanish.xml Transformed to a PDF using XSL:FO."

A manual font size change generates the `inline font-size` element, which controls in-line font changes in body text. In-line fonts are fonts that may change inside a text block. For example, *italics* in a sentence that is otherwise regular text constitutes two in-line fonts, italic and regular, for that sentence. Because the in-line `font-size` is a single value, it can be inherited from the previously defined `fo:region-body` font value. Note the XML `&apos` entity references, which are converted to single quotes in the final output.

```
<fo:flow flow-name="xsl-region-body">
  <fo:block>
    <fo:inline font-size="inherited-property-value(&apos;
    font-size&apos;) + 4pt">AmazonMacbethSpanish.xml Transformed to
     a PDF using XSL:FO</fo:inline>
```

Next comes the processing of the quotes in the table. An `xsl:for-each` processes all of the quotes, each of which starts with a `quote` element. For each `quote` element encountered, XSL:FO creates a new table row. In each row, for each new element encountered, the FO processor creates a table column.

The select statements contain XPath expressions that iterate through each value under the `quotelist/quote` element in the source XML document. A three-column table header is created, and columns are defined to contain values from the XML document.

```
<xsl:for-each select="quotedoc">
  <fo:block>
    <fo:leader leader-pattern="space"/>
  </fo:block>
  <xsl:for-each select="quotelist">
    <xsl:for-each select="quote">
      <xsl:if test="position()=1">
        <fo:table width="100%" space-before.optimum="4pt"
         space-after.optimum="4pt">
          <fo:table-column/>
          <fo:table-column/>
          <fo:table-column/>
          <fo:table-header>
            <fo:table-row>
```

For each table column, a `table-cell` is defined. Table cell borders are solid black and match the white background of the page.

```
<fo:table-cell background-color="white" padding-
  after="5pt" padding-before="5pt" padding-
  end="5pt" padding-start="5pt" border-
  style="solid" border-width="1pt" border-
  color="black">
```

Each `table-cell` contains a `block`, which contains information about the formatting of that `block`. Next, content is placed in the block. The first row of the table is the table header, so a hard-coded text description is passed to the table header row. The first two headings have values (`source` and `author`).

```
<fo:block>
  <fo:inline background-color="white" font-
    size="inherited-property-value(&apos;font-
    size&apos;) - 2pt">source</fo:inline>
</fo:block>
</fo:table-cell>
<fo:table-cell background-color="white" padding-
 after="5pt" padding-before="5pt" padding-
 end="5pt" padding-start="5pt" border-
 style="solid" border-width="1pt" border-
 color="black">
 <fo:block>
   <fo:inline background-color="white" font-
     size="inherited-property-value(&apos;font-
     size&apos;) - 2pt">author</fo:inline>
 </fo:block>
</fo:table-cell>
```

The third column heading is intentionally left blank. There is a definition for the `table-cell`, but the `block` is blank. The `block` tag still needs to be included to meet XSL:FO requirements, even if it is empty.

```
<fo:table-cell background-color="white" padding-
  after="5pt" padding-before="5pt" padding-
  end="5pt" padding-start="5pt" border-
  style="solid" border-width="1pt" border-
  color="black">
  <fo:block/>
</fo:table-cell>
 </fo:table-row>
</fo:table-header>
<fo:table-body>
```

Next, another row is defined for the table using the `table-row` element.

```
<xsl:for-each select="../quote">
  <fo:table-row>
```

This row matches the characteristics of the heading row, but this time referenced values from the original XML document are passed instead of hard-coded values.

```
<fo:table-cell background-color="white"
 padding-after="5pt" padding-before="5pt"
 padding-end="5pt" padding-start="5pt"
 height="24pt" border-style="solid" border-
 width="1pt" border-color="black">
```

The value of the `source` attribute is placed in the `table-cell` using the XPath `@source` reference expression to get the value of the attribute (`value-of-select=.`). The block defines the display for the cell, and inherits the `font-size` from the previously defined size value.

```
<fo:block>
  <xsl:for-each select="@source">
    <fo:inline background-color="white" font-
     size="inherited-property-
     value(&apos;font-size&apos;) - 2pt">
      <xsl:value-of select="."/>
    </fo:inline>
  </xsl:for-each>
</fo:block>
</fo:table-cell>
```

The value of the author attribute is placed in the `table-cell` using the XPath `@author` reference expression. Font attributes are unchanged from the previous cell.

```
<fo:table-cell background-color="white"
 padding-after="5pt" padding-before="5pt"
 padding-end="5pt" padding-start="5pt"
 height="24pt" border-style="solid" border-
 width="1pt" border-color="black">
  <fo:block>
    <xsl:for-each select="@author">
      <fo:inline background-color="white" font-
       size="inherited-property-
       value(&apos;font-size&apos;) - 2pt">
        <xsl:value-of select="."/>
      </fo:inline>
    </xsl:for-each>
  </fo:block>
</fo:table-cell>
```

The text value of the quote is placed in the `table-cell` using the XPath `text()` reference expression. No `value-of-select` expression is needed this time, because there is only one value returned by `text()` - text. Font attributes are unchanged from the previous cell.

```
<fo:table-cell background-color="white"
 padding-after="5pt" padding-before="5pt"
 padding-end="5pt" padding-start="5pt"
 height="24pt" border-style="solid" border-
 width="1pt" border-color="black">
  <fo:block>
    <fo:inline background-color="white" font-
    size="inherited-property-value(&apos;font-
    size&apos;) - 2pt">
      <xsl:apply-templates select="text()"/>
    </fo:inline>
  </fo:block>
</fo:table-cell>
```

Once all of the quotes in the source XML document have been added to their own row in the three-column table, the `table` tags and the `for-each` are closed, ending this table in the XSL:FO output.

```
          </fo:table-row>
        </xsl:for-each>
      </fo:table-body>
    </fo:table>
  </xsl:if>
  </xsl:for-each>
  </xsl:for-each>
</xsl:for-each>
```

Next comes the processing of the book listing values from the original XML document. An `xsl:for-each` processes all of the book listings, each of which starts with a `quotedoc` element. XSL:FO creates a new table row for each book listing, which is located under the `quotedoc/catalog/amazon/product` or `quotedoc/catalog/elcorteingles/product` element. In each row, for each new element encountered, the FO processor creates a table column. The table rows and columns repeat in the same pattern for the rest of the stylesheet, except for one graphic reference, which we will point out a little later.

The select statements contain XPath expressions that iterate through each value under the `quotedoc/catalog/amazon/product` or `quotedoc/catalog/elcorteingles/product` element in the source XML document. As in the previous table, a table header is created for each of the nine columns in the new table. Columns are defined to contain values from the XML document.

```
<xsl:for-each select="quotedoc">
  <xsl:for-each select="catalog">
    <xsl:for-each select="amazon">
```

```
<xsl:for-each select="product">
  <xsl:if test="position()=1">
    <fo:table width="100%" space-before.optimum="4pt"
     space-after.optimum="4pt">
      <fo:table-column column-width="148pt"/>
      <fo:table-column/>
      <fo:table-column/>
      <fo:table-column/>
      <fo:table-column/>
      <fo:table-column/>
      <fo:table-column/>
      <fo:table-column/>
      <fo:table-column/>
      <fo:table-header>
        <fo:table-row>
```

For each column in the table, a `table-cell` is defined. To match the previous table, cell borders are solid black and match the white background of the page.

```
<fo:table-cell background-color="white"
 padding-after="5pt" padding-before="5pt"
 padding-end="5pt" padding-start="5pt"
 height="36pt" width="148pt" border-
 style="solid" border-width="1pt" border-
 color="black">
```

Each `table-cell` contains a `block`, which contains information about the formatting of that `block`. The first row of the table is the table header, so a hard-coded text description is passed to each column heading in the row. The first column heading is `title`.

```
<fo:block>
  <fo:inline background-color="white" font-
    size="inherited-property-value(&apos;font-
    size&apos;) - 2pt">title</fo:inline>
</fo:block>
</fo:table-cell>
<fo:table-cell background-color="white"
 padding-after="5pt" padding-before="5pt"
 padding-end="5pt" padding-start="5pt"
 height="36pt" border-style="solid" border-
 width="1pt" border-color="black">
  <fo:block>
```

The second column heading is `asin`.

```
<fo:inline background-color="white" font-
  size="inherited-property-value(&apos;font-
  size&apos;) - 2pt">asin</fo:inline>
</fo:block>
</fo:table-cell>
```

```
<fo:table-cell background-color="white"
 padding-after="5pt" padding-before="5pt"
 padding-end="5pt" padding-start="5pt"
 height="36pt" border-style="solid" border-
 width="1pt" border-color="black">
```

The third column heading is author.

```
<fo:block>
  <fo:inline background-color="white" font-
   size="inherited-property-value(&apos;font-
   size&apos;) - 2pt">author</fo:inline>
</fo:block>
</fo:table-cell>
<fo:table-cell background-color="white"
 padding-after="5pt" padding-before="5pt"
 padding-end="5pt" padding-start="5pt"
 height="36pt" border-style="solid" border-
 width="1pt" border-color="black">
```

The fourth column heading is image.

```
<fo:block>
  <fo:inline background-color="white" font-
   size="inherited-property-value(&apos;font-
   size&apos;) - 2pt">image</fo:inline>
</fo:block>
</fo:table-cell>
<fo:table-cell background-color="white"
 padding-after="5pt" padding-before="5pt"
 padding-end="5pt" padding-start="5pt"
 height="36pt" border-style="solid" border-
 width="1pt" border-color="black">
```

The fifth column heading is small_image.

```
<fo:block>
  <fo:inline background-color="white" font-
   size="inherited-property-value(&apos;font-
   size&apos;) - 2pt">small_image</fo:inline>
</fo:block>
</fo:table-cell>
<fo:table-cell background-color="white"
 padding-after="5pt" padding-before="5pt"
 padding-end="5pt" padding-start="5pt"
 height="36pt" border-style="solid" border-
 width="1pt" border-color="black">
```

The sixth column heading is `list_price`.

```
<fo:block>
  <fo:inline background-color="white" font-
    size="inherited-property-value(&apos;font-
    size&apos;) - 2pt">list_price</fo:inline>
</fo:block>
</fo:table-cell>
<fo:table-cell background-color="white"
 padding-after="5pt" padding-before="5pt"
 padding-end="5pt" padding-start="5pt"
 height="36pt" border-style="solid" border-
 width="1pt" border-color="black">
```

The seventh column heading is `release_date`.

```
<fo:block>
  <fo:inline background-color="white" font-
    size="inherited-property-value(&apos;font-
    size&apos;)-2pt">release_date</fo:inline>
</fo:block>
</fo:table-cell>
<fo:table-cell background-color="white"
 padding-after="5pt" padding-before="5pt"
 padding-end="5pt" padding-start="5pt"
 height="36pt" border-style="solid" border-
 width="1pt" border-color="black">
```

The eighth column heading is `binding`.

```
<fo:block>
  <fo:inline background-color="white" font-
    size="inherited-property-value(&apos;font-
    size&apos;) - 2pt">binding</fo:inline>
</fo:block>
</fo:table-cell>
<fo:table-cell background-color="white"
 padding-after="5pt" padding-before="5pt"
 padding-end="5pt" padding-start="5pt"
 height="36pt" border-style="solid" border-
 width="1pt" border-color="black">
```

The ninth column heading is `availability`.

```
<fo:block>
  <fo:inline background-color="white" font-
    size="inherited-property-value(&apos;font-
    size&apos;) -
    2pt">availability</fo:inline>
</fo:block>
```

```
        </fo:table-cell>
      </fo:table-row>
    </fo:table-header>
```

Next, a `table-body` is defined for the table. Each value that matches the `.../product` XPath expression creates a new row in the `table-body`.

```
<fo:table-body>
  <xsl:for-each select="../product">
```

A new row is defined for the table using the `table-row` element. This row matches the characteristics of the heading row, but as in the last table; referenced values from the original XML document are passed instead of hard-coded heading values. The values that appear under each column heading are selected using XPath expressions and placed in their cell blocks.

```
<fo:table-row>
  <fo:table-cell background-color="white"
    padding-after="5pt" padding-before="5pt"
    padding-end="5pt" padding-start="5pt"
    width="148pt" border-style="solid" border-
    width="1pt" border-color="black">
    <fo:block>
      <xsl:for-each select="title">
        <fo:inline background-color="white"
          font-size="inherited-property-
          value(&apos;font-size&apos;) - 2pt">
          <xsl:apply-templates/>
        </fo:inline>
      </xsl:for-each>
    </fo:block>
  </fo:table-cell>
  <fo:table-cell background-color="white"
    padding-after="5pt" padding-before="5pt"
    padding-end="5pt" padding-start="5pt"
    border-style="solid" border-width="1pt"
    border-color="black">
    <fo:block>
      <xsl:for-each select="asin">
        <fo:inline background-color="white"
          font-size="inherited-property-
          value(&apos;font-size&apos;) - 2pt">
          <xsl:apply-templates/>
        </fo:inline>
      </xsl:for-each>
    </fo:block>
  </fo:table-cell>
```

```
<fo:table-cell background-color="white"
 padding-after="5pt" padding-before="5pt"
 padding-end="5pt" padding-start="5pt"
 border-style="solid" border-width="1pt"
 border-color="black">
  <fo:block>
    <xsl:for-each select="author">
      <fo:inline background-color="white"
       font-size="inherited-property-
       value(&apos;font-size&apos;) - 2pt">
        <xsl:apply-templates/>
      </fo:inline>
    </xsl:for-each>
  </fo:block>
</fo:table-cell>
```

We've removed a few of the table-cell and block references for the rest of this table because they are all the same, with different values, and we're pretty sure you get the idea by now. All of the cell references in this table are basically the same, except for the next one. In this case, we are passing the literal value of URLs to the output as image references. The image references in this case link to the Amazon Website and display a small graphic of the book cover in the output. This is facilitated through the `fo:external-graphic` element, which creates a `src` attribute for the image. The `src` attribute refers to the source for the graphic reference, which in this case is the value of the content in the cell, accessed via the `xsl:value-of-select` element.

```
<fo:table-cell background-color="white"
 padding-after="5pt" padding-before="5pt"
 padding-end="5pt" padding-start="5pt"
 border-style="solid" border-width="1pt"
 border-color="black">
  <fo:block>
    <xsl:for-each select="image">
      <fo:external-graphic space-
       before.optimum="4pt" space-
       after.optimum="4pt">
        <xsl:attribute
         name="src">url('<xsl:value-of
         select="."/>')</xsl:attribute>
      </fo:external-graphic>
    </xsl:for-each>
  </fo:block>
</fo:table-cell>
```

The actual stylesheet continues on for several hundred more lines and is a repeat of what you've seen so far. The complete file can be downloaded at http://www. XMLProgrammingBible.com.

Summary

In this chapter, you were introduced to XSL:FO and the Apache FOP server, and learned about:

✦ The difference between the 1999 XSLT and 2001 XSL W3C recommendations

✦ The history of XSL:FO

✦ FOP servers

✦ The Apache FOP Server

✦ Output formats for XSL:FO

✦ Using XSL and XSL:FO to produce PDF output

✦ Formatting options for XSL:FO output documents

This chapter concludes the introduction to XML concepts. Now that you have a solid understanding of the fundamentals of XSML, DTD, Schemas, Parsing, XSL, and XSL:FO, you will move on to apply these concepts to practical use. The next part of the book covers the use of XML in Microsoft Windows applications, including more details on the Microsoft Core Services (MSXML), and working with XML in MS office applications. After that, we'll cover the "other" side of XML: working with XML in J2EE.

✦   ✦   ✦

Microsoft Office and XML

Part II provides examples of generating XML from MS access data as well as creating an Excel spreadsheet from an XML data source. These examples illustrate MS-Specific techniques for parsing and generating MS-Derived XML. We review the sample code in the chapters line-by line so that previous VBA/VB code knowledge is not necessary to understand and work with the examples.

Microsoft XML Core Services

♦   ♦   ♦   ♦

In This Chapter

How to install MSXML

How to implement side-by-side versions

Basic features and an introduction to the DOM

New objects added to MSXML

♦   ♦   ♦   ♦

Microsoft is a strong presence in both its use and promotion of XML for building business and consumer applications. Many if not all of the applications Microsoft develops for the software market use XML in some way. In like manner, Microsoft has crafted its Windows platform and development tools while giving XML an increasingly prominent role.

This chapter is about the services Microsoft has provided for working with XML on Windows, its MSXML component library. The focus here is on Microsoft's pre-.NET software development environment, COM. The .NET XML toolset is extensive enough to require a separate discussion, which it does in other chapters of this book. In this chapter you will learn about how to install MSXML and get started using its core features. You will learn about how MSXML is versioned and how to keep things straight when side-by-side versions are installed. You will learn about how it parses and what new objects have been most recently added.

Getting Started

Early on, Microsoft introduced its XML parser and made it available via download. However, it was really an adjunct utility. Additionally, its faithful adherence to the evolving W3 standard XML was sometimes not without error. As time has passed, Microsoft has worked with other major software vendors in the evolution of the XML standard itself and its uses. Microsoft has also made significant advances to the simple XML parser that was once an optional download. In this chapter, we will take a closer look at the Microsoft XML parser contained in MSXML (version 4.1 as of this writing). The latest version of the parser offers significant advances over the previous versions. We will not explore a complete side-by-side comparison of the versions here, because our focus is mainly on the latest, greatest version of the parser itself. However, we will point out a few significant issues as they arise in order to save you time when either installing or upgrading your MSXML version.

Microsoft's MSXML supplies a generous class library that makes it possible to do a lot of things with XML. At the heart of XML is the capability to easily read and manipulate data. But the changing nature of Web applications means that a decent XML toolset must make it possible to send XML content to a variety of displays and to convert it to a variety of structures. At the same time, the need for data integrity is critical to any serious application. Additionally, the toolset must be approachable, easy to use, and straightforward in its implementation. Given these and other requirements in the real world, MSXML provides the following:

✦ A rich Document Object Model (DOM) for doing simple and advanced operations with XML

✦ An XSLT processor that allows you to write code for converting XML content

✦ Support of schemas using XSD, DTDs, and XDR

✦ Support for SAX (Simple XML API)

✦ New objects for using XML on the Web

But first things first. Before any of these benefits are accessible, you need to get MSXML installed.

System requirements and installation

With newer versions of the Windows operating system, MSXML comes installed. This should tell you something about what customers have requested to be pre-installed and what dependencies Windows programs have on XML. Windows XP comes with MSXML installed as does Windows.NET. Nonetheless, you may want to install MSXML on an operating system that does not yet have it installed, or you may want to explicitly update the version running on your operating system. It may seem obvious, but just in case someone out there is still running a 16-bit Microsoft OS, you need a 32-bit OS to run the MSXML services. That's the bare minimum requirement. Candidates for an MSXML installation include:

✦ Windows 98

✦ Windows Millennium

✦ Windows NT 4.0

✦ Windows XP

✦ Windows.NET

Installing Microsoft Core XML Services (MSXML) is pretty easy. You need to download MSXML from Microsoft's MSDN Website (http://msdn.microsoft.com). Go to the Downloads area of the site to find the download for Microsoft XML Core Services. This download (fortunately provided in many languages) will contain both the core MSXML files and the MSXML SDK. When you run the installation package, you will be able to choose what you want to install. To do this, you will need to choose a custom installation (a good choice no matter what you install on your computer) instead of using the standard installation set. If you decide to customize, you will be presented with two main features of the installation as shown in Figure 10-1. On your development workstation, it is a good idea to install the SDK, which includes documentation and an IDL and header files for use with C++.

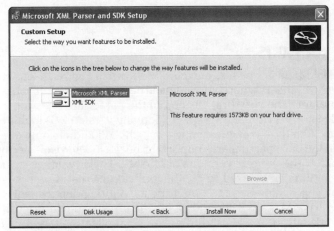

Figure 10-1: Choosing to install the SDK and/or the XML parser

While these files are useful for developer workstations, you would not want to use this installation package for deployments on production servers and workstations. If you build an application that depends on MSXML, you should use the redistributable package titled "CAB File for Redistribution" on the Microsoft Website. This package will contain the bare minimum files you need on a production machine to leverage MSXML. Figure 10-2 shows the list of files contained in the redistributable cab file.

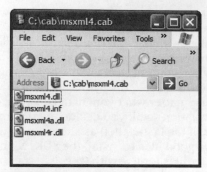

Figure 10-2: Files found in the redistributable cab file

Core files and versions

The heart and soul of MSXML is in one file: msxml.dll (shown in Figure 10-2 as the versioned msxml4.dll). Now, this is where knowing a little about Microsoft's versioning for XML is important. The very first version of the parser includes the file msxml.dll. The second major version of the parser (actually version 2.6) includes msxml2.dll, the third and fourth — you guessed it — msxml3.dll and msxml4.dll, respectively. These versions are particularly important because Microsoft permits side-by-side installations of the various versions of MSXML. The advantage is that a single developer workstation can be used to create applications that target the different parsers. Thus, an application used to target the accounting department where the workstations have MSXML 3.0 installed for the foreseeable future can be created on the same workstation that is used to create an application targeting the corporate Web servers that have MSXML 4.0 installed. This flexibility, while quite useful, also introduces a few complexities about which you should know. The chief potential problem occurs when developers decide to use version-independent ProgIDs and GUIDs.

You should be aware that if you want to load a DOMDocument in MSXML 4.0 and you want to use that specific version of the class when you load it, then you should use the version class name, like this: DOMDocument40, even though there is also another class name, DOMDocument, available to you. In other words, unexpected things can happen when creating an instance of the MSXML DOM using a version independent ProgID, as shown in Listing 10-1.

Listing 10-1: **Creating an Instance of an Object in MSXML**

```
Dim oDOM as Object
Set oDOM=new MSXML2.DOMDocument
```

The result of this code would be that oDOM would contain an instance, not of DOMDocument40 but of a DOMDocument for version 3.0 or lower. In other words, referencing the generic component class name, DOMDocument, does not actually reveal what class is actually being used. What would happen if the developer thought the target machine only had MSXML 2.0 installed, but the machine really had version 3.0 installed? With either version installed, the above statement will work. However, if version 3.0 is installed but the developer really intended the code to use only the features of version 2.0, the above instancing statement would actually pick up whatever the latest installed version is and use that. On one hand, there is a benefit to this. Developers can write code that automatically starts employing the latest, greatest MSXML version on a target machine without having to update the code libraries they have installed to use MSXML. But this adaptability comes at a price. As you can imagine, this automatic sensing of the newest version could also cause to break; for example, if the version 2.0 compatible code tries to use a method or property that has a different signature in the newer version or that has been removed altogether. While this can happen in a compiled Windows program, it is actually more likely in ASP applications where developers are forced to exclusively use late-bound objects in a scripted environment. Many ASP developers were disappointed to find that after installing MSXML 3.0, their code broke, and they could not immediately tell why.

With MSXML 4.0, Microsoft responded to the concerns that version-independent ProgID's and GUIDs introduced, so they drew the line and made MSXML 4.0 ProgID and GUID version dependent. What this means is that if you go to version 4.0, you need to make it clear in the language you are using, even if you are using late-bound objects. To be sure, some developers have complained about having to do a little more work, but at the end of the day, it makes for cleaner, more explicit code and reduces the chance for unexpected results in a production environment. Our discussion will focus on this version of the parser, and you should keep these versioning issues in mind as you develop applications and consider their deployment on different workstations.

One last aspect of this issue to keep in mind is the tight integration between MSXML and Microsoft Internet Explorer. Internet Explorer relies on MSXML for processing XML that it requests and retrieves. Microsoft Internet Explorer 4.0 was the first browser to have XML support built right in. In version 4.0 of the browser, Microsoft shipped a very basic DOM-based XML parser called MSXML 1.0. As XML standards evolved, Microsoft added and improved MSXML features, and today it is much more than just a parser. The default parser for Internet Explorer is MSXML 2.0. Installing IE 5.5 means that you are also installing MSXML 2.0. In other words, IE 5.5 has a built-in dependency on this version of the parser, and just installing the newer parser will not change this. Fortunately, Microsoft has provided a nice little utility to help you point your browser to a newer version of the parser. It is called xmslinst.exe. However, this is not supported with respect to version 4.0 of the parser. In other words, when you install IE, it will not automatically use the latest version, and, while you can make it dependent, Microsoft does not recommend doing so.

Figure 10-2 also shows two other libraries. The msxml4a.dll file is an ANSI resource file. This file is installed only on Windows 98 or Windows ME because they both lack the ANSI support upon which MSXML depends. In a similar way, the Msxml4r.dll is the Unicode equivalent version of the resource file, and would not be installed on Windows 98 or Windows ME platforms as it is used mainly for Windows NT platform machines. If you are running Windows 2000 or Windows XP, you typically will need just the MSXML4.dll on the target machine to run your code.

As just mentioned, the main workhorse of MSXML is the msxml4.dll. The standard MSXML 4.0 installation will place the DLL in the following location: %SystemRoot%\System32\msxml4.dll. The library is actually comparatively small, just 1.7MB, but it actually does quite a few things. Using this parser, you have the ability to parse XML, use XSL and XSLT. You can send XML documents using the HTTP protocol and use the SAX API. As you can tell from reading this book, the bread and butter of XML is just parsing, searching, and transforming structured data. That is what this parser does well.

Identifying components

Before introducing the core classes of MSXML, it is important to know how to reference them in code. Basically, there are three main ways to access a component on the Windows platform: ProgIDs, GUIDs, and component class names (defined in the actual IDL by the original developers). If you are programming in Visual Basic 6 or earlier (or are using COM Interop in .NET), the language will expose all public objects using the component class name that the original creators of MSXML 4.0 put in the IDL when they wrote it. In other words, the creators of MSXML 4.0 at Microsoft called their object DOMDocument40 for MSXML 4.0, DOMDocument30 for version 3.0, and so on. That means you can address that object in VB 6 as DOMDocument40 or Msxml2.DOMDocument40. Additionally, MSXML2 was the library name given in the IDL. You only need the latter notation when you need to resolve ambiguity with another object of the same name in another library (or within your own project). This is the naming convention, accessing the actual component class names, when you are using a language that can bind to the type library information or the header files create by the IDL. However, there are times when this is not possible. For example, VBScript is not a typed language, and all objects are late-bound, meaning that the type library information is not accessible until the script is interpreted and runs. Traditional ASP applications are typically coded in VBScript, and so using the component class name, DOMDocument40, when instancing an object is not permitted. The same is true when using JScript in an ASP application. Simply put, these languages know nothing about the names you used in the IDL. We need another naming convention then.

While one can always use the component's GUID (Globally Unique Identifier) to access the class, these are long and make for hideous code. Fortunately, Microsoft also provides another name called the ProgID. A ProgID is a name found in the Windows registry (found in HKEY_CLASSES_ROOT) that maps over to the GUID representing the component class. So, for example, the ProgIDs for MSXML are "Msxml2.DOMDocument.4.0" and so on. In a scripted environment, you can gain access to a desired component by using this ProgID name.

Keep in mind that the version-independent issues already mentioned apply whether one is using the component class name, the GUID, or the ProgID. In other words, irrespective of what mechanism you choose to access a class, if you do not specifically target version 4.0 of that class, you will have no guarantee that the resulting object instance will be of the correct version.

Parsing and Features Overview

With each release of its MSXML services, Microsoft offers new features and fixes some of the known bugs. Some of the improvements in MSXML 4.0 include support for XML schemas. In previous versions of MSXML, schemas were not supported. This is not all that surprising given that XML schemas had not yet become even a W3 recommendation until the spring of 2001. Thus, there was still no widely accepted standard way, either an official standard or a practical standard, to validate XML documents. DTDs were reasonably popular, but with known limitations (see Chapter 3 for more on XML validation). XDR did not look like it could provide the full breadth of features that XML schemas have come to provide, so it has not been fully embraced either. Given the nascent stage of XML and the lack of a clear winner in the schema department, and probably for other reasons as well, Microsoft did not add schema support until version 4.0 of MSXML. The XML schema support in MSXML 4.0 is pretty thorough. Of course, XSDs can be used for validating in the DOM, but they can also be used with XPATH and XSLT (see Chapter 4).

Another improvement made in version 4 is in performance. Microsoft claims a four-fold increase in performance for XSLT processing. This is because they made significant enhancements to the XSLT engine that ships with MSXML. Microsoft also claims a two-fold increase in performance when doing normal parsing of documents. This is the result of changes made to the parser that ships with MSXML. These changes accompany fixes for known problems, and extended support for the SAX2 API. Additionally, so that C++ developers can make SAX components more easily, there is the SaxAppWizard utility for Microsoft Visual Studio. The primary benefit of the wizard is that it sets up the main structure SAX applications just as console or WFC applications are developed when creating a new project.

Parsing

The MSXML parser is chiefly responsible for parsing XML in the DOM, parsing XSL instructions, and validating XML structures using schemas. If a parser is doing its job, developers will not give it much thought. The API should be all developers need to think about as they work with XML content. In this way, you can focus on how an application works and interacts with the data, thus being insulated, to some extent, from the innerworkings of the XML content. In this light, there are two basic types of XML parsing modes to accommodate different development needs: validating or nonvalidating. Simply put, nonvalidating parsing means that the parser does not validate the document structure against a DTD, even though the parser may know there is a DTD present. As a generality, you typically want to validate the XML in a business application so as to ensure its integrity. This is one of the main functions of parsing and can be specified using the new validateOnParse property of the DOM.

The job of the MSXML parser, then, is to get the content out of the XML document and make it accessible via the appropriate API. Figure 10-3 shows this relationship.

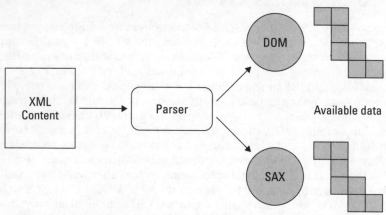

Figure 10-3: The MSXML parser consumes the XML data so they can be used via the DOM or SAX.

You notice here how both APIs are referenced. This is because parsing XML is really just confirming the content's intelligibility. This is only half of the story. The other half is actually getting to the intelligible data in code. That is the job of the API. You will use the fundamental classes of MSXML to do this, and this is where you focus your energy as a developer.

Fundamental classes

Before looking at some of the lesser-known features of MSXML 4.0, we will first look at the bread-and-butter classes it offers. There are many classes defined in the library that support 27 COM interfaces, five major XML-related technologies, and a host of utility features. Our focus is on the DOM, SAX, XSL, XSD, and some new classes recently added.

Document Object Model

The root object in the XML object model, according to the specification, is the DOMDocument40 object. This is the one you will use most often to do the bulk of your work with XML. The MSXML DOM (Document Object Model) implements both fundamental and extended interfaces and also provides additional methods to support XSL Transformations (XSLT), XPath, namespaces, and data types. In essence, the fundamental interfaces are those required for adherence to the XML 1.0 standard. However, fidelity to the standard need not get in the way of making some of the functions in the specification easier to use for developers. Hence, designers of a parser are at liberty to implement extended interfaces, ones that make it easier to access some of the basic functions of the XML specification. Microsoft's parser does implement some of these, and most developers agree that they are welcome additions.

Gaining access to the various classes in MSXML is fairly straightforward. The class names in MSXML are specified in this way: MSXML2.*classname*. For example, the principal class in the entire library, the DOMDocument40, is accessible via this name: MSXML2.DOMDocument40. But this name cannot be used when coding an ASP application in script. Not only this, but in both the scripted and non-scripted environments, the name you choose can give you unexpected results if you use a version-independent class name or ProgID. Earlier, we discussed how Microsoft dropped version-independent ProgIDs and GUIDs from MSXML 4.0, but there is a little more to the story, especially in a scripted environment. Understanding better how Microsoft's naming schemes work for component class libraries will be very beneficial and eliminate confusion when you are coding both in a compiled language or in script.

The main interfaces that give you access to various aspects of the DOM are as follows:

- ✦ DOMDocument40
- ✦ IXMLDOMNode
- ✦ IXMLDOMNodeList
- ✦ IXMLDOMNamedNodeMap

Using an instance of the DOMDocument40 class you can create new documents from scratch, load existing XML strings or streams, load XML documents from the file system or a URL, transform one XML file into another, and save XML content to the file system or a URL. The DOM object then exposes instances of IXMLDOMNode, which can be accessed via instances of IXMLDOMNodeList. IXMLDOMNamedNodeMap permits you to gain access to node attributes by using the name of the attribute instead of its ordinal number. All of the MSXML classes under the hood take care of the W3 XML standard compliance for you.

While Chapter 11 delves into the DOM more fully, a brief introduction is useful here. First, let's load a DOMDocument40 object using a simple file. Listing 10-2 shows the code used to get an instance of the object and fill it with the contents of the local file.

Listing 10-2: Loading XML Content

```
Dim oDOM As DOMDocument40
Set oDOM = New DOMDocument40
oDOM.Load ("c:\XMLBible\quotes.xml")
```

Once loaded, all of the functions and features provided by DOMDocument40 are accessible to your code. You could also reference the file using a valid URL instead of the local file path. UNC paths are equally acceptable. You can use the Save method to persist XML to a file, URL, or UNC path as well. When the MSXML parser loads an XML document into a DOM, it reads it from start to finish and creates a logical model of nodes from the structures and content contained in the XML document. The document itself is a node that contains all of the other nodes, primarily the root element, which, in turn, contains all the rest of the content in the document. If there are errors in the source XML, the Document object cannot parse the entire file properly, and it posts parsing errors. Unless you look for the errors, all you will notice is that the Document object will be empty. However, the object does expose an object that lets you figure out precisely what caused the error, the parseError object. Figure 10-4 shows the output from the parseError object after an error has occurred.

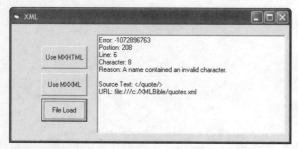

Figure 10-4: Error information provided by the MSXML parser

Listing 10-3 is the code used to post this error information to a Windows form application.

Listing 10-3: Discovering and Reporting Parse Errors

```
Dim oDOM As DOMDocument40
Set oDOM = New DOMDocument40
```

```
oDOM.Load ("c:\XMLBible\quotes.xml")
With oDOM.parseError
    txtResult.Text = "Error: " & _
        CStr(.errorCode) & vbCrLf
    txtResult.Text = txtResult.Text & _
        "Postion: " & CStr(.filepos) & vbCrLf
    txtResult.Text = txtResult.Text & _
        "Line: " & CStr(.Line) & vbCrLf
    txtResult.Text = txtResult.Text & _
        "Character: " & CStr(.linepos) & vbCrLf
    txtResult.Text = txtResult.Text & _
        "Reason: " & CStr(.reason) & vbCrLf
    txtResult.Text = txtResult.Text & _
        "Source Text: " & CStr(.srcText) & vbCrLf
    txtResult.Text = txtResult.Text & _
        "URL: " & CStr(.url) & vbCrLf
End With
```

While accessing files is common, it is becoming increasingly common to use XML in memory. XML can be loaded from streams and output to streams rather than to and from actual files. Listing 10-4 displays the code used to create a new XML document entirely from scratch using methods of the Document object.

Listing 10-4: **Creating XML Content from Scratch**

```
Dim oDOM As DOMDocument40
Dim oElRoot As IXMLDOMElement
Dim oNode As IXMLDOMNode
Dim oNode2 As IXMLDOMNode

Set oDOM = New DOMDocument40

oDOM.insertBefore _
    oDOM.createProcessingInstruction("xml", _
        "version=""1.0"""), _
        oDOM.childNodes.Item(0)

Set oElRoot = oDOM.createNode( _
    NODE_ELEMENT, "quotes", "")
Set oDOM.documentElement = oElRoot

Set oNode = oDOM.createNode( _
    NODE_ELEMENT, "quote", "")

oElRoot.appendChild oNode
```

The resulting XML, however simple, is well-formed XML and is shown here:

```
<?xml version="1.0"?>
<quotes><quote/></quotes>
```

Notice how the processing instruction contains double quotes. The MSXML parser will actually permit single quotes here, but it is preferable to use double quotes whenever possible. This is worth mentioning because, in the code sample, you can see how double sets of double quotes are used so that the resulting XML loaded in the document contain a single set of double quotes. Keep this fact in mind when using strings as names for elements or for text when loading from a database or some other source.

Another feature of the DOMDocument40 class is the ability to use schema definitions using XSDs and transforming XML data structures and output formatting using XSL stylesheets. Support for XSDs was added with version 4.0, while support for XSL did exist in previous versions. However, the performance of XSL and XSLT was improved in this version of MSXML, and the output of transformation has become more reliable. Support for DTDs continues as part of MSXML.

Other objects

There are many other classes available in MSXML. Notably, there is support for SAX, XSD, and XSL. SAX, as explained in Chapter 9, is an event-based way of getting at XML content. SAX is particularly useful when the content being accessed is quite large or when the code you are writing wants to have greater distance from the source XML structure. The key with SAX is to remember that it merely produces events as it steps through the XML source content. You must provide code and objects that listen to and respond to these events. Listing 10-5 shows using SAX to create an XML document that gets loaded into a DOM object.

Listing 10-5: **Using SAX to Produce a Content in the DOM**

```
Dim oDOM As New MSXML2.DOMDocument40
oDOM.validateOnParse = True
Dim oXMLWriter As New MXXMLWriter40
Dim oSAXEvents As IVBSAXContentHandler
Dim oSAXAttributes As New SAXAttributes40
Set oSAXEvents = oXMLWriter
oXMLWriter.output = oDOM
oXMLWriter.indent = True
oSAXEvents.startDocument
oSAXEvents.startElement "", "", "quotes", oSAXAttributes
oSAXAttributes.addAttribute "", "", "type", "CDATA", "general"
oSAXEvents.startElement "", "", "quote", oSAXAttributes
oSAXAttributes.Clear
oSAXEvents.startElement "", "", "source", oSAXAttributes
```

```
oSAXEvents.characters "Mark Twain"
oSAXEvents.endElement "", "", "source"
oSAXEvents.startElement "", "", "text", oSAXAttributes
oSAXEvents.characters "When in doubt, tell the truth."
oSAXEvents.endElement "", "", "text"
oSAXEvents.endElement "", "", "quote"
oSAXEvents.endElement "", "", "quotes"
oSAXEvents.endDocument
```

In this listing, there are other objects being used, but don't worry about them just yet. The focus here is on the events raised by the use of the SAX event handler. As elements and attributes are added and completed, the events are raised to whatever is listening for these events. In this case, it is an instance of the `MXXMLWriter` class. It receives the events and hands its output off to the DOM. To be truthful, all of this content can be created with the DOM directly, but using SAX is in some ways a simpler manner of doing so.

The ability to change the way XML is presented or structured is made possible via MSXML's support for XSL. Chapter 11 deals with XSL using Microsoft's XML Core Services in greater detail, but suffice it to say here that MSXML is able to transform XML content because it has a powerful XSL processor on board. The easiest way to begin using XSL is to reference a stylesheet in your XML source file, in this way: `<?xml-stylesheet type="text/xsl" href="quotes01.xsl"?>`. This statement should follow the initial processing instruction in your source XML file. As the file is parsed by MSXML, the XSL file will be accessed, and the instructions in the XSL file will be applied to the XML file as it is processed.

Schema files, for validating XML content according to your own rules, are referenced in much the same way. The difference is that the XSD reference is usually made inside the root element of the XML document. For example, this statement `<quotes xmlns="po.xsd">` references an XSD in the same directory as the source XML file. As the parser processes the source XML, it will look to the schema definition in the XSD and report an error if the XML does not conform to the rules of the XSD.

New objects

There are new objects in MSXML 4.0, such as the `MXHTMLWriter`, `MXNamespace Manager`, and `MXXMLWriter`. The first is used to create HTML output from an XML source. The `MXNamespaceManager` class defines methods that let you manage and track namespace declarations in your documents and resolve them either in the current context or in the context of a specific DOM node. The latter one, `MXXML Writer`, was used in the sample that showed how to use the SAX API. It was used to produce XML content which was then loaded into the DOM. Let's take another look in Listing 10-6 at the code and focus on how `MXXMLWriter` was used, represented as the `oXMLWriter` object.

Listing 10-6: **Outputting XML Using MXXMLWriter**

```
Set oSAXEvents = oXMLWriter
oXMLWriter.output = oDOM
oXMLWriter.indent = True
oSAXEvents.startDocument
oSAXEvents.startElement "", "", "quotes", oSAXAttributes
oSAXAttributes.addAttribute "", "", "type", "CDATA", "general"
oSAXEvents.startElement "", "", "quote", oSAXAttributes
oSAXAttributes.Clear
oSAXEvents.startElement "", "", "source", oSAXAttributes
oSAXEvents.characters "Mark Twain"
oSAXEvents.endElement "", "", "source"
oSAXEvents.startElement "", "", "text", oSAXAttributes
oSAXEvents.characters "When in doubt, tell the truth."
oSAXEvents.endElement "", "", "text"
oSAXEvents.endElement "", "", "quote"
oSAXEvents.endElement "", "", "quotes"
oSAXEvents.endDocument
```

What makes the instance of MXXMLWriter work is that it is set equal to an instance of a SAX event handler. Therefore, as new elements are created and other content is added, the respective events are handed off to MXXMLWriter so that a more accessible representation of the data becomes available. The MXXMLWriter can only produce parsable XML, not HTML. But producing HTML is a common need, so MSXML also provides the MXHTMLWriter.

The MXHTMLWriter lets applications create HTML output directly using a stream of SAX events, much in the same way that the `<xsl:output>` element in XSLT can generate HTML from a result tree. The main benefit of this is that Active Server Pages can be developed that read XML using a SAX reader and then send the data to the buffer as HTML in one smooth operation. Of course, the MXHTMLWriter can also be used to create HTML manually.

Following, in Listing 10-7, is a simple example that uses this object to write out HTML. In this sample, an instance of the MXHTMLWriter40 class is used to dynamically assemble both the HTML elements with some actual page data. The `oContent` object is defined as an instance of the `IVBSAXContentHandler` class and is used to actually construct the content.

Listing 10-7: **Producing HTML Using the MXHTMLWriter**

```
Dim oXMLWriter As MXHTMLWriter40
Dim oSAXEvents As IVBSAXContentHandler
Dim oSAXReader As SAXXMLReader40
'Create the object instances
```

```
Set oXMLWriter = New MXHTMLWriter40
Set oSAXReader = New SAXXMLReader40
Set oSAXEvents = oXMLWriter
'Begin creating a document from scratch
oSAXEvents.startDocument
oSAXEvents.startElement "", "", "HTML", Nothing
oSAXEvents.characters "this is dynamically written HTML"
oSAXEvents.endElement "", "", "HTML"
oSAXEvents.endDocument
oSAXReader.parse oXMLWriter.output
```

In this example, the output is not XML at all, although it could have been made XML using the MXXMLWriter instead. Selecting HTML as the output demonstrates the flexibility of the objects. The SAXXMLReader object is used to actually do the final parsing before the content is rendered.

Summary

In this chapter, you have been introduced to the Microsoft Core XML Services, commonly referred to as MSXML. There are some specific system requirements you need to know before you install MSXML, the main one being which operating system can support the different versions. If you are running Windows 2000 or greater, things are much easier, and upgrading to a newer OS is recommended if you are running Windows 9x or Windows ME anyway. You also learned in this chapter about the various versions of MSXML. You saw how the files that provide the core services have changed as versions have been released, and you learned about the significant changes Microsoft made with version 4.0. The main one to remember is that version-independent GUIDs and ProgIDs are no longer possible with version 4.0 and above.

This chapter introduced you to how Microsoft uses GUIDs, ProgIDs, and component names as ways to correctly address classes when you are using instances of them in code. You learned the correct way to code your applications to ensure that you get object instances of the correct underlying version if you have side-by-side versions of MSXML installed. You also learned about the registry entries and other Windows-related details that will help you troubleshoot applications that use MSXML.

With this kind of housekeeping out of the way, the chapter introduced you to parsing and the main features of MSXML. Without a doubt, the DOM is the object you will most likely use with the greatest frequency. However, there are other very useful features such as the SAX event handler, support for XSL, and XSD. Furthermore, you have learned about a couple of new classes introduced with version 4.0, MXXMLWriter and MXHTMLWriter, for aiding in working with XML on the Web.

✦　　✦　　✦

Working with the MSXML DOM

In order for your programs to access the content of XML documents, the parser must read the XML and make sense of them. If the content is in a file, the parser processes the file and converts it into an XML document object in memory by the XML parser. The resulting document object contains a hierarchical tree that contains the data and structure of the information contained in the XML document. This tree of information can be accessed and modified using the DOM API.

In Microsoft's COM world, the Document Object Model (DOM) is your vehicle to process XML documents using compiled applications or scripts. The DOM allows programs and scripts to dynamically access and update the content, structure, and style of documents.

The main function of MSXML's DOM implementation lets you load existing XML from file or in memory. You can then access and work with the data structures contained within the document. Finally, you can complete the cycle of working with XML by saving the document as a file or sending to another application as a stream or in-memory structure. It is not an understatement to say that nearly everything you will ever do with MSXML will use the DOM.

In this chapter, you will learn how to work with the DOM in applications, the most commonly used methods and properties of the DOM, how to load XML, and how to persist it for use in other systems or for later consumption.

Introduction

It has already been said that the DOM is the focus of working with XML. The DOM is what gives you access to the members of the IXMLDOMDocument interface. In the previous introduction to MSXML, it was mentioned that the component class name for the DOM is DOMDocument40, with the version number included so as to make clear in your code which underlying version of MSXML you are using. Keep in mind that in a compiled-language environment, this is the preferable manner in which you should gain reference to the DOM. However, you can also use the ProgID in a scripted environment or when using code where the type library information is not accessible to the application. For the most part, the listings in this chapter will use the component class name. Now let's look at how to use the DOM.

DOM members

The object model of the DOM is fairly extensive, exhibiting a large number of properties and methods, but only two events. The properties list shown in Figure 11-1 contains a number of simple properties and others that are collections. For example, the attributes, child nodes, namespaces, and schemas are properties that return collections of their respective items.

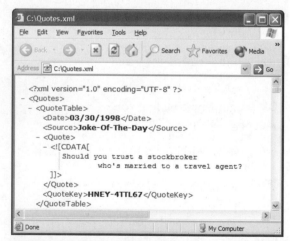

Figure 11-1: The node structure of an XML file that will be searched using selectNodes

Other notable properties include:

- ✦ **documentElement:** The root element of the entire XML document
- ✦ **errorCode:** Reveals the error code of the last encountered parsing error
- ✦ **filepos:** The precise position in the file where an error occurred

✦ **firstChild:** Returns the very first child node of a node in the document

✦ **lastChild:** Returns the very last child node of a node in the document

✦ **line:** Specifies the line where an error occurred

✦ **linepos:** Specifies the character position in a line where an error occurred

✦ **nodeType:** Specifies the type of a node (attribute, element, text, and so on)

✦ **nodeValue:** Sets or returns the value of a node

✦ **ownerDocument:** Returns the overall parent document in which a node is contained

✦ **text:** Returns the text content of a node

✦ **xml:** Returns the XML of a node and all of its descendants

Which properties are of greatest use to you will, of course, depend on the type of applications you are creating. You should consult the XML SDK document for the meaning and purpose of some of the more obscure properties as you encounter them.

There are a number of methods exposed by the DOM, and for the most part they are designed to help you manipulate and navigate the content of an XML document. Some of the more prominent methods are summarized as follows:

✦ **appendChild:** Appends a new child node to a target node

✦ **createAttribute:** Creates a new attribute for a specified element

✦ **createElement:** Creates a new element node with a specified name. The element must then be appended as a child of another node.

✦ **createNode:** Creates a new node which can be appended to another node. This node can be of different types (attribute, element, text, and so on).

✦ **createProcessingInstruction:** Creates a processing instruction such as <? xml version="1.0"?>

✦ **createTextNode:** Creates a new node, but it is only of the text type.

✦ **getElementsByTagName:** Gets all of the elements in a document that have the tag name passed to the method. They are returned as a collection of elements in an IXMLDOMNodeList.

✦ **hasChildNodes:** Specifies whether the target node has children or not

✦ **load:** Loads XML content from a persistent source

✦ **loadXML:** Loads XML content from a source in memory

✦ **removeChild:** Removes and returns a node from a list of child nodes

✦ **save:** Persists XML content of the DOM to a file

✦ **selectNodes:** Returns a collection of nodes from a starting point. You must provide a pattern to look for in the descendants of the target node.

✦ **selectSingleNode:** Returns a single node from a starting point. You must provide a pattern to look for in the descendants of the target node. It returns the first node to match the pattern.

✦ **transformNode:** Transforms a target node and all of its descendants using provided XSL instructions and returns the result as a string

✦ **transformNodeToObject:** Transforms a target node and all of its descendants using provided XSL instructions and returns the result as an object

We are going to explore detailed examples of loading, selecting, and transforming XML content using methods of the DOM as these are probably the most common tasks you will want to perform with the DOM. Before doing so, however, this is a good time to mention the two events that can be raised by the DOM: `ondataavailable` and `onreadystatechanged`.

The first event, `ondataavailable`, is useful when loading XML content asynchronously. You may want to begin processing the data as soon as they are available in the DOM. This event will let your code know when the data can be accessed for processing. The second method, `onreadystatechanged`, fires whenever the state of the `readystate` property has changed. The `readystate` property tells you what the current state of the document is. Its possible values are:

✦ **Loading:** The loading process is under way. You cannot do much with the document at this point.

✦ **Loaded:** The document is ready to be parsed, and the object model is not yet available.

✦ **Interactive:** The data have been partially read and parsed, and what has been read and parsed can now be accessed in the object model as read only.

✦ **Completed:** The document is completely ready in the object model.

Loading XML content

Two methods, `Load` and `loadXML`, are ones that make many of the other properties and methods meaningful. The `Load` function populates the XML document from a location you specify. The location can refer to a UNC pathname, a URL, or a local file system path. Listing 11-1 shows accessing an XML file using a URL.

Listing 11-1: **Loading XML Content in the DOM**

```
Dim oDOM As DOMDocument40
Set oDOM = New DOMDocument40
oDOM.Load ("http://localhost/xmlbible" _
    & "/chapter11/quotes.xml")
txtResult.Text = oDOM.xml
```

The alternative approach is to use the loadXML method, which loads the document using a string. In Listing 11-2, a string is used to load the document. In this case, the string is loaded dynamically as records are retrieved from a database. You need not worry too much about the data access code included here as it may differ depending on the type of database you are accessing. In this listing, a Microsoft SQL Server database is accessed to retrieve quote data.

Listing 11-2: **Loading XML Content from a Database**

```
Dim rs As Recordset
Dim cn As Connection
Dim oDOM As DOMDocument40
Dim str As String
Set rs = New Recordset
Set cn = New Connection

cn.Open "Provider=SQLOLEDB;" _
    & "Data Source=(local);" _
    & "Initial Catalog=quotes;" _
    & "User ID=User;Password=7Secret9x;"
rs.Open "SELECT Date,Source," _
    & "Quote FROM QuoteTable", _
        cn, adOpenForwardOnly, _
            adLockReadOnly
If Not rs.EOF Then
    str = "<?xml version=""1.0"" ?><quotes>"
    While Not rs.EOF
        str = str & "<quote>"
        str = str & "<date>" _
            & rs("Date").Value _
            & "</date>"
        str = str & "<source>" _
            & rs("Source").Value _
            & "</source></quote>"
        rs.MoveNext
    Wend
    str = str & "</quotes>"
    rs.Close
    cn.Close
End If
Set rs = Nothing
Set cn = Nothing
Set oDOM = New DOMDocument40
oDOM.loadXML str
```

Taking a closer look at the XML-oriented aspects of the code, you see that a simple string variable is used to hold all of the XML tags and data that will be assembled along the way. The first item that must be included is the XML declaration. Notice how the double quotes are used around the version number in this string. Of course, each language will differ, but here, in Visual Basic 6.0, the two double quotes are needed to ensure that when the XML is loaded into the DOM, there will be a single set of quotes around the version number. This technique applies to all cases where a single set of double quotes is needed in the final XML output.

Next the code adds a root element to the XML file, in this case `<quotes>`. One of the most common problems is forgetting to include this root element with an accompanying close tag somewhere else in the code. Because the XML content is being assembled as part of a logical loop, it is sometimes difficult to keep things straight, so making sure you thoroughly test your code before deploying it will help in detecting omissions of this sort.

The code enters a loop that begins to load the bulk of the data. These data are the main quotes contained in the data table. In this example, a Microsoft ADO recordset is used to retrieve data values. Keep in mind that you are assembling a large string, and some of the data types of fields being retrieved may not be string data types. You should take care to convert values when necessary. In Listing 11-2, implicit conversions are used so that the code is less cluttered, thus making it easier to see the XML operations. However, the best practice for production code is to handle the data type conversions explicitly. Additionally, you should trap errors and recover from problems in the code gracefully so that, despite problems that may arise, you still end up with a well-formed XML file when the code finishes executing.

In the code you have just seen, the string is assembled from data retrieved directly from the database, and the names of the elements are hard coded. However, even the names of the elements could be dynamic by making a slight adjustment to the structured code loop, as shown in Listing 11-3.

Listing 11-3: **Generate XML Content from Any Table**

```
If Not rs.EOF Then
  str = "<?xml version=""1.0"" ?><" & _
    rs(1).Properties("BASETABLENAME").Value _
    & "s>"
While Not rs.EOF
  str = str & "<" & _
    rs(1).Properties("BASETABLENAME").Value _
    & ">"
  str = str & "<" & rs(1).Name & ">" _
    & rs(1).Value _
    & "</" & rs(1).Name & ">"
```

```
    str = str & "<" & rs(2).Name & ">" _
      & rs(2).Value _
      & "</" & rs(2).Name & "></" _
        & rs(1).Properties("BASETABLENAME").Value _
        & ">"
    rs.MoveNext
  Wend
    str = str & "</" _
      & rs(1).Properties("BASETABLENAME").Value _
      & "s>"
    rs.Close
    cn.Close
  End If
```

What makes code like this particularly powerful is that it can produce well-formed XML by using records from many different types of queries or data sources without altering the code. Taking a closer look, you can see that no names for the elements are included in the code. Instead, a property of the ADO recordset is used to retrieve the table name. It is probable that other data access technologies provide a similar technique to acquire this information when accessing a data source. Here, the BASETABLENAME property is used to acquire the table name. This will become the root element for the XML content. As the code progresses, fields are referenced ordinally in the recordset rather than by name as in Listing 11-2. The flexibility of this code can be tested by changing the statement used to retrieve the data from the database. Different field names can be used there, or a different table in a different database can be referenced altogether.

One of the challenges in loading code in this fashion is that the XML content could be very, very large. Unfortunately, in Visual Basic 6.0, while the string data type can contain a lot of data, it is not very efficient in doing so. Each language differs, so be aware of how well your code performs.

Selecting nodes

Once XML content is loaded into the DOM, you will want to get to certain areas of the data hierarchy as quickly and as easily as possible. Two wonderfully flexible methods, selectNodes and selectSingleNode, will help you do so. The first of these methods is accessible via a target node. From that node, the method will return all descendant nodes that can be found to match a pattern you provide to the method. In the following example in Listing 11-4, the method is used to find all nodes that have a name of Source. Keep in mind that these searches are case sensitive, as is always the case when working with XML elements. You can also use more sophisticated search expressions to find nodes that match irrespective of case, using wild-card searches and much, much more.

Listing 11-4: **Selecting Specific Nodes in the DOM**

```
Dim oDOM As Msxml2.DOMDocument40
Dim oNL As IXMLDOMNodeList
Set oDOM = New DOMDocument40
oDOM.Load "C:\Quotes.xml"
oDOM.setProperty _
  "SelectionLanguage", "XPath"
Set oNL = oDOM.documentElement. _
  selectNodes("//Source")
```

In this code sample, the source file has the structure shown earlier in Figure 11-1. The root node is Quotes, and there are a number of child nodes named QuoteTable. Each QuoteTable node contains a Source element that contains the text of a quote.

A portion of the result of the method search in Listing 11-4 is shown in Listing 11-5. Notice how the list shows only nodes with the name of Source.

Listing 11-5: **Results of the selectNodes Method**

```
<Source>Joke-Of-The-Day</Source>
<Source>Pat Newberry</Source>
<Source>Tammy Vanoss</Source>
<Source>Joke-Of-The-Day</Source>
<Source>Tammy Vanoss</Source>
<Source>Joke-Of-The-Day</Source>
```

But what would happen if the structure of the XML were not so regular? In other words, notice how the current structure is very predictably Quotes/QuoteTable/Source. Each QuoteTable element contains elements for Date, Source, Quote, and QuoteKey. However, Figure 11-2 shows a revised structure where one of the QuoteKey elements in just one of the QuoteTable nodes contains an additional Source element. Without changing the code, this irregularly placed element can still be found, and it will be grouped with the rest of the nodes that follow the more predictable structure.

The list of nodes containing Source elements is shown in shortened form in Listing 11-6. Notice how the results do not distinguish where a node came from in the source hierarchy. All that matters is whether the node matched the search pattern.

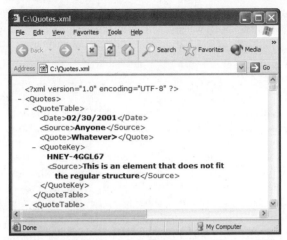

Figure 11-2: Revised XML structure with an oddly placed element

Listing 11-6: **Results of a selectNodes Search Including an Irregularly Structured Element**

```
<Source>Anyone</Source>
<Source>This is an element that does not fit the regular
structure</Source>
<Source>Joke-Of-The-Day</Source>
<Source>Tammy Vanoss</Source>
<Source>Joke-Of-The-Day</Source>
<Source>Tammy Vanoss</Source>
```

The reason why this irregularity in the hierarchy is returned is because in the pattern passed to the selectNodes method, we used the double-slash, like this: "//Source. Double-slashes are a way of telling the query processor that we want to find matches to our pattern irrespective of structure. If we changed it like this: QuoteTable/Source, the irregular element would not be found. This is because we are deliberately telling the DOM to only find Source elements directly below QuoteTable elements. If we changed the pattern like this, QuoteTable//Source, our element would once again be found. Any descendant of QuoteTable that is named Source would be found.

Similar to the `selectNodes` method is the `selectSingleNode` method. The pattern-matching rules are the same in both cases. The main difference is that with the latter method, the first node that matches the search pattern is returned, and the process stops right there.

Transforming using XSL

One of the strengths of the code that loads data from into the DOM from a database (as in the earlier section on loading XML) is that the final XML output can be pretty much of any structure you desire. The code does the work of transforming the data in the database into a different structure and format. But what if the data were not in a database and were in a file instead? This is a common occurrence, and XML would truly lose a lot of its strength if it were unable to provide the capability to do with XML files what we have done here with a database table. Fortunately, the DOM object exposes a set of methods and objects that make it possible to transform XML content from one structure to another or from one structure to a completely different mechanism of display. Chapter 4 deals with XSL specifically, whereas here we will look at how to use MSXML to transform XML files.

There are two fundamental ways to tell the MSXML XSLT processor to do a transformation. One is to use the `TransformNode` or `TransformNodeToObject` methods of the DOM. The second is to reference a valid XSL document in an XML file. To start, take a look at the XML in Listing 11-7. It shows a portion of the XML file that will be transformed using the DOM.

Listing 11-7: **Resulting XML from XSL Instructions**

```
<Quotes>
 <QuoteTable>
  <Date>03/30/1998</Date>
  <Source>Joke-Of-The-Day</Source>
  <Quote><![CDATA[Should you trust a stockbroker
  who's married to a travel agent?]]></Quote>
  <QuoteKey>HNEY-4TTL67</QuoteKey>
 </QuoteTable>
 <QuoteTable>
  <Date>03/30/1998</Date>
  <Source>Tammy Vanoss</Source>
  <Quote>Each day I try to enjoy something
  from each of the four food groups:
  the bonbon group, the salty-snack group</Quote>
  <QuoteKey>HNEY-4TTL6G</QuoteKey>
 </QuoteTable>
</Quotes>
```

The actual XML file contains many more quotes than are shown here, and we have another system that will consume these data. However, in order to use the data, they need to be in a different structure. Listing 11-8 shows the contents of the XSL.

Listing 11-8: Stylesheet Content to Transform XML

```
<xsl:stylesheet version="1.0"
  xmlns:xsl="http://www.w3.org/1999/XSL/Transform">
<xsl:template match="Quotes">
<citations>
<xsl:apply-templates select="QuoteTable" />
</citations>
</xsl:template>
<xsl:template match="QuoteTable"><citation>
<quote_date><xsl:value-of select="Date"/></quote_date>
<text><xsl:value-of select="Quote"/></text>
</citation>
</xsl:template>
</xsl:stylesheet>
```

The XSL here looks for the root node and transforms it into a new node `<citations>`. Then the second template creates new element names with the same data in the original file. Listing 11-9 shows how the DOM is used to transform the XML into the new structure.

Listing 11-9: Transforming Using the DOM

```
Dim DOM1 As MSXML2.DOMDocument40
Dim DOM2 As MSXML2.DOMDocument40
Dim DOM3 As MSXML2.DOMDocument40
Set DOM1 = New MSXML2.DOMDocument40
Set DOM2 = New MSXML2.DOMDocument40
Set DOM3 = New MSXML2.DOMDocument40
DOM1.Load ("C:\QuoteTable_plain.XML")
DOM2.Load ("C:\Quotes02.xsl")
DOM1.transformNodeToObject DOM2, DOM3
DOM3.save "C:\QuoteTable_02.xml"
```

This code creates three instances of the DOM. The first loads the content of the XML data file. The second loads the content of the XSL file. The third file is merely a container to hold the results of the transformation of the XML. The resulting XML is shown in Listing 11-10.

Listing 11-10: Resulting XML from a Transformation

```xml
<?xml version="1.0" encoding="UTF-16"?>
<citations>
  <citation>
  <quote_date>03/30/1998</quote_date>
  <text>Should you trust a stockbroker
  who's married to a travel agent?</text>
  </citation>
  <citation>
  <quote_date>03/30/1998</quote_date>
  <text>Each day I try to enjoy something
  from each of the four food groups:
  the bonbon group, the salty-snack grou</text>
  </citation>
  <citation>
  <quote_date>03/30/1998</quote_date>
  <text>Is boneless chicken considered to be an
invertebrate?</text></citation></citations>
```

The second primary technique for processing files using XSLT with MSXML is to reference the style sheet in the XML data file. There is nothing notably different in the syntax with Microsoft's parser. You'll need to reference the XSL file using a statement such as this: `<?xml-stylesheet type="text/xsl" href="quotes01.xsl"?>`. When the XML file loads, instead of loading the XML data directly, the contents of the source will be processed according to the instructions of the XSL file. Other than that, there is no resultant difference between using this technique or using the DOM's `TransformNodeToObject` method.

As Chapter 4 explains, you can use XSL stylesheets not only to transform XML structure, but also to alter the final presentation output. Listing 11-11 shows XSL that produces HTML as the final output. The source XML file contains a reference to this stylesheet, so the final output is as shown in Figure 11-1.

Listing 11-11: Stylesheet for Transforming Content

```xml
<xsl:stylesheet version="1.0"
  xmlns:xsl="http://www.w3.org/1999/XSL/Transform">
<xsl:output indent="yes" omit-xml-declaration="yes" />
<xsl:template match="Quotes">
<html xmlns="http://www.w3.org/1999/xhtml">
<head><title>Quotes
</title></head><body>
<table BORDER="1" CELLPADDIUNG="0" CELLSPACING="1">
```

```
<tr bgcolor="blue"><th>Date</th><th>Quote</th></tr>
<xsl:apply-templates select="QuoteTable" />
</table></body></html>
</xsl:template>
<xsl:template match="QuoteTable">
<tr><td><xsl:value-of select="Date"/></td>
<td><xsl:value-of select="Quote"/></td></tr>
</xsl:template>
</xsl:stylesheet>
```

Building XML-Based Applications

Now that you are more familiar with the DOM, it's time to leverage the object model in a more comprehensive way. The following example is a browser-based solution that uses XML, XSL, and HTML to produce a simple, dynamic menu. The scripting is all done with JavaScript, and there is some HTML style usage. There are a few different files that make up the solution. They are as follows:

✦ **WorkWithMenus.html:** Contains the HTML and JavaScript routines

✦ **menus.xml:** Contains menu elements that contain information for standard menus on our Web page

✦ **menuitems.xml:** Contains menu elements that contain information for custom menus

✦ **transform_menus.xsl:** Contains XSL instructions to transform the XML menu elements into standard HTML that can be displayed on the Web page

The Web page HTML content is as shown in Listing 11-12. Essentially, the HTML contains one `TextArea` element that is used to show the content of the XML after a new element has been dynamically added to it. Also, there are two SPAN elements contained in a separate column. The initial view of the page is shown in Figure 11-3.

Listing 11-12: **HTML Content in Browser-Based Solution**

```
<body>
<table>
 <tr>
  <td><span id="menu"></td>
  <td>
   <table>
    tr>
```

Continued

Listing 11-12 *(continued)*

```
     <td colspan="2"
     onclick="ConfigureMenus('Information')"  id="Information"
     name="Information">
     <SPAN CLASS="menuprompt">Information</SPAN></td>
   </tr>
   <tr>
     <td colspan="2"
     onclick="ConfigureMenus('Contact')" id="Contact"
     name="Contact">
     <SPAN CLASS="menuprompt">Contact</SPAN></td>
   </tr>
  </table>
  <br>
   <textarea cols="80" id="txtXML" name="txtXML"
   rows="11"></textarea>
   </td>
  </tr>
 </table>
</body>
```

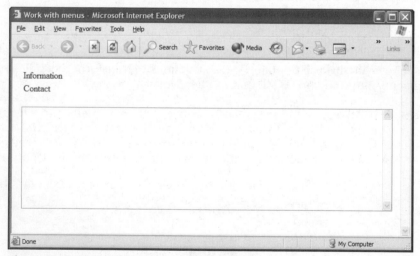

Figure 11-3: Initial view of example Web page

What is significant about the SPAN elements is that when they are clicked, they call a function defined in JavaScript called `ConfigureMenus`. This function accepts one parameter that is the ID of the SPAN that was clicked.

The script of the `ConfigureMenus` procedure is shown here in Listing 11-13. This procedure loads the menus.xml file into a DOM object. This file contains elements that hold the data we will use for standard menus (see Listing 11-14).

Listing 11-13: **Script of the ConfigureMenus Function**

```
function ConfigureMenus(menuItem)
{
  var objNode;
  var objDOM=new ActiveXObject("Msxml2.DOMDocument");
  var objChildNode;
  var nIndex;
  var strElementName;
  var strElementValue;
  var root;
  var str;
  var objTransformedDOM=
        new ActiveXObject("Msxml2.DOMDocument");
  objDOM.async = false;
  objDOM.load("menus.xml");
  nIndex =  2;
  root = objDOM.documentElement;
  objNode=GetMenuItem(menuItem);
  objChildNode =
        root.insertBefore(objNode,
root.childNodes.item(nIndex));
  txtXML.value=root.xml;
  str=GetTransformed(objDOM);
  menu.outerHTML =str
}
```

The XML file is rather simple, containing a root element with two child elements. Each child element has `menuID`, `menucaption`, and `href` attributes. These attributes are useful for the final HTML display on the Web page. The `href` attribute will be used as the hyperlink in an anchor tag. The `menucaption` attribute is used as the text of the anchor tag.

Listing 11-14: **Contents of the menus.xml File**

```
<menus>
  <menu menuID="getdata" menucaption="Get Data"
        href="http://http://www.wiley.com"/>
  <menu menuID="sendmessage" menucaption="Send Message"
        href="http://http://www.wiley.com"/>
</menus>
```

After loading the menus.xml file, the ConfigureMenus function calls another procedure, GetMenuItem, to get an xml node that will contain XML data that correspond to which item was clicked on the page. For example, if the user clicks on the SPAN with the text Information, the GetMenuItem procedure will find an XML element in another file and return that element as a node to the ConfigureMenus procedure. The text of GetMenuItem function is shown in Listing 11-15.

Listing 11-15: **Script of the GetMenuItem Function**

```
function GetMenuItem(menuItem)
{
  var objNode;
  var objDOM=new ActiveXObject("Msxml2.DOMDocument");
  var objChildNode;
  var nIndex;
  var strElementName;
  var strElementValue;
  var root;
  objDOM.async = false;
  objDOM.load("menuitems.xml");
  objNode =
        objDOM.selectSingleNode
             ("menus/menu[@menuID = '" + menuItem + "']");
  return(objNode);
}
```

The GetMenuItem functions loads the content of the menuitems.xml file. This file is nearly identical to the menus.xml file, but the data are different. The premise is that this file contains elements that are not used as part of the standard menus. Rather than returning all of the elements in the document, however, the function only returns the one that matches a search criteria. The function uses the selectSingleNode method and looks for only the menu item whose menuID attribute matches the value passed to the procedure. This value is the same as the text in the SPAN attribute.

With the XML node returned, the ConfigureMenus function calls another function, GetTransformed, and passes the DOM object to it. The function returns an HTML string that is then appended to the Web page. The GetTransformed procedure is shown in Listing 11-16.

Listing 11-16: **Contents of the GetTransformed Function**

```
function GetTransformed(objDOM)
{
var objXSL=new ActiveXObject("Msxml2.DOMDocument");
objXSL.load("transform_menus.xsl");
str = objDOM.transformNode(objXSL);
return (str);
}
```

This procedure loads the contents of the transform_menus.xsl file whose contents are shown in Listing 11-17. What is significant in this file is that it does not output XML. It actually produces HTML by using a couple of simple templates.

Listing 11-17: **Contents of the transform_menus.xsl Instructions**

```
<?xml version="1.0"?>
<xsl:stylesheet version="1.0"
  xmlns:xsl="http://www.w3.org/1999/XSL/Transform">
  <xsl:output indent="yes" omit-xml-declaration="yes" />
<xsl:template match="menus">
<TABLE CELLPADDING='1' CELLSPACING='0' BORDER='1'>
<xsl:apply-templates select="menu"/>
</TABLE>
</xsl:template>
<xsl:template match="menu">
  <xsl:variable name="hrefvalue" select="./@href"/>
<TR><TD><A href="{$hrefvalue}">
<xsl:value-of select="./@menucaption"/></A>
</TD></TR>
</xsl:template></xsl:stylesheet>
```

The XSL instructions include the declaration of a variable, "hrefvalue", which is used by the template to embed the value of the href attribute of the element as an attribute of the HTML anchor tag. The result of a transformation is shown in Listing 11-18. The actual data will differ, of course, depending on what a user has clicked.

Listing 11-18: Results of an XSL Transformation in the Browser Example

```
<TABLE CELLPADDING="1" CELLSPACING="0" BORDER="1">
<TR><TD><A href="http://http://www.wiley.com">Get Data</A>
</TD></TR>
<TR><TD><A href="http://www.sharepointzealot.com">Get Info</A>
</TD></TR>
<TR><TD><A href="http://http://www.wiley.com">Send Message</A>
</TD></TR>
</TABLE>
```

Once the `GetTransformed` function returns the string containing the HTML result of the transformation, a simple DHTML method is used to display the HTML. Figure 11-4 shows the resulting Web page after choosing the `"Contact"` SPAN on the page. Once this is clicked, the `ConfigureMenus` procedure loads the supplemental XML element and transforms the entire XML content to produce an HTML table.

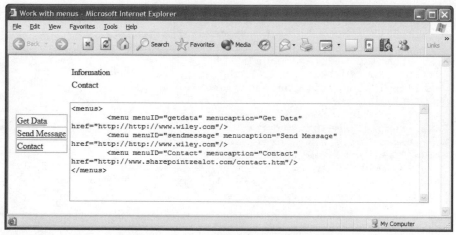

Figure 11-4: View of Web page after making a selection

Notice how the content of the XML is also shown on the Web page, providing you with a peek at what the JavaScript has assembled along the way. What this example shows is how MSXML can be used to create dynamic content in a Web page using methods of the DOM and simple JavaScript.

Summary

This chapter has introduced you to the MSXML DOM object library. Clearly there are many properties and methods, and these have been explained to you. However, a particular emphasis has been placed on loading XML, finding specific elements in the content, and transforming the content to produce new XML or HTML. The reason these characteristics of the DOM have been favored over others is because they are most likely targets of your code in the bulk of your applications.

Undoubtedly, if you create enough XML applications, you will use an increasing number of the properties and methods that have received less emphasis here. As you do, you will find that the DOM object model is surprisingly flexible and easy to use. You will want to use its ability to reports errors so that your applications can gracefully handle problems that arise. You will also want to use more sophisticated search expressions when selecting nodes, and you may want to persist XML as part of a complete solution.

✦   ✦   ✦

Generating XML from MS Access Data

◆ ◆ ◆ ◆

In This Chapter

Importing and
exporting data with
Microsoft Access

Working with
elements and
attributes

Validating and
displaying data

Using Access XML
data with other
applications like
Excel or remote
systems

◆ ◆ ◆ ◆

Microsoft's XML support in its Office technologies continues to grow, and Microsoft Access has XML support that reflects the changing use of Access and databases
generally. With Office XP, Access enhanced its capability to
export and import data by fully embracing the XML standard
and embedding XML support in its application features and
programmability features.

> **Note** This chapter will deal exclusively with Access 2002, the ver-
> sion released with Office XP. It was possible to cause previ-
> ous versions to work with XML, but this was exclusively
> through means that were not directly part of Access. In
> other words, it was possible to use the DOM in your Access
> code, but Access itself had no built-in features to work with
> XML as a native data exchange mechanism. This capability
> is the exclusive province of Access 2002 and later editions.

This chapter looks at the XML features in Access and shows
how they can be used to create more flexible and more full-
featured applications. You will learn about how XML data can
be imported and exported both using the user interface as
well as through code. You will learn how XSDs can be used to
ensure data integrity for imports and exports. You will also
learn more about leveraging XSL to convert XML data that is
not structured properly for import into data that can be
directly consumed by Access.

Introduction

With this version, Access allows you to export XML data, including XML schema information and XSL stylesheets for displaying Access data. You can also import XML data directly into tables and leverage XSDs to ensure that imported data possess the correct characteristics for your data structures in the database. Not surprisingly, each of the features available in the user interface is also available via the Access object model.

When MS Access was first introduced, most developers created single-tier solutions. Access went a long way to popularizing the use of databases for ad hoc data-driven applications. As a result, many organizations witnessed a bloom of small, tightly focused database applications in many departments. Often, these applications became mission-critical applications, serious dependencies for the success of their businesses. Small businesses fully adopted Access as a means for driving the core applications of their business. As small businesses grew to become large businesses or were purchased by other, larger, businesses, the needs of Access applications also changed. In like manner, as small ad hoc database applications became more powerful, the possibility of connecting them to other systems and data became more promising and more necessary. Another need that became increasingly important is the requirement that the database applications make their data available to the ever-expanding legion of Web applications companies have created. As a result of these and other changes, Access has had to become more conversant with other systems and with the Web.

The focus of Access XML support is on exporting, importing, and displaying Access objects using XML. In all cases, nearly, if not all, XML features accessible via the UI can be done in code as well, and there are a few features that can be done in code only. We will look at these features, starting with importing and exporting, and then show how they can be used in more complete applications that reach beyond the borders of Access.

Exporting and Importing Data

Exporting and importing data from the Access user interface is a fairly straightforward affair. First we will look at the overall process, then we will see how to do the same things and more in code.

Exporting

The simplest example of exporting XML from Access is to right-click on a table. An export menu appears on the pop-up menu (see Figure 12-1). Access will then prompt you for a location where it can place the XML file containing the data from the table. In addition to tables you can export the data from a query, datasheet, form, or report into an XML file. In this example, all of the table data will be exported. In a moment, you will see how you can export filtered data using queries. But, first, as you export data you need to give the file a name when you specify the location. If the file name already exists, you will not be prompted to overwrite the file at this time. That will come later. You can save the XML file to any valid path that Windows can recognize. This includes a valid URL to a Web server.

Figure 12-1: Exporting XML via the user interface

Note
More needs to be said about posting XML files to a Web server or to other locations than a typical file path. First, not just any old Web server will do. This is because the file is posted using special features within Microsoft's Web publishing world: a server that has the FrontPage Server Extensions installed. We can also export to a .NET Web Service or to a SQL Server, all techniques we will look at more closely in turn. Initially, we will set up the export so that the resulting files are placed on the local file system. However, in later examples, we will look at using more sophisticated techniques to export and import XML with Access.

Before the objects are exported, you are given the chance to configure how the export will occur and what its results will be. Figure 12-2 shows the initial dialog box where you can choose to configure these settings. The resulting XML file contents will depend upon the options you have selected. The advanced options, configurable in the export settings dialog box, allow you to include the schema information, either embedded within the XML document or as a separate XSD document. You can also have Access create a separate XSL document containing formatting information so your page can be displayed as HTML.

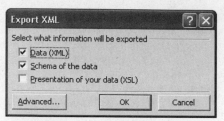

Figure 12-2: Export settings with the user interface

Let's look at the contents of these files. First, the XML file itself. This file contains the data contents of the object exported from Access. Figure 12-3 shows some of the final XML from the export.

```
<?xml version="1.0" encoding="UTF-8" ?>
- <dataroot xmlns:od="urn:schemas-microsoft-com:officedata"
    xmlns:xsi="http://www.w3.org/2000/10/XMLSchema-instance"
    xsi:noNamespaceSchemaLocation="QuoteTable.xsd">
- <QuoteTable>
    <Date>03/30/1998</Date>
    <Source>Joke-Of-The-Day</Source>
- <Quote>
    <![CDATA[ Should you trust a stockbroker who's married to a
    travel agent? ]]>
    </Quote>
    <QuoteKey>HNEY-4TTL67</QuoteKey>
  </QuoteTable>
- <QuoteTable>
    <Date>03/30/1998</Date>
    <Source>Tammy Vanoss</Source>
    <Quote>Each day I try to enjoy something from each of the four food
    groups: the bonbon group, the salty-snack grou</Quote>
    <QuoteKey>HNEY-4TTL6G</QuoteKey>
  </QuoteTable>
```

Figure 12-3: A view of the XML exported from Access

Now, look at the design of the data table in Access shown in Figure 12-4 and notice how the fields relate one to the other. You can see that the same data elements are there, but more than just the data are present. Access has also exported and thus preserved the definition of the data themselves in the XSD schema file.

The schema information will include datatypes, field lengths, and other characteristics that allow your data to conform to the structure defined in Access. As you saw previously in Figure 12-3, the XSD file is referenced as QuoteTable.xsd. By default XSD file names, and the file names of the XSL and HTML (ASP) files generated by Access, will have the same name as the XML file, differing only by the file extension. In Figure 12-5, you can see a portion of the XSD exported by Access. Notice how the schema information communicates the structure that Access preserves in the table design (as shown previously in Figure 12-4).

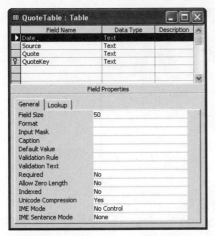

Figure 12-4: Design of table exported from Access

```
<?xml version="1.0" encoding="UTF-8" ?>
- <xsd:schema xmlns:xsd="http://www.w3.org/2000/10/XMLSchema" xmlns:od="urn:schemas-microsoft-
    com:officedata">
  - <xsd:element name="dataroot">
    - <xsd:complexType>
      - <xsd:choice maxOccurs="unbounded">
          <xsd:element ref="QuoteTable" />
        </xsd:choice>
      </xsd:complexType>
    </xsd:element>
  - <xsd:element name="QuoteTable">
    - <xsd:annotation>
      - <xsd:appinfo>
          <od:index index-name="PrimaryKey" index-key="QuoteKey" primary="yes" unique="yes"
            clustered="no" />
          <od:index index-name="QuoteKey" index-key="QuoteKey" primary="no" unique="no"
            clustered="no" />
        </xsd:appinfo>
      </xsd:annotation>
    - <xsd:complexType>
      - <xsd:sequence>
        - <xsd:element name="Date" minOccurs="0" od:jetType="text" od:sqlSType="nvarchar">
          - <xsd:simpleType>
            - <xsd:restriction base="xsd:string">
                <xsd:maxLength value="50" />
              </xsd:restriction>
            </xsd:simpleType>
          </xsd:element>
```

Figure 12-5: XSD information exported from Access

As you can see, the XSD contains information such as whether there is a key constraint on the database table, whether the key enforces uniqueness, what the field names are, their datatypes, and lengths.

The other files exported by Access relate to how the data are displayed. Access uses an XSL file to create instructions so that the XML data can be displayed as HTML. You have your choice to create an HTML or ASP file. In either case, the content is the same, and the only difference is the file extension. You can see how the page looks in Figure 12-6.

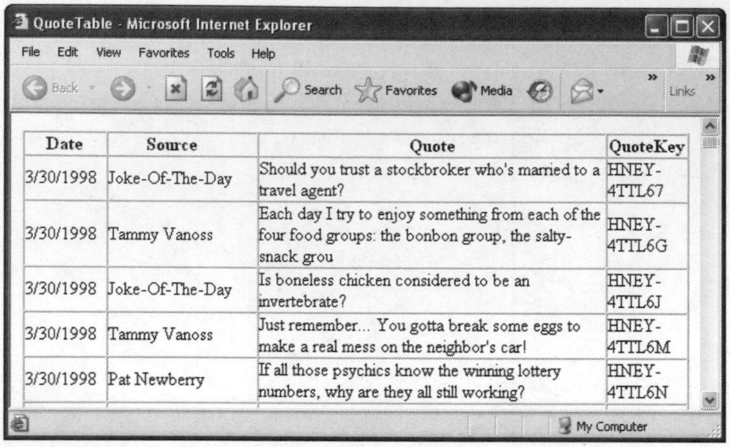

Date	Source	Quote	QuoteKey
3/30/1998	Joke-Of-The-Day	Should you trust a stockbroker who's married to a travel agent?	HNEY-4TTL67
3/30/1998	Tammy Vanoss	Each day I try to enjoy something from each of the four food groups: the bonbon group, the salty-snack grou	HNEY-4TTL6G
3/30/1998	Joke-Of-The-Day	Is boneless chicken considered to be an invertebrate?	HNEY-4TTL6J
3/30/1998	Tammy Vanoss	Just remember... You gotta break some eggs to make a real mess on the neighbor's car!	HNEY-4TTL6M
3/30/1998	Pat Newberry	If all those psychics know the winning lottery numbers, why are they all still working?	HNEY-4TTL6N

Figure 12-6: Final HTML output from Access export

The HTML is pretty simple; it merely references the XSL file, as you can see in Listing 12-1.

Listing 12-1: **HTML Content of Exported Display File**

```
<HTML xmlns:signature="urn:schemas-microsoft-
com:office:access">
<HEAD>
<META HTTP-EQUIV="Content-Type" CONTENT="text/html;charset=UTF-
8"/>
</HEAD>
<SCRIPT event=onload for=window>
  objData = new ActiveXObject("MSXML.DOMDocument");
  objData.async = false;
  objData.load("QuoteTable.xml");
  if (objData.parseError.errorCode != 0)
    alert(objData.parseError.reason);

  objStyle = new ActiveXObject("MSXML.DOMDocument");
  objStyle.async = false;
  objStyle.load("QuoteTable.xsl");
  if (objStyle.parseError.errorCode != 0)
    alert(objStyle.parseError.reason);
  document.open("text/html","replace");
  document.write(objData.transformNode(objStyle));
</SCRIPT>
</HTML>
```

You can easily see that there are no data in this file nor are there any explicit instructions for how the data are supposed to be displayed. What you do see are references to two external files. The first is to the XML file that contains the exported data (refer to Figure 12-3). The second relevant file is to the XSL stylesheet that contains the display instructions. Figure 12-7 shows a portion of those instructions.

```
<?xml version="1.0" ?>
- <xsl:stylesheet xmlns:xsl="http://www.w3.org/TR/WD-xsl" language="vbscript">
  - <xsl:template match="/">
    - <HTML>
      - <HEAD>
          <META HTTP-EQUIV="Content-Type" CONTENT="text/html;charset=UTF-8" />
          <TITLE>QuoteTable</TITLE>
          <STYLE TYPE="text/css" />
        </HEAD>
      - <BODY link="#0000ff" vlink="#800080">
        - <TABLE BORDER="1" BGCOLOR="#ffffff" CELLSPACING="0" CELLPADDING="0">
          - <TBODY>
            - <xsl:for-each select="/dataroot/QuoteTable">
                <xsl:eval>AppendNodeIndex(me)</xsl:eval>
              </xsl:for-each>
            - <xsl:for-each select="/dataroot/QuoteTable">
                <xsl:eval>CacheCurrentNode(me)</xsl:eval>
              - <xsl:if expr="OnFirstNode">
                - <TR>
                    <TH style="width: 0.9375in">Date</TH>
                    <TH style="width: 1.1979in">Source</TH>
                    <TH style="width: 7.0208in">Quote</TH>
                    <TH style="width: 0.9375in">QuoteKey</TH>
                  </TR>
                </xsl:if>
```

Figure 12-7: XSL display instructions for exported data

The XSL templates produce, by default, a fairly simple but nonetheless pleasant HTML display of the data. It also includes a lengthy script block that is used to walk the XML nodes of the source data file and format dates, strings, and do other more sophisticated operations than can be reasonably accomplished using straight XSL commands. Obviously, the strength of the entire XML support model in Access is that you can create your own XSL or XSD files to use with the data and customize the export process.

When you export an object in Access, if you click the advanced button (as shown previously in Figure 12-2) you are presented with a dialog box so you can choose the file names and locations of each of the files discussed thus far (see Figure 12-8).

This dialog lets you choose to export the data from the selected object and place the resulting file in the location of your choosing. You can choose whether you want UTF-8 (the default) or UTF-16 encoding. If you do not need any special characters, leaving the default will suffice. The other two tab sheets are shown in Figure 12-9. Here you can see that you can export the schema as a separate file or just embed the schema information in the XML file itself. On the presentation side, you can export an HTML or ASP file. The section for images is only relevant if you are exporting an object, such as a form or report, which uses images for buttons and so forth.

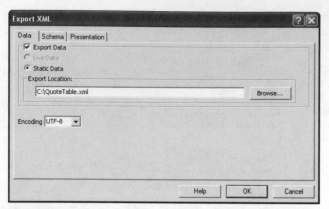

Figure 12-8: First tab of the advanced export dialog box

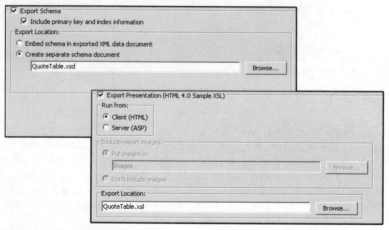

Figure 12-9: Other tabs of the advanced export dialog

One of the tricky things of this dialog box is that the file paths are not all the same. For instance, just because you choose to put the XML data file in one directory, the paths for the other files are not relative to this main file path. You must explicitly tell Access where you want the other files to be placed.

Exporting programmatically

Now that we have seen the overall process and how to do these tasks in the user interface, it's time to look at some code. The `Application` object, representing the Access application itself, has a method called `ExportXML`. This method is the entry point for the entire XML exporting process. It accepts eight different parameters, of which only two are actually required. These two are the type of object you are exporting and the path for the file that will result from the export. The parameters and their explanation are shown in Table 12-1.

Parameter	Description
Table 12-1	
Parameters for the ExportXML Method	
Parameter	*Description*
ObjectType	The type of Access object that will be exported
DataSource	The name of the Access object to export
DataTarget	The file name and path for the exported data
SchemaTarget	The file name and path for the exported schema information
PresentationTarget	The file name and path for the exported presentation information
ImageTarget	The path for exported images
Encoding	The text encoding to use for the exported XML
OtherFlags	Specifies additional options for exporting XML

The `ObjectType` parameter is specified using an `AcExportXMLObjectType` constant. The possible values include:

✦ `acExportDataAccessPage`

✦ `acExportForm`

✦ `acExportFunction`

✦ `acExportQuery`

✦ `acExportReport`

✦ `acExportServerView`

✦ `acExportStoredProcedure`

✦ `acExportTable`

These actual Access objects to which these values refer are fairly obvious. It is likely you will export queries, reports, and tables. There is also the possibility that you will export Data Access Pages (DAPs), functions, views, stored procedures, and forms. The final parameter, OtherFlags, bears mentioning as well. This parameter is useful for permitting other advanced behaviors when exporting data. They are described in Table 12-2.

Table 12-2
Values for the OtherFlags Parameter

Value	Description
1	Embed schema: Writes schema information into the document specified by the DataTarget argument; this value takes precedence over the SchemaTarget argument.
2	Exclude primary key and indexes: Does not export primary key and index schema properties.
4	Run from server: Creates an Active Server Pages (ASP) wrapper; otherwise, the default is an HTML wrapper. Only applies when exporting reports.
8	Live report source: Creates a live link to a remote Microsoft SQL Server 2000 database. Only valid when exporting reports bound to Microsoft SQL Server 2000.
16	Persist ReportML: Persists the exported object's ReportML file.

Well, let's put it to work. Listing 12-2 shows using the ExportXML method in code. What this code does is to export a single query object from the Access database. The resulting file is called output.xml. The schema information is also exported, as are the XSLT instructions and an accompanying ASP. This one line of instruction encapsulates all the basic features shown in the user interface.

Listing 12-2: **Using the ExportXML Method**

```
Application.ExportXML _
    ObjectType:=acExportQuery, _
    DataSource:="QuoteTable", _
    DataTarget:="C:\output.xml", _
    SchemaTarger:="C:\QuoteTable.xsd", _
    PresentationTarget:="C:\QueryTable.xsl", _
    OtherFlags:=4
```

Now, let's put things together for a more realistic application. It would be useful if we could have Access export its data as XML so we can apply an XSL stylesheet so that the results are formatted for use in Excel 2002. The final result, in Excel, is shown in Figure 12-10.

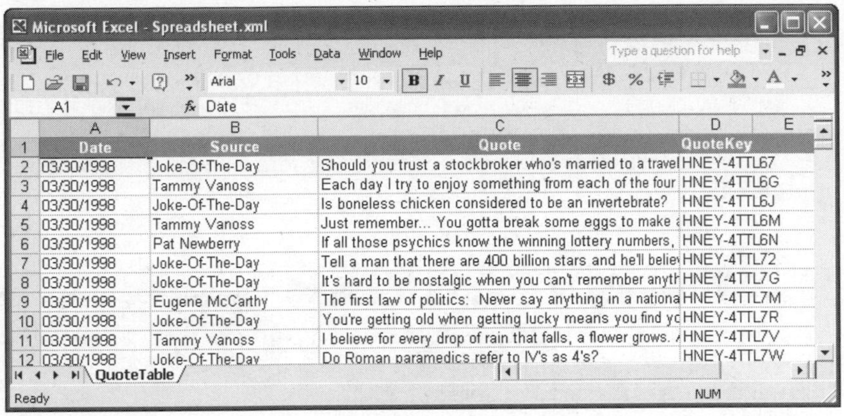

Figure 12-10: XML spreadsheet shown in Excel 2002 after an XML export from Access

The code to export the XML has only one essential difference from the code in Listing 12-2 in that the OtherFlags parameter has a value of 1 instead of 4. This means that the schema information will come embedded in the XML file rather than being separate. The XSL information is optional, because we are going to apply our own XSL stylesheet to the XML content.

In Listing 12-3 you can see the code used to convert the XML output from Access into an Excel spreadsheet. This code applies a special XSL file to produce the final XML file. A portion of code for the XSL is shown in Listing 12-4.

Listing 12-3: Converting an XML from the Standard Access Output to Excel

```
Dim oDOM1 As DOMDocument40
Dim oDOM2 As DOMDocument40
Dim oDOM3 As DOMDocument40
Set oDOM1 = New DOMDocument40
Set oDOM2 = New DOMDocument40
Set oDOM3 = New DOMDocument40
oDOM1.Load "C:\output.xml"
oDOM2.Load "C:\excel_transform.xsl"
oDOM1.transformNodeToObject oDOM2, oDOM3
oDOM3.Save "C:\Spreadsheet.xml"
```

The XSL instructions are actually based on an XSL file that ships with the Microsoft XML Spreadsheet Add-In for Microsoft Access 2002. The add-in can be downloaded from the Microsoft MSDN Website (`http://msdn.microsoft.com/code/default.asp?url=/code/sample.asp?url=/msdn-files/027/001/691/msdncompositedoc.xml`). This add-in leverages an XSL stylesheet called od2ss.xsl. You can modify this sheet as needed to produce Excel spreadsheets that suit your liking.

Listing 12-4: A View of the XSL to Convert Access Output to an Excel Spreadsheet

```
<xsl:template match="xsd:element">
<xsl:variable name="worksheetName" select="@name"/>
<xsl:value-of
  select="ss:init( xsd:complexType/xsd:sequence/xsd:element[
not(xsd:complexType)],xsd:complexType/
xsd:sequence/xsd:element[
not(xsd:complexType)]/@od:jetType)"/>
<Worksheet xmlns =
"urn:schemas-microsoft-com:office:spreadsheet">
  <xsl:attribute name="ss:Name"><xsl:value-of
    select="ss:truncateWorksheetName(ss:replaceHex(@name))"/>
      </xsl:attribute>
  <Table>
  <xsl:for-each
    select="xsd:complexType/xsd:sequence/
      xsd:element[not(xsd:complexType)]">
  <Column>
  <xsl:attribute name="ss:StyleID">
    <xsl:value-of select="ss:colstyle()"/></xsl:attribute>
  </Column>
  </xsl:for-each>
  <Row ss:StyleID="Header">
  <xsl:for-each
    select="xsd:complexType/xsd:sequence/
      xsd:element[not(xsd:complexType)]">
  <Cell>
  <Data ss:Type="String"><xsl:value-of
    select="ss:replaceHex(@name)"/></Data>
  </Cell>
  </xsl:for-each>
  </Row>
  <!--
  <Row><Cell><Data ss:Type="String">
    <xsl:value-of select="ss:debug()"/></Data></Cell></Row>
  -->
  <xsl:for-each
    select="/root/dataroot//*[name()=$worksheetName]">
```

```
<xsl:value-of select="ss:initRow()"/>
<Row>
<xsl:for-each select="*">
<xsl:if test="ss:showcell(.)">
<Cell>
<xsl:if test="ss:iscellstyleid()">
<xsl:attribute name="ss:StyleID">
  <xsl:value-of select="ss:cellstyleid()"/>
    </xsl:attribute>
</xsl:if>
<xsl:if test="ss:iscellhyperlink()">
<xsl:attribute name="ss:HRef">
  <xsl:value-of
      select="ss:cellhyperlink()"/></xsl:attribute>
</xsl:if>
<xsl:if test="ss:iscellindex()">
<xsl:attribute name="ss:Index">
  <xsl:value-of select="ss:cellindex()"/></xsl:attribute>
</xsl:if>
<Data>
<xsl:attribute name="ss:Type">
  <xsl:value-of select="ss:celltype()"/></xsl:attribute>
<xsl:value-of select="ss:cellvalue()"/></Data>
</Cell>
</xsl:if>
</xsl:for-each>
</Row>
</xsl:for-each>
</Table>
</Worksheet>
</xsl:template>
```

What you can see in this XSL stylesheet is that a new worksheet is added to the workbook. The name of the worksheet is set to match the name of the exported object from Access. Also, column headers are added and some styles are applied. Then, the XSL adds the row and cell data to the spreadsheet. Fortunately, Excel 2002 has native support for XML, so the results of the transformation can be saved as an XML file that can then be opened directly in Excel.

What this example shows is one way in which the results of Access XML exports can be sent to other applications to suit other purposes. Access XML files can be transformed for Excel, Visio 2002, Web Services, BizTalk Server processes, custom component applications, and any other system that can parse XML. Moreover, Access can import XML from these sources by using a companion method to the ExportXML method.

Importing

The full strength of the XML support in Access is brought to bear with the fact that data can make a round-trip from Access to another system and back into an Access table or other object once again. As was the case with XML exports, there is the ability to import XML in the user interface, but you can also do so programmatically. First, let's look at the XML to import. Listing 12-5 shows some XML that needs to be inserted into an Access database. These data will be added to a table.

Listing 12-5: XML to Be Imported into Access 2002

```
<QuoteTable>
<Date>12/22/2002</Date>
<Source>Jim Morrison</Source>
<Quote>Some of the worst mistakes of
my life have been haircuts.</Quote>
<QuoteKey>HNEY-1TTJRD</QuoteKey>
</QuoteTable>
```

Notice how the structure of the data in the XML file conforms to the structure of the database table. What is not shown in Listing 12-5 is the equally important schema information. The schema information would help ensure that the structure of the data in the XML import meet the requirements of the data definition in the table itself.

If Access encounters a problem when inserting data into Access, it will place the errors in a new table called ImportErrors (see Figure 12-11). If the table does not exist, Access will create it; otherwise, new errors will be appended to the table.

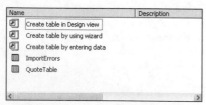

Figure 12-11: ImportErrors table in table list of Access database

To see the kind of information that Access places in the ImportErrors, let's try to add a record to the database where a field value exceeds the maximum allowed in Access. The record in the ImportErrors table for the error is shown in Figure 12-12.

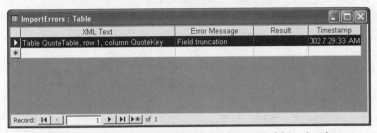

Figure 12-12: Error reported in Access when a field in the data violates a field constraint in the database

To begin an attempted import, you can choose the File | Get External Data | Import menu in Access, or you can choose a pop-up menu when right-clicking in the pane that lists tables, queries, or other objects in Access. Either way, you will be presented with a dialog box to let you navigate to the XML file that contains the data you wish to import. After selecting the file and clicking the button to import the file, you will see the dialog box shown in Figure 12-13.

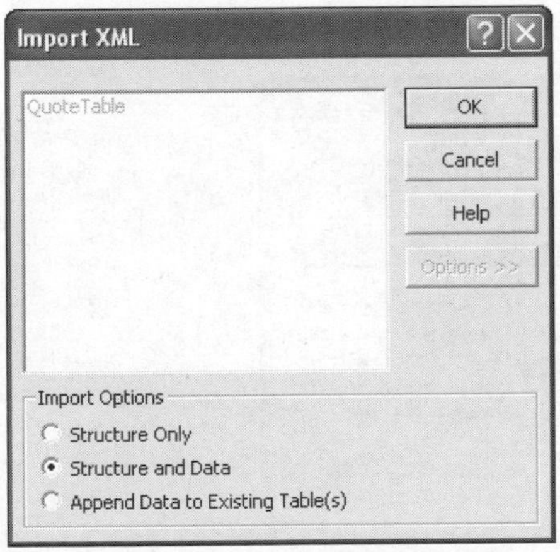

Figure 12-13: Import dialog box

This dialog box presents you with three options. Your import behavior can be altered according to the setting you choose. The possible choices are:

✦ **Structure Only:** This imports the table structure only. If the table does not exist, it will be created. If the table already exists, a new one will be added with a number appended to distinguish it from the pre-existing table of the same name.

✦ **Structure and Data:** This imports the table and the data into the database. If the table exists, a new one will be added with a number appended. The difference between this and the previous option is that this one tells Access to import the data as well.

✦ **Append Data to Existing Table(s):** This option tells Access to merely append data to existing tables. If the tables do not exist, the import will fail.

Another aspect of the import is that Access can figure out if you are importing data for a single table or for multiple tables. For example, if you have an XML file that contains hierarchically structured XML that really should be structured as separate tables, such as customer and order information in a single file, these will be split into two tables in Access. You should make sure you include the appropriate schema information with the file so that Access does not try to figure out the structure implicitly. Access should be given instructions on how the file is to be understood by using an XSD file.

Figure 12-14 shows the result of importing the XML of Listing 12-5.

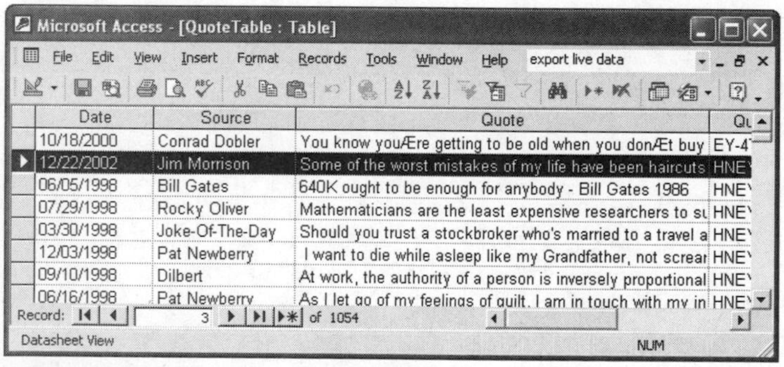

Figure 12-14: Result of the XML import

Importing programmatically

Using the user interface is fine, but, as with all things, programmability is what makes a feature truly powerful. The `Application` object has a single method for XML imports, `ImportXML`. The method accepts three parameters. They are:

✦ **DataSource:** This is the name and path of the XML file you are going to import.

✦ **DataTransform:** This is the name of an XSL file you can apply to the incoming XML data.

✦ **OtherFlags:** A bitmask which specifies other behaviors associated with importing from XML. Table 12-3 describes the behavior that results from specific values; values can be added to specify a combination of behaviors.

Table 12-3
Values for the OtherFlags Parameter

Value	Description
1	**Overwrite** — With this setting, Access overwrites the target table if it already exists.
2	**Don't create structure** — By default, Access will create a new structure for the object being imported. If you have not also added the Overwrite value to the bitmask, a message box will appear asking the user for permission to overwrite.
4	**Don't import data** — A schema will be used to create the structure, and the data will be imported as well, unless you add this value to the bitmask.

To put it together, let's take an Excel spreadsheet and import its data into an Access table. A portion of the XML spreadsheet contents is shown in Listing 12-6.

Listing 12-6: **A Portion of the XML Spreadsheet Contents**

```
<Row>
 <Cell><Data ss:Type="String">12/22/2002Jimi Hendrix</Data>
  <NamedCell ss:Name="Quote"/></Cell>
 <Cell ss:Index="3"><Data ss:Type="String">Imagination is
    the key to my lyrics. The rest is painted
    with a little science fiction. </Data>
    <NamedCell ss:Name="Quote"/></Cell>
 <Cell><Data ss:Type="String">HNEY-2TTJRD</Data>
    <NamedCell ss:Name="Quote"/></Cell>
</Row>
```

As you can see, the structure of this file is not at all in conformity with the structure needed for input into the Access database. Hence, a transformation must be applied to the XML spreadsheet before it can be imported. Listing 12-7 shows the XSL used to accomplish the transformation.

Listing 12-7: XSL Used to Prepare XML for Import into Access

```
<?xml version='1.0'?>
<xsl:stylesheet version="1.0"
 xmlns:xsl="http://www.w3.org/1999/XSL/Transform"
 xmlns:d="urn:schemas-microsoft-com:office:spreadsheet"
 xmlns:o="urn:schemas-microsoft-com:office:office"
 xmlns:x="urn:schemas-microsoft-com:office:excel"
 xmlns:ss="urn:schemas-microsoft-com:office:spreadsheet"
 xmlns:html="http://www.w3.org/TR/REC-html40">

  <xsl:output indent="yes" omit-xml-declaration="no" />
  <xsl:template match="d:Workbook">
    <QuoteTable>
      <Date><xsl:value-of select=
      "Worksheet/Table/Row/Cell
  [NamedCell[@ss:Name='Date']]"/></Date>
      <Source><xsl:value-of select=
  "Worksheet/Table/Row/Cell
  [NamedCell[@ss:Name='Source']]"/></Source>
      <Quote><xsl:value-of select=
  "Worksheet/Table/Row/Cell
  [NamedCell[@ss:Name='Quote']]"/></Quote>
      <QuoteKey><xsl:value-of select=
  "Worksheet/Table/Row/Cell
  [NamedCell[@ss:Name='QuoteKey']]"/></QuoteKey>
    </QuoteTable>
</xsl:template>
</xsl:stylesheet>
```

With the transformation complete, the data are ready to be imported into Access. What this example shows is how external applications and processes can be used as valid sources for new Access data. As long as all of the parties involved use XML, the data are candidates for import. One thing that must be mentioned is regarding the use of namespaces. The source XML file for the import in the previous example was an XML spreadsheet from Microsoft Office. As such, it will reference a Microsoft Office namespace: `xmlns:d="urn:schemas-microsoft-com:office:spreadsheet`. This is important because without it, the XSL will not be able to find the elements of the source XML file. The lesson is, if your source XML files contain essential namespaces, make sure your XSL also knows about them.

Summary

Access has long been a favorite for both large and small organizations. It is highly programmable, and it is fairly easy to administer. As the demands of the marketplace have changed, so have the features of Access. XML support is high on the list for any database environment. Access has support for native XML operations. Data can be exported and imported, all using standard XML and no strings attached. Additionally, Access makes it easy to build applications that consume the XML by providing a mechanism for exporting schema information and display characteristics. Data interaction with another environment becomes more likely as well because schema and/or data can be imported into Access. What heightens the power of Access is that it allows you to do all of these things programmatically so that your application can silently accomplish full round-trips of data using XML.

✦   ✦   ✦

Creating an Excel Spreadsheet from an XML Data Source

Excel is a perennial favorite for report writing, and, as time has passed, it has come to do so much more. It is now a full development platform for applications. Initially, Excel was used for ad hoc reporting, and the sources were comparatively limited. Now, data sources for Excel are very diverse, and its ability to consume data from non-ODBC sources and simple HTML has had to expand.

While it was possible to integrate XML into earlier versions of Microsoft Excel, the release of Excel 2002 with Office XP made it much easier. This version of Excel has built-in native support for XML. Microsoft Excel 2002 now recognizes and opens XML documents including XSL processing instructions. The Range object has also been amended so that developers can access data in a spreadsheet using XML-based access. In addition, Microsoft Excel spreadsheets can be persisted as an XML file while preserving the format, structure, and data through the XML spreadsheet file format. In this chapter, you will learn about how Excel can consume and produce XML. You will learn about the XML spreadsheet file format and the XML Spreadsheet Schema (XML-SS). You will see some of the different source and destination types for the XML that Excel uses. You will also learn how to build applications that use XML. You'll also see how to use Excel programmatically to export data to XML and how XML-SS can work with scripts or Web pages to produce alternate displays of Excel.

Introduction

One of the most important things to keep in mind when integrating XML with Excel is that the XML needs no special tags, styles, or instructions to be used. Excel can use any data and structure, as long as it is well-formed. Let's first look at opening XML files in Excel. Then we will look at how to export XML from spreadsheets. We will also take a look under the hood to see how Excel does its work. We will also see how to use Web queries to acquire XML from URLs before taking a look at how to consume data from SQL Server using features SQL-XML.

Importing XML

When Excel attempts to open an XML file, it has no idea about the source from which the XML came or what its ultimate purposes may be. In the end, the application is left to try to display the data in the spreadsheet format, which is the only format available to a user once the data is loaded. What makes it possible to interpret and then alter the XML so that the data can be viewed as a spreadsheet is what is known as the XML Flattener. The Flattener contains processing logic so that the data in an XML file can be converted into a two-dimensional spreadsheet. The exception to this is when the file is already saved in the XML spreadsheet format. In this case, no flattening is required because the file is already in the Microsoft Excel native XML file format. This means that the XML stylesheet is being used to make sure that the XML is in a structure that Excel can understand. Figure 13-1 shows when the Flattener is invoked depending on the XML being opened.

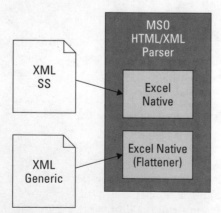

Figure 13-1: The Flattener is used when the source XML is not in a structure that can be used in Excel's spreadsheet structure.

The Flattener is used when you use code to open a workbook or an XML spreadsheet using the `Workbooks.Open` or `Workbooks.OpenXML` methods to open XML files. As already stated, the XML file must be well-formed. If it is not, an error will result and the file will not be opened (or saved if attempting to save the XML). When an XML file is opened and the Flattener is used, the original file is opened as a read-only file so that the flattened file does not replace the original file. You then have the choice of saving the flattened file under a different name.

There are a few different ways you can get XML data into Excel. There are user interface features to facilitate this, and there are programmatic methods you can use to import XML as well. The easiest user interface method is to go to the File⇨Open menu and navigate to an XML file. Figure 13-2 shows the result of navigating to and opening a file containing a shortened view of the XML shown in Listing 13-1.

Listing 13-1: **Source XML for an Excel Spreadsheet**

```
<?xml version="1.0" encoding="UTF-8"?>
<?xml-stylesheet type="text/xsl" href="quotes01.xsl"?>
<Quotes>
<QuoteTable>
<Date>03/30/1998</Date>
<Source>Joke-Of-The-Day</Source>
<Quote><![CDATA[Should you trust a
    stockbroker who's married to a travel agent?]]></Quote>
<QuoteKey>HNEY-4TTL67</QuoteKey>
</QuoteTable>
<QuoteTable>
<Date>03/30/1998</Date>
<Source>Tammy Vanoss</Source>
<Quote>Each day I try to enjoy something
   from each of the four food groups:
   the bonbon group, the salty-snack grou</Quote>
<QuoteKey>HNEY-4TTL6G</QuoteKey>
</QuoteTable>
</Quotes>
```

One of the things that is notable in these data is the reference to a stylesheet. Without the stylesheet, the resulting worksheet in Excel will look like Figure 13-2. The result with the stylesheet applied when importing is shown in Figure 13-3.

	A	B	C	D
1	/Quotes			
2	/QuoteTable/Date	/QuoteTable/Quote	/QuoteTable/QuoteKey	/QuoteTable/Source
3	03/30/1998	Should you trust a sto	HNEY-4TTL67	Joke-Of-The-Day
4	03/30/1998	Each day I try to enjoy	HNEY-4TTL6G	Tammy Vanoss
5	03/30/1998	Is boneless chicken c	HNEY-4TTL6J	Joke-Of-The-Day
6	03/30/1998	Just remember... You	HNEY-4TTL6M	Tammy Vanoss
7	03/30/1998	If all those psychics k	HNEY-4TTL6N	Pat Newberry
8	03/30/1998	Tell a man that there a	HNEY-4TTL72	Joke-Of-The-Day
9	03/30/1998	It's hard to be nostalgi	HNEY-4TTL7G	Joke-Of-The-Day
10	03/30/1998	The first law of politics	HNEY-4TTL7M	Eugene McCarthy
11	03/30/1998	You're getting old whe	HNEY-4TTL7R	Joke-Of-The-Day
12	03/30/1998	I believe for every drop	HNEY-4TTL7V	Tammy Vanoss
13	03/30/1998	Do Roman paramedic	HNEY-4TTL7W	Joke-Of-The-Day
14	03/30/1998	Atheism is a nonprofit	HNEY-4TTL84	Pat Newberry
15	03/30/1998	Sooner or later, doesn	HNEY-4TTL88	Joke-Of-The-Day
16	03/30/1998	Middle age is having a	HNEY-4TTL8B	Joke-Of-The-Day
17	03/30/1998	Why doesn't Tarzan h	HNEY-4TTL8D	Joke-Of-The-Day
18	03/30/1998	How come Superman	HNEY-4TTL8G	Joke-Of-The-Day
19	03/30/1998	If man evolved from m	HNEY-4TTL8J	Pat Newberry
20	03/30/1998	Isn't the best way to s	HNEY-4TTL8P	Joke-Of-The-Day
21	03/30/1998	The aging process co	HNEY-4TTL99	Joke-Of-The-Day
22	03/30/1998	No one will believe yo	HNEY-4TTL9A	Dilbert

Figure 13-2: View of imported XML not using a stylesheet

	A	B
1		
2	3/30/1998	Should you trust a stockbroker who's married to a travel agent?
3	3/30/1998	Each day I try to enjoy something from each of the four food groups: the bonbon group, the salty-snack grou
4	3/30/1998	Is boneless chicken considered to be an invertebrate?
5	3/30/1998	Just remember... You gotta break some eggs to make a real mess on the neighbor's car!
6	3/30/1998	If all those psychics know the winning lottery numbers, why are they all still working?
7	3/30/1998	Tell a man that there are 400 billion stars and he'll believe you. Tell him a bench has wet paint and he ha
8	3/30/1998	It's hard to be nostalgic when you can't remember anything.
9	3/30/1998	The first law of politics: Never say anything in a national campaign that anyone might remember.

Figure 13-3: View of imported XML using a stylesheet

Remember, Excel needs to constrain the structure of the XML into a structure it can display in a typical spreadsheet. Notice how in Figure 13-2, Excel figures out what should be represented as rows and what should be represented as columns pretty well. It even applies some default formatting to the XML by bolding and coloring the column headings. When you import XML into Excel, you can choose to apply any stylesheet referenced in the XML. However, if more than one stylesheet is referenced, only one can be used. When opening a workbook from an XML file that has a stylesheet, a dialog appears (see Figure 13-4).

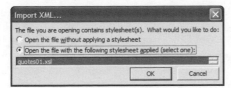

Figure 13-4: Dialog to choose a stylesheet when importing XML in Excel

It's hard to see, but there is actually a scrollable list box containing the names of the stylesheets referenced in the source XML file. If you choose to not use the stylesheets, the XML is imported as shown in Figure 13-5.

Programmatically, these same capabilities are possible. Using the `OpenXML` method from the Workbooks object in Excel, you can import XML content. The method accepts two parameters:

✦ **FileName:** A string containing the name of the file to open.

✦ **Stylesheets:** This is either a single value or an array of values that tell Excel which XSLT stylesheet processing instructions to apply.

Previously, we mentioned how Excel can only apply one of the stylesheets it finds referenced in the source XML file. However, this policy only applies to activities in the user interface. If you import XML programmatically, you can apply multiple stylesheets. For example, if the XML file references two stylesheets, they can be both used when importing if you call the `OpenXML` method this way: `Workbooks.OpenXML "C:\Source.XML", Array(1, 2)`. The use of the array tells Excel to apply the first referenced stylesheet first, then reference the second stylesheet. However, this sequential application of stylesheets will only work if the first stylesheet produces XML. In other words, if the first stylesheet produces non-XML output (such as HTML) or not well-formed XML output, then the second stylesheet cannot be applied.

Once the XML has been loaded into Excel, the normal capabilities of Excel can be brought to bear on the data as you would expect. At this point, Excel has no knowledge that the data in the spreadsheet actually came from an XML source of some kind. This does not mean, however, that the data cannot be represented as XML once again. Before looking at how to export data in an XML spreadsheet, it is worthwhile to look at another feature in Excel for representing spreadsheet data as XML: the use of the Range object.

The Range object is one of the most commonly used objects in the Excel object model. Much of the work Excel programmers do with Excel involves using this object because it allows us to isolate areas in a spreadsheet, transform them, copy them, format them, calculate them, and do many other things. If this is so, it would be extra convenient if the data in a range could be easily changed into XML. Thus, a specific range of cells, say a named range, could be extracted from the spreadsheet and used in another process that requires XML. The code in Listing 13-2 shows how to load an XML file into Excel while applying a stylesheet. Then, a range is populated with the cells in the worksheet that contain data. The value of this range is subsequently retrieved as an XML string. This is accomplished by using the `xlRangeValueXMLSpreadsheet` option when retrieving the range value. This constant tells Excel to dump the range contents as a fully well-formed XML string. The string is used as the source for an instance of a DOM object. If the DOM successfully loads the string, it is saved as an XML file.

Listing 13-2: **Working with XML Data in a Range Object**

```
Dim oDoc As DOMDocument40
Dim oSheet As Worksheet
Dim oRange As Range
    Workbooks.OpenXML Filename:= _
        "C:\QuoteTable.xml"

Set oDoc = New DOMDocument40
Set oSheet = Application.ActiveWorkbook.ActiveSheet
Set oRange = oSheet.Cells.SpecialCells(xlCellTypeConstants)
oDoc.loadXML (oRange.Value(xlRangeValueXMLSpreadsheet))
oDoc.Save ("C:\Destination.xml")
```

Ultimately, this is really doing the same thing that will be possible by simply saving the spreadsheet as an XML spreadsheet, a technique that will be explained when we delve more into exporting XML. What is important to see right now is that if even the XML data have been imported into Excel spreadsheet format, they can still be easily accessed as well-formed XML.

Another way of importing XML into Excel is by using a special feature known as Web queries. A Web query is a way to import data into Excel using a URL. With a Web query, you can import data from any page that is served up and parsed by the Web browser. This excludes components and other display elements that are rendered by something other than the browser, such as a Shockwave component or something of that sort. One of the greatest benefits of Web queries is that they free users and developers from having to worry about hard-coded paths to XML files. URLs are easier to remember, and they are more accessible.

To see how they work, let's load the XML file we imported using the `OpenXML` method in Listing 13-2. Web queries are accessible from the Data⇨Import External Data⇨New Web query menu. When you click this menu, a dialog box (Figure 13-5) will appear that will let you navigate to the Web file you want to import. Remember, these files can be XML, HTML, or any other parsable combination of files that the browser can interpret.

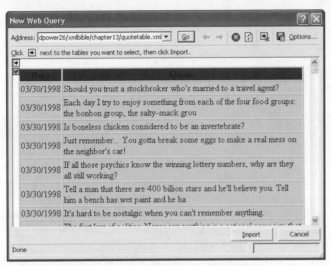

Figure 13-5: Web query dialog

As you can see, the Web query dialog has an address bar so that a user can navigate to a Web file just as one would in a typical Web browser. The browser will attempt to locate and load the page, and if it encounters errors, it will provide error messages in the normal way. If it can load the page, it will do so and place a small yellow box containing a black arrow next to certain portions of the file. These boxes indicate which portions Excel identifies as candidates for imports into a spreadsheet. Areas that cannot be imported will still display in the dialog window, but they will not be accompanied by an arrow. As one clicks on an arrow, the box turns green and the arrow changes to a check, as you can see in Figure 13-5. Notice how what is being imported here is a portion of an XML file that was altered using an XSL stylesheet. With a section checked, just clicking the Import button will import the section, but there are more options that can be selected to alter the behavior of the import.

If you click on the Options button on the Web query dialog, you will see the dialog shown in Figure 13-6. First, you have the option of importing the content with no formatting, rich text formatting, or full HTML formatting. There are settings for pre-formatted HTML blocks, and two additional settings. The first of the two additional settings is to disable date recognition in the source data. For example, a string of characters such as "1/3" will be interpreted as "January 3." If this is not a correct interpretation (say, if the characters really mean "one third"), then checking this box will ensure that the characters will not be turned into dates.

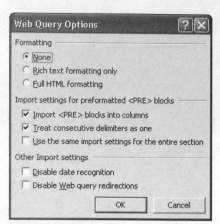

Figure 13-6: Options for new Web queries

The second of the two additional attributes has to do with Web query redirections. With Microsoft Excel 2002, you can create a Web query to a specific HTML page that additionally retrieves data from another Web location by using special commands in the HTML file. For example, if an HTML page contains data for current projects in your organization, a table of data in that page can contain a command to retrieve data from another data source. Here is an example of the special command used for Web query redirections:

```
<TABLE NAME="ProjectStatus"
o:WebQuerySourceHRef="http://localhost/Projects/ProjectStatus.
XML">.
```

One of the main reasons for this feature is that the Web page you are accessing can be formatted for viewing as a Web page, but the accompanying data can be optimized for analysis (for example, in XML format). Another advantage is that the HTML page can be optimized for paged viewing (say, ten rows at a time), whereas the data table that the Web query accesses can retrieve the entire data sample at once. Sometimes you will not want to use this redirection, so it can be disabled by checking the box in the Options dialog box.

With the options set, you can click the Import button to begin the import. When you do, you will see the dialog box shown in Figure 13-7. This lets you specify where you want the import results to go. You can import them into an existing spreadsheet or to a new spreadsheet entirely.

Figure 13-7: Import Data dialog box

There are other options that can be set at this point. There is a Properties button that can be clicked to show the External Data Range Properties dialog box (see Figure 13-8). The first option allows you to save the query definition. This is important because if you choose to save the query definition, the Web query can be refreshed on a button of a small toolbar later on (see Figure 13-9). If you choose to not save the query definition, the data are imported, and the spreadsheet retains no knowledge that the data came from a Web query at all. Web queries can be refreshed after the import by clicking on the exclamation point icon on the Web query toolbar. The dialog box shows settings for the refresh frequency. A background refresh means that the data can be refreshed without the user initiating the process manually. The refresh frequency can be set to a number of minutes (up to 99), and the data can be set to refresh as the file is opened. As the data are refreshed, there may be times when new cells are added.

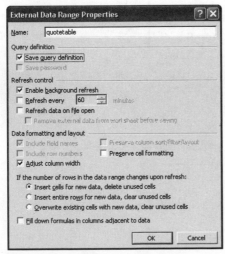

Figure 13-8: External Data Range
Properties dialog box

There are settings in the dialog box to tell Excel what to do when it encounters new rows as well as what to do when existing imported rows are no longer needed.

Another important aspect of the process is to set how the data will be formatted. Settings can be configured so that the column widths of the spreadsheet automatically adjust to the size of the data in the source. Also, a check box allows you to tell Excel to apply its default formatting or not. If you preserve cell formatting, Excel will attempt to apply the original cell formatting; otherwise, Excel will use formatting directives in the template being used. For example, this can specify that column headings will be automatically bolded and their background color changes as the data are imported. The last setting to be mentioned is one that tells Excel what to do if new data are added and there are formulas in the spreadsheet.

The result of the import is shown in Figure 13-9. You can see that the full HTML formatting was preserved. You can also see that there is a small toolbar for refreshing the Web query. This is because Excel was told to save the Web query definition with the spreadsheet. This means that when the spreadsheet is saved and opened again, the Web query will still be present so that it can be refreshed.

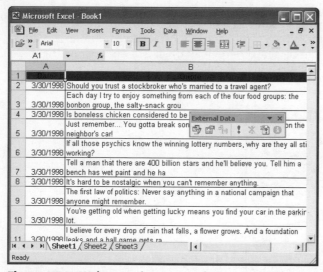

Figure 13-9: Web query import results

The Web query can also be edited by clicking on the toolbar (Figure 13-10). This will reopen the Web query dialog box so that a new URL can be specified, or other settings can be configured.

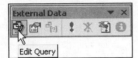

Figure 13-10: Initiating the edit of an existing Web query

This is a lot of information about Excel, but it is only to help us understand how to exploit its ability to work with XML. As the example shown in Figure 13-9 demonstrates, an XML file can be imported. This particular XML file referenced an XSL stylesheet, so the actual results were formatted as HTML. However, Excel could just as easily import the results from an XML file that has no formatting specified at all. Figure 13-11 shows the Web query dialog box for initiating an import of pure XML. Notice how the entire XML content can be imported, or just specific data sections. Figure 13-12 shows the results of the final import.

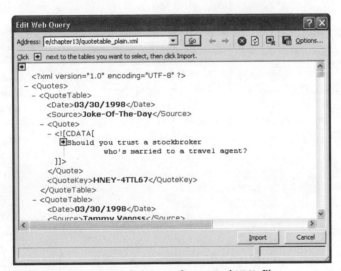

Figure 13-11: Importing an unformatted XML file

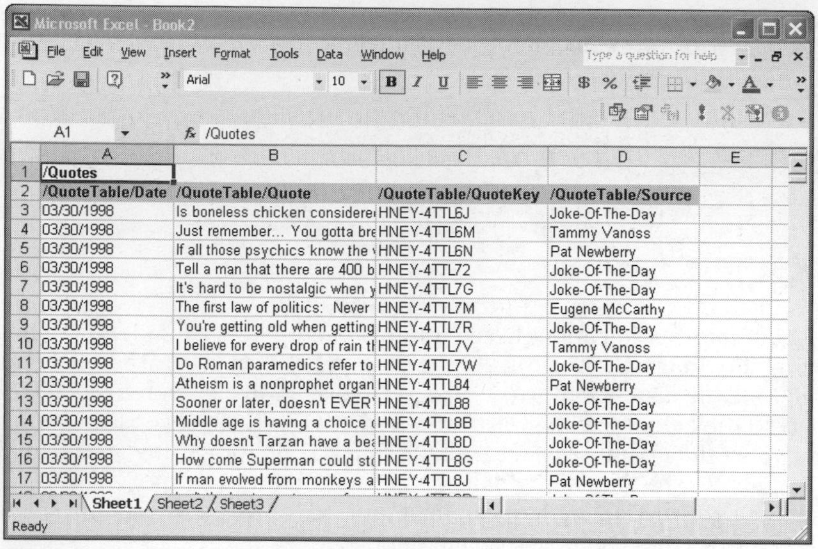

Figure 13-12: Results of the final XML import

Excel 2002 supports creating Web query to an XML file that contains a schema. However, the schema does not have some of the benefits one would expect. For example, the data types in the schema are not directly meaningful to Excel. The alternative is to open an XML spreadsheet. This format is unique to Excel in that it is a complete XML representation of a spreadsheet. All of the data, formatting, and other aspects of the Excel spreadsheet are persisted in the XML. A Web query can be directed to an XML spreadsheet, and in doing so, there are unique benefits. This means that the XML file can:

✦ Preserve data types

✦ Preserve formulas for ad hoc analysis

✦ Preserve named ranges

✦ Preserve Excel-specific formatting

Regular XML files are not the only source for the Web query. XML can be brought in using other techniques. For example, XML can be returned from Microsoft SQL Server as a direct response to a database query. Here is the URL used to return the XML:

```
http://localhost/nwind?sql=SELECT+*+FROM+Authors+FOR+XML+AUTO&
root=root
```

This query will return XML that can be imported and then placed in an Excel spreadsheet. The results are shown in Figure 13-13.

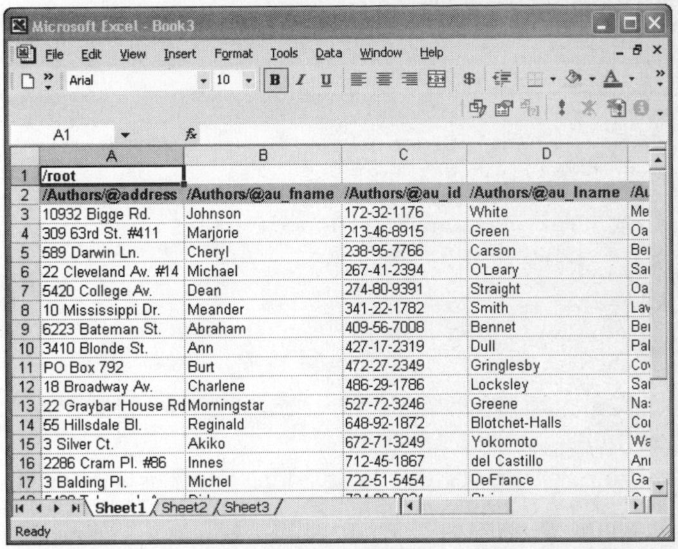

Figure 13-13: Importing XML from Microsoft SQL Server

The next thing to see is how to accomplish the XML/HTML import through a Web query using Excel's programmability. VBA code can be used to do this, and the object that represents a Web query is called the `QueryTable` object. A `QueryTable` can be accessed through a worksheet, and all of the settings of the user interface dialogs are available through it. Listing 13-3 shows how to use a `QueryTable` in code that accesses the Northwind database.

Listing 13-3: **Creating a Web Query Programmatically**

```
With ActiveSheet.QueryTables.Add(Connection:= _
"URL;http://dpower26/nwind?sql=SELECT+*+FROM+Authors+FOR+XML+AU
TO&root=root", _
  Destination:=Range("A1"))
  .Name = "Authors"
  .FieldNames = True
  .RowNumbers = False
  .FillAdjacentFormulas = False
  .PreserveFormatting = False
  .RefreshOnFileOpen = False
```

Continued

Listing 13-3 *(continued)*

```
    .BackgroundQuery = True
    .RefreshStyle = xlInsertDeleteCells
    .SavePassword = False
    .SaveData = True
    .AdjustColumnWidth = True
    .RefreshPeriod = 0
    .WebSelectionType = xlEntirePage
    .WebFormatting = xlWebFormattingNone
    .WebPreFormattedTextToColumns = True
    .WebConsecutiveDelimitersAsOne = True
    .WebSingleBlockTextImport = False
    .WebDisableDateRecognition = False
    .WebDisableRedirections = False
    .Refresh BackgroundQuery:=False
End With
```

This code imports XML from SQL Server, just as was done previously through the user interface. Based on certain conditions in the code, a different URL could be used, or other settings could be changed depending on the conditions. This code can be used in VBA code in the application or through an external program that animates the Excel object model. What all of the examples shown demonstrate is how easy it is to import XML into Excel, through the File | Open menu or through Web queries.

Exporting XML

XML can be exported from Excel as a native format. This means that the entire contents of an Excel spreadsheet can be retained in a fully well-formed Excel file. This is a major step forward in the evolution of end-user productivity and reporting solutions. As Excel has become so integral to business processes, it has become increasingly necessary that the data in Excel become more approachable once outside of the application itself. A spreadsheet saved in this special format is called an XML spreadsheet.

The easiest way to export the XML is to save the spreadsheet from the File➪Save menu. The first part of this XML is shown in Listing 13-4. Notice how the first part of the XML contains information such as what the Window size should be when the spreadsheet is opened in the application. Listing 13-5 reveals that the source of the spreadsheet data was actually an Excel Web query. The Web query will be available when the spreadsheet is reopened in Excel, and all of its features will be restored.

Listing 13-4: Processing Instruction and Initial Data in Content Stored As XML Spreadsheet

```xml
<?xml version="1.0"?>
<Workbook xmlns="urn:schemas-microsoft-com:office:spreadsheet"
 xmlns:o="urn:schemas-microsoft-com:office:office"
 xmlns:x="urn:schemas-microsoft-com:office:excel"
 xmlns:ss="urn:schemas-microsoft-com:office:spreadsheet"
 xmlns:html="http://www.w3.org/TR/REC-html40">
 <DocumentProperties xmlns="urn:schemas-microsoft-
com:office:office">
  <Author>Administrator</Author>
  <LastAuthor>Administrator</LastAuthor>
  <Created>2003-01-03T10:16:42Z</Created>
  <Company>Microsoft Corporation</Company>
  <Version>10.2625</Version>
 </DocumentProperties>
 <OfficeDocumentSettings xmlns="urn:schemas-microsoft-
com:office:office">
  <DownloadComponents/>
  <LocationOfComponents HRef="file:///C:\OfficeXP\"/>
 </OfficeDocumentSettings>
 <ExcelWorkbook xmlns="urn:schemas-microsoft-com:office:excel">
  <WindowHeight>5130</WindowHeight>
  <WindowWidth>8475</WindowWidth>
  <WindowTopX>120</WindowTopX>
  <WindowTopY>75</WindowTopY>
  <ProtectStructure>False</ProtectStructure>
  <ProtectWindows>False</ProtectWindows>
 </ExcelWorkbook>
```

Listing 13-5: Web Query Information Is Also Saved in the XML Spreadsheet

```xml
<QueryTable xmlns="urn:schemas-microsoft-com:office:excel">
 <NoPreserveFormatting/>
 <Name>nwind?sql=SELECT+*+
 FROM+Authors+FOR+XML+AUTO&amp;root=root</Name>
 <AutoFormatFont/>
 <AutoFormatPattern/>
 <QuerySource>
  <QueryType>Web</QueryType>
  <EnableRedirections/>
  <RefreshedInXl9/>
```

Continued

Listing 13-5 *(continued)*

```
<EntirePage/>
<URLString
    x:HRef="http://dpower26/nwind?
    sql=SELECT+*+FROM+Authors+
    FOR+XML+AUTO&amp;root=root"/>
<VersionLastEdit>1</VersionLastEdit>
<VersionLastRefresh>1</VersionLastRefresh>
<VersionRefreshableMin>1</VersionRefreshableMin>
</QuerySource>
</QueryTable>
```

Some of the things that using the XML spreadsheet format will not preserve include any VBA project code and embedded OLE objects. Keep this in mind as you persist your XML in this way. Another way to export the XML content of a spreadsheet is to use the MSXML library and the XML support of Excel to send the XML elsewhere. In Listing 13-6, you see code that loads the content of a spreadsheet to export it to a remote source.

Listing 13-6: Sending the Contents of a Range to a Web Application As XML

```
Dim str As String
Dim oDoc As DOMDocument40
Dim oDoc2 As DOMDocument40
Dim oNode As MSXML2.IXMLDOMNode
Dim oXSL As MSXML2.DOMDocument40
Dim oRng As Range
Dim osvc As clsws_addauthor1

Set oDoc = New DOMDocument40
Set oDoc2 = New MSXML2.DOMDocument40
Set objRng = ActiveWorkbook.Worksheets("Authors") _
.Range("Author")
str = objRng.Value(xlRangeValueXMLSpreadsheet)
oDoc.loadXML str
oXSL.Load ActiveWorkbook.Path & "\AuthorTransform.xsl"
oDoc.transformNodeToObject oXSL, oDoc2
Set osvc = New clsws_addauthor1
osvc.wsm_AddAuthor (oDoc.XML)
```

This code uses three instances of the DOM to get the job done (two could be used, but three are used for clarity here). The first DOM is loaded with the content of the spreadsheet itself. However, it only loads the content of a named range, `"Author"`, within the spreadsheet. This spreadsheet is shown in Figure 13-14 with the named range highlighted to reveal the name. The value of the named range is exported as a fully well-formed XML string and loaded into a string variable. Then the string is used as the source for the first instance of the DOM, and another DOM is loaded with the instructions of an XSL stylesheet. That DOM is used to transform the XML content to a different structure. The contents of the newly created XML document are then shipped off to a .NET Web Service that receives the XML and does some additional processing after loading the XML into an XML document on the server.

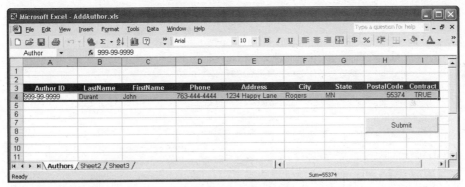

Figure 13-14: The Excel spreadsheet content to be exported to a remote system

You can imagine that this technique could be used to augment the kinds of things that Excel is so good at doing. For example, if Excel is used as a tool for creating new invoices, the invoice data could be exported to either a database system or a remote system (like the Web Service used here). The advantage would be that the XML sent to the remote system need not be cognizant of the way Excel works or structures XML. The remote system can be generic enough to receive invoice data from any system, as long as it conforms to the structure it expects. Excel is an excellent candidate for setting up data interchanges with these types of systems because of its powerful XML support.

Summary

In this chapter, we have taken a close look at working with XML in Microsoft Excel 2002. Excel is capable of importing and exporting XML natively. This means that no special instructions or steps need to be taken to begin using any well-formed XML file with Excel. We saw how Excel can take advantage of XML stylesheets both when importing and exporting. We saw that when importing XML programmatically we have the ability to apply more than one stylesheet when importing, whereas when using the user interface, only one stylesheet is supported. We also took a good look at Web queries, a feature in Excel that lets you import browser-parsed content from any Website. This includes XML. We could see that Web queries could be used to import and automatically format XML data from files located on a Website. We also saw how to import XML directly from SQL Server 2000, which has the capability to export database data as pure XML. We then looked at how to do these types of things programmatically. We probed the XML export features of Excel and saw how to work with XML a little more in VBA code. This included a survey of the XML spreadsheet format, a format used by Excel to persist spreadsheet data as fully well-formed document data. We finished off by looking at how to export Excel data to a .NET Web Service using the MSXML DOM object.

✦   ✦   ✦

XML Web Applications Using J2EE

P A R T

III

✦   ✦   ✦   ✦

In This Part

Chapter 14
XML Tools for J2EE:
IBM, Apache, Sun,
and Others

Chapter 15
Xerces

Chapter 16
Xalan

Chapter 17
XML APIs from Sun

✦   ✦   ✦   ✦

Part III builds on the basic concepts that were introduced in Parts I and II, showing readers how to create XML Web Applications using J2EE. We review sample code line-by-line, so previous Java/J2EE knowledge is not necessary to understand and work with the examples. Open source libraries for working with Java tools are referenced and specific code examples are provided for working with Xalan and Xerces. We also provide examples for the XML APIs in the Sun Java Web services Developer Pack (WSDP), including the Java API for XML Processing (JAXP), Java Architecture for XML Binding (JAXB), and Java Server Pages Standard Tag Library (JSTL) APIs.

XML Tools for J2EE: IBM, Apache, Sun, and Others

When you're working with XML in J2EE applications, you're working with code. Unfortunately for J2EE developers, the core Java classes, methods, and properties have absolutely nothing to do with XML. Fortunately for J2EE developers, however, J2EE does support a great deal of functionality when working with text, and XML is, after all, text. Even more fortunately for J2EE developers, there are several J2EE tools and code libraries that an XML developer can take advantage of to help develop and deploy J2EE XML applications in a timely and efficient manner. In this chapter, I'll review the tools and code libraries that turn Java developers into J2EE code powerhouses. (J2EE code powerhouses? Wow, I should be writing ad copy! But they really are good tools, and I'll show you why later in the chapter.)

Java and J2EE development tools have come a long way since I tried to develop XML code in Java way back in 1997. I say *tried*, because in those days, most Java development was done using Notepad. Compiling took place by calling batch files from the command line.

A couple of years later, Symantec Café and a few worthy competitors emerged on the scene. These integrated UI tools helped developers generate and compile code from GUI templates. But for those of you who used these tools to any extent, you probably remember that point in your application when you had to generate a flawed piece of code in the developer tool, copy it to Notepad, then debug it and compile it from the command line, again. And these tools were usually geared toward Java applets and sometimes applications, but rarely supported new J2EE features such as servlets.

Fortunately for today's developers, Java development environments have evolved into rock-solid code tools that generate and debug J2EE code, compile it, and let you test it on the J2EE application server of your choice. Unfortunately, prices for these tools have evolved along with their feature set, and they can be pricey for a feature set that meets the needs of professional developers. In this chapter I'll briefly cover the two most prominent developer tools: the IBM WebSphere Studio Application Developer and the Sun ONE Studio. I used WebSphere Studio Application Developer while developing most of the examples in this book.

Help for developing XML has evolved as well. Back in 1998, not only was XML code developed in Notepad, if you needed something to parse or generate XML documents, you created the parser or generator yourself. Today there are several excellent J2EE code libraries available for free that support basic functions such as parsing and transforming XML documents. Some of these come with source code, and some don't. In this chapter I'll review the offerings from IBM, Eclipse, Sun, and Apache. There are literally hundreds of other offerings that come and go over the years, but these providers offer consistency and reliability in their offerings, which are pretty good things if you want to base your applications on them. Many of the things I list here, and others, are also listed at `http://www.xmlsoftware.com/utilities.html`.

In subsequent chapters I'll show examples of the Xerces and Xalan libraries, the IBM XML Toolkit, and the XML parts of the Java Web Services Developer Pack (WSDP), formerly known as the Sun Java XML Pack.

IBM Tools

IBM provides one of the two prominent J2EE development tools, WebSphere Studio Application Developer. They also provide a lot of J2EE software for free download from the AlphaWorks Website. In addition to this, Free XML tutorials, articles and sample code are available from the IBM DeveloperWorks XML Zone.

WebSphere Studio Application Developer and Workbench

IBM's J2EE developer environment is based on the Eclipse platform and is called WebSphere Studio. WebSphere Studio is actually the name that is used to describe several "product configurations" of the base tool. The last time that I checked the

WebSphere Studio Website, there were nine configurations listed, all with similar-sounding and confusing names, but all starting with the WebSphere Studio prefix. However, there are really only two configuration options that XML developers need to focus on: WebSphere Studio Application Developer or WebSphere Studio Workbench.

The fist choice is *WebSphere Studio Application Developer (WSAD)*, which is a rich J2EE developer UI combined with tools and wizards to simplify XML and Web development tasks. Aside from J2EE, WSAD also supports JavaScript, Dynamic HTML, and Cascading Style Sheets. It also provides visual layout tools to create dynamic Websites with Java servlet or JavaServer Pages. WASD also includes a built-in XML development environment with support for Xerces, Xalan, and other code libraries, support for Rational ClearCase LT for software configuration management, and Apache AXIS-based Web service functionality for the creation, deployment, and publishing of Web services. IBM has even published a very good series of free online tutorials that cover building XML applications using WebSphere Studio application developer, which can be found at `http://www7b.software.ibm.com/wsdd/techjournal/0111_lau/lau.html`.

This advanced functionality does not come cheap, however. The good news is that there is a 60-day trial version that can be downloaded at the IBM DeveloperWorks WebSphere Studio Zone at `http://www7b.software.ibm.com/wsdd/zones/studio/`.

If WebSphere Studio Application Developer is simply too expensive and/or you take pride in coding your J2EE applications by hand, the second choice is *WebSphere Studio Workbench*. IBM has added several plug-ins to the base Eclipse Workbench platform and re-branded it as WebSphere Studio Workbench, which they offer as a free download at `http://www-3.ibm.com/software/ad/workbench`. (A free registration is required to download the software.) WebSphere Studio Workbench provides an efficient, if basic, developer UI for J2EE applications. The plug-in architecture of Eclipse-based products makes the platform easy to upgrade with customized tools and interfaces. Based on this architecture, it's possible to assemble a reasonable facsimile of WebSphere Studio Application Developer by downloading code libraries from Apache and SUN and free plug-ins from the Eclipse site. This approach, however, will take time and patience, and will never be as seamless as the WebSphere Studio Application Developer. But if you're a build-it-yourself developer on a tight budget, WebSphere Studio Workbench may be the way for you to go.

IBM AlphaWorks

IBM AlphaWorks (`http://alphaworks.ibm.com`) is a very important resource for anyone who has to code XML applications in J2EE. For those unfamiliar with the site, it contains a wealth of free tools and utilities that can be downloaded and integrated into an XML and J2EE developer's arsenal. The AlphaWorks Site also helps to dispel the notion of free tools as something in which you get what you pay for, or more specifically, don't get what you don't pay for. My experience to date with the

AlphaWorks tools is that they work well in most cases, and the only thing missing from comparative paid products are documentation, which is often compensated for with working examples. I've listed some of my favorites below, but there are many more, organized into XML subsections such as *XML-database* and *XML-DTD*. One caveat: Developers who want to work with these tools should download them as soon as possible, as the best AlphaWorks technologies are eventually rolled into commercial products and no longer offered as free downloads. For example, one of the most popular AlphaWorks downloads was the IBM XML toolkit, which included a number of great resources and examples for XML developers. Now parts of the XML Toolkit have been rolled into the WebSphere Studio Application Developer and the Eclipse Modeling Framework that I cover later in this chapter.

XML Parser for Java (XML4J)

XML Parser for Java is a validating XML parser and processor for parsing and generating XML data. It's based on Apache Xerces code, and supports several W3C XML-related recommendations through Java class methods and properties. These include the W3C XML Schema Recommendation 1.0, DOM Level 1, 2, and some of the DOM Level 3 Core and Load/Save Working Drafts. It also supports non-W3C standards and tools such as SAX 1 and 2, Sun's Java API for XML Processing (JAXP), and multilingual error messages. XML4J includes compiled classes and Java source code.

XML Integrator (XI)

One of the most difficult tasks in developing relation XML applications is providing a flexible platform for mapping constantly changing relational data structures to XML elements and attributes. XML Integrator is a tool for converting XML and relational data formats. It also processes conversions between LDAP data and XML. Developers can map structured data formats using Document Type Definition with Source Annotation (DTDSA) or XML Relational Transformation (XRT). DTDSA is a DTD with additional markup for mapping XML elements to rows and columns in a relational database. XRT is a scripting language based on XSL that uses SQL syntax to map elements to rows and columns of data.

The XI engine parses the DTDSA or the XRT and creates run-time objects that are cached for reuse. The run-time engine is contained in a JAR file and can be integrated with Xerces, Xalan, and JDBC drivers.

XML Security Suite

XML Security Suite Adds W3C-defined security features such as digital signature, encryption, and access control to XML documents and XML applications. These features have always been a challenge for XML developers, because they are transporting text over standard protocols that don't support advanced security features. The XML Security Suite includes support for the W3C *XML-Signature Syntax and Processing* and *XML Encryption Syntax and Processing Recommendations*. There is also support for XML Access Control functionality, partly supported by the W3C *Canonical XML Version 1.0 Working Draft*. The free download includes a .jar file containing supporting classes and a number of examples of the XML Security Suite code in use. A good introductory article can be found at the IBM DeveloperWorks XML Zone at `http://www-106.ibm.com/developerworks/security/library/x-xmlsecuritysuite/?dwzone=security`.

XML TreeDiff

XML TreeDiff is old technology (last updated in 1999) but is still extremely useful for comparing two XML documents to check for changes. TreeDiff consists of Java beans that enable differentiation of XML document DOMs. Differences are described as changes to nodes and tell you if a specific node has been changed, deleted, or inserted. XML TreeDiff uses an algorithm that enables a fast tree-matching procedure. Access to the code is either from the command line, or the code can be integrated into Java applications. TreeDiff includes tools for checking XML document differences and updating XML documents. There is also a GUI for displaying tree differences. TreeDiff also supports a reporting function, which writes result files in XML format.

Eclipse Tools

The eclipse.org Website (`http://www.eclipse.org`) is the central product of the Eclipse consortium. Eclipse is an open-source, freely distributable platform for tool integration. In essence, it provides a "lowest common denominator" for developers to integrate functionality into a development UI. IBM provided most of the code for the startup, and since then other large players have joined in at the board level, including Borland, MERANT, QNX Software Systems, Rational Software, Red Hat, SuSE, TogetherSoft, and Webgain2. Several other very large players have also joined as non-board members, including Sybase, Fujitsu, Hitachi, Oracle, SAP, and the Object Management Group (OMG).

Eclipse projects are broken down into three groups:

✦ **The Eclipse Project** is the original open-source software development project that is developing open-source developer UI platform.

✦ **The Eclipse Tools Project** was developed to provide services and support to tools developers who want to integrate their tools into the eclipse platform.

✦ **The Eclipse Technology Project** provides support for Eclipse project research, incubators, and education. Research projects explore programming languages, tools, and development environments applicable to the Eclipse project. Incubators implement new capabilities on the Eclipse platform and may or may not be based on research. Education projects develop educational materials, teaching aids, and courseware.

The Eclipse Modeling Framework

The tools project is probably the most interesting to XML developers, because this is where the *Eclipse Modeling Framework* is located. The Eclipse Modeling Framework (EMF) is composed of pieces taken from what used to be the IBM XML toolkit, and a few other places.

EMF is a framework for generating applications based on class models. EMF uses Java and XML to generate Java code from application models. The intention is to provide the same sort of functionality that is found in other, more expensive application architecture and modeling tools. In addition to a Java code generator, EMF saves objects as XML documents that can be transformed and adapted for use with other tools and applications. In addition, an updated model can regenerate the Java code, and updated Java code can be used to update the model.

Here's a listing of the EMF framework components:

✦ The EMF framework core includes a set of tools for describing models using metadata. The metadata starts with an instance of an object, and then describes all of the features of that object, including properties, methods, and so on. The framework core is implemented as a plug-in to the Eclipse platform UI.

✦ The EMF.Edit component contains reusable classes that developers can use to build of EMF model editors. Classes include support for class content, labels and source code. Also included is support for display of the classes in the Eclipse platform UI.

✦ The EMF.Codegen component generates J2EE code from an EMF model. Classes include support for a developer UI for specifying generation options and calling generators. Code can be generated for EMF models, implementation classes for editing and display of the model in the Eclipse Platform UI, and editors that manage the editing and display of the model in the Eclipse Platform UI.

Sun Tools

Sun owns the Sun One Studio Developer, which is the biggest competitor to IBM's WebSphere Studio Application Developer. Like IBM, Sun also provides a huge amount of J2EE and XML resources for free download from Sun's Java site. In addition, Free XML tutorials, articles, and sample code are available from the Sun Developer Services Website.

Sun ONE

Sun's open-source, free distribution offering is based on the former Forte Tools for Java. As with the IBM WebSphere Studio offerings, the plug-in architecture of Sun ONE-based products makes the platform easy to customize to a developer's tastes. Also like the IBM offering, Sun's developer tools offer a robust but expensive option and a simpler but free option. The Free Sun ONE Community Edition is the base platform for the very uncheap Sun ONE Enterprise edition. Like WebSphere Studio Workbench, Sun ONE Community Edition has some very good, if basic, features that can be updated for dedicated do-it-yourself types. All Sun One products are based on the open-source but sun-controlled NetBeans platform. Both flavors of Sun ONE studio can be downloaded from `http://www.sun.com/software/sundev`.

The Java Web Services Developer Pack

Sun's Java Web Services Developer Pack is a great tool for J2EE developers working with XML and Web service applications. Based on JCP (Java Community Process) API initiatives for XML, the Java Web Services Developer Pack contains several XML interface APIs that act as proxies between compliant tools such as parsers and transformation engines. These APIS are designed to shield developers from having to recode Java when a new version of a J2EE tool comes out. For example, a J2EE developer using the Java API for XML Processing (JAXP) API to access a DOM1 parser could theoretically move to a DOM2 or SAX parser with no change to their Java source code. The updated parser is accessible by changing the pluggable interface reference from DOM1 to any other JAXP-compliant parser.

The Java Web Services Developer Pack is downloadable from Sun at `http://java.sun.com/xml/`.The following sections outline the XML components and their associated benefits. I'll cover the Web services components of the Java Web Services Developer Pack in the Web services part of this book.

Cross-Reference   Examples of using the XML components of the Java Web Services Developer Pack (listed below) are covered in Chapter 17. The Web service components are covered in Chapter 33.

JAXP (Java API for XML Processing)

The Java API for XML Processing (JAXP) supports processing of XML documents using DOM 1, 2, and some of DOM 3, SAX 1 and 2, and XSLT. JAXP enables applications to change the processor that is used to parse and transform XML documents without changing the underlying source code for the application that is doing the parsing or transformation. JAXP also supports the W3C XML Schema 1.0 Recommendation and an XSLT compiler (XSLTC).

JAXB (Java Architecture for XML Binding)

JAXB automates mapping between XML documents and Java objects. It makes elements and attributes classes as well as properties and methods by marshalling and unmarshalling them in a customized XML document.

JAXM (Java API for XML Messaging)

JAXM provides an Interface for SOAP messages, including SOAP with attachments. Because JAXM is based on XML, the messaging format can be changed to other message standards that support XML formats.

JAX-RPC (Java API for XML-Based RPC)

JAX-RPC provides an Interface for XML messages using an RPC transport, including, but not limited to, SOAP calls over RPC to Web Services.

JAXR (Java API for XML Registries)

JAXR provides an interface for XML registries, supporting UDDI and OASIS/U.N./CEFACT ebXML Registry and Repository standards, among others.

SAAJ (SOAP with Attachments API for Java)

SAAJ provides support for producing, sending, and receiving SOAP messages with attachments. Sun's SAAJ library provides an interface to the features and capabilities described in the W3C SOAP 1.1 attachment note, which have not changed much in their current form. The current W3C specification is the W3C SOAP 1.2 Attachment Feature, currently in the Working Draft stage of the W3C Recommendation process.

The W3C SOAP 1.2 Attachment Feature Working Draft states that a SOAP message may include attachments directly in the W3C SOAP body structure. The SOAP body and header may contain only XML content. Non-XML data must be contained in an attachment under the SOAP body. This provides facilities for providing binary information and non-XML data in a SOAP envelope.

 SOAP and SOAP attachments are covered in more detail in Chapters 23 and 24, respectively.

Apache Tools

The Apache XML Project is part of the Apache Software Foundation, a nonprofit consortium that provides organizational, legal, and financial support for Apache open-source software projects. Apache XML Projects are documented at `http://xml.apache.org/`. The goal of the Apache XML projects is to provide high-quality standards-based XML solutions that are developed in an open and cooperative fashion. Apache also provides implementation classes of many W3C specifications, such as Xerces for DOM, Xalan for XSLT, and AXIS for SOAP. Because of this, the Apache projects and participants are in a unique position to provide feedback to the W3C XML working group. Feedback usually involves implementation issues that result from W3C Recommendation implementation attempts. I'm listing the most relevant XML projects here, and anything that has been updated in the last six months. For a full list of Apache XML projects, go to http://xml.apache.org/.

Xerces: XML parser in Java and C++, Perl and COM

The Xerces parser is a validating parser that is available in Java and C++. Apparently, the parser was named after the now extinct Xerces blue butterfly, a native of the San Francisco peninsula.

Xerces the parser fully supports the W3C XML DOM (Level 1 and 2) standards, the DOM3 standards when they finally become a W3C recommendation, and SAX version 2. Xerces is a validating parser and provides support for XML Document validation against W3C Schemas and DTDs. The C++ version of the Xerces parser also includes a Perl wrapper and a COM wrapper that works with the MSXML parser.

Xalan: XSL stylesheet processors in Java & C++

One of the first Java transformation engines was the LotusXSL engine, which IBM donated to the Apache Software Group, where it became the Xalan Transformation engine. Since then, Apache has developed Xalan version 2, which implements a pluggable interface into Xalan 1 and 2, as well as integrated SAX and DOM parsers. Both of the Java versions of XALAN implement the W3C Recommendations XSLT and XPath. Xalan is currently available in Java and C++.

FOP: XSL Formatting Object processor in Java

The Apache FOP server is the original and most popular FOP server. The engine can be run from a command prompt, integrated with J2EE code, or plugged in to one of several XSL:FO editors on the market, a partial list of which can also be found at http://www.xmlsoftware.com/xslfo.html. FOP is written in Java 1.2 and is mainly used for converting XML documents into PDF documents. The source XML document can be an XML document or a passed DOM document or set of SAX events.

Cross-Reference For an example of a XSL:FO stylesheet that uses the Apache FOP server to convert an XML document to a PDF, please refer to Chapter 9.

AXIS: The Apache Implementation of the W3C SOAP Recommendation

IBM donated the SOAP4J code library to the Apache XML project, where it became the Apache SOAP project, with a full implementation of the W3C SOAP 1.1 Recommendation. The latest implementation of the Apache SOAP project has been renamed AXIS, just to keep us on our toes. *AXIS* stands for *Apache eXtensible Interaction System*, but is still based the W3C SOAP Recommendation, with the equally inscrutable acronym of Simple Object Access Protocol. AXIS supports all of the W3C SOAP 1.1 Recommendation, and most of the SOAP 1.2 Working Draft.

Cross-Reference   SOAP is covered in more detail in Chapters 23 and 24, respectively.

Xindice: A native XML database

Apache Xindice (pronounced *zeen-dee-chay*) is a database implemented in XML to store XML data. The idea is that XML data that is already in XML format doesn't need to be converted to another format. But it probably does need to be transformed to another XML structure, or parsed into a destination format. It is an interesting cutting-edge implementation. The Xindice query language is XPath. The XML:DB API(http://www.xmldb.org/xapi/) is used for record updates and for Java development. This enables other applications and languages to access Xindice via XML-RPC.

XML Parsing Code: XML4J, Xerces, and JAXP: What Is What?

The latest versions of Apache Xerces, IBM XML for Java (XML4J), and Sun's JAXP parser are all validating parsers that support almost identical functionality. All of these downloads also support both the DOM and SAX interfaces for XML document parsing. So the logical question is, which parser should you use: XML4J, Xerces, or JAXP?

The answer is, if you're using one, you're probably using them all. Java parsers tend to reuse parts of other Java parsers to implement their functionality. For example, the parser in XML4J is an implementation of the Xerces parser, which IBM heavily contributes to, and has subsequently reused for the DOM parser in XML4J. Consequently, Java developers have to keep a close watch of the version of parser they are using to ensure compatibility with their current code implementations. Xerces is usually the most up-to-date parser code, and XML4J usually adopts new versions of Xerces a month or two after they are issued.

JAXP is another case entirely. JAXP is a "pluggable" interface that provides access to functionality, but doesn't technically provide the functionality. JAXP changes the processor that is used to parse and transform XML documents without changing the underlying source code for the application that is doing the parsing or transformation.

Summary

In this chapter, you were introduced to XML tools for J2EE developers:

✦ An introduction to IBM WebSphere Studio

✦ IBM AlphaWorks Offerings:

- IBM XML for Java (XML4J)
- XML Integrator (XI)
- IBM XML Security Suite

✦ Eclipse Offering:

- The Eclipse Modeling Framework

✦ Sun ONE Studio

✦ The XML components of the Java Web Services Developer Pack

✦ The Apache XML Project: Xalan, Xerces, and others

✦ The Difference between XML4J, Xerces, and JAXP|BM WebSphere Studio

In the next few chapters, we'll be putting many of these tools to use in practical examples. We'll start with a review of Xerces and parsing XML documents with J2EE in Chapter 15. Chapter 16 will cover Xalan and transforming XML documents with J2EE. Chapter 17 will cover the XML components of the Java Web Services Developer Pack in great detail, with examples and documentation.

✦   ✦   ✦

Xerces

As I said in the introduction to Chapter 14, when you're working with XML in J2EE applications, you're working with text. The Apache Xerces API, along with Xalan, AXIS, and a few other Apache offerings, ease the burden of J2EE XML developers by providing "canned" code that can be reused in J2EE XML applications. In this chapter, I'll introduce you to Apache Xerces, what it is, where it came from, and how to integrate Xerces functionality into your applications.

The Apache XML Project (`http://xml.apache.org/`) is part of the Apache Software Foundation, a non-profit consortium that provides organizational, legal, and financial support for Apache open-source software projects, all of which can be seen at `http://www.apache.org/`.

Xerces is a set of Java classes, properties, and methods that supports XML document parsing. Xerces is also an implementation and reference code library for the W3C XML DOM (Level 1 and 2) standards. It also provides classes, properties, and methods that keep up with the current Working Draft of the W3C DOM Level 3 standards, in preparation for the day that DOM Level 3 attains W3C Recommendation status. Xerces also supports SAX version 2. Xerces parser classes are available in Java and C++. Xerces is a validating parser, and provides support for XML document validation against W3C Schemas and DTDs. The C++ version of the Xerces parser also includes a Perl wrapper and a COM wrapper.

Xerces ships as a set of compiled classes in a .jar file. There is an optional source code download as well. The source code and classes can be reused and rewritten, in the spirit of open source software and according to the Apache Software Foundation license, which can be found at `http://xml.apache.org/LICENSE`.

Cross-Reference This chapter will focus on the code required to make XML document parsing work. For a full reference on XML document parsing fundamentals, including listings of DOM and SAX documentation, please refer to Chapters 4, 5, and 6.

For those of you working with IBM's XML for Java classes (XML4J), the parser in XML4J is an implementation of the Xerces parser, which IBM heavily contributes to, and has subsequently reused for the DOM parser in XML4J. Xerces is usually the most up-to-date parser code available, and XML4J usually adopts new versions of Xerces a month or two after they are issued. Information on the current version of Xerces that is embedded in XML4J can be found listed at `http://alphaworks.ibm.com/tech/xml4j`.

Sun's Java API for XML Processing (JAXP) API can also be used to access Xerces via its "pluggable interface" architecture. JAXP provides access to Xerces functionality, but doesn't technically provide that functionality. JAXP can change the processor that is used to parse and transform XML documents without changing the underlying source code for the application that is doing the parsing or transformation.

For more information on JAXP, please refer to Chapter 17.

Downloading and Installing Xerces

If your J2EE IDE doesn't ship with Xerces parser pre-installed (most do), the most recent Java version can be downloaded from `http://xml.apache.org/xerces2-j/index.html`. Xerces is contained in a compressed zip file format (tar for non-Windows users) and is currently around 5MB in size. You also have an option of downloading just the .jar files (referred to as the "binaries" download) or the .jar files and the source code (referred to as the "source" download). Once downloaded, Xerces can be decompressed and copied to the directory of your choice. Table 15-1 shows the Xerces component files and default subdirectory locations for the "binary" download version.

Table 15-1 Xerces Components	
Interface Name	**Description**
xercesImpl.jar	Contains implementation classes for all of the supported Xerces parsers. Currently this includes DOM Level 1 and 2, some of the DOM W3C DOM Level 3 Working Draft specifications, and SAX version 2.
xmlParserAPIs.jar	Contains the Core Java API classes.
xercesSamples.jar	Sample class files.
data/	Directory containing sample XML data, DTD, and Schema.

Interface Name	Description
docs/	Directory containing Xerces API and implementation class documentation.
samples/	Directory containing sample source code. Source for samples is included in the binary and the source distribution.

Once the Xerces distribution file is downloaded, decompressed, and copied to its destination, the documentation for the distribution can be read by opening the index.html file in the /docs directory.

Parsing XML Documents in J2EE

As I outlined in Chapters 4, 5, and 6, there are two options for parsing XML documents, Document Object Model (DOM), and Simple API for XML (SAX). Xerces supports both methods in J2EE.

DOM builds a representation of the XML document as a node tree in memory. DOM methods navigate through the XML document, as shown in Chapter 5. Node properties supply node values. DOM node trees stay resident in memory as long as the application that created the node tree is in memory, and DOM nodes are available to an application at any time.

SAX parses documents sequentially, based on events in an XML document. SAX methods are used to track document events, such as the start and end of an element. SAX methods also return values from XML document objects during an event, which provides XML document values to a calling program. Unlike DOM, SAX events are only in memory as long as the event is in memory. This means that XML document values that are returned from events have to be recorded to variables to be used by an application.

In the examples for this chapter, I'll show J2EE code for parsing a small and simple XML document into a DOM node tree. We'll also show an example of parsing a more complex XML document using SAX events.

Parsing XML documents with DOM

I'll be parsing the same very simple XML document for the DOM and SAX examples. Aside from being easy to follow, the very simple XML document in Listing 15-1 is also a generalized example of the type of document that is practical for DOM parsing. The document is so small and simple that performance will not be an issue, and I may want to reuse nodes in the document, a feature that SAX can't provide.

The Java source code and the XML document used in this chapter are available for download from the www.XMLProgrammingBible.com Website.

Listing 15-1: A Very Simple XML Document

```xml
<?xml version="1.0" encoding="UTF-8"?>
<rootelement>
   <firstelement position="1">
      <level1 children="0">This is level 1 of the nested
      elements</level1>
   </firstelement>
   <secondelement position="2">
      <level1 children="1">
         <level2>This is level 2 of the nested
         elements</level2>
      </level1>
   </secondelement>
</rootelement>
```

Listing 15-2 shows us the code used to parse the simple XML document. I'll show the code in its entirety, and then break it up to explain the most important parts. The code reads through an XML document, parses the document into org.w3c.dom nodes using the org.apache.xerces DOM parser, and prints output to the screen about the types of nodes and values that are in the source XML document.

Listing 15-2: Code for Parsing the Very Simple XML Document: SimpleParsingWithDOM.java

```java
import java.io.*;
import org.w3c.dom.*;
import org.apache.xerces.parsers.DOMParser;
import org.xml.sax.SAXException;

public class SimpleParsingWithDOM {

    public static void main(String[] args) {
        SimpleParsingWithDOM SPWD = new SimpleParsingWithDOM();
    }

    public SimpleParsingWithDOM() {
        String XMLToParse =
        "C:/jdk1.3.1_01/bin/XMLBookSource/XMLDocs/verysimpleXML.xml";
        DOMParser parser = new DOMParser();
```

```
        try {
            parser.parse(XMLToParse);
            Document document = parser.getDocument();
            nodeReader(document);

        } catch (IOException ie) {
            System.err.println(ie);
        }
        catch (SAXException se) {
            System.err.println(se);
        }
    }


    private void nodeReader(Node node) {

        if(node.hasChildNodes()) {
            NodeList children = node.getChildNodes();
            if (children != null) {
                for (int i=0; i< children.getLength(); i++) {
                    Node ThisNode= children.item(i);
                    String name = children.item(i).getNodeName();
                    String localName = ThisNode.getLocalName();
                    String uri       = ThisNode.getNamespaceURI();
                    String prefix    = ThisNode.getPrefix();
                    String value     = ThisNode.getNodeValue();
                    String NodeText=null;
                    int type = ThisNode.getNodeType();


                    switch (type) {
                        case 1: NodeText = "Node type 1: Element Constant:
                        ELEMENT_NODE \r\n";break;
                        case 2: NodeText = "Node type 2: Attribute
                        Constant: ATTRIBUTE_NODE \r\n";break;
                        case 3: NodeText = "Node type 3: Text Constant:
                        TEXT_NODE \r\n";break;
                        case 4: NodeText = "Node type 4: CDATA Section
                        Constant: CDATA_SECTION_NODE \r\n";break;
                        case 5: NodeText = "Node type 5: Entity Reference
                        Constant: ENTITY_REFERENCE_NODE \r\n";break;
                        case 6: NodeText = "Node type 6: Entity Constant:
                        ENTITY_NODE \r\n";break;
                        case 7: NodeText = "Node type 7: Processing
                        Instruction Constant: PROCESSING_INSTRUCTION_NODE
                        \r\n";break;
                        case 8: NodeText = "Node type 8: Comment Constant:
                        COMMENT_NODE \r\n";break;
                        case 9: NodeText = "Node type 9: Document Constant:
                        DOCUMENT_NODE \r\n";break;
```

Continued

Listing 15-2 *(continued)*

```
        case 10: NodeText = "Node type 10: Document Type
        Declaration Constant: DOCUMENT_TYPE_NODE
        \r\n";break;
        case 11: NodeText = "Node type 11: Document
        Fragment Constant: DOCUMENT_FRAGMENT_NODE
        \r\n";break;
        case 12: NodeText = "Node type 12: Notation
        Constant: NOTATION_NODE \r\n";break;
        //Remove this comment when DOM supports the
        XPATH_NAMESPACE_NODE Constant
        //case 13: NodeText = "Node type 13: W3C DOm Level
        3 XPathNamespace Constant:
        XPATH_NAMESPACE_NODE";break;
        default: NodeText = "Not a valid W3C Node type
        \r\n";

    }

    String nodeString = NodeText;

    nodeString += ("Name: " + name + "\r\n");
    if (localName != null) {
        nodeString += ("Local Name: " + localName +
    "\r\n");
    }
    if (prefix != null) {
        nodeString += ("Prefix: " + prefix + "\r\n");
    }
    if (uri != null) {
        nodeString += ("Namespace URI: " + uri + "\r\n");
    }

    if (type == ThisNode.ELEMENT_NODE) {

        if (ThisNode.hasAttributes())  {
            String Attributes = null;
            NamedNodeMap AttributesList =
            node.getAttributes();
            for(int j = 0; j < AttributesList.getLength();
            j++) {
            nodeString +=("Attribute Name: " +
            AttributesList.item(j).getNodeName() +
            "\r\nAttribute Value: " +
            AttributesList.item(j).getNodeValue()+"\r\n" );
            }
        }
    }
```

```
            if (value != null) {

                nodeString += ("Value: " + value + "\r\n");
            }

            System.out.println(nodeString);

            if(children.item(i).hasChildNodes()) {
                nodeReader(children.item(i));

            }
        }
      }
    }
  }


}
```

Let's break down what the code is doing piece by piece. The first part of the code imports classes that you need for this Java class to function. `java.io` classes are used to write output to the screen. `org.w3c.dom` classes are used to track nodes that are produced when parsing takes place. Parsing is facilitated through the org.apache.xerces.parser classes. It may seem a little odd to use `org.xml.sax` classes in a DOM parsing example, but it's actually very normal. The event-based `SAXException` class is used to catch parsing events from all types of parsing in Xerces.

```
import java.io.*;
import org.w3c.dom.*;
import org.apache.xerces.parsers.DOMParser;
import org.apache.xerces.dom.*;
import org.xml.sax.SAXException;
```

Next, the code creates a class, which implements a main method, which calls a constructor, which creates a new instance of the `SimpleParsingWithDOM` class.

```
public class SimpleParsingWithDOM {

    public static void main(String[] args) {
        SimpleParsingWithDOM SPWD = new SimpleParsingWithDOM();
    }

    public SimpleParsingWithDOM() {
```

The `SimpleParsingWithDOM` class identifies a new document to parse. In this case, the XML document has to be in the same directory as this code, and is named `verysimpleXML.xml`. The code parses the XML document into W3C nodes using the parse method of the `org.apache.xerces.parsers.DOMParser.parser` class. Next, the `nodeReader` class is called, which reads through the nodes and analyzes them. Note that the code catches an `ioException` if there are any errors associated with reading or writing to the output that is produced, and a SAX exception if there are any parsing errors.

```
String XMLToParse = "verysimpleXML.xml";
DOMParser parser = new DOMParser();

try {
    parser.parse(XMLToParse);
    Document document = parser.getDocument();
    nodeReader(document);

} catch (IOException ie) {
    System.err.println(ie);
}
catch (SAXException se) {
    System.err.println(se);
}
}
```

The `NodeReader` class analyzes each node and builds output that is printed to the screen. The `SimpleParsingWithDOM` class passes the parsed document to the `NodeReader` class as a parameter. The XML document contains a document node, which is the first node in the DOM node tree. The first thing that the `NodeReader` class does is check to see if the document tree has any nodes using the `getChildNodes()` method. If there are children, they are put into a Node list. Next, a loop iterates through each of the child nodes and gathers information about that node, using Xerces node methods.

```
private void nodeReader(Node node) {

    if(node.hasChildNodes()) {
        NodeList children = node.getChildNodes();
        if (children != null) {
            for (int i=0; i< children.getLength(); i++) {
                Node ThisNode= children.item(i);
                String name = children.item(i).getNodeName();
                String localName = ThisNode.getLocalName();
                String uri       = ThisNode.getNamespaceURI();
                String prefix     = ThisNode.getPrefix();
                String value      = ThisNode.getNodeValue();
```

After information about the node has been gathered, values can be assigned to the node based on node type. The node numbers and constants listed below are part of the DOM recommendation, and map to the values assigned. I've added the DOM 3 XPathNamespace node type, but commented it out for now. It can be uncommented when Xerces recognizes it as a valid node type; until then, the XPathNamespace node type generates a compiler error.

Cross-Reference For more information on DOM constants, properties, and methods, please refer to Chapter 5.

```
String NodeText=null;
int type = ThisNode.getNodeType();


switch (type) {
    case 1: NodeText = "Node type 1: Element Constant:
    ELEMENT_NODE \r\n";break;
    case 2: NodeText = "Node type 2: Attribute
    Constant: ATTRIBUTE_NODE \r\n";break;
    case 3: NodeText = "Node type 3: Text Constant:
    TEXT_NODE \r\n";break;
    case 4: NodeText = "Node type 4: CDATA Section
    Constant: CDATA_SECTION_NODE \r\n";break;
    case 5: NodeText = "Node type 5: Entity Reference
    Constant: ENTITY_REFERENCE_NODE \r\n";break;
    case 6: NodeText = "Node type 6: Entity Constant:
    ENTITY_NODE \r\n";break;
    case 7: NodeText = "Node type 7: Processing
    Instruction Constant: PROCESSING_INSTRUCTION_NODE
    \r\n";break;
    case 8: NodeText = "Node type 8: Comment Constant:
    COMMENT_NODE \r\n";break;
    case 9: NodeText = "Node type 9: Document Constant:
    DOCUMENT_NODE \r\n";break;
    case 10: NodeText = "Node type 10: Document Type
    Declaration Constant: DOCUMENT_TYPE_NODE
    \r\n";break;
    case 11: NodeText = "Node type 11: Document
    Fragment Constant: DOCUMENT_FRAGMENT_NODE
    \r\n";break;
    case 12: NodeText = "Node type 12: Notation
    Constant: NOTATION_NODE \r\n";break;
    //Remove this comment when DOM supports the
    XPATH_NAMESPACE_NODE Constant
    //case 13: NodeText = "Node type 13: W3C DOm Level
    3 XPathNamespace Constant:
    XPATH_NAMESPACE_NODE";break;
    default: NodeText = "Not a valid W3C Node type
    \r\n";

}
```

Next, optional values are assigned to a string that displays information about the node in the output. The node name is always part of a node. The node local name, prefix, and URI are for objects with namespace values.

```
String nodeString = NodeText;

nodeString += ("Name: " + name + "\r\n");
if (localName != null) {
    nodeString += ("Local Name: " + localName +
"\r\n");
}
if (prefix != null) {
    nodeString += ("Prefix: " + prefix + "\r\n");
}
if (uri != null) {
    nodeString += ("Namespace URI: " + uri + "\r\n");
}
```

Next, the code gathers a little more information if the node is an element type node and has any associated attributes. The attributes of an element are loaded into a `NamedNodeMap`, which is then iterated through to gather attribute names and values.

```
if (type == ThisNode.ELEMENT_NODE) {

    if (ThisNode.hasAttributes())  {
        String Attributes = null;
        NamedNodeMap AttributesList =
        node.getAttributes();
        for(int j = 0; j < AttributesList.getLength();
        j++) {
        nodeString +=("Attribute Name: " +
        AttributesList.item(j).getNodeName() +
        "\r\nAttribute Value: " +
        AttributesList.item(j).getNodeValue()+"\r\n" );
        }
    }
}
```

The `nodeString` is the string that has been gathering text values from the node for displaying the output. The last thing that is gathered is the node value, if there is any. The gathered node information is then sent to the screen using `System.out.println`.

```
if (value != null) {

    nodeString += ("Value: " + value + "\r\n");
```

```
        }

        System.out.println(nodeString);
```

The next part of the code checks to see if the current node has any child nodes. If it does, the `nodeReader` class calls itself again, and repeats the process to read nodes as deep as it needs to go in the node level nesting.

```
        if(children.item(i).hasChildNodes()) {
            nodeReader(children.item(i));
```

Listing 15-3 shows the resulting output when the `SimpleParsingWithDOM` class is applied to the VerySimpleXML document.

Listing 15-3: The Results of the SimpleParsingWithDOM Class When Applied to the VerySimpleXML Document

```
Node type 1: Element Constant: ELEMENT_NODE
Name: rootelement
Local Name: rootelement
Node type 1: Element Constant: ELEMENT_NODE
Name: firstelement
Local Name: firstelement
Node type 1: Element Constant: ELEMENT_NODE
Name: level1
Local Name: level1
Attribute Name: position
Attribute Value: 1
Node type 3: Text Constant: TEXT_NODE
Name: #text
Value: This is level 1 of the nested elements
Node type 1: Element Constant: ELEMENT_NODE
Name: secondelement
Local Name: secondelement
Node type 1: Element Constant: ELEMENT_NODE
Name: level1
Local Name: level1
Attribute Name: position
Attribute Value: 2
Node type 1: Element Constant: ELEMENT_NODE
Name: level2
Local Name: level2
Node type 3: Text Constant: TEXT_NODE
Name: #text
Value: This is level 2 of the nested elements
```

Parsing XML documents with SAX

For the SAX example, I'll use the same source XML document, which is shown in Listing 15-1. Normally, you would use SAX to parse a more complicated and longer XML document. The general idea is that larger and more complex documents are more quickly parsed if SAX is used. Listing 15-4 shows the SAX document parsing example. I'll break down the code after the full listing, as I did with the DOM example.

Listing 15-4: Parsing XML Documents with SAX: SimpleParsingWithSAX.java

```java
import java.io.*;
import org.xml.sax.*;
import org.xml.sax.helpers.DefaultHandler;
import org.apache.xerces.parsers.SAXParser;

public class SimpleParsingWithSAX extends DefaultHandler {
    String eventString = "";

    public static void main(String[] args) {
        SimpleParsingWithSAX SPWS = new SimpleParsingWithSAX();
    }

    public SimpleParsingWithSAX(){
        String XMLToParse =
        "C:/jdk1.3.1_01/bin/XMLBookSource/XMLDocs/verysimpleXML.xml";

        SAXParser parser = new SAXParser();
        parser.setContentHandler(this);

        try{
            parser.parse(XMLToParse);
        } catch (SAXException e) {
            System.err.println(e);
        } catch (IOException e) {
            System.err.println(e);
        }
    }

    public void processingInstruction( String target, String instruction ){
        eventString +="ProcessingInstruction() Event - Target:" + target +
        " Instruction:" + instruction + "\r\n";
    }

    public void startDocument() {
        eventString +="StartDocument() Event \r\n";
    }
```

```java
    public void startPrefixMapping( String prefix, String uri ) {
        eventString +="startPrefixMapping() Event - Prefix:" + prefix + "
        URI:" + uri + "\r\n";
    }

    public void startElement(String uri, String localname, String qname,
    Attributes attributes){
        eventString += "startElement() Event: " + localname + "\r\n";

        for (int i = 0; i < attributes.getLength(); i++) {
            eventString +=  "Attribute Name: "+
            attributes.getLocalName(i)+"\r\n";
            eventString += "Attribute Value: " +
            attributes.getValue(i)+"\r\n";

        }
    }

    public void endPrefixMapping( String prefix ) {
        eventString += "endPrefixMapping() Event - Prefix:" + prefix +
        "\r\n";
    }

    public void characters(char[] cdata, int start, int length){
        String textvalue = new String(cdata, start, length);
        if (!textvalue.trim().equals("")){
            eventString += "Text: "+ textvalue + "\r\n";
        }
    }

    public void ignorableWhitespace( char[] cdata, int start, int end ) {
        eventString += "ignorableWhitespace() Event \r\n";
    }

    public void endElement(String uri, String local, String qName){
        eventString += "endElement() Event: " + local + "\r\n";
    }

    public void skippedEntity( String name ) {
        eventString += "skippedEntity() Event(): " + name;
    }

    public void endDocument(){
        eventString += "endDocument() Event";
        System.out.println(eventString);
    }
}
```

Let's break down what the SAX code is doing piece by piece. As in the DOM example, the first part of the code imports classes that you need for this Java class to function. `java.io` classes are used to write output to the screen. Parsing is facilitated through the `org.apache.xerces` parser classes. `org.xml.sax` contains the classes that manage all of the SAX events.

```
import java.io.*;
import org.xml.sax.*;
import org.xml.sax.helpers.DefaultHandler;
import org.apache.xerces.parsers.SAXParser;
```

The `DefaultHandler` class is a grab bag of properties and methods in various SAX 2 interfaces with all having one thing in common: They are all *callback* methods. SAX callback methods return something when they are triggered by an event. The event actions are predefined in the application code using these methods. When a SAX parser encounters an event, the method is triggered. This invokes an action in the code. `DefaultHandler` is very useful for developers who are developing a bare-bones parsing solution using SAX. `DefaultHandler` implements access to the key methods of `ContentHandler`, `DTDHandler`, `EntityResolver`, and `ErrorHandler` in one class.

Next, the code creates a class and defines the `eventString` string. This string is used to gather event data while the document is being parsed.

The `SimpleParsingWithSAX` class implements a main method, which calls a constructor, which creates a new instance of the `SimpleParsingWithSAX` class.

```
public class SimpleParsingWithSAX extends DefaultHandler {
    String eventString = "";

    public static void main(String[] args) {
        SimpleParsingWithSAX SPWS = new SimpleParsingWithSAX();
    }
```

Next, the document is parsed by calling the `setContentHandler` method. `ContentHandler` is the main interface for a SAX 2 document's content. `XMLReader` uses `ContentHandler` to track all of the SAX events for an XML document. When a document is parsed, `ContentHandler` tracks all of the events that are being caught while the document is being parsed. As in the last example, an `ioException` catches any errors associated with the output that is produced, and a SAX exception catches parsing errors.

```
    public SimpleParsingWithSAX(){
        String XMLToParse = "verysimpleXML.xml";

        SAXParser parser = new SAXParser();
        parser.setContentHandler(this);
```

```
        try{
            parser.parse(XMLToParse);
        } catch (SAXException e) {
            System.err.println(e);
        } catch (IOException e) {
            System.err.println(e);
        }
    }
```

Next the events that `ContentHandler` is watching for are defined. I've organized them in the same approximate order that they would be encountered by a parser in an XML document. `processingInstruction` is triggered when the parser encounters a processing instruction. `startDocument` is triggered when the root element is encountered in an XML document. `startPrefix` explicitly maps a prefix to a URI. This is used with the `startElement` and `endElement` events to map a prefix to a URI at time of parsing. The prefix and/or URI do not need to be in the original XML document.

Note `processingInstruction` is not triggered for XML declarations, which are technically a processing instruction. It's only triggered for processing instructions located between the `startDocument()` and `endDocument()` events.

```
public void processingInstruction( String target, String instruction ){
    eventString +="ProcessingInstruction() Event - Target:" + target +
    " Instruction:" + instruction + "\r\n";
}

public void startDocument() {
    eventString +="StartDocument() Event \r\n";
}

public void startPrefixMapping( String prefix, String uri ) {
    eventString +="startPrefixMapping() Event - Prefix:" + prefix + "
    URI:" + uri + "\r\n";
}
```

`startElement` is triggered when the parser encounters the beginning of an element. Attributes are part of the `startElement` event.

Note There are no `startAttribute` and `endAttribute` events in SAX. On first look at SAX, handling attribute events like other document content events may seem logical, but attributes are only associated with elements, and there are enough exceptions when working with groups of attributes to warrant that they have their own interface. Attributes in SAX are returned by the `startElement` event in their own Attributes object, which is manipulated using the attributes interface, as shown here.

```
public void startElement(String uri, String localname, String qname,
Attributes attributes){
    eventString += "startElement() Event: " + localname + "\r\n";

    for (int i = 0; i < attributes.getLength(); i++) {
        eventString +=  "Attribute Name: "+
        attributes.getLocalName(i)+"\r\n";
        eventString += "Attribute Value: " +
        attributes.getValue(i)+"\r\n";

    }
}
```

endPrefixMapping is triggered when the ending of the explicit mapping of a pre-fix to a URI is encountered. characters is triggered when the parser encounters text data. ignorableWhitespace is triggered when the parser encounters text that it considers ignorable. Usually this is spaces, carriage returns, line feeds, and tabs.

```
public void endPrefixMapping( String prefix ) {
    eventString += "endPrefixMapping() Event - Prefix:" + prefix +
    "\r\n";
}

public void characters(char[] cdata, int start, int length){
    String textvalue = new String(cdata, start, length);
    if (!textvalue.trim().equals("")){
        eventString += "Text: "+ textvalue + "\r\n";
    }
}

public void ignorableWhitespace( char[] cdata, int start, int end ) {
    eventString += "ignorableWhitespace() Event \r\n";
}
```

endElement is triggered when the end of an element is encountered. skipped Entity is triggered when the parser encounters a skipped entity. Skipped entities are entity values that were not resolved by a DTD reference, either because the parser did not validate against a DTD or resolve entities, or the parser couldn't resolve an entity for whatever reason. This condition triggers a skippedEntity event.

```
public void endElement(String uri, String local, String qName){
    eventString += "endElement() Event: " + local + "\r\n";
}

public void skippedEntity( String name ) {
    eventString += "skippedEntity() Event(): " + name;
}
```

endDocument is always the last event in a SAX parse. In this case, we use this fact to print the eventString string to the screen. eventString has been collecting information on events and XML document data using the parse, and now the data is dumped to the screen. I prefer collecting all output data and sending it to the screen at once over the regular method, which is printing each line from each event individually. The first reason for this approach is that if you collect the data in a single string, you have the option to pass the string to another class or to a file, as well as to the screen. Second, the data in the string can be further manipulated before being displayed. The third reason is that the data does not need to be shown if an error occurs during event processing. Instead, an error message string can be created that incorporates the incomplete SAX output.

```
public void endDocument(){
    eventString += "endDocument() Event";
    System.out.println(eventString);
```

Once the last event in the XML document is encountered (the endDocument() event), the collected string is passed to the screen. Listing 15-5 shows the results of the Sax parsing.

Listing 15-5: Results for the SAX Parsing Example When Applied to the VerySimpleXML Document

```
StartDocument() Event
startElement() Event: rootelement
startElement() Event: firstelement
Attribute Name: position
Attribute Value: 1
startElement() Event: level1
Attribute Name: children
Attribute Value: 0
Text: This is level 1 of the nested elements
endElement() Event: level1
endElement() Event: firstelement
startElement() Event: secondelement
Attribute Name: position
Attribute Value: 2
startElement() Event: level1
Attribute Name: children
Attribute Value: 1
startElement() Event: level2
Text: This is level 2 of the nested elements
endElement() Event: level2
endElement() Event: level1
endElement() Event: secondelement
endElement() Event: rootelement
endDocument() Event
```

Summary

In this chapter, you were introduced to the Apache Xerces API for XML document parsing:

✦ An introduction to Apache Xerces

✦ How to download and install Xerces

✦ Parsing XML documents in J2EE

✦ An example of parsing an XML document with DOM

✦ An example of parsing an XML document with SAX

In the next chapter, I cover Xalan and show some examples of transforming XML documents with J2EE. I'll be applying the techniques covered in the example XSL stylesheets that you learned about in Chapters 7 and 8. Chapter 17 will cover the XML APIs that are included in the Sun Java Web Services Developer Pack (WSDP) in great detail, with some very detailed transformation code examples, including examples of using the Java API for XML Processing (JAXP) to switch between DOM and SAX parsers without changing your underlying application code.

✦   ✦   ✦

Xalan

The Apache Xalan API facilitates XSL Transformations in J2EE applications. The Apache XML Project (`http://xml.apache.org/`) is part of the Apache Software Foundation, a non-profit consortium that provides organizational, legal, and financial support for Apache open-source software projects, all of which can be seen at `http://www.apache.org/`. Xalan contains Apache's J2EE implementation classes for the W3C *XSL Transformations (XSLT) Version 1.0* Recommendation (`http://www.w3.org/TR/xslt`) and the *XML Path Language (XPath) Version 1.0* Recommendation (`http://www.w3.org/TR/xpath`). Xalan is currently available in Java and C++.

Cross-Reference
This chapter will focus on the J2EE code required to make XML Transformations work using Apache Xalan. For a full reference of XSL Transformation stylesheet techniques, including XSL and XPath documentation and XSL stylesheet examples, please refer to Chapters 7 and 8.

By default, Xalan uses SAX to parse stylesheets and process transformations. The SAX 2 `XMLReader` class parses XML documents and implements a `ContentHandler` to track SAX events during parsing. Xalan handles SAX parsing as part of the transformation process. Xerces also implements Sun's Transformation API for XML (TRAX), which I will cover in the next chapter. Xalan accepts a stream of SAX or DOM input, and produces output formatted as a stream, SAX events, or a DOM node tree. Because of this, transformation output can be accepted from the results of a DOM or SAX parse and sent to another SAX or DOM parsing process. Output can also be sent to another transformation process that accepts stream, SAX or DOM input.

Cross-Reference
For more information on SAX parsing, please refer to Chapter 6. For more information on parsing XML documents in J2EE using Apache Xerces, please refer to Chapter 15. For more information on TRAX, please refer to Chapter 17.

Downloading and Installing Xalan

The Xalan download includes part of Xerces, the xercesImpl.jar file. The Xalan core is contained in the xalan.jar and xml-apis.jar files, which will need to be added to your workstation classpath.

If your Java IDE doesn't already include Xalan as part of the installation (most do), or you want to update to the latest version of Xalan, Xalan-Java can be downloaded from `http://xml.apache.org/xalan-j/downloads.html`. Xalan is contained in a compressed .zip file format (or a tar for non-Windows users) and is currently around 12MB in size. You also have an option of downloading just the Jar files (referred to as the "binaries") or the source and binaries (referred to as the "source"). Once downloaded, Xalan can be decompressed and copied to the directory of your choice. The \bin directory is where the .jar files are located. Table 16-1 shows the Xalan component files and subdirectories for the binary download file.

Table 16-1 Xalan Components	
Interface Name	**Description**
\bin\xalan.jar	Contains the implementation classes for the W3C XSL Transformations (XSLT) Version 1.0 Recommendation and the XML Path Language (XPath) Version 1.0 Recommendation.
\bin\xml-apis.jar	Contains APIs for SAX, DOM, and JAVAX interfaces.
\bin\xercesImpl.jar	Contains implementation classes for all of the supported Xerces parsers. Currently this includes DOM Level 1 and 2, some of the DOM W3C DOM Level 3 Working Draft specifications, and SAX version 2.
\docs	Directory containing Xalan API and implementation class documentation.
\samples	Directory containing Sample source code. Source for samples is included in the binary and the source distribution.

Tip   Once the Xalan distribution file is downloaded, decompressed, and copied to its destination, the documentation for the distribution can be read by opening the index.html file in the \docs directory.

Transforming XML Documents in J2EE

In the examples for this chapter, I'll show J2EE code for transforming an example XML document. The same code can be used to transform XML to XML, HTML, or text. Xalan is not the only transformation engine available for J2EE, but it is the most widely used and is a good performer. A full list of XML transformation engines can be found at http://www.xmlsoftware.com/xslt.html.

 The sample XML documents and the J2EE code used in this chapter can be downloaded from the XML Programming Bible Website, at http://www.XML ProgrammingBible.com.

Using Xalan to transform XML documents

All of the examples in this chapter will use the same source XML file. I'm using the sample XML document I have used in previous chapters. The example XML document starts with a list of selected quotes from William Shakespeare, then goes on to list three books that contain the quotes that are available for purchase from Amazon.com, and a Spanish translation of *Macbeth*, *Romeo and Juliet*, *Hamlet*, and other volumes that are available from http://www.elcorteingles.es. Amazon.com provides a service that returns XML documents based on a URL query, and the format nested under the Amazon element is based on this format. I've added the elcorteingles.com book listing format and the quote listing, as well as other parts of the document to illustrate several features of XML element and attributes.

Listing 16-1 shows the XML document, named AmazonMacbethSpanish.xml, which I will refer back to in the next few examples.

Listing 16-1: **An Example XML Document for Xalan Transformations**

```
<?xml version="1.0" encoding="ISO-8859-1"?>
<quotedoc>
  <quotelist author="Shakespeare, William" quotes="4">
    <quote source="Macbeth" author="Shakespeare, William">When the
    hurlyburly's done, / When the battle's lost and won.</quote>
    <quote source="Macbeth" author="Shakespeare, William">Out, damned spot!
    out, I say!-- One; two; why, then 'tis time to do't ;--Hell is murky!-
    -Fie, my lord, fie! a soldier, and afeard? What need we fear who knows
    it, when none can call our power to account?--Yet who would have
    thought the old man to have had so much blood in him?</quote>
```

Continued

Listing 16-1 *(continued)*

```
  <quote source="Macbeth" author="Shakespeare, William">Is this a dagger
  which I see before me, the handle toward my hand? Come, let me clutch
  thee: I have thee not, and yet I see thee still. Art thou not, fatal
  vision, sensible to feeling as to sight? or art thou but a dagger of
  the mind, a false creation, proceeding from the heat-oppressed
  brain?</quote>
  <quote source="Macbeth" author="Shakespeare, William">To-morrow, and
  to-morrow, and to-morrow, creeps in this petty pace from day to day, to
  the last syllable of recorded time; and all our yesterdays have
  lighted fools the way to dusty death. Out, out, brief candle! Life's
  but a walking shadow; a poor player, that struts and frets his hour
  upon the stage, and then is heard no more: it is a tale told by an
  idiot, full of sound and fury, signifying nothing. </quote>
  <quote/>
</quotelist>
<catalog items="4">
  <Amazon items="3">
    <product>
      <ranking>1</ranking>
      <title>Hamlet/MacBeth</title>
      <asin>8432040231</asin>
      <author>Shakespeare, William</author>
      <image>http://images.Amazon.com/images/P/
       8432040231.01.MZZZZZZZ.jpg</image>
      <small_image>http://images.Amazon.com/images/P/
       8432040231.01.TZZZZZZZ.jpg</small_image>
      <list_price>$7.95</list_price>
      <release_date>19910600</release_date>
      <binding>Paperback</binding>
      <availability/>
      <tagged_url>http://www.Amazon.com:80/exec/obidos/redirect?tag=
       associateid&amp;benztechnologies=9441&amp;camp=1793&amp;link_code=
       xml&amp;path=ASIN/8432040231</tagged_url>
    </product>
    <product>
      <ranking>2</ranking>
      <title>MacBeth</title>
      <asin>1583488340</asin>
      <author>Shakespeare, William</author>
      <image>http://images.Amazon.com/images/P/
       1583488340.01.MZZZZZZZ.jpg</image>
      <small_image>http://images.Amazon.com/images/P/
       1583488340.01.TZZZZZZZ.jpg</small_image>
      <list_price>$8.95</list_price>
      <release_date>19991200</release_date>
      <binding>Paperback</binding>
```

```
        <availability/>
        <tagged_url>http://www.Amazon.com:80/exec/obidos/redirect?tag=
          associateid&amp;benztechnologies=9441&amp;camp=1793&amp;link_code=
          xml&amp;path=ASIN/1583488340</tagged_url>
      </product>
      <product>
        <ranking>3</ranking>
        <title>William Shakespeare: MacBeth</title>
        <asin>8420617954</asin>
        <author>Shakespeare, William</author>
        <image>http://images.Amazon.com/images/P/
          8420617954.01.MZZZZZZZ.jpg</image>
        <small_image>http://images.Amazon.com/images/P/
          8420617954.01.TZZZZZZZ.jpg</small_image>
        <list_price>$4.75</list_price>
        <release_date>19810600</release_date>
        <binding>Paperback</binding>
        <availability/>
        <tagged_url>http://www.Amazon.com:80/exec/obidos/redirect?tag=
          associateid&amp;benztechnologies=9441&amp;camp=1793&amp;link_code=
          xml&amp;path=ASIN/8420617954</tagged_url>
      </product>
    </Amazon>
    <elcorteingles items="1">
      <product xml:lang="es">
        <titulo>Romeo y Julieta/Macbeth/Hamlet/Otelo/La fierecilla
          domado/El sueño de una noche de verano/ El mercader de
          Venecia</titulo>
        <isbn>8484036324</isbn>
        <autor>Shakespeare, William</autor>
        <imagen>http://libros.elcorteingles.es/producto/
          verimagen_blob.asp?ISBN=8449503639</imagen>
        <precio>7,59 &#x20AC;</precio>
        <fecha_de_publicación>6/04/1999</fecha_de_publicación>
        <Encuadernación>Piel</Encuadernación>
        <librourl>http://libros.elcorteingles.es/producto/
          libro_descripcion.asp?CODIISBN=8449503639</librourl>
      </product>
    </elcorteingles>
  </catalog>
</quotedoc>
```

Listing 16-2 shows the code used to transform the XML document shown in Listing 16-1. The code reads through an XML document using SAX and transforms the data using a specified stylesheet.

Listing 16-2: **Code for Transforming an XML Document Using Xalan - XalanSimpleTransform.java**

```java
import javax.xml.transform.*;
import javax.xml.transform.stream.*;

public class XalanSimpleTransform {

    public static void main(String[] args) {
        XalanSimpleTransform XST = new XalanSimpleTransform();
    }

    public XalanSimpleTransform() {
        try {

            TransformerFactory tFactory = TransformerFactory.newInstance();
            String XMLSource =
            "C:/jdk1.3.1_01/bin/XMLBookSource/XMLDocs/
            AmazonMacbethSpanish.xml";
            String XSLSource = "C:/jdk1.3.1_01/bin/XMLBookSource/XMLDocs/
            XMLtoQuotes.xsl";
            String ResultOutput = "C:/temp/ResultOutput.XML";

            Transformer transformer = tFactory.newTransformer(new
            StreamSource(XSLSource));

            transformer.transform(new StreamSource(XMLSource), new
            StreamResult(ResultOutput));

            System.out.println("Transform Successful.
            Output saved to file: C:/temp/ResultOutput.XML");          }

        catch (TransformerException e) {
            System.err.println("Error: " + e);
        }
    }
}
```

This code is relatively short and simple because it's the stylesheet that does most of the work. In this case, the stylesheet creates a new XML document that lists the quotes from the original XML document. Listing 16-3 shows the result of the transformation.

Listing 16-3: **The ResultOutput.xml Document**

```
<?xml version="1.0" encoding="ISO-8859-1"?>
<transformedquotes>
  <quote source="Macbeth" author="Shakespeare, William">When the
  hurlyburly's done, / When the battle's lost and won.</quote>
  <quote source="Macbeth" author="Shakespeare, William">Out, damned spot!
  out, I say!-- One; two; why, then 'tis time to do't ;--Hell is murky!--
  Fie, my lord, fie! a soldier, and afeard? What need we fear who knows
  it, when none can call our power to account?--Yet who would have thought
  the old man to have had so much blood in him?</quote>
  <quote source="Macbeth" author="Shakespeare, William">Is this a dagger
  which I see before me, the handle toward my hand? Come, let me clutch
  thee: I have thee not, and yet I see thee still. Art thou not, fatal
  vision, sensible to feeling as to sight? or art thou but a dagger of the
  mind, a false creation, proceeding from the heat-oppressed
  brain?</quote>
  <quote source="Macbeth" author="Shakespeare, William">To-morrow, and to-
  morrow, and to-morrow, creeps in this petty pace from day to day, to the
  last syllable of recorded time; and all our yesterdays have lighted
  fools the way to dusty death. Out, out, brief candle! Life's but a
  walking shadow; a poor player, that struts and frets his hour upon the
  stage, and then is heard no more: it is a tale told by an idiot, full of
  sound and fury, signifying nothing. </quote>
  <quote/>
</transformedquotes>
```

Let's break down what the transformation code is doing. The first part of the code imports classes that you need for transformation and file reading and writing. Transformation is facilitated through the `javax.xml.transform` classes. Xalan accepts javax stream, SAX or DOM input, and produces output to a javax stream, SAX, or DOM. In this case, javax streams are used for input and for output. The files are accessed by string reference. The strings represent the XSLSource, XMLSource, and ResultOutput files on the file system. The files are converted to streams using the `javax.xml.transform.stream` class. Next, the code creates a class, which implements a main method, which calls a constructor, which creates a new instance of the `XalanSimpleTransform` class.

```
import javax.xml.transform.*;
import javax.xml.transform.stream.*;


public class XalanSimpleTransform {
```

```
public static void main(String[] args) {
    XalanSimpleTransform XST = new XalanSimpleTransform();
}

public XalanSimpleTransform() {
    try {
```

Next, the code creates an instance of `TransformerFactory`, and three strings are defined. An XSL processor needs three things to perform a transformation: an XML source document, a stylesheet, and a transformation output destination. The `XMLSource` string defines the location of the source XML file. The `XSLSource` string defines the location of the source XSL file. The `ResultOutput` defines the location that the transformation output will be sent to. If there is already a `ResultOutput` file at the location specified by the string, the transformer overwrites the contents of the file with the results of this transformation. The file references in the strings are designed on the assumption that the XML and XSL files are in the same directory as the J2EE code.

```
TransformerFactory tFactory = TransformerFactory.newInstance();
String XMLSource = "AmazonMacbethSpanish.xml";
String XSLSource = "XMLtoQuotes.xsl";
String ResultOutput = "C:/temp/ResultOutput.XML";
```

Next, a transformer is created. The stylesheet is passed as one of the input parameters. Behind the scenes, the XSL stylesheet is parsed into a template object that is used to transform the XML source document.

```
Transformer transformer = tFactory.newTransformer(new
StreamSource(XSLSource));
```

Next, the transformer uses the transform method to load the `XMLSource` as a stream and create an empty `ResultOutput` stream for XSL processor output. Inside the method, the code defines two new streams to pass the values to the transformer. I could have separated out the stream creation into separate lines, but inline creation of the stream objects was just as easy, and in my opinion it's a little easier to follow one compound method with inline stream creation than three separate statements. Note that the streams are slightly different. The XML Source document is passed in a `StreamSource` object, while `ResultOutput` is passed in a `StreamOutput` object.

```
transformer.transform(new StreamSource(XMLSource), new
StreamResult(ResultOutput));
```

If the transform is successful, a message is displayed in the Java output indicating where the transformation results can be found. If a transformation error is encountered, an error message displays instead.

```
        System.out.println("Transform Successful.
        Output saved to file: C:/temp/ResultOutput.XML");          }

    catch (TransformerException e) {
        System.err.println("Error: " + e);
```

Sending transformation output to the screen and using an XML stylesheet reference

The previous Xalan code is a simple example of creating a Java document from a source file and sending transformation output to another source file. There may be times when you want to send transformation output directly to the Web or another interface. There also may be times when you want to use a stylesheet reference in the source XML document for the XSL transformation stylesheet. Listing 16-4 shows how to do both. This time I use an XML document that contains a processing instruction that points to an XSL stylesheet. The code uses the XML document reference to access the stylesheet this time, instead of explicitly specifying a stylesheet to use for the transformation. This way the stylesheet reference can be flexible, based on the XML document, not the code. The stylesheet produces HTML from the source XML document. Instead of storing the output as a file, the HTML is sent directly to the screen.

Listing 16-4: Code for Transforming an XML Document Using Xalan - XalanSImpleTransformToScreen.java

```java
import javax.xml.transform.*;
import javax.xml.transform.stream.*;

public class XalanSimpleTransformToScreen {

    public static void main(String[] args) {
        XalanSimpleTransformToScreen XST = new
        XalanSimpleTransformToScreen();
    }

    public XalanSimpleTransformToScreen() {
        try {

            TransformerFactory tFactory = TransformerFactory.newInstance();
            String XMLSource = "AmazonMacbethSpanishforxsl.xml";
            Source XSLstylesheet = tFactory.getAssociatedStylesheet(new
            StreamSource(XMLSource),null, null, null);

            Transformer transformer =
            tFactory.newTransformer(XSLstylesheet);
```

Continued

Listing 16-4 *(continued)*

```
        transformer.transform(new StreamSource(XMLSource), new
        StreamResult(System.out));

    } catch (Exception e) {
        System.err.println("Error: " + e);
    }
  }

}
```

The first part of the code is the same as the previous example. Transformation is facilitated through the javax.xml.transform classes. Xalan accepts Javax stream, SAX, or DOM input, and produces output to a Javax stream, SAX, or DOM. In this case, streams are used for input and for output. The files are located by the strings that represent the XSLSource, XMLSource, and ResultOutput files on the file system. The files are converted to streams using the `javax.xml.transform.stream` class. Next, the code creates a class, which implements a main method, which calls a constructor, which creates a new instance of the `XalanSimpleTransformToScreen` class.

```
import javax.xml.transform.*;
import javax.xml.transform.stream.*;
public class XalanSimpleTransformToScreen {

    public static void main(String[] args) {
        XalanSimpleTransformToScreen XST = new
        XalanSimpleTransformToScreen();
    }

    public XalanSimpleTransformToScreen() {
        try {
```

Next, the code creates an instance of `TransformerFactory`, and a string is defined. The `XMLSource` string defines the location of the source XML file. The `XSLSource` string defines the location of the source XSL file. The file references this string on the assumption that the `AmazonMacbethSpanishforxsl.xml` file is in the same directory as the J2EE code.

```
        TransformerFactory tFactory = TransformerFactory.newInstance();
        String XMLSource = "AmazonMacbethSpanishforxsl.xml";
```

Instead of specifying a string for the stylesheet as I did in the last example, this time I use the `getAssociatedStylesheet` method of the `TransformerFactory` class to retrieve the stylesheet reference from the XML document. XML documents can contain a reference to a stylesheet in a processing instruction reference that looks like this:

```
<?xml-stylesheet type="text/xsl" href="XMLtoHTML.xslt"?>
```

This is a stylesheet reference that is contained in the AmazonMacbethSpanishforxsl.xml file. It tells the XSL processor that the stylesheet is called XMLtoHTML.xslt and is located in the same directory as the source XML document. The getAssociatedStylesheet method returns a stream containing a stylesheet. The three null parameters are for attributes that can be included in the stylesheet processing instruction. The attribute names are media, title, and charset. The getAssociatedStylesheet method uses these optional attributes to match specific attributes in a stylesheet to qualify that it is the correct stylesheet to use for a transformation. In this case, I'm not picky about the content of these attributes, and set them all to null.

```
Source XSLstylesheet = tFactory.getAssociatedStylesheet(new
StreamSource(XMLSource),null, null, null);
```

Next, the code processes the transformation. In the previous example, a StreamResult was defined to pass transformation output to a file on the file system. In this case, I just want to redirect the HTML output directly to the screen, so I simply use System.out to do that. If there is any kind of error in this class, it is passed to the screen instead of the output.

```
Transformer transformer =
tFactory.newTransformer(XSLstylesheet);
transformer.transform(new StreamSource(XMLSource), new
StreamResult(System.out));

} catch (Exception e) {
    System.err.println("Error: " + e);
```

Figure 16-1 shows the HTML output that was generated by the transformation.

Passing transformation output to DOM and SAX

As I've mentioned a couple of times so far in this chapter, Xalan accepts Javax stream, SAX, or DOM input, and produces output to a Javax stream, SAX, or DOM object. So far I've show the stream interface in this chapter's examples, which is the most common type of XSL processing input and output.

There may be times when you want to process a transformation that comes from a SAX or DOM object and/or pass the results to another SAX or DOM object.

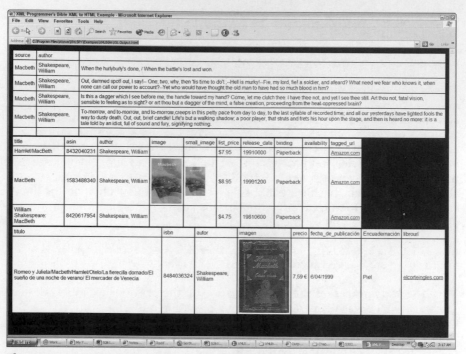

Figure 16-1: HTML output that was generated by the transformation from Listing 16-4

Transforming XSL output to DOM

The example code in Listing 16-5 transforms the source XML document into a DOM object, and then passes it to a parser class to display the parsed DOM document nodes.

Cross-Reference   For more information on parsing XML documents with DOM in J2EE applications, please refer to Chapter 15 (Xerces).

Listing 16-5: Code for Transforming an XML Document to DOM Using Xalan - XalanSimpleTransformToDOM.java

```java
import org.w3c.dom.*;
import javax.xml.transform.*;
import javax.xml.transform.stream.*;
import javax.xml.transform.dom.DOMResult;

public class XalanSimpleTransformToDOM {
```

```
    public static void main(String[] args) {
        XalanSimpleTransformToDOM XSTTD = new XalanSimpleTransformToDOM();
    }

    public XalanSimpleTransformToDOM() {
        try {

            TransformerFactory tFactory = TransformerFactory.newInstance();
            String XMLSource = AmazonMacbethSpanish.xml";
            String XSLSource = XMLtoQuotes.xsl";
            DOMResult domResult = new DOMResult();

            Transformer transformer = tFactory.newTransformer(new
            StreamSource(XSLSource));

            transformer.transform(new StreamSource(XMLSource), domResult);

            nodeReader(domResult.getNode());
        } catch (TransformerException e) {
            System.err.println("Error: " + e);
        }
    }



    private void nodeReader(Node node) {

        if(node.hasChildNodes()) {
            NodeList children = node.getChildNodes();
            if (children != null) {
                for (int i=0; i< children.getLength(); i++) {
                    Node ThisNode= children.item(i);
                    String name = children.item(i).getNodeName();
                    String localName = ThisNode.getLocalName();
                    String uri       = ThisNode.getNamespaceURI();
                    String prefix    = ThisNode.getPrefix();
                    String value     = ThisNode.getNodeValue();
                    String NodeText=null;
                    int type = ThisNode.getNodeType();


                    switch (type) {
                        case 1: NodeText = "Node type 1: Element Constant:
                        ELEMENT_NODE \r\n";break;
                        case 2: NodeText = "Node type 2: Attribute
                        Constant: ATTRIBUTE_NODE \r\n";break;
                        case 3: NodeText = "Node type 3: Text Constant:
                        TEXT_NODE \r\n";break;
                        case 4: NodeText = "Node type 4: CDATA Section
                        Constant: CDATA_SECTION_NODE \r\n";break;
                        case 5: NodeText = "Node type 5: Entity Reference
                        Constant: ENTITY_REFERENCE_NODE \r\n";break;
```

Continued

Listing 16-5 *(continued)*

```
        case 6: NodeText = "Node type 6: Entity Constant:
        ENTITY_NODE \r\n";break;
        case 7: NodeText = "Node type 7: Processing
        Instruction Constant: PROCESSING_INSTRUCTION_NODE
        \r\n";break;
        case 8: NodeText = "Node type 8: Comment Constant:
        COMMENT_NODE \r\n";break;
        case 9: NodeText = "Node type 9: Document Constant:
        DOCUMENT_NODE \r\n";break;
        case 10: NodeText = "Node type 10: Document Type
        Declaration Constant: DOCUMENT_TYPE_NODE
        \r\n";break;
        case 11: NodeText = "Node type 11: Document
        Fragment Constant: DOCUMENT_FRAGMENT_NODE
        \r\n";break;
        case 12: NodeText = "Node type 12: Notation
        Constant: NOTATION_NODE \r\n";break;
        //Remove this comment when DOM supports the
        XPATH_NAMESPACE_NODE Constant
        //case 13: NodeText = "Node type 13: W3C DOm Level
        3 XPathNamespace Constant:
        XPATH_NAMESPACE_NODE";break;
        default: NodeText = "Not a valid W3C Node type
        \r\n";

    }

    String nodeString = NodeText;

    nodeString += ("Name: " + name + "\r\n");
    if (localName != null) {
        nodeString += ("Local Name: " + localName +
    "\r\n");
    }
    if (prefix != null) {
        nodeString += ("Prefix: " + prefix + "\r\n");
    }
    if (uri != null) {
        nodeString += ("Namespace URI: " + uri + "\r\n");
    }

    if (type == ThisNode.ELEMENT_NODE) {

        if (ThisNode.hasAttributes())  {
            String Attributes = null;
            NamedNodeMap AttributesList =
            node.getAttributes();
```

```
                    for(int j = 0; j < AttributesList.getLength();
                    j++) {
                    nodeString +=("Attribute Name: " +
                    AttributesList.item(j).getNodeName() +
                    "\r\nAttribute Value: " +
                    AttributesList.item(j).getNodeValue()+"\r\n" );
                    }
                }
            }

        if (value != null) {

            nodeString += ("Value: " + value + "\r\n");
        }

        System.out.println(nodeString);

        if(children.item(i).hasChildNodes()) {
            nodeReader(children.item(i));


        }
    }
            }
        }
    }
}
```

The code in this example is almost identical to the code in the XalanSimpleTransform.
java example shown in Listing 16-2. I've added a class from the example in Listing 15-2
in Chapter 15 to the end. In the interest of brevity, I'll just point out the code that has
changed.

 The sample XML documents and the J2EE code used in this chapter, including a
full listing of this code, can be downloaded from the XML Programming Bible
Website, at http://www.XMLProgrammingBible.com.

A new instance of TransformerFactory is created. This time, however, the
parameters for the transform method have changed. Instead of a StreamResult
object, I define a DOMResult object. The DOMResult object is used to contain the
transformation output instead of a Javax stream. Next, I pass the results of the
transformation in the DOMResult object via the getNode method to the
nodeReader class (from the example in Chapter 15). The nodeReader class prints
out all of the nodes in a node tree to the screen.

```
        TransformerFactory tFactory = TransformerFactory.newInstance();
        String XMLSource = AmazonMacbethSpanish.xml";
        String XSLSource = XMLtoQuotes.xsl";
```

```
DOMResult domResult = new DOMResult();

Transformer transformer = tFactory.newTransformer(new
StreamSource(XSLSource));

transformer.transform(new StreamSource(XMLSource), domResult);

nodeReader(domResult.getNode());
```

Transforming XSL output to SAX

As with the previous XSL to DOM example, the code in the example in Listing 16-6 is almost identical to the code in the XalanSimpleTransform.java example shown in Listing 16-2, with a class from the example in Listing 15-3 in Chapter 15 tacked on to the end. After the full listing, I'll point out the code that has changed.

Listing 16-6: Code for Transforming an XML Document to SAX Using Xalan - XalanSimpleTransformToSAX.java

```
import org.xml.sax.*;
import javax.xml.transform.*;
import javax.xml.transform.sax.*;
import javax.xml.transform.stream.*;

public class XalanSimpleTransformToSAX {
    String eventString = "";

    public static void main(String[] args) {
        XalanSimpleTransformToSAX XSTTS = new XalanSimpleTransformToSAX();
    }

    public XalanSimpleTransformToSAX() {
        try {

            TransformerFactory tFactory = TransformerFactory.newInstance();
            String XMLSource = "AmazonMacbethSpanish.xml";
            String XSLSource = "XMLtoQuotes.xsl";

            SAXTransformerFactory saxTFactory = ((SAXTransformerFactory)
            tFactory);
            TransformerHandler tHandler =
            saxTFactory.newTransformerHandler(new
            StreamSource("XMLtoQuotes.xsl"));
            SAXResult saxResult = new SAXResult(tHandler);
            Transformer transformer = tFactory.newTransformer(new
            StreamSource(XSLSource));
            transformer.transform(new StreamSource(XMLSource), saxResult);
```

```
        } catch (TransformerException e) {
            System.err.println("Error: " + e);
        }
    }

    public void processingInstruction( String target, String
    instruction ){
        eventString +="ProcessingInstruction() Event - Target:" + target +
        " Instruction:" + instruction + "\r\n";
    }

public void startDocument() {
    eventString +="StartDocument() Event \r\n";
}

public void startPrefixMapping( String prefix, String uri ) {
    eventString +="startPrefixMapping() Event - Prefix:" + prefix + "
    URI:" + uri + "\r\n";
}

public void startElement(String uri, String localname, String qname,
Attributes attributes){
    eventString += "startElement() Event: " + localname + "\r\n";

    for (int i = 0; i < attributes.getLength(); i++) {
        eventString +=  "Attribute Name: "+
        attributes.getLocalName(i)+"\r\n";
        eventString += "Attribute Value: " +
        attributes.getValue(i)+"\r\n";


    }
}

public void endPrefixMapping( String prefix ) {
    eventString += "endPrefixMapping() Event - Prefix:" + prefix +
    "\r\n";
}

public void characters(char[] cdata, int start, int length){
    String textvalue = new String(cdata, start, length);
    if (!textvalue.trim().equals("")){
        eventString += "Text: "+ textvalue + "\r\n";
    }
}

public void ignorableWhitespace( char[] cdata, int start, int end ) {
    eventString += "ignorableWhitespace() Event \r\n";
}

public void endElement(String uri, String local, String qName){
    eventString += "endElement() Event: " + local + "\r\n";
}
```

Continued

Listing 16-6 *(continued)*

```
public void skippedEntity( String name ) {
    eventString += "skippedEntity() Event(): " + name;
}

public void endDocument(){
    eventString += "endDocument() Event";
    System.out.println(eventString);
}


}
```

For the SAX example, a new instance of `TransformerFactory` is created. Because the transformation code is dealing with SAX for this example, it needs to contain a `ContentHandler`, which will catch SAX events. To do this, the code explicitly casts the `TransformerFactory` to an instance of `SAXTransformerFactory`. The `ContentHandler` that is defined in the `SAXResult` cannot be null, so the `TransformerHandler` lets us create a `ContentHandler` that the `SAXResult` can use in the transformation. Next, the transformation is processed, passing data to the `SAXResult`. The `ContentHandler` that is contained in the `SAXResult` object reacts to the transformation just as it would an `XMLReader` class, and passes through the document, catching events as it encounters them in the `SAXResult` object.

```
TransformerFactory tFactory = TransformerFactory.newInstance();
String XMLSource = "AmazonMacbethSpanish.xml";
String XSLSource = "XMLtoQuotes.xsl";

SAXTransformerFactory saxTFactory = ((SAXTransformerFactory)
tFactory);
TransformerHandler tHandler =
saxTFactory.newTransformerHandler(new
StreamSource("XMLtoQuotes.xsl"));
SAXResult saxResult = new SAXResult(tHandler);
Transformer transformer = tFactory.newTransformer(new
StreamSource(XSLSource));
transformer.transform(new StreamSource(XMLSource), saxResult);
```

The rest of the classes that gather information about SAX events are the same as the classes that were reviewed in Listing 15-3 in Chapter 15.

Summary

In this chapter, you were introduced to Xalan:

✦ An introduction to Apache Xalan

✦ How to download and install Xalan

✦ Transforming XML documents in J2EE

✦ Passing transformed data to the screen

✦ Passing transformed data to the file system

✦ Using the stylesheet reference in XML documents for transformation

✦ Transforming XML documents to DOM objects

✦ Transforming XML documents to SAX objects

In the next chapter, I get into the XML APIs that are included as part of the Sun Java Web Services Developer Pack (WSDP). I've actually included Java API for XML Processing (JAXP) code in this chapter, but haven't called your attention to it because I wanted to focus on Xalan. Sun's Java Web Services Developer Pack forms the basis of many tools and code libraries, and I'll explain each component and illustrate the highlights with examples.

✦   ✦   ✦

XML APIs from Sun

Sun's Java Web Services Developer Pack (Java WSDP) is a great tool for J2EE developers working with any XML applications, not just Web services. Most of the APIs in the Web Services Developer Pack started as XML JCP (Java Community Process) API initiatives. JCPS are projects created by Sun to standardize popular and often used interfaces for common tasks in J2EE. The APIs that were developed as a result of the XML JCPS were originally rolled into the Sun Java XML Pack. The XML Pack has not been updated since summer 2002, but it can still be downloaded from `http://java.sun.com/xml/downloads/javaxmlpack.html`. The APIs in the Java XML Pack were then rolled into the Java Web Services Developer Pack in the fall of 2002. The Java Web Services Developer Pack contains several interface APIs for XML functionality from the Java XML Pack, and some new APIs specifically for Web Service Functions. In this chapter we'll show examples of the Java API for XML Processing (JAXP), Java Architecture for XML Binding (JAXB), and the Java Server Pages Standard Tag Library (JSTL). We'll dive into the details of each API and provide Java code examples (and JSP page examples for the JSTL). In addition, we'll be using these APIs in examples in the rest of the J2EE XML parts of this book.

We'll also introduce you to the Web Service APIs in the Java Web Services Developer Pack. These are the Java API for XML Messaging (JAXM), the Java API for XML Registries (JAXR), Java WSDP Registry Server, Java API for XML-Based RPC (JAX-RPC), and the SOAP with Attachments API for Java (SAAJ). We cover the Web Service APIs in more detail and provide Web Service API code examples in Chapter 33.

About the Java Community Process

The Java Community Process (JCP) is where all of Sun's non-core Java specifications are developed. The JCP process develops Java language specifications based on public input. The specification development process is very similar to the W3C process, with the exception that W3C Recommendations are language-neutral and JCP specifications are specific to Java. JCP Specifications begin life as Java Specification Requests (JSRs). JSRs are descriptions of proposed new and changed features that evolve into final specifications. More information on JSP proposals and JCP involvement can be found at http://www.jcp.org/en/participation/overview.

There are five development stages and one maintenance stage that a JSR goes through in its lifetime:

✦ **Review**: After a new JSR is submitted, it is posted on the Web. The first stage is a brief period when anyone can review and comment on a new JSR Web posting. The result of this process is a draft specification.

✦ **Community Review**: After the initial review is complete, members review and comment on the draft specification. A Java Community Process Member is a company, organization, or individual that has signed the Java Specification Participation Agreement (JSPA), an agreement between Sun Microsystems and the company, organization or individual under which participation in the Java Community Process is permitted.

✦ **Public Review**: After the Community review, the public can review and comment on the draft Specification.

✦ **Final Draft Proposal**: The Review, Community Review and Public Review produce a draft Specification that is used to build a Reference Implementation (RI) and a Technology Compatibility Kit (TCK). A Reference Implementation is a "proof of concept" implementation of a Specification in Java, and a Technology Compatibility Kit contains development tools, documentation, and implementation tests to ensure compatibility with a specification.

✦ **Final Release**: Final Draft Proposals are approved by an Executive Committee (EC) EC members are nominated and elected by JCP members. A current listing of EC members can be found at http://www.jcp.org/en/participation/committee.

✦ **Maintenance Review**: At the time that a Specification is approved, a Maintenance Lead is appointed to oversee ongoing maintenance of a specification. An e-mail address is published with the specification that JCP members and the public can send information about errata and request clarification, interpretation, and enhancements to the Specification. It's up to the maintenance lead to decide if any further information or development requires a new version of the specification as part of the Maintenance Review process.

There are hundreds of JSRs currently at various stages of completion. A listing of JSRs by development stage can be found at `http://www.jcp.org/en/jsr/overview`. Each JSR includes a reference implementation. In the Case of the Java Web Services Developer Pack, the Java APIs that have been developed as components in the pack are a result of the reference implementation.

Some of the JSRs have their own specific and unique functionality. Other JSRs such as the Java API for XML Processing (JAXP) specification act as proxies between supported tools such as parsers and transformation engines and are designed to shield developers from having to recode Java when a new version of a J2EE tool comes out. For example, a J2EE developer that has written a parsing interface to a DOM 1 parser could theoretically move to a DOM 2 or SAX parser with no change to their Java source code, changing the JAXP pluggable reference from DOM1 to any other JAXP-compliant parser could facilitate the move.

Introduction to the Sun Java Web Services Developer Pack

The Java Web Service Developer Pack (WSDP) is downloadable from Sun at `http://java.sun.com/webservices/webservicespack.html`. The current version of the WSDP is compatible with JDK 1.3.1 and higher. It is has been tested on Solaris 8 and 9, Windows 2000 Professional, Windows XP Professional, and RedHat Linux 7.2. Check the readme file for issues regarding configuration, compatibility, and enhancements to your existing JDK environment. Outlined below are WSDP, the APIs, and their associated benefits.

JAXP (Java API for XML Processing)

The Java API for XML Processing (JAXP) supports processing of XML documents using DOM 1, 2, and some of DOM 3, SAX 1 and 2, and XSLT. JAXP enables applications to change the processor that is used to parse and transform XML documents without changing the underlying source code for the application that is doing the parsing or transformation. JAXP also supports the W3C XML Schema 1.0 Recommendation and an XSLT compiler (XSLTC).

JAXB (Java Architecture for XML Binding)

JAXB automates mapping between XML documents and Java objects, making elements and attributes classes, properties and methods by marshalling and unmarshalling them in a customized XML document.

JAXM (Java API for XML Messaging)

JAXM provides an Interface for SOAP messages, including SOAP with attachments. Because JAXM is based on XML, the messaging format can be changed to other message standards that support XML formats.

JSTL (Java Server Pages Standard Tag Library)

JSTL consists of four custom Java Server Page (JSP) tag libraries called the core, XML, I18N & Formatting and database access libraries. All are based on the JSP 1.2 API. The core JSP library supports basic HTM page generation features. The XML library contains support for XML functionality, such as transformations and parsing. The database access library contains support for database access functions, and the I18N & Formatting library contains functionality for internationalization and formatting of Web pages.

JAX-RPC (Java API for XML-Based RPC)

JAX-RPC provides an Interface for XML messages using an RPC transport, including, but not limited to, SOAP calls over RPC to Web Services.

JAXR (Java API for XML Registries)

JAXR provides an interface for XML registries, supporting UDDI and OASIS/U.N./ CEFACT ebXML Registry and Repository standards, among others.

Java WSDP Registry Server

The Java WSDP Registry Server implements Version 2 of the UDDI (Universal Description, Discovery and Integration) specification. It provides a registry that is compatible with JAXR (Java API for XML Registries). The Java WSDP Registry Server can be used as a standalone UDDI server and also as a testing tool for JAXR applications.

SAAJ (SOAP with Attachments API for Java)

SAAJ provides support for producing, sending, and receiving SOAP messages with attachments. Sun's SAAJ library provides an interface to the features and capabilities described in the W3C SOAP 1.1 attachment note, which have not changed much in their current form. The current W3C specification is the W3C SOAP 1.2 Attachment Feature, currently in the Working Draft stage of the W3C Recommendation process. The W3C SOAP 1.2 Attachment Feature Working Draft states that a SOAP message may include attachments directly in the W3C SOAP body structure. The SOAP body and header may contain only XML content. Non-XML data must be contained in an attachment under the SOAP body. This provides facilities for providing binary information and non-XML data in a SOAP envelope.

SOAP and SOAP attachments are covered in more detail in Chapter 23, "Web Service Concepts," and Chapter 24, "SOAP."

Developing with JAXP (Java API for XML Processing)

As mentioned in the introduction, the Java API for XML Processing (JAXP) supports processing of XML documents using DOM 1, 2, and some of DOM 3, SAX 1 and 2, and XSLT.

If you're using JDK 1.4 or higher, JAXP is included in the distribution of the JDK, and may be older than the Web Services Developer Pack (WSDP) version. To overwrite the JDK version of JAXP with the WSDP version of JAXP, copy the files in C:\<jwsdp install drive>\jaxp-1.2.2\lib\endorsed to <JAVA_HOME>\jre\lib\endorsed. To change the reference in the JDK to the WSDP version without overwriting the JDK JAXP distribution files, set the java.endorsed.dirs system property to C:\<jwsdp install drive>\jaxp-1.2.2\lib\endorsed.

JAXP enables applications to change the processor that is used to parse and transform XML documents without changing the underlying source code for the application that is doing the parsing or transformation.

To show you how this actually happens, let's refer back to the first Xalan example in Chapter 16. I actually used JAXP code, which Xalan supports, to process the transformation. Listing 17-1 shows the code used to extract a subset of the XML document shown in Listing 16-1 using XSL transformation. The code reads through an XML document using SAX behind the scenes and transforms the data using the specified stylesheet. The code also instantiates `TransformerFactory` for the transformation, which is a JAXP class for integration with a transformation engine. By default in Xalan, the JAXP "pluggable" interface connects to the Xalan transformation engine, and the Xerxes SAX parser to facilitate Xalan transformations.

Listing 17-1: **Code for Transforming an XML Document Using Xalan - XalanSimpleTransform.java**

```java
import javax.xml.transform.*;
import javax.xml.transform.stream.*;

public class XalanSimpleTransform {

    public static void main(String[] args) {
        XalanSimpleTransform XST = new XalanSimpleTransform();
    }

    public XalanSimpleTransform() {
        try {

            TransformerFactory tFactory = TransformerFactory.newInstance();
            String XMLSource =
            "C:/jdk1.3.1_01/bin/XMLBookSource/XMLDocs/
            AmazonMacbethSpanish.xml";
            String XSLSource = "C:/jdk1.3.1_01/bin/XMLBookSource/XMLDocs/
            XMLtoQuotes.xsl";
            String ResultOutput = "C:/temp/ResultOutput.XML";

            Transformer transformer = tFactory.newTransformer(new
            StreamSource(XSLSource));

            transformer.transform(new StreamSource(XMLSource), new
            StreamResult(ResultOutput));

            System.out.println("Transform Successful.
            Output saved to file: C:/temp/ResultOutput.XML");        }

        catch (TransformerException e) {
            System.err.println("Error: " + e);
        }
    }
}
```

We first reviewed this code in Chapter 16 from a Xalan and XSLT perspective. This time we'll review the same code from a JAXP perspective. The first part of the code imports classes that you need for this Java class to function. Transformation is facilitated through the JAXP javax.xml.transform class. The files are located by the strings that represent the XSLSource, XMLSource, and ResultOutput files on the file system. The files are converted to streams using the javax.xml.transform.stream class. Next, the code creates a class, which implements a main method, which calls a constructor, which creates a new instance of a class that creates a new JAXP TransformerFactory object, which is the JAXP interface to the Xalan transformation engine.

Note   JAXP by itself is not a XSLT processor or a XML parser. The default implementation of JAXP uses Xalan as the XSLT processor and the Xerces SAX parser as the default parser.

```
import javax.xml.transform.*;
import javax.xml.transform.stream.*;


public class XalanSimpleTransform {

    public static void main(String[] args) {
        XalanSimpleTransform XST = new XalanSimpleTransform();
    }

    public XalanSimpleTransform() {
        try {
```

The new instance of `TransformerFactory` is defined along with three strings; XMLSource, XSLSource and ResultOutput. A JAXP Transformer created with TransformerFactory needs the objects represented by these three strings to perform a transformation. The `XMLSource` string defines the location of the source XML file. The `XSLSource` string defines the location of the source XSL file, and is used to create the new instance of the transformer. The file represented by the XSLSource string becomes the template object when an instance of the transformer is created. The `ResultOutput` defines the location that the transformation output will be sent to, in this case c:\temp\ResultOutput on the file system. The file references for the source XML and XSL files do not contain path information because the files should be located in the same directory as this J2EE code.

```
TransformerFactory tFactory = TransformerFactory.newInstance();
String XMLSource = "AmazonMacbethSpanish.xml";
String XSLSource = "XMLtoQuotes.xsl";
String ResultOutput = "C:/temp/ResultOutput.XML";
```

Swapping processors and parsers with JAXP

From a JAXP perspective, it's interesting to note what's going on behind the scenes when a new instance of the TransformerFactory is created. JAXP contains facilities for one XSLT processor to be swapped out for another XSLT processor, without changing this code. The parser that is used to parse the XSL stylesheet into a template object and the XML source document into something that the XSLT processor can digest (usually a DOM node tree or a set of SAX events) can also be substituted.

The JAXP specification details how to swap one XSTP processor and/or parser for another. The full JAXP specification and all other XML JCP specifications can be found on the JCP Website at `http://jcp.org/en/jsr/tech?listBy=1&listByType=tech`. we'll summarize them for you here and show examples of how to make the swaps.

Tip

Always check for more than one JCP listing if you're looking for a specification at jcp.org. The jcp.org Website can be a little difficult to navigate to the latest release of a specification. Instead of reusing the original specification number and document when publishing updates, new versions of a JCP specification use new numbers in separate documents, unless they are a maintenance release. Compounding the problem, JSRs that represent different versions of the same specification are often located in different sections of the site. For example, JAXP 1.0 was JSR 5, and JAXP 1.1 was JSR 63. JAXP 1.2 is a maintenance release of JAXP 1.1 and has the same number (63). JAXP 1.3 is JSR 206.

JAXP system properties

JAXP identifies the parser and the XSL processor to be used in the Transformer Factory in system properties. The system property for the XSLT processor is `javax.xml.transform.TransformerFactory` and the default setting is `org.apache.xalan.processor.TransformerFactoryImpl`.

There are two settings for JAXP parser functionality, depending on whether you are using SAX or DOM parsing. The `javax.xml.parsers.SAXParserFactory` system property tells JAXP which SAX parser to use. The default setting is `org.apache.xerces.jaxp.SAXParserFactoryImpl`. This represents the Xerces SAX parser that is downloaded with JAXP. If you want to use a specific DOM parser in your code, the `javax.xml.parsers.DocumentBuilderFactory` system property defines the `DocumentBuilder` that is used for DOM parsing. The default setting is `org.apache.xerces.jaxp.DocumentBuilderFactoryImpl`. This represents the Xerces DOM parser that is downloaded with JAXP.

How JAXP swaps XSL processors and parsers

JAXP JSRs describe three checks that a new instance of `TransformerFactory` needs to perform before creating a new transformer:

1. Check for a hard-coded system property reference. This is set by passing the system property from the command line when calling the class.

2. Check for a system property in {JAVA_HOME}/lib/ jaxp.properties. JAVA_HOME is an environment variable that designates the location of the root of the JDK jaxp.properties is the name of the file containing the XSLT processor and/or parser settings.

3. Check the system property entry in {JAXP Xalan Source Directory}/src/META-INF/services/(xalan.jar or xercesImpl.jar).

If none of these settings exist and/or have been updated from their defaults, the default Xalan XSLT processor and Xerces SAX parser are used to form the functionality of the JAXP transformer object.

Passing a hard-coded system property reference

Passing the system property from the command line is the most flexible way to substitute a parser. It's good for testing because of the command-line flexibility, but not practical if you're calling JAXP from another class. Using the command-line specification for a system property takes precedence over system properties specified in a jaxp.properties file or a META-INf/services file. Here's an example of passing a command-line transformation property with a class from a DOS command line:

```
java -Djavax.xml.transform.TransformerFactory=<name and location of your
JAXP compatible XSLT processor >
-D javax.xml.parsers.DocumentBuilderFactory=<name and location of your JAXP
compatible DOM parser >
-Djavax.xml.parsers.SAXParserFactory=<name and location of your JAXP
compatible SAX parser >  XalanSimpleTransform
```

This command tells Java to run the `XalanSimpleTransform` class in Listing 17-1. The `-D` tells JAXP to use the value pair to override a system property value when a new instance of `TransformerFactory` is created. The `-Djavax.xml.transform.TransformerFactory=` system property setting tells `TransformerFactory` to use the JAXP compatible implementation class listed in the reference value as the XSLT processor. The `-D javax.xml.parsers.DocumentBuilderFactory` system property setting tells `TransformerFactory` to use the JAXP compatible implementation class listed in the reference value as the DOM parser. The `-Djavax.xml.parsers.SAXParserFactory=` system property setting tells `Transformer Factory` to use the JAXP compatible implementation class listed in the reference value as the SAX parser.

Changing the system properties in {JAVA_HOME}/lib/ jaxp.properties

Global changes of the JAXP system properties can also be specified in the JAVA_HOME}/lib/ jaxp.properties file. JAVA_HOME is a system environment variable that designates the location of the root of the JDK that you are using on the system. jaxp.properties is the name of the file containing the XSLT processor and/or parser settings. The file is not created by default when JAXP is installed. If jaxp.properties does not exist, the JAXP TransformerFactory uses the default values. The jaxp.properties file can be created manually when global JAXP parsers and an XSLT processor need to be specified. The downside of using the jaxp.properties file is that all JAXP parsing and transformation processes will have to use the processor and parsers specified. Using the command-line specification for a system property takes precedence over the settings in a jaxp.properties file. The values in a jaxp.properties file take precedence over system properties specified in a META-INf/services file. Here are the contents of a sample jaxp.properties file, with default values.

Note   Unlike the command-line references, the jaxp.properties references do not need an = to specify the value of the system properties.

```
javax.xml.transform.TransformerFactory
org.apache.xalan.processor.TransformerFactoryImpl
javax.xml.parsers.DocumentBuilderFactory
org.apache.xerces.jaxp.DocumentBuilderFactoryImpl
javax.xml.parsers.SAXParserFactory
org.apache.xerces.jaxp.SAXParserFactoryImpl
```

Changing the system property entry in {JAXP Source Directory}/src/META-INF/services

The last option can be the most flexible of the three options, but it requires a lot more work. You have to download the JAXP source code distribution, and the ANT builder tool. Both of these are part of the full download of the Web Services Developer Pack. If a command-line system property is not used, and a JAR file specification includes a way to locate a subclass of TransformerFactory, which is located in the META-INF/services subdirectory of the jaxp-api.jar file. The compiled file for the XSLT processor is located in javax/xml/transform/TransformerFactory.class. The compiled DOM parser is in javax.xml/parsers/DocumentBuilderFactory.class. The compiled SAX parser is in javax.xml/parsers/SaxParserFactory.class. You can rewrite the code to suit your needs, or specify another class to be used in substitution for your XSLT processor and/or your SAX and DOM parsers. At runtime, the command line specification of a system property takes precedence over the settings in a jaxp.properties file and the class located in a META-INF/services file.

Working with JAXP and Xalan JAXP examples

We won't get into any more of the JAXP details in this chapter, because the JAXP download contains complete and very easy to understand documentation and some very good sample files. The documentation is located in the \docs subdirectory of your JAXP install directory. The samples are located in the \samples subdirectory of your JAXP install directory. We also use JAXP in several working examples later in the book.

In addition, if you're looking for examples of swapping parsers for use with the Xalan XSLT processor, or using DOM and SAX objects for sources and output, the Xalan sample files and related documentation have complete examples. All of the Xalan examples use JAXP to access the Xalan XSLT processor and parsers. The samples are located in the \samples subdirectory of your Xalan install directory.

 For more information about Xalan, including download and installation instructions, please refer to Chapter 16.

Developing with JAXB (Java Architecture for XML Binding)

JAXB automates mapping between XML documents and Java objects. JAXB marshalling generates an XML document from a Java object that represents an XML document. JAXB unmarshalling turns an XML document into a Java object. JAXB relies on Schemas to specify marshalling and unmarshalling formats for XML documents.

You may be wondering what the difference is between JAXB unmarshalling and XML parsing. Both render objects that can be used by Java code to access specific parts of an XML document. Both JAXB unmarshalling and XML parsing (using a validating parser) use Schemas to parse documents. However, the difference between parsing and unmarshalling is that while validating parsers use schemas to enforce a structure of an XML document, JAXB can use the same schema as a set of instructions for converting Java objects to an XML document and an XML document to Java objects. JAXB allows easier access to Java objects than either SAX or DOM parsing can provide. It also allows Java objects that represent XML document objects to be validated before they become XML document objects.

The flexibility of JAXB does come at a price. It would be great if you could feed a schema to JAXB at runtime and have it build XML document object classes on the fly, but that's not the way that JAXB works (for now, anyway). There are two steps to enabling XML document data binding with JAXB. The first step is to generate a set of classes that are used to handle XML document objects. A Java class is created for each object in a schema. The object classes are generated by JAXB processes and are based on a W3C schema that you provide. The second step uses the generated classes to handle marshalling, manipulation, and unmarshalling of XML documents, with optional schema validation.

Practical applications for JAXB

Despite the two-step process, JAXB can be very useful for many applications. The most practical implementation of a JAXB solution is to provide a set of classes for XML document development in a team development environment. One team member can develop the XML document structure and use JAXB to create a Java .jar file containing handler classes for the XML document. The .jar file can be passed to a Java development team and used for generating XML documents that have a reasonable expectation of being valid.

One pleasant side-effect of JAXB is that after the XML schema document structure has been broken down into a set of Java classes, the javadoc API can be used to provide documentation of the schema to Java developers. This comes in very handy for a development team who may not know anything about the XML document structure. It's also a fast way for an XML schema developer to create an easy-to-follow record of the schema structure for future reference. We'll show you an example of the generated Java docs for a sample schema later in this chapter.

Setting up JAXB

The first step to setting up JAXB is downloading the JAXB files. If you haven't already done so, we recommend downloading the full Web Services Developer Pack (WSDP) from `http://java.sun.com/xml`. If for some reason you don't want to download the entire WSDP, you can download just the JAXB code from the same page, which includes a couple of necessary files from the JAXP and WSDP packages as well. The JAXP and WSDP packages are only needed for the schema binding and class generation process. Once the classes are generated, you only need the JAXB packages to marshal and unmarshal XML documents.

Next, you have a few options for setting up a CLASSPATH that will be used by the binding process and run-time XML document manipulation. It would be great if the WSDP InstallShield process created the necessary environment variables for CLASS-PATH and path settings, but it doesn't.

Tip
The JAXB documentation provides elaborate and well-documented instructions on how to set up environment variable references to base directories like JAXB_HOME, JAXB_LIBS, JWSDP_HOME, etc., and then refer to these directories in other environment variables such as CLASSPATHS. Personally, I find this too easy to mess up when the references are added manually, and the nested references are hard to follow when you're trying to find a problem. On top of this, not all system administrators will let developers have access to servers to update environment variables. The idea behind the environment variable references accessing other environment variable references is to point to different versions of a package from a central point. This is because the package version number is usually part of the base directory for the packages.

We have a different approach that I find easier to follow, and you might too. We usually download the package into its default directory, and then create a new reference without the version numbers in the directory name. This way we have a copy of the old version and the new version if we need it. We also know without a doubt that the version we are using now is the one in our non-versioned directory for those packages. This makes it much easier for us to trace package reference issues.

For example, we downloaded the Web Service Developer Pack to its default directory (jwsdp-1.1), then made a copy of it to a non-versioned directory (jwsdp). We edited all subdirectories for JAXP, JAXB, etc., in a similar way. Our environment variable reference points to the jwsdp directory. This environment variable only has to be created once, and never edited. When we download the next WSDP version, we will copy the new files into the jwsdp directory, where they are immediately accessible to our programs without having to update any environment variables.

You'll need to manually add references to your system CLASSPATH or your Java IDE CLASSPATH before you can use JAXB. Below is a sample of the package references you need in your CLASSPATH, based on a WSDP installation directory of C:\jwsdp, and a standard WSDP installation.

```
C:\jwsdp\jaxb\lib\jaxb-api.jar;
C:\jwsdp\jaxb\lib\jaxb-ri.jar;
C:\jwsdp\jaxb\lib\jaxb-xjc.jar;
C:\jwsdp\jaxb\lib\jaxb-libs.jar;
C:\jwsdp\jaxp\lib\endorsed\dom.jar;
C:\jwsdp\jaxp\lib\endorsed\sax.jar;
C:\jwsdp\jaxp\lib\endorsed\xalan.jar;
C:\jwsdp\jaxp\lib\endorsed\xercesimpl.jar;
C:\jwsdp\jaxp\lib\endorsed\xsltc.jar;
C:\jwsdp\jwsdp-shared\lib\jax-qname.jar;
C:\jwsdp\jwsdp-shared\lib\namespace.jar
```

Creating JAXB classes from a Schema

Once the CLASSPATH settings are set up correctly, you are ready for Step 1 of the
JAXB process. Step 1 generates Java classes into a package that can be used for
marshalling, unmarshalling, XML document object manipulation and validation. You
need the JAXB packages installed on your system, your system environment set up
as shown above, and the Schema and batch file that is part of the downloads for
this chapter.

Listing 17-2 shows the W3C Schema for the sample XML document used in this
chapter. The schema and XML document are similar to examples that we have
shown in previous chapters. The only difference is that schema and XML document
references that used an xml: namespace prefix have been removed.

Tip
JAXB 1.0 appears not to recognize xml: prefixes on attribute names such as
xml:lang and others, even though they are well-formed and valid XML with correct
namespace references. Hopefully this is a JAXB 1.0 issue and will be fixed in future
versions. You will need to remove any schema references and XML document
objects with an xml: prefix of you get the following message when JAXB generates
classes:

"The prefix "xml" cannot be bound to any namespace other than its usual namespace; neither can the namespace for "xml" be bound to any prefix other than
"xml""

**Listing 17-2: The JAXB Example W3C Schema -
AmazonMacbethSpanish.xsd**

```
<?xml version="1.0" encoding="UTF-8"?>
<!--W3C Schema generated by XMLSPY v5 rel. 2 U (http://www.xmlspy.com)-->
<xs:schema xmlns:xs="http://www.w3.org/2001/XMLSchema"
elementFormDefault="qualified">
  <xs:element name="Encuadernación" type="xs:string"/>
  <xs:complexType name="amazonType">
    <xs:sequence>
```

Continued

Listing 17-2 *(continued)*

```xml
    <xs:element name="product" type="productType" maxOccurs="unbounded"/>
  </xs:sequence>
  <xs:attribute name="items" type="xs:string" use="required"/>
</xs:complexType>
<xs:element name="asin" type="xs:string"/>
<xs:element name="author" type="xs:string"/>
<xs:element name="autor" type="xs:string"/>
<xs:element name="availability" type="xs:string"/>
<xs:element name="binding" type="xs:string"/>
<xs:complexType name="catalogType">
  <xs:sequence>
    <xs:element name="amazon" type="amazonType"/>
    <xs:element name="elcorteingles" type="elcorteinglesType"/>
  </xs:sequence>
  <xs:attribute name="items" type="xs:string" use="required"/>
</xs:complexType>
<xs:complexType name="elcorteinglesType">
  <xs:sequence>
    <xs:element name="product" type="productType"/>
  </xs:sequence>
  <xs:attribute name="items" type="xs:string" use="required"/>
</xs:complexType>
<xs:element name="fecha_de_publicación" type="xs:string"/>
<xs:element name="image" type="xs:string"/>
<xs:element name="imagen" type="xs:string"/>
<xs:element name="isbn" type="xs:string"/>
<xs:element name="librourl" type="xs:string"/>
<xs:element name="list_price" type="xs:string"/>
<xs:element name="precio" type="xs:string"/>
<xs:complexType name="productType">
  <xs:sequence>
    <xs:element ref="ranking" minOccurs="0"/>
    <xs:choice maxOccurs="unbounded">
      <xs:element ref="title"/>
      <xs:element ref="titulo"/>
    </xs:choice>
    <xs:choice maxOccurs="unbounded">
      <xs:element ref="asin"/>
      <xs:element ref="isbn"/>
    </xs:choice>
    <xs:choice maxOccurs="unbounded">
      <xs:element ref="author"/>
      <xs:element ref="autor"/>
    </xs:choice>
    <xs:choice maxOccurs="unbounded">
      <xs:element ref="image"/>
      <xs:element ref="imagen"/>
    </xs:choice>
```

```xml
      <xs:element ref="small_image" minOccurs="0"/>
      <xs:choice maxOccurs="unbounded">
        <xs:element ref="list_price"/>
        <xs:element ref="precio"/>
      </xs:choice>
      <xs:choice maxOccurs="unbounded">
        <xs:element ref="release_date"/>
        <xs:element ref="fecha_de_publicación"/>
      </xs:choice>
      <xs:choice maxOccurs="unbounded">
        <xs:element ref="binding"/>
        <xs:element ref="Encuadernación"/>
      </xs:choice>
      <xs:element ref="availability" minOccurs="0"/>
      <xs:choice maxOccurs="unbounded">
        <xs:element ref="tagged_url"/>
        <xs:element ref="librourl"/>
      </xs:choice>
    </xs:sequence>
  </xs:complexType>
  <xs:complexType name="quoteType">
    <xs:simpleContent>
      <xs:extension base="xs:string">
        <xs:attribute name="source" type="xs:string"/>
        <xs:attribute name="author" type="xs:string"/>
      </xs:extension>
    </xs:simpleContent>
  </xs:complexType>
  <xs:element name="quotedoc">
    <xs:complexType>
      <xs:sequence>
        <xs:element name="quotelist" type="quotelistType"/>
        <xs:element name="catalog" type="catalogType"/>
      </xs:sequence>
    </xs:complexType>
  </xs:element>
  <xs:complexType name="quotelistType">
    <xs:sequence>
      <xs:element name="quote" type="quoteType" maxOccurs="unbounded"/>
    </xs:sequence>
    <xs:attribute name="author" type="xs:string" use="required"/>
    <xs:attribute name="quotes" type="xs:string" use="required"/>
  </xs:complexType>
  <xs:element name="ranking" type="xs:string"/>
  <xs:element name="release_date" type="xs:string"/>
  <xs:element name="small_image" type="xs:string"/>
  <xs:element name="tagged_url" type="xs:string"/>
  <xs:element name="title" type="xs:string"/>
  <xs:element name="titulo" type="xs:string"/>
</xs:schema>
```

Generating JAXB classes from a W3C Schema

As you can see, this is a fairly complex schema. There are several complex types, and valid XML documents are broken down into several segments under the root element. JAXB uses this schema to generate several Java classes, one representing each object in the schema. The JAXB documentation has very good, elaborate, and detailed instructions on how to do the same thing with the Ant build tool. The Ant build tool ships with the WSDP, and example Ant xml configuration files are included with the JAXB examples if you prefer to use that method. We use a simpler method, which is a batch file to generate JAXB code from the command line. We call the `jaxb-xjc.jar` directory, and pass it two parameters:

```
java -jar C:\jwsdp\jaxb\lib\jaxb-xjc.jar AmazonMacbethSpanish.xsd
-p jaxbexample1
```

The `jaxb-xjc.jar` contains the classes that generate the XML document classes. The first parameter is the name of the schema on which to base class generation on (AmazonMacbethSpanish.xsd). The second parameter is the name of the package that the classes will be created under (jaxbexample1). Both parameters assume that the schema and the output directory are in the same directory as the batch files. You can also optionally include a CLASSPATH reference from the command line:

```
-classpath C:\jwsdp\jaxb\lib\jaxb-api.jar;C:\jwsdp\jaxb\lib\jaxb-
ri.jar;C:\jwsdp\jaxb\lib\jaxb-xjc.jar;C:\jwsdp\jaxb-1.0\lib\jaxb-
libs.jar;C:\jwsdp\jaxp\lib\endorsed\dom.jar;C:\jwsdp\jaxp\lib\endorsed\sax.
jar;C:\jwsdp\jaxp\lib\endorsed\xalan.jar;C:\jwsdp\jaxp\lib\endorsed\xercesi
mpl.jar;C:\jwsdp\jaxp\lib\endorsed\xsltc.jar;C:\jwsdp\jwsdp-shared\lib\jax-
qname.jar;C:\jwsdp\jwsdp-shared\lib\namespace.jar
```

JAXB uses this batch file to generate a single class of each XML document object described in the schema. These classes are used to marshal and unmarshal XML documents. They are also used to access specific objects in an XML document that adheres to the schema, or to create a document from scratch using Java code, then marshal that document into XML.

Compiling JAXB classes

Once the JAXB classes have been generated, they need to be compiled. I use another batch file from the command line for this:

```
javac jaxbexample1\*.java jaxbexample1\impl\*.java
```

This code compiles all of the files in the jaxbexample1 and jaxbexample1\impl directories. The same optional -classpath value that was used in the generation batch file can be passed in the batch file to compile the code as well.

Figure 17-1 shows generated and compiled classes in the jaxbexample1 directory. Each class matches an XML document object. The classes and their XML document objects are listed in Table 17-1.

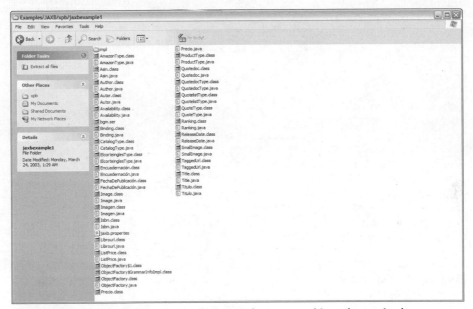

Figure 17-1: Generated and compiled XML document object classes in the jaxbexample1 directory

Generating documentation for JAXB classes

As we mentioned earlier in this chapter, you can also easily generate javadoc documentation for the generated JAXB classes. Not only does this provide documentation for Java developers to use when writing Java code that will create valid XML documents, but it also generates fairly good documentation of the original schema for the future reference of the schema developer. Here's the command that is used to generate Java documentation using the javadoc API from the command prompt. The javadoc API is part of the JDK.

```
javadoc -package jaxbexample1 -d javadoc
```

This tells the javadoc API to generate Java documentation for the jaxbexample1 package, and put the documentation in the javadoc subdirectory of the current directory.

Figure 17-2 shows the index for the javadocs that were generated by the preceding command.

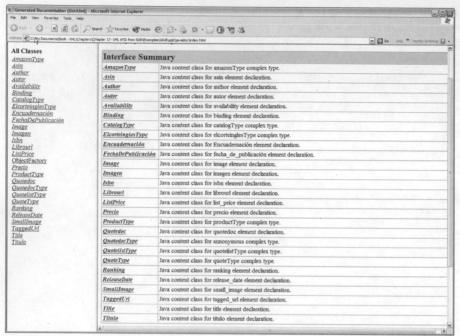

Figure 17-2: Class listing and Interface summary for the jaxbexample1 class files

In the javadoc HTML interface that is shown in Figure 17-2, the class names link to more detailed explanations of each object.   For example, Figure 17-3 shows the generated Javadoc for the AmazonType interface.

The Generated JAXB classes

Table 17-1 shows the interfaces generated and their javadoc descriptions. JAXB generated 27 interfaces and a handler class based on my example schema. The interfaces provide access to XML document objects directly from Java code. The JAXB ObjectFactory handler class provides facilities for creating new instances of each interface, which become new XML document objects when the JAXB document representation is marshalled into an XML document. As you can see from this table, the class names are a little easier to follow than their counterparts in the schema.

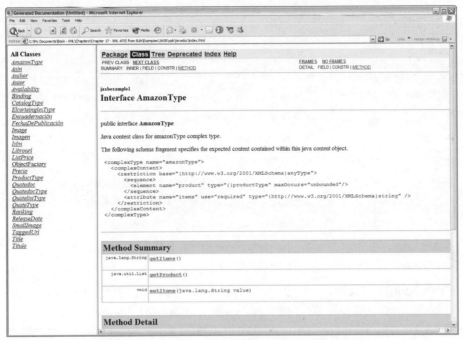

Figure 17-3: Javadoc documentation for the AmazonType Interface

Table 17-1
Classes Generated by AmazonMacbethSpanish.xsd

Name	Description
ObjectFactory	This object contains factory methods for each Java content interface and Java element interface generated in the jaxbexample1 package.
AmazonType	Java content class for amazonType complex type.
Asin	Java content class for asin element declaration.
Author	Java content class for author element declaration.
Autor	Java content class for autor element declaration.
Availability	Java content class for availability element declaration.
Binding	Java content class for binding element declaration.
CatalogType	Java content class for catalogType complex type.
ElcorteinglesType	Java content class for elcorteinglesType complex type.

Continued

Table 17-1 *(continued)*

Name	Description
Encuadernación	Java content class for Encuadernación element declaration.
FechaDePublicación	Java content class for fecha_de_publicación element declaration.
Image	Java content class for image element declaration.
Imagen	Java content class for imagen element declaration.
Isbn	Java content class for isbn element declaration.
Librourl	Java content class for librourl element declaration.
ListPrice	Java content class for list_price element declaration.
Precio	Java content class for precio element declaration.
ProductType	Java content class for productType complex type.
Quotedoc	Java content class for quotedoc element declaration.
QuotedocType	Java content class for anonymous complex type.
QuotelistType	Java content class for quotelistType complex type.
QuoteType	Java content class for quoteType complex type.
Ranking	Java content class for ranking element declaration.
ReleaseDate	Java content class for release_date element declaration.
SmallImage	Java content class for small_image element declaration.
TaggedUrl	Java content class for tagged_url element declaration.
Title	Java content class for title element declaration.
Titulo	Java content class for titulo element declaration.

Working with the created JAXB classes

Once the JAXB classes are generated and documented, you can start working with the classes in your Java code. Listing 17-3 shows an example XML that validated to the schema in Listing 17-2.

Listing 17-3: The Example XML Document – AmazonMacbethSpanish.xml

```
<?xml version="1.0" encoding="ISO-8859-1"?>
<quotedoc>
  <quotelist author="Shakespeare, William" quotes="4">
    <quote source="Macbeth" author="Shakespeare, William">When the
    hurlyburly's done, / When the battle's lost and won.</quote>
```

```
    <quote source="Macbeth" author="Shakespeare, William">Out, damned spot!
    out, I say!-- One; two; why, then 'tis time to do't ;--Hell is murky!-
    -Fie, my lord, fie! a soldier, and afeard? What need we fear who knows
    it, when none can call our power to account?--Yet who would have
    thought the old man to have had so much blood in him?</quote>
    <quote source="Macbeth"  author="Shakespeare, William">Is this a dagger
    which I see before me, the handle toward my hand? Come, let me clutch
    thee: I have thee not, and yet I see thee still. Art thou not, fatal
    vision, sensible to feeling as to sight? or art thou but a dagger of
    the mind, a false creation, proceeding from the heat-oppressed
    brain?</quote>
    <quote source="Macbeth" author="Shakespeare, William">To-morrow, and
    to-morrow, and to-morrow, creeps in this petty pace from day to day, to
    the last syllable of recorded time; and all our yesterdays have
    lighted fools the way to dusty death. Out, out, brief candle! Life's
    but a walking shadow; a poor player, that struts and frets his hour
    upon the stage, and then is heard no more: it is a tale told by an
    idiot, full of sound and fury, signifying nothing. </quote>
    <quote/>
</quotelist>
<catalog items="4">
  <Amazon items="3">
    <product>
      <ranking>1</ranking>
      <title>Hamlet/MacBeth</title>
      <asin>8432040231</asin>
      <author>Shakespeare, William</author>
      <image>http://images.Amazon.com/images/P/
        8432040231.01.MZZZZZZZ.jpg</image>
      <small_image>http://images.Amazon.com/images/P/
        8432040231.01.TZZZZZZZ.jpg</small_image>
      <list_price>$7.95</list_price>
      <release_date>19910600</release_date>
      <binding>Paperback</binding>
      <availability/>
      <tagged_url>http://www.Amazon.com:80/exec/obidos/redirect?tag=
        associateid&amp;benztechnologies=9441&amp;camp=1793&amp;link_code=
        xml&amp;path=ASIN/8432040231</tagged_url>
    </product>
    <product>
      <ranking>2</ranking>
      <title>MacBeth</title>
      <asin>1583488340</asin>
      <author>Shakespeare, William</author>
      <image>http://images.Amazon.com/images/P/
        1583488340.01.MZZZZZZZ.jpg</image>
      <small_image>http://images.Amazon.com/images/P/
        1583488340.01.TZZZZZZZ.jpg</small_image>
      <list_price>$8.95</list_price>
      <release_date>19991200</release_date>
      <binding>Paperback</binding>
      <availability/>
```

Continued

Listing 17-3 *(continued)*

```
      <tagged_url>http://www.Amazon.com:80/exec/obidos/redirect?tag=
        associateid&amp;benztechnologies=9441&amp;camp=1793&amp;link_code=
        xml&amp;path=ASIN/1583488340</tagged_url>
    </product>
    <product>
      <ranking>3</ranking>
      <title>William Shakespeare: MacBeth</title>
      <asin>8420617954</asin>
      <author>Shakespeare, William</author>
      <image>http://images.Amazon.com/images/P/
        8420617954.01.MZZZZZZZ.jpg</image>
      <small_image>http://images.Amazon.com/images/P/
        8420617954.01.TZZZZZZZ.jpg</small_image>
      <list_price>$4.75</list_price>
      <release_date>19810600</release_date>
      <binding>Paperback</binding>
      <availability/>
      <tagged_url>http://www.Amazon.com:80/exec/obidos/redirect?tag=
        associateid&amp;benztechnologies=9441&amp;camp=1793&amp;link_code=
        xml&amp;path=ASIN/8420617954</tagged_url>
    </product>
  </Amazon>

  <elcorteingles items="1">
    <product>
      <titulo>Romeo y Julieta/Macbeth/Hamlet/Otelo/La fierecilla
        domado/El sueño de una noche de verano/ El mercader de
        Venecia</titulo>
      <isbn>8484036324</isbn>
      <autor>Shakespeare, William</autor>
      <imagen>http://libros.elcorteingles.es/producto/
        verimagen_blob.asp?ISBN=8449503639</imagen>
      <precio>7,59 &#x20AC;</precio>
      <fecha_de_publicación>6/04/1999</fecha_de_publicación>
      <Encuadernación>Piel</Encuadernación>
      <librourl>http://libros.elcorteingles.es/producto/
        libro_descripcion.asp?CODIISBN=8449503639</librourl>
    </product>
  </elcorteingles>
  </catalog>
</quotedoc>
```

Because we created both the XML document and the schema as examples for this book, we know that this XML document validates against the schema. However, in the real world, it's seldom the case that you would know this up front. You could use a validating parser to check for validation. But this section of the chapter is about JAXB, so we're going to use JAXB to check the document for validity by unmarshalling it into a set of JAXB objects. We also add a new quote to the quote list, and then check the new quote to see if it's valid, based on the schema. Once that's done, we marshal the new document. Listing 17-4 shows the code in its entirety, and then we break it down after the listing.

Listing 17-4: Code for Working with the Generated JAXB Classes - JAXBExample.java

```java
import java.io.*;
import java.util.*;
import javax.xml.bind.*;
import jaxbexample1.*;

public class JAXBExample {

    public static void main(String[] args) {
        JAXBExample JBE = new JAXBExample();
    }

    public JAXBExample() {

        try {
            JAXBContext JBC = JAXBContext.newInstance( "jaxbexample1" );
            Unmarshaller u = JBC.createUnmarshaller();
            u.setValidating( true );

            Quotedoc QD = (Quotedoc)u.unmarshal( new FileInputStream( "
AmazonMacbethSpanish.xml" ) );
            QuotelistType QuoteList = QD.getQuotelist();
            List Qlist = QuoteList.getQuote();

            System.out.println("Original List of Quotes in QuoteDoc:");
            for( Iterator i = Qlist.iterator(); i.hasNext(); ) {
                QuoteType Qitem = (QuoteType)i.next();
                System.out.println(  "Author: " + Qitem.getAuthor() +"\n" +
                "Source: " + Qitem.getSource() +"\n" +
                Qitem.getValue());
            }

            ObjectFactory OF = new jaxbexample1.ObjectFactory();
            QuoteType newQuote = OF.createQuoteType();
            newQuote.setAuthor("Shakespeare, William");
            newQuote.setSource("Macbeth");
            newQuote.setValue("Sleep shall neither night nor day Hang upon
his penthouse lid; He shall live a man forbid: Weary . . .");
```

Continued

Listing 17-4 *(continued)*

```
        Validator val = JBC.createValidator();
        boolean validQuote = val.validate(newQuote);
        if (validQuote=true) {
            System.out.println("New Quote is Valid"+"\n");
        }

        Qlist.add(newQuote);

        QuoteList = QD.getQuotelist();
        Qlist = QuoteList.getQuote();

        System.out.println("New List of Quotes in QuoteDoc:");
        for( Iterator i = Qlist.iterator(); i.hasNext(); ) {
            QuoteType Qitem = (QuoteType)i.next();
            System.out.println(  "Author: " + Qitem.getAuthor() +"\n" +
            "Source: " + Qitem.getSource() +"\n" +
            Qitem.getValue());
        }

        Marshaller m = JBC.createMarshaller();
        m.setProperty( Marshaller.JAXB_FORMATTED_OUTPUT, Boolean.TRUE
        );
        OutputStream OS = new FileOutputStream(
        " AmazonMacbethSpanish1.xml" );
        m.marshal( QD, OS );

    }
    catch( JAXBException je ) {
        je.printStackTrace();
    }
    catch( IOException ioe ) {
        ioe.printStackTrace();
    }


    }


}
```

The first piece of code is the imports. `java.io.*` and `java.util.*` provide us with a way to read and write XML documents and work with lists. `javax.xml.bind.*` provides access to JAXB functionality. `jaxbexample1.*` pulls in all of the custom JAXB classes that were generated earlier in this chapter. The classes in the jaxbexample1 package could be compressed into a .jar file for easier distribution, but since this is an example, we've left them uncompressed so they are easier to access and review. Next, the code creates a class, which implements a main method, which calls a constructor, which creates a new instance of the JAXBExample class.

```
import java.io.*;
import java.util.*;
import javax.xml.bind.*;
import jaxbexample1.*;

public class JAXBExample {

    public static void main(String[] args) {
        JAXBExample JBE = new JAXBExample();
    }

    public JAXBExample() {

        try {
```

A new instance of JAXBContext is created, which provides access to the JAXB classes. Next, a new unmarshaller is created, which is used to unmarshal the XML document. When the XML document is unmarshalled, it will be validated, because the setValidating property of the unmarshaller is set to true. If there is a validation error, the code will stop execution and a JAXB error will be returned via the catch below.

```
JAXBContext JBC = JAXBContext.newInstance( "jaxbexample1" );
Unmarshaller u = JBC.createUnmarshaller();
u.setValidating( true );
```

Next, a FileInputStream is used to get the XML document from the file system. The XML document is assumed to be in the same directory as this class. Quotedoc represents the root element in the XML document. A QuotelistType object is created using one of the generated JAXB classes. QuotelistType is a class that represents the QuotelistType complex type from the schema. The QuotelistType contains one or more QuoteTypes, which represent quoteType complex types from the schema. A list is used to contain the quotes. Quotes are loaded into the list by extracting them from the QuotelistType using the getQuote method.

```
Quotedoc QD = (Quotedoc)u.unmarshal( new FileInputStream
( "AmazonMacbethSpanish.xml" ) );
QuotelistType QuoteList = QD.getQuotelist();
List Qlist = QuoteList.getQuote();
```

Now that the quotes are in a list, they can be traversed with an Iterator. We use an Iterator to display the current list of quotes to System.out. The getAuthor, getSource, and getValue methods are used to return the Quote author, source, and the quote, which is represented by the text value associated with the quote element.

```
System.out.println("Original List of Quotes in QuoteDoc:");
for( Iterator i = Qlist.iterator(); i.hasNext(); ) {
    QuoteType Qitem = (QuoteType)i.next();
    System.out.println( "Author: " + Qitem.getAuthor() +"\n" +
    "Source: " + Qitem.getSource() +"\n" +
    Qitem.getValue());
}
```

So far so good — the code is still running at this point, which confirms that the document has been successfully unmarshalled and validated, and access to objects is working. The next piece of code writes to the XML document using a new instance of `ObjectFactory`. The `createQuoteType` method of `ObjectFactory` creates a new empty quote object. The `setAuthor`, `setSource`, and `setValue` methods of `QuoteType` fills in the quote object with string values.

```
ObjectFactory OF = new jaxbexample1.ObjectFactory();
QuoteType newQuote = OF.createQuoteType();
newQuote.setAuthor("Shakespeare, William");
newQuote.setSource("Macbeth");
newQuote.setValue("Sleep shall neither night nor day Hang upon
his penthouse lid; He shall live a man forbid: Weary . . .");
```

The quote object is now populated with new values, but is not part of the XML document object yet. Before it is made a part of the XML document, the JAXB `Validator` class can be used to validate the QuoteType object. This is a handy and quick way to validate an object without having to validate the entire XML document, which was already validated when the XML document was unmarshalled.

 Note   The `if (validQuote=true)` statement is added for clarity, but is not necessary. If the `Validator` encounters a validation error, the code stops and a JAXB exception is thrown. Therefore, we could have left the `if` statement out — if the code is still running after validation, then the validation is a success.

```
Validator val = JBC.createValidator();
boolean validQuote = val.validate(newQuote);
if (validQuote=true) {
    System.out.println("New Quote is Valid"+"\n");
}
```

If the new object is valid according to the schema, the Java List `add` method is used to add the new quote to the end of the quote list. Next, the quote listing is displayed to the `System.out` again to confirm that the new quote is added. This code is the same as the previous code for iteration of the list and display to `System.out`. Normally, we would write redundant code like this to a separate subclass, but that messes up the flow of examples, so we've repeated the code here.

```
Qlist.add(newQuote);
QuoteList = QD.getQuotelist();
Qlist = QuoteList.getQuote();
```

```
System.out.println("New List of Quotes in QuoteDoc:");
for( Iterator i = Qlist.iterator(); i.hasNext(); ) {
    QuoteType Qitem = (QuoteType)i.next();
    System.out.println( "Author: " + Qitem.getAuthor() +"\n" +
    "Source: " + Qitem.getSource() +"\n" +
    Qitem.getValue());
}
```

Next, the code saves a new XML document with the added quote to the file system using a new instance of the JAXBContext Marshaller. The JAXB_FORMATTED_OUTPUT property tells the Marshaller to format the output with indents and line feeds. Other Marshaller properties set the encoding and a schema reference. These are left at their default values. The new document is marshalled to a FileOutputStream, which saves the new XML document as AmazonMacbethSpanish1.xml. QD refers to the original Quotedoc that was created when the original XML document was unmarshalled.

```
Marshaller m = JBC.createMarshaller();
m.setProperty( Marshaller.JAXB_FORMATTED_OUTPUT, Boolean.TRUE
);
OutputStream OS = new FileOutputStream(
" AmazonMacbethSpanish1.xml" );
m.marshal( QD, OS );
```

If the class encounters any marshalling or validation errors, JAXBException is caught. IOException catches and file read and/or write errors.

```
    }
catch( JAXBException je ) {
    je.printStackTrace();
}
catch( IOException ioe ) {
    ioe.printStackTrace();
}
```

There are two results from this class, a new XML document called AmazonMacbethSpanish1.xml, and status output written to System.out. Listing 17-5 shows the output that is written to System.out.

Listing 17-5: **Output from JAXBExample,java**

```
Original List of Quotes in QuoteDoc:
Author: Shakespeare, William
Source: Macbeth
When the hurlyburly's done, / When the battle's lost and won.
Author: Shakespeare, William
Source: Macbeth
```

Continued

Listing 17-5 *(continued)*

Out, damned spot! out, I say!-- One; two; why, then 'tis time to do't ;--Hell is
murky!--Fie, my lord, fie! a soldier, and afeard? What need we fear who knows
it, when none can call our power to account?--Yet who would have thought the old
man to have had so much blood in him?
Author: Shakespeare, William
Source: Macbeth
Is this a dagger which I see before me, the handle toward my hand? Come, let me
clutch thee: I have thee not, and yet I see thee still. Art thou not, fatal
vision, sensible to feeling as to sight? or art thou but a dagger of the mind, a
false creation, proceeding from the heat-oppressed brain?
Author: Shakespeare, William
Source: Macbeth
To-morrow, and to-morrow, and to-morrow, creeps in this petty pace from day to
day, to the last syllable of recorded time; and all our yesterdays have lighted
fools the way to dusty death. Out, out, brief candle! Life's but a walking
shadow; a poor player, that struts and frets his hour upon the stage, and then
is heard no more: it is a tale told by an idiot, full of sound and fury,
signifying nothing.

New Quote is Valid

New List of Quotes in QuoteDoc:
Author: Shakespeare, William
Source: Macbeth
When the hurlyburly's done, / When the battle's lost and won.
Author: Shakespeare, William
Source: Macbeth
Out, damned spot! out, I say!-- One; two; why, then 'tis time to do't ;--Hell is
murky!--Fie, my lord, fie! a soldier, and afeard? What need we fear who knows
it, when none can call our power to account?--Yet who would have thought the old
man to have had so much blood in him?
Author: Shakespeare, William
Source: Macbeth
Is this a dagger which I see before me, the handle toward my hand? Come, let me
clutch thee: I have thee not, and yet I see thee still. Art thou not, fatal
vision, sensible to feeling as to sight? or art thou but a dagger of the mind, a
false creation, proceeding from the heat-oppressed brain?
Author: Shakespeare, William
Source: Macbeth
To-morrow, and to-morrow, and to-morrow,creeps in this petty pace from day to
day, to the last syllable of recorded time; and all our yesterdays have lighted
fools the way to dusty death. Out, out, brief candle! Life's but a walking
shadow; a poor player, that struts and frets his hour upon the stage, and then
is heard no more: it is a tale told by an idiot, full of sound and fury,
signifying nothing.

```
Author: Shakespeare, William
Source: Macbeth
Sleep shall neither night nor day Hang upon his penthouse lid; He shall live a
man forbid: Weary . . .
```

Developing with JSTL (JavaServer Pages Standard Tag Library)

The JavaServer Pages Standard Tag Library (JSTL) lets Web developers generate servlet code using Java objects without having to code, compile, and deploy servlets, and with very little knowledge of the Java classes that are being used. In this way the design of Web pages can be somewhat separated from Web content and Web applications. JSTL documents are a lot easier to create and edit than servlets that produce the same content.

Introduction to JSPs

Java Server Pages (JSPs) are a way of integrating server-side functionality with HTML element tags to create dynamic content for the Web while separating content from display in a J2EE world. Most developers know by now that HTML pages are static files that can be edited and saved on a server's file system. JSPs are a way of generating servlets on the fly. JSPs are calculated HTML pages that are generated at runtime by a servlet, which is in turn generated by a JSP. JSP tags are formatted much like HTML tags, but are actually references to servlet functionality that generates an HTML page at runtime, before it is sent to a browser.

JSPs can therefore be described as a meta-language for developing servlets without having to code, debug, and compile Java source code then deploy servlet class files. All a developer needs is an HTML editor tool and a reference describing any necessary JSP tag's syntax. Instead of saving the HTML page as an .htm page, a developer saves the page as a .jsp page, and deploys the page to a JSP-compatible Web server. The Web server creates and compiles a servlet based on tags in the .jsp page. When the .jsp page is called on the Web server, the servlet runs. The servlet output usually generates a static HTML page containing dynamic content that was added to the page at runtime.

JSP Tag Syntax: Declarations, directives, expressions, and scriptlets

It's important to understand different types of tags and how they affect JSP output. Table 17-2 describes directives and three other standard JSP scripting elements that JSP developers need to know about.

Table 17-2
JSP Tag Syntax: Declarations, Directives, Expressions, and Scriptlets

Scripting Element	Description
Expressions	Expressions are included as part of a generated servlet's response.
Declarations	Declarations are inserted into the servlet outside of method calls.
Directives	Directives come in three flavors: Include, page and taglib. Include inserts a file from the file system when a servlet is generated by a JSP. Page defines attributes for a page, including imports, output encoding, error handling, session support, and packages to import. The taglib directive is used to define custom tag libraries. The JSTL uses taglib directives to include JSTL tags in JSP pages. I'll show examples of this later in the chapter.
Scriptlets	Actual pieces of Java code to be inserted in the generated Servlet. Scriptlets are inserted into a special methods created for JSP servlets called _jspService

Expressions, declarations, directives, and scriptlets can be formatted as JSP tags or as XML tags. Table 17-3 shows the standard JSP and XML formats.

Table 17-3
JSP and XML Tag Formats

Standard Tag Format	XML Format
Expressions : <%=expression%>	<jsp:expression> tag expression </jsp:expression>
Declarations: <%!declaration%>	<jsp:declaration> tag declaration </jsp:declaration>
Directives: <%@ directive attr1="value1" attr2="value2"%>	<jsp:directive.(include | page | taglib) attr1=value1 attr2=value2 />
Scriptlets: <%scriptlet%>	<jsp:scriptlet> scriptlet code </jsp:scriptlet>

JSP predefined variables

JSP pages can use several predefined variables that are outside the scope of the JSTL, so a brief introduction is in order. The list of variables also provides a good overview of the objects that can be accessed and manipulated by a JSP page. Table 17-4 shows the eight predefined JSP variables.

Table 17-4
Predefined Variables

Variable	Description
application	application provides access to variables stored in a ServletContext object. Variables that are stored in the ServletContext object can be shared between servlets that are part of the same application.
config	config represents a ServletConfig object for a JSP page. ServletConfig objects contain initialization parameters via a jspInit method. Initialization parameters are parameters that are passed from a JSP server instance to a JSP page at page initialization. Initialization parameters are defined in the WEB-INF/web.xml page for a JSP server instance.
out	out is a buffered PrintWriter called JspWriter. JSP page buffering is controlled by setting a buffer size attribute using a JSP page directive. Buffering is enabled by default, and the default page buffer is 8kb. Out is not needed for JSP expressions, because they are automatically sent to the JspWriter. Scriptlets (Java Code embedded on a JSP page) and other objects can explicitly refer to the out variable to pass output to the JspWriter.
page	page provides a placeholder for a page object. Intended for use with non-scripting languages, so not commonly used with standard JSP pages.
pageContext	pageContext contains JSP page-specific objects and functionality, such as JspWriter. pageContext provides access to all page-related classes in this table through a single interface.
request	request represents a JSP page request. It provides access to parameters, HTTP header information, cookies, and initialization parameters.
response	response represents the HTTP response to a JSP page request. HTTP status codes and header information can be manipulated using response, unless buffering has been disabled. JSP page buffering is controlled by setting a buffer size attribute using a JSP page directive. Buffering is enabled by default, and the default page buffer is 8kb.
session	session represents an HTTP session object associated with a JSP page request. Sessions are enabled by default on JSP pages. JSP sessions can be disabled by using a JSP page directive to set session="false".

Tag library descriptors (TLDs) and JSTL

JSP tags are described in XML format in a Tag Library Descriptor file (TLD). TLDs are very useful for storing and sharing JSP tags in a portable format and are part of the JSP specification. Tags defined in the TLDs access Java classes in accompanying .jar files when creating servlets from JSP pages.

JSP tag libraries are contained in tag library descriptor (TLD) files. TLDs describe a tag library by providing documentation on a library and its tags, actions that each tag represents, and compatibility information for JSP servers based on the tag version number. TLDs are well-formed XML documents, and can be viewed as such.

The JavaServer Pages Standard Tag Library (JSTL) ships with eight TLD files and four .jar files. The eight TLD files support two types of tag structures: Request Time Expression Values (RT) and Expression Language Values (EL). JSP specifications are published and maintained by Sun via the JCP process. Request Time Expression (RT) is part of the JSP 1.2 specification. Expression Language (EL) is part of the JSP 1.3 Specification, and is designed to supplant the Java-based RT tag format in future specifications. We'll explain the Expression Language in more detail later in this chapter. For now, you just need to know that both the legacy RT tags and newer EL tags ship with the JSTL, and tag formats can be mixed on a page, but it is not recommended. The RT tags maintain backward compatibility with older JSP pages, but we don't recommend using them for new development. Future JSP versions may drop the RT tags in favor of EL tags exclusively. Full documentation of current JSP specifications can be found at http://java.sun.com/products/jsp/docs.html. The version that we are working with for this chapter is JSTL 1.0.3, which is part of the WSDP 1.1. Currently, JSP 2.0 is in the works, having just reached the second working draft as we write this.

Table 17-5 shows the four JSTL tag libraries, represented by eight TLD files.

Table 17-5
JSTL Libraries, TLD Files, Prefixes, and URIs.

Library Name	TLD File	Prefix	URI
Core	c.tld	c	http://java.sun.com/jstl/core
	c-rt.tld	c_rt	http://java.sun.com/jstl/core_rt
SQL Database access	sql.tld	sql	http://java.sun.com/jstl/sql
	sql-rt.tld	sql_rt	http://java.sun.com/jstl/sql_rt
Internationalization with I18N formatting	Fmt.tld	fmt	http://java.sun.com/jstl/fmt
	fmt-rt.tld	fmt_rt	http://java.sun.com/jstl/fmt_rt
XML processing	x.tld	x	http://java.sun.com/jstl/xml
	x-rt.tld	x_rt	http://java.sun.com/jstl/xml_rt

The core JSTL library contains support for common servlet tasks such as iteration, conditional expressions such as `if` and `choose`, and many others. The SQL library supports SQL access to databases via JDBC 2.0. The Internationalization library supports tags for JSTL internationalization functions, including text encoding and locale-sensitive formatting. The XML library supports several functions for XML document processing. The tags and their associated attributes are covered in great detail in the JSTL documentation, which can be downloaded from `http://java.sun.com/products/jsp/jstl/`. I will cover the XML tag library in detail later in this chapter.

Table 17-6 shows the four .jar files that represented by eight TLD files. The classes in the .jar files do not directly correspond to a single tag library. The .tld file for each library points to one or more of the .jar files for Java reference classes. Parsing is a big part of JSP pages, because JSP tags are parsed before they are converted to servlets on a JSP server.

Table 17-6
JSTL Libraries, TLD Files, Prefixes, and URIs.

Library Name	Description
Jaxen jaxen-full.jar	Evaluates Xpath expressions.
JSTL jstl.jar	Contains the JSTL API classes.
JSTL implementation classes standard.jar	Contains the JSTL implementation classes.
Saxpath saxpath.jar	Provides support for Xpath expressions with SAX parsing.

Using the JSP Expression Language (EL) with JSTL

EL is developed on a base of ECMAScript and Xpath, so developers with basic understanding of Script Languages and XPath will probably be comfortable with the basic syntax of Expression Language (EL) expressions. EL expressions start with `${` and end with `}`. For example, a property of an object is accessed with `${object.property}`. Here's a simple transform tag that we use in a JSP later in this chapter. It contains two EL variable references:

```
<x:transform xml="${xmlSource}" xslt="${xsltSource}" />
```

The `x:transform` tag performs an XSLT transformation on a source document defined by the EL reference `xml="${xmlSource}"` using a stylesheet defined by the EL reference `xslt="${xsltSource}`. Both the `xmlSource` and the `xsltSource` variables reference XML documents. The XML documents are imported earlier in the page and passed to the transform tag as XML document objects.

EL supports five literal object types: Boolean, floating point, integer, null, and string. Variables can be tested and manipulated with standard mathematical operators +, -, /, %, <, <=, >, and >=. EL also supports other operators that are similar to JavaScript syntax, shown in Table 17-7.

Table 17-7
JSP Expression Language Operators

Operator	Description
["element"] or [elementVariable] or ["property"] or [propertyVariable]	Get an element of an array, map or list, or the property of an object by property name. Literal element or property references can be in single or double quotes. Quotes within quotes have to be single quotes nested in double quotes, double quotes nested in single quotes, or escaped as part of the text value (\' or \").
.	Get a property of an object.
=	Variable assignment
(== or eq)	Equal
(!= or ne)	Not equal
()	Expression Grouping
(&& or and)	Logical AND
(|| or or)	Logical OR
(! or not) boolean	Reverse Boolean reference
empty	Null value, empty string, or empty collection

The Expression Language also makes several predefined variables available for processing. The predefined variables are referred to as *implicit* objects, because they map to objects that can be present on a page, and are retrieved as Java objects instead of text-based attribute values. JSP objects that contain one or more value usually take the form of `java.util.lists`, or `java.util.arrays`, or `java.util.maps`. Maps, lists, and arrays contain one or more Java objects, called elements. Maps contain a grouping of keys and values in each element. Map values can be duplicated but map keys have to be unique. Lists contain multiple single-dimension elements that are accessible by an index number, based on the order of the list. Lists can have duplicate elements. Arrays are like lists, but can be multi-dimensional. Except for pageContext, implicit objects take the form of java.util.maps. For more information on maps, lists, and arrays, start with the JDK 1.4 API Collections interface documentation at `http://java.sun.com/j2se/1.4/docs/api/java/util/Collection.html`.

The first six implicit objects are associated with page requests. A JSP page request can have associated cookies, headers, URL parameter values, and initialization parameters. For example, if a JSP page is accessed with the URL `http://www.JSPHost.com/ExamplePage.jsp?ParameterName=ParameterValue` and includes a cookie as part of the page request, then parameter, cookie, and header information is available to be processed by the JSP page. The parameter represented by `ParameterName` is available to the `param` and `paramValues` implicit objects. HTTP Header information is available via the `header` and `headerValues` objects. Cookie information is available from the `cookie` object.

Initialization parameters are parameters that are passed from a JSP server instance to a JSP page at page initialization. Initialization parameters are defined in the WEB-INF/web.xml page for a JSP server instance, and look like this for JSPs:

```
<init-param>
<param-name>name</param-name>
<param-value>value</param-value>
</init-param>
```

Table 17-8 shows the five implicit objects for page requests, and one object for initialization parameters:

Table 17-8	
JSP Expression Language Page Request Variables	
Implicit Object	*Description*
cookie value="${cookie.name}"	A java.util.map of JSP page request cookies. Each cookie element has a key representing the name of the cookie and returns a javax.servlet.http.Cookie object for a corresponding cookie name.
header value="${header.name}"	A java.util.map of HTTP request header values. Each header element has a key representing the name of the header element and a string value. If a header element value has multiple values, it is returned as a single string.

Continued

Table 17-8 *(continued)*

Implicit Object	Description
headerValues value="${headerValues.name}"	A java.util.map of JSP page request header values. Similar to header, but designed for multiple value headers. Each header element has a key representing the name of the header element, and a value in a string array. Header values are returned as string arrays.
initParam value="${initParam.name}"	A java.util.map of JSP page initialization parameters. Each initialization parameter element has a key representing the name of the parameter and a string value. If an initialization parameter has multiple values, it is returned as a single string.
param value="${param.name}"	A java.util.map of JSP page request parameters. Each parameter element has a key representing the name of the parameter and a string value. If a parameter has multiple values, it is returned as a single string.
paramValues value="${paramValues.name}"	A java.util.map of JSP page request parameters. Similar to param, but designed for multiple value parameters. Each parameter element has a key representing the name of the parameter, and a value in a string array. Parameters are returned as string arrays.

Table 17-9 shows the remaining implicit objects that are used for a pageContext object and several scoped objects. A *scope* defines a level at which an object or variable will be available for processing. These are translated into specific locations in a servlet when the servlet is generated from the JSP page. When a new object is created on a JSP page, the object must specify a page, request, session, or application scope that the object belongs to. Page-scoped objects are stored in the PageContext object of a servlet. Request-scoped objects are stored in a servlet's ServletRequest object. A session-scoped object becomes part of the HttpSession object in a servlet. An application-scoped object becomes part of a servlet's ServletContext object, and is available to all JSP pages that are defined as part of the same application.

Table 17-9
JSP Expression Language Page Request Variables

Implicit Object	Description
pageContext	pageContext provides access to all page-related classes in the JSTL through a single interface, including application, config, out, request, response, and session objects.
pageScope	A java.util.map of JSP objects associated with a JSP page. Represented by the PageContext object in a servlet.
requestScope	A java.util.map of JSP objects associated with a JSP page Request. Represented by the ServletRequest object in a servlet.
sessionScope	A java.util.map of JSP objects associated with a JSP session. Represented by the HttpSession object in a servlet.
applicationScope	A java.util.map of JSP objects associated with a JSP application. Represented by the ServletContext object in a servlet. ServletContext is available to all JSP pages defined as part of an application.

Downloading and installing the JSTL

Earlier in this chapter we introduced you to the eight Tag Library Descriptor files (TLDs) and the four .jar files that are used in the JSTL. Each of the tags in the TLD files links to a class in a .jar file. JSP pages are parsed and servlets are generated on a server that supports a *JSP container*. JSP containers are part of most J2EE Web applications servers, such as IBM's WebSphere application server, Bea WebLogic Application Server, Sun One Application Server, and Apache Tomcat. You'll need one of these servers to use JSP functionality and the JSTL. Many J2EE IDEs come with an integrated J2EE Web application server that is pre-configured with a JSP container. These implementations are usually fine for JSP development and testing, before the JSP is deployed to an application server. J2EE IDES that support JSPs include IBM's WebSphere Studio Application Developer, and the Sun ONE Studio. Check your IDE documentation to see if it provides JSP support.

Note The JSP container that you are using for JSTL-based JSP pages must support JSP 1.2 or higher. Check the application server and/or IDE documentation for supported versions.

The first step to setting up JSTL is downloading the JSTL files. If you haven't already done so, we recommend downloading the full Web Services Developer Pack (WSDP) from `http://java.sun.com/xml`. If for some reason you don't want to download the entire WSDP, you can download just the JSTL code from the same page, which includes all necessary .jar and .tld files, very brief documentation, and several samples.

The CLASSPATH for the JSP workstation or the IDE environment must include references to the following .jar files, with the addition of path information based on your JSTL installation configuration:

```
jaxen-full.jar, jstl.jar, standard.jar, saxpath.jar
```

Customizing a J2EE server instance to support JSTL

J2EE servers can have more than one instance of a server running at a time. Each instance of the server is supported by a WEB-INF directory, which contains all of the files that are used to run that instance, including .jar files, .tld files, .class files, and .jsp files.

Note   Many application servers and IDEs have automatic processes to import tag libraries by importing .jar files and .tld files and updating the web.xml file to support the tags. Check your documentation to see if these features are supported. Others just have an integrated process for checking the well-formedness and validity of a web.xml file. In any case, it's good to know about the manual process in case there is a configuration problem with a J2EE server instance. We find server JSP support configuration to be at least 50 percent of the headaches when developing JSP pages.

The .jar and .tld files must be placed in the WEB-INF directory or a subdirectory. Typically, the .jar files are installed into WEB-INF/classes. .tld files are usually installed directly into WEB-INF. For the purposes of this example, we've followed that convention, but when we set up a server, we usually like to install the .jar and .tld files in their own unique subdirectory on the server. That way the files associated with a specific tag library installation and version are easily identifiable. Also, the possibility of confusion over two .tld files or .jar files with the same name is eliminated if every installation is in its own directory.

Next, the web.xml file for the JTSL instance of the J2EE server must be edited. The web.xml file contains support and configuration information for servlets, jsps, initialization variables, and customized functionality for a J2EE server instance. References to a JSP implementation and its associated files can be changed by editing the CLASSPATH and the web.xml files for a J2EE server instance. The order of placement of tags in the web.xml file can often be important. In general, they should be placed at the end of the file, just above the `</web-app>` closing tag. Listing 17-6 shows references to the JSTL .tld files must be added to web.xml. The example includes the complete reference to the RT and the EL tag libraries. If you don't need one or the other, the references can be omitted.

Listing 17-6: taglib References for the web.xml File

```xml
<taglib>
    <taglib-uri>http://java.sun.com/jstl/fmt</taglib-uri>
    <taglib-location>/WEB-INF/fmt.tld</taglib-location>
</taglib>
<taglib>
    <taglib-uri>http://java.sun.com/jstl/fmt_rt</taglib-uri>
    <taglib-location>/WEB-INF/fmt-rt.tld</taglib-location>
</taglib>

<taglib>
    <taglib-uri>http://java.sun.com/jstl/core</taglib-uri>
    <taglib-location>/WEB-INF/c.tld</taglib-location>
</taglib>
<taglib>
    <taglib-uri>http://java.sun.com/jstl/core_rt</taglib-uri>
    <taglib-location>/WEB-INF/c-rt.tld</taglib-location>
</taglib>

<taglib>
    <taglib-uri>http://java.sun.com/jstl/sql</taglib-uri>
    <taglib-location>/WEB-INF/sql.tld</taglib-location>
</taglib>
<taglib>
    <taglib-uri>http://java.sun.com/jstl/sql_rt</taglib-uri>
    <taglib-location>/WEB-INF/sql-rt.tld</taglib-location>
</taglib>

<taglib>
    <taglib-uri>http://java.sun.com/jstl/x</taglib-uri>
    <taglib-location>/WEB-INF/x.tld</taglib-location>
</taglib>
<taglib>
    <taglib-uri>http://java.sun.com/jstl/x_rt</taglib-uri>
    <taglib-location>/WEB-INF/x-rt.tld</taglib-location>
</taglib>
```

Referencing JSTL tag libraries in JSP pages using the taglib Directive

Once a server or IDE environment is set up and configured to support JSTL, you access JSTL functionality by including *taglib directives* in your JSP pages. Taglib directives reference the .tld files that are specified in the uri attribute. Once a tag library is referenced using a directive, the prefix specified in the prefix attribute of the directive is used to refer to the tag library. Listing 17-7 shows a complete list of JSTL tag library references to the RT and the EL tag libraries. If you don't need one or the other, the references can be omitted. Technically, the prefixes defined in the taglib directives can be anything you want them to be, but the prefixes show here are the recommended prefixes for JSTL taglib references.

Listing 17-7: **Complete RT and EL JSP Page References for JSTL Libraries**

```
<%-- JSTL Core --%>
<%@ taglib uri="/WEB-INF/tld/c.tld" prefix="c" %>
<%@ taglib uri="/WEB-INF/tld/c-rt.tld" prefix="c_rt" %>
<%-- JSTL Internationalization (I18N Formatting) --%>
<%@ taglib uri="/WEB-INF/tld/fmt.tld" prefix="fmt" %>
<%@ taglib uri="/WEB-INF/tld/fmt-rt.tld" prefix="fmt_rt" %>
<%-- JSTL SQL --%>
<%@ taglib uri="/WEB-INF/tld/sql.tld" prefix="sql" %>
<%@ taglib uri="/WEB-INF/tld/sql-rt.tld" prefix="sql_rt" %>
<%-- JSTL XML --%>
<%@ taglib uri="/WEB-INF/tld/x.tld" prefix="x" %>
<%@ taglib uri="/WEB-INF/tld/x-rt.tld" prefix="x_rt" %>
```

Working with the JSTL XML Processing Library

Because this is, after all, an XML book, we'll focus on the JSTL tag library for XML. By way of introduction to the JSTL XML tag library, we'll take you through the x.tld file line by line. Examining the TLD for the XML tag library provides detail on the xml tag library tags and attributes, as well as a good overview of how .tld files are structured, in case you ever want to develop your own tag library. We'll also show some examples later in this chapter that showa few core library tags and XML tags in action. For the latest detailed documentation of the core, I18N, and SQL libraries, the bet place to look is Sun's JSTL page at `http://java.sun.com/products/jsp/jstl`.

The XML Tag Library Header

The first item in the tag library is an XML declaration, which indicates that this tag library document is a well-formed XML document. Next, the Document Type Declaration (DOCTYPE) indicates that this document must not only be well formed, but valid when tested against the DTD at `java.sun.com/dtd/web-jsp-taglibrary_1_2.dtd`. This DTD makes sure that the tag library conforms to the JSP 1.2 specification. Next, the `tlib-version` tag is an indicator of the version of this tag library, which is part of JSTL 1.0. The `jsp-version` tag is an indicator of the JSP version that this tag library supports. The `short-name` and `uri` tags are used by IDES to designate a default prefix and uri for the tag library. `Short-name` and `uri` are used to programmatically update a `web.xml` file and JSP page `taglib` directive auto-complete and syntax checking (for IDES that support automatic installation of a tag library).

`Short-name` and `uri` can be overridden when developing a JSP page by manually including a `taglib` directive with a custom uri and prefix. Most of the time, however, it's recommended to go with the default specified in the .tld file, unless you have a very good reason to change it.

The `display-name` tag is another IDE setting, which can be used to name the tag library in the IDE. The `description` tag is used to include brief documentation of the tag library.

```
<?xml version="1.0" encoding="ISO-8859-1"?>
<!DOCTYPE taglib PUBLIC "-//Sun Microsystems, Inc.//DTD JSP Tag Library 1.2//EN"
  "http://java.sun.com/dtd/web-jsptaglibrary_1_2.dtd">
<taglib>
  <tlib-version>1.0</tlib-version>
  <jsp-version>1.2</jsp-version>
  <short-name>x</short-name>
  <uri>http://java.sun.com/jstl/xml</uri>
  <display-name>JSTL XML</display-name>
  <description>JSTL 1.0 XML library</description>
```

The `validator` tag can be used to specify a validation class. Validation classes are extensions of the `javax.servlet.jsp.tagext.TagLibraryValidator` class, and are used to test specific tags on a JSP page for validity before a JSP page generates a servlet. In this case, the `validator-class` element specifies the class that is used to validate the .tld file. The `init-param` specifies initialization parameters that are part of the validator. The tags and attributes in the `init-param` list are checked for validity before the servlet is generated.

```
<validator>
  <validator-class>
  org.apache.taglibs.standard.tlv.JstlXmlTLV
  </validator-class>
  <init-param>
    <param-name>expressionAttributes</param-name>
    <param-value>
    out:escapeXml
    parse:xml
    parse:systemId
    parse:filter
    transform:xml
    transform:xmlSystemId
    transform:xslt
    transform:xsltSystemId
    transform:result
    </param-value>
    <description>
    Whitespace-separated list of colon-separated token pairs
    describing tag:attribute combinations that accept expressions.
    The validator uses this information to determine which
```

```
        attributes need their syntax validated.
    </description>
      </init-param>
    </validator>
```

The XML Tag Library Tags

At this point in the JSP the tag library has finished housekeeping, and moves on to the actual tags that will do things on the page. Each tag specifies a `name` and an associated `tag-class`, which maps to a class in a JSTL .jar file. Some tags also have references to a `tei-class`. This is a tag reference containing classes that can be shared among several tags. These classes contain common processing classes that supplement the main `tag-class`.

The `body-content` tag specifies if the body is empty or not. For example, a JSP declaration in XML format has a body-content value of "JSP" because it contains text associated with the declaration, and a separate closing tag:

```
<jsp:declaration>tag declaration</jsp:declaration>
```

However, a JSP declaration in XML has a body-content value of "empty" because the tag is a container for attributes and has no separate closing tag:

```
<jsp:directive.page attr1="value1" attr2="value2" />
```

The description tag provides brief documentation for each tag in the JSTL XML tag library. Optional attribute tags define attributes that are associated with a tag.

x:choose

The first tag is the `choose` tag, which provides functionality for a choose/when/ otherwise conditional expression. Contents of a nested `when` tag are processed if a when expression evaluates to true. Contents of a nested `otherwise` tag are processed if no when expressions are satisfied. The when tag and otherwise tag are defined later in this TLD.

```
<tag>
  <name>choose</name>
  <tag-class>
  org.apache.taglibs.standard.tag.common.core.ChooseTag
  </tag-class>
  <body-content>JSP</body-content>
  <description>
      Simple conditional tag that establishes a context for
      mutually exclusive conditional operations, marked by
      &lt;when&gt; and &lt;otherwise&gt;
  </description>
</tag>
```

x.out

The out tag passes the result of an expression to the JspWriter object. Most JSP page output passes directly to the JspWriter implicitly. The out tag is used to explicitly pass Xpath expression results to the JspWriter. All output passed to the JspWriter using the out tag is passed as a string. The select attribute contains the Xpath expression to evaluate. The escapeXml attribute contains a Boolean value that tells out to convert illegal XML characters such as > and < to entity reference values such as > and <.

```
<tag>
  <name>out</name>
  <tag-class>org.apache.taglibs.standard.tag.el.xml.ExprTag</tag-class>
  <body-content>empty</body-content>
  <description>
   Like &lt;%= ... &gt;, but for XPath expressions.
  </description>
  <attribute>
    <name>select</name>
    <required>true</required>
    <rtexprvalue>false</rtexprvalue>
  </attribute>
  <attribute>
    <name>escapeXml</name>
    <required>false</required>
    <rtexprvalue>false</rtexprvalue>
  </attribute>
</tag>
```

x:if

The if tag is used to evaluate a conditional expression. If the expression in the statement evaluates to a Boolean true, the contents of the tag are processed. The select attribute contains an optional Xpath expression. The var attribute provides the option of defining a variable name and value destination for the expression output. The scope attribute specifies in which scope the new variable will be available: application, page, request, or session.

```
<tag>
  <name>if</name>
  <tag-class>org.apache.taglibs.standard.tag.common.xml.IfTag</tag-class>
  <body-content>JSP</body-content>
  <description>
    XML conditional tag, which evaluates its body if the
    supplied XPath expression evaluates to 'true' as a boolean
  </description>
  <attribute>
    <name>select</name>
    <required>true</required>
    <rtexprvalue>false</rtexprvalue>
```

```
      </attribute>
      <attribute>
        <name>var</name>
        <required>false</required>
        <rtexprvalue>false</rtexprvalue>
      </attribute>
      <attribute>
        <name>scope</name>
        <required>false</required>
        <rtexprvalue>false</rtexprvalue>
      </attribute>
    </tag>
```

x:forEach

The `forEach` tag is used to loop through the nodes of a result of an Xpath expression. The body text of a `forEach` tag is processed for each node in the result. The `select` attribute contains the Xpath expression. The `var` attribute provides the option of defining a variable for the results.

```
    <tag>
      <name>forEach</name>
      <tag-class>
        org.apache.taglibs.standard.tag.common.xml.ForEachTag
      </tag-class>
      <body-content>JSP</body-content>
      <description>
        XML iteration tag.
      </description>
      <attribute>
        <name>var</name>
        <required>false</required>
        <rtexprvalue>false</rtexprvalue>
      </attribute>
      <attribute>
        <name>select</name>
        <required>true</required>
        <rtexprvalue>false</rtexprvalue>
      </attribute>
    </tag>
```

x:otherwise

The `otherwise` tag is always nested under the `choose` tag, which provides functionality for a choose/when/otherwise conditional expression. Contents of a nested `when` tag are processed if a when expression evaluates to true. Contents of a nested `otherwise` tag are processed if no when expressions are satisfied. The `when` tag is defined later in this TLD.

```
    <tag>
      <name>otherwise</name>
      <tag-class>
        org.apache.taglibs.standard.tag.common.core.OtherwiseTag</tag-class>
```

```
  <body-content>JSP</body-content>
  <description>
Subtag of &lt;choose&gt; that follows &lt;when&gt; tags
and runs only if all of the prior conditions evaluated to
'false'
  </description>
</tag>
```

x:param

The param tag passes a parameter value to an XSL stylesheet. It is used as part of the transform tag, defined later in the TLD. The name and value attributes define the name and value of the parameter.

```
<tag>
  <name>param</name>
  <tag-class>org.apache.taglibs.standard.tag.el.xml.ParamTag</tag-class>
  <body-content>JSP</body-content>
  <description>
      Adds a parameter to a containing 'transform' tag's Transformer
  </description>
  <attribute>
    <name>name</name>
    <required>true</required>
    <rtexprvalue>false</rtexprvalue>
  </attribute>
  <attribute>
    <name>value</name>
    <required>false</required>
    <rtexprvalue>false</rtexprvalue>
  </attribute>
</tag>
```

x:parse

The parse tag parses an XML document. By default, parse renders the output as a org.w3c.dom.Document object. The var attribute is the variable name to assign to the resulting parsed DOM document. The varDom attribute is the variable name to assign to the resulting parsed DOM object. The scope attribute sets the scope of the parsed DOM document. The scopeDom attribute sets the scope of the parsed DOM object. The xml attribute contains the XML document object to be parsed. The XML document must be defined as a string or a Reader object. The optional systemId attribute is used to define a uri that can be referenced for entity resolution. The filter attribute applies a SAX filter to the XML document before it is parsed. We show an example of parsing later in this chapter.

```
<tag>
  <name>parse</name>
  <tag-class>org.apache.taglibs.standard.tag.el.xml.ParseTag</tag-class>
  <tei-class>org.apache.taglibs.standard.tei.XmlParseTEI</tei-class>
  <body-content>JSP</body-content>
  <description>
    Parses XML content from 'source' attribute or 'body'
```

```
    </description>
    <attribute>
      <name>var</name>
      <required>false</required>
      <rtexprvalue>false</rtexprvalue>
    </attribute>
    <attribute>
      <name>varDom</name>
      <required>false</required>
      <rtexprvalue>false</rtexprvalue>
    </attribute>
    <attribute>
      <name>scope</name>
      <required>false</required>
      <rtexprvalue>false</rtexprvalue>
    </attribute>
    <attribute>
      <name>scopeDom</name>
      <required>false</required>
      <rtexprvalue>false</rtexprvalue>
    </attribute>
    <attribute>
      <name>xml</name>
      <required>false</required>
      <rtexprvalue>false</rtexprvalue>
    </attribute>
    <attribute>
      <name>systemId</name>
      <required>false</required>
      <rtexprvalue>false</rtexprvalue>
    </attribute>
    <attribute>
      <name>filter</name>
      <required>false</required>
      <rtexprvalue>false</rtexprvalue>
    </attribute>
  </tag>
```

x:set

The set tag assigns a variable to an expression result. The `select` attribute contains an Xpath expression. The `var` attribute defines the name of the variable. The `scope` attribute specifies in which scope the new variable will be available: application, page, request, or session.

```
  <tag>
    <name>set</name>
    <tag-class>org.apache.taglibs.standard.tag.common.xml.SetTag</tag-class>
    <body-content>empty</body-content>
    <description>
Saves the result of an XPath expression evaluation in a 'scope'
    </description>
    <attribute>
```

```
      <name>var</name>
      <required>true</required>
      <rtexprvalue>false</rtexprvalue>
    </attribute>
    <attribute>
      <name>select</name>
      <required>false</required>
      <rtexprvalue>false</rtexprvalue>
    </attribute>
    <attribute>
      <name>scope</name>
      <required>false</required>
      <rtexprvalue>false</rtexprvalue>
    </attribute>
  </tag>
```

x:transform

The transform tag uses an XSLT stylesheet to transform an XML source document. By default, transformation results are sent to the JspWriter. The transformation output can also be sent to a variable using the `var` attribute. The `scope` attribute sets the scope of the new variable. Transformation output can also be sent to a `javax.xml.transform.Result` object by specifying a `result` attribute. The `xml` attribute specifies a source XML document for the transformation. The optional `xmlSystemId` attribute specifies the uri for the XML document. The `xslt` attribute specifies a stylesheet for the transformation. The optional `xsltSystemId` attribute specifies the uri of the XSLT stylesheet. We show an example of transformation later in this chapter.

```
  <tag>
    <name>transform</name>
    <tag-class>
     org.apache.taglibs.standard.tag.el.xml.TransformTag
    </tag-class>
    <tei-class>org.apache.taglibs.standard.tei.XmlTransformTEI</tei-class>
    <body-content>JSP</body-content>
    <description>
     Conducts a transformation given a source XML document
     and an XSLT stylesheet
    </description>
    <attribute>
      <name>var</name>
      <required>false</required>
      <rtexprvalue>false</rtexprvalue>
    </attribute>
    <attribute>
      <name>scope</name>
      <required>false</required>
      <rtexprvalue>false</rtexprvalue>
    </attribute>
    <attribute>
      <name>result</name>
```

```
        <required>false</required>
        <rtexprvalue>false</rtexprvalue>
      </attribute>
      <attribute>
        <name>xml</name>
        <required>false</required>
        <rtexprvalue>false</rtexprvalue>
      </attribute>
      <attribute>
        <name>xmlSystemId</name>
        <required>false</required>
        <rtexprvalue>false</rtexprvalue>
      </attribute>
      <attribute>
        <name>xslt</name>
        <required>false</required>
        <rtexprvalue>false</rtexprvalue>
      </attribute>
      <attribute>
        <name>xsltSystemId</name>
        <required>false</required>
        <rtexprvalue>false</rtexprvalue>
      </attribute>
    </tag>
```

x:when

The when tag is always nested under the choose tag, which provides functionality for a choose/when/otherwise conditional expression. Contents of a nested when tag are processed if a when expression evaluates to true. Contents of a nested otherwise tag are processed if no when expressions are satisfied. The choose and otherwise tags are defined earlier in this TLD.

```
    <tag>
      <name>when</name>
      <tag-class>
       org.apache.taglibs.standard.tag.common.xml.WhenTag
      </tag-class>
      <body-content>JSP</body-content>
      <description>
          Subtag of &lt;choose&gt; that includes its body if its
          expression evalutes to 'true'
      </description>
      <attribute>
        <name>select</name>
        <required>true</required>
        <rtexprvalue>false</rtexprvalue>
      </attribute>
    </tag>
</taglib>
```

Example 1: A simple XML transformation using JSTL

In this simple example, an XML document called AmazonMacbethSpanish.xml is transformed using a stylesheet called XMLtoQuotes.xsl. The XML document is the same one that was used for the JAXB example earlier in this chapter, and several other examples in the book. The XSL stylesheet was used as an example in Chapter 8 — "XSL Transformations."

Cross-Reference   In this chapter we focus on JSP pages and the JSTL XML tag library, so we won't get into the details of how an XSL transformation works. For more information on XSLT and XSL stylesheets, please refer to Chapter 8.

The JSP in Listing 17-8 starts with a page directive that sets the page output format to text/html. Next, the JSTL core and JSTL XML libraries are defined using two taglib directives, each of which defines a uri and a prefix. The c prefix is used for core library actions such as c:import. The x prefix is used for XML library actions such as x:transform. Next, an HTML page is created and a simple HTML page head with a page title is defined. Next, the HTML body of the page begins with the import of an XML document. The XML document is assigned a variable name of xmlSource. The XSL Stylesheet is imported next, and assigned a variable name of xsltSource. The XSL transformation takes place using the transform tag. The two required attributes for the transform tag are xml for the xml source document, and xslt for the XSL stylesheet. Each attribute value is passed as an object to the transform tag using expression language references. Lastly, the body and the html tags are closed. Transformation output is automatically sent to a JspWriter, so there is no need to specify an output for the transformation. When the JSP is called the transformation output is automatically sent to a browser screen.

Listing 17-8: A JSP Page for XML Transformation

```
<%@page contentType="text/html"%>
<%@ taglib uri="http://java.sun.com/jstl/core" prefix="c" %>
<%@ taglib uri="http://java.sun.com/jstl/xml" prefix="x" %>

<html>
<head><title>JSP PageTransformation Example</title></head>
<body>

<c:import var="xmlSource" url="AmazonMacbethSpanish.xml" />
<c:import var="xsltSource" url="XMLtoQuotes.xsl" />
<x:transform xml="${xmlSource}" xslt="${xsltSource}" />

</body>
</html>
```

This relatively simple JSP page generates a much larger servlet when loaded on a JSP server. Going though the generated servlet is a good way to become intimately acquainted with how all JSPs work, stating with the imports. The imports are noticeably different in a JSP servlet vs. a regular servlet, because of the import of the org.apache.jsp classes as well as the jasper run-time classes. The Apache Foundation provides the implementation classes for the JSTL specification, including org.apache.jsp and the org.apache.jasper classes. The org.apache.jsp class is used to extend HttpJspBase, which is an extension of javax.servlet.http.HttpServlet.

```
package org.apache.jsp;

import javax.servlet.*;
import javax.servlet.http.*;
import javax.servlet.jsp.*;
import org.apache.jasper.runtime.*;


public class JSPExample1$jsp extends HttpJspBase {


    static {
    }
    public JSPExample1$jsp( ) {
    }

    private static boolean _jspx_inited = false;
```

_jspx_init is where any initialization parameters are defined in the servlet. In this simple example there was no need for initialization parameters, so this section is blank.

```
    public final void _jspx_init() throws
    org.apache.jasper.runtime.JspException {
    }
```

_jspService includes basic object setup for a servlet created by a JSP. Most of the classes and methods in a JSP servlet are JSP-specific extensions of javax.servlet classes and methods, just in case the servlet classes are already being used in Scriptlets or other code passed from the JSP. The JspFactory helps set up page context. The PageContext is an extension of javax.servlet.ServletRequest. HttpSession track sessions for a page, if there are any. ServletContext is an extension of javax.servlet.ServletContext. ServletConfig handles initialization parameters. JspWriter is the class for the browser output.

```
    public void _jspService(HttpServletRequest request, HttpServletResponse
    response)
        throws java.io.IOException, ServletException {
```

```
JspFactory _jspxFactory = null;
PageContext pageContext = null;
HttpSession session = null;
ServletContext application = null;
ServletConfig config = null;
JspWriter out = null;
Object page = this;
String  _value = null;
try {
```

The _jspx_inited variable tracks threads in the servlet. The conditional statement opens a new thread if no thread is open so far. Servlets have to have at least one explicitly opened thread to function.

```
if (_jspx_inited == false) {
    synchronized (this) {
        if (_jspx_inited == false) {
            _jspx_init();
            _jspx_inited = true;
        }
    }
}
```

This segment sets the output type for the JspWriter and gets the current JSP page. After the request and response definitions, the first true parameter defines a session, 8192 is a default buffer size for reading the JSP page, and the second true parameter automatically unloads the page when finished.

```
_jspxFactory = JspFactory.getDefaultFactory();
response.setContentType("text/html");
pageContext = _jspxFactory.getPageContext(this, request,
response, "", true, 8192, true);
```

Next, objects are pulled from the pageContext and the servletConfig. Once the servlet context is defined, and a session and an output method is created, the servlet can start writing output to the browser screen.

```
application = pageContext.getServletContext();
config = pageContext.getServletConfig();
session = pageContext.getSession();
out = pageContext.getOut();
```

The comments in this code are generated by an Apache TomCat 4.04 application server while generating the servlet. Other application servers and versions may differ in the way the code is generated, but all have to conform to JSP specifications, so most of the pieces are in very similar places. The comments refer to the original lines that the original JSP tags were in the JSP page. The first number is the line number, and the second number is the characters from the left, starting at 0. The

Java code generated for each line or line segment is just below the commented JSP page reference. The first few lines are direct copies of the HTML tags to create the HTML head and define the HTML body.

```
// HTML // begin [file="/JSPExample1.jsp";from=(0,33);to=(1,0)]
    out.write("\r\n");
    out.write("");
// end
// HTML // begin [file="/JSPExample1.jsp";from=(1,60);to=(2,0)]
    out.write("\r\n");
    out.write("");
// end
// HTML // begin [file="/JSPExample1.jsp";from=(2,59);to=(8,0)]
    out.write("\r\n");
    out.write("\r\n");
    out.write("<html>\r\n");
    out.write("<head><title>JSP PageTransformation
    Example</title></head>\r\n");
    out.write("<body>\r\n");
    out.write("\r\n");
    out.write("");
// end
```

This is where the code imports the XML source document using the `org.apache.taglibs.standard.tag.el.core.ImportTag` class. The `ImportTag.setVar` method sets the variable name and the `ImportTag.setUrl` method defines the location of the XML document.

```
// begin [file="/JSPExample1.jsp";from=(8,0);to=(8,59)]
    /* ---- c:import ---- */
    org.apache.taglibs.standard.tag.el.core.ImportTag
    _jspx_th_c_import_0 = new
    org.apache.taglibs.standard.tag.el.core.ImportTag();
    _jspx_th_c_import_0.setPageContext(pageContext);
    _jspx_th_c_import_0.setParent(null);
    _jspx_th_c_import_0.setVar("xmlSource");
    _jspx_th_c_import_0.setUrl("AmazonMacbethSpanish.xml");
    try {
```

The `doStartTag()` method imports the XML document as a string.

```
    int _jspx_eval_c_import_0 =
    _jspx_th_c_import_0.doStartTag();
```

The rest of the code does the work of evaluating the JSP tag and converting the content in the XML document to a string. All of the methods here are accessed through the `BodyContent` interface, which implements methods for converting tag contents into a String. The `BodyContent` interface is a subclass of `JspWriter`.

```
            if (_jspx_eval_c_import_0 !=
        javax.servlet.jsp.tagext.Tag.SKIP_BODY) {
            try {
                if (_jspx_eval_c_import_0 !=
                javax.servlet.jsp.tagext.Tag.EVAL_BODY_INCLUDE)
                {
```

The `pushBody()` method of the page context loads the tag for evaluation and reading.

```
                    out = pageContext.pushBody();
                    _jspx_th_c_import_0.setBodyContent(
                    (javax.servlet.jsp.tagext.BodyContent) out);
                }
                _jspx_th_c_import_0.doInitBody();
                do {
                // end
                // begin
                [file="/JSPExample1.jsp";from=(8,0);to=(8,59)]
                } while (_jspx_th_c_import_0.doAfterBody() ==
            javax.servlet.jsp.tagext.BodyTag.EVAL_BODY_AGAIN);
            } finally {
                if (_jspx_eval_c_import_0 !=
                javax.servlet.jsp.tagext.Tag.EVAL_BODY_INCLUDE)
```

The `popBody()` method of the page context unloads the tag for evaluation and reading.

```
                out = pageContext.popBody();
            }
        }
        if (_jspx_th_c_import_0.doEndTag() ==
        javax.servlet.jsp.tagext.Tag.SKIP_PAGE)
            return;
    } catch (Throwable _jspx_exception) {
        _jspx_th_c_import_0.doCatch(_jspx_exception);
    } finally {
        _jspx_th_c_import_0.doFinally();
        _jspx_th_c_import_0.release();
    }
// end
// HTML // begin [file="/JSPExample1.jsp";from=(8,59);to=(9,0)]
    out.write("\r\n");
    out.write("");
// end
```

This code imports the XSL Stylesheet document using the same `org.apache.taglibs.standard.tag.el.core.ImportTag` class as the XML document import. The `ImportTag.setVar` method sets the variable name and the

`ImportTag.setUrl` method defines the location of the XML document. The rest of the process is identical to the previous XML document import, with the exception of the variable name and the URL of the file to import.

```
// begin [file="/JSPExample1.jsp";from=(9,0);to=(9,51)]
    /* ---- c:import ---- */
    org.apache.taglibs.standard.tag.el.core.ImportTag
    _jspx_th_c_import_1 = new
    org.apache.taglibs.standard.tag.el.core.ImportTag();
    _jspx_th_c_import_1.setPageContext(pageContext);
    _jspx_th_c_import_1.setParent(null);
    _jspx_th_c_import_1.setVar("xsltSource");
    _jspx_th_c_import_1.setUrl("XMLtoQuotes.xsl");
    try {
        int _jspx_eval_c_import_1 =
        _jspx_th_c_import_1.doStartTag();
        if (_jspx_eval_c_import_1 !=
        javax.servlet.jsp.tagext.Tag.SKIP_BODY) {
            try {
                if (_jspx_eval_c_import_1 !=
                javax.servlet.jsp.tagext.Tag.EVAL_BODY_INCLUDE) {
                    out = pageContext.pushBody();
                    _jspx_th_c_import_1.setBodyContent(
                    (javax.servlet.jsp.tagext.BodyContent) out);
                }
                _jspx_th_c_import_1.doInitBody();
                do {
                // end
                // begin
                [file="/JSPExample1.jsp";from=(9,0);to=(9,51)]
                } while (_jspx_th_c_import_1.doAfterBody() ==
                javax.servlet.jsp.tagext.BodyTag.EVAL_BODY_AGAIN);
            } finally {
                if (_jspx_eval_c_import_1 !=
                javax.servlet.jsp.tagext.Tag.EVAL_BODY_INCLUDE)
                    out = pageContext.popBody();
            }
        }
        if (_jspx_th_c_import_1.doEndTag() ==
        javax.servlet.jsp.tagext.Tag.SKIP_PAGE)
            return;
    } catch (Throwable _jspx_exception) {
        _jspx_th_c_import_1.doCatch(_jspx_exception);
    } finally {
        _jspx_th_c_import_1.doFinally();
        _jspx_th_c_import_1.release();
    }
// end
// HTML // begin [file="/JSPExample1.jsp";from=(9,51);to=(10,0)]
    out.write("\r\n");
    out.write("");
// end
```

This code handles the XSL transformation using the `org.apache.taglibs.standard.tag.el.xml.TransformTag` class. The `TransformTag.setXml` method sets the XML Source document for the transformation. The `TransformTag.setXxslt` method defines the XSL stylesheet. The EL values for the XML document and the stylesheet are passed directly to the `TransformTag` class, which performs the transformation. The rest of the code is the same tag evaluation code that was used in the XML document and XSL stylesheet imports, to load, evaluate, and unload the tag.

```
// begin [file="/JSPExample1.jsp";from=(10,0);to=(10,55)]
    /* ---- x:transform ---- */
    org.apache.taglibs.standard.tag.el.xml.TransformTag
    _jspx_th_x_transform_0 = new
    org.apache.taglibs.standard.tag.el.xml.TransformTag();
    _jspx_th_x_transform_0.setPageContext(pageContext);
    _jspx_th_x_transform_0.setParent(null);
    _jspx_th_x_transform_0.setXml("${xmlSource}");
    _jspx_th_x_transform_0.setXslt("${xsltSource}");
    try {
        int _jspx_eval_x_transform_0 =
        _jspx_th_x_transform_0.doStartTag();
        if (_jspx_eval_x_transform_0 !=
        javax.servlet.jsp.tagext.Tag.SKIP_BODY) {
            try {
                if (_jspx_eval_x_transform_0 !=
                javax.servlet.jsp.tagext.Tag.EVAL_BODY_INCLUDE) {
                    out = pageContext.pushBody();
                    _jspx_th_x_transform_0.setBodyContent(
                    (javax.servlet.jsp.tagext.BodyContent) out);
                }
                _jspx_th_x_transform_0.doInitBody();
                do {
                // end
                // begin
                [file="/JSPExample1.jsp";from=(10,0);to=(10,55)]
                } while (_jspx_th_x_transform_0.doAfterBody() ==
                javax.servlet.jsp.tagext.BodyTag.EVAL_BODY_AGAIN);
            } finally {
                if (_jspx_eval_x_transform_0 !=
                javax.servlet.jsp.tagext.Tag.EVAL_BODY_INCLUDE)
                    out = pageContext.popBody();
            }
        }
        if (_jspx_th_x_transform_0.doEndTag() ==
        javax.servlet.jsp.tagext.Tag.SKIP_PAGE)
            return;
    } finally {
        _jspx_th_x_transform_0.release();
    }
// end
```

```
// HTML // begin [file="/JSPExample1.jsp";from=(10,55);to=(14,0)]
    out.write("\r\n");
    out.write("\r\n");
    out.write("</body>\r\n");
    out.write("</html>\r\n");
    out.write("");
// end
```

The balance of the code is standard error catching, and a command to release the
pageContext, which flushes the JSP page from memory, based on the previously
defined getPageContext method.

```
    } catch (Throwable t) {
        if (out != null && out.getBufferSize() != 0)
            out.clearBuffer();
        if (pageContext != null) pageContext.handlePageException(t);
    } finally {
        if (_jspxFactory != null)
        _jspxFactory.releasePageContext(pageContext);
    }
  }
}
```

The output from the JSP produces an html 4.01-compliant document. Listing 17-9
shows what the source of that html document looks like.

Listing 17-9: **The HTML Document Output from the JSP Page**

```
<?xml version="1.0" encoding="ISO-8859-1"?>
<transformedquotes>
  <quote source="Macbeth" author="Shakespeare, William">When the
  hurlyburly's done, / When the battle's lost and won.</quote>
  <quote source="Macbeth" author="Shakespeare, William">Out, damned spot!
  out, I say!-- One; two; why, then 'tis time to do't ;--Hell is murky!--
  Fie, my lord, fie! a soldier, and afeard? What need we fear who knows
  it, when none can call our power to account?--Yet who would have thought
  the old man to have had so much blood in him?</quote>
  <quote source="Macbeth" author="Shakespeare, William">Is this a dagger
  which I see before me, the handle toward my hand? Come, let me clutch
  thee: I have thee not, and yet I see thee still. Art thou not, fatal
  vision, sensible to feeling as to sight? or art thou but a dagger of the
  mind, a false creation, proceeding from the heat-oppressed
  brain?</quote>
```

```
<quote source="Macbeth" author="Shakespeare, William">To-morrow, and to-
  morrow, and to-morrow, creeps in this petty pace from day to day, to the
  last syllable of recorded time; and all our yesterdays have lighted
  fools the way to dusty death. Out, out, brief candle! Life's but a
  walking shadow; a poor player, that struts and frets his hour upon the
  stage, and then is heard no more: it is a tale told by an idiot, full of
  sound and fury, signifying nothing. </quote>
  <quote/>
</transformedquotes>
```

Example 2: Parsing an XML document using JSTL

In this example, the same AmazonMacbethSpanish.xml document is parsed, and a segment of the document that contains quotations is selected. A forEach tag is used to loop through each instance of a quote and display the results in a table on an HTML page. If you followed along through the previous example, much of the startup code is repeated. Because the servlet is generated and not hand-coded, the patterns in the code are largely the same, with core code towards the end of the servlet making the JSP unique. If you were comfortable with the setup code from the previous servlet example, you can skip down to the part of the code that defines the `org.apache.taglibs.standard.tag.el.xml.ParseTag` and begins parsing the document.

The JSP in Listing 17-10 starts with two taglib directives that define the JSTL core and JSTL XML libraries. Each taglib directive defines a uri and a prefix. As in the previous example, the `c` prefix is used for core library actions such as `c:import`. The `x` prefix is used for the XML library `x:parse` action. Next, an HTML page is created and a simple HTML page head with a page title is defined. Next, the HTML body of the page begins with the import of an XML document. The XML document is assigned a variable name of `xmlToParse`. Parsing the XML document is facilitated through the `parse` tag, and the parsed `org.w3c.dom.Document` object is assigned to a variable named `parsedXML`. Next, an HTML table is defined and Author, Source, and Quotation headings are defined in the table.

The `forEach` tag uses an EL expression to pass the `org.w3c.dom.Document` object into the `select` attribute. The rest of the `select` attribute retrieves all of the nested elements under the `/quotedoc/quotelist/*` XPath expression. The results of a `select` are not implicitly sent to the `JspWriter`, which is actually a good thing, because we only want to send some of the `select` statement results out to the browser screen. The `Author` attribute, `Source` attribute (Defined by the @ XPath Expression), and the contents of the text associated with each element (defined by the . XPath expression) are sent to the `JspWriter` using the out tag.

Listing 17-10: A JSP Page for XML Parsing

```
<<%@ taglib prefix="c" uri="http://java.sun.com/jstl/core" %>
<%@ taglib prefix="x" uri="http://java.sun.com/jstl/xml" %>

<html>
<head>
  <title>JSP Page Parsing Example</title>
</head>

<c:import var="xmlToParse" url="AmazonMacbethSpanish.xml" />
<x:parse var="parsedXML"  xml="${xmlToParse}" />


<table border="1" width="100%">
 <tr>
 <th>Author</th>
 <th>Source</th>
 <th>Quotation</th>
 </tr>
 <tr>

<x:forEach select="${parsedXML}/quotedoc/quotelist/*" var="quotes">
  <td><x:out select="@Author"/></td>
  <td><x:out select="@Source"/></td>
  <td><x:out select="."/></td></tr>
</x:forEach>
</table>


</body>
</html>
```

As we did with the previous example, we'll run through the servlet generated by the JSP page to show how JSPs work behind the scenes. The imports start with the import of the `org.apache.jsp` classes as well as the jasper run-time classes. The Apache Foundation provides the implementation classes for the JSTL specification, including org.apache.jsp and the org.apache.jasper classes. The `org.apache.jsp` class is used to extend `HttpJspBase`, which is an extension of `javax.servlet.http.HttpServlet`.

```
package org.apache.jsp;

import javax.servlet.*;
import javax.servlet.http.*;
import javax.servlet.jsp.*;
import org.apache.jasper.runtime.*;
```

```
public class JSPExample2$jsp extends HttpJspBase {


    static {
    }
    public JSPExample2$jsp( ) {
    }


    private static boolean _jspx_inited = false;
```

`_jspx_init` is where any initialization parameters are defined in the servlet. In this simple example there was no need for initialization parameters, so this section is blank.

```
public final void _jspx_init() throws
org.apache.jasper.runtime.JspException {
    }
```

`_jspService` includes basic object setup for a servlet created by a JSP. Most of the classes and methods in a JSP servlet are JSP-specific extensions of `javax.servlet` classes and methods, just in case the servlet classes are already being used in Scriptlets or other code passed from the JSP. The `JspFactory` helps set up page context. The `PageContext` is actually an extension of `javax.servlet.ServletRequest`. `HttpSession` tracks sessions for a page, if there are any. `ServletContext` is an extension of `javax.servlet.ServletContext`. `ServletConfig` handles initialization parameters. `JspWriter` is the class for the browser output.

```
public void _jspService(HttpServletRequest request, HttpServletResponse
response) throws java.io.IOException, ServletException {

        JspFactory _jspxFactory = null;
        PageContext pageContext = null;
        HttpSession session = null;
        ServletContext application = null;
        ServletConfig config = null;
        JspWriter out = null;
        Object page = this;
        String  _value = null;
        try {
```

The `_jspx_inited` variable tracks threads in the servlet. The conditional statement opens a new thread if no thread is open so far. Servlets have to have at least one explicitly opened thread to function.

```
            if (_jspx_inited == false) {
                synchronized (this) {
                    if (_jspx_inited == false) {
```

```
              _jspx_init();
              _jspx_inited = true;
          }
      }
  }
```

This segment sets the output type for the `JspWriter` and gets the current JSP page. After the request and response definitions, the first true parameter defines a session, `8192` is a default buffer size for reading the JSP page, and the second true parameter automatically unloads the page when finished. Next, objects are pulled from the `pageContext` and the `servletConfig`. Once the servlet context is defined, and a session and an output method are created, the servlet can start writing output to the browser screen.

```
_jspxFactory = JspFactory.getDefaultFactory();
response.setContentType("text/html;charset=ISO-8859-1");
pageContext = _jspxFactory.getPageContext(this, request,
response, "", true, 8192, true);
application = pageContext.getServletContext();
config = pageContext.getServletConfig();
session = pageContext.getSession();
out = pageContext.getOut();
```

The comments in this code are generated by an Apache TomCat 4.04 application server while generating the servlet. The comments refer to the original lines that the original JSP tags were in the JSP page. The first number is the line number and the second number is the characters from the left, starting at 0. The Java code generated for each line or line segment is just below the commented JSP page reference. The first few lines are direct copies of the HTML tags to create the HTML head and define the HTML body.

```
// HTML // begin [file="/JSPExample2.jsp";from=(0,0);to=(0,1)]
    out.write("<");
// end
// HTML // begin [file="/JSPExample2.jsp";from=(0,61);to=(1,0)]
    out.write("\r\n");
    out.write("");
// end
// HTML // begin [file="/JSPExample2.jsp";from=(1,59);to=(8,0)]
    out.write("\r\n");
    out.write("\r\n");
    out.write("<html>\r\n");
    out.write("<head>\r\n");
    out.write("  <title>JSP Page Parsing Example</title>\r\n");
    out.write("</head>\r\n");
    out.write("\r\n");
    out.write("");
// end
```

This is where the code imports the XML source document using the `org.apache.taglibs.standard.tag.el.core.ImportTag` class. The `ImportTag.setVar` method sets the variable name and the `ImportTag.setUrl` method defines the location of the XML document.

```
// begin [file="/JSPExample2.jsp";from=(8,0);to=(8,60)]
    /* ----   c:import ---- */
    org.apache.taglibs.standard.tag.el.core.ImportTag
    _jspx_th_c_import_0 = new
    org.apache.taglibs.standard.tag.el.core.ImportTag();
    _jspx_th_c_import_0.setPageContext(pageContext);
    _jspx_th_c_import_0.setParent(null);
    _jspx_th_c_import_0.setVar("xmlToParse");
    _jspx_th_c_import_0.setUrl("AmazonMacbethSpanish.xml");
    try {
```

The `doStartTag()` method imports the XML document as a string.

```
int _jspx_eval_c_import_0 =
_jspx_th_c_import_0.doStartTag();
if (_jspx_eval_c_import_0 !=
javax.servlet.jsp.tagext.Tag.SKIP_BODY) {
    try {
```

The rest of the code does the work of evaluating the JSP tag and converting the content in the XML document to a string. All of the methods here are accessed through the `BodyContent` interface, which implements methods for converting tag contents into a String. The `BodyContent` interface is a subclass of `JspWriter`.

```
if (_jspx_eval_c_import_0 !=
javax.servlet.jsp.tagext.Tag.EVAL_BODY_INCLUDE) {
```

The `pushBody()` method of the page context loads the tag for evaluation and reading.

```
out = pageContext.pushBody();
_jspx_th_c_import_0.setBodyContent(
(javax.servlet.jsp.tagext.BodyContent) out);
}
_jspx_th_c_import_0.doInitBody();
do {
// end
// begin [file="/JSPExample2.jsp";
from=(8,0);to=(8,60)]
} while (_jspx_th_c_import_0.doAfterBody() ==
javax.servlet.jsp.tagext.BodyTag.EVAL_BODY_AGAIN);
```

The `popBody()` method of the page context unloads the tag for evaluation and reading.

```
        } finally {
            if (_jspx_eval_c_import_0 !=
            javax.servlet.jsp.tagext.Tag.EVAL_BODY_INCLUDE)
                out = pageContext.popBody();
        }
    }
    if (_jspx_th_c_import_0.doEndTag() ==
    javax.servlet.jsp.tagext.Tag.SKIP_PAGE)
        return;
} catch (Throwable _jspx_exception) {
    _jspx_th_c_import_0.doCatch(_jspx_exception);
} finally {
    _jspx_th_c_import_0.doFinally();
    _jspx_th_c_import_0.release();
}
// end
// HTML // begin [file="/JSPExample2.jsp";from=(8,60);to=(9,0)]
    out.write("\r\n");
    out.write("");
// end
```

This code handles the XML document parsing using the `org.apache.taglibs.standard.tag.el.xml.ParseTag` class. The `ParseTag.setXml` method sets the XML Source document for parsing. The `ParseTag.setVar` method sets a variable name that the `org.w3c.dom.Document` object resulting from the parse is sent to. The EL value for the XML document is passed directly to the `ParseTag` class, which performs the parsing. The rest of the code is the same tag evaluation code that was used in the XML document import, to load, evaluate, and unload the tag.

```
// begin [file="/JSPExample2.jsp";from=(9,0);to=(9,48)]
    /* ----  x:parse ---- */
    org.apache.taglibs.standard.tag.el.xml.ParseTag
    _jspx_th_x_parse_0 = new
    org.apache.taglibs.standard.tag.el.xml.ParseTag();
    _jspx_th_x_parse_0.setPageContext(pageContext);
    _jspx_th_x_parse_0.setParent(null);
    _jspx_th_x_parse_0.setVar("parsedXML");
    _jspx_th_x_parse_0.setXml("${xmlToParse}");
    try {
        int _jspx_eval_x_parse_0 =
        _jspx_th_x_parse_0.doStartTag();
        if (_jspx_eval_x_parse_0 !=
        javax.servlet.jsp.tagext.Tag.SKIP_BODY) {
            try {
```

```
                   if (_jspx_eval_x_parse_0 !=
                   javax.servlet.jsp.tagext.Tag.EVAL_BODY_INCLUDE) {
                       out = pageContext.pushBody();
                       _jspx_th_x_parse_0.setBodyContent(
                       (javax.servlet.jsp.tagext.BodyContent) out);
                   }
                   _jspx_th_x_parse_0.doInitBody();
                   do {
                   // end
                   // begin [file="/JSPExample2.jsp";
                   from=(9,0);to=(9,48)]
                   } while (_jspx_th_x_parse_0.doAfterBody() ==
                 javax.servlet.jsp.tagext.BodyTag.EVAL_BODY_AGAIN);
               } finally {
                   if (_jspx_eval_x_parse_0 !=
                   javax.servlet.jsp.tagext.Tag.EVAL_BODY_INCLUDE)
                       out = pageContext.popBody();
               }
           }
           if (_jspx_th_x_parse_0.doEndTag() ==
           javax.servlet.jsp.tagext.Tag.SKIP_PAGE)
               return;
       } finally {
           _jspx_th_x_parse_0.release();
       }
   // end
```

Next, the HTML table is defined and headings in the table are set up, using HTML code passed directly from the JSP to the JspWriter object of the servlet.

```
   // HTML // begin [file="/JSPExample2.jsp";from=(9,48);to=(20,0)]
       out.write("\r\n");
       out.write("\r\n");
       out.write("\r\n");
       out.write("<table border=\"1\" width=\"100%\">\r\n");
       out.write("  <tr>\r\n");
       out.write("  <th>Author</th>\r\n");
       out.write("  <th>Source</th>\r\n");
       out.write("  <th>Quotation</th>\r\n");
       out.write("  </tr>\r\n");
       out.write("  <tr>\r\n");
       out.write("\r\n");
       out.write("");
   // end
```

The forEach starts by using the org.apache.taglibs.standard.tag. common.xml.ForEachTag class. The ForEachTag.setSelect method is used to create a select statement from the JSP page select attribute. The ForEachTag. setVar class is used to define a variable that contains the select results. The rest of the code is the same tag evaluation code that was used in the XML document import, to load, evaluate, and unload the tag.

```
// begin [file="/JSPExample2.jsp";from=(20,0);to=(20,67)]
    /* ----  x:forEach ---- */
    org.apache.taglibs.standard.tag.common.xml.ForEachTag
    _jspx_th_x_forEach_0 = new
    org.apache.taglibs.standard.tag.common.xml.ForEachTag();
    _jspx_th_x_forEach_0.setPageContext(pageContext);
    _jspx_th_x_forEach_0.setParent(null);
    _jspx_th_x_forEach_0.setSelect(
    "${parsedXML}/quotedoc/quotelist/*");
    _jspx_th_x_forEach_0.setVar("quotes");
    try {
        int _jspx_eval_x_forEach_0 =
        _jspx_th_x_forEach_0.doStartTag();
        if (_jspx_eval_x_forEach_0 ==
        javax.servlet.jsp.tagext.BodyTag.EVAL_BODY_BUFFERED)
        throw new JspTagException("Since tag handler class
        org.apache.taglibs.standard.tag.common.xml.ForEachTag
        does not implement BodyTag, it can't return
        BodyTag.EVAL_BODY_TAG");
        if (_jspx_eval_x_forEach_0 !=
        javax.servlet.jsp.tagext.Tag.SKIP_BODY) {
            do {
            // end
            // HTML // begin
            [file="/JSPExample2.jsp";from=(20,67);to=(21,6)]
                out.write("\r\n");
                out.write("  <td>");
            // end
            // begin
            [file="/JSPExample2.jsp";from=(21,6);to=(21,31)]
```

The next code segment represents the first line in the forEach statement, which retrieves the Author attribute from the result of the forEach select XPath expression. The org.apache.taglibs.standard.tag.el.xml.ExprTag class is used for this line. The ExprTag class writes results of the expression directly to the JspWriter. The parent is set to the forEach object, _jspx_th_x_forEach_0, using the ExprTag .setParent() method. The select is set to the Author attribute (@Author) for the current DOM node using the ExprTag.setSelect. The rest of the code is the same tag evaluation code that was used in the other lines of this servlet to load, evaluate, and unload the tag.

```
/* ----  x:out ---- */
org.apache.taglibs.standard.tag.el.xml.ExprTag
_jspx_th_x_out_0 = new
org.apache.taglibs.standard.tag.el.xml.ExprTag();
_jspx_th_x_out_0.setPageContext(pageContext);
```

```
                _jspx_th_x_out_0.setParent(_jspx_th_x_forEach_0);
                _jspx_th_x_out_0.setSelect("@Author");
                try {
                    int _jspx_eval_x_out_0 =
                    _jspx_th_x_out_0.doStartTag();
                    if (_jspx_eval_x_out_0 ==
                    javax.servlet.jsp.tagext.BodyTag.
                    EVAL_BODY_BUFFERED)
                    throw new JspTagException("Since tag handler
                    class org.apache.taglibs.standard.tag.el
                    .xml.ExprTag does not implement BodyTag, it
                    can't return BodyTag.EVAL_BODY_TAG");
                    if (_jspx_eval_x_out_0 !=
                    javax.servlet.jsp.tagext.Tag.SKIP_BODY) {
                        do {
                    // end
                    // begin
                    [file="/JSPExample2.jsp";from=(21,6);to=(21,31)]
                        } while (_jspx_th_x_out_0.doAfterBody() ==
                    javax.servlet.jsp.tagext.BodyTag.EVAL_BODY_AGAIN);
                }
                    if (_jspx_th_x_out_0.doEndTag() ==
                    javax.servlet.jsp.tagext.Tag.SKIP_PAGE)
                    return;
            } finally {
                    _jspx_th_x_out_0.release();
            }
    // end
    // HTML // begin
    [file="/JSPExample2.jsp";from=(21,31);to=(22,6)]
        out.write("</td>\r\n");
        out.write("  <td>");
    // end
    // begin [file="/JSPExample2.jsp";from=(22,6);to=(22,31)]
```

The next code segment represents the second line in the `forEach` statement, which is almost identical to the first line. This line retrieves the Source attribute from the result of the `forEach` select XPath expression. The `org.apache.taglibs.standard.tag.el.xml.ExprTag` class is used for this line. The `ExprTag` class writes results of the expression directly to the `JspWriter`. The parent is set to the `forEach` object, `_jspx_th_x_forEach_0`, using the `ExprTag.setParent()` method. The select is set to the Source attribute (`@Source`) for the current DOM node using the `ExprTag.setSelect`. The rest of the code is the same tag evaluation code that was used in the other lines in this servlet to load, evaluate, and unload the tag.

```
                /* ----  x:out ---- */
                org.apache.taglibs.standard.tag.el.xml.ExprTag
                _jspx_th_x_out_1 = new
                org.apache.taglibs.standard.tag.el.xml.ExprTag();
```

```
_jspx_th_x_out_1.setPageContext(pageContext);
_jspx_th_x_out_1.setParent(_jspx_th_x_forEach_0);
_jspx_th_x_out_1.setSelect("@Source");
try {
    int _jspx_eval_x_out_1 =
    _jspx_th_x_out_1.doStartTag();
    if (_jspx_eval_x_out_1 ==
    javax.servlet.jsp.tagext.BodyTag.EVAL_BODY_BUFFERED)
        throw new JspTagException("Since tag handler
        class org.apache.taglibs.standard.tag.el.xml.
        ExprTag does not implement BodyTag, it can't
        return BodyTag.EVAL_BODY_TAG");
    if (_jspx_eval_x_out_1 !=
    javax.servlet.jsp.tagext.Tag.SKIP_BODY) {
        do {
        // end
        // begin
        [file="/JSPExample2.jsp";from=(22,6);to=(22,31)]
        } while (_jspx_th_x_out_1.doAfterBody() ==
        javax.servlet.jsp.tagext.BodyTag.EVAL_BODY_AGAIN);
    }
    if (_jspx_th_x_out_1.doEndTag() ==
    javax.servlet.jsp.tagext.Tag.SKIP_PAGE)
        return;
} finally {
    _jspx_th_x_out_1.release();
}
// end
// HTML // begin
    [file="/JSPExample2.jsp";from=(22,31);to=(23,6)]
    out.write("</td>\r\n");
    out.write("    <td>");
// end
// begin [file="/JSPExample2.jsp";from=(23,6);to=(23,25)]
```

The next code segment represents the third line in the forEach statement, which is almost identical to the first and second lines. This line retrieves the text data associated with the current DOM node from the result of the forEach select XPath expression. The `org.apache.taglibs.standard.tag.el.xml.ExprTag` class is used for this line. The `ExprTag` class writes results of the expression directly to the `JspWriter`. The parent is set to the `forEach` object, `_jspx_th_x_forEach_0`, using the `ExprTag.setParent()` method. The select is set to the text data using the XPath context expression (.) for the current DOM node. The rest of the code is the same tag evaluation code that was used in the other lines in this servlet to load, evaluate, and unload the tag.

```
/* ----  x:out ---- */
org.apache.taglibs.standard.tag.el.xml.ExprTag
_jspx_th_x_out_2 = new
org.apache.taglibs.standard.tag.el.xml.ExprTag();
```

```
                    _jspx_th_x_out_2.setPageContext(pageContext);
                    _jspx_th_x_out_2.setParent(_jspx_th_x_forEach_0);
                    _jspx_th_x_out_2.setSelect(".");
                    try {
                        int _jspx_eval_x_out_2 =
                        _jspx_th_x_out_2.doStartTag();
                        if (_jspx_eval_x_out_2 ==
                        javax.servlet.jsp.tagext.BodyTag.EVAL_BODY_BUFFERED)
                        throw new JspTagException("Since tag handler class
                        org.apache.taglibs.standard.tag.el.xml.ExprTag does
                        not implement BodyTag, it can't return
                        BodyTag.EVAL_BODY_TAG");
                        if (_jspx_eval_x_out_2 !=
                        javax.servlet.jsp.tagext.Tag.SKIP_BODY) {
                            do {
                            // end
                            // begin
                            [file="/JSPExample2.jsp";from=(23,6);to=(23,25)]
                            } while (_jspx_th_x_out_2.doAfterBody() ==
                            javax.servlet.jsp.tagext.BodyTag.EVAL_BODY_AGAIN);
                        }
                        if (_jspx_th_x_out_2.doEndTag() ==
                        javax.servlet.jsp.tagext.Tag.SKIP_PAGE)
                            return;
                    } finally {
                        _jspx_th_x_out_2.release();
                    }
                // end
                // HTML // begin
                [file="/JSPExample2.jsp";from=(23,25);to=(24,0)]
                    out.write("</td></tr>\r\n");
                    out.write("");
                // end
                // begin [file="/JSPExample2.jsp";from=(24,0);to=(24,12)]
                } while (_jspx_th_x_forEach_0.doAfterBody() ==
                  javax.servlet.jsp.tagext.BodyTag.EVAL_BODY_AGAIN);
            }
            if (_jspx_th_x_forEach_0.doEndTag() ==
                javax.servlet.jsp.tagext.Tag.SKIP_PAGE)
                return;
        } catch (Throwable _jspx_exception) {
            _jspx_th_x_forEach_0.doCatch(_jspx_exception);
        } finally {
            _jspx_th_x_forEach_0.doFinally();
            _jspx_th_x_forEach_0.release();
        }
    // end
    // HTML // begin [file="/JSPExample2.jsp";from=(24,12);to=(30,0)]
        out.write("\r\n");
        out.write("</table>\r\n");
        out.write("\r\n");
```

```
        out.write("</body>\r\n");
        out.write("</html>\r\n");
        out.write("\r\n");
        out.write("");
   // end
```

The balance of the code is standard error catching, and a command to release the pageContext, which flushes the JSP page from memory, based on the previously defined getPageContext method.

```
} catch (Throwable t) {
   if (out != null && out.getBufferSize() != 0)
       out.clearBuffer();
   if (pageContext != null) pageContext.handlePageException(t);
} finally {
   if (_jspxFactory != null) _jspxFactory.releasePageContext(pageContext);
}
}

   }
```

Summary

In this chapter, you were introduced to the XML tools included in the Sun Web Services Developer Pack (WSDP):

✦ Sun's Java Web Services Developer Pack

✦ The Java API for XML Messaging (JAXM), the Java API for XML Registries (JAXR) and the Java WSDP Registry Server, the Java API for XML-Based RPC (JAX-RPC), and the SOAP with Attachments API for Java (SAAJ)

✦ Documentation and examples of developing with the Java API for XML Processing (JAXP)

✦ Documentation and examples of developing with the Java Architecture for XML Binding Examples for the (JAXB)

✦ Documentation and examples of developing with the Java Server Pages Standard Tag Library (JSTL)

In the next few chapters, we'll show you how to put many of these tools to use in practical examples. We'll cover extraction of data from SQL Server, Oracle, and DB2 to XML and vice versa. We'll also show you how to create Web and J2EE applications that facilitate XML extraction from relation databases. After that, we'll show you a few tips on transforming native and custom relation data from one XML format to another.

✦   ✦   ✦

Relational Data and XML

Part IV provides examples of Web applications that use relational XML data. There are many relational XML formats, but most developers work with either SQL Server, DB2, or Oracle, each of which have their own XML output and interactive XML features. We provide an overview of each RDBMS XML access methods, output options, associated unique features and quirks. After we explain each format, we provide working examples for transforming data from one RDBMS XML format to another.

Accessing and Formatting XML from SQL Server Data

SQL Server support for XML started in 2000 with SQL Server 7. Microsoft provided a separate download called the *Microsoft SQL Server XML Technology Preview*. Microsoft Internet Information Server (IIS) had to be loaded on the target machine, and queries were passed to the server via URL with a FOR XML extension tacked onto the end of an SQL statement. Results were returned to the browser as an XML document. The XML Technology Preview used an IIS ISAPI extension via a dynamic-link library (DLL) to provide HTTP access to SQL Server and support for XML data formatting and updating capabilities. It shipped with fairly complete documentation and samples.

XML support on SQL Server 2000 is facilitated via Downloadable SQLXML (XML for SQL Server) add-ons.

Note MS SQL Server's proprietary SQLXML functionality should not be confused with SQL/XML functions that Oracle, IBM, and other RDBMS vendors use (we cover SQL/XML functions for DB2 and Oracle in Chapters 18 and 19). SQL/XML functions are based on the SQL/XML standard, which is a combination of XML and SQL functionality. The SQL/XML standard is maintained by the International Committee for Information Technology Standards (INCITS). Microsoft's SQLXML functionality, while very good, has nothing to do with this standard.

Support for XML queries and results are extended to the Enterprise Manager and to the Query Analyzer. XML access via HTTP is still supported, via the same FOR XML clause, and a few other ways. OPENXML is a feature that permits developers to update a SQL Server with XML documents. This permits SQL Server and related applications to access XML documents like any other type of SQL Server data. XML documents can also be used to process queries. Schema-based XPath expressions can also be used to query data. XML Updategrams permit updating and insertion of XML document data into SQL Server tables. XML bulk-load facilities batch-type insertion of a large volume of XML data. A SQLXMLOLEDB data-access component supports client-side and server-side XML formatting against query results using XPath or SQL, to provide client-side OPENXML functionality.   For .NET developers, SQLXML managed classes use the Microsoft .NET Framework class libraries to access .NET Framework classes. These classes can be used to insert XML data and retrieve XML results, including XPath queries and XML templates. I'll cover XML Templates later in this chapter. DiffGrams can also be used from the SQLXML managed classes. These use the DataSet class of the .NET Framework object model. The latest version of SQLXML also supports Web Services via SOAP HTTP requests that can execute stored procedures, user-defined functions (UDFs), and XML templates.

> **Note** A trial version of SQL server can be downloaded at `http://www.microsoft.com/sql/evaluation/trial/`.

As you can see from this list of features, there are almost too many options for manipulating SQL Server data with XML. The most important options, and the ones that we will be covering in detail in this chapter, are the FOR XML T-SQL extension, adding XML documents to a database, handling the data from the document as relational data set using OPENXML, and using XPath expressions to retrieve that data as XML documents.

The XML Programming Bible Example Tables

All of the tables in this chapter and this part of the book use the same data structure. For SQL Server, the data is structured into five tables (Tables 18-1, 18-2, 18-3, 18-4, and 18-5, respectively). All five tables are contained in a database called XMLProgrammingBible. Table 18-1 lists the structure of the AmazonListings table. This is the table that contains all of the Amazon book listings for our relational data examples and applications.

> **On The Web** We've included SQL code that creates these tables and inserts sample data as part of the downloads for this chapter. Downloads for the XML Programming Bible can be retrieved from `http://www.XMLProgrammingBIble.com`, in the downloads section.

Table 18-1
Structure of the AmazonListings Table

Table Column	Data Type	Maximum Size
ProductID (Primary Key)	int	
Ranking	int	
Title	char	200
ASIN	char	10
AuthorID (Foreign Key - Authors)	int	
Image	char	100
Small_Image	char	100
List_price	money	
Release_date	datetime	
Binding	char	50
Availability	char	10
Tagged_URL	char	200

Table 18-2 lists the structure of the Authors table. This is the table that contains information about the book and quotation authors. It is related to the AuthorID field in the AmazonListings, ElcorteinglesListings, and the Quotations tables.

Table 18-2
Structure of the Authors Table

Table Column	Data Type	Maximum Size
AuthorID (Primary Key)	Int	
AuthorName	Char	50

Table 18-3 lists the structure of the ElcorteinglesListings table. This is the table that contains all of the Spanish Language Elcorteingles Website book listings for our relational data examples and applications.

Table 18-3
Structure of the ElcorteinglesListings Table

Table Column	Data Type	Maximum Size
ProductID (Primary Key)	int	
titulo	char	200
ISBN	char	20
AuthorID (Foreign Key - Authors)	int	
Imagen	char	100
Precio	money	
fecha_de_publicación	datetime	
Encuadernación	char	50
librourl	char	200

Table 18-4 lists the structure of the Quotations table. This is the table that contains all of the Quotations related to books, authors, and sources in the relational data examples and applications.

Table 18-4
Structure of the Quotations Table

Table Column	Data Type	Maximum Size
QuotationID (Primary Key)	int	
SourceID (Foreign Key - Sources)	int	
AuthorID (Foreign Key - Authors)	int	
Quotation	char	300

Table 18-5 lists the structure of the Sources table. This is the table that contains information about the book and quotation authors. It is related to the AuthorID field in the AmazonListings and Quotations tables.

	Table 18-5	
	Structure of the Sources Table	
Table Column	*Data Type*	*Maximum Size*
SourceID (Primary Key)	Int	
SourceName	Char	50

Installing and Configuring SQLXML

You can download the latest version of SQLXML from `http://www.microsoft.com/sql/techinfo/xml/default.asp`. You will need at least version 3.0 SP1 for the examples in this chapter. Once the file is downloaded and installed via a simple InstallShield process, XML functionality is available via the Enterprise Manager and the Query Analyzer. You can also set up optional HTTP support for SQL Server XML queries by setting up Using IIS Virtual Directory Management. HTTP server access to SQL Server requires that Microsoft Internet Information Server (IIS) be running on the same machine as the SQL Server and the SQLXML installation. Developers that don't want to configure IIS for their development workstation can still work with SQLXML features via the Enterprise Manager and the Query Manager. You will, however, need to configure your Query Analyzer client to handle display and format of XML documents, as we outline in the next section.

Tip

Installing a new version of SQLXML does not remove the DLLs installed from previous versions (SQLXML 1.0 or SQLXML 2.0). This means that each version can be run independently on the same machine if needed, and is handy for rollback if there are any problems.

Viewing XML Results in Query Analyzer

When a FOR XML query is executed on SQL Server 2000, results returned contain a single text column and one or more rows. The text column contains a Unique ID that the SQL Server recognizes as a stream of XML data. When output is sent to an application or a Web browser, the unique ID is used to identify the output request and XML is assembled one row at a time. This means that the display of XML is organized into rows of data formatted by the stream as a single column.

Query Analyzer uses ODBC for query results instead of the streaming interface. The ODBC driver has a default Maximum Characters per Column of 256 characters, which is much shorter than most XML document's output. For example, a basic FOR XML AUTO query like this:

```
SELECT * FROM [XMLProgrammingBible].[dbo].[AmazonListings] FOR XML AUTO
```

Results in a very incomplete XML document like this in Query Analyzer and Enterprise Manager:

```
<XMLProgrammingBible.dbo.AmazonListings ProductID="1001" Ranking="1"
Title="Hamlet/MacBeth
```

To fix this, update the Maximum Characters per Column setting via the Tools ⇨ Options ⇨ Results option in the main menu of Query Analyzer. I set mine to 5000 characters, which is usually enough to display a full XML document in the results.

There is also an undocumented "pretty print" XML feature in Query Analyzer that can help you to review XML results. Set trace tag 257 on with this statement before the SELECT:

```
DBCC traceon(257)
SELECT * FROM [XMLProgrammingBible].[dbo].[AmazonListings] FOR XML AUTO
```

This produces indentation and line-end formatting of XML Document output, which makes it much more readable.

Accessing SQL Server Using HTTP

Before you can create SQL Server queries via HTTP, you have to set up a virtual root for Web access using the IIS Virtual Directory Management for SQL Server utility. If you already are running SQLXML via HTTP older than version 3.0, you may also have to update your SQL virtual directories to the latest version. The Microsoft Management Console (MMC) snap-in for the SQL Server Virtual Directory Management utility contains a tab in the properties dialog box for upgrading virtual directories to the latest SQLXML format.

Configuring IIS Virtual Directory Management for SQL Server

The IIS Virtual Directory Management for SQL Server utility can be accessed by selecting "Configure SQL XML Support in IIS" from the SQL Server start menu options. The utility creates an association between a virtual directory on the IIS server and SQL Server. A URL containing the IIS server address, the virtual directory, and an SQL expression can be passed from a Web browser or an application over HTTP to the IIS Server. The IIS server will route the request to the SQL Server based on the virtual directory name. Security, database port information that is pre-configured in the virtual directory connects the request to a database for execution. The help associated with the configuration tool covers all of the setup details. I do, however, have a few additional tidbits that may be useful for the setup:

✦ TCPIP must be enabled via the network utility, and the port must be configured to port 1433.

✦ Windows and SQL Server login support must be enabled (the default is "Windows Only").

✦ A version of SQLXML must be loaded and installed. For the examples in this chapter, SQLXML 3.0 SP1 should be installed. The examples may work with previous examples, but have not been tested with anything other than the most recent version.

Calling the Virtual Directory using URLs

Once the configuration is set up, HTTP commands can be used to access tables via URLS containing HTTP-formatted SQL or XPath expressions. Here's an example of a simple URL that calls the BenzTech IIS server to return all rows of the AmazonListings table of the XMLProgrammingBible Database:

```
http://iis.benztech.com/XMLProgrammingBible?sql=SELECT+*+FROM+AmazonListings+FOR
+XML+AUTO
```

Note   Spaces are replaced by + in the URL. This is because URLs cannot contain spaces. The escape character for a space (%20) can also be used to format the spaces. The IIS server reformats the SQL query and replaces the spaces before the query gets to the SQL Server. Also, the URL query does not have to be qualified by a database name, because the virtual directory contains the information about which database to access.

Parameters for SQL Server URLs

Table 18-6 lists optional parameters that can be used with a SQL Server query string. Parameters are added to the end of an SQL Server query URL. They are separated from the rest of the query and each other by an ampersand (&).

Table 18-6
Parameters for SQL Server URLs

Parameter	Description
&contenttype=	The Multipurpose Internet Mail Extension (MIME) content-type of the returned document. Example values are "text/XML," "text/html," "text/plain," and "image/jpeg." The default value is "text/XML." A full listing of registered MIME types can be found at the Internet Assigned Numbers Authority, at http://www.iana.org.
&outputencoding=	The encoding character set to use for the resulting output. The default is UTF-8.
&root=	If multiple rows of data are returned in an XML document, they result in multiple root elements in the document, which is not well-formed XML. The root parameter specifies a root element that is used to contain multiple rows of XML results in a well-formed XML document format.
&xsl=	The XSL stylesheet file specified in the xsl parameter value is used to transform results before they are displayed in the browser.

SQL Server templates

An SQL Server template is a valid XML document that is stored in an SQL Server virtual directory. Templates can contain one or more formatted SQL statements that are returned as a single result XML document. Templates can also be used to return more than one query result as a single XML document and store default parameters. Templates also have security advantages, because the calling URL containing the SQL Server query is not directly readable by an HTML page. Here's an example of the same query, but this time the query contains a reference to a template called MultiQueryExample1.xml instead of a query:

```
http://iis.benztech.com/XMLProgrammingBible/template/MultiQueryExample1.xml
```

The name of the virtual directory for this example is template. When you set up an IIS virtual directory, you can specify directories under the virtual directory that will contain templates and schemas. In this case, URL queries are sent to the XMLProgrammingBible directory via the virtual directory settings. URLs that use a template reference are sent to the /XMLProgrammingBible/template directory. URLs that use an XDR or W3C schema reference to process queries with XPath expressions are sent to the /XMLProgrammingBible/schema directory (we'll cover schema references and XPath queries in more detail later in the chapter). The template and schema directories were set up when we created the virtual directory for XMLProgrammingBible. They can be named anything, and you can have more than one of each. The virtual directory settings specify if a directory is a schema directory or a template directory. A directory can be a schema or template directory, but not both.

Note   For security reasons, the directories have to already exist when you set up the virtual directory settings. The Virtual Directory Configuration Utility does not create new directories from names specified in the virtual directory settings.

Elements for SQL Server templates

SQL Server XML templates can contain several optional elements. The only two elements required by the XML template are the root element, which can be named anything, and the namespace, `xmlns:sql="urn:schemas-microsoft-com:xml-sql`, which can have any namespace prefix. Most templates use a root element name of `ROOT` and a namespace prefix of `sql`. Table 18-7 contains the rest of the legal elements of a SQL Server template file.

Table 18-7
Elements of a SQL Server Template File

Element	Description
sql:xsl <root xmlns:sql= 'urn:schemas-microsoft-com: xml-sql' sql:xsl= 'stylesheet.xsl >	The `sql:xsl` attribute of a template root tag specifies an XSL stylesheet that is applied to an XML result document. Any path relative to the virtual directory root can be specified for the stylesheet. This is a default value that can be overwritten by a `?xsl=stylesheet` parameter in a URL that calls a template.
sql:header <sql:header> <sql:param .... </sql:header>	This is a container for one or more parameters, which are text values associated with the `<sql:param>` tag. The header tag is designated for expanded but unspecified use, in future versions of SQLXML.

sql:param
<sql:param name=
'name'>DefaultValue
</sql:param>
	This tag defines parameters that can be passed to a template query. Parameters are children of the `<sql:header>` tag. Multiple parameters can be specified, but each parameter has to be enclosed in a `<sql:param>` tag. Parameter names and default values can be stored in the `<sql:param>` tag, and values that override the default value can be passed from a URL using a URL parameter in this format:
	
	`http://serverURL/template/template.xml?`
	`ParameterName=ParameterValue`

Continued

Table 18-7 *(continued)*	
Element	*Description*
sql:query <sql:query> SELECT * FROM X </sql:query>	Contains SQL queries, which are text values associated with the <sql:query> tag. Multiple queries can be specified in a template, but each parameter has to be enclosed in a <sql:query> tag. Results from multiple queries are assembled into a single XML document.
sql:xpath-query <sql:xpath-query> (XPathExpression) </sql:xpath-query>	Specifies an XPath query that is processed against an annotated XDR or W3C schema.
mapping-schema	The mapping-schema attribute of the <sql:xpath-query> element identifies a schema that is located in a template file by the schema's id attribute. You can also identify external schemas from a template by relative path and file name. XPath queries in the <sql:xpath-query> element use the XDR or W3C schema that is referenced to access SQL Server data.

Using XML templates to store SQL queries

Here's an example of a very simple template that illustrates the combination of two queries into one XML result document. In this case, the same query runs twice via two sql:query tags, returning the first row (TOP 1) of the XMLProgramming Bible.dbo.AmazonListings table twice in the same result XML document.

Note   The query is accessed by HTTP, but because the template is already on the server and does not travel by HTTP. Therefore, the spaces in the SQL statements do not have to be reformatted with + or %20.

```
<QueryRoot xmlns:sql="urn:schemas-microsoft-com:xml-sql">
  <sql:query>
   SELECT TOP 1 * FROM XMLProgrammingBible.dbo.AmazonListings FOR XML AUTO
  </sql:query>
  <sql:query>
   SELECT TOP 1 * FROM XMLProgrammingBible.dbo.AmazonListings FOR XML AUTO
  </sql:query>
</QueryRoot>
```

When you save the template with a file name of MultiQueryExample1.xml in the template subdirectory of the virtual directory, you can call the template via this URL:

```
http://iis.benztech.com/XMLProgrammingBible/template/MultiQueryExample1.xml
```

An XML document is returned, which contains a result set of two SQL Server rows.

Transforming XML results with an XSL stylesheet

SQL Server also has a couple of ways to automatically transform XML results using an XSL stylesheet. A stylesheet reference can be contained in a URL that references a template with a parameter like this:

```
http://iis.benztech.com/XMLProgrammingBible/template/MultiQueryExample1.xml?xsl=
ResultTransform.xsl
```

In this example, the `ResultTransform.xsl` stylesheet is stored in the stylesheets subdirectory of the virtual directory. This is not an official directory for stylesheets, just a directory that I chose to create and store stylesheets in. It could be contained anywhere under the virtual directory and be named anything. The relative path reference branches from the virtual directory root.

You can also reference default stylesheets inside a template file using the sql:xsl attribute of a template's root tag. This has the same effect as the URL parameter.

<root xmlns:sql='urn:schemas-microsoft-com:xml-sql'
sql:xsl='/stylesheets/ResultTransform.xsl'>

> **Note**   The stylesheet reference stored in the template file is a *default* value. This means that any valid stylesheet reference that is passed as a parameter in a URL overrides the default stylesheet.

XPath queries, W3C schemas, and templates

XPath queries can be used to access and update SQL server data. Combined with Updategrams and OPENXML, SQL Server 2000 becomes a very flexible and robust XML document repository. XPath queries do require some setup, however. You have to create a schema subdirectory under your virtual root using the IIS Virtual Directory Management for SQL Server utility. You also have to create what Microsoft calls an "annotated schema" to map XML data elements and attributes to relational data tables and columns.

> **Note**   You need to download and install SQLXML 2.0 or higher to use annotated W3C schemas. Please refer to my SQLXML download and installation instructions earlier in this chapter. Annotated XDR schemas, an older and proprietary schema format based on a 1999 W3C schema working draft, can be used with SQLXML 1.0 or above. However, because it's an older non-standard industry schema format, I don't recommend using it if you can use W3C Schemas for the same purpose.

Annotated schemas are simply regular W3C schemas that use the W3C annotation element (`<xsd:annotation>`) to contain information about relationships between tables. To facilitate the elements and attributes inside the annotation, an additional namespace must also be added to the schema, `xmlns:sql="urn:schemas-microsoft-com:mapping-schema`. Under normal circumstances, W3C annotations are used to contain documentation about a certain element or attribute in a

W3C schema. For SQL Server annotated schemas, the annotation is located immediately after the root element and namespace declarations.

Cross-Reference   For more information on W3C Schemas, please refer to Chapter 3.

You can also map schema attributes and elements to relational data tables and columns using the `sql:relation` and `sql:field` attributes. This is only required if the schema element and attribute names do not match the table and column names in a SQL Server table. An SQL Server table name automatically maps to a complex element type with the same name in the schema. An SQL Server column in a table automatically maps to a simple element or attribute with the same name in the schema.

Here's an example of a very simple annotated schema. This is actually just a regular W3C schema for a table with the `urn:schemas-microsoft-com:mapping-schema` namespace added. That was the only change I had to make, because the first complex element, `<xs:element name="AmazonListings">`, contains the same name as the table, AmazonListings, and the attributes in the schema all correspond to column names in the AmazonListings table. The schema represents a single table, so I didn't need to add an annotation for database relationships either.

```
<?xml version="1.0" encoding="UTF-8"?>
<xs:schema xmlns:sql="urn:schemas-microsoft-com:mapping-schema"
xmlns:xs="http://www.w3.org/2001/XMLSchema">
  <xs:element name="AmazonListings">
    <xs:complexType>
      <xs:attribute name="ProductID" type="xs:short" use="required"/>
      <xs:attribute name="Ranking" type="xs:boolean" use="required"/>
      <xs:attribute name="Title" type="xs:string" use="required"/>
      <xs:attribute name="ASIN" type="xs:long" use="required"/>
      <xs:attribute name="AuthorID" type="xs:short" use="required"/>
      <xs:attribute name="Image" type="xs:string" use="required"/>
      <xs:attribute name="Small_Image" type="xs:string" use="required"/>
      <xs:attribute name="List_price" type="xs:decimal" use="required"/>
      <xs:attribute name="Release_date" type="xs:dateTime" use="required"/>
      <xs:attribute name="Binding" type="xs:string" use="required"/>
      <xs:attribute name="Tagged_URL" type="xs:anyURI" use="required"/>
    </xs:complexType>
  </xs:element>
</xs:schema>
```

You can use the sql:relation attribute to explicitly specify the SQL Server table name that the AmazonListings element maps to:

```
xsd:element name="Alist" sql:relation="AmazonListings"
```

You can also use the sql:field attribute to specify the SQL Server column name that the AmazonListings attribute maps to:

```
<xs:attribute name="PID" sql:field="ProductID" type="xs:short" use="required"/>
```

There are many other SQL Server annotated schema elements and attributes. I'll cover some of them later in this chapter. The others are well documented in the documentation that comes with the SQLXML download.

Now that the schema is defined, it can be saved in the virtual directory that you set up for schemas. I named mine AmazonListings.xsd to match the table that the schema refers to, and saved it in the XMLProgrammingBible\schemas directory.

Once the schema is saved, XPath expressions that refer to the schema can be passed from a URL like this:

```
http://iis.benztech.com/XMLProgrammingBible/schema/AmazonListing.xsd/AmazonListi
ngs[@ProductID=1001]
```

The XPath expression in the above URL is AmazonListings[@ProductID= 1001]. The XPath refers to the ProductID attribute of the AmazonListings element with a value of 1001 which maps to rows in the ProductID column in the AmazonListings table that contains a value of 1001.

Cross-Reference

For more information on XPath expressions, please refer to Chapter 7. For more information on the latest subset of XML expressions that are available with SQL Server, please refer to the SQLXML documentation that was included with your SQLXML download.

XPath expressions and references to schemas can also be passed from template files.

Here's a template file that contains an external schema reference and the same XPath expression that I used in the previous URL example. The template file is saved in the virtual template directory with a file name of XPathExample1.xml, and the schema file is located in the /schema subdirectory of the root, hence the relative path for the schema file:

```
<XPathRoot xmlns:sql="urn:schemas-microsoft-com:xml-sql">
  <sql:xpath-query mapping-schema=".\schema\AmazonListings.xsd">
  AmazonListings[@ProductID=1001]
  </sql:xpath-query>
</XPathRoot>
```

The template-based XPath results are accessible via this URL:

```
http://iis.benztech.com/XMLProgrammingBible/template/XPathExample1.xml
```

You can also include a schema in a template file, and refer to the schema with an ID reference instead of a relative path to another file. However, I find this approach leads to very large and complicated template files that quickly become unwieldy. I recommend separating the schema files from the template files whenever possible. Please refer to the SQLXML documentation for more details on including inline schemas in template files if you want to follow this approach.

Retrieving XML Data Using FOR XML

Now that SQLXML is set up, Query Analyzer displays XML output in a readable way, and I've explained all of the different ways that you can get at SQL Server data from a Web browser, let's get into the details of the FOR XML clause, and what data looks like when FOR XML modes are used. FOR XML includes three modes; RAW, AUTO, or EXPLICIT.

Using RAW mode

For example, this SELECT statement retrieves information from Customers and Orders table in the Northwind database. This query specifies the RAW mode in the FOR XML clause:

```
SELECT TOP 1 * FROM AmazonListings FOR XML RAW
```

This query returns the first row in the AmazonListings table. Here's what the results look like:

```
<row ProductID="1001" Ranking="1" Title="Hamlet/MacBeth" ASIN="8432040231"
AuthorID="1001"
Image="http://images.amazon.com/images/P/8432040231.01.MZZZZZZZ.jpg"
Small_Image="http://images.amazon.com/images/P/8432040231.01.TZZZZZZZ.jpg"
List_price="7.95" Release_date="1991-06-01T00:00:00" Binding="Paperback"
Tagged_URL="http://www.amazon.com:80/exec/obidos/redirect?tag=associateid&benzte
chnonogies=9441&camp=1793&link_code=xml&path=ASIN/8432040231"/>
```

As you can see from this example, RAW is a pretty good description of the format of data that comes back. It's certainly not very readable by human eyes. The row that is retuned is defined by a single element called `row`, and all of the columns in that row are defined by an attribute with the format `columnName="value"`. This result also points out an important problem with RAW mode—:the returned value does not convert illegal XML characters to XML-formatted legal characters. For example, the `Tagged_URL` attribute at the end of the result element contains several ampersands (&) that are used to parse parameters when the URL is sent to the Amazon Website. RAW mode does not encode them to the ampersand entity reference (&). If you need that functionality, you'll have to use AUTO or EXPLICIT mode.

The XMLDATA option

Using the XMLDATA option in RAW mode returns the row of data as an XML-Data schema. This includes all of the information in the previous example, plus a couple of XML-data schema names and the data type of each column associated with each attribute. This can be very handy for data sharing or producing schemas.

Using AUTO mode

Let's look at the same URL, but this time with the AUTO mode:

```
SELECT TOP 1 * FROM AmazonListings FOR XML AUTO
```

The only difference between AUTO and RAW in this example is that the `row` element name has been replaced by the name of the table, `AmazonListings`, and the ampersands (&) in the `tagged_URL` attribute have been converted to entity references (&).

```
<AmazonListings ProductID="1001" Ranking="1" Title="Hamlet/MacBeth"
ASIN="8432040231" AuthorID="1001"
Image="http://images.amazon.com/images/P/8432040231.01.MZZZZZZZ.jpg"
Small_Image="http://images.amazon.com/images/P/8432040231.01.TZZZZZZZ.jpg"
List_price="7.95" Release_date="1991-06-01T00:00:00" Binding="Paperback"
Tagged_URL="http://www.amazon.com:80/exec/obidos/redirect?tag=associateid&amp;be
nztechnonogies=9441&amp;camp=1793&amp;link_code=xml&amp;path=ASIN/8432040231" />
```

AUTO mode is very handy for queries that use related tables, GROUP BY, or aliased tables in the SQL statement. If there were more tables in the query and they were related to AmazonListings, each row from the related table would be a child element of the AmazonListings element. Table alias names are returned in the results used, and GROUP BY also has its own elements that are retuned with the result set.

The ELEMENTS option

One of the most interesting features of AUTO mode is the ELEMENTS option, which returns results from table columns as elements instead of attributes. A query like this:

```
SELECT TOP 1 * FROM AmazonListings FOR XML AUTO,ELEMENTS
```

returns this format:

```
<AmazonListings>
  <ProductID>1001</ProductID>
  <Ranking>1</Ranking>
  <Title>Hamlet/MacBeth</Title>
  <ASIN>8432040231</ASIN>
  <AuthorID>1001</AuthorID>
```

```
<Image>
http://images.amazon.com/images/P/8432040231.01.MZZZZZZZ.jpg
</Image>
<Small_Image>
http://images.amazon.com/images/P/8432040231.01.TZZZZZZZ.jpg
</Small_Image>
<List_price>7.95</List_price>
<Release_date>1991-06-01T00:00:00</Release_date>
<Binding>Paperback</Binding>
<Tagged_URL>
http://www.amazon.com:80/exec/obidos/redirect
?tag=associateid&amp; benztechnonogies=9441&amp;
camp=1793&amp;link_code=xml&amp;path=ASIN/8432040231
</Tagged_URL>
</AmazonListings>
```

The ELEMENTS option makes the data much easier to read, and may be more compatible with formats that use an element for each data column rather than an attribute. Readers who have been following through the book chapter by chapter will probably notice that this format looks a lot like the Amazon listings that are part of the XML AmazonMacbethSpanish.xml document that we've been using as an example in many places in the book.

Using Explicit mode

The EXPLICIT mode offers the most control of XML document formatting returned from an SQL Server URL query. The cost of this flexibility is development and debugging time. EXPLICIT mode is so very explicit that it may even be considered its own XML document formatting language. Because of the uniqueness of the syntax, FOR XML EXPLICIT queries are one of the most difficult parts of SQLXML to master. It's worth the work, however, because of the control that you have over XML output. FOR XML EXPLICIT queries always start with the following two column assignments:

```
SELECT 1 as Tag, 0 as Parent
```

Tag designates the column number of a tag for nesting purposes. Parent designates the nesting level of the column. A Parent value of 0 indicates that there are no parents for this select statement. Both are required values in a FOR XML EXPLICIT query, and both are integers.

The next line formats the first element in a FOR XML EXPLICIT query, and refers to a table column. This example line formats an explicitly named amazon column as an element, with the column value as the text value of the element:

```
ProductID AS [amazon!1!ProductID!element]
```

The ProductID AS expression is regular T-SQL, but the rest is part of the FOR XML EXPLICIT syntax. The Exclamations marks separate the FOR XML EXPLICIT arguments in the syntax. amazon is the name of the parent element. 1 denotes the nesting level (1 level below the amazon element). ProductID is the name of the new element. Element tells SQL Server to render the output as an element. Here's how the output looks:

```
<amazon>
    <ProductID>1001</ProductID>.......
```

A similar syntax is used to produce attribute output instead of element output:

```
ProductID AS [amazon!1!ProductID]
```

The only thing different between this attribute syntax and the previous element syntax is the removal of the !element directive from the end of the argument. This produces the following output format:

<amazon ProductID="1001">

This time, the ProductID becomes an attribute of the amazon element, instead of a nested element.

There are several other arguments and directives. Table 18-8 shows all of the FOR XML EXPLICIT arguments and directives, based on this syntax:

```
Parent!Tag!(attribute or element name)!(Optional Directives)
```

Table 18-8	
FOR XML EXPLICIT Arguments and Directives	
Element	*Description*
Parent (Argument)	An element defines a parent element by name. If the expression creates an attribute, the attribute becomes part of the element. If the expression creates an element, the new element is nested under the Parent element.
Tag (Argument)	Is the tag number of the element or attribute to be created? Always an integer value. Tag indicates the level of nested XML elements. Elements are nested according to tag number. Attributes are created as part of the element named at a specific tag level.

Continued

Table 18-8 *(continued)*

Element	Description
(attribute or element) name (Argument)	The name of an Is either the name of the XML attribute (if Directive is not specified) or the name of the contained element (if Directive is either xml, cdata, or element). If Directive is specified, AttributeName can be empty. In this case, the value contained in the column is directly contained by the element with the specified ElementName.
element (Optional Directive)	If the element directive is included in an expression, the output is formatted as an element. Otherwise, output is formatted as an attribute.
XML (Optional Directive)	If the XML directive is included in an expression, the output is formatted as an element, and no entity reference conversions take place (& is not converted to &, for example). Otherwise, output is formatted as an attribute. If the XML directive is used, the hide directive must be used as well to remove the unconverted element from the output.
hide (Optional Directive)	Used in UNIONS, JOINS, and/or ORDER BY, GROUP BY to structure output based on an attribute or element that will not be sent to the final XML output.
xmltext (Optional Directive)	`xmltext` is only used with hide in the same expression. Stored left-over column data from an OPENXML statement in a single element. The `xmltext` directive can be used with an attribute too, but only under very restricted conditions. Refer to the SQLXML documentation for details.
cdata (Optional Directive)	Can only be used with hide and with elements, not attributes. `cdata` stores column data in CDATA section without making any entity reference conversions or checking if the data is well formed.
ID (Optional Directive)	ID designates an attribute as an ID attribute. Used with the FOR XML EXPLICIT, XMLDATA Option.
IDREF (Optional Directive)	IDREF designates an attribute as an IDREF attribute. Used with the FOR XML EXPLICIT, XMLDATA Option.
IDREFS (Optional Directive)	IDREFS designates an attribute as an IDREFS attribute. Used with the FOR XML EXPLICIT, XMLDATA Option.

That's the overall syntax. We find that examples help a lot when dealing with FOR XML EXPLICIT queries. Listing 18-1 contains an XML template that contains two fairly simple FOR XML EXPLICIT queries. We've combined the queries in a template file. This creates a single output document that starts with a root catalog element, then a nested amazon element. Next, the second query produces an elcorteingles element with nested elements. We've used TOP 1 in the queries to return the first rows only of each result, just to make the results smaller. We saved the query in the template virtual directory on our IIS server, with a name of MultiQueryExample2.xml.

Listing 18-1: **The MultiQueryExample2.xml Template**

```xml
<?xml version="1.0" encoding="UTF-8"?>
<catalog>
  <sql:query>
    SELECT TOP 1 1 as Tag, 0 as Parent,
    ProductID AS [amazon!1!ProductID!element],
    Ranking AS [amazon!1!Ranking!element],
    Title AS [amazon!1!Title!element],
    ASIN AS [amazon!1!ASIN!element],
    AuthorID AS [amazon!1!AuthorID!element],
    Image AS [amazon!1!Image!element],
    Small_Image AS [amazon!1!Small_Image!element],
    List_Price AS [amazon!1!List_price!element],
    Release_Date AS [amazon!1!Release_date!element],
    Binding AS [amazon!1!Binding!element],
    Availability AS [amazon!1!Availablilty!element],
    Tagged_URL AS [amazon!1!Tagged_URL!element]
    FROM [XMLProgrammingBible].[dbo].[AmazonListings] FOR XML EXPLICIT
  </sql:query>
  <sql:query>
    SELECT TOP 1 1 as Tag, 0 as Parent,
    ProductID AS [elcorteingles!1!ProductID!element],
    titulo AS [elcorteingles!1!titulo!element] ,
    ISBN AS [elcorteingles!1!ISBN!element],
    AuthorID AS [elcorteingles!1!AuthorID!element],
    Imagen AS [elcorteingles!1!Imagen!element],
    Precio AS [elcorteingles!1!Precio!element],
    fecha_de_publicación AS [elcorteingles!1!fecha_de_publicación!element],
    Encuadernación AS [elcorteingles!1!Encuadernación!element],
    librourl AS [elcorteingles!1!librourl!element]
    FROM [XMLProgrammingBible].[dbo].[ElcorteinglesListings] FOR XML
    EXPLICIT
  </sql:query>

  </catalog>
```

The queries in the MultiQueryExample2.xml template file produce the output in Listing 18-2. The output is formatted as two XML document segments, one for `amazon` and one for `elcorteingles`. Each column name in the original query table is formatted into an element name, and the column value is a text value for each element.

> ### Listing 18-2: **Output from the MultiQueryExample2.xml Template**

```
<?xml version="1.0" encoding="UTF-8"?>
<catalog>
  <amazon>
    <ProductID>1001</ProductID>
    <Ranking>1</Ranking>
    <Title>Hamlet/MacBeth</Title>
    <ASIN>8432040231</ASIN>
    <AuthorID>1001</AuthorID>
    <Image>
    http://images.amazon.com/images/P/8432040231.01.MZZZZZZZ.jpg
    </Image>
    <Small_Image>
    http://images.amazon.com/images/P/8432040231.01.TZZZZZZZ.jpg
    </Small_Image>
    <List_price>7.95</List_price>
    <Release_date>1991-06-01T00:00:00</Release_date>
    <Binding>Paperback</Binding>
    <Tagged_URL>
     http://www.amazon.com:80/exec/obidos/
     redirect?tag=associateid&amp;benztechnonogies=9441
     &amp;camp=1793&amp;link_code=xml&amp;path=ASIN/8432040231
     </Tagged_URL>
  </amazon>
  <elcorteingles>
    <ProductID>1001</ProductID>
    <titulo>Romeo y Julieta/Macbeth/Hamlet/Otelo/
    La fierecilla domado/El sueño de una noche de verano/ El mercader de
    Venecia</titulo>
    <ISBN>8484036324</ISBN>
    <AuthorID>1001</AuthorID>
    <Imagen>
    http://libros.elcorteingles.es/producto/
    verimagen_blob.asp?ISBN=8449503639
    </Imagen>
    <Precio>759</Precio>
    <fecha_de_publicación>1999-06-04T00:00:00</fecha_de_publicación>
    <Encuadernación>Piel</Encuadernación>
    <librourl>http://libros.elcorteingles.es/producto/
    libro_descripcion.asp?CODIISBN=8449503639</librourl>
  </elcorteingles>
</catalog>
```

Updating SQL Server Data with XML

SQL Server 2000 data can be updated by XML documents using OPENXML, XML Updategrams, and XML Bulk Load.

XML Bulk Load is designed to batch-load XML document data into SQL server tables. Behind the scenes, it used the BULK INSERT command to update tables from parsed XML document data. Bulk Load uses MSXML to process streams of XML, which enables it to handle large amounts of XML data relatively quickly and efficiently. While Bulk Load is for large-scale data insertions, XML Updategrams are more suited for small-scale XML data inserts, deletions, or updates. They can be used at runtime, and handle loading of smaller XML documents into tables via very simple SQL Server templates. OPENXML is a flexible option for manipulating XML document data using T-SQL commands.

Updating relational data using OPENXML

Like the FOR XML EXPLICIT mode shown earlier in this chapter, OPENXML is a language unto itself. OPENXML is a keyword that can be added to T-SQL commands to map and manipulate XML data represented by SQL Server tables and columns. OPENXML is mostly used for updating, deleting, or inserting SQL server data from an XML document data source. It can also be used to select and view XML documents in SQL Server tables.

There are many options for mapping XML documents to SQL Server tables. You can also integrate ADO with OPENXML to provide a very flexible way for SQL server to communicate with applications using XML instead of regular rowsets. The techniques and syntax for this functionality is covered in great detail in the documentation that comes with SQL Server.

Note   The help documentation for OPENXML is in the main SQL Server documentation, not the SQLXML Documentation.

In this chapter we'll focus on some of the most useful T-SQL functions of OPENXML; inserting and updating SQL server tables based on table formats, and using OPENXML with SELECT queries to produce edge tables.

Working with OPENXML edge tables

Let's start with edge tables, because they need the smallest query and the results provide insight into the structure of OPENXML. Despite the name, edge tables are not something you find at IKEA. Edge tables are actually parsed representations of an XML document that is formatted in an OPENXML format and inserted into a temporary table for display. Microsoft says that the edge in edge table refers to "edges" of the data in the XML document, whatever that means. We say that columns in the edge table refer to parsed nodes from an XML document.

Listing 18-3 shows a simple OPENXML query that formats one row of data in the AmazonListings table as an Edge table. The code is only five lines long, but the XML document in the middle makes it look more complicated than it is.

```
DECLARE @iDoc int, @cDoc varchar (5000)

SET @cDoc = '<AmazonListings ProductID="1001" Ranking="1" Title="Hamlet/MacBeth"
ASIN="8432040231"
Image="http://images.amazon.com/images/P/8432040231.01.MZZZZZZZ.jpg"
Small_Image="http://images.amazon.com/images/P/8432040231.01.TZZZZZZZ.jpg"
List_price="$7.95" Release_date="2001-12-17T09:30:47-05:00"
Binding="Paperback" Availability=""
Tagged_URL="http://www.amazon.com:80/exec/obidos/redirect?tag=associateid&a
mp;benztechnonogies=9441&amp;camp=1793&amp;link_code=xml&amp;path=ASIN/8432
040231"/>'

EXEC sp_xml_preparedocument @iDoc OUTPUT, @cDoc
SELECT * FROM OPENXML (@iDoc, '/AmazonListings', 1)
EXEC sp_xml_removedocument @idoc
```

The first line declares two variables. The iDoc variable is used by the sp_xml_preparedocument stored procedure to parse a provided XML document. The cDoc variable contains the XML document that is parsed.

```
DECLARE @iDoc int, @cDoc varchar (5000)
```

The XML document that is parsed by the sp_xml_preparedocument stored procedure is usually passed via a parameter to the OPENXML command. For this introductory example, we've explicitly added the document in the code to make it easier to follow the flow. The XML document is the result of a FOR XML AUTO query on the first row of the AmazonListings table:

```
SET @cDoc = '<AmazonListings ProductID="1001" Ranking="1" Title="Hamlet/MacBeth"
ASIN="8432040231"
Image="http://images.amazon.com/images/P/8432040231.01.MZZZZZZZ.jpg"
Small_Image="http://images.amazon.com/images/P/8432040231.01.TZZZZZZZ.jpg"
List_price="$7.95" Release_date="2001-12-17T09:30:47-05:00"
Binding="Paperback" Availability=""
Tagged_URL="http://www.amazon.com:80/exec/obidos/redirect?tag=associateid&a
mp;benztechnonogies=9441&amp;camp=1793&amp;link_code=xml&amp;path=ASIN/8432
040231"/>'
```

sp_xml_preparedocument accepts the integer variable iDoc and the XML document in the cDoc variable and returns a handle that is used to access the parsed document.

```
EXEC sp_xml_preparedocument @iDoc OUTPUT, @cDoc
```

The SELECT command uses the handle passed back from sp_xml_preparedocument to access the parsed XML document. An XPath expression is used to select the AmazonListings element. The last parameter designates the mapping style of the source XML document to the output in the edge table. The most important values are 1 and 2. A value of 1 maps attributes in the source XML document to nodes in the edge table. This is also the default value if the attribute is omitted. A value 2 of two maps attributes in the source XML document to nodes in the edge table. You can also add values together to provide mapping combinations. A value of 3 denotes attribute and element mapping in the same document.

```
SELECT * FROM OPENXML (@iDoc, '/AmazonListings', 1)
```

The last parameter also handles left-over values from the OPENXML expression. When OPENXML queries process an XML document, the results are returned based on XPath. For example, if we wanted to just return the List_price attribute in the code listed in Listing 18-3, the SELECT statement would look like this:

```
SELECT * FROM OPENXML (@iDoc, '/AmazonListings[@List_price]', 1)
```

The rest of the document that is not accessed by XPath is considered unprocessed or overflow values in the OPENXML node tree. These overflow values are stored in a variable called @mp:xmltext, and can be referred to for further processing. Any variable with a @mp: prefix is an OPENXML metaproperty. Metaproperties contain values that are assigned to reserved keywords and describe information about an XML document such as schema data type, and so on. The @mp:xmltext is a specialized variable for handling overflow text from OPENXML expressions. The numeric parameter at the end of the OPENXML expression accommodates the formatting of the overflow. Eight is the base number, and the 1, 2, and 3 values are added together with 8 to get values 9 through 11. A value of 8 or 9 (8+1) stores overflow values in the @mp:xmltext variable mapped as attributes. A value of 10 (8+2) stores overflow values in the @mp:xmltext variable mapped as elements. A value of 11 (8+3) stores overflow values in the @mp:xmltext variable mapped as mixed elements and attributes.

The next line in the code resets the connection and removes the handle created by sp_xml_preparedocument using the sp_xml_removedocument stored procedure with a passed parameter of the XML document handle (iDoc).

```
EXEC sp_xml_removedocument @idoc
```

Figure 18-1 shows the results of the query in grid format. The results are worth reviewing because edge tables provide a good introduction to OPENXML syntax and structure.

	id	parentid	nodetype	localname	prefix	namespaceuri	datatype	prev	text
1	0	NULL	1	AmazonListings	NULL	NULL	NULL	NULL	NULL
2	2	0	2	ProductID	NULL	NULL	NULL	NULL	NULL
3	13	2	3	#text	NULL	NULL	NULL	NULL	1001
4	3	0	2	Ranking	NULL	NULL	NULL	NULL	NULL
5	14	3	3	#text	NULL	NULL	NULL	NULL	1
6	4	0	2	Title	NULL	NULL	NULL	NULL	1
7	15	4	3	#text	NULL	NULL	NULL	NULL	Hamlet/MacBeth
8	5	0	2	ASIN	NULL	NULL	NULL	NULL	NULL
9	16	5	3	#text	NULL	NULL	NULL	NULL	8432040231
10	6	0	2	Image	NULL	NULL	NULL	NULL	NULL
11	17	6	3	#text	NULL	NULL	NULL	NULL	http://images.amazon.com/images/P/8432040231.01.MZZZZZZZ.jpg
12	7	0	2	Small_Image	NULL	NULL	NULL	NULL	NULL
13	18	7	3	#text	NULL	NULL	NULL	NULL	http://images.amazon.com/images/P/8432040231.01.TZZZZZZZ.jpg
14	8	0	2	List_price	NULL	NULL	NULL	NULL	NULL
15	19	8	3	#text	NULL	NULL	NULL	NULL	$7.95
16	9	0	2	Release_date	NULL	NULL	NULL	NULL	NULL
17	20	9	3	#text	NULL	NULL	NULL	NULL	2001-12-17T09:30:47-05:00
18	10	0	2	Binding	NULL	NULL	NULL	NULL	NULL
19	21	10	3	#text	NULL	NULL	NULL	NULL	Paperback
20	11	0	2	Availablilty	NULL	NULL	NULL	NULL	NULL
21	12	0	2	Tagged_URL	NULL	NULL	NULL	NULL	NULL
22	22	12	3	#text	NULL	NULL	NULL	NULL	http://www.amazon.com:80/exec/obidos/redirect?tag=associateid&ben...

Figure 18-1: The edge table created as a result of the OPENXMLExample1.sql query

The structure and information in an edge table help analyze the parsed nodes of an XML document as SQL Server sees it, based on the results of your OPENXML expression. I usually start any OPENXML query by sending output based on an XPath expression that returns the root element of an XML document to an edge table. That way I can have a look at the data as SQL Server sees it, and shape the output based on attribute and element settings. Edge tables are also good to check before you do an insert or update with an OPENXML expression, to see what the effect will be on the data before you point the expression at a table. Table 18-9 shows the columns in the edge table with descriptions.

Table 18-9 Columns in an Edge Table	
Column	**Description**
id	There is one unique ID for each parsed document node. Node counts start at 0 for the root element.
parented	Refers to the node id number of the parent node. Parents of attributes and text are their elements. Parents of element are other elements. Root elements have null parent ids.
nodetype	Based on the W3C DOM node types 1 to 12. The three most common node types are listed in this edge table; elements (1), attributes (2), and text (3). Table 5-3 in Chapter 5 has a full listing of DOM Node types and descriptions.

Column	Description
localname	The local name of the element or attribute. #text for text data, and null for non-named nodes.
prefix	The namespace prefix of the node. null if there is no namespace.
namespaceuri	The namespace uri of the node. null if there is no namespace.
datatype	W3C schema data type for the node. Since I am not using schemas in this XML document, all values are null.
prev	The node id number of the previous sibling. Since this is a single-element XML document, all sibling values are null.
text	If the node is an element, the attribute value is in this column. If the node is a text node, the text value is in this column. Otherwise, null.

OPENXML provides many ways to explicitly map the format of an SQL Server table as part of an OPENXML expression. While explicit mapping of XML data to SQL Server data may be useful for some applications, I prefer to use the features in OPENXML that let me map my XML document to an existing SQL Server table structure when possible. That way, if my SQL Server table changes, I only have to change the XML document structure, and not the explicit mapping in all of my OPENXML expressions. Also, I find it a little easier to follow code that maps XML document objects to SQL Server table objects with the same names, instead of having to follow the mapping in a piece of intermediary code. Of course, in reality sometimes you have to explicitly map XML documents to SQL Server tables. I'll cover table mapping in this part of the chapter, including how to insert and update XML documents while maintaining referential integrity in SQL Server tables. I'll also show you an example of a common situation where you have to bite the bullet and explicitly map SQL Server table columns to XML document data. For all of the OPENXML examples, I'm using the following XML document. The document starts with an XML document declaration, followed by a root element of XMLProgrammingBible. The root element can be named anything. Because it contains representations of all of the tables and relationships in the XMLProgrammingBible database, I named it XMLProgrammingBible.

```
<?xml version="1.0" encoding="UTF-8"?>
<XMLProgrammingBible>
```

Note that the element for the Quotations table is nested inside the elements for the Sources and Authors tables. This is to represent foreign key relationships between the tables. The Authors and Sources tables contain primary keys. The Quotations table contains foreign key relationships with Authors and Sources. Nesting the Quotations table inside the Sources and Authors table represents the foreign key relationships.

```
<Authors AuthorID="1001" AuthorName="Shakespeare, William">
  <Sources SourceID="1001" Source_Name="Macbeth">
```

The nested elements don't contain references to the `AuthorID` or `SourceID` columns, even though these values are part of the SQL Server tables represented by the nested elements. This information is supplied by the foreign key relationships in the tables and represented by the way that the elements are nested. It's implied by the element nesting that, for example, the `AuthorID` and the `SourceID` for the `Quotations` data should be supplied by the `AuthorID` in the `Authors` parent element.

```
    <Quotations QuotationID="1001" Quotation="When the hurlyburly's done,
      / When the battle's lost and won."/>
  </Sources>
 </Authors>
</XMLProgrammingBIble>
```

Using OPENXML to insert XML data

I've show you what XML document node trees look like when they are created by OPENXML in an edge table, and I've provided an overview of the XML document that I am using for the OPENXML examples. Now I can use OPENXML expressions to insert data into related tables. The code in Listing 18-4 inserts data into three tables from a single XML document.

Listing 18-4: **Inserting Data into SQL Server Tables Using OPENXML - OPENXMLExample2.sql**

```
DECLARE @iDoc int, @cDoc varchar (5000)
SET @cDoc =
'<XMLProgrammingBible>
 <Authors AuthorID="1001" AuthorName="Shakespeare, William">
  <Sources SourceID="1001" Source_Name="Macbeth">
   <Quotations QuotationID="1001" Quotation="When the hurlyburlys done,
    When the battles lost and won."/>
  </Sources>
 </Authors>
</XMLProgrammingBible>'
EXEC sp_xml_preparedocument @iDoc OUTPUT, @cDoc

INSERT INTO [XMLProgrammingBible].[dbo].[Authors]([AuthorID], [AuthorName])
(SELECT [AuthorID], [AuthorName] FROM OPENXML (@iDoc,
'/XMLProgrammingBible/Authors') WITH Authors)

INSERT INTO [XMLProgrammingBible].[dbo].[Sources]([SourceID], [Source Name])
(SELECT [SourceID], [Source Name] FROM OPENXML (@iDoc,
'/XMLProgrammingBible/Authors/Sources') WITH Sources)

INSERT INTO [XMLProgrammingBible].[dbo].[Quotations]([QuotationID], [SourceID],
[AuthorID], [Quotation])
```

```
(SELECT QuotationID, SourceID, AuthorID, Quotation FROM OPENXML (@iDoc,
'/XMLProgrammingBible') WITH (
QuotationID int './Authors/Sources/Quotations/@QuotationID',
SourceID int './Authors/Sources/@SourceID',
AuthorID int './Authors/@AuthorID',
Quotation char(300) './Authors/Sources/Quotations/@Quotation'))

EXEC sp_xml_removedocument @idoc
```

As with the previous OPENXML example, the first line declares two variables. The iDoc variable is used by the sp_xml_preparedocument stored procedure to parse a provided XML document. The cDoc variable contains the XML document that is parsed.

```
DECLARE @iDoc int, @cDoc varchar (5000)
```

The XML document that is parsed by the sp_xml_preparedocument stored procedure is usually passed via a parameter to the OPENXML command. As with the first example, I've explicitly added the document in the code to make it easier to follow the flow.

```
SET @cDoc =
'<XMLProgrammingBible>
 <Authors AuthorID="1001" AuthorName="Shakespeare, William">
  <Sources SourceID="1001" Source_Name="Macbeth">
   <Quotations QuotationID="1001" Quotation="When the hurlyburlys done,
   When the battles lost and won."/>
  </Sources>
 </Authors>
</XMLProgrammingBible>'
```

sp_xml_preparedocument accepts the integer variable iDoc and the XML document in the cDoc variable and returns a handle that is used to access the parsed document.

```
EXEC sp_xml_preparedocument @iDoc OUTPUT, @cDoc
```

Next is the first INSERT command. This insert uses a very simple OPENXML SELECT statement to retrieve the AuthorID and AuthorName attributes from the Authors element in the source XML document. The XPath expression locates the element in the XML document. The WITH Authors command at the end of the OPENXML expression tells OPENXML to use the Authors table as a guide when formatting the node tree.

```
INSERT INTO [XMLProgrammingBible].[dbo].[Authors]([AuthorID], [AuthorName])
(SELECT [AuthorID], [AuthorName] FROM OPENXML (@iDoc,
'/XMLProgrammingBible/Authors') WITH Authors)
```

The Sources INSERT command is almost identical to the Authors INSERT command. This time, the SourceID and Source_Name attributes from the Sources element in the source XML document are retrieved. The WITH Sources command at the end of the OPENXML expression tells OPENXML to use the Sources table as a guide when formatting the node tree.

```
INSERT INTO [XMLProgrammingBible].[dbo].[Sources]([SourceID], [Source Name])
(SELECT [SourceID], [Source Name] FROM OPENXML (@iDoc,
'/XMLProgrammingBible/Authors/Sources') WITH Sources)
```

The Quotations INSERT command has to gather attributes from several elements in the XML document, so unfortunately it can't use the WITH (table) mapping like Sources and Authors did. Instead, the WITH command contains explicit data typing and mapping. OPENXML explicit mappings gather the Quotation, SourceID, AuthorID, and Quotation attributes from several elements in the XML document. XPath expressions point to positions relative to the root /XMLProgrammingBible element in the XML document.

```
INSERT INTO [XMLProgrammingBible].[dbo].[Quotations]([QuotationID], [SourceID],
[AuthorID], [Quotation])
(SELECT QuotationID, SourceID, AuthorID, Quotation FROM OPENXML (@iDoc,
'/XMLProgrammingBible') WITH (
QuotationID int './Authors/Sources/Quotations/@QuotationID',
SourceID int './Authors/Sources/@SourceID',
AuthorID int './Authors/@AuthorID',
Quotation char(300) './Authors/Sources/Quotations/@Quotation'))
```

The last line in the code resets the connection and removes the handle created by sp_xml_preparedocument using the sp_xml_removedocument stored procedure with a passed parameter of the XML document handle (iDoc).

```
EXEC sp_xml_removedocument @idoc
```

Using OPENXML to update XML data

Updating XML data with OPENXML is very similar to OPENXML data insertion. The code Listing 18-5 updates a row of data in the Sources table with a value provided in an XML document.

Listing 18-5: Updating Data in SQL Server Tables Using OPENXML - OPENXMLExample3.sql

```
DECLARE @iDoc int, @cDoc varchar (5000)
SET @cDoc =
'<XMLProgrammingBible>
```

```
  <Sources SourceID="1001" Source_Name="McBeth">
  </Sources>
</XMLProgrammingBible>'
EXEC sp_xml_preparedocument @iDoc OUTPUT, @cDoc

UPDATE Sources
    SET [Source Name] = XS.Source_Name
    FROM [XMLProgrammingBible].[dbo].[Sources] S, (SELECT [SourceID],
[Source_Name] FROM OPENXML (@iDoc, '/XMLProgrammingBible/Authors/Sources')
WITH Sources) XS
WHERE S.[Source Name] = 'Macbeth'

EXEC sp_xml_removedocument @idoc
```

This code starts with the same variable declarations as the previous two examples. The XML document that is passed for the update contains a single row of data to update the Sources table. The SourceID stays the sane, but the Source_Name changes.

```
DECLARE @iDoc int, @cDoc varchar (5000)
SET @cDoc =
'<XMLProgrammingBible>
  <Sources SourceID="1001" Source_Name="McBeth">
  </Sources>
</XMLProgrammingBible>'
EXEC sp_xml_preparedocument @iDoc OUTPUT, @cDoc
```

The UPDATE command contains a nested SELECT statement that pulls the new value out of the attributes in the XML source document and parses them into nodes. The UPDATE command takes the value of the Source_Name attribute and updates the [Source Name] value in the SQL Server table row. The last line in the code resets the connection and removes the handle created by sp_xml_prepare document using the sp_xml_removedocument stored procedure with a passed parameter of the XML document handle (iDoc).

```
UPDATE Sources
    SET [Source Name] = XS.Source_Name
    FROM [XMLProgrammingBible].[dbo].[Sources] S, (SELECT [SourceID],
[Source_Name] FROM OPENXML (@iDoc, '/XMLProgrammingBible/Authors/Sources')
WITH Sources) XS
WHERE S.[Source Name] = 'Macbeth'

EXEC sp_xml_removedocument @idoc
```

Creating an annotated W3C schema for SQL Server data

The next part of this chapter will cover XML Bulk Load and Updategram functionality, both of which rely heavily on annotated SQL Server schemas. We provided an introduction to five example tables and a simple single-table annotated schema earlier in this chapter. Now we'll produce a single annotated schema that represents the five example SQL Server tables. To create an MS SQL Server Annotated schema, you have a few options. The first option is to hand code a schema using an XML developer tool. This is undesirable for obvious reasons, when using a very large, complex schema. The second option is to use Visual Studio.NET to produce a schema base on the tables. This is the fastest option, but we find that the VS.NET output does not always adhere to the standards of a well-formed W3C schema. In those cases you have to use an editing tool to edit the schema, and hope that it still works with SQL server. The third option is the one that we use the most. Altova's XMLSpy (a free trial download is available from `http://www.xmlspy.com`) has a tool that can connect to an SQL Server via OLE and create a W3C schema based on tables that you select. The result is a W3C-compatible schema based on the tables, but without the relationship annotation at the top of the schema. We then manually code the relationship annotation, which took me about five minutes for the four relationship annotations in the example database.

The five tables are represented by pieces of a W3C Schema. The relationships between the tables are represented in the annotation at the top of the schema. The rest of the schema is a standard W3C schema format, because we can use the schema defaults to map tables to elements of complex type and attributes of simple type. In other words, because all of the table columns match up to XML document attributes in the schema, the basic, unmapped W3C schema meets our needs. Below is an annotated schema for the five tables in the `XMLProgrammingBible` database.

The first part of the Schema includes an XML document declaration and the W3C and Microsoft namespaces that are used in the schema. The `<xs:appinfo>` tag in the `<xs:annotation>` indicates that the annotation has specific information that is reserved for an application that uses the schema. In this case, The relationships between the SQL Server tables are stored in the `<xs:appinfo>` tag.

```
<?xml version="1.0" encoding="UTF-8"?>
<xs:schema xmlns:xs="http://www.w3.org/2001/XMLSchema" xmlns:sql="urn:schemas-
microsoft-com:mapping-schema">
  <xs:annotation>
    <xs:appinfo>
```

The first reference is a foreign key relationship between The `Authors` table and the `AmazonListings` table. The primary key is the AuthorID in the Authors table, which is represented by the parent-key and parent attributes in the relationship element. The foreign key is the AuthorID in the AmazonListings table, which is represented by the child-key and child attributes in the relationship element. Naming the attributes primary-table, primary-key, foreign-table and foreign-key was too easy, we guess....

```
<sql:relationship name="FK_AmazonListings_Authors" parent="Authors"
 parent-key="AuthorID" child="AmazonListings" child-key="AuthorID"/>
```

The three remaining relationship elements represent other foreign key relationships. The Authors table is also connected to the Quotations table and the ElcorteinglesListings table by a foreign key reference. The Sources table is connected to the Quotations table using another foreign key relationship.

```
<sql:relationship name="FK_ElcorteinglesListings_Authors"
parent="Authors" parent-key="AuthorID" child="ElcorteinglesListings"
child-key="AuthorID"/>
<sql:relationship name="FK_Quotations_Authors" parent="Authors"
 parent-key="AuthorID" child="Quotations" child-key="AuthorID"/>
<sql:relationship name="FK_Quotations_Sources" parent="Sources"
 parent-key="SourceID" child="Quotations" child-key="SourceID"/>
  </xs:appinfo>
 </xs:annotation>
```

The first table in the schema is the AmazonListings table. The table is represented by an element containing a W3C schema complex data type. Nested inside the complex data type are attributes, some of which contain a W3C schema simple data type.

```
<xs:element name="AmazonListings">
  <xs:complexType>
    <xs:attribute name="ProductID" type="xs:integer"/>
    <xs:attribute name="Ranking" type="xs:integer"/>
```

XMLSPY automatically reproduces field constraints and data types based on SQL server constraints and data types in schemas that are generated from SQL Server databases. For example, the `Title` column is a W3C schema string data type, and has a maximum length of 200.

```
<xs:attribute name="Title">
  <xs:simpleType>
    <xs:restriction base="xs:string">
      <xs:maxLength value="200"/>
    </xs:restriction>
  </xs:simpleType>
</xs:attribute>
<xs:attribute name="ASIN">
  <xs:simpleType>
    <xs:restriction base="xs:string">
```

```
          <xs:maxLength value="10"/>
        </xs:restriction>
      </xs:simpleType>
    </xs:attribute>
    <xs:attribute name="AuthorID" type="xs:integer"/>
    <xs:attribute name="Image">
      <xs:simpleType>
        <xs:restriction base="xs:string">
          <xs:maxLength value="100"/>
        </xs:restriction>
      </xs:simpleType>
    </xs:attribute>
    <xs:attribute name="Small_Image">
      <xs:simpleType>
        <xs:restriction base="xs:string">
          <xs:maxLength value="100"/>
        </xs:restriction>
      </xs:simpleType>
    </xs:attribute>
    <xs:attribute name="List_price" type="xs:integer"/>
    <xs:attribute name="Release_date" type="xs:dateTime"/>
    <xs:attribute name="Binding">
      <xs:simpleType>
        <xs:restriction base="xs:string">
          <xs:maxLength value="50"/>
        </xs:restriction>
      </xs:simpleType>
    </xs:attribute>
    <xs:attribute name="Availablilty">
      <xs:simpleType>
        <xs:restriction base="xs:string">
          <xs:maxLength value="10"/>
        </xs:restriction>
      </xs:simpleType>
    </xs:attribute>
    <xs:attribute name="Tagged_URL">
      <xs:simpleType>
        <xs:restriction base="xs:string">
          <xs:maxLength value="200"/>
        </xs:restriction>
      </xs:simpleType>
    </xs:attribute>
  </xs:complexType>
```

XMLSPY doesn't create the relationship annotation at the top of the schema, but it does create W3C Schema `key` and `keyref` elements representing the relationships via XPath. The `keyref` element below refers to the foreign key relationship between The `AuthorID` in the `AmazonListings` table and the `AuthorID` in the Authors table. The `refer` attribute refers to a unique key listed in the Authors table in this schema. The `xs:selector` and the `xs:field` elements contain a reference to XPath expressions for the reference in the current `AmazonListings` table. The `keyref` value represents the foreign key, and the `key` value represents the primary key.

```
<xs:keyref name="AmazonListings_AuthorID" refer="Authors_AuthorID">
  <xs:selector xpath="."/>
  <xs:field xpath="@AuthorID"/>
</xs:keyref>
</xs:element>
```

The Authors table contains the same representational data types and constraints as the AmazonListings table.

```
<xs:element name="Authors">
  <xs:complexType>
    <xs:attribute name="AuthorID" type="xs:integer"/>
    <xs:attribute name="AuthorName">
      <xs:simpleType>
        <xs:restriction base="xs:string">
          <xs:maxLength value="50"/>
        </xs:restriction>
      </xs:simpleType>
    </xs:attribute>
  </xs:complexType>
```

The AuthorID field in the Authors table is the primary key for three relationships in the sample tables. The foreign key relationships are represented by W3C schema `keyref` elements with a refer attribute back to the `Authors_AuthorID` key shown here. The `field` element refers to the authored attribute with an XPath expression (`@AuthorID`), and the `selector` element refers to the value in the `AuthorID` attribute to select with another XPath expression (`.`).

```
<xs:key name="Authors_AuthorID">
  <xs:selector xpath="."/>
  <xs:field xpath="@AuthorID"/>
</xs:key>
</xs:element>
```

The ElcorteinglesListings table repeats the same data typing and constraints shown in the previous tables.

```
<xs:element name="ElcorteinglesListings">
  <xs:complexType>
    <xs:attribute name="ProductID" type="xs:integer"/>
    <xs:attribute name="titulo">
      <xs:simpleType>
        <xs:restriction base="xs:string">
          <xs:maxLength value="200"/>
        </xs:restriction>
```

```
            </xs:simpleType>
          </xs:attribute>
          <xs:attribute name="ISBN">
            <xs:simpleType>
              <xs:restriction base="xs:string">
                <xs:maxLength value="20"/>
              </xs:restriction>
            </xs:simpleType>
          </xs:attribute>
          <xs:attribute name="AuthorID" type="xs:integer"/>
          <xs:attribute name="Imagen">
            <xs:simpleType>
              <xs:restriction base="xs:string">
                <xs:maxLength value="100"/>
              </xs:restriction>
            </xs:simpleType>
          </xs:attribute>
          <xs:attribute name="Precio" type="xs:integer"/>
          <xs:attribute name="fecha_de_publicación" type="xs:dateTime"/>
          <xs:attribute name="Encuadernación">
            <xs:simpleType>
              <xs:restriction base="xs:string">
                <xs:maxLength value="50"/>
              </xs:restriction>
            </xs:simpleType>
          </xs:attribute>
          <xs:attribute name="librourl">
            <xs:simpleType>
              <xs:restriction base="xs:string">
                <xs:maxLength value="200"/>
              </xs:restriction>
            </xs:simpleType>
          </xs:attribute>
        </xs:complexType>
```

This `keyref` refers back to the `Authors_AuthorID` key element in the Authors table. Like the `key` element in the `Authors` table, the `field` element of the `keyref` element refers to the authored attribute with an XPath expression (`@AuthorID`), and the `selector` element refers to the value in the `AuthorID` selection expression with another XPath expression (`.`). It also represents a foreign key relationship between the ElcorteinglesListings table and the Authors table.

```
      <xs:keyref name="ElcorteinglesListings_AuthorID"
      refer="Authors_AuthorID">
        <xs:selector xpath="."/>
        <xs:field xpath="@AuthorID"/>
      </xs:keyref>
    </xs:element>
```

The Quotations table contains two keyrefs, one to the Authors_AuthorID key element in the Authors table, and the Sources_SourceID key element in the Sources table. These references represent foreign key relationships between the Authors and Sources tables and the current Quotations table. The Authors table is used to contain the author of a quotation, and the Sources table is used to store sources of the quotation (book title, etc.).

```
<xs:element name="Quotations">
  <xs:complexType>
    <xs:attribute name="QuotationID" type="xs:integer"/>
    <xs:attribute name="SourceID" type="xs:integer"/>
    <xs:attribute name="AuthorID" type="xs:integer"/>
    <xs:attribute name="Quotation">
      <xs:simpleType>
        <xs:restriction base="xs:string">
          <xs:maxLength value="300"/>
        </xs:restriction>
      </xs:simpleType>
    </xs:attribute>
  </xs:complexType>
  <xs:keyref name="Quotations_AuthorID" refer="Authors_AuthorID">
    <xs:selector xpath="."/>
    <xs:field xpath="@AuthorID"/>
  </xs:keyref>
  <xs:keyref name="Quotations_SourceID" refer="Sources_SourceID">
    <xs:selector xpath="."/>
    <xs:field xpath="@SourceID"/>
  </xs:keyref>
</xs:element>
```

The Sources table contains data types and constraints of the SQL Server table, and one key element.

```
<xs:element name="Sources">
  <xs:complexType>
    <xs:attribute name="SourceID" type="xs:integer"/>
    <xs:attribute name="Source_Name">
      <xs:simpleType>
        <xs:restriction base="xs:string">
          <xs:maxLength value="50"/>
        </xs:restriction>
      </xs:simpleType>
    </xs:attribute>
  </xs:complexType>
```

The SourceID field in the Authors table is the primary key for the foreign key relationship between the Sources table and the Quotations table. The foreign key relationship is represented by a W3C schema keyref element in the Quotations table with a refer attribute back to the Sources_SourceID key shown here. The `field` element refers to the authored attribute with an XPath expression (`@SourceID`), and the `selector` element refers to the value in the `SourceID` attribute to select with another XPath expression (`.`).

```
    <xs:key name="Sources_SourceID">
      <xs:selector xpath="."/>
      <xs:field xpath="@SourceID"/>
    </xs:key>
  </xs:element>
</xs:schema>
```

Using schemas to specify SQL Server table relationships

For the Schema mapping examples, we're using a document that is similar to the one used for the OPENXML insert and update examples. The document starts with an XML document declaration, followed by a root element of `XMLProgramming Bible`. The root element can be named anything. Because it contains representations of all of the tables in the `XMLProgrammingBible` database, we named it `XMLProgrammingBible`.

```
<?xml version="1.0" encoding="UTF-8"?>
<XMLProgrammingBIble>
```

Note that the elements for the `Quotations`, `AmazonListings`, and `Elcorte inglesListings` tables are nested inside the elements for the `Sources` and `Authors` tables. This is to accommodate the way that SQL Server parses relationships when it loads XML documents into tables. The parsing process refers to the schema, which contains several relationship elements in the annotation. When an XML document is parsed, it loads XML document objects into memory until it reaches an end tag for a table element. Nesting the `Quotations`, `AmazonListings`, and `ElcorteinglesListings` table elements inside of the `Sources` and `Authors` table elements ensures that all related fields are available for the SQL server table load.

```
  <Authors AuthorID="1001" AuthorName="Shakespeare, William">
    <Sources SourceID="1001" Source_Name="Macbeth">
```

The other thing to note in this XML document representation of SQL Server data is that the nested elements don't contain references to the `AuthorID` or `SourceID` columns. This information is supplied by the schema relationships and the way that the elements are nested. It's implied by the element nesting that, for example, the

AuthorID and the SourceID for the Quotations data should be supplied by the AuthorID in the Authors parent element. This is specified by the Foreign Key relationship between Authors and Quotations in the Schema.

```
    <Quotations QuotationID="1001" Quotation="When the hurlyburly's done,
    / When the battle's lost and won."/>
    <AmazonListings ProductID="1001" Ranking="1" Title="Hamlet/MacBeth"
    ASIN="8432040231" Image="http://images.amazon.com/images/P/
    8432040231.01.MZZZZZZZ.jpg"
    Small_Image="http://images.amazon.com/images/
    P/8432040231.01.TZZZZZZZ.jpg" List_price="$7.95"
    Release_date="2001-12-17T09:30:47-05:00" Binding="Paperback"
    Availability="" Tagged_URL="http://www.amazon.com:80/exec/
    obidos/redirect?tag=associateid&amp;benztechnonogies=9441&amp
    ;camp=1793&amp;link_code=xml&amp;path=ASIN/8432040231"/>
    <ElcorteinglesListings ProductID="1001" titulo="Romeo y
    Julieta/Macbeth/Hamlet/Otelo/La fierecilla domado/El sueño de una
    noche de verano/ El mercader de Venecia" ISBN="8484036324"
    Imagen="http://libros.elcorteingles.es/producto/
    verimagen_blob.asp?ISBN=8449503639" Precio="7,59 &#x20AC;"
    fecha_de_publicación="1991-12-17T09:30:47-05:00"
    Encuadernación="Piel"
    librourl="http://libros.elcorteingles.es/producto/
    libro_descripcion.asp?CODIISBN=8449503639"/>
  </Sources>
 </Authors>
</XMLProgrammingBIble>
```

Using XML Bulk Load

Bulk Load uses MSXML to process large amounts of data in XML-to-SQL insertions via a streaming interface, which means that XML documents are parsed as they are fed into tables. Streaming avoids having to load very large XML documents in their entirety before parsing and table insertion, greatly increasing the maximum size of a source XML document and the performance of the parsing and insertion. However, as with any batch-style process, don't expect stellar performance with XML Bulk Load, because it's not designed to be a run-time tool that is optimized for speed.

Unfortunately there is no command-line or Query Analyzer tool for running an XML Bulk Load. The easiest way to activate XML Bulk Load is through the Data Transformation Services (DTS) interface. You can write Visual basic code to designate the source XML file, the schema to be used to map the XML document to tables and column, and then activate the bulk load. Listing 18-6 shows a simple Visual Basic ActiveX Script that runs a simple Bulk Load.

Listing 18-6: **Output from the MultiQueryExample2.xml Template**

```
'****************************************************************************
'  Visual Basic ActiveX Script
'****************************************************************************
Function Main()
    Set blObject = CreateObject("SQLXMLBulkLoad.SQLXMLBulkLoad")

    blObject.ConnectionString = "provider=SQLOLEDB.1;data
        source=(local);database=XMLProgrammingBible;Integrated Security=SSPI"
        blObject.ErrorLogFile = "C:\XMLProgrammingBible\BulkXMLErrors.log"

    blObject.Execute "C:\XMLProgrammingBible\XMLProgrammingBible.xsd,
        C:\XMLProgrammingBible\XMLProgrammingBibleWithRelationalData.xml"

    Set blObject=Nothing
    Main = DTSTaskExecResult_Success

End Function
```

The first thing that this script does is create the SQLXMLBulkload.3.0 object, denoting the fact that this object is using SQLXML 3. The name of the new Bulk Load object is blObject.

```
    Set blObject = CreateObject("SQLXMLBulkLoad.SQLXMLBulkLoad")
```

Next, connection string is defined to connect to the SQL server instance on the local machine. The database name is specified and the security for the connection is set to Windows integrated authentication (SSPI).

```
    blObject.ConnectionString = "provider=SQLOLEDB.1;data
        source=(local);database=XMLProgrammingBible;Integrated Security=SSPI"
```

Any errors that are generated by the Bulk Load procedure are routed to the C:\XMLProgrammingBible\BulkXMLErrors.log file. There are two modes of XML Bulk load, transacted and non-transacted. If the load mode is set to non-transacted (the default value), the error log can be useful to see where the load stopped and where the new load has to pick up from, or which tables you need to roll back to their pre-load condition. Transacted mode cancels the entire load if there is any error, so logs are not necessary to track updates.

```
    blObject.ErrorLogFile = "C:\XMLProgrammingBible\BulkXMLErrors.log"
```

Next, the Bulk Load is executed. The schema and the source XML document are loaded. Behind the scenes, the XML Bulk load process actually parses the XML document into column values organized by table, then preforms BULK INSERT SQL commands to insert data for each table.

```
blObject.Execute "C:\XMLProgrammingBible\XMLProgrammingBible.xsd,
    C:\XMLProgrammingBible\XMLProgrammingBibleWithRelationalData.xml"
```

Next, assuming all the inserts went as planned, the object is cleaned up. The DTSTaskExecResult_Success constant indicates a successful completion of the XML Bulk Load task.

```
Set blObject=Nothing
Main = DTSTaskExecResult_Success
```

There are several properties and methods that can be used with XML Bulk Loads, all of which are well documented in the SQLXML documentation that cones with the download.

Updategrams

Updategrams are very handy for inserting, updating, and deleting table data over the Web. Updategrams are stored in XML templates and XML document data. Updategrams can handle this functionality without using schemas. For example, here's an example of an Updategram that adds an author authors table:

```
<ROOT xmlns:updg="urn:schemas-microsoft-com:xml-updategram">
  <updg:sync >
    <updg:before>
    </updg:before>
    <updg:after>
        <Authors AuthorID="9999" AuthorName="Miller, Henry">
    </updg:after>
  </updg:sync>
</ROOT>
```

The value in the `after` element is added to the Authors table.

The XML in the next example is saved as an XML template in the XMLProgramming Bible virtual directory. That way the database doesn't have to be designated, as it's already part of the virtual directory properties. All that has to be specified is the table name and the columns to add. Here's one that changes the author name:

```
<ROOT xmlns:updg="urn:schemas-microsoft-com:xml-updategram">
  <updg:sync >
    <updg:before>
        <Authors AuthorID="9999" AuthorName="Miller, Henry">
```

```
    </updg:before>
    <updg:after>
       <Authors AuthorID="9999" AuthorName="Mailer, Norman">
    </updg:after>
  </updg:sync>
</ROOT>
```

This is very similar to the previous example, except that the Author name is replaced in an existing document instead of an insertion of a new row in the table. The row is located using the value in the `before` element.

Now let's delete the row:

```
<ROOT xmlns:updg="urn:schemas-microsoft-com:xml-updategram">
  <updg:sync >
    <updg:before>
       <Authors AuthorID="9999" AuthorName="Mailer, Norman">
    </updg:before>
    <updg:after>
    </updg:after>
  </updg:sync>
</ROOT>
```

Nothing in the `after` element means that a deletion command is generated by SQL Server. Because these are templates, the real value is in specifying parameters from URL queries that are passed to the before and after elements. The SQLXML documentation that cones with the download covers this in detail. Let's move on to using Updategrams with schemas, which is another good way to get relational data into SQL Server from XML documents.

This example uses the same schema as the XML Bulk Load example, named XMLProgrammingBible.xsd. The schema is located in the `schemas` subdirectory of the XMLProgrammingBible virtual directory on the IIIS server. The schema enables table relationships to be maintained without having to be specified in the template. This time, instead of a raw insert of bulk data, we're adding a Quotation in the quotations table. Note that the Authors and Sources hierarchy must be defined in the before and the after. The `AuthorID` attribute from the `Authors` element and the `SourceID` from the `Sources` element are automatically added to the new quotation in the `Quotations` table. This is because a foreign key relationship is established n the schema that specifies the `Quotations` table as a foreign key table for each relationship.

```
<ROOT xmlns:sql="urn:schemas-microsoft-com:xml-sql" xmlns:updg="urn:schemas-
microsoft-com:xml-updategram">
  <updg:sync mapping-schema="=".\schema\XMLProgrammingBible.xsd">
    <updg:before>
      <Authors AuthorID="1001">
        <Sources SourceID="1001">
```

```
        </Sources>
      </Authors>
    </updg:before>
    <updg:after>
      <Authors AuthorID="1001">
        <Sources SourceID="1001">
          <Quotations QuotationID="1001" Quotation="Is this a dagger which
          I see before me, the handle toward my hand? Come, let me clutch
          thee: I have thee not, and yet I see thee still. Art thou not,
          fatal vision, sensible to feeling as to sight? or art thou but a
          dagger of the mind, a false creation, proceeding from the heat-
          oppressed brain?"/>
        </Sources>
      </Authors>
    </updg:after>
  </updg:sync>
</ROOT>
```

Summary

In this chapter, you were introduced to the XML tools associated with SQL Server:

✦ An introduction to the sample relational data structure

✦ XML Templates and Schemas in SQL Server

✦ For XML RAW, AUTO and EXPLICIT

✦ Inserting relational data with OPENXML

✦ Updating data with OPENXML

✦ Creating Annotated Schemas

✦ Using Annotated Schemas with XML Bulk Load

✦ Using Annotated Schemas with Updategrams

In the next two chapters, we'll show you how to work XML using DB2 and Oracle. After that, we'll show you how to create Web and J2EE applications that generate XML data from relational data in Chapter 21. In Chapter 22 we'll show you how to transform relation data from one relational database's XML format to another.

✦   ✦   ✦

Accessing and Formatting XML from Oracle Data

Oracle support for XML started with Oracle 8i database. XML documents could be included in an Oracle database file system (iFS) and manipulated like a folder-based file system. XML documents could be broken down and reassembled from Oracle data based on Oracle's iFS Document Type Definition, which is a proprietary format of the W3C Document Type Definition (DTD). Parsing and reassembly of XML documents was facilitated through Oracle's own XML document parser, which supported DOM and SAX. The third feature supported in Oracle 8i was XML-based searching in the ConText full-text search engine. Content rating retrieved XML document content and ignores tags, but searches could be tag-based.

Oracle9i has extended these capabilities with more advanced XML database features, such as SQL/XML query support and compatibility with W3C schemas. Also included is a Java application server based on the Apache HTTP Server.

Oracle9i standard edition has everything that a developer needs to create XML database solutions. The Enterprise Edition includes more advanced capabilities, such as online analytical processing (OLAP) server support and several features that enable sophisticated data mining, partitioning, and clustering.

Oracle8i XML features enabled developers to store XML in Oracle databases or parse it into tabular data. Oracle9i extends these capabilities to support full DOM 2 and DOM 3 features such as comments and namespaces. Additional support for W3C schemas helps enforce element and attribute ordering, and other granular XML document structures. Also, performance is enhanced by more advanced support for XML indexes.

Oracle has split XML DB functionality into two groups: Structured XML and unstructured XML. Unstructured data features cater to developers who need to develop XML document repositories for applications that work with unstructured data such as pages on a Website. Structured data features meet the needs of developer who are working with traditional tabular relational data, but need to manipulate that data as XML.

The Oracle9i XML DB contains a set of special SQL functions that allows XML data to be manipulated as relational data. A new data type called XMLType enables storage of XML data as a plain XML document or as a format based on a DOM. XMLType tables and views can be defined using annotated W3C Schemas. The schemas can control how an XML document maps to Oracle data. Windows Explorer can be used with the XML DB Repositories (formerly iFS) to view an XML database as a drive on the file system.

A combination of XPath and SQL can also be used to manipulate XML documents. You can also retrieve regular relational data in XML formats and perform an XSLT transformation of the data to text, HTML, or custom formats of XML.

In this chapter we'll show you how to work with SQL/XML and Oracle XML functions using Oracle XML DB. We'll also introduce you to the XMLType data type and show you how to store data as XMLType and how to map relational data as XMLType data using W3C Schemas. I'll also show you how to store XML documents as relational data using W3C Schemas. PL/SQL developers will see how to use DBMS_XMLGEN() as part of a PL/SQL solution. We'll also show you how to use the XDK, XSQL, and the XML SQL Utility (XSU) in Java.

The XML Programming Bible Example Tables

All of the tables in this chapter and this part of the book use the same data structure. For Oracle9i, the data is structured into five tables. All five tables are contained in a database called XMLPB1. Table 19-1 lists the structure of the AMAZONLISTINGS table. This is the table that contains all of the Amazon book listings for our relational data examples and applications.

 On The Web   We've included SQL code that creates these tables and inserts sample data as part of the downloads for this chapter. Downloads for the XML Programming Bible can be retrieved from `http://www.XMLProgrammingBible.com`, in the downloads section.

Table 19-1
Structure of the AMAZONLISTINGS Table

Table Column	Data Type	Maximum Size
PRODUCTID (Primary Key)	NUMBER	10
RANKING	NUMBER	10
TITLE	CHAR	200
ASIN	CHAR	10
AUTHORID (Foreign Key - AUTHORS)	NUMBER	10
IMAGE	CHAR	100
SMALL_IMAGE	CHAR	100
LIST_PRICE	NUMBER	10.2
RELEASE_DATE	DATE	
BINDING	CHAR	50
AVAILABILITY	CHAR	10
TAGGED_URL	CHAR	200

Table 19-2 lists the structure of the AUTHORS table. This is the table that contains information about the book and quotation authors. It is related to the AUTHORID field in the AMAZONLISTINGS, ELCORTEINGLESLISTINGS, and the QUOTATIONS tables.

Table 19-2
Structure of the Authors Table

Table Column	Data Type	Maximum Size
AUTHORID (Primary Key)	NUMBER	10
AUTHORNAME	CHAR	50

Table 19-3 lists the structure of the ELCORTEINGLESLISTINGS table. This is the table that contains all of the Spanish Language Elcorteingles Website book listings for our relational data examples and applications.

Table 19-3
Structure of the ElcorteinglesListings Table

Table Column	Data Type	Maximum Size
PRODUCTID (Primary Key)	NUMBER	10
TITULO	CHAR	200
ISBN	CHAR	20
AUTHORID (Foreign Key - AUTHORS)	NUMBER	10
IMAGEN	CHAR	100
PRECIO	NUMBER	10.2
FECHA_DE_PUBLICACION	DATE	
ENCUADERNACION	CHAR	50
LIBROURL	CHAR	200

Table 19-4 lists the structure of the QUOTATIONS table. This is the table that contains all of the Quotations related to books, authors, and sources in the relational data examples and applications.

Table 19-4
Structure of the Quotations Table

Table Column	Data Type	Maximum Size
QUOTATIONID (Primary Key)	NUMBER	10
SOURCEID (Foreign Key - SOURCES)	NUMBER	10
AUTHORID (Foreign Key - AUTHORS)	NUMBER	10
QUOTATION	CHAR	300

Table 19-5 lists the structure of the SOURCES table. This is the table that contains information about the book and quotation authors. It is related to the AUTHORID field in the AMAZONLISTINGS and QUOTATIONS tables.

Table 19-5
Structure of the Sources Table

Table Column	Data Type	Maximum Size
SOURCEID (Primary Key)	NUMBER	10
SOURCENAME	CHAR	50

Installing and Configuring the Oracle Database and the Oracle XDK

You can download the latest version of the database for evaluation and development purposes from `http://otn.oracle.com/software/products/oracle9i/content.html`. The examples in this chapter were developed using Oracle database is Oracle9i database release 2.

The downloads are large, so plan for some download waiting time, even with a good connection. For the bandwidth-challenged, there is also a trial download available for a fee from the same site. Once the files are downloaded and installed, XML functionality is available via the Oracle Enterprise Manager Console and the SQL Scratchpad.

About Oracle XML DB

Oracle XML DB is a grouping of XML and XPath functions combined with SQL extensions. XML DB features facilitate the manipulation of Oracle data as XML. They also enable XML documents to be stored and queried as Oracle data using the XMLTYPE data type. The Oracle XDK is not required for XML DB functions if you just want to query XML documents from the Enterprise Manager Console or a third-party query tool. Using XML DB functionality in your applications requires the XDK.

About the Oracle XDK

The latest version of the Oracle XDK is available at `http://otn.oracle.com/tech/xml/xdk`. The XDK is available in Java, C, C++, and PL/SQL versions. At time of this writing, I'm working with the beta release of the version 10 XDK. The Oracle XDK is a set of XML APIS that can be used by developers to incorporate Oracle data into their applications. I'll cover the XDK in more detail later in this chapter.

Note The Oracle9i database and the Oracle XDK are made available to developers for evaluation and development use only. Any other use of the Oracle9i database or XDK must be backed by an Oracle software license.

Developing Oracle XML Solutions with XML DB

Oracle developers who are new to XML development are usually under the impression that the Oracle XDK is the only way to access and manipulate XML in Oracle. In fact, there are several options for retrieving XML from Oracle tables, and for storing and retrieving XML documents in Oracle as XML. In this section I'll review the XML DB functions that read and write between Oracle data and XML. I'll also show you how to manipulate and store XML documents using the XMLType data type.

Working with XML DB

Oracle9i supports several core SQL functions, as well as core SQL/XML functions, several SQL/XML extensions, and a PL/SQL package called DBMS_XMLGEN. Core Oracle XML functions are unique to Oracle and are accessible via SQL*Plus queries. SQL/XML functions are based on the SQL/XML standard, which is a combination of XML and SQL functionality. The SQL/XML standard is maintained by the International Committee for Information Technology Standards (INCITS). INCITS maintains a grab-bag of international hardware, media, and other standards, including the original SQL standard in the United States. Specific information on SQL/XML can be found at `http://sqlx.org`. More information about INCITS can be found at `http://www.ncits.org`.

Note Oracle XML documentation often refers to forests of XML documents, especially when working with the XMLFOREST() function. At the highest level, a forest is a grouping of XML documents. The forest concept is based on the same concept in SGML, called groves. Single XML documents follow a tree structure, so logically multiple document tree structures are a forest. In the case of elements, one or more elements that are nested at the same level in an XML document are considered forests, made up of single-element trees. In the extreme extension of this logic, a single element can also be referred to as a forest, made up of single-character trees. Oracle and SQL/XML documentation refers to XML document fragments (XML elements grouped together but without a root element) nested at the same level as a forest.

Table 19-6 shows all of the Oracle9i XML functions, and a brief description of each.

Table 19-6
Oracle XML Functions

Function	Description
DBMS_XMLGEN() PL/SQL package	A PL/SQL package that generates an XML document from an SQL query.
SYS_XMLGEN() Oracle XML DB Function	SYS_XMLGEN() returns an XML document or document fragment when passed an expression that evaluates to a particular row and column of a table. The data type of the row and column can be anything, but SYS_XMLGEN() works best when retrieving XML documents from a column formatted as the XMLType data type. Use the SQL/XML functions (covered below) for formatting regular relational data types as XML.
SYS_XMLAGG() Oracle XML DB Function	SYS_XMLAGG() returns an aggregated XML document from one or more rows of data. The rows of data are created and formatted by a contained expression. Returned values are automatically nested in a root element named ROWSET.
XMLSEQUENCE() Oracle SQL/XML Extension	Used to produce XML document fragments that are parsed into relational table rows. The functionality is essentially the opposite of the XMLCONCAT() function. The output format is an array of XMLType data types, called an XMLSequenceType. If used with a cursor, XMLSEQUENCE() can also be used to extract fragments of an XML document and parse them into multiple XML documents formatted as XMLType data.
XMLTRANSFORM() Oracle SQL/XML Extension	Performs an XSLT transformation on an XML Document using an XSL Stylesheet. The XSL stylesheet and the source XML document are passed as XMLType data types. The transformation result is returned as another XMLType data object.
EXTRACT() Oracle SQL/XML Extension	Returns an XML document fragment in an XMLType data type format from an XPath expression.
ExtractValue() Oracle SQL/XML Extension	Returns a scalar value from an XPath expression.
EXISTSNODE() Oracle SQL/XML Extension	If the result of an XPath expression returns any nodes, EXISTSNODE() is true.
UPDATEXML()	Returns an XMLType object when passed a valid XPath expression representing an element (as an XMLType), an attribute, or a text node (as any scalar data type).

Continued

Table 19-6 *(continued)*

Function	Description
XMLELEMENT() SQL/XML	Creates XML document fragments from relational data. Element names are hard-coded into the expression. Column values become text values of the element. Nested instances of XMLELEMENT are used to create well-formed XML documents. Can be used with XML.
XMLATTRIBUTES() SQL/XML	A nested expression of XMLELEMENT(). Provides a list of attributes for an element as value pairs. Attribute names can be hard-coded into the expression. By default, column names become attribute names and column values become attribute values.
XMLFOREST() SQL/XML	Creates XML document fragments from relational data. By default, each column name becomes an element name and each column value becomes a text value. Nested instances of XMLELEMENT and XMLFOREST() are used to create well-formed XML documents.
XMLCONCAT() SQL/XML	Concatenates multiple XMLType objects into a single XML document. If the result of an XMLSEQUENCE() function is passed, a single XMLType object is created from the multiple instances in the XMLSequenceType array.
XMLAGG() SQL/XML	Creates an aggregated XML document fragment from a collection of separate XMLType objects. SYS_XMLAGG() nests results inside a ROWSET root element, XMLAGG() does not.
XMLCOLATTVAL() Oracle SQL/XML Extension	XMLCOLATTVAL() creates an XML document fragment containing an element for each column with specified column values as attributes. Each element in the fragment is named `column`. Column names are stored in the `name` attribute of the element. Column values become text values of the `column` element.

Working with XMLFOREST()

For this section, I'll extract data from the AmazonListings table using XML. The easiest way to start is with the `XMLFOREST()` function. In this query, I retrieve all of the columns in the first row of the AMAZONLISTINGS table:

```
SELECT XMLFOREST(
PRODUCTID,
RANKING,
TITLE,
ASIN,
AUTHORID,
IMAGE,
SMALL_IMAGE,
LIST_PRICE,
RELEASE_DATE,
BINDING,
AVAILABILITY,
TAGGED_URL) as  "RESULT"
FROM   AmazonListings
WHERE  rownum = 1;
```

The following XML document fragment is returned by the XMLFOREST() function. All of the elements are nested at the same level. As you may recall from Chapter 1, an XML document needs a single, unique root element to be well-formed XML. Therefore, XMLFOREST() is an easy way to return a fragment that will become part of an aggregated or concatenated XML document, but is not useful for creating XML documents all by itself.

```
<PRODUCTID>1001</PRODUCTID>
<RANKING>1</RANKING>
<TITLE>Hamlet/MacBeth</TITLE>
<ASIN>8432040231</ASIN>
<AUTHORID>1001</AUTHORID>
<IMAGE>http://images.amazon.com/images/P/8432040231.01.MZZZZZZZ.jpg</IMAGE>
<SMALL_IMAGE>http://images.amazon.com/images/P/8432040231.01.TZZZZZZZ.jpg
</SMALL_IMAGE>
<LIST_PRICE>7.95</LIST_PRICE>
<RELEASE_DATE>01-JUN-91</RELEASE_DATE>
<BINDING>Paperback</BINDING>
<TAGGED_URL>http://www.amazon.com:80/exec/obidos/redirect?tag=associateid&a
mp;benztechnonogies=9441&amp;camp=1793&amp;link_code=xml&amp;path=ASIN/8432
040231</TAGGED_URL>
```

Creating a well-formed XML document using SYS_XMLAGG()

The easiest way to return a completely well-formed XML document is to nest the XMLFOREST() function inside of the SYS_XMLAGG() function like this:

```
SELECT SYS_XMLAGG(XMLFOREST(
PRODUCTID,
RANKING,
TITLE,
ASIN,
AUTHORID,
```

```
IMAGE,
SMALL_IMAGE,
LIST_PRICE,
RELEASE_DATE,
BINDING,
AVAILABILITY,
TAGGED_URL)) as  "RESULT"
FROM   AmazonListings
WHERE  rownum = 1;
```

This query returns the following XML Document. The addition of the
`SYS_XMLAGG()` function creates an element called `ROWSET`. The nesting in the SQL
query nests the XML document fragment returned by `XMLFOREST()` under the
`ROWSET()` element.

```
<ROWSET>
  <PRODUCTID>1001</PRODUCTID>
  <RANKING>1</RANKING>
  <TITLE>Hamlet/MacBeth</TITLE>
  <ASIN>8432040231</ASIN>
  <AUTHORID>1001</AUTHORID>
  <IMAGE>http://images.amazon.com/images/P/8432040231.01.MZZZZZZZ.jpg
  </IMAGE>
  <SMALL_IMAGE>http://images.amazon.com/images/P/8432040231.01.TZZZZZZZ.jpg
  </SMALL_IMAGE>
  <LIST_PRICE>7.95</LIST_PRICE>
  <RELEASE_DATE>01-JUN-91</RELEASE_DATE>
  <BINDING>Paperback</BINDING>
  <TAGGED_URL>http://www.amazon.com:80/exec/obidos/redirect?
  tag=associateid&amp;benztechnonogies=9441&amp;camp=1793&amp;
  link_code=xml&amp;path=ASIN/8432040231</TAGGED_URL>
</ROWSET>
```

Specifying a root element using XMLELEMENT()

If you want to give the root element a specific name, instead of the default `ROWSET`
element name, use the `XMLELEMENT()` function and provide a hard-coded name:

```
SELECT XMLELEMENT("RootElement", XMLFOREST(
PRODUCTID,
RANKING,
TITLE,
ASIN,
AUTHORID,
IMAGE,
SMALL_IMAGE,
LIST_PRICE,
RELEASE_DATE,
BINDING,
AVAILABILITY,
```

```
TAGGED_URL)) as  "RESULT"
FROM   AmazonListings
WHERE  rownum = 1;
```

This returns the same set of results, but with the customized root element name of RooElement:

```
<RootElement>
  <PRODUCTID>1001</PRODUCTID>
  <RANKING>1</RANKING>
  <TITLE>Hamlet/MacBeth</TITLE>
  <ASIN>8432040231</ASIN>
  <AUTHORID>1001</AUTHORID>
  <IMAGE>http://images.amazon.com/images/P/8432040231.01.MZZZZZZZ.jpg
  </IMAGE>
  <SMALL_IMAGE>http://images.amazon.com/images/P/8432040231.01.TZZZZZZZ.jpg
  </SMALL_IMAGE>
  <LIST_PRICE>7.95</LIST_PRICE>
  <RELEASE_DATE>01-JUN-91</RELEASE_DATE>
  <BINDING>Paperback</BINDING>
  <TAGGED_URL>http://www.amazon.com:80/exec/obidos/redirect?
  tag=associateid&amp;benztechnonogies=9441&amp;camp=1793&amp;
  link_code=xml&amp;path=ASIN/8432040231</TAGGED_URL>
</RootElement>
```

Creating attributes using XMLATTRIBUTES()

One of the additional advantages of using a nested XMLELEMENT() function to create a root element is that the XMLATTRIBUTES() function can be used. XMLATTRIBUTES() creates a set of attributes for an element specified as apparent via the XMLELEMENT() function. This time we reuse the query from the last example, but just replace the XMLFOREST() function with an XMLATTRIBUTES() function:

```
SELECT XMLELEMENT("RootElement", XMLATTRIBUTES(
PRODUCTID,
RANKING,
TITLE,
ASIN,
AUTHORID,
IMAGE,
SMALL_IMAGE,
LIST_PRICE,
RELEASE_DATE,
BINDING,
AVAILABILITY,
TAGGED_URL)) as  "RESULT"
FROM   AmazonListings
WHERE  rownum = 1;
```

The result is a single XML element with an attribute for each column in the first row of the AMAZONLISTINGS table:

```
RootElement PRODUCTID="1001" RANKING="1" TITLE="Hamlet/MacBeth"
ASIN="8432040231" AUTHORID="1001"
IMAGE="http://images.amazon.com/images/P/8432040231.01.MZZZZZZZ.jpg"
SMALL_IMAGE="http://images.amazon.com/images/P/8432040231.01.TZZZZZZZ.jpg"
LIST_PRICE="7.95" RELEASE_DATE="01-JUN-91" BINDING="Paperback"
TAGGED_URL="http://www.amazon.com:80/exec/obidos/redirect?tag=associateid&a
mp;benztechnonogies=9441&amp;camp=1793&amp;link_code=xml&amp;path=ASIN/8432
040231"/>
```

Creating elements and attributes using XMLCOLATTVAL()

The XMLCOLLATVAL() function also produces attributes for column data, but with an important difference. XMLCOLATTVAL() produces an element named `column` for each column value and an element named `name` for each column name. The value of the column is the text value for the element. In this example I reuse the query from the last example, but just replace the XMLATTRIBUTES() function with an XMLCOLATTVAL() function:

```
SELECT XMLELEMENT("RootElement", XMLCOLATTVAL(
PRODUCTID,
RANKING,
TITLE,
ASIN,
AUTHORID,
IMAGE,
SMALL_IMAGE,
LIST_PRICE,
RELEASE_DATE,
BINDING,
AVAILABILITY,
TAGGED_URL)) as  "RESULT"
FROM   AmazonListings
WHERE  rownum = 1;
```

The resulting combination of elements, attributes and text data could be created with nested XMLELEMENT() and XMLATTRIBUTES() functions, but using XMLCOLLATVAL() is much easier to code:

```
<RootElement>
  <column name="PRODUCTID">1001</column>
  <column name="RANKING">1</column>
  <column name="TITLE">Hamlet/MacBeth</column>
  <column name="ASIN">8432040231</column>
  <column name="AUTHORID">1001</column>
  <column name="IMAGE">
      http://images.amazon.com/images/P/8432040231.01.
      MZZZZZZZ.jpg</column>
```

```
<column name="SMALL_IMAGE">
    http://images.amazon.com/images/P/8432040231.01.
    TZZZZZZZ.jpg</column>
<column name="LIST_PRICE">7.95</column>
<column name="RELEASE_DATE">01-JUN-91</column>
<column name="BINDING">Paperback</column>
<column name="AVAILABILITY"/>
<column name="TAGGED_URL">
    http://www.amazon.com:80/exec/obidos/redirect?tag=associateid
    &amp;benztechnonogies=9441&amp;camp=1793&amp;link_code=xml
    &amp;path=ASIN/8432040231</column>
</RootElement>
```

Working with multiple data rows using XML DB

So far we've shown you how to use the XMLFOREST(), SYS_XMLAGG(), XMLELEMENT(), and XMLATTRIBUTES() functions to work with single rows of data. Multiple row result sets are more of a challenge, because each row should be defined in the XML document. Also, in most cases the XML document has to be well formed, while containing the multiple row definitions. However, if more than one row is contained in the previous SYS_XMLAGG() example, all elements are contained at the same nesting level. The result is a jumble of row data as elements, with no clear definition of the start and end of a row of results in the XML document. The previous XMLELEMENT() and XMLATTRIBUTES() examples return an XML document fragment with a RootElement for each row, but no XML document root element.

Aggregating multiple rows of data using XMLAGG()

The XMLAGG() function aggregates multiple rows of data into a single XML document. For example, the query below uses nested XMLELEMENT() and XMLFOREST() functions to create well-formed XML document fragments for each row of data:

```
SELECT XMLELEMENT("RowElement", XMLFOREST(
PRODUCTID,
RANKING,
TITLE)) as  "RESULT" FROM   AmazonListings
```

The XML result is not a well-formed XML document, but a set of document fragments for each row of data:

```
<RowElement>
  <PRODUCTID>1001</PRODUCTID>
  <RANKING>1</RANKING>
  <TITLE>Hamlet/MacBeth</TITLE>
</RowElement>
```

```
<RowElement>
  <PRODUCTID>1002</PRODUCTID>
  <RANKING>2</RANKING>
  <TITLE>MacBeth</TITLE>
</RowElement>

<RowElement>
  <PRODUCTID>1003</PRODUCTID>
  <RANKING>3</RANKING>
  <TITLE>William Shakespeare: MacBeth</TITLE>
</RowElement>
```

The XMLAGG() function aggregates multiple rows of results into a single XML document when you use a query like this:

```
SELECT XMLELEMENT("RootElement", XMLAGG(XMLELEMENT("RowElement", XMLFOREST(
PRODUCTID,
RANKING,
TITLE)))) as  "RESULT" FROM   AmazonListings
```

The result is a well-formed XML document with a root element and a definition of each row of data. Data rows are children of the RowElement element:

```
<RootElement>
  <RowElement>
    <PRODUCTID>1001</PRODUCTID>
    <RANKING>1</RANKING>
    <TITLE>Hamlet/MacBeth</TITLE>
  </RowElement>
  <RowElement>
    <PRODUCTID>1002</PRODUCTID>
    <RANKING>2</RANKING>
    <TITLE>MacBeth</TITLE>
  </RowElement>
  <RowElement>
    <PRODUCTID>1003</PRODUCTID>
    <RANKING>3</RANKING>
    <TITLE>William Shakespeare: MacBeth</TITLE>
  </RowElement>
</RootElement>
```

A combination of XMLAGG(), XMLELEMENT(), XMLATTRIBUTES(), XMLFOREST(), and XMLCOMMATTVAL() are the most common ways to represent relational Oracle data as XML.

Working with the XMLTYPE data type

As of Oracle9i the XMLType data type can be used to store an XML data in Oracle databases. Before Oracle9i, LOBS and text were used to store XML documents as text. At the base level, CLOB and XMLType data is not very different. However, there are several useful methods in the XMLType API that can be used to manipulate XML documents stored as XMLType data types.

When relational data tables are mapped to XML document data via W3C schemas, data in the tables becomes available as an XMLType data type. Columns in a regular table can also be XMLType data types, and XMLType views can be used to mask relational data as XMLType data. For more information about XMLType, please refer to the Oracle9i XML Database Developer's Guide—:Oracle XML DB Chapter 4.

Getting data into XMLType columns

XMLType columns can be added to any Oracle table (in Oracle9i or above). In this example, we create a table called XMLONLY, which consists of one column, called XMLDOC. We assign the data type for XMLDOC as XMLTYPE:

```
CREATE TABLE XMLONLY (XMLDOC SYS.XMLTYPE);
```

With the new XMLONLY table, we can insert XMLType data from any source. In the example below, we select the first three columns of the AMAZONLISTINGS table using nested XMLELEMENT() and XMLFOREST() functions. The query selection is inserted into a variable called XMLTypeVal, which is an in-memory XMLType object. Next, we insert the XMLType object into the XMLDOC column of the XMLONLY table.

Tip   XMLType data type columns only accept well-formed XML documents, not document fragments. For example, if you try to insert an XML document fragment resulting from an XMLFOREST expression, Oracle returns the ORA-19010: Cannot insert XML fragments error message. Adding the XMLELEMENT() function wraps a root element around the XMLFOREST result, and the insert is accepted.

```
DECLARE
   XMLTYpeVal    SYS.XMLTYPE;
BEGIN
   SELECT XMLELEMENT("RootElement", XMLFOREST(
   PRODUCTID,
   RANKING,
   TITLE)) as "result"
   INTO   XMLTYpeVal
   FROM   AmazonListings
   WHERE  rownum = 1;
   INSERT INTO XMLONLY (XMLDOC) VALUES (XMLTYpeVal);
   COMMIT;
END;
```

Using SQL and SYS_XMLGEN with XMLType columns

Now that we have some XMLType data in XMLDOC column of the XMLONLY table, we can extract the data with regular SQL functions. For example, this simple select will return the XML document stored in XMLDOC:

```
SELECT XMLDOC from XMLONLY
```

Here are the results of the query:

```
<RootElement>
    <PRODUCTID>1001</PRODUCTID>
    <RANKING>1</RANKING>
    <TITLE>Hamlet/MacBeth</TITLE>
</RootElement>
```

SYS_XMLGEN() is an Oracle SQL function that returns a single column of a table as an XML element. The Element name is based on the column name. This can be used in limited situations on regular data, but is really useful for XMLType columns. Here's an example of SYS_XMLGEN() returning an XML element from regular table data:

```
SELECT SYS_XMLGEN(PRODUCTID) from AMAZONLISTINGS where rownum=1
```

And here's the result of the query:

```
<PRODUCTID>1001</PRODUCTID>
```

The same query is very useful when applied against XMLType columns. In this example, we query the XMLDOC column of the XMLONLY table and return a single XML document:

```
SELECT SYS_XMLGEN(XMLDOC) from XMLONLY where rownum=1
```

SYS_XMLGEN() wraps the column name around the results as an element name:

```
<XMLDOC>
  <RootElement>
    <PRODUCTID>1001</PRODUCTID>
    <RANKING>1</RANKING>
    <TITLE>Hamlet/MacBeth</TITLE>
  </RootElement>
</XMLDOC>
```

You may have noticed that there is no XML document declaration at the top of the XML document. This is on purpose. As you may recall from Chapter 1, XML declarations are optional; only a root element is required to create a well-formed XML document structure. It's much better to store the XML document without the optional declaration and create a declaration as part of a query. XML documents without the declaration can be added together to make a larger XML document. If you store the XML declaration as part of the data, it takes up more space, and makes it harder to aggregate XML results into a larger document. Here's an example of a query that prepends an XML document declaration to the SYS_XMLGEN() results from the previous example:

```
SELECT '<?xml version="1.0"?>', SYS_XMLGEN(XMLDOC) from XMLONLY
```

And here are the results, with the XML document declaration added:

```
<?xml version="1.0"?>
<XMLDOC>
  <RootElement>
    <PRODUCTID>1001</PRODUCTID>
    <RANKING>1</RANKING>
    <TITLE>Hamlet/MacBeth</TITLE>
  </RootElement>
</XMLDOC>
```

Creating relational data from XML documents

The Oracle Enterprise manager has facilities for registering generated schemas and mapping XML document data to relational data. XMLType Views can also be used to map XML document data to relational data, and act as an XML interface for legacy data structures without having to alter the tables themselves. In this section we'll cover both methods. we'll also cover some of the SQL commands that facilitate data updates.

Generating W3C schemas from Oracle Database schemas

Oracle can generate W3C Schemas from relational data using XDK functions, the PL/SQL DBMS_XMLSCHEMA.generateSchema() package, or a third-party tool such as XMLSpy (a free evaluation is available at http://www.xmlspy.com). In Listing 19–1, we used XMLSpy, which can connect to Oracle data via an ADO string using an Oracle OLE DB provider. XMLSpy automatically creates a W3C schema for all tables in a database without needing an object type to be created or referenced. The generated schema can be chopped up and reused. Below is the generated W3C schema for the AMAZONLISTINGS table. The table is represented by an element containing a W3C schema complex data type. Nested inside the complex data type are attributes, some of which contain a W3C schema simple data type. XMLSpy automatically reproduces field constraints and data types based on Oracle constraints and data types in schemas that are generated from Oracle databases. For example, the Title column is a W3C schema string data type, and has a maximum length of 200.

Listing 19-1: **A Sample Schema from Oracle Data**

```
<?xml version="1.0" encoding="UTF-8"?>
<!-- edited with XMLSPY v5 rel. 4 U (http://www.xmlspy.com) by Brian Benz
(Wiley) -->
<xs:schema xmlns:xs="http://www.w3.org/2001/XMLSchema">
  <xs:element name="AMAZONLISTINGS">
    <xs:complexType>
      <xs:sequence>
        <xs:element name="PRODUCTID" type="xs:decimal"/>
        <xs:element name="RANKING" type="xs:decimal"/>
        <xs:element name="TITLE">
          <xs:simpleType>
            <xs:restriction base="xs:string">
              <xs:maxLength value="200"/>
            </xs:restriction>
          </xs:simpleType>
        </xs:element>
        <xs:element name="ASIN">
          <xs:simpleType>
            <xs:restriction base="xs:string">
              <xs:maxLength value="10"/>
            </xs:restriction>
          </xs:simpleType>
        </xs:element>
        <xs:element name="AUTHORID" type="xs:decimal"/>
        <xs:element name="IMAGE">
          <xs:simpleType>
            <xs:restriction base="xs:string">
              <xs:maxLength value="100"/>
            </xs:restriction>
          </xs:simpleType>
        </xs:element>
        <xs:element name="SMALL_IMAGE">
          <xs:simpleType>
            <xs:restriction base="xs:string">
              <xs:maxLength value="100"/>
            </xs:restriction>
          </xs:simpleType>
        </xs:element>
        <xs:element name="LIST_PRICE" type="xs:decimal"/>
        <xs:element name="RELEASE_DATE" type="xs:dateTime"/>
        <xs:element name="BINDING">
          <xs:simpleType>
            <xs:restriction base="xs:string">
              <xs:maxLength value="50"/>
            </xs:restriction>
```

```
        </xs:simpleType>
      </xs:element>
      <xs:element name="AVAILABILITY">
        <xs:simpleType>
          <xs:restriction base="xs:string">
            <xs:maxLength value="10"/>
          </xs:restriction>
        </xs:simpleType>
      </xs:element>
      <xs:element name="TAGGED_URL">
        <xs:simpleType>
          <xs:restriction base="xs:string">
            <xs:maxLength value="200"/>
          </xs:restriction>
        </xs:simpleType>
      </xs:element>
    </xs:sequence>
  </xs:complexType>
</xs:element>
</xs:schema>
```

Registering W3C schemas in Oracle

A wonderful recent development in the Oracle enterprise manager is the ability to interactively register an XML schema in a database and generate an Oracle table based on the Schema. This used to be a laborious process of creating and/or running several sets of very complicated SQL commands to create a database, generate a schema, and register the schema. With XMLSpy and the Oracle Enterprise Manager registration dialog, we were able to create the schema, register the schema, create the table for the schema, generate a sample document and test the new table in a fraction of the time it would take for a hand-coded solution.

To register a W3C schema, expand the User Types node in the enterprise manager navigator, and then select the XML Schemas node. Right-click on the node and choose "create" from the pop-up menu options. You have the option of selecting the source for the W3C schema from the file system, a database, or a URL. You can also cut and paste the source directly into the dialog window. The advanced tab gives you the option of generating object types, tables, and Java beans from the registered schema. You also have the option of overriding any errors and saving the schema, which we do not recommend, because improperly created schemas and partially created object types can sometimes be difficult to remove from the database. For this example, we generated object types and a table based on the schema. Figure 19-1 shows the schema registration dialog box.

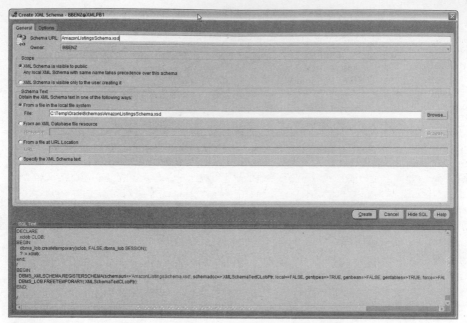

Figure 19-1: Registering a schema using the Enterprise Manager

The SQL*Plus code for registering the schema can be cut and pasted from the "show SQL" window at the bottom of the dialog box. Here's the code in its entirety:

```
DECLARE
   xclob CLOB;
BEGIN
   dbms_lob.createtemporary(xclob, FALSE,dbms_lob.SESSION);
   ? := xclob;
end;
/
BEGIN
DBMS_XMLSCHEMA.REGISTERSCHEMA(schemaurl=>'AmazonListingsSchemaTable.xsd',
schemadoc=>:XMLSchemaTextCLobPtr, local=>FALSE, gentypes=>TRUE, genbean=>FALSE,
gentables=>TRUE, force=>FALSE, owner=>'BBENZ');
   DBMS_LOB.FREETEMPORARY(:XMLSchemaTextCLobPtr);
END;
/
```

Because the `gentables=>TRUE` option is set, the registration process creates a new table called AmazonListingsSchemaTable that is used by the schema to map XML data from XML documents to relational table formats.

Tip Make sure that the schema name that you are using does not match any table names that already exist in the database. If the schema name matches an existing table name, a new table is created with a cryptic database name, which does not match the schema name. This will inevitably create maintenance issues and confusion in the future. To create mapping from existing relational structures to XML documents, use an XMLType view, which we cover in detail later in this chapter.

SQL INSERT commands using XMLType.createXML()

Now that the schema is registered in the database and a table is created based on the schema, we can test the new table by sending it a sample XML document. XMLSpy has a menu option for generating a sample document, which we use as a guide to build a real test document. Next, we wrap an SQL INSERT command around the XML document like this:

```
INSERT INTO 'AMAZONLISTINGSSCHEMATABLE VALUES(sys.XMLType.createXML(
'<?xml version="1.0" encoding="UTF-8"?>
<AMAZONLISTINGS xmlns:xsi="http://www.w3.org/2001/XMLSchema-instance"
      xsi:noNamespaceSchemaLocation="'AmazonListingsSchemaTable.xsd">
 <PRODUCTID>1004</PRODUCTID>
 <RANKING>4</RANKING>
 <TITLE>Ulysses</TITLE>
 <ASIN>0679722769</ASIN>
 <AUTHORID>1002</AUTHORID>
 <IMAGE>http://images.amazon.com/images/P/0679722769.01._PE30_PIdp-
      schmoo2,TopRight,7,-26_TCMZZZZZZZ_.jpg</IMAGE>
 <SMALL_IMAGE>http://images.amazon.com/images/P/0679722769.01._PE30_PId
      p-schmoo2,TopRight,7,-26_SCMZZZZZZZ_.jpg</SMALL_IMAGE>
 <LIST_PRICE>11.90</LIST_PRICE>
 <RELEASE_DATE/>
 <BINDING>Paperback</BINDING>
 <AVAILABILITY/>
 <TAGGED_URL>http://www.amazon.com/exec/obidos/ASIN/0679722769/qid=1050
      987099/sr=2-1/ref=sr_2_1/104-2508041-6900765</TAGGED_URL>
</AMAZONLISTINGS>'));
```

The XML document is accepted into the database and stored as relational data. At the same time, the XML schema checks to see if the document is valid, and issues an error if it is not. For example, if the TITLE exceeds 200 characters, the INSERT command returns the `ORA-22814: attribute or element value is larger than specified in type` error message.

You can extract XML using a regular XML expression, provided you return all of the columns in a row. For example, this query returns the first row of data as an XML document:

```
select * from AmazonListingsSchemaTable WHERE  rownum = 1;
```

However, because the database is based on a schema and not a regular table structure, a regular query that returns less than a full XML document is not permitted.
For example, a query to return the PRODUCTID column:

```
select PRODUCTID from AmazonListingsSchemaTable WHERE  rownum = 1;
```

Returns an error message that says `ORA-00904: "PRODUCTID": invalid
identifier`. Because the XML data is based on a schema, the entire table looks
like an XMLType object to queries. XMLType objects can be queried using XPath
expressions, which are part of the `EXTRACT()`, `EXISTSNODE()`, and `UPDATEXML()`
functions.

Querying XMLType Objects using EXTRACT() and EXTRACTVALUE()

In order to retrieve one or more columns from an XMLType column or table, use the
`EXTRACT()` command.

Cross-Reference   For more information on XPath expressions, please refer to Chapter 7.

This example extracts the PRODUCTID column using the `EXTRACT()` command and
an XPath expression from the AmazonListingsSchemaTable.

```
select extract(value(x), '/AMAZONLISTINGS/PRODUCTID') from
AmazonListingsSchemaTable x WHERE  rownum = 1;
```

Just the PRODUCTID column of row 1 is returned, as an element:

```
<PRODUCTID>1004</PRODUCTID>
```

The same query and XPath expression using the `EXTRACTVALUE()` command
returns the value of the column without the XML formatting:

```
select extract(value(x), '/AMAZONLISTINGS/PRODUCTID') from
AmazonListingsSchemaTable x WHERE  rownum = 1;
```

The value returned by the above expression is `1004`.

Selecting data based on values using EXISTSNODE() and EXTRACT()

You can conditionally select XML documents from an XMLType object using the
`EXTRACTVALUE()` command in a Where expression:

```
select extract(value(x), '/AMAZONLISTINGS/PRODUCTID') from AMAZONLISTINGS70_TAB
x WHERE extractValue(value(x),'/AMAZONLISTINGS/PRODUCTID') = 1004;
```

You can also extract data conditionally using XPath expressions and the EXISTS NODE() command. The following example extracts the row of data that has a PRODUCTID value of 1004:

```
select extract(value(x), '/AMAZONLISTINGS/PRODUCTID') from
AmazonListingsSchemaTable x WHERE  existsNode(value(x),'
/AMAZONLISTINGS[PRODUCTID="1004"]') = 1;
```

Both queries produce the same XML Document Fragment results:

```
<PRODUCTID>1004</PRODUCTID>
```

Using UPDATEXML to update XMLType objects

Because the AmazonListingsSchemaTable table is an XMLType object, it can be updated using XPath expressions and the UPDATEXML() command. The following example updates the Availability column in the table by updating the Availability element in the XMLType representation of the column:

```
UPDATE AmazonListingsSchemaTable x SET value(x) =
UPDATEXML(value(x), '/AMAZONLISTINGS/AVAILABILITY', 'Out of Stock')
WHERE  existsNode(value(x),' /AMAZONLISTINGS[PRODUCTID="1004"]') = 1;
```

XMLType views

XMLType views are similar to XMLType tables, but do not require the tables represented by the view to be changed to accommodate XMLType queries. You can use a table for regular data processing, and have the option of viewing the same data as XML via the XMLType view. XMLType views can be created using most of the functions that we have covered so far in this chapter, such as XMLELEMENT() and XMLFOREST(). To create an XMLType view without a schema, use the CREATE OR REPLACE VIEW <view name> OF XMLTYPE SQL command. You can also map an XMLType view to a W3C schema. Schemas can validate XML data going in and format XML data coming out of the view.

 Note Before creating an XMLType view based on a W3C schema, you must register the schema in the database. See the "Registering W3C Schemas in Oracle" section earlier in this chapter for instructions on schema registration.

To create XML Views that map to a W3C schema, it's much easier to use the Oracle Enterprise Manager than is to code the view creation and query processes. Select a View node in the enterprise manager navigator. Right click on the node and choose "create" from the pop-up menu options. In the general window, add the view name and the query that produces the view. Figure 19-2 shows the general view creation window for the XMLTYPEVIEW1 view.

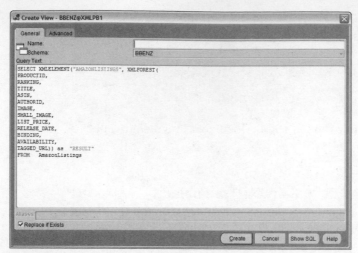

Figure 19-2: The General View Creation Window for the XMLTYPEVIEW1 View

Mapping data in the query to a schema and setting constraints for the View is handled in the advanced view creation window. For the XMLTYPEVIEW1 example, we specified the BBENZ database schema, the previously registered W3C schema called AmazonListingsXMLTable, and chose the root element for the schema, which is AMAZONLISTINGS. Figure 19-3 shows the advanced view creation window for the XMLTYPEVIEW1 view.

When the create button is pressed, the view is created and mapped to the chosen W3C schema. Here's the SQL that is generated by the Enterprise Manager:

```
CREATE OR REPLACE VIEW "BBENZ"."" OF SYS.XMLTYPE
 XMLSCHEMA
"http://xmlns.oracle.com/xdb/schemas/BBENZ/AmazonListingsXMLTable.xsd" ELEMENT
"AMAZONLISTINGS"  WITH OBJECT IDENTIFIER ('/') AS SELECT
XMLELEMENT("AMAZONLISTINGS", XMLFOREST(
PRODUCTID,
RANKING,
TITLE,
ASIN,
AUTHORID,
IMAGE,
SMALL_IMAGE,
LIST_PRICE,
RELEASE_DATE,
BINDING,
AVAILABILITY,
TAGGED_URL)) as  "RESULT"
FROM   AmazonListings
```

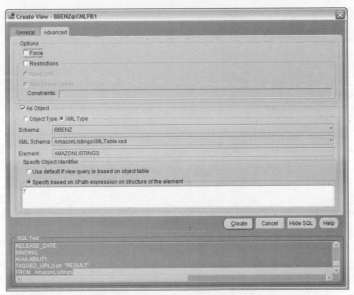

Figure 19-3: The Advanced View Creation Window for the XMLTYPEVIEW1 View

Once the view is set up, the AMAZONLISTINGS table can be queried and updated via normal SQL queries, or queried and updated as an XMLType table via the XML-TYPE1 view.

Managing XMLType objects using XML DB repositories

Another interesting feature of the Oracle XML DB is the ability to present XML Type data objects as folders and files in a hierarchy over standard protocols such as HTTP, WebDAV, and FTP. XMLType objects can be queried and updated via XMLType-compatible SQL commands. For more information on setting up the server, client, and databases for this feature, please refer to the Oracle9i XML Database Developer's Guide—:Oracle XML DB Chapter 13.

Formatting XML documents with XMLFormat

The SYS_XMLAGG() and SYS_XMLGEN() functions accommodate XML document format definitions using the XMLFormat object type.

If you are using SYS_SMLAGG and have a W3C schema created for your XML data, you can create an XMLFormat object using the createFormat() function. Here's an example of a query that formats output from the AMAZONLISTINGS table based on a W3C Schema named AmazonListingsSchemaTable.xsd:

```
SELECT SYS_XMLAGG(XMLFOREST(
PRODUCTID,
RANKING,
TITLE)) as "RESULT"
FROM   AmazonListings
WHERE  rownum = 1
XMLFORMAT.CREATEFORMAT('AZLIST',
'http://schemas.benztech.com/'AmazonListingsSchemaTable.xsd'));
```

You can also use the `createFormat()` function to specify the root tag of a SYS_XMLGEN result. In this example, the XMLONLY table contains one XMLType column called XMLDOC. The results of this query returns the AZLIST parameter as the root element for the SYS_XMLGEN() XML document output.

```
SELECT SYS_XMLGEN(XMLDOC,
XMLFORMAT.CREATEFORMAT('AZLIST')) FROM XMLONLY WHERE  rownum = 1;
```

You can also create a hard-coded XMLFormat object using `createFormat()` and several related attributes. Table 19-7 describes the XMLFormat object type attributes, and which Oracle SQL functions support them. As you can see from the attribute listings, hard-coding the XMLFormat object type is useful for generating an `ObjectType` that references a schema. The only exception to this would be to create XML document output form an XMLType data type that includes a processing instruction. In this case, the instruction can be added to the XML output using the `processingIns` attribute of the XMLFormat object.

Note   XMLFormat schemas are W3C schemas, not Oracle database schemas. As of Oracle 9.2, XMLSEQUENCE() also has partial support for XMLFormat, but does not accommodate schemas. Instead, XMLSEQUENCE() uses an XMLFormat object created with the createFormat() function using attributes in Table 19-7 to build an XMLType data type.

Table 19-7
XMLFormat Object Type Attributes

Attribute	Description
schemaType SYS_XMLGEN(), SYS_XMLAGG(), and XMLSEQUENCE()	Indicates whether to use a W3C schema for formatting or not. The options are 'NO_SCHEMA' (default) and 'USE_GIVEN_SCHEMA'. Currently, XMLSEQUENCE() does not support the 'USE_GIVEN_SCHEMA' option. XMLFormat objects are passed to XMLSEQUENCE() as part of call that contains a REF CURSOR. If 'NO_SCHEMA' is specified, the XMLFormat object is created using the createFormat object.

Attribute	Description
schemaName SYS_XMLGEN() and SYS_XMLAGG()	The name of the target schema when the schemaType is set to 'USE_GIVEN_SCHEMA'.
enclTag SYS_XMLGEN()	The name of the enclosing tag for the single-column result of the SYS_XMLGEN function. If no hard-coded or schema value is provided, the element name defaults to the column name.
targetNameSpace SYS_XMLGEN() and SYS_XMLAGG()	The target namespace when the schemaType is set to 'USE_GIVEN_SCHEMA'.
Dburl SYS_XMLGEN() and, SYS_XMLAGG()	The URL to the database to use when the schemaType is set to 'USE_GIVEN_SCHEMA'. Default is a relative URL reference from the current database instance.
processingIns SYS_XMLGEN() and SYS_XMLAGG()	Processing instructions to be added to the XML document output.

XML resources for PL/SQL developers

Oracle9i maintains a very complete set of XML DB functions for PL/SQL, Java, and C++ in the XDK. However, PL/SQL developers who don't want to use the XDK are definitely not neglected. Many XDK XML document functions have comparable PL/SQL functionality. For example, the XMLType API includes the `createXML()` function for generating XML from a string and 20 other functions for manipulating XMLType data types.

There is also a PL/SQL DOM Parser (DBMS_XMLDOM), a fast validating parser for XMLType and CLOB data types (DBMS_XMLPARSER), and an XSLT Processor (DBMS_XSLPROCESSOR). Oracle also includes packages for registering W3C schemas (DBMS_XMLSCHEMA) and several views for reviewing schemas and their user assignments (Oracle XML DB XML Schema Catalog Views). Administrators and developers alike will appreciate the Resource API for PL/SQL (DBMS_XDB) for managing XML DB security, and the DBMS_XDB_VERSION API for managing version control. The RESOURCE_VIEW and PATH_VIEW views accommodate access to Oracle data via third party tools using JNDI, FTP, or WebDAV. The DBMS_XDBT API facilitates maintenance of ConText indexes for an XML DB instance.

All of these APIS and associated functions are well documented in Appendix F of the Oracle9i XML Database Developer's Guide — :Oracle XML DB. For this reason, we won't drill down any deeper into these APIS. Instead I'll show you several important tips and tricks for writing XML documents to the file system using another important PL/SQL package: DBMS_XMLGEN().

Generating multi-row XML using DBMS_XMLGEN()

DBMS_XMLGEN() is a subset of the XML SQL Utility (XSU), which as originally a Java servlet in Oracle8i. In Oracle9i, DBMS_XMLGEN() functions are part of the database kernel to improve performance. Because DBMS_XMLGEN() is a PL/SQL package, it contains several sub-functions that shape XML output. Table 19-8 shows all of the DBMS_XMLGEN() functions.

Table 19-8
Oracle XML Functions

Function	Description
getXML()	Returns an XMLType or CLOB object from the results of an SQL query.
newContext()	Accepts an SQL query and returns a new context handle.
closeContext()	Closes the named context.
setRowSetTag ()	Set the root tag for the XML document fragment that is returned by getXML(). The default value is ROWSET.
setRowTag()	Set the tag that defines each row of an XML document returned by getXML(). The default value is ROWSET.
useItemTagsForColl()	an _ITEM suffix is added collection element names in the XML document. The default value is the object name.
setMaxRows()	Limits the maximum number of rows to be fetched each time. The default value is unlimited. Useful when combined with setSkipRows() and getNumRowsProcessed() for pagination of results.
setSkipRows()	Skip x rows before returning results as XML. The default is value 0. Useful when combined with setMaxRows() and getNumRowsProcessed() for pagination of results.
getNumRowsProcessed()	Returns the number of rows that were returned by the latest query in the context. Useful for checking to see if there are results to process. Also useful when combined with setMaxRows() and setSkipRows() for pagination of results.
setConvertSpecialChars()	By default, non-XML characters are converted to their escaped values. Conversion can be disabled with this function.
convert()	Manually converts non-XML characters to their escaped values and vice versa.
restartQUERY()	Resets the context to restart the query.

A DBMS_XMLGEN example

As you can see from the list of sub-functions in Table 19-6, DBMS_XMLGEN() can be a language unto itself. Listing 19-2 shows an example procedure that uses DBMS_XMLGEN() and many of its functions. The result is a single well-formed XML document containing two rows of data from the AMAZONLISTINGS table. The output is saved to a file named DBMS_XMLGENEXAMPLE.xml.

Listing 19-2: **A DBMS_XMLGEN Example**

```
SET SERVEROUTPUT ON
CREATE OR REPLACE PROCEDURE printClobOut(result IN OUT NOCOPY CLOB) is
xmlstr varchar2(32767);
line varchar2(10000);
begin
  xmlstr := dbms_lob.SUBSTR(result,32767);
  loop
    exit when xmlstr is null;
    line := substr(xmlstr,1,instr(xmlstr,chr(10))-1);
    dbms_output.put_line('| '||line);
    xmlstr := substr(xmlstr,instr(xmlstr,chr(10))+1);
  end loop;
end;
/


DECLARE
  currentContext  DBMS_XMLGen.ctxHandle;
  XMLFile  Utl_File.File_Type;
  XMLCLOB    CLOB;
BEGIN

  currentContext := DBMS_XMLGen.newContext('SELECT PRODUCTID, RANKING,
  TITLE FROM   AmazonListings');

  DBMS_XMLGen.setRowsetTag(currentContext, 'RootElement');
  DBMS_XMLGen.setRowTag(currentContext, 'RowElement');
  DBMS_XMLGEN.setMaxRows(currentContext,3);
  DBMS_XMLGEN.setSkipRows(currentContext,1);

  XMLCLOB := DBMS_XMLGen.GetXML(currentContext);
  printClobOut(XMLCLOB);
  DBMS_XMLGen.closeContext(currentContext);

  XMLFile := Utl_File.FOpen('C:Temp', 'DBMS_XMLGENEXAMPLE.xml', 'W');
  Utl_File.Put(XMLFile, XMLCLOB);
  Utl_File.FClose(XMLFile);
END;
/
```

Let's review the DBMS_XMLGEN() code line by line to see how the XML document output was created. The first line sets the server output to on. That way, if you're running this example in the SQL*Plus Worksheet, results will be displayed on the screen. The printClobOut procedure prints out CLOBS to the screen as well. The procedure writes output from a CLOB to the screen one line at a time.

Tip

The printClobOut procedure is copied from the Oracle9i XML Developer's Kits Guide - XDK, Chapter 23. Even though the procedure is in the XDK documentation, it's pure PL/SQL, and does not require the XDK to run. We find it a very handy tool for interactively developing and debugging PL/SQL functions that write CLOBS to a file.

```
SET SERVEROUTPUT ON

CREATE OR REPLACE PROCEDURE printClobOut(result IN OUT NOCOPY CLOB) is
xmlstr varchar2(32767);
line varchar2(10000);
begin
  xmlstr := dbms_lob.SUBSTR(result,32767);
  loop
    exit when xmlstr is null;
    line := substr(xmlstr,1,instr(xmlstr,chr(10))-1);
    dbms_output.put_line('| '||line);
    xmlstr := substr(xmlstr,instr(xmlstr,chr(10))+1);
  end loop;
end;
/
```

The next procedure (the / signifies the end of the printClobOut procedure) does the work of generating XML from relational data using DBMS_XMLGEN(). The context handle is called currrentContext. The file to write to is called XMLFile. The CLOB is created by the getXML() function. We're using a CLOB for this example so that we can print results to the screen with the printClobOut procedure. You can return the results of getXML() function directly into an XMLType data type. You can also convert the CLOB to an XMLType later in the code using the PL/SQL XMLType() function, which is part of the XMLType API.

```
DECLARE
  currentContext  DBMS_XMLGen.ctxHandle;
  XMLFile  Utl_File.File_Type;
  XMLCLOB  CLOB;
```

A hard-coded SQL query is passed to the current context, which returns the result set. Before the result set data is generated as XML, we set the root element name to RootElement for the document using DBMS_XMLGen.setRowsetTag(). The element that defines the rows of data is named RowElement using DBMS_XMLGen. setRowTag(). We also set the maximum rows to three, and change the default setSkipRows() function of 0 to 1. This means that the getXML() function will read through the result set starting at the second row, skipping row 1, and return a maximum of three rows. In this case, there are only three rows in the AMAZONLISTINGS table, so `getXML()` skips the first row and returns the last two rows.

Tip The `newContext()` function can accept a hard-coded SQL query or a reference cursor (REF CURSOR) as a parameter. REF CURSORS are great for interactive queries, because parameters can be passed to the procedure in the contents of the cursor, and variables defined in REF CURSORS can be shared with more than one query. The contents of the cursor can be manipulated by PL/SQL, Java, or other applications, and a state between the application and the procedure can be maintained. This way, you can use `DBMS_XMLGEN()` to interactively paginate results using a single query and REF CURSOR. we'll talk about this technique a little later in the XSU section.

```
BEGIN
  currentContext := DBMS_XMLGen.newContext('SELECT PRODUCTID, RANKING,
  TITLE FROM  AmazonListings');

  DBMS_XMLGen.setRowsetTag(currentContext, 'RootElement');
  DBMS_XMLGen.setRowTag(currentContext, 'RowElement');
  DBMS_XMLGEN.setMaxRows(currentContext,3);
  DBMS_XMLGEN.setSkipRows(currentContext,1);
```

Next, the CLOB is created containing the XML document. The `getXML()` function creates the XML document using any previously defined functions that limit the scope or shape the output. Because this is an example, we also print the contents of the CLOB out to the screen using the `printClobOut` procedure. Once the CLOB is created that contains all of the required data from the result set, we can drop the current context object using the `closeContext()` function.

```
  XMLCLOB := DBMS_XMLGen.GetXML(currentContext);
  printClobOut(XMLCLOB);
  DBMS_XMLGen.closeContext(currentContext);
```

Now that we have the CLOB and its XML document context, we can write the `DBMS_XMLGEN()` output to a file. To do that, we use the `Utl_File.FOpen` function to open a file, with a reference to the directory and file name. The third parameter can be W for write, R for read, or A for append. Next, we use the `Utl_File.Put()` function to write the CLOB to the open file, and then finish up the procedure by closing the file using `Utl_File.FClose()`.

Tip If this procedure returns an error `ORA-29280: invalid directory path`, you probably need to set file system security rights in Oracle for the output directory (in this case, `C:\temp`). To do this, you have to log in to the database instance with an ID that has sys admin rights and type the following commands at the SQL prompt:

```
create or replace directory dbdir as 'C:\Temp\';
Grant read on directory dbdir to <your user name>;
```

```
XMLFile := Utl_File.FOpen('C:\Temp', 'DBMS_XMLGENEXAMPLE.xml', 'W');
Utl_File.Put(XMLFile, XMLCLOB);
Utl_File.FClose(XMLFile);

END;
/
```

Below are the contents of the DBMS_XMLGENEXAMPLE.xml file. DBMS_XMLGEN()
automatically creates the XML document declaration in XML document output. The
root element is defined by the DBMS_XMLGen.setRowsetTag() function, and the
element that separates row data is defined by the DBMS_XMLGen.setRowTag()
function. The rest of the data is formatted with the column name as the element
name and the column value as the text value for the element.

```
<?xml version="1.0"?>
 <RootElement>
  <RowElement>
   <PRODUCTID>1002</PRODUCTID>
   <RANKING>2</RANKING>
   <TITLE>MacBeth</TITLE>
  </RowElement>
  <RowElement>
   <PRODUCTID>1003</PRODUCTID>
   <RANKING>3</RANKING>
   <TITLE>William Shakespeare: MacBeth</TITLE>
  </RowElement>
 </RootElement>
```

Working with the Oracle XDK

The Oracle XDK includes DOM and SAX Parsers with support for W3C Schemas, and
a customized high-performance XSLT Processor. Java and C++ developers can use
the XML Class Generator to generate classes from DTDs and Schemas. The generated classes can be used to send XML documents to Oracle databases. XML Java
Beans provide a visual tool for exploring and transforming XML documents. Java
developers can use the XML SQL Utility to create XML documents, from SQL
queries. You can also create DTDs and Schemas for XML result sets. The XSQL
Servlet can be used with the Oracle Java VM or another application server, including the Oracle AS (Application Server) to manipulate XML using SQL and XSLT. The
XML Pipeline processor enables the combination of queries and other Java processes, and the TransX Utility facilitates XML document to Oracle data loading.

For more information on parsing and transforming XML using Java, please refer to Chapters 15 and 16. The parsing and transformation code examples for Xalan and Xerces can be reused with the Oracle Java XDK. The only modification required is the substitution of Oracle XDK transformation and parsing packages in the import statements.

Oracle and Java integration: JDBC and SQLJ

Although the XDK is available in Java, C, C++, and PL/SQL versions, the most complete feature set is in the Java XDK. The Oracle JDBC API is the standard way to access Oracle data from J2EE applications. JDBC supports reading and writing of data from Java to external data sources. JDBC is based on the X/Open SQL call level interface (CLI) specification. More information on the X/Open SQL CLI can be found at http://www.opengroup.org.

For more details on JDBC and an example of a JDBC application, please refer to Chapter 21.

Oracle9i also supports SQLJ. SQLJ supports embedded SQL queries in Java code, based on SQLJ syntax. A key component of SQLJ is a code generator that converts SQLJ statements in Java source code with calls to the Oracle JDBC driver. The generated Java code can call Oracle database objects and return results via JDBC. This saves some time in coding, but requires a SQLJ run-time engine to run on the Oracle server. More information about SQLJ can be found at http://www.sqlj.org.

Developing with XSQL

The XSQL servlet processes SQL queries that are formatted in XML documents and returns results as XML. XSQL functionality can be combined with the Oracle XML Parser for Java, the XML- SQL Utility (XSU), and the Oracle XSL Transformation (XSLT) Engine to produce complex XML and HTML pages. This combination of tools is known as the XSQL Pages Publishing Framework. XSQL is compatible with most J2EE application servers. JSP pages can also include calls to the XSQL servlet via <jsp:forward> and <jsp:include> tags. For more details on XSQL including installation, setup and configuration instructions, please refer to the Oracle9i XML Developer's Kits Guide — :XDK Chapter 9.

XSQL queries are stored in XSQL page template files, which are defined by the .xsql file extension. Here's an example of a basic XSQL page template, called GetProduct.xsql:

```
<?xml version="1.0"?>
<xsql:query connection="xsqlconnect" bind-params="PRODUCTID"
xmlns:xsql="urn:oracle-xsql">
SELECT PRODUCTID, RANKING, TITLE
FROM AmazonListings
WHERE PRODUCTID = ?
</xsql:query>
```

Once the `GetProduct.xsql` file is created and stored under your Web server's virtual directory hierarchy, you can access the template via URL:

```
http://<J2EE server URL>/GetProduct.xsql?PRODUCTID=1001
```

The servlet registers the `.xsql` file and creates a servlet parameter from the `PRODUCTID` URL parameter. The data is automatically formatted as XML. Here's an example of default XML output from the XSQL servlet:

```
<?xml version="1.0"?>
<ROWSET>
  <ROW num="1">
    <PRODUCTID>1001</PRODUCTID>
    <RANKING>1</RANKING>
    <TITLE>Hamlet/MacBeth</TITLE>
  </ROW>
</ROWSET>
```

Changing the default SQLX-generated element names to something other than `ROWSET` and `ROW`, or changing the XML output to another document format or HTML requires XSL transformation. To automatically transform XSQL servlet output using a stylesheet, add the following link to the page template file, just above the `xsql:query` element:

```
<?xml-stylesheet type="text/xsl" href="<URI reference to the stylesheet>"?>
```

Developing with the XML SQL Utility (XSU)

The XSQL servlet uses the XML SQL Utility (XSU) to generate XML document output. XSU functionality can also be added to any other servlet on a J2EE application server. The XSU is an API that can run on a J2EE server. Other interfaces to XSU run on a command line and through PL/SQL. The XSU can generate XML output from SQL queries, generate DTDs and W3C schemas, and perform XSL transformations on XML document output. XSU query output can be returned as an XML document, a DOM node tree representation, or a series of SAX events.

Listing 19-3 shows a sample Java class that uses the XSU API `OracleXMLQuery` class to create a simple XML document from the AMAZONLISTINGS table.

Listing 19-3: **An XSU Example - GetAmazonListings.java**

```
import java.sql.*;
import oracle.jdbc.driver.*;
import oracle.xml.sql.query.*;

class GetAmazonListings {
```

```
public static void main(String[] argv)
{

  try{

    DriverManager.registerDriver(new oracle.jdbc.driver.OracleDriver());
    Connection conn =  new
    oracle.jdbc.driver.OracleDriver().defaultConnection ();

    OracleXMLQuery qry = new OracleXMLQuery(conn, "SELECT PRODUCTID,
    RANKING, TITLE FROM AMAZONLISTINGS WHERE ROWNUM = 1");
    String str = qry.getXMLString();
    System.out.println(str);
    qry.close();

  } catch(SQLException e){
    System.out.println(e.toString());
  }
}

}
```

The code starts by importing the standard Java SQL package, then the Oracle JDBC driver classes, and the XSU classes, including the `OracleXMLQuery` class:

```
import java.sql.*;
import oracle.jdbc.driver.*;
import oracle.xml.sql.query.*;

class GetAmazonListings {

  public static void main(String[] argv)
  {
```

This JDBC connection illustrates the connection string required for code that will run in the Java server on the Oracle server. The JDBC driver on the Oracle server runs on a default session, so no name and password are required as part of the connection string. The `defaultConnection()` method of the `oracle.jdbc.driver.OracleDriver` class retrieves the default session information. The XSU `OracleXMLQuery` class uses JDBC to make the connection to the Oracle server instance, and then returns the data as XML when it receives the result set from the JDBC driver.

```
  try{

    DriverManager.registerDriver(new oracle.jdbc.driver.OracleDriver());
    Connection conn =  new
```

```
oracle.jdbc.driver.OracleDriver().defaultConnection ();
OracleXMLQuery qry = new OracleXMLQuery(conn, "SELECT PRODUCTID,
RANKING, TITLE FROM AMAZONLISTINGS WHERE ROWNUM = 1");
```

Once the result set is retrieved and converted to XML by the `OracleXMLQuery` class, the resulting XML document can be retrieved via the `getXMLString()` method. Next, the `OracleXMLQuery` is closed to complete the class.

```
String str = qry.getXMLString();
System.out.println(str);
qry.close();
```

Summary

In this chapter, we showed you how to work with XML in Oracle:

✦ Working with the Oracle XML DB —:SQL functions that create XML

✦ Working with the XMLType data Type —:in columns, tables, and views

✦ Registering and using W3C Schemas in Oracle

✦ PL/SQL solutions using DBMS_XMLGEN()

✦ Working with the XDK —:key features

✦ Servlet solutions using XSQL and the XSQL Pages Publishing Framework

✦ An example of using the XML SQL Utility (XSU) in Java

In the next chapter, we'll show you how to work XML using DB2. After that, in Chapter 21, we'll show you how to create Web and J2EE applications and Websites that generate XML data from relational data. In Chapter 22, we'll show how to convert and transform relation data from one RDBMS XML format to another.

✦   ✦   ✦

Accessing and Formatting XML from DB2

XML functionality in DB2 is facilitated through several core XML functions for queries. Additional functions and data types are available as part of the IBM DB2 Universal Database (UDB) XML Extender. The XML extender preserves the scalability and security of DB2 databases, while allowing additional interfaces between XML and relational data.

Like Oracle and MS SQL Server, XML documents can be stored in DB2 databases as CLOB data. You can also store XML documents on the DB2 server file system. File system documents can be added to DB2 indexes and queries.

In this chapter we'll show you how to retrieve XML documents from DB2 as whole documents.we'll also show you techniques for extracting XML documents and document fragments from relational and CLOB data. We'll also show you how to use the DB2 XML Extender to store and retrieve XML documents in their original formats and as relational data.

Installing DB2 and the DB2 XML Extender

You can download a free developer version of the DB2 for evaluation and development purposes from `http://www-3.ibm.com/software/data/db2`. The examples in this chapter were developed using DB2 version 8.1 and DB2 XML Extender is version 7 Fixpack 9. As of DB2 version 8, the XML Extender is part of the download file set.

If you already have DB2 installed and just want to download the latest version of the XML extender, it's available for free at `http://www-3.ibm.com/software/data/db2/extenders/xmlext`. We recommend installing the DB2 XML Extender Administration Assistant as well to smooth the process of setting up XML extender.

The downloads for DB2 developer edition, the XML extender, and associated files are well over 1GB, so plan for some download waiting time, even with a good connection. Once the files are downloaded and installed, XML functionality is available via the DB2 Command Center Console and the DB2 Development Center UI.

The XML Programming Bible Example Tables

All of the tables in this chapter and this part of the book use the same data structure. For DB2, the data is structured into five tables. All five tables are contained in a database called XMLPB.

 On The Web I've included SQL code that creates these tables and inserts sample data as part of the downloads for this chapter. Downloads for the XML Programming Bible can be retrieved from `http://www.XMLProgrammingBible.com`, in the downloads section.

Table 20-1 lists the structure of the AMAZONLISTINGS table. This is the table that contains all of the Amazon book listings for our relational data examples and applications.

Table 20-1		
Structure of the AMAZONLISTINGS Table		
Table Column	*Data Type*	*Maximum Size*
PRODUCTID (Primary Key)	INTEGER	
RANKING	INTEGER	
TITLE	CHARACTER	200
ASIN	CHARACTER	10
AUTHORID (Foreign Key - AUTHORS)	INTEGER	
IMAGE	CHARACTER	100
SMALL_IMAGE	CHARACTER	100
LIST_PRICE	DECIMAL	Precision 2
RELEASE_DATE	DATE	

Table Column	Data Type	Maximum Size
BINDING	CHARACTER	50
AVAILABILITY	CHARACTER	10
TAGGED_URL	CHARACTER	200

Table 20-2 lists the structure of the AUTHORS table. This is the table that contains information about the book and quotation authors. It is related to the AUTHORID field in the AMAZONLISTINGS, ELCORTEINGLESLISTINGS, and the QUOTATIONS tables.

Table 20-2 Structure of the Authors Table		
Table Column	Data Type	Maximum Size
AUTHORID (Primary Key)	INTEGER	
AUTHORNAME	CHARACTER	50

Table 20-3 lists the structure of the ELCORTEINGLESLISTINGS table. This is the table that contains all of the Spanish Language Elcorteingles Website book listings for our relational data examples and applications.

Table 20-3 Structure of the ElcorteinglesListings Table		
Table Column	Data Type	Maximum Size
PRODUCTID (Primary Key)	INTEGER	
TITULO	CHARACTER	200
ISBN	CHARACTER	20
AUTHORID (Foreign Key - AUTHORS)	INTEGER	
IMAGEN	CHARACTER	100
PRECIO	DECIMAL	Precision 2

Continued

Table 20-3 *(continued)*		
Table Column	**Data Type**	**Maximum Size**
FECHA_DE_PUBLICACION	DATE	
ENCUADERNACION	CHARACTER	50
LIBROURL	CHARACTER	200

Table 20-4 lists the structure of the QUOTATIONS table. This is the table that contains all of the Quotations related to books, authors and sources in the relational data examples and applications.

Table 20-4 **Structure of the Quotations Table**		
Table Column	**Data Type**	**Maximum Size**
QUOTATIONID (Primary Key)	INTEGER	
SOURCEID (Foreign Key - SOURCES)	INTEGER	
AUTHORID (Foreign Key - AUTHORS)	INTEGER	
QUOTATION	CHARACTER	300

Table 20-5 lists the structure of the SOURCES table. This is the table that contains information about the book and quotation authors. It is related to the AUTHORID field in the AMAZONLISTINGS and QUOTATIONS tables.

Table 20-5 **Structure of the Sources Table**		
Table Column	**Data Type**	**Maximum Size**
SOURCEID (Primary Key)	INTEGER	
SOURCENAME	CHARACTER	50

DB2 XML Functions

DB2 developers who are new to XML development are usually under the impression that the DB2 XML Extender is the only way to access and manipulate XML in DB2. The XMLELEMENT, XMLATTRIBUTES, XMLAGG, REC2XML, COLATTVAL and XML2CLOB functions are part of the DB2 core and do not need XML Extender to function. These core functions are also SQL/XML functions, with the exception of COLATTVAL, which is an SQL/XML extension function. SQL/XML functions are based on the SQL/XML standard, which is a combination of XML and SQL functionality. The SQL/XML standard is maintained by the International Committee for Information Technology Standards (INCITS). INCITS maintains a grab-bag of international hardware, media and other standards, including the original SQL standard in the USA. Specific information on SQL/XML can be found at http://sqlx.org. More information about INCITS can be found at http://www.ncits.org.

The DB2 XML Extender adds the XMLVarcharFromFile, XMLCLOBFromFile, XMLFileFromVarchar, XMLFileFromCLOB, svalidate, and dvalidate functions to the core functions. It also adds some XML data types for storage of XML documents. We will cover the XML Extender functions and data types later in this chapter.

 Note DB2 documentation often refers to XML forests. At the highest level, a forest is a grouping of XML documents. The forest concept based on the same concept in SGML, called groves. Single XML documents follow a tree structure, so logically; multiple document tree structures are a forest. In the case of elements, one or more elements that are nested at the same level in an XML document are considered forests, made up of single-element trees. In the extreme extension of this logic, a single element can also be referred to as a forest, made up of single-character trees. DB2 and SQL/XML documentation refers to XML document fragments (XML elements grouped together but without a root element) nested at the same level as a forest.

Table 20-6 shows all of the DB2 core XML functions, and a brief description of each.

Table 20-6
DB2 Core XML Functions

Function	Description
REC2XML() DB2	Creates a well-formed XML document fragment. The COLATTVAL parameter creates an XML document fragment containing an element for each column with specified column values as attributes. Each element in the fragment is named column. Column names are stored in the name attribute of the element. Column values become text values of the column element.

Continued

	Table 20-6 *(continued)*
Function	**Description**
XML2CLOB() DB2	Returns XML data types as CLOB data. The XMLELEMENT, XMLATTRIBUTES, and XMLAGG functions return data as an XML data type.
XMLELEMENT() DB2 SQL/XML	Creates an XML document fragment from relational data. Element names are hard-coded into the expression. Column values become text values of the element. Nested instances of XMLELEMENT are used to create well-formed XML documents. Can be used with XMLATTRIBUTES() to construct custom XML element and attribute formats.
XMLATTRIBUTES() DB2 SQL/XML	A nested expression of XMLELEMENT(). Provides a list of attributes for an element as value pairs. Attribute names can be hard-coded into the expression. By default, column names become attribute names and column values become attribute values.
XMLAGG() DB2 SQL/XML	Creates an aggregated XML document fragment from a collection of separate XMLType objects. SYS_XMLAGG() nests results inside a ROWSET root element, XMLAGG() does not.

Creating a well-formed XML document using REC2XML()

The easiest way to return an XML document fragment is to use the REC2XML() function. There are three parameters that are part of the RE2XML() function. The first parameter is a number between 1 and 6, and specifies an expansion value for characters columns in the original table. The second parameter is COLATTVAL or XML_COLATTVAL. These values are case sensitive, and one of the options has to be chosen. By default, all illegal XML characters in generated element names are converted to their entity reference equivalents (< to <, > to >, " to ", & to &, and ' to '). The COLATTVAL and XML_COLATTVAL parameters determine if illegal characters in element values are converted as well. COLATTVAL converts illegal characters to their entity reference values, while XML_COLLATVAL leaves them in their original state. The third parameter specifies a root element name for the document fragment. For example, if you want to return an XML document fragment with no root element, the following query will do the job:

```
SELECT REC2XML(1.0, 'COLATTVAL', ' ',
PRODUCTID,
RANKING,
TITLE,
ASIN) as XMLTRESULTS
from AMAZONLISTINGS
FETCH FIRST ROW ONLY
```

This query returns the following XML document fragment.:

```
<column name="PRODUCTID">1001</column>
<column name="RANKING">1</column>
<column name="TITLE">Hamlet/Macbeth</column>
<column name="ASIN">8432040231</column>
```

As you may recall from Chapter 1, an XML document needs a single, unique root element to be well-formed XML. Therefore, this format of REC2XML() is an easy way to return a fragment that will become part of an aggregated or concatenated XML document, but is not useful for creating XML documents all by itself. To add a root element with the DB2 default row element name, you just have to change the space in the third parameter to a null value like this:

```
SELECT REC2XML(1.0, 'COLATTVAL', '',
PRODUCTID,
RANKING,
TITLE,
ASIN) as XMLTRESULTS
from AMAZONLISTINGS
FETCH FIRST ROW ONLY
```

This format creates a root element. DB2 provides a default ROW element name to create a well-formed XML document:

```
<row>
  <column name="PRODUCTID">1001</column>
  <column name="RANKING">1</column>
  <column name="TITLE">Hamlet/Macbeth</column>
  <column name="ASIN">8432040231</column>
</row>
```

You can also add your own name for the root element by replacing the null value in the third parameter with legal XML element text:

```
SELECT REC2XML(1.0, 'COLATTVAL', 'RowElement',
PRODUCTID,
RANKING,
TITLE,
ASIN) as XMLTRESULTS
from AMAZONLISTINGS
FETCH FIRST ROW ONLY
```

This creates an XML document fragment with the root element name of your choice:

```
<RowElement>
  <column name="PRODUCTID">1001</column>
  <column name="RANKING">1</column>
```

```
<column name="TITLE">Hamlet/Macbeth</column>
<column name="ASIN">8432040231</column>
</RowElement>
```

As you can see from these examples, REC2XML is a great way to quickly produce XML document fragments from DB2 table data. However, you have very little control over the format of the XML that is returned. Next, we show you the XMLELEMENT, XMLATTRIBUTES, and XMLAGG functions. These DB2 core XML functions give you more control, but are also more complex to code into queries.

Working with XML2CLOB()

The XMLELEMENT, XMLATTRIBUTES, and XMLAGG functions return data as an XML data type. The XML data type is used in DB2 for manipulating and combining data from XML function results. However, the XML data type is a DB2 data type that only exists in DB2 memory. The XML data type can not be stored in a regular DB2 table column. It also can not be displayed interactively in the command center or command-line processor. In order to remedy this, wrap any XMLELEMENT, XMLATTRIBUTES, or XMLAGG functions in an XML2CLOB function, like this:

```
SELECT XML2CLOB (XMLELEMENT(........)) AS "XMLResult" FROM AMAZONLISTINGS
```

We'll show XML2CLOB in use as we cover the next examples, for the XMLELEMENT, XMLATTRIBUTE, and XMLAGG functions.

Note

If you omit the XML2CLOB function from an SQL expression that returns an XML data type, you will receive the following very misleading error message:

```
    DBA2191E SQL execution error.
com.ibm.db.DataException: A database manager error occurred. :
[IBM][CLI Driver][DB2/NT] SQL0270N  Function not supported (Reason
code = "58"). SQLSTATE=42997
```

The "Function not supported" phrase leads many developers to assume that the XMLELEMENT, XMLATTRIBUTES, and XMLAGG commands are part of the XML extender function set, and that XML extender needs to be installed and enabled on the DB2 database instance before these functions will work. This is not the case. The error is returned because the XML data type cannot be displayed on the screen. Wrapping the query with a XML2CLOB function fixes the error.

Specifying a Row element using XMLELEMENT()

If you want to create a custom element structure from column and row data, use the XMLELEMENT() function and provide a hard-coded name for each column of data. You can also provide a hard-coded element name to define each row result by nesting XMLELEMENT() functions. Here's an example:

```
SELECT XML2CLOB(
XMLELEMENT(NAME "RowElement",
XMLELEMENT(NAME "PRODUCTID", PRODUCTID),
XMLELEMENT(NAME "RANKING", RANKING)))
AS "XMLResult" FROM AMAZONLISTINGS
```

This query returns the same row data as the REC2XML() function example did, but this time the result is formatted in a custom element structure. Each row of data is defined by the element named RowElement. RowElement is the result of the first nested XMLELEMENT() function in the query:

```
<RowElement><PRODUCTID>1001</PRODUCTID><RANKING>1</RANKING></RowElement>
<RowElement><PRODUCTID>1002</PRODUCTID><RANKING>2</RANKING></RowElement>
<RowElement><PRODUCTID>1003</PRODUCTID><RANKING>3</RANKING></RowElement>
```

Creating attributes using XMLATTRIBUTES()

One of the additional advantages of using a nested XMLELEMENT() function to create a root element is that the XMLATTRIBUTES() function can be used. XMLATTRIBUTES() creates a set of attributes for an element specified as apparent via the XMLELEMENT() function. This time we reuse the query from the last example, but just replace the XMLFOREST() function with an XMLATTRIBUTES() function:

```
SELECT XML2CLOB(
XMLELEMENT(NAME "RowElement",
XMLATTRIBUTES("PRODUCTID", "RANKING")))
AS "XMLResult" FROM AMAZONLISTINGS
```

The result is a single XML element for each row of data. Attributes in the element define the column data:

```
<RowElement PRODUCTID ="1001" RANKING="1"></RowElement>
<RowElement PRODUCTID ="1002" RANKING="2"></RowElement>
<RowElement PRODUCTID ="1003" RANKING="3"></RowElement>
```

You can also specify the attribute name for each attribute this way:

```
SELECT XML2CLOB(
XMLELEMENT(NAME "RowElement",
XMLATTRIBUTES(PRODUCTID as "PID", RANKING as "RANK")))
AS "XMLResult" FROM AMAZONLISTINGS
```

The above query produces these results:

```
<RowElement PID ="1001" RANK="1"></RowElement>
<RowElement PID ="1002" RANK="2"></RowElement>
<RowElement PID ="1003" RANK="3"></RowElement>
```

You may have noticed that the results here are not well-formed XML documents, because the row data is not nested inside of a root element. In order to add a root element to XMLELEMENT and XMLATTRIBUTES results, you need to use the XMLAGG function, which we will cover next.

Aggregating multiple rows of data using XMLAGG()

The XMLAGG() function aggregates multiple rows of data into a single XML document. For example, one might think that the following query would produce a well-formed XML document, with a root element name of RootElement and rows of data defined by RowElement elements:

```
SELECT XML2CLOB(
XMLELEMENT(NAME "RootElement",
XMLELEMENT(NAME "RowElement",
XMLELEMENT(NAME "PRODUCTID", PRODUCTID),
XMLELEMENT(NAME "RANKING", RANKING))))
AS "XMLResult" FROM AMAZONLISTINGS
```

However, the concatenated result is a set of sibling XML document fragments with no root element:

```
<RootElement><RowElement><PRODUCTID>1001</PRODUCTID><RANKING>1</RANKING>
</RowElement></RootElement>
<RootElement><RowElement><PRODUCTID>1002</PRODUCTID><RANKING>2</RANKING>
</RowElement></RootElement>
<RootElement><RowElement><PRODUCTID>1003</PRODUCTID><RANKING>3</RANKING>
</RowElement></RootElement>
```

When the XMLAGG function is added between the XMLELEMENT() functions that define RootElement and RowElement in the query, like this:

```
SELECT XML2CLOB(
XMLELEMENT(NAME "RootElement",
XMLAGG(
XMLELEMENT(NAME "RowElement",
XMLELEMENT(NAME "PRODUCTID", PRODUCTID),
XMLELEMENT(NAME "RANKING", RANKING)))))
AS "XMLResult" FROM AMAZONLISTINGS
```

The result is a single, aggregated, well-formed XML document, as shown here:

```
<RootElement>
  <RowElement>
    <PRODUCTID>1001</PRODUCTID>
    <RANKING>1</RANKING>
  </RowElement>
  <RowElement>
    <PRODUCTID>1002</PRODUCTID>
```

```
    <RANKING>2</RANKING>
  </RowElement>
  <RowElement>
    <PRODUCTID>1002</PRODUCTID>
    <RANKING>2</RANKING>
  </RowElement>
</RootElement>
```

The same technique can be used for nested attributes in a query. In this example, we replace the elements in the row results with attributes, and aggregate the results using XMLAGG():

```
SELECT XML2CLOB(
XMLELEMENT(NAME "RootElement",
XMLAGG(
XMLELEMENT(NAME "RowElement",
XMLATTRIBUTES("PRODUCTID", "RANKING")))))
AS "XMLResult"
FROM AMAZONLISTINGS
```

The result is a well-formed XML document structures in a custom element and attribute format:

```
<RootElement>
  <RowElement PRODUCTID ="1001" RANKING="1"></RowElement>
  <RowElement PRODUCTID ="1002" RANKING="2"></RowElement>
  <RowElement PRODUCTID ="1003" RANKING="3"></RowElement>
</RootElement>
```

Adding an XML document declaration

As you may recall from Chapter 1, an XML document declaration is an optional processing instruction that is positioned at the top of the XML document. The XML document declaration indicates the version of XML used to create a document and the data encoding of the contents, among other things. To add an optional declaration to the top of a XML document created with XMLAGG(), simply hard-code the value into the query. The declaration should be positioned above the XMLAGG() function expression. Here's an example including an XML document declaration:

```
SELECT '<?xml version="1.0" encoding="UTF-8"?>',
XML2CLOB (
XMLELEMENT(NAME "RootElement",
XMLAGG(XMLELEMENT(NAME "RowElement",
XMLELEMENT(NAME "PRODUCTID", PRODUCTID),
XMLELEMENT(NAME "RANKING", RANKING)))))
AS "XMLResult" FROM AMAZONLISTINGS
```

The resulting XML document declaration is appended to the top of a well-formed XML document:

```
<?xml version="1.0" encoding="UTF-8"?>
<RootElement>
  <RowElement>
    <PRODUCTID>1001</PRODUCTID>
    <RANKING>1</RANKING>
  </RowElement>
  <RowElement>
    <PRODUCTID>1002</PRODUCTID>
    <RANKING>2</RANKING>
  </RowElement>
  <RowElement>
    <PRODUCTID>1002</PRODUCTID>
    <RANKING>2</RANKING>
  </RowElement>
</RootElement>
```

Grouping and ordering XML with XMLAGG()

You can also use the GROUP BY and ORDER BY SQL clauses to group and sort the display of XML elements and attributes. When The XMLAGG function is applied, the results are formatted as individual well-formed XML documents for each group. Grouping and sorting is processed before the data is converted to XML. This example produces three XML documents, with the highest ranking document listed first:

```
SELECT XML2CLOB(
XMLELEMENT(NAME "RootElement",
XMLAGG(XMLELEMENT(NAME "RowElement",
XMLELEMENT(NAME "PRODUCTID", PRODUCTID),
XMLELEMENT(NAME "RANKING", RANKING)))))
AS "XMLResult" FROM AMAZONLISTINGS
GROUP BY RANKING ORDER BY RANKING DESC
```

And here is what the results of the query look like, with the highest ranking at the top and each XML document fragment grouped by ranking:

```
<RootElement>
  <RowElement PRODUCTID ="1003" RANKING="3"></RowElement>
</RootElement>
<RootElement>
  <RowElement PRODUCTID ="1002" RANKING="2"></RowElement>
</RootElement>
<RootElement>
  <RowElement PRODUCTID ="1001" RANKING="1"></RowElement>
</RootElement>
```

So far we've shown you XML functionality that is part of the core DB2 SQL functions. Next, we'll show you how to use the DB2 XML extender to add more flexible options for getting XML data you of DB2 and some new techniques for storing data as XML in DB2 databases.

Developing XML Solutions with the DB2 XML Extender

XML Extender adds several functions and data types to the core DB2 XML functionality that we've covered so far in the chapter. D2 XML extender adds several options for storing data in DB2 tables, and several functions for reading, writing, and updating that data. The XML extender also includes a DTD and W3C schema repository in a database. DTDs that are part of the database can be used to validate XML documents before they are converted to relational data and stored in tables. You can also store and manipulate Data access Definition (DAD) files, which map XML document structures to relational data structures.

Binding and enabling databases for XML Extender

In order to access DB2 XML Extender data types and functions, you have to "bind" DB2 XML Extender classes to existing DB2 databases. Once bound, the database also needs to be "enabled" to create tables for storing DTDs, schemas, and DADs. This is done via the DB2 Command Line Processor. See the first section of this chapter to download the DB2 XML extender if it's not already installed on the same computer as your DB2 server.

Binding a database to DB2 XML Extender

Access the Command Line processor. In Windows, under the Start menu, go to IBM DB2 ⇨ Command Line Tools ⇨ Command Line Processor.

Note   Use the Command Line processor to bind to DB2 extensions, not the DB2 Command Center. My experience (and the experience of others) is that not all extension binding and enabling functions work as expected in Command Center, but they always work in the Command Processor window.

Connect to the database to which you want to bind XML extender. For example, to bind the XMLPB database to XML extender, use this command:

```
C:\Program Files\IBM\SQLLIB\BIN>db2 connect to XMLPB
```

You should get a similar response to this, depending on your DB2 version:

```
Database Connection Information
Database server      = DB2/NT 8.1.0
SQL authorization ID = OWNER
Local database alias = XMLPB
```

Next, bind XML Extender to the connected database using the following command. Change the path to your DB2 XML Extender path if you didn't use the default of c:\dxx\.

```
C:\Program Files\IBM\SQLLIB\BIN>db2 bind "c:\dxx\bnd\@dxxbind.lst"
```

You should get the following response:

```
LINE    MESSAGES FOR dxxbind.lst
SQL0061W  The binder is in progress.
LINE    MESSAGES FOR dxxcomp.bnd
1994    SQL0204N  "DB2XML.XML_USAGE" is an undefined name.
              SQLSTATE=01532
LINE    MESSAGES FOR dxxbind.lst
        SQL0091N  Binding was ended with "0" errors and "1" warnings.
```

The warning above is displayed when you bind DB2 XML Extender for the first time to a database that you have not yet enabled. That's expected, because you haven't enabled it yet.

Next, disconnect from the database with the following command:

```
C:\Program Files\IBM\SQLLIB\BIN>db2 terminate
```

To which you should get this response:

```
DB20000I  The TERMINATE command completed successfully.
```

Once disconnected, you can enable the database for use with the DB2 XML Extender with this command:

```
C:\Program Files\IBM\SQLLIB\BIN>c:\dxx\bin\dxxadm enable_db XMLPB
```

This is the response you should get:

```
DXXA002I  Connecting to database XMLPB.
DXXA005I  Enabling database XMLPB.  Please wait.
DXXA006I  The database "XMLPB" was enabled successfully.
C:\Program Files\IBM\SQLLIB\BIN>
```

The database is now bound and enabled for DB2 XML Extender.

Working with Document Access Definitions (DAD)

XML Extender uses Document Access Definition (DAD) documents to map XML elements and attributes to DB2 tables. DADs are used to translate selected XML document data to "side tables," which are tables that contain elements and attributes as table columns.

Despite the name, side tables are not something you can find at IKEA (For those of you who may have noticed — yes, we used the same joke in the SQL Server chapter — relational data jokes are hard to come by, we have to reuse them when we can!). Side tables are relation tables that are mapped to XML documents. They are used to index XML data for fast searches without all of the XML document clutter.

DADs can also be used to translate data from XML documents to relational tables, and vice versa. There are three types of DADs: XML column, XML collection SQL mapping, and SQL collection RDB node mapping. SQL column DADs are used to map an XML document column to side tables. XML collection SQL mapping is used to map an SQL query statement to XML document output. SQL mapping is used for queries only, not updates or inserts. XML collection RDB node mapping is used to map XML documents elements, attributes, and text nodes to column data in relational tables. RDB node mapping provides a little more information than SQL collection mapping. It uses the additional information to handle both SQL queries and relational data updates and inserts.

Working with XML columns

XML Extender-enabled databases can use XML columns to store XML documents in a DB2 column. XML documents are stored in their original format inside an XMLCLOB or XMLVARCHAR column. XMLCLOB and XMLVARCHAR are DB2 XML Extender user defined data types that are based on core DB2 data types. XMLCLOB is based on CLOB and XMLVARCHAR is based on VARCHAR(3000). A third data type, XMLFILE, is used to store a reference to a file on the file system. XMLFILE is used to include XML documents on the file system in text indexes. XMLFILE is also a DB2 XML Extender user defined data type. It's based on VARCHAR(512).

XML column data can be retrieved a whole XML document using cast functions. There are also several functions that can retrieve XML document fragments from stored XML documents using XPath functions.

Table 20-7
DB2 XML Extender Casting Functions

Function	Description
XMLVARCHAR(VARCHAR)	Returns an XMLVARCHAR from a VARCHAR
XMLCLOB(CLOB)	Returns an XMLCLOB from a CLOB or a CLOB locator
XMLFILE(VARCHAR)	Stores the file name of an XML document on the file system.

In addition to the three core casting functions in Table 20-7, there are also five XML Extender user defined functions (UDFS) that can cast the XML extender User Defined Types. These UDFS are used to read and write XML documents to and from the file system on the server. Table 20-8 shows the user defined functions for casting.

Table 20-8
DB2 XML Extender Casting UDFS

UDF	Description
XMLVarcharFromFile(file)	Creates an XMLVARCHAR data type object from a file on the file system. The parameter is a file name and path.
XMLCLOBFromFile(file)	Creates an XMLCLOB data type object from a file on the file system. The parameter is a file name and path.
XMLFileFromVarchar(file, encoding)	Writes an XMLVARCHAR data type to a file on the file system. The parameters are a file name and path, and optional encoding for the XML document file. Returns the file name in XMLFILE format.
XMLFileFromCLOB(file, encoding)	Writes an XMLCLOB data type to a file on the file system. The parameters are a file name and path, and optional encoding for the XML document file. Returns the file name in XMLFILE format.

XML column mapping example

If a database has been enabled for use with DB2 XML, table columns can be formatted a mixture of regular DB2 data types and XML data types.

For this example, we've created a table with one column. The column is formatted as an XMLCLOB data type using this SQL command:

```
CREATE TABLE OWNER.XMLONLY ( XMLDOC DB2XML.XMLCLOB NOT LOGGED    ) ;
```

 Note   The NOT LOGGED condition is needed because columns with a potential size of 1GB or more (XMLCLOBS can go up to 2GB) cannot be logged. You have to either limit the size of the XMLCLOB to less than 1GB, or turn logging off for that column.

We'll use the column to access book records as XML, rather than having to generate and shred XML documents from relational data. We also create a very simple DAD file, which will be used by the table to validate incoming XML documents and index certain fields in the XML document for text searches. The dtdid element in the example below tells DB2 XML Extender functions to validate incoming XML documents against the AmazonListings DTD. The DAD elements that are nested inside the Xcolumn element tell DB2 to extract and index the PRODUCTID and the TITLE elements from XML documents for fast text searches. The element locations are defined by XPath expressions.

```
<DAD>
  <dtdid>AmazonListings</dtdid>
  <validation>YES</validation>
  <Xcolumn>
    <table name="XMLONLY_side_tab">
      <column name="PRODUCTID" type="integer"
       path="/AMAZONLISTINGS/PRODUCTID" multi_occurrence="NO"/>
      <column name="TITLE" type="CHARACTER(200)"
       path="/AMAZONLISTINGS/TITLE" multi_occurrence="NO"/>
    </table>
  </Xcolumn>
</DAD>
```

The DTD reference is based on a unique ID. DB2 databases that have been enabled for XML Extender store DTDs in a table called DTD_REF with a unique ID. A reference in a DAD file to a unique ID returns the matching DTD. Here's the DTD:

```
<?xml version="1.0" encoding="UTF-8"?>
<!ELEMENT AMAZONLISTINGS (PRODUCTID, RANKING, TITLE, ASIN, AUTHORID, IMAGE,
SMALL_IMAGE, LIST_PRICE, RELEASE_DATE, BINDING, AVAILABILITY, TAGGED_URL)>
<!ELEMENT PRODUCTID (#PCDATA)>
<!ELEMENT RANKING (#PCDATA)>
<!ELEMENT TITLE (#PCDATA)>
<!ELEMENT ASIN (#PCDATA)>
<!ELEMENT AUTHORID (#PCDATA)>
<!ELEMENT IMAGE (#PCDATA)>
<!ELEMENT SMALL_IMAGE (#PCDATA)>
<!ELEMENT LIST_PRICE (#PCDATA)>
<!ELEMENT RELEASE_DATE (#PCDATA)>
<!ELEMENT BINDING (#PCDATA)>
<!ELEMENT AVAILABILITY (#PCDATA)>
<!ELEMENT TAGGED_URL (#PCDATA)>
```

The DTD is very basic, just specifying the elements that should be present in the XML document, and the order in which they should be structured.

Tip   We used XMLSpy (free trial download available at `http://www.xmlspy.com`) to generate the DTD instead of hand-coding it. XMLSpy can automatically connect to DB2 databases using an included IBM OLE DB provider for DB2. XMLSpy generates a W3C Schema from a database schema. We based the schema on the AMAZONLISTINGS table, and generated the schema. Next, we converted the W3C Schema to the DTD you see here with another XMLSpy menu option. After that, we created a sample document for use with the DTD. We made sure that the DTD was valid by adding AMAZONLISTINGS table data to the XML document, then testing the sample XML document against the DTD. The entire process to a few minutes, a fraction of the time it would have taken to hand-code and test a DTD.

Once the DTD is ready , you can register it in the XMLPB database using the DB2 Administration Wizard, which is available from the Windows start menu at DB2 XML Extender⇨XML Extender Administration Wizard. If you're at the console of the DB2 server, you can log on to the database using a local JDBC connection string like this:

```
jdbc:db2:XMLPB
```

Next, choose the file containing the DTD and specify an ID for the DTD. You can refer to the ID when using DADS that are associated with the same database. Figure 20-1 shows the "Import a DTD Wizard" screen that registers a DTD. The screen is part of the DB2 XML Extender Administration Wizard.

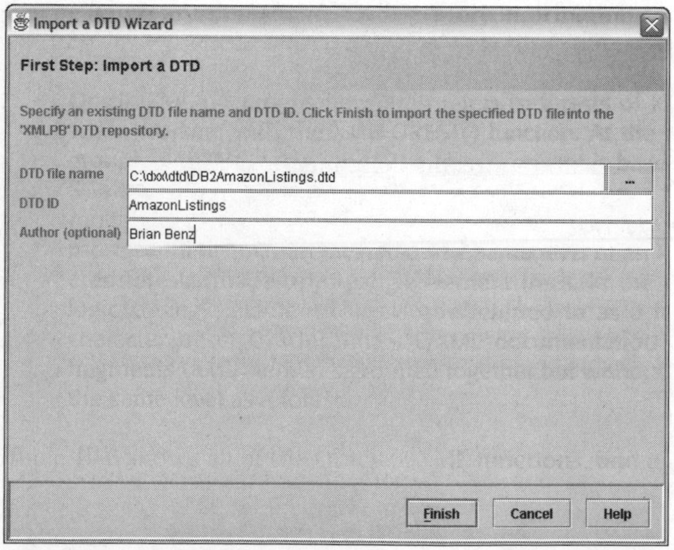

Figure 20-1: The Import a DTD Wizard, part of the DB2 XML Extender Administration Wizard

Once the DTD is registered, the next step is to enable the XMLDOC column for use with XML extender. This is done through the same screen as the DTD registration. Select the "Work with XML Columns" button. In the screen that appears (Figure 20-2), choose the table (XMLONLY), the column name (XMLDOC), and the location of the DAD file. The file is automatically registered with the column.

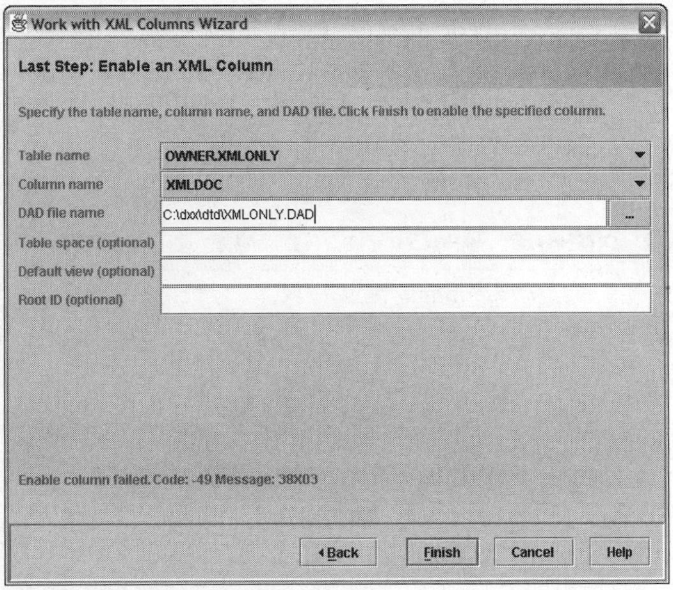

Figure 20-2: The Work with XML Columns Wizard, part of the DB2 XML Extender Administration Wizard

Getting data into an XMLCLOB column

With the new XMLONLY table, we can insert XML document data from any file system or in-memory XML document source. In the example below, we select a file that contains XML document from the file system and store it in the XMLDOC column:

```
INSERT INTO XMLONLY(XMLDOC)
VALUES(XMLCLOBFromFile('C:/dxx/samples/xml/newbook.xml'))
```

This example imports the XML document from the file named `C:/dxx/samples/xml/newbook.xml` into the XMLDOC column of the XMLONLY table.

Updating elements and attributes in Stored XML documents

The XML extender UPDATE UDF provides a way to update the values of selected attributes or text values in an XML document that is stored in DB2. The following

example updates the value of the AVAILABILITY element of a book with a
PRODUCTID of 1004 to Out of Stock:

```
UPDATE XMLONLY set XMLDOC = Update(XMLDOC, '/AMAZONLISTINGS/AVAILABILITY', 'Out
of Stock')
WHERE PRODUCTID = 1004
```

There are several other functions that can be used to extract and manipulate XML
documents stored in DB2 XML columns. Table 20-9 shows additional XML functions
for XML Columns.

<table>
<tr><td colspan="2" align="center">Table 20-9
DB2 XML Extender Functions for XML Columns</td></tr>
<tr><td>*Function*</td><td>*Description*</td></tr>
<tr><td>**extractInteger(XPath)**</td><td>Extracts the value returned by XPath as an integer.</td></tr>
<tr><td>**extractSmallint(XPath)**</td><td>Extracts the value returned by XPath as a smallint.</td></tr>
<tr><td>**extractDouble(XPath)**</td><td>Extracts the value returned by XPath as a double.</td></tr>
<tr><td>**extractReal(XPath)**</td><td>Extracts the value returned by XPath as real.</td></tr>
<tr><td>**extractChar(XPath)**</td><td>Extracts the value returned by XPath as a character.</td></tr>
<tr><td>**extractVarchar(XPath)**</td><td>Extracts the value returned by XPath as a varchar.</td></tr>
<tr><td>**extractCLOB(XPath)**</td><td>Extracts the value returned by XPath as a CLOB.</td></tr>
<tr><td>**extractDate(XPath)**</td><td>Extracts the value returned by XPath as a date.</td></tr>
<tr><td>**extractTime(XPath)**</td><td>Extracts the value returned by XPath as a time.</td></tr>
<tr><td>**extractTimestamp(XPath)**</td><td>Extracts the value returned by XPath as a timestamp.</td></tr>
</table>

XML collection SQL mapping DAD example

Let's go through an XML collection SQL mapping DAD that is used to map an XML
document format to the AMAZONLISTINGS table. DAD documents are actually well-
formed XML, with a .DAD file extension. The !DOCTYPE processing instruction
refers to a DTD that is stored on the file system and is used to make sure that the
XML document follows a valid DAD file format. The next element contains the root
element for the XML document, DAD.

```
<?xml version="1.0"?>
<!DOCTYPE DAD SYSTEM "c:\dxx\dtd\dad.dtd">
<DAD>
```

The `dtdid` element refers to a DTD that incoming XML documents can be validated against. The validation tag toggles validation against the DTD on (`YES`) or off (`NO`). XML collection SQL mapping DADs manage queries only, so DTD validation is not required. However, the elements have to be present for a valid DAD file.

```
<dtdid>c:\dxx\dtd\DB2AmazonListings.dtd</dtdid>
<validation>NO</validation>
```

The `Xcollection` tag tells DB2 that this DAD is describing a DB2 XML collection instead of an XML column. The `SQL_stmt` element defines the SQL statement that will be used to define the mapping between the rows in a table and the elements in an output XML document. Subsequent elements in the DAD refer back to columns in this query. The text values of the `prolog` and `doctype` elements are appended to XML documents that are generated using the DAD.

```
<Xcollection>
   <SQL_stmt>SELECTPRODUCTID, RANKING, TITLE, ASIN, AUTHORID, IMAGE,
SMALL_IMAGE,
   LIST_PRICE, RELEASE_DATE, BINDING, AVAILABILITY,TAGGED_URL
   </SQL_stmt>
   <prolog>?xml version="1.0"?</prolog>
   <doctype>!DOCTYPE AMAZONLISTINGS SYSTEM
   "c:\dxx\dtd\DB2AmazonListings.dtd"</doctype>
```

Next, the DAD identifies the root node of the XML document with the `root_node` element. The element node directly under that provides the name of the root element, AMAZONLISTINGS.

```
<root_node>
   <element_node name="AMAZONLISTINGS">
```

Next, the DAD maps the text value of the `PRODUCTID` element to the `PRODUCTID` column in the SQL query. This is done my nesting the `text_node` element inside the `PRODUCTID` element. If there were any attributes for the PRODUCTID element, they would be nested under the `element_node` as an `attribute_node`.

```
        <element_node name="PRODUCTID">
          <text_node>
              <column name="PRODUCTID" type="INTEGER"/>
          </text_node>
        </element_node>
```

The `RANKING` element is mapped to the RANKING column of the AMAZONLISTINGS table in the same way. The data type is specified as `INTEGER` to match the data type in the table. The source XML document does not have to specify a data type; this is solely for the purpose of DB2.

```
        <element_node name="RANKING">
          <text_node>
```

```
          <column name="RANKING" type="INTEGER"/>
     </text_node>
</element_node>
```

The rest of the element-to-column mappings follow the same pattern, mapping all of the XML document values to table column values, with the correct data types.

```
<element_node name="TITLE">
  <text_node>
     <column name="TITLE" type="CHARACTER"/>
  </text_node>
</element_node>
<element_node name="ASIN">
  <text_node>
     <column name="ASIN" type="CHARACTER"/>
  </text_node>
</element_node>
<element_node name="AUTHORID">
  <text_node>
     <column name="AUTHORID" type="INTEGER"/>
  </text_node>
</element_node>
<element_node name="IMAGE">
  <text_node>
     <column name="IMAGE" type="CHARACTER"/>
  </text_node>
</element_node>
<element_node name="SMALL_IMAGE">
  <text_node>
     <column name="SMALL_IMAGE" type="CHARACTER"/>
  </text_node>
</element_node>
<element_node name="LIST_PRICE">
  <text_node>
     <column name="LIST_PRICE" type="DECIMAL(10,2)"/>
  </text_node>
</element_node>
<element_node name="RELEASE_DATE">
  <text_node>
     <column name="RELEASE_DATE" type="DATE"/>
  </text_node>
</element_node>
<element_node name="BINDING">
  <text_node>
     <column name="BINDING" type="CHARACTER"/>
  </text_node>
</element_node>
<element_node name="AVAILABILITY">
  <text_node>
     <column name="AVAILABILITY" type="CHARACTER"/>
```

```
        </text_node>
    </element_node>
    <element_node name="TAGGED_URL">
      <text_node>
          <column name="TAGGED_URL" type="CHARACTER"/>
      </text_node>
    </element_node>
```

Once all of the elements have been mapped to columns, the root element node is closed, the XML collection is closed, and the DAD root element closing finishes the DAD file.

```
      </element_node>
    </root_node>
  </Xcollection>
</DAD>
```

XML Collection RDB Node example

Earlier in this chapter we showed you an XML collection SQL Mapping DAD that is used for queries only. An XML Collection RDB Node Mapping DAD can also be used to translate data from XML documents to relational tables, and vice versa. Below is a DAD that is used to insert an XML document into the AMAZONLISTINGS table. The tSQL Mapping and RDB node DAD files are very similar. We have to repeat myself a bit to fully explain both DADS. We'll point out the additional elements in a RDB node DAD as we go along.

DAD documents are well-formed XML, with a .DAD file extension. The !DOCTYPE processing instruction refers to a DTD that is stored on the file system and is used to make sure that the XML document is a valid DAD file. The next element contains the root element for the XML document, DAD.

```
<?xml version="1.0"?>
<!DOCTYPE DAD SYSTEM "c:\dxx\dtd\dad.dtd">
<DAD>
```

The current version of DB2 and DB2 XML Extender support *automatic* validation of incoming XML documents against a DTD, but not against a W3C schema. You can still validate incoming XML documents against a schema, but you have to explicitly add validation to your SQL expressions. The XML DB2 Extender and SVALIDATE() function explicitly validates data against a schema. The DVALIDATE() function explicitly validates against a DTD. The dtdid element refers to a DTD that incoming XML documents can be validated against. The validation tag toggles validation against the DTD on (YES) or off (NO).

```
<dtdid>c:\dxx\dtd\DB2AmazonListings.dtd</dtdid>
<validation>YES</validation>
```

The `Xcollection` tag tells DB2 that this DAD is describing a DB2 XML collection instead of an XML column. XML columns are used for storing XML documents as a single unit in a single column. XML collections split up XML document elements, attributes, and text values into relational data columns, then reassemble the XML document when data is queried. XML columns are best used for data that doesn't neatly fit into relational table structures, such as raw Website content. XML columns can also be used for improving performance by storing frequently accessed XML documents. If the data is already formatted as an XML document, there is no overhead associated with shredding and building the document, as there is with XML document collections.

The text values of the `prolog` and `doctype` elements are appended to XML documents that are generated using the DAD.

```
<Xcollection>
  <prolog>?xml version="1.0"?</prolog>
  <doctype>!DOCTYPE AMAZONLISTINGS SYSTEM
  "c:\dxx\dtd\DB2AmazonListings.dtd"</doctype>
```

Next, the DAD identifies the root node of the XML document with the `root_node` element. The element node directly under that provides the name of the root element, AMAZONLISTINGS. The multi-occurrence attribute specifies that all of the elements nested under the current element should be treated as a single row of relational data. This means that the nested element values in the DAD are added to the same row in the relational table, until another sibling occurrence of the AMAZONLISTINGS element is found.

```
<root_node>
  <element_node name="AMAZONLISTINGS" multi_occurrence="YES">
```

Nested under the `root_node` are all of the elements that are contained in the row of relational data. The `RDB_node` element defines a mapping from a relational database object to an XML document object. The first mapping defines the PRODUCTID element of an XML document as a primary key in the relational database using a `condition` element..

```
<RDB_node>
  <table name="AMAZONLISTINGS" key="PRODUCTID"/>
  <condition>
   AMAZONLISTINGS.PRODUCTID =AMAZONLISTINGS.PRODUCTID
  </condition>
</RDB_node>
```

Next, the DAD maps the text value of the PRODUCTID element to the PRODUCTID column in the AMAZONLISTINGS table. This is done my nesting the `text_node` element inside the PRODUCTID element. If there were any attributes for the PRODUCTID element, they would be nested under the `element_node` as an `attribute_node`.

```
<element_node name="PRODUCTID">
  <text_node>
    <RDB_node>
      <table name="AMAZONLISTINGS"/>
      <column name="PRODUCTID" type="INTEGER"/>
    </RDB_node>
  </text_node>
</element_node>
```

The RANKING element is mapped to the RANKING column of the AMAZONLISTINGS table in the same way. The data type is specified as INTEGER to match the data type in the table. The source XML document does not have to specify a data type, this is solely for the purpose of DB2.

```
<element_node name="RANKING">
  <text_node>
    <RDB_node>
      <table name="AMAZONLISTINGS"/>
      <column name="RANKING" type="INTEGER"/>
    </RDB_node>
  </text_node>
</element_node>
```

The rest of the element-to-column mappings follow the same pattern, mapping all of the XML document values to table column values, with the correct data types.

```
<element_node name="TITLE">
  <text_node>
    <RDB_node>
      <table name="AMAZONLISTINGS"/>
      <column name="TITLE" type="CHARACTER"/>
    </RDB_node>
  </text_node>
</element_node>
<element_node name="ASIN">
  <text_node>
    <RDB_node>
      <table name="AMAZONLISTINGS"/>
      <column name="ASIN" type="CHARACTER"/>
    </RDB_node>
  </text_node>
</element_node>
<element_node name="AUTHORID">
  <text_node>
    <RDB_node>
      <table name="AMAZONLISTINGS"/>
      <column name="AUTHORID" type="INTEGER"/>
    </RDB_node>
  </text_node>
</element_node>
```

```
<element_node name="IMAGE">
  <text_node>
    <RDB_node>
      <table name="AMAZONLISTINGS"/>
      <column name="IMAGE" type="CHARACTER"/>
    </RDB_node>
  </text_node>
</element_node>
<element_node name="SMALL_IMAGE">
  <text_node>
    <RDB_node>
      <table name="AMAZONLISTINGS"/>
      <column name="SMALL_IMAGE" type="CHARACTER"/>
    </RDB_node>
  </text_node>
</element_node>
<element_node name="LIST_PRICE">
  <text_node>
    <RDB_node>
      <table name="AMAZONLISTINGS"/>
      <column name="LIST_PRICE" type="DECIMAL(10,2)"/>
    </RDB_node>
  </text_node>
</element_node>
<element_node name="RELEASE_DATE">
  <text_node>
    <RDB_node>
      <table name="AMAZONLISTINGS"/>
      <column name="RELEASE_DATE" type="DATE"/>
    </RDB_node>
  </text_node>
</element_node>
<element_node name="BINDING">
  <text_node>
    <RDB_node>
      <table name="AMAZONLISTINGS"/>
      <column name="BINDING" type="CHARACTER"/>
    </RDB_node>
  </text_node>
</element_node>
<element_node name="AVAILABILITY">
  <text_node>
    <RDB_node>
      <table name="AMAZONLISTINGS"/>
      <column name="AVAILABILITY" type="CHARACTER"/>
    </RDB_node>
  </text_node>
</element_node>
<element_node name="TAGGED_URL">
  <text_node>
    <RDB_node>
```

```
            <table name="AMAZONLISTINGS"/>
            <column name="TAGGED_URL" type="CHARACTER"/>
        </RDB_node>
      </text_node>
    </element_node>
```

Once all of the elements have been mapped to columns, the root element node is closed, the XML collection is closed, and the DAD root element closing finishes the DAD file.

```
      </element_node>
    </root_node>
  </Xcollection>
</DAD>
```

Checking your RDB Node DAD with the DAD Checker

The DAD checker is a tool from IBM that checks the validity of a DAD. It checks the data constraints of the DAD document and returns errors and warnings, if there are any. It can be downloaded from http://www-3.ibm.com/software/data/db2/extenders/xmlext.

Note   The DAD checker only validates XML collection DAD files, not XML Column.

Here's an example of a DAD file session. As per the setup instructions, go to the install directory and type the following command:

```
C:\Temp\Db2\dadchk\bin>java dadchecker.Check_dad_xml -dad AmazonListings.DAD
```

If all goes well, you should get a message like this, listing all of the errors that were checked. The documentation that cones with the tool has a full explanation of the messages. If there are any problems with the DAD format, the line number of the error will display, along with a possible cause:

```
Checking DAD document: AmazonListings.DAD
No duplicated tags were found.
No type attributes are missing for <column> tags.
All <RDB_node> tags are properly enclosed.
The 'name' attributes for the <table> and <column> tags are all non empty
strings.
No <element_node> tags have been found with the same names and different
mappings.
No <attribute_node> tags have been found with the same names and different
mappings.
No missing multi_occurrence="YES" has been found.
FIXPAK 3 or earlier only:
no <attribute_node> tag mapping order problems were found.
```

Adding DADS and DTDs to the database

When we introduced XML Columns to you earlier in this chapter, we showed you how to register DTDs and DADs with a database. Behind the scenes, the DB2 XML Extender Administration Wizard provides a user-friendly interface to the dxxEnableCollection() stored procedure. This procedure accepts a DAD file name and a collection name, then registers the structure of the DAD as an XML collection in the database. DTDs can be registered there as well. Once the connection is registered, DB2 XML Extender stored procedures can be used to retrieve, store, and manipulate XML documents and relational data. These are well covered in DB2 XML Extender documentation.

Table 20-10	
DB2 XML Extender Stored Procedures	
Procedure	*Description*
dxxEnableCollection()	Registers a DAD file in a DB2 XML Extender-enabled database, and names a collection. The collection can be referenced when extracting or shredding XML documents.
dxxDisableCollection()	Disables a registered DAD file in a DB2 XML Extender-enabled database, and removes the collection name reference.
dxxGenXML()	Returns a table-based result set from a query and a supplied DAD file. The DAD file does not have to be registered in the database as a named XML collection.
dxxRetrieveXML()	Returns a table-based result set from a query and a named XML collection that is registered in the database.
dxxShredXML()	Creates relational data from a supplied XML document based on a specified DAD file. The DAD file does not have to be registered in the database as a named XML collection.
dxxInsertXML()	Creates relational data from a supplied XML document and a named XML collection that is registered in the database.

Summary

In this chapter, we showed you how to work with XML in DB2:

✦ Working with the DB2 Core SQL functions that create XML

✦ Introduction to the DB2 XML Extender

✦ Creating and editing DADs

✦ XML Column DADs

✦ XML Collection Node Mapping DADs

✦ XML Collection RDB Node DADs

✦ Checking Collection DADS with the DAD Checker

✦ Validating XML document data with DTDs and schemas

In the next chapter, we'll show you how to create Web and J2EE applications and Websites that generate XML data from relational data. In Chapter 22, we'll show you tips and tricks for converting and transforming native and custom relation data from one relational database's XML format to another.

✦   ✦   ✦

Building XML-Based Web Applications with JDBC

In this chapter we'll apply much of the tools and techniques that have been reviewed so far in the book. First, we'll show you how to create a J2EE application that accesses relational data via JDBC. Next, we'll show you how to adapt the J2EE application into a multi-tier application. The multi-tier application uses servlets and JDBC to serve relational data via XML to Web browsers and/or J2EE applications, depending on parameters that are sent to the servlet.

These examples are a great way to show you how to create applications that generate XML, parse XML, and transport XML between servers and client applications. Examples also include formatting considerations for displaying XML on the Web, how to call servlets from Web browsers and custom applications, and how to parse XML documents in a Web browser and client application.

About Java Database Connectivity (JDBC)

The JDBC specification and its reference implementation classes are Sun products. Like other specifications such as those included in the Sun Web Services Developer Pack (JAXP, JAXB, JAXM, and so on), the JDBC specification is part of the Java Community Process (JCP). At the time of this writing, the latest version of JDBC is the JDBC 3.0 API. JDBC contains classes that are stored in the `java.sql` and `javax.sql` packages. Java's JDK 1.4 and up bundle JDBC as part of the JDK, so no additional packages are needed. Otherwise, you'll have to download JDBC support from `http://java.sun.com/ products/jdbc/download.html` and follow the instructions for setting up the packages to use the examples in this chapter.

JDBC supports reading and writing of data from Java to external data sources. Even though JDBC is a Sun product, it's based on the X/Open SQL call level interface (CLI) specification, which is the same specification that Microsoft's Open Database Connectivity (ODBC) offerings are based on. Because of this, JDBC and ODBC functionality is closely related, and some JDBC drivers use ODBC as their connection service. More information on the X/Open SQL CLI can be found at `http://www. opengroup.org`.

JDBC is based on the `java.sql` and `javax.sql` packages for JDBC support coding access to a JDBC driver. JDBC drivers are not included in the JDK or the JDBC downloads. Most relational database vendors have created JDBC drivers for their database offerings. Aside from vendor-provided drivers, there are dozens of third-party JDBC drivers. Sun hosts a page that lists JDBC drivers and vendors at `http://industry.java.sun.com/products/jdbc/drivers`.

Besides the three JDBC specification versions, there are four *types* of JDBC drivers:

✦ Type 1 JDBC drivers function as a *JDBC-ODBC bridge*. Just like a real bridge, Type 1 drivers connect two things together. On one side, a Java interface is used to map a connection to an ODBC driver. The ODBC driver does all of the work of connecting to the database, and feeding information between the relational data source and the Java interface on the other side of the bridge.

✦ Type 2 drivers rely on external code to function. That code may be written in Java or any other language, as long as it provides access to the driver through Java.

✦ Type 3 drivers are written completely in Java. They can be downloaded and configured at runtime, and talk to relational databases and middleware servers via custom protocols.

✦ Type 4 drivers are Java-like Type 3 drivers. They handle connections directly to database servers without any conversion protocols between the server and the RDBMS.

The Microsoft SQL Server, Oracle, and DB2 (via the IBM DB2 Connect product) all provide JDBC 3 Type 4 drivers with their RDBMS products. Even though all JDBC drivers claim to fully support JDBC specifications, we've found that each provider had interpreted the JDBC specifications in different ways. This means that while there are significant compatibilities between provided JDBC drivers, you will find that there are differences in functionality. The promise of being able to access any database using the same J2EE code by swapping out one JDBC driver for another is a good one, but not quite there yet.

For the examples in this chapter, we'll use the SQL Server JDBC driver from Microsoft. You can download the JDBC driver and installation instructions, as well as all other SQL Server-related downloads, from `http://msdn.microsoft.com/ library/default.asp?url=/downloads/list/sqlserver.asp`.

The JDBC driver should be installed on the same machine as SQL server, and the SQL server should have URL access set up. The following conditions must be met on the SQL server:

✦ TCPIP must be enabled via the network utility, and the port must be configured to port 1433.

✦ Windows and SQL server login support must be enabled, (the default is "Windows Only").

Note
Because SQL server data is accessed via JDBC, SQLXML and IIS are not needed for the examples in this chapter. For the example that shows browser access with a servlet, you will need a J2EE application server such as Tomcat or WebSphere to run the servlet examples. I'll briefly cover setup and deployment of the servlets later in the chapter.

The most important part of the setup is the Setting up the CLASSPATH environment variable for the machine you are running the JDBC driver on.

Once the JDBC drivers have been downloaded and installed, you need to set up your CLASSPATH environment variable. In Windows 2000 and Windows XP, the CLASSPATH is contained in the environment variable settings (control panel⇨ system⇨advanced).

Tip
One of the problems we had while setting up the latest version of the MS JDBC drivers had to do with the order of .jar files in my CLASSPATH. We weren't able to get our J2EE application server (WebSphere) to recognize the JDBC driver, which is in mssqlserver.jar. After some trial and error, we rearranged the references one by one in the CLASSPATH until we got to the order shown below, with mssqlserver.jar, then msutil.jar, then msbase.jar before the other .jar files in the CLASSPATH. Once this order had been established, everything worked fine. We have since seen similar problems outlined in MS SQL Server forums, with the same solution, but no explanation of the cause. I recommend that if you have the same trouble, you set the order as shown here:

```
CLASSPATH=.;c:\sqljdbc\mssqlserver.jar;c:\sqljdbc\msu
til.jar;c:\sqljdbc\msbase.jar;...(Other .jar files in
your CLASSPATH.)
```

Introduction to the Sample Java Application – XMLPBXMLApp.java

The first example in this chapter is a fully functional Java Application that uses Swing Classes and AWT events to generate a UI, JDBC to access SQL Server data, and Java classes to generate customized XML formats. Let's jump right into the application with a look at the screen. Figure 21-1 shows the Java Application (Quote XML Generator) screen, with William Shakespeare selected as the Quote Author, the first quote selected as the output, "Element XML (Table=Root, Field Name= Element)" selected as the output format, and the resulting XML output displayed in the lower pane of the screen.

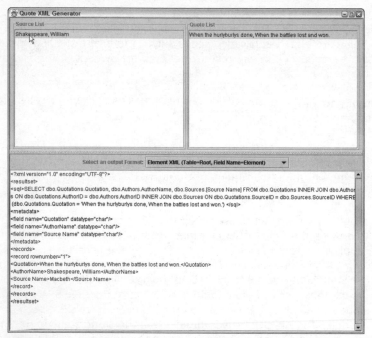

Figure 21-1: The XMLPBXMLApp.java (Quote XML Generator) application screen

How the application works

When the application window is opened, a class is called that retrieves a list of unique quote authors from the Authors SQL Server Database via JDBC. The application then draws the various Swing panels on the page and attaches AWT events to the panels. Users can scroll up and down the list of quote authors in the author List panel, and select a single author by clicking on it in the list. Clicking on a quote author name triggers another query to retrieve all the quotes attributed to the selected author. The quotes are displayed in the quote list panel on the top right of the screen. When a user clicks on one of the quotes in the quote list panel, another Java class is called to generate output for the selected quote and display it in the output panel in the lower half of the application window. In the middle of the screen is a combo box that can be used to select output format options. Table 21-1 lists the four options and what they produce:

Table 21-1
Quote Output Formatting Options

Just the Quote	Generates plain quote text in the output window.
Element XML (Table=Root, Field Name=Element)	JDBC metadata and columns of a table represented as elements nested in a parent `record` element.
Attribute XML (Table=Element, Field Name=Attribute)	JDBC metadata and columns of a table represented as attributes in a `record` element.

Aside from being a good Java Application prototype, the Quote XML Application is a good example of creating an alternative user interface to SQL Server data using JDBC and Java GUI Classes. It contains examples of accessing and displaying SQL Server tables in several different ways, including strings, arrays, and XML documents.

About the example SQL Server database

In this chapter we're reusing tables from the XMLProgrammingBible SQL Server database. Setup instructions for the database can be found in Chapter 18.

Creating the Java Application User Interface

Because the source code for this application is more than 400 lines, and occupies more than 15 pages of this book, we have broken down the source code into segments that relate to a specific topic, rather than showing the source code in its entirety on the pages. All of the examples contained in this chapter can be downloaded from the XMLProgrammingBible.com Website, in the Downloads section. Please see the Website for installation Instructions.

Defining public variables and the application window

Let's look under the hood of the Java Application by breaking down the Java Application source code into topical sections with detailed explanations of the code, starting with the introductory application setup Listing 21-1.

This Java Application imports the `java.io` classes for writing to the screen, `javax.swing` classes to handle UI features, and selected `java.awt` classes to manage action events. The `java.sql` classes manage access to the Microsoft SQL server JDBC classes. The `java.util` classes handle list and array formatting.

The rest of this code sets up a `Jframe` window, which becomes the application window, and creates an instance of an `actionlistener` to watch for the window to be closed. When the window is closed, the application exits.

Listing 21-1: Defining the Public Variables and the Application Window

```
import javax.swing.*;
import javax.swing.event.*;
import java.util.*;
import java.awt.*;
import java.awt.event.*;
import java.io.*;
import java.sql.*;

public class XMLPBXMLApp extends JPanel {
    JTextArea output;
    JList authorList;
    JList QuoteList;
    ListSelectionModel authorListSelectionModel;
    ListSelectionModel QuotelistSelectionModel;
    public String[] listData;
    JComboBox comboBox;

    public static void main(String[] args) {
        JFrame frame = new JFrame("Quote XML Generator");
        frame.addWindowListener(new WindowAdapter() {
            public void windowClosing(WindowEvent e) {
                System.exit(0);
            }
        });

        frame.setContentPane(new XMLPBXMLApp());
        frame.pack();
        frame.setVisible(true);
    }
```

Setting objects in the Window and implementing ActionListeners

Listing 21-2 shows the code that is used to define the main UI on top of the application Window. The first task is to retrieve a unique list of quote authors from the SQL Server Authors table calling the `GetAuthorList()` class, which we will cover a bit later.

Once this is done, the `AuthorList` object is created, and an `AuthorList SelectionHandler` object is attached to the list. When users click on a quote author, the `AuthorListSelectionHandler` class is called to handle the action. Next, a `JscrollPane` called `SourcePane` is created for the list object, and the pane is placed in the top left of the application window.

The instantiation steps are repeated for the `QuoteList` object, which will be used to display quotes for a selected author on the top right of the application window. A `QuoteListSelectionHandler` object is attached to the quote list.

Next, a drop-down combo box containing the application output options is created, which will be located in the center of the Application window, just below the author list and quote list panes. The hard-coded output options are defined and the default is set to the first object.

The last step is for a `JtextArea` object to be defined and placed in the bottom half of the application window. This is where the XML and text output is sent when a user selects a quote from the quote list.

The balance of the code in Listing 21-2 is Swing and AWT class housekeeping to create the details of the layout that the user interface needs.

Listing 21-2: **Setting Objects in the Window and Implementing ActionListeners**

```
public XMLPBXMLApp() {
    super(new BorderLayout());


    listData = GetAuthorList();
    String[] WelcomeMessage={"Click on a Source in the Left Pane to
    Retrieve Quotes"};

    authorList = new JList(listData);

    authorListSelectionModel = authorList.getSelectionModel();
    authorListSelectionModel.addListSelectionListener(
```

Continued

Listing 21-2 *(continued)*

```java
new authorListSelectionHandler());
JScrollPane SourcePane = new JScrollPane(authorList);

QuoteList = new JList(WelcomeMessage);
QuotelistSelectionModel = QuoteList.getSelectionModel();
QuotelistSelectionModel.addListSelectionListener(
new QuoteListSelectionHandler());
JScrollPane QuotePane = new JScrollPane(QuoteList);

JPanel OutputSelectionPane = new JPanel();
String[] OutputFormats = { "Just the Quote", "Element XML
(Table=Root, Field Name=Element)",
"Attribute XML (Table=Element, Field Name=Attribute)"};

comboBox = new JComboBox(OutputFormats);
comboBox.setSelectedIndex(0);
OutputSelectionPane.add(new JLabel("Select an output Format:"));
OutputSelectionPane.add(comboBox);

output = new JTextArea(1, 10);
output.setEditable(false);
output.setLineWrap(true);
JScrollPane outputPane = new JScrollPane(output,
ScrollPaneConstants.VERTICAL_SCROLLBAR_ALWAYS,
ScrollPaneConstants.HORIZONTAL_SCROLLBAR_AS_NEEDED);

JSplitPane splitPane = new JSplitPane(JSplitPane.VERTICAL_SPLIT);
add(splitPane, BorderLayout.CENTER);

JPanel TopPanel = new JPanel();
TopPanel.setLayout(new BoxLayout(TopPanel, BoxLayout.X_AXIS));
JPanel SourceContainer = new JPanel(new GridLayout(1,1));
SourceContainer.setBorder(BorderFactory.createTitledBorder(
"Source List"));
SourceContainer.add(SourcePane);
SourcePane.setPreferredSize(new Dimension(300, 100));
JPanel QuoteContainer = new JPanel(new GridLayout(1,1));
QuoteContainer.setBorder(BorderFactory.createTitledBorder(
"Quote List"));
QuoteContainer.add(QuotePane);
QuotePane.setPreferredSize(new Dimension(300, 500));
TopPanel.setBorder(BorderFactory.createEmptyBorder(5,5,0,5));
TopPanel.add(SourceContainer);
TopPanel.add(QuoteContainer);

TopPanel.setMinimumSize(new Dimension(400, 50));
TopPanel.setPreferredSize(new Dimension(400, 300));
splitPane.add(TopPanel);
```

```
        JPanel BottomPanel = new JPanel(new BorderLayout());
        BottomPanel.add(OutputSelectionPane, BorderLayout.NORTH);
        BottomPanel.add(outputPane, BorderLayout.CENTER);
        BottomPanel.setMinimumSize(new Dimension(400, 50));
        BottomPanel.setPreferredSize(new Dimension(800, 400));
        splitPane.add(BottomPanel);
    }
```

Listings 21-3 and 21-4 show the AWT Class `ActionListeners`, which facilitates the UI functionality in the application.

Defining the action for the source list

Listing 21-3 shows the code that is called when a user clicks on a quote author. When the `ActionListener` detects that the user has selected a quote author, the `GetSingleAuthorList` class is called, which returns a single-column listing of quotes for that author. The quotes are displayed in the quote list object on the top right of the application window.

Listing 21-3: **Defining the Action for the Author List**

```
class authorListSelectionHandler implements ListSelectionListener {
        public void valueChanged(ListSelectionEvent se) {
            ListSelectionModel slsm = (ListSelectionModel)se.getSource();
            String [] s =
            GetSingleAuthorList(authorList.getSelectedValue().toString());
            QuoteList.setListData(s);

        }
    }
```

Defining the action for the quote list

When a user selects a quote by clicking on a selection in the quote list, the code in Listing 21-4 is called. When the `ActionListener` detects that the user has selected a Quote, the `QuoteListSelectionHandler` checks the combo box to see which output format is selected by the user.

If `"Just the Quote"` is selected, the quote is sent to the output object as text. If the `"Element XML (Table=Root, Field Name=Element)"` option is chosen, the GetSingleQuoteElement class is called to generate Custom XML for the output, with SQL Server table column values formatted as elements in the XML document. If "Attribute XML (Table=Element, Field Name=Attribute)" is chosen, the GetSingleQuoteAttribute is called to generate result set table column values as attributes.

Listing 21-4: Defining the Actions for the Quote List

```
class QuoteListSelectionHandler implements ListSelectionListener {
    public void valueChanged(ListSelectionEvent qe) {
        ListSelectionModel qlsm = (ListSelectionModel)qe.getSource();
        String OutputFormatChoice = (String)comboBox.getSelectedItem();

        if (OutputFormatChoice.equals("Just the Quote")) {
            output.setText(QuoteList.getSelectedValue().toString());
        }

        else if (OutputFormatChoice.equals("Element XML (Table=Root,
        Field Name=Element)")) {
            output.setText(GetSingleQuoteElement
            (QuoteList.getSelectedValue().toString(
            ))); }
        else if (OutputFormatChoice.equals("Attribute XML
        (Table=Element, Field Name=Attribute)")) {
            output.setText(GetSingleQuoteAttribute
            (QuoteList.getSelectedValue().toString()));}
        else {
            output.setText(QuoteList.getSelectedValue().toString());
        }

    }
}
```

Retrieving a list of authors from the Authors table via JDBC

The code in Listing 21-5 returns a unique listing of quote authors from the Authors table of the XMLProgrammingBible SQL Server database. The code starts by defining an array for the list of authors and a string containing a hard-coded SQL Server query. Next, an MS SQL Server JDBC driver instance is created. A connection is defined to the SQL Server instance. In this case, we're running the SQL Server instance and the J2EE application on the same machine, so the IP address is the home IP address of the machine - 127.0.0.1. The JDBC user and password for the database are set up in the connection string. Because the XMLProgramming Bible database is specified in the connection string, we don't need to explicitly name the database in our SQL server query.

A JDBC result set object is created, which is the result of the query string passed to the SQL server. An array is built from the result set with the buildArray class, which we'll show you in the next listing. Once the result set is processed, the connection and the result set are dropped. The contents of the author list object are created by the array and passed to the application window.

Note The port (1433) is designated, and the User and Password are predefined. Review the setup section earlier in this chapter for instructions on preparing to run SQL server and the JDBC driver if you have not already done so.

Listing 21-5: Retrieving a List of Authors from the SQL Server Authors Table

```
public String [] GetAuthorList() {
    String authorList [] = null;
    String sql = "select AuthorName from Authors";

    try {

        Class.forName("com.microsoft.jdbc.sqlserver.SQLServerDriver");
        Connection conn = DriverManager.getConnection("jdbc:microsoft:
        sqlserver://127.0.0.1:1433;User=jdbcUser;Password=jdbcUser;
        DatabaseName=XMLProgrammingBible");
        Statement s = conn.createStatement();
        ResultSet rs = s.executeQuery(sql);
        authorList = buildArray(rs);

        rs.close();
        conn.close();
    } catch(Exception e) {
        e.printStackTrace();
    }

    return authorList ;

}
```

Listing 21-6 shows the buildArray class that is used by the GetAuthorList and GetSingleAuthorList classes to build an array from an SQL Server JDBC result set. An ArrayList is created, which is an implementation of the List interface. The most important feature of ArrayLists for the purposes of this code is that they are automatically resizable, via the add() method.

Note   We have explicitly specified `java.util.List` because the `java.awt` package also has a List interface.

The JDBC specification contains a `.toArray()` method for result sets, which would be great for this purpose. However, not all JDBC drivers implement a complete set of methods for JDBC classes. The code in the `buildArray` class can be used when the `toArray()` method is not supported, as is the case with the MS SQL Server JDBC driver, or when you want all JDBC result set array output to be the same regardless of driver-specific formatting.

An SQL Server result set is passed from the calling object and an `ArrayList` is defined called `arrayResults`. The code loops through the result set and retrieves the current result set row value as a string. SQL Server result set values returned by the SQL Server JDBC driver sometimes contain leading and trailing blanks, so the trim() method is sued to trim spaces off the string as it is created. The string is added to the `arrayResults` object using the `ArrayList.add()` method. Next, a string array called `sarray` is created, and the value of the `ArrayList` is passed to the string array using the `ArrayList.toArray()` method.

Listing 21-6: Building an Array for the Source and Quote lists

```
String[] buildArray(ResultSet rs) {
    java.util.List arrayResults = new ArrayList();
    try {
        int rownumber= 0;
        String rowvalue = new String();
        while(rs.next()) {
            rownumber++;
            rowvalue = rs.getString(rownumber++);
            arrayResults.add(rowvalue.trim());
        }
    }catch(Exception e) {}
    String[] sarray = (String[]) arrayResults.toArray(new
    String[arrayResults.size()]);
    return sarray;
}
```

Retrieving a list of quotes from a selected author

When a user clicks on a quote author, the `ActionListener` for the author list object passes the author name as a string value to the `GetSingleAuthorList` Class, shown in Listing 21-7. This class uses the passed value, called `CategoryName`, to retrieve all the quotes for an author using an SQL query passed to the server via JDBC. A single-dimension array based on the quotes for the author is passed to the quote list object using the `buildArray` class, which is shown in Listing 21-7. The contents of the quote list object are then created by the array and the quote list object is displayed in the upper-right panel of the application window.

Listing 21-7: Retrieving Quotes for an Author

```
public String [] GetSingleAuthorList(String CategoryName) {
    String singleauthorList [] = null;
    String sql = "SELECT dbo.Quotations.Quotation FROM dbo.Quotations
    INNER JOIN dbo.Authors ON dbo.Quotations.AuthorID =
    dbo.Authors.AuthorID INNER JOIN dbo.Sources ON
    dbo.Quotations.SourceID = dbo.Sources.SourceID WHERE
    (dbo.Authors.AuthorName = '"+CategoryName+"')";
    String fromrow="1";
    String torow="50";
    String threshold="50";

    try {

        Class.forName("com.microsoft.jdbc.sqlserver.SQLServerDriver");
        Connection conn =  DriverManager.getConnection
        ("jdbc:microsoft:sqlserver://127.0.0.1:1433;
        User=jdbcUser;Password=jdbcUser;DatabaseName=XMLProgrammingBible");
        Statement s = conn.createStatement();
        ResultSet rs = s.executeQuery(sql);
        singleauthorList = buildArray(rs);

        rs.close();
        conn.close();
    } catch(Exception e) {
        e.printStackTrace();
    }

    return singleauthorList ;

}
```

Generating Custom XML Output

Users clicking on one of the quotes trigger a call to the `QuoteListSelection Handler`, which is outlined in Listing 21-4. This triggers one of three actions, depending on the output format chosen in the combo box. The first action is to send the plain text directly to the output object. The code in Listing 21-8 is called when a quote is selected in the quote list object and the `Element XML (Table=Root, Field Name=Element)` option is chosen from the output format combo box. The Quote text is passed to the GetSingleQuoteElement class. This class generates another JDBC query to the SQL Server instance. The query returns a result set containing all of the columns in the quotations table related to the selected quote.

Next, the result set and the SQL query string are passed to the `buildElementXML` class, which is used to build an XML document. The `buildElementXML` class is shown in Listing 21-9.

Listing 21-8: **The GetSingleQuoteElement Class**

```
public String GetSingleQuoteElement(String PassedQuote) {
        String XMLDoc=null;

        String sql = "SELECT dbo.Quotations.Quotation,
        dbo.Authors.AuthorName, dbo.Sources.[Source Name] FROM
        dbo.Quotations INNER JOIN dbo.Authors ON dbo.Quotations.AuthorID =
        dbo.Authors.AuthorID INNER JOIN dbo.Sources ON
        dbo.Quotations.SourceID = dbo.Sources.SourceID WHERE
        (dbo.Quotations.Quotation = '"+PassedQuote+"')";


        try {

            Class.forName("com.microsoft.jdbc.sqlserver.SQLServerDriver");
            Connection conn =  DriverManager.getConnection
            ("jdbc:microsoft:sqlserver://127.0.0.1:1433;
             User=jdbcUser;Password=jdbcUser;
             DatabaseName=XMLProgrammingBible");
            Statement s = conn.createStatement();
            ResultSet rs = s.executeQuery(sql);
            XMLDoc = buildElementXML(rs, sql);

            rs.close();
            conn.close();
        } catch(Exception e) {
            e.printStackTrace();
        }

        return XMLDoc ;

    }
```

Listing 21-9 shows the buildElementXML class that is used to create a custom element-based XML document for the SQL Server output. We could have used an SQLXML format for our output at this point. Producing SQLXML output would have needed less code, but would probably result in maintenance issue when a new version of SQLXML is released that changes the format of the output passed to this application. Also, if for some reason we want to change the data source from SQL Server to Oracle, DB2, or another RDBMS, we would have to figure out how to format the XML from the server to meet my needs. By manually writing XML at the application level based on a JDBC result set, you have complete control over the format of the XML that is produced.

The first thing the `buildElementXML` class does is create a new `StringBuffer` in which to store the XML document. An XML document declaration is sent to the `StringBuffer`, along with a root element, called `resultset`. Next, an element called `sql` is created, which contains the SQL Server query that was used to generate the result set. We also retrieve the metadata into the XML document, which can be used by applications that work with the XML document to parse the XML values by data type and column name. We also use the metadata column name to name the elements that represent columns in the XML document.

Row data is returned as children of a records element. Because this example returns a single row, a single record element contains the column values. Column values are stored in text data, and column names are represented as element names. The entityRefs class converts any illegal XML characters in the text data (&, ', >, <, and ") into legal entity references for those values.

The `buildElementXML` class retrieves the XML document from the `String Buffer` and returns the XML document to the calling object as a string.

Listing 21-9: **The buildElementXML Class**

```
String buildElementXML(ResultSet rs, String sql) {
      StringBuffer strResults = new StringBuffer("<?xml version=\"1.0\"
      encoding=\"UTF-8\"?>\r\n<resultset>\r\n");
      try {
            strResults.append("<sql>" + sql +" </sql>\r\n");
            ResultSetMetaData rsMetadata = rs.getMetaData();
            int intFields = rsMetadata.getColumnCount();
            strResults.append("<metadata>\r\n");
            for(int h =1; h <= intFields; h++) {
                  strResults.append("<field name=\"" +
                  rsMetadata.getColumnName(h) + "\" datatype=\"" +
                  rsMetadata.getColumnTypeName(h) + "\"/>\r\n");
            }
            strResults.append("</metadata>\r\n<records>\r\n");

            int rownumber= 0;
```

Continued

Listing 21-9 *(continued)*

```
        while(rs.next()) {
            rownumber++;
            strResults.append("<record
            rownumber=\""+rownumber+"\">\r\n");
            for(int i =1; i <= intFields; i++) {
                strResults.append("<" + rsMetadata.getColumnName(i) +
                ">" + entityRefs(rs.getString(i).trim()) +
                "</"+rsMetadata.getColumnName(i) +">\r\n");
            }
            strResults.append("</record>\r\n");
        }
    }catch(Exception e) {}
    strResults.append("</records>\r\n</resultset>");
    System.out.println(strResults.toString());
    return strResults.toString();
}
```

Listing 21-10 shows the entityRefs and the stringReplace classes. These classes are used to format text output from SQL Server into legal XML characters by replacing non-XML characters with entity references. Two string arrays are created. The first array contains illegal XML characters. The second array contains equivalent entity references. The entityRefs class calls the stringReplace class to replace any characters found with their entity reference equivalents.

Listing 21-10: **The entityRefs and the stringReplace Classes**

```
String entityRefs(String XMLString) {
    String[] before = {"&","\'",">","<","\""};
    String[] after = {"&amp;","&apos;","&gt;","&lt;","&quot;"};
    if(XMLString!=null) {
        for(int i=0;i<before.length;i++) {
            XMLString = stringReplace(XMLString, before[i], after[i]);
        }
    }else {XMLString="";}
    return XMLString;
}

String stringReplace(String stringtofix, String textstring,
String xmlstring) {
    int position = stringtofix.indexOf(textstring);
    while (position > -1) {
        stringtofix = stringtofix.substring(0,position) + xmlstring +
        stringtofix.substring(position+textstring.length());
```

```
        position = stringtofix.indexOf
          (textstring,position+xmlstring.length());
      }
      return stringtofix;
  }
```

Listing 21-11 shows what the Element XML output looks like for a quote in the application:

Listing 21-11: Custom XML Output Generated by the GetSingleQuoteElement Class

```xml
<?xml version="1.0" encoding="UTF-8"?>
<resultset>
  <sql>SELECT dbo.Quotations.Quotation, dbo.Authors.AuthorName,
  dbo.Sources.[Source Name] FROM dbo.Quotations INNER JOIN dbo.Authors ON
  dbo.Quotations.AuthorID = dbo.Authors.AuthorID INNER JOIN dbo.Sources ON
  dbo.Quotations.SourceID = dbo.Sources.SourceID WHERE
  (dbo.Quotations.Quotation = 'When the hurlyburlys done, When the battles
  lost and won.') </sql>
  <metadata>
    <field name="Quotation" datatype="char"/>
    <field name="AuthorName" datatype="char"/>
    <field name="Source Name" datatype="char"/>
  </metadata>
  <records>
    <record rownumber="1">
      <Quotation>When the hurlyburlys done, When the battles lost and
      won.</Quotation>
      <AuthorName>Shakespeare, William</AuthorName>
      <SourceName>Macbeth</SourceName>
    </record>
  </records>
</resultset>
```

Listing 21-12 is called when a user clicks on a quote and the `Attribute` XML (`Table=Element, Field Name=Attribute`) option is chosen from the output format combo box. The Quote text is passed to the `GetSingleQuoteAttribute` class. This class generates another JDBC query to the SQL Server instance. The query returns a result set containing all of the columns in the quotations Table related to the selected quote.

Next, the result set and the SQL query string are passed to the `buildAttribute` `XML` class, which is used to build an XML document. The `buildAttributeXML` class is shown in Listing 21-13.

Listing 21-12: **The GetSingleQuoteAttribute Class**

```
public String GetSingleQuoteAttribute(String PassedQuote) {
     String XMLDoc=null;

     String sql = "SELECT dbo.Quotations.Quotation,
     dbo.Authors.AuthorName, dbo.Sources.[Source Name] FROM
     dbo.Quotations INNER JOIN dbo.Authors ON dbo.Quotations.AuthorID =
     dbo.Authors.AuthorID INNER JOIN dbo.Sources ON
     dbo.Quotations.SourceID = dbo.Sources.SourceID WHERE
     (dbo.Quotations.Quotation = '"+PassedQuote.trim()+"')";

     try {

         Class.forName("com.microsoft.jdbc.sqlserver.SQLServerDriver");
         Connection conn = DriverManager.getConnection
         ("jdbc:microsoft:sqlserver://127.0.0.1:1433;
          User=jdbcUser;Password=jdbcUser;
          DatabaseName=XMLProgrammingBible");
         Statement s = conn.createStatement();
         ResultSet rs = s.executeQuery(sql);
         XMLDoc = buildAttributeXML(rs, sql);

         rs.close();
         conn.close();
     } catch(Exception e) {
         e.printStackTrace();
     }

     return XMLDoc ;


    }


}
```

Listing 21-13 shows the `buildAttributeXML` class that is used to create a custom element-based XML document for the SQL Server output. It's very similar to the `buildElementXML` class, but this time the code produces row data as attributes of a single element, instead of nested elements under a `records` element.

The first thing the buildAttributeXML class does is create a new StringBuffer in which to store the XML document. An XML document declaration is sent to the StringBuffer, along with a root element, called resultset. Next, an element called sql is created, which contains the SQL Server query that was used to generate the result set. We also retrieve the metadata into the XML document, which can be used by applications that work with the XML document to parse the XML values by data type and column name. We also use the metadata column name to name the elements that represent columns in the XML document.

Row data is returned in a single records element. Because this example returns a single row, a single element contains all of the column values as attributes. Column values are stored in text data, and column names are represented as element names. The entityRefs class converts any illegal XML characters in the text data (&, ', >, <, and ") into legal entity references for those values.

The buildAttributeXML class retrieves the XML document from the String Buffer and returns the XML document to the calling object as a string.

Listing 21-13: **The buildAttributeXML Class**

```
String buildAttributeXML(ResultSet rs, String sql) {
        StringBuffer strResults = new StringBuffer("<?xml version=\"1.0\"
        encoding=\"UTF-8\"?>\r\n<resultset>\r\n");
        try {
            strResults.append("<sql>" + sql +" </sql>\r\n");

            ResultSetMetaData rsMetadata = rs.getMetaData();
            int intFields = rsMetadata.getColumnCount();
            strResults.append("<metadata>\r\n");
            for(int h =1; h <= intFields; h++) {
                strResults.append("<field name=\"" +
                rsMetadata.getColumnName(h) + "\" datatype=\"" +
                rsMetadata.getColumnTypeName(h) + "\"/>\r\n");
            }
            strResults.append("</metadata>\r\n<records>\r\n");


            int rownumber= 0;

            while(rs.next()) {
                rownumber++;
                strResults.append("<record rownumber=\""+rownumber+"\"");
                for(int i =1; i <= intFields; i++) {
                    strResults.append(" "+rsMetadata.getColumnName(i) + " =
                    \"" + entityRefs(rs.getString(i).trim()) + "\"");
                }
```

Continued

Listing 21-13 *(continued)*

```
            strResults.append("/>\r\n");
        }
    }catch(Exception e) {}
    strResults.append("</records>\r\n</resultset>");
    System.out.println(strResults.toString());
    return strResults.toString();

}
```

Listing 21-14 shows what the Attribute XML output looks like for a quote in the application:

Listing 21-14: **Custom XML Output Generated by the GetSingleQuoteAttribute Class**

```
<?xml version="1.0" encoding="UTF-8"?>
<resultset>
  <sql>SELECT dbo.Quotations.Quotation, dbo.Authors.AuthorName,
  dbo.Sources.[Source Name] FROM dbo.Quotations INNER JOIN dbo.Authors ON
  dbo.Quotations.AuthorID = dbo.Authors.AuthorID INNER JOIN dbo.Sources ON
  dbo.Quotations.SourceID = dbo.Sources.SourceID WHERE
  (dbo.Quotations.Quotation = 'When the hurlyburlys done, When the battles
  lost and won.') </sql>
  <metadata>
    <field name="Quotation" datatype="char"/>
    <field name="AuthorName" datatype="char"/>
    <field name="Source Name" datatype="char"/>
  </metadata>
  <records>
    <record rownumber="1" Quotation="When the hurlyburlys done, When the
    battles lost and won." AuthorName="Shakespeare, William"
    SourceName="Macbeth"/>
  </records>
</resultset>
```

XML Servlets

In general, Java has had some adoption issues in the IT marketplace, with the exception of Servlets. Java Applets have not lived up to the promise of universal, platform-independent application delivery using Web browsers as a front-end, because of performance, reliability, and compatibility issues. Java Applications require a JDK or a JVM to be loaded on a client's machine to provide any meaningful functionality, and unfortunately share the performance, reliability, and compatibility characteristics of Java Applets. Servlets, however, are a different story. Java Servlets are quickly becoming the method of choice for implementing Java solutions in enterprise environments, mainly because of the high-performance Servlet Application servers on the market that support high-volume, high-capacity transactional Websites. Servlets are a natural fit for the middle tiers of multi-tier application architectures because of their relatively good security model and multi-thread performance characteristics. Because the Java in this case is running exclusively on a server, there are less performance, distribution, and compatibility issues than the Applet and Java Application Models.

Servlets are Java Code that extends the HTTPServlet Java Class, which is the core of the Sun Java Servlet Development Kit (JSDK). Servlet class files are loaded onto a Servlet Application server and are called via Web browser requests. Every Servlet has a call method, which receives Servlet requests, and a response, which returns Servlet responses. Because of this structure and functionality, Servlets are a great tool for quickly and flexibly generating XML.

Note

We will provide some insight into how servlets work in this chapter as we go through the sample servlet code, but the chapter will focus more on XML than servlets. If you're new to servlets and would like more information, the best place to start is the servlets.com Web page, at http://servlets.com. Also, Servlets are a Java Community Process (JCP) Specification. The latest Java Specification Request (JSR) document covers the Servlets 2.4 specification, and can be found at http://web1.jcp.org/en/jsr/detail?id=154.

Example: A Three-Tier System Combining Java Applications, Servlets, and SQL Server

In this section we'll break up the Java Application that we showed you in Listings 21-1 to 21-14 and create two multi-tier servlet applications from the pieces.

The first application is a Web browser implementation that provides an HTML interface to SQL Server data. The first tier is a Web browser, which provides the client user interface to the data. The second tier is made up of four Java Servlets that use JDBC to handle requests for data from the browser and retrieve data from the third tier, which is SQL Server and its associated databases. The Web application has a more basic user interface than the Java Application. The servlets are called via URLs from a Web page and response data is directed back to a browser window instead of a Java Application Object.

The second application is a Java Application implementation that provides the same Swing and AWT interface to SQL Server data as the first application in this chapter did. The difference this time is that the first tier is a Java Application that only handles the user interface. That means that you don't need to load MS SQL Server JDBC drivers on the machine that is running the application. The JDBC drivers are used by the four application servlets on the second tier, so they only need to be loaded on the server. The third tier is SQL Server.

Prerequisites for Servlet Development

It probably goes without saying that multi-tier applications are harder to develop than single-tier applications. The biggest factor is all of the "moving parts." You usually need a client platform, one or more middle-tier platforms, and a server tier.

Servlets run on a J2EE application server. Examples of J2EE application servers are IBM's WebSphere application server, Bea WebLogic Application Server, Sun One Application Server, and Apache Tomcat. You'll need one of these servers to use the example servlets in this chapter. The servlets need to be deployed onto the J2EE application server. Many J2EE IDEs come with an integrated J2EE Web application server that makes development, deployment, and testing of servlets much faster and easier. IDES with integrated J2EE servers include IBM's WebSphere Studio Application Developer, and the Sun ONE Studio. Check your IDE documentation to see if it provides an integrated J2EE server for servlet development and testing.

The application and servlets for this example were developed and tested using IBM's WebSphere Studio Application Developer (WSAD) 5, which is available as a trial download from http://www7b.software.ibm.com/wsdd/zones/studio. WSAD includes an integrated J2EE application server, so servlets can be developed, tested, and deployed on the same machine. We are also running Microsoft SQL Server 2000 on the same machine with the JDBC driver loaded.

 WebSphere Studio Application Developer is discussed in more detail in Chapter 36.

Introducing the XML example servlets and client application

The following files are available for download from the XMLProgrammingBible.com Website. Check with the documentation of your J2EE server for instructions on deployment and setup. Check with your JDK setup instructions for information on running the Java client application on a client machine.

 All the servlets in this example, as well as the Java Application and T-SQL commands for producing the SQL Server data, can be downloaded from the XMLProgrammingBible.com Website, in the Downloads section.

The Web example application in this chapter uses four servlets:

✦ **XMLPBWebServletGetAuthorList** gets a list of quote authors from the SQL Server Authors table.

✦ **XMLPBWebServletGetSingleAuthorList** gets a list of quotes for a single quote author that a user selects via a URL.

✦ **XMLPBWebServletBuildElementXML** returns a Quote in XML format with nested elements from row data to a Web browser.

✦ **XMLPBWebServletBuildAttributeXML** returns a Quote in XML format with attributes created from row data to a Web browser.

The multi-tier Java Application uses four servlets and one client application:

✦ **XMLPBAppServletGetAuthorList** gets a list of quote authors from the SQL Server Authors table.

✦ **XMLPBAppServletGetSingleAuthorList** gets a list of quotes for a single quote author that a user selects in the Java Application.

✦ **XMLPBAppServletBuildElementXML** returns a Quote in XML format with nested elements from row data to the Java Application.

✦ **XMLPBAppServletBuildAttributeXML** returns a Quote in XML format with attributes created from row data to the Java Application.

✦ **XMLPBServletApp** is a Java Application that calls the above servlets to retrieve SQL Server data via JDBC.

Running the Web Example Application

Once the Web servlets have been deployed on a J2EE server, the MS SQL Server JDBC driver has been installed, and the JDBC driver is configured to access SQL Server data, start up any browser and open the following URL:

```
http://<server IP address>/servlet/XMLPBWebServletGetAuthorList
```

Caution   Most J2EE application servers are case sensitive. URLs must match file name and path case exactly. This is the first thing to check when having trouble with servlets in a Web browser environment.

It may take 10-15 seconds for the Servlet to load the first time due to servlet initialization. If everything is configured properly, you should get results like those in Figure 21-2. The `XMLPBWebServletGetAuthorList` Servlet displays a unique list of quote authors, formatted as URL links.

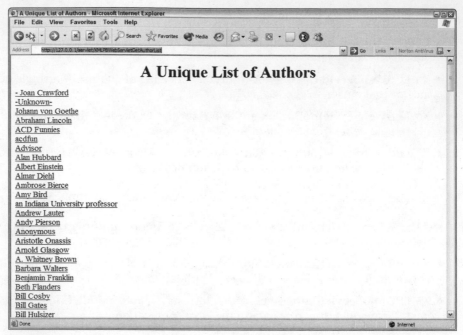

Figure 21-2: The output for the XMLPBWebServletGetAuthorList servlet, displaying a list of authors as links

Clicking on one of the links calls the XMLPBWebServletGetSingleAuthorList Servlet that generates a list of quotes for a specific author. The author is determined by a value that is passed in the link to the servlet. The links look like this to a Browser:

```
<A HREF=/servlet/XMLPBWebServletGetSingleAuthorList?CategoryName=Dave+Barry
>Dave Barry</A>
```

Figure 21-3 shows the links for Dave Barry.

Under each quote are two links, Element XML to Screen, and Attribute XML to Screen. The Element XML to Screen option calls the XMLPBWebServlet BuildElementXML Servlet to return the associated quote in a Custom XML Format. This is what the link looks like for the first Quote in Figure 21-3:

```
<A HREF=/servlet/ XMLPBWebServletBuildElementXML?PassedQuote=There+is+a
very+fine+line+between+hobby+and+mental+illness.>Element XML to Screen</A>
```

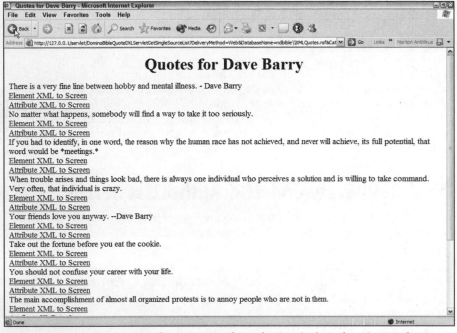

Figure 21-3: The output for the XMLPBWebServletGetSingleAuthorList Servlet, displaying a list of quotes for Dave Barry

The `Attribute XML to Screen` option calls the `XMLPBWebServletBuild AttributeXML` Servlet to return the associated Quote in another form of custom XML format. Here's what this link looks like:

```
<A HREF=/servlet/ XMLPBWebServletBuildAttributeXML?PassedQuote=There+is+a
very+fine+line+between+hobby+and+mental+illness.>Element XML to Screen</A>
```

Removing spaces from parameters

You may have noticed that the URL parameter references have a + where spaces usually are. When a value is passed as a parameter via HTTP, the parser in the application that receives the information stops at the first space it encounters, because it is expecting a constant stream of data, and a space indicates the end of a value. Therefore, spaces have to be removed from passed parameters. For example, `Dave+Barry` is received by a servlet as `Dave+Barry` and the spaces can be replaced using a simple one-line `String.replace` method in Java. However, `Dave Barry` (without the +) is parsed as just `Dave`, and will not match the correct value when re-sent as a parameter to a servlet.

Under the Hood of the Web Application Servlets

The four servlets that make up the Web application that retrieves and displays quotes from SQL Server data are adaptations of the classes that we created for the regular Java Application earlier in this chapter. In this section we'll go under the hood of each servlet to show how they work. After that we'll introduce you to the servlets that are part of the multi-tier Java Application and point out the key differences between the servlets.

The XMLPBWebServletGetAuthorList Servlet

The servlet in Listing 21-15 returns a unique listing of quote authors from the Authors table in the SQL Server XMLProgrammingBible database.

Listing 21-15: The XMLPBWebServletGetAuthorList Servlet Code

```
import java.util.*;
import java.io.*;
import javax.servlet.*;
import javax.servlet.http.*;
import java.sql.*;

public class XMLPBWebServletGetAuthorList extends HttpServlet {


    public void doGet(HttpServletRequest request,
    HttpServletResponse response)
    throws IOException, ServletException {

        String [] AuthorList = GetAuthorList();

        response.setContentType("text/html");
        PrintWriter out = response.getWriter();
        String title = "A Unique List of Quote Sources";
        out.println("<HTML><HEAD><TITLE>"+ title +"</TITLE></HEAD>");
        out.println("<BODY><H1 ALIGN=CENTER>" + title + "</H1>");
        for (int i= 0 ; i < AuthorList.length; i++) {
            String sl=AuthorList[i].replace(' ','+');
            out.print("<A
            HREF=/servlet/XMLPBWebServletAppGetSingleAuthorList");
            out.print("?CategoryName="+sl+">"+AuthorList[i]+"</A><br>");
        }
```

```java
        out.println("</BODY></HTML>");
        out.close();
    }

    public String [] GetAuthorList() {
        String authorList [] = null;
        String sql = "select AuthorName from Authors";

        try {

            Class.forName("com.microsoft.jdbc.sqlserver.SQLServerDriver");
            Connection conn =
            DriverManager.getConnection("jdbc:microsoft:sqlserver:
            //127.0.0.1:1433;User=jdbcUser;Password=jdbcUser;DatabaseName
            =XMLProgrammingBible");
            Statement s = conn.createStatement();
            ResultSet rs = s.executeQuery(sql);

            authorList = buildArray(rs);

            rs.close();
            conn.close();
        }catch(Exception e) {
            e.printStackTrace();
        }

        return authorList ;

    }


    String[] buildArray(ResultSet rs) {
        java.util.List arrayResults = new ArrayList();
        try {
            int rownumber= 0;
            String rowvalue = new String();
            while(rs.next()) {
                rownumber++;
                rowvalue = rs.getString(rownumber++);
                arrayResults.add(rowvalue.trim());
            }
        }catch(Exception e) {}
        String[] sarray = (String[]) arrayResults.toArray(new
        String[arrayResults.size()]);
        return sarray;
    }


}
```

This servlet starts with standard servlet code constructs. A doGet creates the request and response object that is used to retrieve parameters and return data. The next step is to call the `GetAuthorList` class, which returns an array of unique quote authors. This is actually just a copy of the array that was used in the previous Java Application example, but this time the class returns data that will be formatted as HTML.

```
public String [] GetAuthorList() {
```

For Web browser output, the `response.setContentType` is set to "text/html." Next, an instance of the `PrintWriter` class is created. Next, the code generates HTML to add a Browser window title from the HTML head object, then an HTML title for the Web page.

```
response.setContentType("text/html");
PrintWriter out = response.getWriter();
String title = "A Unique List of Quote Sources";
out.println("<HTML><HEAD><TITLE>"+ title +"</TITLE></HEAD>");
out.println("<BODY><H1 ALIGN=CENTER>" + title + "</H1>");
```

Once the basic page layout is set up, The code cycles through the array that was created by the `GetAuthorList` class to generate a URL for each of the unique quote authors in the array and display the URL as a link on the page. Each link calls the `XMLPBWebServletAppGetSingleAuthorList` servlet and passes the author displayed in the link as a parameter named `CategoryName`. CategoryName is based on the unique author name. It is used to retrieve a list of quotes for that author from the SQL Server `Quotations` table.

```
for (int i= 0 ; i < AuthorList.length; i++) {
        String sl=AuthorList[i].replace(' ','+');
        out.print("<A
        HREF=/servlet/XMLPBWebServletAppGetSingleAuthorList");
        out.print("?CategoryName="+sl+">"+AuthorList[i]+"</A><br>");
}
        out.println("</BODY></HTML>");
        out.close();

}
```

The XMLPBWebServletAppGetSingleAuthorList Servlet

The `XMLPBWebServletAppGetSingleAuthorList` Servlet (Listing 21-16) is called when a user clicks on an Author link from a Web browser. The URL that is sent to the Servlet passes the `CategoryName` as a parameter, and returns an array of quotes for an author back to the Web browser.

Listing 21-16: The XMLPBWebServletAppGetSingleAuthorList Servlet Code

```java
import java.util.*;
import java.io.*;
import javax.servlet.*;
import javax.servlet.http.*;
import java.sql.*;

public class XMLPBWebServletGetSingleAuthorList extends HttpServlet {


    public void doGet(HttpServletRequest request,
    HttpServletResponse response)
    throws IOException, ServletException {

        String CategoryName=request.getParameter("CategoryName");

        String [] SingleAuthorList = GetSingleAuthorList(CategoryName);

        response.setContentType("text/html");
        PrintWriter out = response.getWriter();
        String title = "Quotes for "+CategoryName.replace('+',' ');
        out.println("<HTML><HEAD><TITLE>"+ title +"</TITLE></HEAD>");
        out.println("<BODY><H1 ALIGN=CENTER>" + title + "</H1>");
        for (int i= 0 ; i < SingleAuthorList.length; i++) {
            String sl=SingleAuthorList[i].replace(' ','+');
            out.print(SingleAuthorList[i]+"<br>");

            out.print("<A HREF=/servlet/XMLPBWebServletBuildElementXML");
            out.print("?PassedQuote="+sl+">Element XML to Screen</A><br>");

            out.print("<A HREF=/servlet/XMLPBWebServletBuildAttributeXML");
            out.print("?PassedQuote="+sl+">Attribute XML To
            Screen</A><br>");


        out.println("</BODY></HTML>");
        out.close();
    }


}

public String [] GetSingleAuthorList(String CategoryName) {
    String singleauthorList [] = null;
```

Continued

Listing 21-16 *(continued)*

```
String sql = "SELECT dbo.Quotations.Quotation FROM dbo.Quotations INNER
JOIN dbo.Authors ON dbo.Quotations.AuthorID = dbo.Authors.AuthorID
INNER JOIN dbo.Sources ON dbo.Quotations.SourceID =
dbo.Sources.SourceID WHERE (dbo.Authors.AuthorName =
'"+CategoryName+"')";

    try {

        Class.forName("com.microsoft.jdbc.sqlserver.SQLServerDriver");
        Connection conn =
        DriverManager.getConnection("jdbc:microsoft:sqlserver:
        //127.0.0.1:1433;User=jdbcUser;Password=jdbcUser;
        DatabaseName=XMLProgrammingBible");
        Statement s = conn.createStatement();
        ResultSet rs = s.executeQuery(sql);
        singleauthorList = buildArray(rs);

        rs.close();
        conn.close();
    }catch(Exception e) {
        e.printStackTrace();
    }

    return singleauthorList ;

}


String[] buildArray(ResultSet rs) {
    java.util.List arrayResults = new ArrayList();
    try {
        int rownumber= 0;
        String rowvalue = new String();
        while(rs.next()) {
            rownumber++;
            rowvalue = rs.getString(rownumber++);
            arrayResults.add(rowvalue.trim());
        }
    }catch(Exception e) {}
    String[] sarray = (String[]) arrayResults.toArray(new
String[arrayResults.size()]);
    return sarray;
}


}
```

Like the previous servlet, this servlet also returns data to a Web browser as well, but instead of a single link for each quote, this time two links are sent to the screen using the following code:

```
for (int i= 0 ; i < SingleAuthorList.length; i++) {
String sl=SingleAuthorList[i].replace(' ','+');
out.print(SingleAuthorList[i]+"<br>");

out.print("<A HREF=/servlet/XMLPBWebServletBuildElementXML");
out.print("?PassedQuote="+sl+">Element XML to Screen</A><br>");

out.print("<A HREF=/servlet/XMLPBWebServletBuildAttributeXML");
out.print("?PassedQuote="+sl+">Attribute XML To
Screen</A><br>");
```

If the user clicks on the first link, the XMLPBWebServletBuildElementXML is called. If the second link is chosen, the XMLPBWebServletBuildAttributeXML servlet is called. Both are passed the PassedQuote parameter, which represents the actual quote from the Web page. The GetSingleAuthorList class is the same class that was used in the Java Application earlier in this chapter. This class uses the CategoryName to retrieve all the quotes for that quote source. Once the array has been created, it is passed back to the servlet's doGet to be formatted for the Web via the PrintWriter Class.

The SQL Server query string uses the CategoryName parameter to complete the SQL query that will be set to the server:

```
String sql = "SELECT dbo.Quotations.Quotation FROM dbo.Quotations INNER
JOIN dbo.Authors ON dbo.Quotations.AuthorID = dbo.Authors.AuthorID
INNER JOIN dbo.Sources ON dbo.Quotations.SourceID =
dbo.Sources.SourceID WHERE (dbo.Authors.AuthorName =
'"+CategoryName+"')";
```

The XMLPBWebServletBuildElementXML Servlet

The code in Listing 21-17 is called when a Quote is selected by clicking on the "Element XML to Screen" link from a Web browser.

Listing 21-17: **The XMLPBWebServletBuildElementXML Servlet Code**

```
import java.util.*;
import java.io.*;
import javax.servlet.*;
```

Continued

Listing 21-17 *(continued)*

```java
import javax.servlet.http.*;
import java.sql.*;

public class XMLPBWebServletBuildElementXML extends HttpServlet {

    public void doGet(HttpServletRequest request,
    HttpServletResponse response)
    throws IOException, ServletException {

        String PassedQuote=request.getParameter("PassedQuote");
        String XMLQuote = GetSingleQuoteElement(PassedQuote);

        response.setContentType("text/xml");
        PrintWriter out = response.getWriter();
        out.println(XMLQuote);
        out.close();

    }

    public String GetSingleQuoteElement(String PassedQuote) {
        String XMLDoc=null;

        String sql = "SELECT dbo.Quotations.Quotation,
        dbo.Authors.AuthorName, dbo.Sources.[Source Name]
        FROM dbo.Quotations INNER JOIN dbo.Authors ON
        dbo.Quotations.AuthorID = dbo.Authors.AuthorID INNER JOIN
        dbo.Sources ON dbo.Quotations.SourceID = dbo.Sources.SourceID WHERE
        (dbo.Quotations.Quotation = '"+PassedQuote+"')";
        String fromrow="1";
        String torow="50";
        String threshold="50";

        try {

            Class.forName("com.microsoft.jdbc.sqlserver.SQLServerDriver");
            Connection conn =  DriverManager.getConnection
            ("jdbc:microsoft:sqlserver://127.0.0.1:1433;
            User=jdbcUser;Password=jdbcUser;DatabaseName=XMLProgrammingBible");
            Statement s = conn.createStatement();
            ResultSet rs = s.executeQuery(sql);
            XMLDoc = buildElementXML(rs, sql);

            rs.close();
            conn.close();
        } catch(Exception e) {
            e.printStackTrace();
        }
```

```java
        return XMLDoc ;

}


String buildElementXML(ResultSet rs, String sql) {
    StringBuffer strResults = new StringBuffer("<?xml version=\"1.0\"
    encoding=\"UTF-8\"?>\r\n<resultset>\r\n");
    try {
        strResults.append("<sql>" + sql +" </sql>\r\n");
        ResultSetMetaData rsMetadata = rs.getMetaData();
        int intFields = rsMetadata.getColumnCount();
        strResults.append("<metadata>\r\n");
        for(int h =1; h <= intFields; h++) {
            strResults.append("<field name=\"" +
            rsMetadata.getColumnName(h) + "\" datatype=\"" +
            rsMetadata.getColumnTypeName(h) + "\"/>\r\n");
        }
        strResults.append("</metadata>\r\n<records>\r\n");

        int rownumber= 0;
        while(rs.next()) {
            rownumber++;
            strResults.append("<record
            rownumber=\""+rownumber+"\">\r\n");
            for(int i =1; i <= intFields; i++) {
                strResults.append("<" + rsMetadata.getColumnName(i) +
                ">" + entityRefs(rs.getString(i).trim()) +
                "</"+rsMetadata.getColumnName(i) +">\r\n");
            }
            strResults.append("</record>\r\n");
        }
    }catch(Exception e) {}
    strResults.append("</records>\r\n</resultset>");
    System.out.println(strResults.toString());
    return strResults.toString();
}

String entityRefs(String XMLString) {
    String[] before = {"&","\'",">","<","\""};
    String[] after = {"&amp;","&apos;","&gt;","&lt;","&quot;"};
    if(XMLString!=null) {
        for(int i=0;i<before.length;i++) {
            XMLString = stringReplace(XMLString, before[i], after[i]);
        }
    }else {XMLString="";}
    return XMLString;
}
```

Continued

Listing 21-17 *(continued)*

```
String stringReplace(String stringtofix, String textstring, String
xmlstring) {
    int position = stringtofix.indexOf(textstring);
    while (position > -1) {
        stringtofix = stringtofix.substring(0,position) + xmlstring +
        stringtofix.substring(position+textstring.length());
        position =
        stringtofix.indexOf(textstring,position+xmlstring.length());
    }
    return stringtofix;
}

}
```

This time the output is not HTML. The output is formatted as XML for display on the Web browser screen. Consequently, the Web output option is much simpler than the previous two examples. The content type to `text/xml` instead of the previous type, `text/html`. Once this is done the string that was generated by the `GetSingleQuoteElement` class is retrieved and returned to the Web as a string.

```
response.setContentType("text/xml");
PrintWriter out = response.getWriter();
out.println(XMLQuote);
out.close();
```

The BuildElementXML, entityRefs, and stringReplace classes are copied of the classes that were used in the previous Java Application example. They format a quotation that is extracted from the SQL Server quotations table as XML, based on a structure of nested XML elements for each row of data in the result set.

The XMLPBWebServletBuildAttributeXML Servlet

The code in Listing 21-18 is called when a quote is selected by clicking on the "Attribute XML to Screen" link from a Web browser. As in the previous example, the output it text formatted as XML, so the content type is set to "text/xml." Once this is done, a string is generated by the buildAttributeXML class. The new string is returned to the Web as an XML document.

The `buildAttributeXML`, `entityRefs`, and `stringReplace` classes are copies of the classes with the same name from the previous Java example. Once the XML output string has been created, it is passed back to the servlet's `doGet` to be formatted for the Web via the `PrintWriter` class.

Listing 21-18: **The XMLPBWebServletBuildAttributeXML Code**

```java
import java.util.*;
import java.io.*;
import javax.servlet.*;
import javax.servlet.http.*;
import java.sql.*;

public class XMLPBWebServletBuildAttributeXML extends HttpServlet {


    public void doGet(HttpServletRequest request,
    HttpServletResponse response)
    throws IOException, ServletException {

        String PassedQuote=request.getParameter("PassedQuote");

        String XMLQuote = GetSingleQuoteAttribute(PassedQuote);

        response.setContentType("text/xml");
        PrintWriter out = response.getWriter();
        out.println("<?xml version=\"1.0\" encoding=\"UTF-8\" ?>");
        out.println(XMLQuote);
        out.close();

    }

    public String GetSingleQuoteAttribute(String PassedQuote) {
        String XMLDoc=null;

        String sql = "SELECT dbo.Quotations.Quotation,
        dbo.Authors.AuthorName, dbo.Sources.[Source Name] FROM
        dbo.Quotations INNER JOIN dbo.Authors ON dbo.Quotations.AuthorID =
        dbo.Authors.AuthorID INNER JOIN dbo.Sources ON
        dbo.Quotations.SourceID = dbo.Sources.SourceID WHERE
        (dbo.Quotations.Quotation = '"+PassedQuote.trim()+"')";
        String fromrow="1";
        String torow="50";
        String threshold="50";

        try {

            Class.forName("com.microsoft.jdbc.sqlserver.SQLServerDriver");
            Connection conn = DriverManager.getConnection
            ("jdbc:microsoft:sqlserver://127.0.0.1:1433;
             User=jdbcUser;Password=jdbcUser;
             DatabaseName=XMLProgrammingBible");
            Statement s = conn.createStatement();
```

Continued

Listing 21-18 *(continued)*

```java
        ResultSet rs = s.executeQuery(sql);
        XMLDoc = buildAttributeXML(rs, sql);

        rs.close();
        conn.close();
    } catch(Exception e) {
        e.printStackTrace();
    }

    return XMLDoc ;

}

String buildAttributeXML(ResultSet rs, String sql) {
    StringBuffer strResults = new StringBuffer("<?xml version=\"1.0\"
    encoding=\"UTF-8\"?>\r\n<resultset>\r\n");
    try {
        strResults.append("<sql>" + sql +" </sql>\r\n");

        ResultSetMetaData rsMetadata = rs.getMetaData();
        int intFields = rsMetadata.getColumnCount();
        strResults.append("<metadata>\r\n");
        for(int h =1; h <= intFields; h++) {
            strResults.append("<field name=\"" +
            rsMetadata.getColumnName(h) + "\" datatype=\"" +
            rsMetadata.getColumnTypeName(h) + "\"/>\r\n");
        }
        strResults.append("</metadata>\r\n<records>\r\n");


        int rownumber= 0;

        while(rs.next()) {
            rownumber++;
            strResults.append("<record rownumber=\""+rownumber+"\"");
            for(int i =1; i <= intFields; i++) {
                strResults.append(" "+rsMetadata.getColumnName(i) + " =
                \"" + entityRefs(rs.getString(i).trim()) + "\"");
            }
            strResults.append("/>\r\n");
        }
    }catch(Exception e) {}
    strResults.append("</records>\r\n</resultset>");
    System.out.println(strResults.toString());
    return strResults.toString();

}
```

```
String entityRefs(String XMLString) {
    String[] before = {"&","\'",">","<","\""};
    String[] after = {"&amp;","&apos;","&gt;","&lt;","&quot;"};
    if(XMLString!=null) {
        for(int i=0;i<before.length;i++) {
            XMLString = stringReplace(XMLString, before[i], after[i]);
        }
    }else {XMLString="";}
    return XMLString;
}


String stringReplace(String stringtofix, String textstring,
String xmlstring) {
    int position = stringtofix.indexOf(textstring);
    while (position > -1) {
        stringtofix = stringtofix.substring(0,position) + xmlstring +
        stringtofix.substring(position+textstring.length());
        position = stringtofix.indexOf(textstring,position+
        xmlstring.length());
    }
    return stringtofix;
}

}
```

A Multi-Tier Java Application

The second set of servlets that you were introduced to earlier in this chapter work with a Java Application instead of a Web browser. This Java Application example in this chapter is based on the first Java Application example that I showed you earlier in this chapter. It has been adapted as a multi-tier system by adding the ability to call servlets from the application, instead of containing all of the application code and functionality on the server. This eliminates many of the client configuration headaches associated with loading extra support classes on the client machine, such as JDBC drivers. It also provides more control over the data that is accessed, because the SQL queries are stored on the server. It also provides remedial security by moving much of the access and processing of data away from the user and onto a server.

Installing the XMLPBServletApp Java Application

The XMLPBServletApp.java application has to be installed in a directory of a workstation that is accessible to the Java JDK on the same machine, and accessible to the server that is running the servlets over a network. Once the application is downloaded, run the application by typing `java XMLPBServletApp` from a command prompt or the Windows "Run " menu option. The application will appear on the screen in its own Java window. The application is identical in function to the single-tier Java Application shown earlier in this chapter. It's what's happening behind the scenes that is probably of more interest to developers. In this section we'll show you how the servlets interact with the Java Application and SQL Server.

Under the Hood of the Multi-Tier Application Servlets

The Java Application and four servlets that make up the Quote XML Generator – Servlet Edition Application are adaptations of the classes that we created for the regular single-tier Java Application that we showed earlier in this chapter. In this section we'll go under the hood of each servlet and the application to show how they work together.

The XMLPBAppServletGetAuthorList Servlet

The code in Listing 21-19 is a servlet that returns a unique listing of authors to a Java Application. The `buildArray` class is a coy of the `buildArray` class in the single-tier Java Application.

Listing 21-19: The XMLPBAppServletGetAuthorList Servlet Code

```
import java.util.*;
import java.io.*;
import javax.servlet.*;
import javax.servlet.http.*;
import java.sql.*;

public class XMLPBAppServletGetAuthorList extends HttpServlet {


    public void doGet(HttpServletRequest request,
    HttpServletResponse response)
    throws IOException, ServletException {


        String [] AuthorList = GetAuthorList();

                response.setContentType("application/x-java-serialized-
                object");
```

```java
                ObjectOutputStream out = new
                ObjectOutputStream(response.getOutputStream());
                out.writeObject(AuthorList);
                out.flush();
            }


    public String [] GetAuthorList() {
        String authorList [] = null;
        String sql = "select AuthorName from Authors";

        try {

            Class.forName("com.microsoft.jdbc.sqlserver.SQLServerDriver");
            Connection conn =  DriverManager.getConnection(
            "jdbc:microsoft:sqlserver://127.0.0.1:1433;
             User=jdbcUser;Password=jdbcUser;
             DatabaseName=XMLProgrammingBible");
            Statement s = conn.createStatement();
            ResultSet rs = s.executeQuery(sql);

            authorList = buildArray(rs);

            rs.close();
            conn.close();
        }catch(Exception e) {
            e.printStackTrace();
        }

        return authorList ;

    }

    String[] buildArray(ResultSet rs) {
        java.util.List arrayResults = new ArrayList();
        try {
            int rownumber= 0;
            String rowvalue = new String();
            while(rs.next()) {
                rownumber++;
                rowvalue = rs.getString(rownumber++);
                arrayResults.add(rowvalue.trim());
            }
        }catch(Exception e) {}
        String[] sarray = (String[]) arrayResults.toArray(new
        String[arrayResults.size()]);
        return sarray;
    }


}
```

Instead of preparing the response object to return text for Web output, the
`XMLPBAppServletGetAuthorList` servlet returns an object to the calling application that matches the original data format specified in the application. The
`response.setContentType` is set to `application/x-java-serialized-`
`object`, which is a mime type that can support any serializable Java class. Servlets
that access the Java Application are passing arrays and strings back to the application, so this format is perfect for the needs of this application. A new instance of the
`ObjectOutputStream` is created, which in an extension of the Java `Stream` class,
instead of a `PrintWriter` or other type of `Writer` implementation. The calling
application uses an `ObjectInputStream` on the other end, which I will cover in
more detail later in the chapter. Next, the code simply writes the `AuthorList` to
the `ObjectOutputStream`, which is an array that was created by the
`GetAuthorList` class.

```
response.setContentType("application/x-java-serialized-
object");
ObjectOutputStream out = new
ObjectOutputStream(response.getOutputStream());
out.writeObject(AuthorList);
out.flush();
```

The XMLPBAppServletGetSingleAuthorList Servlet

The `XMLPBAppServletGetSingleAuthorList Servlet` in Listing 21-20 is
called when a user clicks on an author name in the Java Application. The call that
is sent to the Servlet passes the `CategoryName` as a parameter and returns an
array of quotes for the selected author. If the Servlet is being called from a Java
Application, the array representing the quote for a single author is passed to
the `ObjectOutputStream`. The `ObjectOutputStream` is passed back to the
servlet's `doGet` and then is sent back to the Java Application as an array via the
`ObjectOutputStream` class.

Listing 21-20: The XMLPBAppServletGetSingleAuthorList
Servlet Code

```
import java.util.*;
import java.io.*;
import javax.servlet.*;
import javax.servlet.http.*;
import java.sql.*;

public class XMLPBAppServletGetSingleAuthorList extends HttpServlet {

    public void doGet(HttpServletRequest request,
```

```java
HttpServletResponse response)
throws IOException, ServletException {

    String CategoryName=request.getParameter("CategoryName");

    String [] SingleAuthorList = GetSingleAuthorList(CategoryName);



        response.setContentType("application/x-java-serialized-
        object");
        ObjectOutputStream out = new
        ObjectOutputStream(response.getOutputStream());
        out.writeObject(SingleAuthorList);
        out.flush();

}

public String [] GetSingleAuthorList(String CategoryName) {
    String singleauthorList [] = null;
    String sql = "SELECT dbo.Quotations.Quotation FROM dbo.Quotations
    INNER JOIN dbo.Authors ON dbo.Quotations.AuthorID =
    dbo.Authors.AuthorID INNER JOIN dbo.Sources ON
    dbo.Quotations.SourceID = dbo.Sources.SourceID WHERE
    (dbo.Authors.AuthorName = '"+CategoryName+"')";
    String fromrow="1";
    String torow="50";
    String threshold="50";

    try {

        Class.forName("com.microsoft.jdbc.sqlserver.SQLServerDriver");
        Connection conn =
        DriverManager.getConnection("jdbc:microsoft:sqlserver://
        127.0.0.1:1433;User=jdbcUser;Password=jdbcUser;
        DatabaseName=XMLProgrammingBible");
        Statement s = conn.createStatement();
        ResultSet rs = s.executeQuery(sql);
        singleauthorList = buildArray(rs);

        rs.close();
        conn.close();
    }catch(Exception e) {
        e.printStackTrace();
    }

    return singleauthorList ;

}
```

Continued

Listing 21-20 *(continued)*

```java
String[] buildArray(ResultSet rs) {
    java.util.List arrayResults = new ArrayList();
    try {
        int rownumber= 0;
        String rowvalue = new String();
        while(rs.next()) {
            rownumber++;
            rowvalue = rs.getString(rownumber++);
            arrayResults.add(rowvalue.trim());
        }
    }catch(Exception e) {}
    String[] sarray = (String[]) arrayResults.toArray(new
    String[arrayResults.size()]);
    return sarray;
}

}
```

The XMLPBAppServletBuildElementXML Servlet

The code in Listing 21-21 is called when a quote is selected by choosing the
`Element XML (Table=Root, Field Name=Element)` option as the quote output format in the Java Application. The content type we set to `text/xml`, indicating that an XML document is being built as the servlet output. The string
representing the Single Quote in XML Format is passed from the `GetSingle`
`QuoteElement` class to the `ObjectOutputStream` via the servlet's `doGet`. Rows
of data are formatted as nested elements in the XML document structure. SQL
Server column names become XML document element names, and column values
become text data values.

**Listing 21-21: The XMLPBAppServletBuildElementXML
Servlet Code**

```java
import java.sql.*;
import java.util.*;
import java.io.*;
import javax.servlet.*;
import javax.servlet.http.*;

public class XMLPBAppServletBuildElementXML extends HttpServlet {
```

```
public void doGet(HttpServletRequest request,
HttpServletResponse response)
throws IOException, ServletException {

    String PassedQuote=request.getParameter("PassedQuote");

    String XMLQuote = GetSingleQuoteElement(PassedQuote);

    response.setContentType("application/x-java-serialized-object");
    ObjectOutputStream out = new
    ObjectOutputStream(response.getOutputStream());
    out.writeObject(XMLQuote);
    out.flush();

}

public String GetSingleQuoteElement(String PassedQuote) {
    String XMLDoc=null;

    String sql = "SELECT dbo.Quotations.Quotation,
    dbo.Authors.AuthorName, dbo.Sources.[Source Name] FROM
    dbo.Quotations INNER JOIN dbo.Authors ON dbo.Quotations.AuthorID =
    dbo.Authors.AuthorID INNER JOIN dbo.Sources ON
    dbo.Quotations.SourceID = dbo.Sources.SourceID WHERE
    (dbo.Quotations.Quotation = '"+PassedQuote+"')";
    String fromrow="1";
    String torow="50";
    String threshold="50";

    try {

        Class.forName("com.microsoft.jdbc.sqlserver.SQLServerDriver");
        Connection conn =
        DriverManager.getConnection("jdbc:microsoft:sqlserver://
        127.0.0.1:1433;User=jdbcUser;Password=jdbcUser;
        DatabaseName=XMLProgrammingBible");
        Statement s = conn.createStatement();
        ResultSet rs = s.executeQuery(sql);
        XMLDoc = buildElementXML(rs, sql);

        rs.close();
        conn.close();
    } catch(Exception e) {
        e.printStackTrace();
    }

    return XMLDoc ;

}
```

Continued

Listing 21-21 *(continued)*

```java
String buildElementXML(ResultSet rs, String sql) {
    StringBuffer strResults = new StringBuffer("<?xml version=\"1.0\"
    encoding=\"UTF-8\"?>\r\n<resultset>\r\n");
    try {
        strResults.append("<sql>" + sql +" </sql>\r\n");
        ResultSetMetaData rsMetadata = rs.getMetaData();
        int intFields = rsMetadata.getColumnCount();
        strResults.append("<metadata>\r\n");
        for(int h =1; h <= intFields; h++) {
            strResults.append("<field name=\"" +
            rsMetadata.getColumnName(h) + "\" datatype=\"" +
            rsMetadata.getColumnTypeName(h) + "\"/>\r\n");
        }
        strResults.append("</metadata>\r\n<records>\r\n");

        int rownumber= 0;
        while(rs.next()) {
            rownumber++;
            strResults.append("<record
            rownumber=\""+rownumber+"\">\r\n");
            for(int i =1; i <= intFields; i++) {
                strResults.append("<" + rsMetadata.getColumnName(i) +
                ">" + entityRefs(rs.getString(i).trim()) +
                "</"+rsMetadata.getColumnName(i) +">\r\n");

            }
            strResults.append("</record>\r\n");
        }
    }catch(Exception e) {}
    strResults.append("</records>\r\n</resultset>");
    System.out.println(strResults.toString());
    return strResults.toString();
}


String entityRefs(String XMLString) {
    String[] before = {"&","\'",">","<","\""};
    String[] after = {"&amp;","&apos;","&gl;","&lt;","&quot;"};
    if(XMLString!=null) {
        for(int i=0;i<before.length;i++) {
            XMLString = stringReplace(XMLString, before[i], after[i]);
        }
    }else {XMLString="";}
    return XMLString;
}


String stringReplace(String stringtofix, String textstring, String
xmlstring) {
    int position = stringtofix.indexOf(textstring);
```

```
        while (position > -1) {
            stringtofix = stringtofix.substring(0,position) + xmlstring +
            stringtofix.substring(position+textstring.length());
            position =
            stringtofix.indexOf(textstring,position+xmlstring.length());
        }
        return stringtofix;
    }

}
```

The XMLPBAppServletBuildAttributeXML Servlet

The code in Listing 21-22 is called when a quote is selected by choosing the
`Attribute XML (Table=Element, Field Name=Attribute)` option as the
quote output format in the Java Application. As with the last example, the content
type is set to `text/xml`, indicating that an XML document is being built as the
servlet output. The string representing the Single Quote in XML Format is passed
from the `GetSingleQuoteAttribute` class to the `ObjectOutputStream` via the
servlet's `doGet`. Rows of data are formatted as attributes in a row element in the
XML document structure. SQL Server column names become XML document
attribute names, and column values become attribute values.

**Listing 21-22: The XMLPBAppServletBuildAttributeXML
Servlet Code**

```
import java.util.*;
import java.io.*;
import javax.servlet.*;
import javax.servlet.http.*;
import java.sql.*;

public class XMLPBAppServletBuildAttributeXML extends HttpServlet {


    public void doGet(HttpServletRequest request,
    HttpServletResponse response)
    throws IOException, ServletException {

        String PassedQuote=request.getParameter("PassedQuote");

        String XMLQuote = GetSingleQuoteAttribute(PassedQuote);

        response.setContentType("application/x-java-serialized-object");
```

Continued

Listing 21-22 *(continued)*

```
        ObjectOutputStream out = new
        ObjectOutputStream(response.getOutputStream());
        out.writeObject(XMLQuote);
        out.flush();
    }

    public String GetSingleQuoteAttribute(String PassedQuote) {
        String XMLDoc=null;

        String sql = "SELECT dbo.Quotations.Quotation,
        dbo.Authors.AuthorName, dbo.Sources.[Source Name] FROM
        dbo.Quotations INNER JOIN dbo.Authors ON dbo.Quotations.AuthorID =
        dbo.Authors.AuthorID INNER JOIN dbo.Sources ON
        dbo.Quotations.SourceID = dbo.Sources.SourceID WHERE
        (dbo.Quotations.Quotation = '"+PassedQuote.trim()+"')";
        String fromrow="1";
        String torow="50";
        String threshold="50";

        try {

            Class.forName("com.microsoft.jdbc.sqlserver.SQLServerDriver");
            Connection conn =
            DriverManager.getConnection("jdbc:microsoft:sqlserver:
            //127.0.0.1:1433;User=jdbcUser;Password=jdbcUser;
            DatabaseName=XMLProgrammingBible");
            Statement s = conn.createStatement();
            ResultSet rs = s.executeQuery(sql);
            XMLDoc = buildAttributeXML(rs, sql);

            rs.close();
            conn.close();
        } catch(Exception e) {
            e.printStackTrace();
        }

        return XMLDoc ;

    }

    String buildAttributeXML(ResultSet rs, String sql) {
        StringBuffer strResults = new StringBuffer("<?xml version=\"1.0\"
        encoding=\"UTF-8\"?>\r\n<resultset>\r\n");
        try {
            strResults.append("<sql>" + sql +" </sql>\r\n");

            ResultSetMetaData rsMetadata = rs.getMetaData();
            int intFields = rsMetadata.getColumnCount();
            strResults.append("<metadata>\r\n");
```

```java
        for(int h =1; h <= intFields; h++) {
            strResults.append("<field name=\"" +
            rsMetadata.getColumnName(h) + "\" datatype=\"" +
            rsMetadata.getColumnTypeName(h) + "\"/>\r\n");
        }
        strResults.append("</metadata>\r\n<records>\r\n");


        int rownumber= 0;

        while(rs.next()) {
            rownumber++;
            strResults.append("<record rownumber=\""+rownumber+"\"");
            for(int i =1; i <= intFields; i++) {
                strResults.append(" "+rsMetadata.getColumnName(i) + " =
                \"" + entityRefs(rs.getString(i).trim()) + "\"");
            }
            strResults.append("/>\r\n");
        }
    }catch(Exception e) {}
    strResults.append("</records>\r\n</resultset>");
    System.out.println(strResults.toString());
    return strResults.toString();

}


String entityRefs(String XMLString) {
    String[] before = {"&","\'",">","<","\""};
    String[] after = {"&amp;","&apos;","&gt;","&lt;","&quot;"};
    if(XMLString!=null) {
        for(int i=0;i<before.length;i++) {
            XMLString = stringReplace(XMLString, before[i], after[i]);
        }
    }else {XMLString="";}
    return XMLString;
}

String stringReplace(String stringtofix, String textstring, String
xmlstring) {
    int position = stringtofix.indexOf(textstring);
    while (position > -1) {
        stringtofix = stringtofix.substring(0,position) + xmlstring +
        stringtofix.substring(position+textstring.length());
        position =
        stringtofix.indexOf(textstring,position+xmlstring.length());
    }
    return stringtofix;
}

}
```

Under the Hood of the XML Quote Generator — Servlet Edition Application

The Java Application in this example is based on the single-tier Java Application that was shown earlier in this chapter. There are only a few changes that need to be made to the original Java Application to adapt it for use a multi-tier application client. The main change is to remove all of the classes that are not located in the servlets. The other change is to adapt the classes that called those classes to call servlets instead. Listing 21-23 shows the changed code in the XMLPBServletApp Java Application.

I can now remove the `java.sql.*` import for the SQL Server JDBC driver classes, because all JDBC driver functionality has been moved to the servlets. This means that the application can be loaded on any workstation that supports Java JDK 1.3.1 or higher, and does not have to have a JDBC driver or any other external support packages installed. The second change is the addition of a variable at the top of the application that specifies the server location and the directory on that server where the servlets are located.

Listing 21-23: **Changed Code in the XMLPBServletApp Java Application**

```
import javax.swing.*;
import javax.swing.event.*;
import java.util.*;
import java.awt.*;
import java.awt.event.*;
import java.io.*;
import java.net.*;

public class XMLPBServletApp extends JPanel {
    JTextArea output;
    JList authorList;
    JList QuoteList;
    ListSelectionModel authorListSelectionModel;
    ListSelectionModel QuotelistSelectionModel;
    public String[] listData;
    JComboBox comboBox;
    String ServletURLBase = "http://127.0.0.1/servlet/";
```

In addition to the two small changes to the application code, there are a few changes to the classes. Instead of containing code that generated lists of authors, quotes, and XML output in the Application code, the classes are now used to call servlets that pass the correct data back to the application in the required format. Listing 21-24 shows the classes that have been changed in the XMLPBServletApp Java Application:

> **Listing 21-24: Changed Classes in the XMLPBServletApp Java Application**

```
public String [] GetAuthorList() {
      String AuthorList [] = null;

      try{
          ObjectInputStream inputFromServlet = null;
          String ServletCall = ServletURLBase +
          "XMLPBAppServletGetAuthorList";
          URL ServletURL = new URL( ServletCall );
          URLConnection ServletConnection = ServletURL.openConnection();
          inputFromServlet = new
          ObjectInputStream(ServletConnection.getInputStream());
          AuthorList = (String []) inputFromServlet.readObject();
      }

      catch(Exception e) {
          e.printStackTrace();
      }
      return AuthorList ;

}

  public String [] GetSingleAuthorList(String CategoryName) {
      String singleAuthorList [] = null;

      try{
          ObjectInputStream inputFromServlet = null;
          String ServletCall = ServletURLBase +
          "XMLPBAppServletGetSingleAuthorList";
          ServletCall += "&CategoryName="+CategoryName.replace(' ','+');
          URL ServletURL = new URL( ServletCall );
          URLConnection ServletConnection = ServletURL.openConnection();
          inputFromServlet = new
          ObjectInputStream(ServletConnection.getInputStream());
          singleAuthorList = (String []) inputFromServlet.readObject();
      }

      catch(Exception e) {
          e.printStackTrace();
      }
```

Continued

Listing 21-24 *(continued)*

```
        return singleAuthorList ;

    }


public String GetSingleQuoteElement(String PassedQuote) {
    String XMLDoc=null;

    try{
        ObjectInputStream inputFromServlet = null;
        String ServletCall = ServletURLBase +
        "XMLPBAppServletBuildElementXML";
        ServletCall += "&PassedQuote="+PassedQuote.replace(' ','+');
        URL ServletURL = new URL( ServletCall );
        URLConnection ServletConnection = ServletURL.openConnection();
        inputFromServlet = new
        ObjectInputStream(ServletConnection.getInputStream());
        XMLDoc = (String) inputFromServlet.readObject();
    }

    catch(Exception e) {
        e.printStackTrace();
    }


    return XMLDoc ;

}

public String GetSingleQuoteAttribute(String PassedQuote) {
    String XMLDoc=null;

    try{
        ObjectInputStream inputFromServlet = null;
        String ServletCall = ServletURLBase +
        "XMLPBAppServletBuildAttributeXML";
        ServletCall += "&PassedQuote="+PassedQuote.replace(' ','+');
        URL ServletURL = new URL( ServletCall );
        URLConnection ServletConnection = ServletURL.openConnection();
        inputFromServlet = new
        ObjectInputStream(ServletConnection.getInputStream());
        XMLDoc = (String) inputFromServlet.readObject();
    }

    catch(Exception e) {
        e.printStackTrace();
    }
```

```
        return XMLDoc ;


    }
```

Each class in the Java Application builds a URL that calls the appropriate servlet and creates a `ObjectInputStream` to receive data from the `ObjectOutputStream` that is generated by the servlet. Below is the code that retrieves the list authors from the Authors table in the SQL Server `XMLProgrammingBible` database:

```
ObjectInputStream inputFromServlet = null;
String ServletCall = ServletURLBase +
"XMLPBAppServletGetAuthorList";
URL ServletURL = new URL( ServletCall );
URLConnection ServletConnection = ServletURL.openConnection();
inputFromServlet = new
ObjectInputStream(ServletConnection.getInputStream());
AuthorList = (String []) inputFromServlet.readObject();
```

In this example, a new instance of the `ObjectInputStream` is created, and a URL is assembled into a string using the `ServletURLBase` variable assigned at the beginning of the application, the servlet name, and any appropriate parameters that need to be passed to the servlet. Next a URL object is created from the string, and a `URLConnection` is created using the newly created URL and the `openConnection()` method. This calls the servlet, which returns an `ObjectOuputStream`. The `ObjectInputStream` on the application side collects the response from the servlet and passes the response back to the application. The response from the servlet that has been collected using the `ObjectInputStream` is assigned to an object in the Java Application via the `ObjectInputStream.readObject` method. There are two formats for responses from the servlets in this application: arrays and strings. An array that contains a list of authors is received using this code:

```
AuthorList = (String []) inputFromServlet.readObject();
```

A Java string that contains custom XML for a single quote is received using this code:

```
XMLDoc = (String) inputFromServlet.readObject();
```

In either case, the object is passed back to the application and used as an element of the application user interface.

Summary

In this chapter we've outlined techniques for building J2EE applications that work with XML documents and relational data:

✦ A J2EE sample application

✦ Using JDBC with J2EE applications that use JDBC

✦ Controlling custom XML formats

✦ A three-tier system combining Java Applications, servlets, and JDBC

✦ Accessing servlets from a Web browser

✦ Accessing servlets from a J2EE application

In the next chapter we'll show you how to transform relational data from one RDBMS format to another using XSL, and relational XML data formats.

✦   ✦   ✦

Transforming Relational XML Output into Other Formats

So far in this section we've shown you how to get XML data out of MS SQL Server, Oracle, and DB2. You can use the generated XML to integrate data with other formats of XML using XSLT transformation. You can also transform the relational XML output directly to HTML, or load the data into an XML data island.

In this chapter we'll review XSL transformation of XML relational data formats that we showed you in Chapters 18, 19, and 20 for MS SQL Server, Oracle, and DB2. We'll start with a comparison of each vendor's approach to transforming XML. Then we'll show you how to transform data structures from each RDBMS platform. We include examples of stylesheets for transforming XML output from MS SQL Server, Oracle and DB2. These can serve as good bases for your own transformation stylesheets.

We'll also show you a way to transform a generalized XML format created by the JDBC-based J2EE application that we showed you in Chapter 21. During the process we'll put together a framework for transforming relational data formats, including tips for converting relational XML output to HTML. We'll finish up the chapter with an XML data islands example that transforms relational data and manipulates the data in a Web browser client using Microsoft XML Core Services (MSXML).

Note   In this chapter we'll cover the ways of formatting relational data as XML, but we won't cover the fundamentals of XSLT. For that information, refer to Chapters 7 and 8.

Transformation Functions in Oracle, DB2, and MS SQL Server

Each RDBMS vendor has its own way of handling XSL transformations, either via SQL functions, or via other languages that receive XML output from the RDBMS. Major software vendors are providing facilities for developers to generate HTML directly to a Web browser using XSLT. While this may be a handy feature for developers, it's a potential security nightmare for RDBMS administrators. Allowing direct access between a Web browser and a relational database is not a recommended solution for most secure IT shops.

We'll show you the easiest ways to generate HTML from relational data via XSL transformations, but flexible application architectures should always use a middle-tier HTTP server such as MS Internet information Server (IIS), a portal server such as IBM WebSphere portal server, an MS SharePoint server, or a J2EE application server. The middle tier takes some of the processing load from the RDBMS server and also acts as a physical and virtual security layer. The middle tier of a multi-tier application separates the Web from your data store. That's a good thing, as Martha would say.

Later in the chapter we'll show you an example of transforming JDBC XML output from the J2EE application in Chapter 21. Because this technique can be used in a multi-tier environment, it may be a more appropriate solution than directly producing HTML from relational data.

Tip   When creating XSL stylesheets to transform relational output to HTML, don't hurt yourself by trying hand-code and test stylesheet. Use an XSLT tool like the XMLSpy stylesheet designer, which is available as a trial download from `http://www.XMLSpy.com`. We used it to create all of the examples in this chapter. Other tools are available from www.xmlsoftware.com, but we've found the XMLSpy Stylesheet designer to be the best, if not the cheapest.

MS SQL Server and XSL

There are two ways to transform data in SQL Server output. An XSL stylesheet can be included in a template file as a default stylesheet. Any XML document output that is created with this template is automatically transformed by a SQL Server before results are sent back to the requestor. You can also specify a stylesheet via URI when making a URL call to a template file.

Cross-Reference   For more information on working with XML in SQL Server, please refer to Chapter 19.

Transforming MS SQL Server XML results with an XSL stylesheet

SQL Server 2000 supports two ways to automatically transform XML results using an XSL stylesheet. In this example, the `ResultTransform.xsl` stylesheet is stored in the `stylesheets` subdirectory of the IIS virtual directory. This is not an official directory for stylesheets, just a directory that we chose to create and store stylesheets in. It could be contained anywhere under the virtual directory and be named anything. The relative path reference branches from the virtual directory root.

You can also reference stylesheets inside a template file using the `sql:xsl` attribute of a template's root tag. Here's an example of a very simple query that transforms a row of XML data to HTML:

```
<?xml version="1.0" encoding="UTF-8"?>
<QueryRoot xmlns:sql="urn:schemas-microsoft-com:xml-sql"
 sql:xsl="/stylesheets/ResultTransform.xsl">
 <sql:query>
  SELECT TOP 1 * FROM XMLProgrammingBible.dbo.AmazonListings FOR XML AUTO
 </sql:query>
</QueryRoot>
```

A stylesheet reference can be contained in a URL that references a template with a parameter like this:

```
http://iis.benztech.com/XMLProgrammingBible/template/MultiQueryExample1.xml?xsl=
/stylesheets/ResultTransform.xsl
```

Note   If a template contains an XSL stylesheet reference and a stylesheet is specified in a URL that calls the template, stylesheet in the URL overrides the template stylesheet reference.

Transforming FOR XML AUTO output to HTML

Here's the output that is generated by the example template shown above. The `QueryRoot` root element is defined in the temple, everything else is created by the SQL command. The row that is retuned is defined by a single element called `AmazonListings`, and all of the columns in that row are defined by an attribute with the format `columnName="value"`. Note that the ampersands (&) in the `tagged_URL` attribute have been converted to entity references (&). This is part of the functionality of the `AUTO` SQL command parameter.

```
<?xml version="1.0" encoding="UTF-8"?>
<QueryRoot>
  <AmazonListings ProductID="1001" Ranking="1" Title="Hamlet/MacBeth"
  ASIN="8432040231" Image="http://images.amazon.com/images/
  P/8432040231.01.MZZZZZZZ.jpg" Small_Image="http://images.amazon.com
  /images/P/8432040231.01.TZZZZZZZ.jpg" List_price="$7.95"
  Release_date="2001-12-17T09:30:47-05:00" Binding="Paperback"
  Availability="" Tagged_URL="http://www.amazon.com:80
  /exec/obidos/redirect?tag=associateid&amp;
  benztechnonogies=9441&amp;camp;camp=1793&amp;
  link_code=xml&amp;path=ASIN/8432040231"/>
</QueryRoot>
```

I used XMLSpy's (`http://www.xmlspy.com`) stylesheet designer to create the
stylesheet that transforms this XML document to an HTML table. The XMLSpy
stylesheet designer uses DTDs or W3C schemas to create XSL stylesheets. I loaded
the XML document shown above into XMLSpy and created a DTD from the XML
document using the `Generate Schema/DTD` menu option. I saved the DTD and
reopened it in Stylesheet designer. All I had to do then was drag and drop the
AmazonListings element into the stylesheet designer window and format the input
as an HTML table. I messed with the fonts a little, and the HTML output in Figure
22-1 is the result.

The stylesheet that is generated by the stylesheet designer is 178 lines and very
repetitive, so we won't show you the whole thing here. Instead we'll just show you
the first few lines, which are repeated for each row in the HTML table.

 On The Web   The examples in this chapter can be downloaded from the XMLprogramming
Bible.com Web site, under the Downloads section.

The stylesheet starts with an XML document declaration, and an XSL transformation namespace declaration as part of the xsl:stylesheet root element. This defines
the XSL elements from any other types of elements such as HTML output. This is
mainly for the benefit of XSLT processors. The XSLT processing is started by a template element with a match attribute. The XPath expression for the source XML
document refers to the root element (/).

```
<?xml version="1.0" encoding="UTF-8"?>
<xsl:stylesheet version="1.0" xmlns:xsl="http://www.w3.org/1999/XSL/Transform">
  <xsl:template match="/">
```

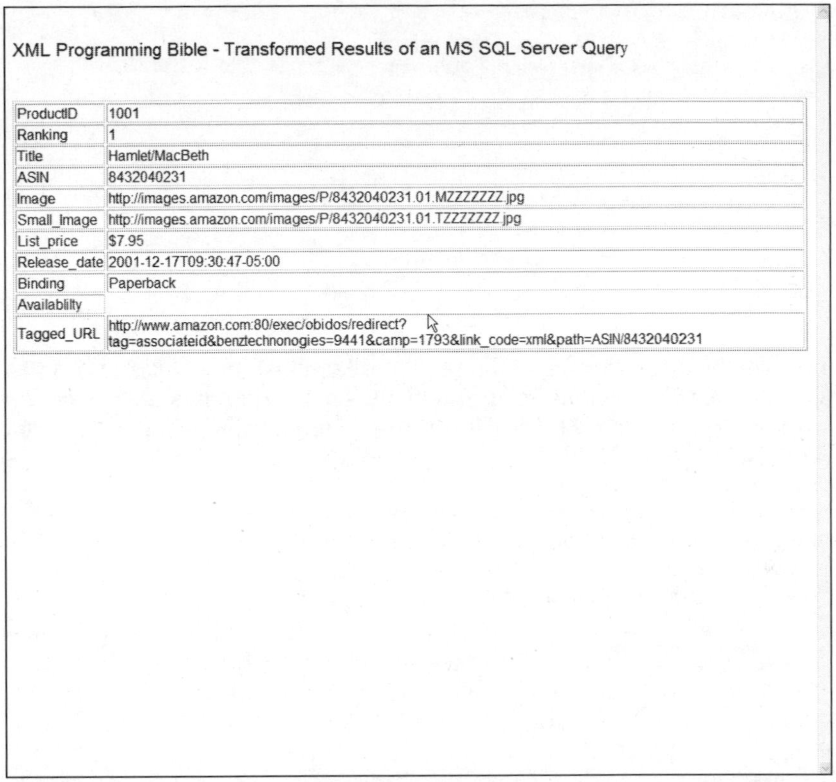

Figure 22-1: The Transformed HTML output from an SQL Server FOR XML
AUTO query

The next few elements are HTML and become part of the Output HTML document,
exactly as you see them here. The span element sets up the style for the display of
the heading on the HTML page.

```
<html>
  <head/>
  <body>
  <br/>
  <span style="font-family:Arial; ">XML Programming Bible -
   Transformed Results of an MS SQL Server Quer</span>y<br/>
  <br/>
  <br/>
```

Next, the XSLT elements define that for each instance of the `QueryRoot/`
`AmazonListings` element in the source document, a new HTML table should be
created on the page. More HTML elements define the first row of the HTML table.

```
<xsl:for-each select="QueryRoot">
  <xsl:for-each select="AmazonListings">
  <xsl:if test="position()=1">
    <table border="1">
    <tbody>
      <tr>
      <td>
        <span style="font-family:Arial; font-size:xx-small;
          ">ProductID</span>
      </td>
      <xsl:for-each select="../AmazonListings">
        <td>
```

Next, a new row is added to the HTML table for each instance of the ProductID attribute inside of the AmazonListings element. The attribute name is used for the left column in the table row. The attribute value becomes the value in the right column in the row.

```
<xsl:for-each select="@ProductID">
  <span style="font-family:Arial; font-size:xx-
    small; ">
  <xsl:value-of select="."/>
  </span>
</xsl:for-each>
</td>
</xsl:for-each>
</tr>
<tr>
```

The rest of the stylesheet repeats this pattern for each attribute in the AmazonListings element. If there is another AmazonListings element, the stylesheet creates another table and starts over.

Oracle and XSL

Oracle supports a number of methods of transforming XML using XSLT. You can use the integrated high-performance parser and transformation engine that is part of the Oracle XDK in a multi-tier environment. You can also use XML DB XMLTRANSFORM function. The XSQL servlet and XSQL Pages Publishing Framework also support XSLT transformation features.

Cross-Reference

For more information on parsing and transforming XML using Java, please refer to Chapters 15 and 16. The parsing and transformation code examples for Xalan and Xerces can be reused with the Oracle Java XDK. The only modification required is the substitution of Oracle XDK transformation and parsing packages in the import statements.

One of the easiest ways to get data out of Oracle is though a combination of the XMLELEMENT and XMLFOREST XML DB functions. Here's the query we am using to create an XML document from Oracle data:

```
SELECT XMLELEMENT("RootElement", XMLFOREST(
PRODUCTID,
RANKING,
TITLE,
ASIN,
AUTHORID,
IMAGE,
SMALL_IMAGE,
LIST_PRICE,
RELEASE_DATE,
BINDING,
AVAILABILITY,
TAGGED_URL)) as  "RESULT"
FROM   AmazonListings
WHERE  rownum = 1;
```

And here's what a sample XML document looks like when it is returned by this query:

```
<RootElement>
  <PRODUCTID>1001</PRODUCTID>
  <RANKING>1</RANKING>
  <TITLE>Hamlet/MacBeth</TITLE>
  <ASIN>8432040231</ASIN>
  <AUTHORID>1001</AUTHORID>
  <IMAGE>http://images.amazon.com/images/P/8432040231.01.MZZZZZZZ.jpg
  </IMAGE>
  <SMALL_IMAGE>http://images.amazon.com/images/P/8432040231.01.TZZZZZZZ.jpg
  </SMALL_IMAGE>
  <LIST_PRICE>7.95</LIST_PRICE>
  <RELEASE_DATE>01-JUN-91</RELEASE_DATE>
  <BINDING>Paperback</BINDING>
  <TAGGED_URL>http://www.amazon.com:80/exec/obidos/redirect?
  tag=associateid&amp;benztechnonogies=9441&amp;camp=1793&amp;
  link_code=xml&amp;path=ASIN/8432040231</TAGGED_URL>
</RootElement>
```

Creating an Oracle table to store stylesheets

In Chapter 19 we showed you how to create a table that contains an XMLType data type. In this chapter we'll create another table in the XMLPB1 database that contains three columns. The table is named STYLESHEETS. The first column is named SHEETNUMBER and is a numeric column used to store an incremental ID for stylesheets. The second column is named SHEETID and is used to store character-based IDs for stylesheets. The third column is named STYLESHEET and contains the XSL stylesheet formatted as an XMLType data type. Here's the SQL that creates the table:

```
CREATE TABLE "BBENZ"."STYLESHEETS" ("SHEETNUMBER" NUMBER(10) NOT
  NULL, "SHEETID" CHAR(50), "STYLESHEET" "SYS"."XMLTYPE")
```

Once the table is created, stylesheets can be stored and retrieved as needed by Oracle applications. This has several advantages over the alternate options, which are storing XSL on the file system or hard-coding a stylesheet into an application. First, you can take advantage of Oracle security for managing stylesheets. Second, the stylesheets are always contained in the database with the XML that is being transformed. Third, application performance is better when retrieving a stylesheet from a table than retrieving the stylesheet from the file system. Here's a sample query for inserting a stylesheet into the STYLESHEETS table:

```
INSERT INTO STYLESHEETS(SHEETNUMBER, SHEETID, STYLESHEET) VALUES(1,
'FirstStyleSheet',
xmltype(
'<?xml version="1.0" encoding="UTF-8"?>
<xsl:stylesheet version="1.0" xmlns:xsl="http://www.w3.org/1999/XSL/Transform">
  <xsl:output method="xml"/>
  <xsl:template match="@*">
  <xsl:element name="{name()}">
    <xsl:value-of select="."/>
  </xsl:element>
  </xsl:template>
  <xsl:template match="*">
  <xsl:copy>
    <xsl:apply-templates select="*|@*"/>
  </xsl:copy>
  </xsl:template>
</xsl:stylesheet>'));
```

This works well for loading stylesheets into a table from the SQL*Plus console. You can also retrieve an XSL document from a document on the file system and load it into the STYLESHEETS table using `DBMS_XMLGEN()` functions. Stylesheets can be retrieved from the database using an SQL subquery like this:

```
SELECT STYLESHEET from STYLESHEETS where SHEETID =
'FirstStyleSheet'
```

 Cross-Reference   For more information on working with XML in Oracle, please refer to Chapter 19.

The XSL Stylesheet is called `OracleXMLElement.xslt`, and has a SHEETID of `OracleXMLElement` in the STYLESHEETS table. Here's what the beginning of the stylesheet looks like. The rest of the stylesheet is repetitive and long, so we'll only show the first part in the book.

The examples in this chapter can be downloaded from the XMLprogramming Bible.com Website, under the Downloads section.

The stylesheet starts with an XML document declaration, and an XSL transformation namespace declaration as part of the xsl:stylesheet root element. This defines the XSL elements from any other types of elements such as HTML output. This is mainly for the benefit of XSLT processors. The XSLT processing is started by a template element with a match attribute. The XPath expression for the source XML document refers to the root element (/).

```
?xml version="1.0" encoding="UTF-8"?>
<xsl:stylesheet version="1.0" xmlns:xsl="http://www.w3.org/1999/XSL/Transform">
  <xsl:template match="/">
```

The next few elements are HTML and become part of the Output HTML document, exactly as you see them here. The span element sets up the style for the display of the heading on the HTML page.

```
<html>
  <head />
  <body>
    <br />
    <span style="font-family:Arial; ">XML Bible - Transformed Results
     of an Oracle Query</span>
    <br />
    <br />
```

Next, the XSLT elements define that for each instance of the RootElement element in the source document, a new HTML table should be created on the page. More HTML elements define the first row of the HTML table.

```
<xsl:for-each select="RootElement">
  <xsl:if test="position()=1">
    <table border="1">
      <tbody>
        <tr>
          <td>
            <span style="font-family:Arial; font-size:xx-small;
             ">PRODUCTID</span>
          </td>
          <xsl:for-each select="../RootElement">
            <td>
```

Next, a new row is added to the HTML table for each instance of the PRODUCT element. The element name is used for the left column in the table row. The text value of the element becomes the value in the right column in the row.

```
<xsl:for-each select="PRODUCTID">
  <span style="font-family:Arial; font-size:xx-small;
   ">
```

```
                    <xsl:apply-templates />
                </span>
            </xsl:for-each>
        </td>
    </xsl:for-each>
</tr>
```

Figure 22-2 shows the transformed HTML output from the combined XMLELEMENT and XMLFOREST query.

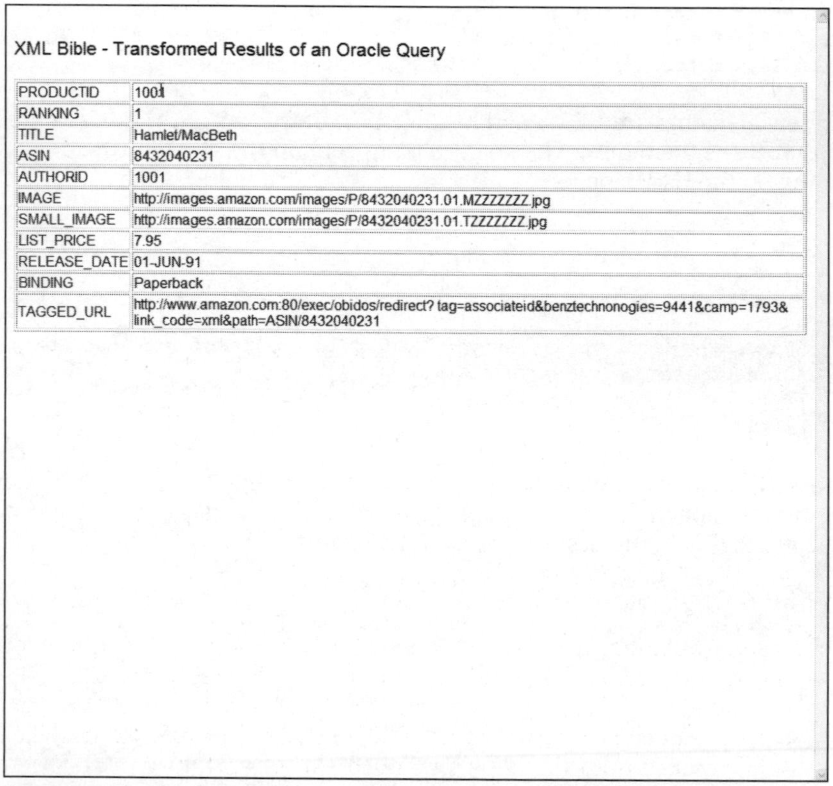

XML Bible - Transformed Results of an Oracle Query

PRODUCTID	1001
RANKING	1
TITLE	Hamlet/MacBeth
ASIN	8432040231
AUTHORID	1001
IMAGE	http://images.amazon.com/images/P/8432040231.01.MZZZZZZZ.jpg
SMALL_IMAGE	http://images.amazon.com/images/P/8432040231.01.TZZZZZZZ.jpg
LIST_PRICE	7.95
RELEASE_DATE	01-JUN-91
BINDING	Paperback
TAGGED_URL	http://www.amazon.com:80/exec/obidos/redirect? tag=associateid&benztechnonogies=9441&camp=1793& link_code=xml&path=ASIN/8432040231

Figure 22-2: The transformed output for the Oracle HTML transformation

Now that you have an understanding of the XSL stylesheet and what the XSL output looks like, let's go through the options for performing an XSL transformation.

Using the XML DB XMLTRANSFORM() function

XMLTRANSFORM() acccpts a source XML document in XMLType data type and an XSLT stylesheet. It applies the stylesheet to the XML document and returns a transformed XML instance. Here's an example of XMLTRANSFORM that returns an XML document as a string. The XML document source in the first subquery is a combination of nested XMLELEMENT and XMLATTRIBUTE functions. The result is a source XML document that is passed to the XMLTRANSFORM function. The second subquery retrieves the OracleXMLElement stylesheet as an XMLType document. The stylesheet becomes the second parameter in the XMLTRANSFORM function. The transformation output is converted to a string using the getStringVal() method.

```
SELECT XMLTRANSFORM(
(SELECT XMLELEMENT("RootElement", XMLFOREST(
PRODUCTID,
RANKING,
TITLE,
ASIN,
AUTHORID,
IMAGE,
SMALL_IMAGE,
LIST_PRICE,
RELEASE_DATE,
BINDING,
AVAILABILITY,
TAGGED_URL)) as  "RESULT"
FROM   AmazonListings
WHERE  rownum = 1;
),
(SELECT STYLESHEET
from STYLESHEETS
where SHEETID =
'OracleXMLElement')).getStringVal()
AS HTMLResult from AMAZONLISTINGS
WHERE  rownum = 1;
```

DB2 and XSL

DB2 supports two DB2 XML Extender functions for transforming XML documents. The XSLTransformToClob() function accepts a stylesheet object and an XML document object and returns a CLOB object. The XSLTransformToFIle () function accepts a stylesheet object and an XML document object and writes a file to the file system. You can use DB2 XML columns to store and retrieve stylesheets from a database.

DB2 has many ways to generate XML data from Relational tables. One of the simplest ways is to use a combination of XMLAGG and XMLELEMENT to build a well-formed XML document from rows of table data. Here's a query that we're using for the DB2 examples in this chapter:

```
SELECT XML2CLOB(
XMLELEMENT(NAME "RootElement",
XMLAGG(
```

```
XMLELEMENT(NAME "RowElement",
XMLELEMENT(NAME "PRODUCTID", PRODUCTID),
XMLELEMENT(NAME "RANKING", RANKING),
XMLELEMENT(NAME"TITLE", TITLE),
XMLELEMENT(NAME"ASIN",ASIN),
XMLELEMENT(NAME"AUTHORID",AUTHORID),
XMLELEMENT(NAME"IMAGE",IMAGE),
XMLELEMENT(NAME"SMALL_IMAGE",SMALL_IMAGE),
XMLELEMENT(NAME"LIST_PRICE",LIST_PRICE),
XMLELEMENT(NAME"RELEASE_DATE",RELEASE_DATE),
XMLELEMENT(NAME"BINDING",BINDING),
XMLELEMENT(NAME"AVAILABILITY",AVAILABILITY),
XMLELEMENT(NAME"TAGGED_URL", TAGGED_URL)
))))
AS "XMLResult" FROM AMAZONLISTINGS
```

And here's what the XML document results look like:

```
<RootElement>
  <RowElement>
    <PRODUCTID>1001</PRODUCTID>
    <RANKING>1</RANKING>
    <TITLE>Hamlet/Macbeth</TITLE>
    <ASIN>8432040231</ASIN>
    <AUTHORID>1001</AUTHORID>
    <IMAGE>http://images.amazon.com/images/P/8432040231.01.
     MZZZZZZZ.jpg</IMAGE>
    <SMALL_IMAGE>http://images.amazon.com/images/P/8432040231.01.
     TZZZZZZZ.jpg</SMALL_IMAGE>
    <LIST_PRICE>07.</LIST_PRICE>
    <RELEASE_DATE>1991-06-01</RELEASE_DATE>
    <BINDING>Paperback</BINDING>
    <AVAILABILITY/>
   <TAGGED_URL>http://www.amazon.com:80/exec/obidos/redirect?
    tag=associateid&amp;benztechnonogies=9441&amp;camp=1793&amp;
    link_code=xml&amp;path=ASIN/8432040231</TAGGED_URL>
  </RowElement>
</RootElement>
```

Creating a DB2 Table to store stylesheets

In Chapter 20 we showed you how to create a table that contains an XML Column in a database that has been enabled for use with DB2 XML Extender. In this chapter we'll create another table in the XMLPB database that contains three columns. The table is named STYLESHEETS. The first column is named SHEETNUMBER, and is an INTEGER column used to store an incremental ID for stylesheets. The second column is named SHEETID and is used to store character-based IDs for stylesheets. The third column is named STYLESHEET and contains the XSL stylesheet formatted as an XML Column. Here's the SQL that creates the table:

```
CREATE TABLE OWNER.STYLESHEETS ( SHEETNUMBER INTEGER , SHEETID CHARACTER (50) ,
STYLESHEET DB2XML.XMLCLOB  ) ;
```

Once the table is created, stylesheets can be stored and retrieved as needed by DB2 functions and applications. This has several advantages over the alternate options, which are storing XSL on the file system or hard-coding a stylesheet into an application. First, you can take advantage of DB2 security for managing stylesheets. Second, the stylesheets are always contained in the database with the XML that is being transformed. Here's a sample query for inserting a stylesheet into the STYLESHEETS table from a file using the DB2 XML Extender `XMLCLOBFromFile()` function:

```
INSERT INTO STYLESHEETS (SHEETNUMBER, SHEETID, STYLESHEET)
VALUES(1, 'Db2XMLElement', DB2XML.XMLCLOBFromFile
('c:\dxx\samples\DB2XMLElement.xsl'))
```

Stylesheets that are stored in DB2 XML columns can be retrieved from the database using an SQL subquery like this:

```
SELECT STYLESHEET from STYLESHEETS where SHEETID =
'Db2XMLElement'
```

Cross-Reference For more information on working with XML in DB2, please refer to Chapter 20.

The DB2 XSL stylesheet is called `DB2XMLElement.xslt`, and has a SHEETID of `DB2XMLElement` in the STYLESHEETS table. Here's what the beginning of the stylesheet looks like. The rest of the stylesheet is repetitive and long, so we'll only show the first part in the book.

On The Web The examples in this chapter can be downloaded from the XMLProgramming Bible.com Website, under the Downloads section.

The DB2 stylesheet starts with an XML document declaration, and an XSL transformation namespace declaration as part of the `xsl:stylesheet` root element. This defines the XSL elements from any other types of elements such as HTML output. This is mainly for the benefit of XSLT processors. The XSLT processing is started by a template element with a match attribute. The XPath expression for the source XML document refers to the root element (/).

```
<?xml version="1.0" encoding="UTF-8"?>
<xsl:stylesheet version="1.0"
xmlns:xsl="http://www.w3.org/1999/XSL/Transform">
    <xsl:template match="/">
```

The next few elements are HTML and become part of the output HTML document, exactly as you see them here. The span element sets up the style for the display of the heading on the HTML page.

```
<html>
    <head />
    <body>
        <br />
        <span style="font-family:Arial; ">XML Bible - Transformed
         Results of a DB2 Query</span>
        <br />
        <br />
```

Next, the XSLT elements define that for each instance of the RootElement element in the source document, a new HTML table should be created on the page. More HTML elements define the first row of the HTML table.

```
<xsl:for-each select="RootElement">
    <xsl:for-each select="RowElement">
      <xsl:if test="position()=1">
        <table border="1">
          <tbody>
            <tr>
              <td>
                <span style="font-family:Arial; font-size:xx-small;
                 ">PRODUCTID</span>
              </td>
              <xsl:for-each select="../RowElement">
                <td>
```

Next, a new row is added to the HTML table for each instance of the PRODUCT element. The element name is used for the left column in the table row. The text value of the element becomes the value in the right column in the row.

```
              <xsl:for-each select="PRODUCTID">
                <span style="font-family:Arial; font-size:xx-
                 small; ">
                  <xsl:apply-templates/>
                </span>
              </xsl:for-each>
            </td>
          </xsl:for-each>
        </tr>
```

Figure 22-3 shows the transformed HTML output from the combined XMLAGG and XMLELEMENT query.

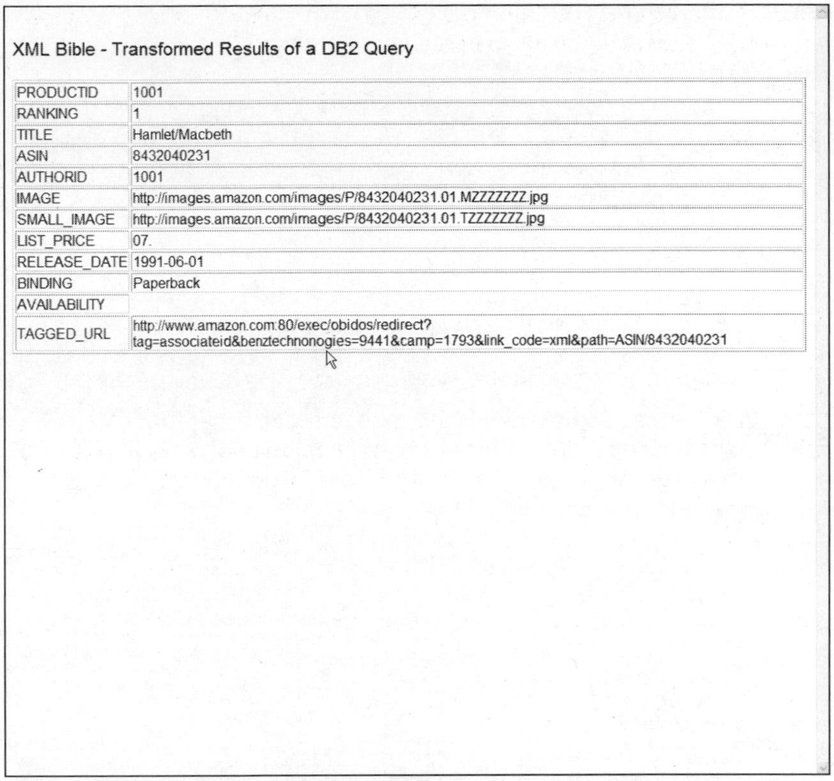
XML Bible - Transformed Results of a DB2 Query

PRODUCTID	1001
RANKING	1
TITLE	Hamlet/Macbeth
ASIN	8432040231
AUTHORID	1001
IMAGE	http://images.amazon.com/images/P/8432040231.01.MZZZZZZZ.jpg
SMALL_IMAGE	http://images.amazon.com/images/P/8432040231.01.TZZZZZZZ.jpg
LIST_PRICE	07.
RELEASE_DATE	1991-06-01
BINDING	Paperback
AVAILABILITY	
TAGGED_URL	http://www.amazon.com:80/exec/obidos/redirect?tag=associateid&benztechnonogies=9441&camp=1793&link_code=xml&path=ASIN/8432040231

Figure 22-3: The transformed output for the DB2 HTML transformation

Using XSLTransformToClob and XSLTransformToFile to transform data to a CLOB

XSLTransformToClob is a handy way to create a CLOB object that contains an HTML page. The XSLTransformToClob function receives two parameters; an XML source document and an XSL stylesheet document. Both parameters must be in CLOB format (hence the `XML2CLOB` function is used). Stylesheets can also be in VARCHAR format. Both input parameters can also be file names with paths to the file system.

```
SELECT XSLTransformToClob(
(SELECT XML2CLOB(
XMLELEMENT(NAME "RootElement",
XMLAGG(
XMLELEMENT(NAME "RowElement",
XMLELEMENT(NAME "PRODUCTID", PRODUCTID),
XMLELEMENT(NAME "RANKING", RANKING),
```

```
XMLELEMENT(NAME"TITLE", TITLE),
XMLELEMENT(NAME"ASIN",ASIN),
XMLELEMENT(NAME"AUTHORID",AUTHORID),
XMLELEMENT(NAME"IMAGE",IMAGE),
XMLELEMENT(NAME"SMALL_IMAGE",SMALL_IMAGE),
XMLELEMENT(NAME"LIST_PRICE",LIST_PRICE),
XMLELEMENT(NAME"RELEASE_DATE",RELEASE_DATE),
XMLELEMENT(NAME"BINDING",BINDING),
XMLELEMENT(NAME"AVAILABILITY",AVAILABILITY),
XMLELEMENT(NAME"TAGGED_URL", TAGGED_URL)
))))
AS "XMLResult" FROM AMAZONLISTINGS),
(SELECT XML2CLOB(STYLESHEET from STYLESHEETS where SHEETID =
'Db2XMLElement')))
```

The `XSLTransformToFile` function is almost identical, except that it uses a third parameter to pass the transformed output to a file instead of a CLOB object. Here's an example that writes the transformed output to a file named `c:\dxx\samples\DB2TransformExample.xml`:

```
SELECT XSLTransformToFile(
(SELECT XML2CLOB(
XMLELEMENT(NAME "RootElement",
XMLAGG(
XMLELEMENT(NAME "RowElement",
XMLELEMENT(NAME "PRODUCTID", PRODUCTID),
XMLELEMENT(NAME "RANKING", RANKING),
XMLELEMENT(NAME"TITLE", TITLE),
XMLELEMENT(NAME"ASIN",ASIN),
XMLELEMENT(NAME"AUTHORID",AUTHORID),
XMLELEMENT(NAME"IMAGE",IMAGE),
XMLELEMENT(NAME"SMALL_IMAGE",SMALL_IMAGE),
XMLELEMENT(NAME"LIST_PRICE",LIST_PRICE),
XMLELEMENT(NAME"RELEASE_DATE",RELEASE_DATE),
XMLELEMENT(NAME"BINDING",BINDING),
XMLELEMENT(NAME"AVAILABILITY",AVAILABILITY),
XMLELEMENT(NAME"TAGGED_URL", TAGGED_URL)
))))
AS "XMLResult" FROM AMAZONLISTINGS),
(SELECT XML2CLOB(STYLESHEET from STYLESHEETS where SHEETID =
'Db2XMLElement'), 'c:\dxx\samples\DB2TransformExample.xml'))
```

Transforming JDBC Result Sets to HTML

As we mentioned at the beginning of this chapter, while facilities exist to produce HTML and XML output from relational data directly from a RDBMS server, we have misgivings about them. This is mainly due to security and performance issues associated with providing a direct connection from the Web to your data store. Also, speaking of performance, the more you as a server to do, the busier it gets, and performance goes down. This is especially true of high volumes of XSL parsing and transformation.

In this part of the chapter, we'll use the XML document output that was generated by the J2EE application in Chapter 21. This is a good example of transforming XML data on a mid-tier in the infrastructure, instead of on the RDBMS server.

After reviewing the SQL Server, Oracle, and DB2 solutions for XSL transformations, you are probably noticing that this gets a bit repetitive. This is actually a good thing; it means that the process of transforming relational XML formats to HTML (and other formats of XML) is somewhat standardized across platforms. Oracle and DB2 are closer together in features than SQL Server, but on the other hand SQL Server has some unique and useful features.

Here's a sample XML document that was produced by the J2EE application in Chapter 21. The XML document consists of three quotes, with the author and source for each quote as siblings of a quotation. Each quotation record is the child of a `record` element, and records are children of the `resultset` root element.

```xml
<?xml version="1.0" encoding="UTF-8"?>
<resultset>
  <metadata>
    <field name="Quotation" datatype="char"/>
    <field name="AuthorName" datatype="char"/>
    <field name="SourceName" datatype="char"/>
  </metadata>
  <records>
    <record rownumber="1">
      <Quotation>When the hurlyburly's done, When the battle's lost and
      won.</Quotation>
      <AuthorName>Shakespeare, William</AuthorName>
      <SourceName>Macbeth</SourceName>
    </record>
    <record rownumber="2">
      <Quotation>Out, damned spot! out, I say!-- One; two; why, then 'tis
       time to do't ;--Hell is murky!--Fie, my lord, fie! a soldier, and
       afeard? What need we fear who knows it, when none can call our power
       to account?--Yet who would have thought the old man to have had so
       much blood in him?</Quotation>
      <AuthorName>Shakespeare, William</AuthorName>
      <SourceName>Macbeth</SourceName>
    </record>
    <record rownumber="3">
```

```
      <Quotation>To-morrow, and to-morrow, and to-morrow, creeps in this
       petty pace from day to day, to the last syllable of recorded time;
       and all our yesterdays have lighted fools the way to dusty death.
       Out, out, brief candle! Life's but a walking shadow; a poor player,
       that struts and frets his hour upon the stage, and then is heard no
       more: it is a tale told by an idiot, full of sound and fury,
       signifying nothing. </Quotation>
      <AuthorName>Shakespeare, William</AuthorName>
      <SourceName>Macbeth</SourceName>
    </record>
  </records>
</resultset>
```

Here's the transformation stylesheet for the JDBC example. As with the three previous examples, the DB2 stylesheet starts with an XML document declaration, and an XSL transformation namespace declaration as part of the xsl:stylesheet root element. This defines the XSL elements from any other types of elements such as HTML output. This is mainly for the benefit of XSLT processors. The XSLT processing is started by a template element with a match attribute. The XPath expression for the source XML document refers to the root element (/).

```
<?xml version="1.0" encoding="UTF-8"?>
<xsl:stylesheet version="1.0" xmlns:xsl="http://www.w3.org/1999/XSL/Transform">
  <xsl:template match="/">
```

The next few elements are HTML and become part of the output HTML document, exactly as you see them here. The span element sets up the style for the display of the heading on the HTML page.

```
  <html>
    <head/>
    <body>
      <br/>
      <br/>
      <span style="font-family:Arial; ">XML Programming Bible - JDBC XML
       Document Transformation Example</span>
      <br/>
      <br/>
```

Next, the stylesheet creates a process for handling each resultset, records, and record element on the page. Next, the table headings are hard-coded into the HTML table as table column headers.

```
      <xsl:for-each select="resultset">
        <xsl:for-each select="records">
          <xsl:for-each select="record">
            <xsl:if test="position()=1">
              <table border="1">
                <thead>
```

```
<tr>
  <td>
    <span style="font-family:Arial; font-size:xx-small;
    ">Author Name</span>
  </td>
  <td>
    <span style="font-family:Arial; font-size:xx-small;
    ">Source Name</span>
  </td>
  <td>
    <span style="font-family:Arial; font-size:xx-small;
    ">Quotation</span>
  </td>
</tr>
</thead>
```

The table body starts with the `tbody` element. The author name, source name, and quotation are defined by the elements with the same names in the source XML document. The parent of these elements is the record element. This code defines the table row values as three columns across the HTML page. When another record element is encountered, a new row is started in the table. The rest of the stylesheet is font formatting and tag closing until the end of the stylesheet is encountered.

```
<tbody>
  <xsl:for-each select="../record">
    <tr>
      <td>
        <xsl:for-each select="AuthorName">
          <span style="font-family:Arial; font-size:xx-
          small; ">
            <xsl:apply-templates/>
          </span>
        </xsl:for-each>
      </td>
      <td>
        <xsl:for-each select="SourceName">
          <span style="font-family:Arial; font-size:xx-
          small; ">
            <xsl:apply-templates/>
          </span>
        </xsl:for-each>
      </td>
      <td>
        <xsl:for-each select="Quotation">
          <span style="font-family:Arial; font-size:xx-
          small; ">
            <xsl:apply-templates/>
          </span>
        </xsl:for-each>
      </td>
```

```
                    </tr>
                  </xsl:for-each>
                </tbody>
              </table>
            </xsl:if>
          </xsl:for-each>
        </xsl:for-each>
      </xsl:for-each>
    </body>
  </html>
  </xsl:template>
</xsl:stylesheet>
```

Figure 22-4 shows the results of the XSL transformation from JDBC XML document output to HTML.

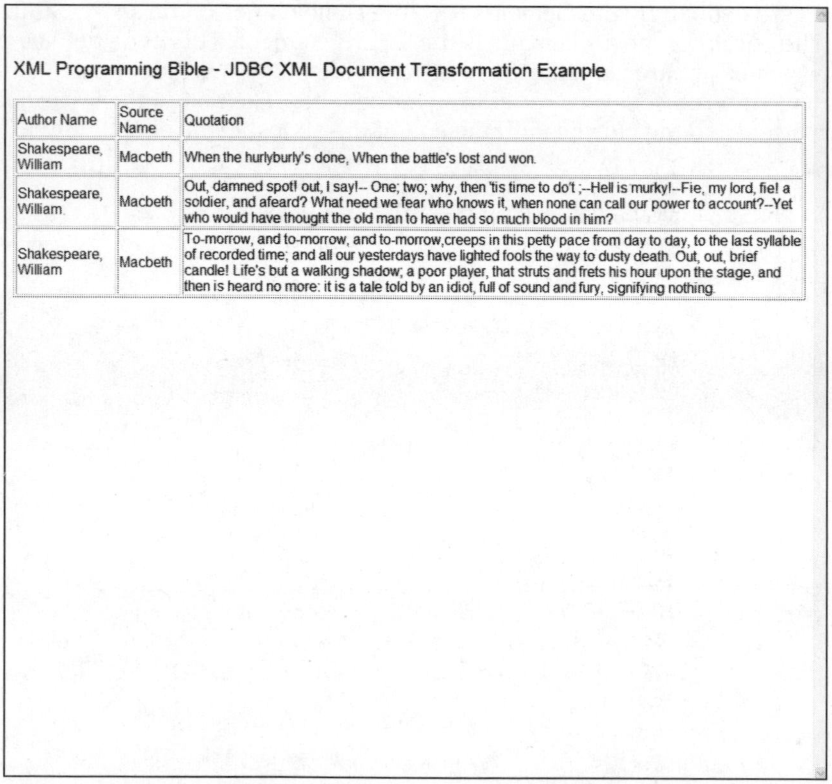

Figure 22-4: The transformed output for the DB2 HTML transformation

Transforming the JDBC XML Output using Java

The example J2EE application in Chapter 21 shows you how to connect MS SQL server data to a J2EE application via a JDBC connection. The connection itself could be swapped out with any other RDBMS product that supplies JDBC drivers. Even if the JDBC connection is altered, the XML document output format should not be affected, because the XML is generated from the result set, not by the RDBMS server. The transformation itself can use any XSLT engine, including Xalan, and if you're using Oracle, the high-performance XSLT processor in the Oracle XDK.

 Please refer to Chapter 16 for examples of XSL transformations using Java.

Another option is client-side processing of XML data. In the next section of this chapter we show you how to manipulate XML data on a Web browser client using XML data islands.

Building Data Islands with the Microsoft XML Core Services (MSXML)

Data islands is a term used to describe tagged data embedded on an HTML page. The data itself can be physically embedded into the HTML. XML data can also be added to an HTML page using a reference to an XML page with a `src='source'` attribute, just like an image. You can also load a separate XML document XML into the page programmatically using JavaScript `XMLDOM` and `XMLHTTP` ActiveX objects. We'll show you an example of loading an `XMLDOM` ActiveX object via JavaScript.

Introduction to XML data islands

XML filtering and sorting is usually faster on a client than via interactive calls to a server. If you use a server to process the sorts and filters, you have to rely on a network connection to process and server each page of filtered or sorted data. Avoiding trips back and forth to the server is usually easier on the server and network. This is why other types of client-side processing, such as JavaScript data validation for forms, produce faster response times for users. The downside is that developers are relying their code to run on a client environment that they have no control over.

 Despite Mozilla and Navigator 6.0 advances in client-side DHTML and XML handling, the JavaScript and client-side XML and XSL examples in this chapter work most reliably on Microsoft Internet Explorer Web browser clients.

The Microsoft XML Core Services (MSXML)

Microsoft XML Core Services (formerly known as the Microsoft XML Parser, which is a little closer to the acronym) is available for free with Internet Explorer 5 and up. The example in this chapter requires the MSXML 4.x parser, which began shipping with IE 6.

If you can't upgrade to IE6, a separate MSXML DLL and related files can be downloaded for free and added to browsers without requiring a full browser upgrade. For developers who are unsure which version they have on their machines, Microsoft provides a free utility for verifying MSXML installation and checking the version of the install. The version checking tool and the latest version of the parser can be downloaded from http://www.microsoft.com/msxml.

The Data Islands Example Page

For this example, I start with an XML document. The XML document is created by the multi-tier J2EE application in Chapter 21. At the top of the XML document is a metadata element, which lists the MS SQL server column names that this XML document is based on. There are three columns: `Quotation`, `AuthorName`, and `SourceName`. Nested inside of the records row is a record element for each row returned by the JDBC query. Listing 22-1 shows the XML document that forms the base of this example.

Listing 22-1: XML Output from the Quote Generator - Servlet Edition

```xml
<?xml version="1.0" encoding="UTF-8"?>
<resultset>
  <metadata>
  <field name="Quotation" datatype="char"/>
  <field name="AuthorName" datatype="char"/>
  <field name="SourceName" datatype="char"/>
  </metadata>
  <records>
  <record rownumber="1">
    <Quotation>When the hurlyburly's done, When the battle's lost and
    won.</Quotation>
    <AuthorName>Shakespeare, William</AuthorName>
    <SourceName>Macbeth</SourceName>
  </record>
  <record rownumber="2">
```

```
    <Quotation>Out, damned spot! out, I say!-- One; two; why,
     then 'tis time to do't ;--Hell is murky!--Fie, my lord, fie! a
     soldier, and afeard? What need we fear who knows it, when none can
     call our power to account?--Yet who would have thought the old man
     to have had so much blood in him?</Quotation>
    <AuthorName>Shakespeare, William</AuthorName>
    <SourceName>Macbeth</SourceName>
  </record>
  <record rownumber="3">
    <Quotation>To-morrow, and to-morrow, and to-morrow, creeps in this
     petty pace from day to day, to the last syllable of recorded time;
     and all our yesterdays have lighted fools the way to dusty death.
     Out, out, brief candle! Life's but a walking shadow; a poor player,
     that struts and frets his hour upon the stage, and then is heard no
     more: it is a tale told by an idiot, full of sound and fury,
     signifying nothing.
    </Quotation>
    <AuthorName>Shakespeare, William</AuthorName>
    <SourceName>Macbeth</SourceName>
  </record>
  </records>
</resultset>
```

The MSXML 4 parser that is part of my IE 6 installation loads the XML document in Listing 22-1 into an HTML page. The XML document is then transformed into a smaller XML document that contains only the Quotation, AuthorName, and SourceName elements, nested inside an element named Quotes. Listing 22-2 shows the transformed data.

Tip   If you are using large XML documents that contain a lot of data that is not needed by the data island, I recommend transforming the data. By performing a transformation to a smaller XML document format when loading the page, you enhance the performance of sorts and filters later. The overhead when loading the page is much less noticeable than when a user clicks on a sort button. If you are using relatively small XML documents as I am here, you probably don't need to perform an XSL transformation.

The new XML document object is parsed into a table that can be sorted by a second XSL stylesheet. The XML document is displayed on the screen as an HTML table with hidden frames. Figure 22-5 shows the HTML page containing the XML data island. The format looks basic, but it contains some very powerful functionality courtesy of the MSXML parser. When the buttons along the top of the screen are clicked, the data dynamically sorts according to instructions sent to the HTML page. The main feature of the page is not the sorting, but the fact that all of the action takes place on the local workstation. No server interaction is needed to filter or sort data once the page is loaded.

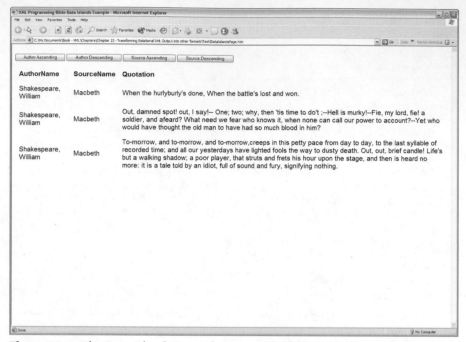

Figure 22-5: The Data Islands Example Page, with buttons for client-side data island sorting

 All of the examples contained in this chapter can be downloaded from the XMLProgrammingBIble.com Website, in the Downloads section. Please see the Web site for installation Instructions.

Creating a data island using JavaScript and MSXML

The HTML page shown in Figure 22-5 calls the getTransformedXML() JavaScript function via the HTML page's onLoad event. The getTransformedXML() function and two deceptively small XSL stylesheets contain most of the functionality for this example. Let's have a look at the getTransformedXML() function in its entirety, then break it down in segments and review each step in more detail. Listing 22-2 shows the code for the getTransformedXML() function.

Listing 22-2: **The Code for the getTransformedXML() Function**

```
var XMLDoc;
var xslSheet;
var transformedXML;
```

```
var sortSheet;
var strResult;

function getTransformedXML()
   {

   XMLDoc = new ActiveXObject("Msxml2.FreeThreadedDOMDocument.4.0");
   XMLDoc.async = false;
   loadSuccess = XMLDoc.load("QuotesExport1.xml");

   xslSheet = new ActiveXObject("Msxml2.FreeThreadedDOMDocument.4.0");
   xslSheet.async = false;
   loadSuccess = xslSheet.load("JDBCXMLtoDIV.xsl");

   sortSheet = new ActiveXObject("Msxml2.FreeThreadedDOMDocument.4.0");
   sortSheet.async = false;
   loadSuccess = sortSheet.load("SortXML.xsl");
   sortSheet.setProperty("SelectionNamespaces",
   "xmlns:xsl='http://www.w3.org/1999/XSL/Transform'");
   transformedXML= new
   ActiveXObject("Msxml2.FreeThreadedDOMDocument.4.0");
   XMLDoc.transformNodeToObject(xslSheet, transformedXML);

   NodeList = transformedXML.documentElement.childNodes;

   var vHTML = "<table
   border=0><tr><thead><th>Author</th><th>Source</th>
   <th>Quote</th></thead>";

   for (var i=0; i<NodeList.length; i++) {

      ChildList = NodeList.item(i).childNodes;
      for (var j=0; j<ChildList.length; j++) {
         Child = ChildList.item(j);
         vHTML += "<td>" + Child.text + "</td>";
      }
    vHTML += "</tr>";
   }
   transformedXMLOutput.innerHTML = vHTML;
   }
```

As mentioned before, we use the Microsoft XML Core Services XMLDOM ActiveX Object to load and parse XML data into the data island. The data island JavaScript code looks deceptively short and simple, because MSXML does most of the work. Let's go through each segment of code and review what's happening when the HTML page is loaded.

Loading the XML document into the data island

The XML document is loaded into the data island by creating a new ActiveX Object. The contents of the XML document are loaded into the XMLDoc object on the page. The async property is set to false, meaning that JavaScript execution is paused until the data is loaded. This doesn't usually represent a noticeable delay and saves developers from having to write code to check and see if a data island has completed population before something is done with the data. The XML document will be transformed once the XMLDoc object is loaded, so it's best to wait for the object to complete loading instead of taking the chance on generating transform errors on an incomplete XML View.

```
XMLDoc = new ActiveXObject("Msxml2.FreeThreadedDOMDocument.4.0");
XMLDoc.async = false;
loadSuccess = XMLDoc.load("QuotesExport1.xml");
```

Loading the stylesheets

The next step is to load each of two XSL stylesheets. The first sheet, represented by the xslSheet object, is used to transform data from the original JDBC result format to a smaller and leaner XML format for sorting and filtering.

The second stylesheet, represented by the sortSheet object, is used to facilitate client-side sorting of data island data. We'll show you how sorting works a little later, but for now let's have a look at how the XML to XML transformation takes place.

```
xslSheet = new ActiveXObject("Msxml2.FreeThreadedDOMDocument.4.0");
xslSheet.async = false;
loadSuccess = xslSheet.load("JDBCXMLtoDIV.xsl");

sortSheet = new ActiveXObject("Msxml2.FreeThreadedDOMDocument.4.0");
sortSheet.async = false;
loadSuccess = sortSheet.load("SortXML.xsl");
```

Transforming an XML document to an XML data island

Once the XML data island source and the XSL stylesheets are loaded, the next step is to transform the XML in the XMLDoc object using the xslSheet stylesheet. To facilitate this, we create a new object called transformedXML. The new object uses the transformNodeToObject method of the XMLDomNode class to apply the xslSheet object and create the new XML document.

The document child nodes are replaced when the document is transformed. The XML transformation can also be sent to a stream, but we're using the transformed data on the same page, so replacing the transformedXML object is more appropriate.

```
transformedXML= new
ActiveXObject("Msxml2.FreeThreadedDOMDocument.4.0");
XMLDoc.transformNodeToObject(xslSheet, transformedXML);
```

The JDBCXMLtoDIV stylesheet is used to facilitate the transformation. The code in the stylesheet starts at the /resultset/records element and adds a new root element for the XML document, called "Quotes." Next, the stylesheet traverses the JDBC result document until it gets to the first /resultset/records/record element. The record element is replaced by the QuoteEntry element in the new XML document. Next, all of the child elements under the record, which represent table columns in the JDBC result, are replaced with simple elements that use their original element names. The contents of the stylesheet are shown in Listing 22-3.

Cross-Reference For more information on XSL transformations and XSL Stylesheets, please refer to Chapters 7 and 8.

Listing 22-3: **The JDBCXMLtoDIV Stylesheet**

```xml
<?xml version="1.0" encoding="UTF-8"?>
<xsl:stylesheet xmlns:xsl="http://www.w3.org/1999/XSL/Transform" version="1.0">
  <xsl:output method="xml"/>
  <xsl:template match="/resultset/records">
  <xsl:element name="Quotes">
    <xsl:apply-templates/>
  </xsl:element>
  </xsl:template>
  <xsl:template match="/resultset/records/record">
  <xsl:element name="QuoteEntry">
    <xsl:apply-templates select="AuthorName"/>
    <xsl:apply-templates select="SourceName"/>
    <xsl:apply-templates select="Quotation"/>
  </xsl:element>
  </xsl:template>
  <xsl:template match="AuthorName">
  <xsl:element name="{name()}">
    <xsl:value-of select="."/>
  </xsl:element>
  </xsl:template>
  <xsl:template match="SourceName">
  <xsl:element name="{name()}">
    <xsl:value-of select="."/>
  </xsl:element>
  </xsl:template>
  <xsl:template match="Quotation">
  <xsl:element name="{name()}">
    <xsl:value-of select="."/>
  </xsl:element>
  </xsl:template>
</xsl:stylesheet>
```

Listing 22-4 shows what the JDBC result set XML document looks like after being transformed to a compact XML format using the stylesheet in Listing 22-3.

Listing 22-4: The Transformed XML Document That Is Loaded into the Data Island

```
<?xml version="1.0" encoding="UTF-8"?>
<Quotes>
  <QuoteEntry>
  <AuthorName>Shakespeare, William</AuthorName>
  <SourceName>Macbeth</SourceName>
  <Quotation>When the hurlyburly's done, When the battle's lost and
won.</Quotation>
  </QuoteEntry>
  <QuoteEntry>
  <AuthorName>Shakespeare, William</AuthorName>
  <SourceName>Macbeth</SourceName>
  <Quotation>Out, damned spot! out, I say!-- One; two; why, then 'tis
   time to do't ;--Hell is murky!--Fie, my lord, fie! a soldier, and
   afeard? What need we fear who knows it, when none can call our power
   to account?--Yet who would have thought the old man to have had so
   much blood in him?</Quotation>
  </QuoteEntry>
  <QuoteEntry>
  <AuthorName>Shakespeare, William</AuthorName>
  <SourceName>Macbeth</SourceName>
  <Quotation>To-morrow, and to-morrow, and to-morrow, creeps in this petty
   pace from day to day, to the last syllable of recorded time; and all
   our yesterdays have lighted fools the way to dusty death. Out, out,
   brief candle! Life's but a walking shadow; a poor player, that struts
   and frets his hour upon the stage, and then is heard no more: it is a
   tale told by an idiot, full of sound and fury, signifying nothing.
   </Quotation>
  </QuoteEntry>
</Quotes>
```

Parsing data island data into a table

Now that the XML document data is in a more compact format, it can be parsed into an HTML table and displayed in a Web browser. The code below iteratively parses the transformed data into DOM nodes, which are then nested in table rows and columns.

```
NodeList = transformedXML.documentElement.childNodes;

    var vHTML = "<table
    border=0><tr><thead><th>Author</th><th>Source</th>
    <th>Quote</th></thead>";

    for (var i=0; i<NodeList.length; i++) {

      ChildList = NodeList.item(i).childNodes;
      for (var j=0; j<ChildList.length; j++) {
         Child = ChildList.item(j);
         vHTML += "<td>" + Child.text + "</td>";
      }
    vHTML += "</tr>";
  }
  transformedXMLOutput.innerHTML = vHTML;
}
```

Once the data has been parsed into HTML table format, it is passed to the `transformedXMLOutput` DIV tag on the screen for display.

Linking XSL with HTML page design elements

At this point the XML document from the J2EE application is transformed and parsed. It's now ready to be filtered and sorted. Now it's time to add design objects to the HTML page to enable data sorting. Four buttons and another JavaScript function are added to the JavaScript to enable the sorting of the data island. It would be great if just adding the buttons enabled sorting on the XML document data, but alas, there is still some work to do before the example is fully functional.

Sorting data islands using JavaScript and XSL

The four buttons along the top of the XML Data Island Example Page call a JavaScript sort function. The buttons also pass parameters with instructions on how to sort the data island data. For example, here's the JavaScript code for the buttons:

```
sort('AuthorName', 'ascending')
sort('AuthorName', 'descending')
sort('SourceName', 'ascending')
sort('SourceName', 'descending')
```

Listing 22-5 shows the sort function, which is added to the header object of the XML Data Island Example HTML code. The JavaScript `sort` function is passed parameters from the JavaScript `button` codes listed above. These parameters become the `strSortBy` and `strOrder` variables in the function. The function calls the `sortSheet` Stylesheet and calls the `selectSingleNode` method of the `XMLDOMNode` class, which returns the first node that matches the value passed by the sort button. Next, the code assigns the `nodeValue` for the XML element and the sort method (either `ascending` or `descending`), and transforms the data using the `transformNode` method of the XMLDOMNode Class.

Listing 22-5: **The JavaScript Sort Function**

```
function sort(strSortBy, strOrder) {

    var objSelect = sortSheet.selectSingleNode("//xsl:sort/@select");
    var objOrder = sortSheet.selectSingleNode("//xsl:sort/@order");

    objSelect.nodeValue = strSortBy;
    objOrder.nodeValue = strOrder;

    strResult = transformedXML.transformNode(sortSheet);

    transformedXMLOutput.innerHTML = strResult;
}
```

The transformation is based on the `SortXML` stylesheet, which is shown in Listing 22-6. The `SortXML` Stylesheet is actually a rough sketch of the entire layout of the XML Data Island Example Page, laid out in an XSL stylesheet. The top half of the code sets up the HTML page title, the fonts and layouts via an embedded cascading style sheet (CSS), and a default display if none is specified for page loading.

When the JavaScript sort function calls this stylesheet, it sets the `nodeValue` for the XML element, which is either `AuthorName` or `SourceName`. The sort method is determined by the `ascending` or `descending`. Once these default nodes are set, the transformation result pivots around the default nodes and produces a sorted XML document, which is rewritten to the `transformedXMLOutput` DIV Tag.

 Cross-Reference For more information on XSL transformations that incorporate HTML, please refer to Chapter 8.

Listing 22-6: **The SortXML Stylesheet**

```
<?xml version="1.0" encoding="UTF-8"?>
<xsl:stylesheet xmlns:xsl="http://www.w3.org/1999/XSL/Transform" version="1.0">
  <xsl:template match="/">
```

```html
<html>
  <head>
  <title>XM Programming BIble Data Islands Example</title>
  </head>
  <body>
  <table border="0" cellpadding="10">
    <tr>
    <th align="left">AuthorName</th>
    <th align="left">SourceName</th>
    <th align="left">Quotation</th>
    </tr>
    <xsl:apply-templates select="/Quotes/QuoteEntry">
    <xsl:sort select="AuthorName" order="ascending"/>
    </xsl:apply-templates>
  </table>
  <p/>
  </body>
</html>
</xsl:template>
<xsl:template match="QuoteEntry">
<tr>
  <td>
  <xsl:value-of select="AuthorName"/>
  </td>
  <td>
  <xsl:value-of select="SourceName"/>
  </td>
  <td>
  <xsl:value-of select="Quotation"/>
  </td>
</tr>
</xsl:template>
</xsl:stylesheet>
```

Summary

In this chapter we've outlined techniques for building transforming relation data to HTML and other formats. We reviewed XSL transformation features in MS SQL Server, Oracle, and DB2. We also showed you how to manipulate XML data from a JDBC result set on a multi-tier application infrastructure using MSXML.

✦ About XSLT

✦ Techniques and tools for building stylesheets

✦ Converting XML to HTML

✦ Support for XSL on MS SQL Server, Oracle, and DB2 RDBMS servers

✦ Manipulating XML data from JDBC result sets

✦ Building data islands

In the next chapter you're introduced to one of the best and most exciting developments in the XML world, Web services. Web services are almost completely based on XML formats, so you'll have plenty of opportunities to apply what you've learned so far.

✦   ✦   ✦

Introducing Web Services

P art V introduces Web services that are based on XML formats and technologies. Web service concepts are introduced, and the three key components of Web services, SOAP, WSDL and UDDI are discussed in detail, with illustrative examples of each technology. Part V ends with a comparison of J2EE and Microsoft Web services, which both use the same underlying technologies but implement them in subtly different ways.

Web Service Concepts

Web services are quickly becoming more than just a promising idea. Countless organizations are implementing them at a surprising rate, even though Web services are still in their relative infancy. At its heart, a Web service is a component-based, self-describing application based on an architecture of emerging standards. Other technologies like CORBA, DCOM, and Java RMI have all targeted the same objective: deliver application functionality as a service-oriented component in a distributed and heterogeneous environment.

This chapter will introduce readers to the concepts of Web services and how they relate to application development, whether the applications leverage XML or not. Nonetheless, we will see how much Web services use XML to make remote interactions possible. We'll start with the basic concepts of Web Services Architectures, SOAP, WSDL, and UDDI. Once we have the basic concepts, we will show how these standards, SOAP, WSDL, and UDDI, can be used in a server-based application and then see how a client can consume the application. These examples are merely introductory as other chapters are specifically dedicated to creating more sophisticated client-server applications using Web services.

Introduction to Web Services

Web services can be defined as a method of integrating data and applications via XML standards across computing platforms and operating systems. Web-service enabled applications make calls and send responses to each other via an XML format called SOAP (Simple Object Access Protocol). Web services are described to clients and other server applications by using another XML format called WSDL (Web Services

Description Language), which is associated with all standard Web services. Registration information and location of a Web service can be published to a UDDI (Universal Description, Discovery, and Integration) directory, which is itself a Web service, and because it's a Web service, each UDDI registry server contains associated WSDL files and SOAP accessibility.

Web services are moving quickly, and new sites that either implement a UDDI registry search tool or provide their own navigational tools to find Web Service Providers (WSPs) are springing up daily. Those that implement UDDI browsing are a little forbidding to the Web service newcomer, but they often have the most detailed and well-organized information. Whether you discover a Web service through an online search or if you just stumble upon one (it does happen), the fundamentals of the service are all the same.

The promise of Web services is not in simple or even complex call-and-response applications, but in having those applications function together as a single entity while accessing many different types of data on several disparate software platforms and operating systems. For example, most readers have probably had the experience of booking a flight, rental car, or hotel on a Website. The promise of Web services is to take this common experience such as travel booking and extend it via a smart client and Web services to coordinate your flight booking with simultaneous hotel and car bookings based on a client's preferences and expense limits, and then update a calendar and expense tracking system with final booking data. Then have the smart Web Services client notify the traveler of any flight delays or schedule changes, incorporating all the data in several back-end and client systems via the smart client. Web services and related emerging technologies promise this kind of seamless functionality and are starting to deliver.

Web Service Building Blocks

It's important to point out that the specifications for the main building blocks for Web services are still very much in development, even though most of the technologies and specifications are based on the W3C (World Wide Web Consortium) XML Standard. There are several organizations that are working on the development of these specifications and tools, hopefully with backward-compatibility for the existing tools that make up many core Web services.

The Web services organization that's grabbing most of the attention these days is the Web Services Interoperability Organization (WS-I). WS-I is an industry organization that represents most of the major players, including Oracle, IBM, Microsoft, BEA System, and many others, including recently, SUN. Their charter is to provide Web services interoperability (hence the name!) across platforms, applications, and programming languages. You may be wondering why such a consortium is needed when the whole idea of Web services is to provide platform-agnostic component interaction. The irony is lost on no one. However, in fairness, the truth of the matter is that nothing is very simple. Even XML, the most critical protocol of Web services, is not *completely* platform-agnostic. If this were not true, some parts of this book would not be necessary.

Aside from providing a forum to hammer out compatibility and standards, there are several WS-I "deliverables" that may be of interest to Web service developers:

✦ **Profiles** are sets of specifications that work together to support specific solutions, like design patterns, but outlining best practices in Web service standards rather than application architectures.

✦ **Sample implementations** are teams that are the result of teams that are put together to assemble and test applications based on profiles, which provide valuable documentation on performance and functionality flashpoints.

✦ **Implementation guidelines** are a result of the sample implementations based on the profiles. They are similar to W3C Recommendations, but also can be based on W3C Recommendations, and are not specifications per se, but more like best practices based on implementation testing.

✦ **Test Materials** are for testing, monitoring, and logging Web service interactions. The monitor tool runs at runtime and produces a log file that the analyzer reads. The monitor and analyzer produce results that are based on implementation guidelines.

More information about the WS-I and the deliverables can be found at `http://www.ws-i.org/`.

Most of the current efforts and implementations at the WS-I are based on specifications that are being developed by the W3C. The WS-I cooperates with the W3C on developing the SOAP and WSDL specifications, and the Universal Description, Discovery and Integration (UDDI) project for UDDI registries.

In general the WS-I provides implementation testing and support for applications based on emerging specifications, and the W3C and UDDI project provide specifications, which are in turn often extended and updated by efforts by the WS-I deliverables.

Now that we have some idea of the players involved in the specification development and implementation of Web service standards, let's have a look at the SOAP, WSDL, and UDDI building blocks that are currently in development.

SOAP (Simple Object Access Protocol)

SOAP enables transportation of Web service calls and responses. SOAP is a messaging format that describes XML data according to W3C standards, and represents call and response data in an envelope and message format. The current W3C specification-in-progress can be viewed at `http://www.w3.org/TR/SOAP/`.

SOAP structure can be compared to a letter or package mailer. SOAP documents are XML documents that contain an envelope, which contains a description of the contents of a message (but not the message yet!), serialization (encoding) rules for application-defined data types, which are represented as text serializations of data according to XML specifications, and optional RPC representation for remote procedure call and response formats, if RPC is the transport being used to send an receive the SOAP document. HTTP and SMTP are other transport options, though RPC is the most common transport method, and SMTP is rarely used.

WSDL (Web Services Description Language)

WSDL is based on the W3C XML standard, and describes what Web services are, what they do, and how they can be accessed to applications that want to access them via SOAP. All standard Web services are described in an associated WSDL document. WSDL can be complicated and verbose, but it enables clients or other Web services to develop or adapt application interfaces based on WSDL document specifications. For example, currently there are several tools that enable developers to create a client and/or server interface to a Web service by parsing a service's WSDL and automatically building code to handle calls and responses to the Web service, including the IBM Web Services Tool Kit (WSTK) for Java interfaces, and several tools from Microsoft for MS and .NET applications (wsdl.exe, disco.exe, and more). Most of these tools create and adapt a proxy class from WSDL. The proxy class can act as a client or server interface to the Web service by handling SOAP calls and responses to and from the client or another Web service via the generated Java classes. The Web services activity group at the W3C is currently developing WSDL, and the working draft of the specification can be seen at `http://www.w3.org/TR/2002/WD-wsdl12-20020709/`.

UDDI (Universal Description, Discovery and Integration)

UDDI is the directory standard for Web services, developed and maintained by the Universal Description, Discovery and Integration (UDDI) project, which is a part of the Organization for the Advancement of Structured Information Standards (OASIS) and is not part of the W3C. There are no auto-indexing or discovery features as are common with Web crawler search engines for HTML pages on the Web. Each Web service provider and each service must be registered on a UDDI server and must be manually registered, either at the one of the two current UDDI Websites, or via a UDDI registry Web service client. Currently IBM, Microsoft, SAP, and NTT Telecom host versions of the UDDI directory, which are kept in sync via replication. URLs for registry sites as well as the latest version of the UDDI specification can be found at `http://uddi.org/`.

Web Services Architecture

Due to the developing nature of the Web services specification and the community, vendors such as IBM and Microsoft, and organizations such as the WS-I have developed several Web service architectures and published specifications. However, the most advanced and complete architecture for general Web services based on current W3C specifications is the specification developed by the W3C Web Services Architecture Working Group. The full specification is described at `http://www.w3.org/2002/ws/arch/`.

Basic Web service architecture

Basic Web services can be described as applications that employ W3C and UDDI standard specifications for SOAP, WSDL, and UDDI to exchange messages, describe Web services, and publish Web service descriptions. The official term for applications that handle Web services is agents. Agents can be consumers or servers of a Web service, but consumers must be able to find descriptions of Web services via WSDL associated with a Web service provider agent.

Added to the mix is the role of the service discovery agency, which uses UDDI to publish registered Web services to Web service consumers, much like a real estate agency puts buyers and sellers together for homes, but (so far!) without the commission. The concept is that a consumer will find a Web service they need at a service discovery agency, then follow the registration information to the service location, and then access the service according to instructions in the published WSDL document. Figure 23-1 shows the layout of a basic Web service architecture, including an optional service discovery agency.

Extended Web service architectures

Extended Web service architectures involve support for more complicated message exchange patterns (MEPs) that create a full multi-layered transaction from simple call and response mechanisms. These transactions can include security and authentication, event chaining to other Web services, and confirmation and roll-back functionality.

Extended Web service architectures also take advantage of more recent developments in W3C and UDDI specifications, such as including attachments in SOAP documents to represent several transactions accumulated or concatenated during a complicated multi-layer transaction, authenticating messages via user ID and password, application authentication tokens, or X.509 certificates.

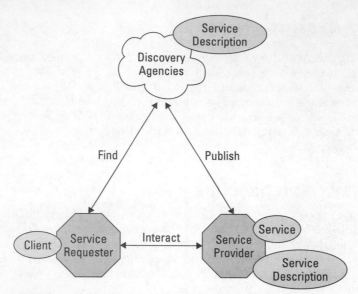

Figure 23-1: The basic Web service architecture

Other initiatives include development of encryption for SOAP messages, digital signatures, fixed message routing, and session handling between messages and services.

Figure 23-2 shows the layout of extended Web service architectures, illustrating how the different components work together. Most of the operational load falls on the SOAP messages, with additional support for authentication and security in the WSDL documents, and no significant changes in the UDDI directory role.

The role of workflow is also currently being developed, with the Business Process Execution Language for Web Service (BPEL4WS) looking like a good but developing way to handle synchronized execution of Web services. BPEL4WS was developed in a joint effort between IBM, Microsoft, and BEA Systems. More information on the specification can be found at `http://www-106.ibm.com/developerworks/library/ws-bpel/`.

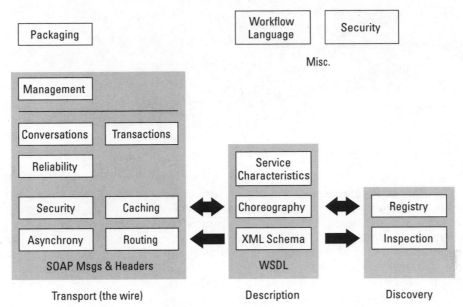

Figure 23-2: Extended Web service architectures

Web Service Models

Beyond the specifications, basic and extended Web service architectures can be broken down into three real-world models: call and response, brokered calls, and chained.

The call and response model

The basic format for a Web service is a default call and response mechanism from one calling agent to a serving agent. In this scenario, the calling agent can either be a Web services client or a Web services provider.

The calling agent in this case has already discovered the serving agent, and the calling agent simply interacts with the serving agent via SOAP calls and responses. The call is made to the serving agent via a dynamic generation of an interface by the calling agent based on the WSDL document of the serving agent, a developer who has read the WSDL and created a compatible interface, or by a non-dynamic WSDL interface generation tool. Figure 23-3 illustrates a basic call and response Web service model, with WDSL being interpreted and SOAP calls and responses generated based on the WSDL.

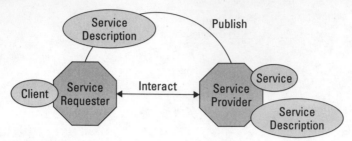

Figure 23-3: The call and response model

This is the most common method of Web service interaction today. Most clients are either Web browsers or smart clients such as Java or Windows applications that access a predetermined Web service at a predetermined location. If interactions with multiple Web services are required for a transaction, as in the travel-booking scenario described in the introduction of this chapter, then the client usually controls the Web service call and response flow by waiting for one Web service to return data before the next Web service is called.

The brokered calls model

The brokered calls model is very similar to the call and response model, but with the addition of a Web service between the calling and providing agents. The function of the "middle man" in this case is not the same as the service discovery agency role described in the basic Web service architecture. Instead of acting as an agent that puts calling agents together with appropriate providing agents, the central Web service in this case acts like an application proxy for the calling agent, processing one or more call and response mechanisms on behalf of the original calling agent to one or more serving agents, and then returning concatenated responses to the calling agent. As with the previous scenario, the calling agent can either be a Web services client or another Web services provider. The central Web service can also be used to centrally enforce security and authentication standards between Web services.

This multi-tier Web services architecture simplifies client application maintenance by simplifying the application requirements for the calling agent and providing a layer for the Web service to adapt to changes in the environment, such as a server move or WSDL change for a serving agent. Figure 23-4 illustrates a brokered calls model, with WDSL being interpreted and SOAP calls and responses generated based on the WSDL, through an intermediate Web service.

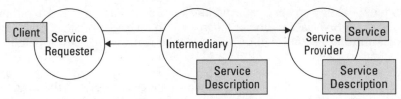

Figure 23-4: The call and response model

The chained model

The chained model is more closely aligned with current architecture specifications, and implements several new features of SOAP and a few features of more recent WSDL specifications, such as support for attachments in SOAP documents to represent several transactions accumulated or concatenated during a complicated multi-layer chained transaction, authenticating messages, digital signatures, commit and rollback functionality, and workflow specifications such as the Business Process Execution Language for Web Service (BPEL4WS).

Web Service interaction is still facilitated through calls and responses, but the calling and responding agents can also call and respond to other agents to get their jobs done, rolling the series of calls and responses into a single network transaction that eventually finds it way back to the calling agent. The chain can start at the client level or at a server level via the brokered calls model. Figure 23-5 illustrates a brokered calls model, with WDSL being interpreted, and SOAP calls and responses are generated based on the WSDL along every link of the chain.

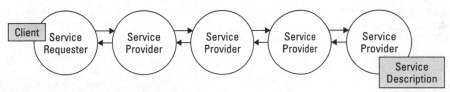

Figure 23-5: The chained model

Serving Web Services

Web services can be served from any platform that can support data binding to the HTTP, RPC, or SMTP protocols and the deployment of a related WSDL document to describe an application as a Web service. Once that's done, the Web service can be registered to a UDDI server (or published at Xmethods.com) for Web service clients to access.

However, in most cases Web service providing agents are implemented in either Java or one of the MS Visual Studio.net languages, to take advantage of platform-specific tools, utilities, and class libraries that make Web service development more of a practical enterprise.

For example, most Java implementations of Web services use one of the UI tools for development, such as WebSphere application Developer, Sun One developer for Java, or the IBM Web Services toolkit to speed up Web service development time. In almost all cases, Java implementation of Web services uses the Apache SOAP class libraries as their SOAP implementation.

Consuming Web Services

As with serving Web services, Web services can be called from any platform that can support data binding to the HTTP, RPC, or SMTP protocols and that is able to read and interpret a Web service provider's WSDL document, either via a dynamic generation of an interface by the calling agent based on the WSDL document of the serving agent, a developer who has read the WSDL and created a compatible interface, or by a non-dynamic WSDL interface generation tool. Once the interface to the Web service has been established, the client can call the Web service as if it were part of the local system.

However, Web services shine when a smart client with a rich UI base and easy integration with tools such as calendars, to-do lists, and e-mail are available. In this case, browsers make very basic Web service clients. The best Web service clients tend to be Windows applications or ASP.NET applications because of the Web service integration features in Windows, Office XP, the .NET Framework, and the ease of development for Web service client applications via Visual Studio.NET tools.

Summary

In this chapter, we provided an introduction to Web services and a description of how Web service standards and specifications are developing. Next, we provided a quick introduction to the Web Service Building Blocks: SOAP, WSDL, and UDDI. We provided an overview of Web service architecture as well, with details on the three most common Web service models: call and response, brokered calls, and chaining. We also covered the basic requirements for serving Web services and consuming Web services. Other chapters get into the building blocks in greater detail. For example, we look at the detail of a SOAP request and response. We also get into WSDL and how it works, and we take a hard look at UDDI and its operations.

✦   ✦   ✦

SOAP

The Simple Object Access Protocol (SOAP) is designed to let you invoke remote applications independent of platform and programming language. It is important for application development to allow applications to communicate over the Internet, irrespective of the platform on which the application is running. Today's applications communicate using Remote Procedure Call (RPC) mechanisms between objects using protocols like DCOM and CORBA. However, HTTP was not really designed to accommodate the sophisticated interactions needed when using these RPCs. Because an RPC carries a request to do something rather important, RPC represents a compatibility and security vulnerability that firewalls and proxy servers will normally block.

The challenge then is to allow this kind of complex application interaction using an RPC without compromising security and without sacrificing platform-agnostic advantages. SOAP is the protocol for packaging these requests when sending method calls over HTTP. SOAP makes it possible to communicate between applications running on different operating systems, with different technologies and programming languages all in play. In this chapter, we will get into the nuts and bolts of SOAP. We will look at the specific structure of SOAP messages, how to send and receive messages, and what is contained in the full payload of a SOAP message.

 Note   For information on the actual SOAP specification go to http://www.w3.org/. For more practical SOAP information and samples you can go to http://www.xmethods.com.

Introduction

SOAP is an evolutionary result of the development of distributed computing over the Web. In recent years, the need has arisen for a method of invoking application calls and responses in a format that will travel easily through corporate firewalls and the Internet, and at the same time describe the often-complicated data that is being delivered in an accurate and detailed way. As most developers know, applications and data usually start out simple and quickly get complicated as layers of complexity are added to systems. For example, here's a fairly simple ASP URL call with some querystring parameters.

```
http://localhost/XMLWeb/GetCustomerData.aspx?Formatting=FullHTM
L&CustomerIDEncoded=1823F3A3948300E4
```

This call passes only two parameters to the URL, which are then passed to the code behind the page. This code returns some customer data based on the parameters that are passed. You are accustomed to seeing this kind of URL when visiting many sites on the Internet, and there is nothing inherently wrong with such things. While this is a very simple example, it is not uncommon to have 20 or 100 parameters passed to a URL in an unreadable string. Where this strategy starts to become cumbersome is when the need arises to start describing the data format of parameters for distributed applications or when needing to send or return complex datatypes to the application. Also, this URL-based strategy is not a component-based solution. No matter what you do, you are still just sending URL requests and getting responses as URLs, not as actual objects in code. It starts to become obvious that a new way is needed to pass values from one distributed application to another, including the description of the data being sent. XML is a natural format for sending this data, because of its transportability and rich formatting capabilities for representing complex data formats in a hierarchy. Add messaging capabilities, encoding for data representation, and RPC descriptors, and you have SOAP.

SOAP format

The W3C SOAP specification is based on XML and used to describe objects that are used to make calls and responses in Web services and other distributed applications over HTTP.

SOAP is formatted in several parts that are used to deliver calls and responses:

✦ **The SOAP endpoint,** which is an HTTP-standard URL, with an optional URI and SoapAction.

✦ **One or more SOAP methods** (for calls via HTTP POST) to be called on a Web service. Each method is identified by a namespace URI (more on namespace URIs a little later).

✦ **The HTTP header** indicating the method being invoked by this call.

✦ **The SOAP envelope** describes what is in a message and what should be done with the message.

✦ **The SOAP encoding rules** describe serializations of data based on general or application-specific data types.

✦ **The optional SOAP RPC representation** can be used to represent remote procedure calls and responses.

✦ **The SOAP body** contains the call or response message that is described by the envelope and encoded according to the encoding rules.

A SOAP request

Let's examine an actual SOAP call and response to a Web service. The examples we are using in this chapter include the "Delayed Quote" example on the Xmethods Website, at `http://www.Xmethods.com` and some custom Web services created for this chapter. The Xmethods Website is a great starting point for developers who want to get familiar with Web services. It provides several practical working examples, tutorials, and a place for Web Service Developers to post and share their Web services.

One thing to keep in mind before looking at these examples is that in all cases here we are using SOAP to bind to HTTP as the transport protocol for the SOAP requests and responses. The advantage is that transport protocol fits the request/response message model providing SOAP request parameters in a HTTP request and SOAP response parameters in an HTTP response.

The HTTP header

The HTTP header is generated based on values in the WSDL file for the Web service, which we will review a little later in this chapter.

Let's look at the HTTP Request and the SOAP envelope that is sent with the request in Listing 24-1.

Listing 24-1: Xmethods Stock Quote SOAP Request HTTP Header

```
HTTP Header:
POST /soap HTTP/1.1
Host: 66.28.98.121:9090
Content-Type: text/xml; charset=utf-8
SOAPAction: "urn:xmethods-delayed-quotes#getQuote"
```

POST and GET

The first line of the HTTP header for the soap request contains three things: the HTTP method (POST), the request Uniform Resource Identifier (/soap), and the HTTP protocol version (1.1). HTTP GET is the regular HTTP method for surfing the Web, which sends a URL and optional parameters such as port number. POST is used to make calls to Web services, which tells the HTTP server to expect more than just a URL as part of the request. The HTTP method is blank when a response is returned.

URIs, URLs, and URNs

Uniform Resource Identifiers are just short strings that identify resources in the Web. You can think of URIs as the general format definition of which URLs are an implementation. URIs point to things like documents, images, files, services, e-mail inboxes, and so on. URIs, as a generalization, do not specify what protocol should be used to access the resource. However, common access methods are HTTP or FTP. Uniform Resource Locators (URLs), with which anyone who uses the Web is probably already familiar, are a type.

Uniform Resource Names (URNs) are different, but they are also URIs. The main difference is that URLs are used to specify a location-specific resource on the Web, such as `http://www.ibm.com`, while URNs are used to describe a value that could be at any Web location. In other words, a URN is the name of a resource that identifies a unit of information independent of its location. URNs are a name that can be mapped to one or more URLs. URNs are usually used to mask a complicated namespace or value for later reference, similar to the way DNS replaces an IP address with a URL. In this case, the request URI (Uniform Resource Identifier) identifies the soap subdirectory as the target of the request. If no URI is specified in an HTTP POST, the default HTTP directory of the server is used.

SOAPAction

Let's see what this discussion of URIs, URLs, and URNs has to do with SOAP. SOAPAction is used with a URL and a URI to further identify the location of the Web service on the server. In most implementations, the URI and the SOAPAction header will have the same value and therefore is optional. However, in this case the SOAPAction is "urn:xmethods-delayed-quotes#getQuote," which indicates the method name of `getQuote` and the URN name of urn:xmethods-delayed-quotes. The HTTP header assembles the URL and URI of the HTTP post to find the Web service endpoint. A Web service endpoint is the place where the Web service calling methods are located. In this case, the endpoint is the /soap directory at 66.28.98.121:9090, and the SOAPAction tells us that we need to use the `getQuote` method of the service in our request.

The SOAP request envelope

Once we have the target of the HTTP Post, we can use the SOAP envelope to make the call to the Web service method listed in the SOAPAction and pass the contents of the SOAP envelope to the Web service for processing. Listing 24-2 shows the SOAP request envelope.

Listing 24-2: **Xmethods Stock Quote SOAP Request**

```
<?xml version="1.0" encoding="UTF-8" standalone="no"?>
<SOAP-ENV:Envelope xmlns:SOAP-
ENV="http://schemas.xmlsoap.org/soap/envelope/"
xmlns:tns="http://www.themindelectric.com/wsdl/net.xmethods.ser
vices.stockquote.StockQuote/"
xmlns:electric="http://www.themindelectric.com/"
xmlns:soap="http://schemas.xmlsoap.org/wsdl/soap/"
xmlns:xsd="http://www.w3.org/2001/XMLSchema"
xmlns:soapenc="http://schemas.xmlsoap.org/soap/encoding/"
xmlns:wsdl="http://schemas.xmlsoap.org/wsdl/"
xmlns:xsi="http://www.w3.org/2001/XMLSchema-instance">

<SOAP-ENV:Body>
<mns:getQuote xmlns:mns="urn:xmethods-delayed-quotes" SOAP-
ENV:encodingStyle="http://schemas.xmlsoap.org/soap/encoding/">
<symbol xsi:type="xsd:string">MSFT</symbol>
</mns:getQuote>
</SOAP-ENV:Body>
</SOAP-ENV:Envelope>
```

SOAP envelope structure

Like the HTTP header in a SOAP request, the SOAP envelope is based on values declared in the WSDL file for the Web service, which provides instructions on how requests and responses to the Web Service are structured. Because SOAP messages are well-formed XML documents, we start with an XML declaration, followed by a single <SOAP-ENV:Envelope> root element. The <SOAP-ENV:Envelope> contains several namespace declarations, which we will cover in the next section of this chapter.

In the mandatory <SOAP-ENV:Body> element, we find the getQuote method call as an element name. The nested value in the getQuote element is the parameter that we will pass to the getQuote method when it is called by the SOAPAction in the HTTP header, the value of which is the stock symbol for Microsoft Corporation. All parameters for a method must be contained in elements inside the procedure call.

One advanced technique that the SOAP structure permits is the passing of what is known as the SOAP header. A SOAP header is an optional element in the overall SOAP envelope structure. The Body element contains the data specific to the message, and the Header element can hold additional information not directly related to the particular method call. Each child element of the Header element is called a SOAP header.

For example, you may want to place authentication information in the SOAP header for some or all methods of a Web service. In this way, the authentication information is passed with the method call and can be verified before the specific target method executes. If the authentication fails, you can throw a new SOAP exception so that the calling program knows why the call failed. Sending back a clear exception will help the calling code know that the error had nothing to do with the target method and was an authentication error.

Although the SOAP headers can contain data related to the message, it is probably not as straightforward to do so. You should control data for a given method call by using parameters rather than using a SOAP header element. The SOAP specification doesn't have any rules about what can be in the header, so you can define its contents any way you wish. A good practice is to define a SOAP header that holds method-independent information that can be processed by the Web service once it is passed; they typically contain information processed by infrastructure within a Web server. Listing 24-3 shows the XML definition of a SOAP envelope that also contains a SOAP header element.

Listing 24-3: **SOAP Request with an Optional SOAP Header**

```
<?xml version="1.0" encoding="utf-8"?>
<soap:Envelope xmlns:xsi="http://www.w3.org/2001/XMLSchema-
instance" xmlns:xsd="http://www.w3.org/2001/XMLSchema"
xmlns:soap="http://schemas.xmlsoap.org/soap/envelope/">
  <soap:Header>
    <CustomerHeader xmlns="http://tempuri.org/">
      <CustomerToken>string</CustomerToken>
    </CustomerHeader>
  </soap:Header>
  <soap:Body>
    <GetAccountDetails xmlns="http://tempuri.org/">
      <accountID>int</accountID>
    </GetAccountDetails>
  </soap:Body>
</soap:Envelope>
```

Notice that there is a new section that you do not see in Listing 24-2. The SOAP header here specifies that we can pass a custom type called CustomerHeader.

That type has a property called `CustomerToken` that is a string. When the client program calls a method of the Web service, like `GetAccountDetails`, it can also pass the SOAP header in the way shown in Listing 24-4.

Listing 24-4: Client Application Calling the Web Service with the SOAP Header

```
Dim oSVC As New CustomerSVC.SoapHeaderDemo()
Dim oHeader As New CustomerSVC.CustomerHeader()
oHeader.CustomerToken = "One"
oSVC.CustomerHeaderValue = oHeader
Dim bln As Boolean = oSVC.GetAccountDetails(ID)
```

Don't worry too much about the language syntax here and other environmental conventions. Rather, look at the way the special SOAP header is used. First, the code gets an instance of the special SOAP header type defined in the WSDL. This is the `CustomerHeader` type. The type has a property called `CustomerToken` that accepts a string value. Then, the instance of the `CustomerHeaderType` is placed in a value container extended by the Web service. At this point, the client application can access the Web service method that uses the SOAP header in a normal fashion.

In the end, the principal benefit of SOAP headers is the ability to pass along to the Web service additional information. This information can be of any sort and can even be contained in complex types. The important thing is that the Web service knows what to do with the SOAP header once it is received.

Namespaces, URNs, and SOAP encoding

Unlike most basic forms of XML, namespaces and schemas are a very important part of Web services XML technologies. Namespaces can be arbitrary in other types of applications. For example, when writing your own object libraries, you can specify your own namespace for components written for your company, such as ourcompany.applications.customers or ourcompany.applications.humanresources. These two namespaces are ones that make sense within the frontiers of your organization. Other namespaces, however, may actually point to specification documents or schemas when the namespace is resolved. The namespaces referenced inside an XSL stylesheet are examples of these, such as `<xsl:stylesheet version="1.0" xmlns:xsl="http://www.w3.org/1999/XSL/Transform">`. This namespace is not arbitrary as it makes it possible to use XSL elements in your stylesheets like `<xsl:if>` or `<xsl:copy>`.

In a similar manner, the namespaces referenced in a SOAP call are not arbitrary. All of the URLs specified by namespaces in the SOAP envelope in Listing 24-2 actually resolve to real Schema documents describing the structure of the elements and attributes represented by that namespace. Each URL namespace is assigned to a smaller URN for use in the SOAP envelope. For example, the URL represented in this line is assigned a namespace of SOAP-ENV that resolves to the SOAP envelope Schema URL:

```
xmlns:SOAP-ENV="http://schemas.xmlsoap.org/soap/envelope/"
```

This way, when we define the body of the envelope, we can use this:

```
<SOAP-ENV:Body>
```

Which is easier to follow than this:

```
< http://schemas.xmlsoap.org/soap/envelope/:Body>
```

Schemas also define SOAP data encoding as well as element and attribute structures. For example, any nested elements in the getQuote method use the namespace xsi, which resolves to http://www.w3.org/2001/XMLSchema-instance, which in turn describes basic data types for elements, such as float and string. Developers can choose between using standard data encoding formats, or developing their own, and an associated schema to go with them.

A SOAP response

Once the SOAP request has been made, the Web service returns a response. The body of the response formatted according to the same SOAP envelope structure and encoding rules, but in this case containing less namespaces and a slight variation on the method name, as shown in Listing 24-5.

Listing 24-5: Xmethods Stock Quote SOAP Response

```
<?xml version="1.0" encoding="UTF-8"?>
<soap:Envelope
xmlns:soap="http://schemas.xmlsoap.org/soap/envelope/"
xmlns:xsi="http://www.w3.org/2001/XMLSchema-instance"
xmlns:xsd="http://www.w3.org/2001/XMLSchema"
xmlns:soapenc="http://schemas.xmlsoap.org/soap/encoding/"
soap:encodingStyle="http://schemas.xmlsoap.org/soap/encoding/">
<soap:Body>
<n:getQuoteResponse xmlns:n="urn:xmethods-delayed-quotes">
<Result xsi:type="xsd:float">56.27</Result>
</n:getQuoteResponse>
</soap:Body>
</soap:Envelope>
```

The single Body element contains the original method name with the word "Response" added to the end of it (getQuote + Response=getQuoteResponse), which makes for easy calculation of the response element name for parsing and transformation of the response data. The response to the request is located in the same nested element of the method as the request was located, using the same encoding namespace, xsi.

Summary

This chapter introduced the SOAP specification. We have seen how SOAP messages are put together and how they are represented. SOAP messages define the points of contact between the Web service and the client application that calls it. SOAP does not care about how the messages are passed between the two parties. Rather, SOAP is concerned with how the messages are put together. Each party, the client and the server-based application, must have the necessary SOAP tools to pick up a message packaged according to the SOAP specification and then pass the information to code that will do the processing. The data are packaged up in a deliberate fashion that includes an envelope, header(s), body, SOAPAction, and how to send requests and receive responses. The next chapter goes deeper into WSDL, the specification that lets the client application know about the methods, headers, and other data interactions that are possible with a Web service.

✦   ✦   ✦

WSDL

So far we have looked at the SOAP message format that is sent to and from Web services. WSDL is the other moving part of a Web Services Architecture, which defines what SOAP calls and responses should look like, and helps Web service calling agents define what an interface should be to a specific Web service.

WSDL Format

In a previous chapter, we used the Stock Quote Web service from the XMethods Website. This service accepts a stock symbol and returns the stock quote that is up to 20 minutes old. Listing 25-1 contains the calling code that gets the stock quote from the service and puts it in a text box.

Listing 25-1: Code from a Calling Application That Uses a Web Service

```
Dim oSvc As New DelayedQuote. _

netxmethodsservicesstockquoteStockQuoteService
()
    Dim sglPrice As Single
    sglPrice = oSvc.getQuote("MSFT")
    txtPrice.Text = CType(sglPrice, String))
```

There is a single class available, one that is inordinately long to be sure, `netxmethodsservicesstockquoteStock QuoteService`, has a method, `getQuote`. If the following conditions are true: 1) a Web service is entirely remote and 2) using a Web service means that no code components or type library information is downloaded to the computer that calls the Web service, then the only way the client application can know about the service's behaviors is by having some kind of type library information. This is provided by WSDL.

Most developers are overwhelmed when they see WSDL for the first time. Web Services Description Language is based on XML, but with the addition of many namespaces, parts, ports, and so on, the format can be intimidating. However, it's important to remember that WSDL is not really meant for humans to read; its purpose is to inform Web service clients and other Web services about how to access the methods in a Web service. The verbosity of WSDL is actually a very good feature for Web services. The detail allows Web services to converse with each other without ambiguity about any aspect of each other's function.

The good news is that most development tools in the Java and Windows application world these days have some sort of WSDL generation tools to free developers from the drudgery of WSDL coding. Also, more advanced tools are currently becoming available that allow clients and other Web services to create and adapt interfaces to other Web services. The theory is that if a Web service changes its data formats, the calling agent should be able to adapt to the function, as long as the serving agent's WSDL is up to date.

WSDL is formatted in several parts that are used to describe a Web service:

✦ **definitions:** WSDL files start with a root definitions element, which defines a Web service. As with SOAP, this is followed by namespace definitions as parameters of the definitions element.

✦ **documentation:** Can be contained under the definitions element in a documentation tag.

✦ **types:** Describe the structures of data to be contained in call and response SOAP messages.

✦ **messages:** Group types together to describe an input, output, or fault message.

✦ **operations:** Group input, output, and fault messages into a unit.

✦ **portTypes:** Can group together or contain one or more operations. All operations have to be contained in at least one portType.

✦ **bindings:** Tie portTypes to a specific protocol.

✦ **ports:** Tie bindings together with specific Web service endpoints.

✦ **Services:** Tie one or more ports together.

It is important to know that as of this writing, WSDL is not yet a full standard, but it will be. Some big companies are behind WSDL as the standard descriptive language for Web services. Companies like Microsoft and IBM are supporting its adoption and development, and it is currently the de facto standard on the Web.

Let's have a look at the WSDL file for the XMethods Stock Quote Web Service, in Listing 25-2.

Listing 25-2: **XMethods Stock Quote WSDL**

```
<wsdl:definitions
xmlns:tns="http://www.themindelectric.com/wsdl/net.xmethods.ser
vices.stockquote.StockQuote/"
xmlns:electric="http://www.themindelectric.com/"
xmlns:soap="http://schemas.xmlsoap.org/wsdl/soap/"
xmlns:xsd="http://www.w3.org/2001/XMLSchema"
xmlns:soapenc="http://schemas.xmlsoap.org/soap/encoding/"
xmlns:wsdl="http://schemas.xmlsoap.org/wsdl/"
xmlns="http://schemas.xmlsoap.org/wsdl/"
targetNamespace="http://www.themindelectric.com/wsdl/net.xmetho
ds.services.stockquote.StockQuote/"
name="net.xmethods.services.stockquote.StockQuote">
<message name="getQuoteResponse1">
<part name="Result" type="xsd:float"/>
</message>
<message name="getQuoteRequest1">
<part name="symbol" type="xsd:string"/>
</message>
<portType
name="net.xmethods.services.stockquote.StockQuotePortType">
<operation name="getQuote" parameterOrder="symbol">
<input message="tns:getQuoteRequest1"/>
<output message="tns:getQuoteResponse1"/>
</operation>
</portType>
<binding
name="net.xmethods.services.stockquote.StockQuoteBinding"
type="tns:net.xmethods.services.stockquote.StockQuotePortType">
<soap:binding style="rpc"
transport="http://schemas.xmlsoap.org/soap/http"/>
<operation name="getQuote">
<soap:operation soapAction="urn:xmethods-delayed-
quotes#getQuote"/>
<input>
<soap:body use="encoded"
encodingStyle="http://schemas.xmlsoap.org/soap/encoding/"
namespace="urn:xmethods-delayed-quotes"/>
</input>
<output>
<soap:body use="encoded"
encodingStyle="http://schemas.xmlsoap.org/soap/encoding/"
namespace="urn:xmethods-delayed-quotes"/>
</output>
```

Continued

Listing 25-2 *(continued)*

```
</operation>
</binding>
<service
name="net.xmethods.services.stockquote.StockQuoteService">
<documentation>net.xmethods.services.stockquote.StockQuote web
service</documentation>
<port name="net.xmethods.services.stockquote.StockQuotePort"
binding="tns:net.xmethods.services.stockquote.StockQuoteBinding
">
<soap:address location="http://66.28.98.121:9090/soap"/>
</port>
</service>
</wsdl:definitions>
```

This may seem like a lot of information, but let's break it down. Figure 25-1 shows the same WSDL file only with the nodes collapsed so we can make a little more sense of it.

```
<?xml version="1.0" encoding="UTF-8" ?>
- <definitions name="net.xmethods.services.stockquote.StockQuote"
    targetNamespace="http://www.themindelectric.com/wsdl/net.xmethods.services.stockquote.StockQuote/"
    xmlns:tns="http://www.themindelectric.com/wsdl/net.xmethods.services.stockquote.StockQuote/"
    xmlns:electric="http://www.themindelectric.com/" xmlns:soap="http://schemas.xmlsoap.org/wsdl/soap/"
    xmlns:xsd="http://www.w3.org/2001/XMLSchema"
    xmlns:soapenc="http://schemas.xmlsoap.org/soap/encoding/"
    xmlns:wsdl="http://schemas.xmlsoap.org/wsdl/" xmlns="http://schemas.xmlsoap.org/wsdl/">
  + <message name="getQuoteResponse1">
  + <message name="getQuoteRequest1">
  + <portType name="net.xmethods.services.stockquote.StockQuotePortType">
  + <binding name="net.xmethods.services.stockquote.StockQuoteBinding"
      type="tns:net.xmethods.services.stockquote.StockQuotePortType">
  + <service name="net.xmethods.services.stockquote.StockQuoteService">
</definitions>
```

Figure 25-1: Collapsed nodes of the WSDL file

The bulk of what you see are Namespace declarations. Then there are five more nodes. Two are for the request and response of the method the service offers. One is for the port (the exposed interfaces), another is for the binding information (the message format and protocol details), and a final one for the name and address of the service itself.

Using WSDL

In this example, several WSDL parts are combined hierarchically, which is the common definition method for defining WSDL elements. Let's break down the elements line by line and review the role of each part.

Definitions

The definition for this example defines several namespaces for structure and data encoding, as in the SOAP examples, then names the class on the XMethods server that is used for the Web service, net.xmethods.services.stockquote.StockQuote.

```
<wsdl:definitions
xmlns:tns="http://www.themindelectric.com/wsdl/net.xmethods.ser
vices.stockquote.StockQuote/"
xmlns:electric="http://www.themindelectric.com/"
xmlns:soap="http://schemas.xmlsoap.org/wsdl/soap/"
xmlns:xsd="http://www.w3.org/2001/XMLSchema"
xmlns:soapenc="http://schemas.xmlsoap.org/soap/encoding/"
xmlns:wsdl="http://schemas.xmlsoap.org/wsdl/"
xmlns="http://schemas.xmlsoap.org/wsdl/"
targetNamespace="http://www.themindelectric.com/wsdl/net.xmetho
ds.services.stockquote.StockQuote/"
name="net.xmethods.services.stockquote.StockQuote">
```

Parts, types, and messages

In this example, the parts described become part of the request and response calls in the SOAP messages that access this Web service. The result parameter is a float, and the symbol parameter is a string. The parts and types are grouped into input and output messages.

```
<message name="getQuoteResponse1">
<part name="Result" type="xsd:float"/>
</message>
<message name="getQuoteRequest1">
<part name="symbol" type="xsd:string"/>
</message>
```

Operations and portTypes

Next, the input and output messages are grouped into an operation, then into a portType, and named net.xmethods.services.stockquote.StockQuotePortType.

```
<portType
name="net.xmethods.services.stockquote.StockQuotePortType">
<operation name="getQuote" parameterOrder="symbol">
<input message="tns:getQuoteRequest1"/>
<output message="tns:getQuoteResponse1"/>
</operation>
</portType>
```

Bindings

Next, we bind the net.xmethods.services.stockquote.StockQuotePortType portType to RPC over HTTP (really SOAP). We also define the Namespace and SoapAction urn:xmethods-delayed-quotes#getQuote that will be used in the HTTP POST header of any SOAP request that calls the Web service, and call the binding net.xmethods.services.stockquote.StockQuoteBinding.

```
<binding
name="net.xmethods.services.stockquote.StockQuoteBinding"
type="tns:net.xmethods.services.stockquote.StockQuotePortType">
<soap:binding style="rpc"
transport="http://schemas.xmlsoap.org/soap/http"/>
<operation name="getQuote">
<soap:operation soapAction="urn:xmethods-delayed-
quotes#getQuote"/>
<input>
<soap:body use="encoded"
encodingStyle="http://schemas.xmlsoap.org/soap/encoding/"
namespace="urn:xmethods-delayed-quotes"/>
</input>
<output>
<soap:body use="encoded"
encodingStyle="http://schemas.xmlsoap.org/soap/encoding/"
namespace="urn:xmethods-delayed-quotes"/>
</output>
</operation>
</binding>
```

Services and ports

Now we bind the net.xmethods.services.stockquote.StockQuoteBinding with the reference to the SOAPAction to the Web service endpoint, and name the port net.xmethods.services.stockquote.StockQuotePort, then bind the port to the service net.xmethods.services.stockquote.StockQuoteService.

```
<service
name="net.xmethods.services.stockquote.StockQuoteService">
<documentation>net.xmethods.services.stockquote.StockQuote web
service</documentation>
```

```
<port name="net.xmethods.services.stockquote.StockQuotePort"
binding="tns:net.xmethods.services.stockquote.StockQuoteBinding
">
<soap:address location="http://66.28.98.121:9090/soap"/>
</port>
</service>
</wsdl:definitions>
```

When the WSDL is read by a client or another Web service, the HTTP header creates references to the endpoint and the SOAPAction from the binding, and generates a SOAP envelope with input and output messages and appropriate nested parameters from the portType.

Updating WSDL

As is obvious by now, WSDL is the type library information for components that run over the Web. But what happens when the component changes? In other words, if the WSDL file is generated and stored locally on a machine, that file can become outdated if the Web service behaviors are changed by the Web service provider (that may or may not be you). Your calling application needs to stay informed about changes that have occurred in the WSDL before it attempts to call a method whose definition may have changed or that no longer exists. In the end, the proxy class that resides on the client machine must reflect the precise characteristics offered by the remote service. This means that there must be a way to generate the proxy class at a point in time *after* the application has been compiled and deployed. Here are some of the effects of this type of dynamic Web services invocation:

✦ This technique frees you from having to know the precise Web service endpoint at design or compile time.

✦ You can point to different Web services to find methods that can be dynamically selection based on the client application logic or user input.

✦ You can dynamically acquire the WSDL from UDDI or a custom location (like XMethods).

To make this possible, you need code in your client application that creates a Web service proxy on the fly. There are no limitations in the standards to prevent you from doing this. The main ones, SOAP, XML, HTTP, and WSDL, will not care when you are building the proxy class. The real dependency is the development environment in which you are creating the client application. Not all runtimes are created equal, so you will need to look within the tools of your development platform to figure out if you can do this. Irrespective of your environment, your code needs to find the location of a desired Web service.

To do this, you can choose from a nearly infinite collection of possibilities here such as loading nodes of an XML file that stores possible Web service addresses, or calling a Web service to get a list of Web services (an intriguing idea actually).

✦ Get the WSDL for the desired Web service

✦ Build the proxy class based on the WSDL

✦ Make a runtime-consumable version of the proxy class

✦ Use an instance of the class and call methods

Some of these techniques for dynamically finding and referencing a Web service are not for beginners, but if you need an application that could consume any number of unknown Web services you will need to go beyond simple referencing and find ways to dynamically generate proxy classes. The very fact that we are even discussing this says something about how far we have come in the world of distributed computing. This kind of thing, especially between remote components on different platforms, is nearly unthinkable without the standards involved with Web services. Yes, it has been done prior to Web services, but not without some very complicated code. Web services make this technique much more accessible to all developers.

Editing WSDL

A word or two must be said about WSDL editors. Any text editor will do. Even though WSDL was not created explicitly for human eyes to read, the fact remains that the more curious developer will want to know what is going on in the WSDL. It is important to read WSDL when troubleshooting applications or when using more advanced techniques with Web services. Even though any text editor will do, if the WSDL file is long because of Web service complexity, then a simple text editor becomes less useful. Fortunately, WSDL files are just XML files, so any XML editor will do. However, things can be taken a step further, and there are editors (not many just yet) that can parse the XML while also knowing that it is a WSDL file. Some of the more notable WSDL editors in existence as of this writing include the following (these may be larger suites that contain a WSDL editor):

✦ XML Spy version 5.0+

✦ OmniOpera

✦ Cape Clear 4 suite (see Figure 25-2)

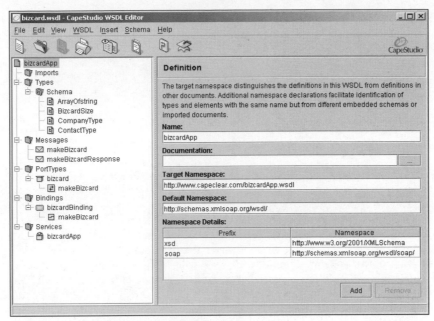

Figure 25-2: An example of a WSDL editor

Because WSDL is good old XML (can "old" be associated with XML yet?), you can also create your own WSDL editor. It could be fun.

Summary

In this chapter, we have dissected a WSDL file. We saw how the file is structured and what information is included therein. We discovered what the elements of WSDL mean and how they are used by the calling application to determine a Web service's behaviors and characteristics. WSDL is arguably the de facto standard on the Internet for making known to consuming client applications what a Web service does. We also learned about how to dynamically create a Web service proxy class at runtime based on WSDL that is not known at design time. Finally, we learned that there are some WSDL editors out there and that one can be created from scratch if desired.

✦　　✦　　✦

UDDI

Web services can be used for interaction between remote systems within a single organization. However, one of the most promising aspects of Web services is that they can be used business-to-business integration. For example, one company might expose an invoicing Web service that the company's suppliers use to send their own internal invoices. Similarly, a company might expose a Web service for placing orders electronically, using special schemas that the customers can use internally for their own purchasing process. Now, if one company wanted to purchase goods from a vendor using a service of this kind, how would it find it? Let's say the company wants to begin ordering office supplies from a John's International Office Supplies (an idea waiting to happen) it would need to search for all vendors who sell office supplies over the Internet and then find ones that sell goods using a Web service.

To do this, the customer needs a directory, a sort of yellow pages-type directory of all businesses that expose Web services. This directory is called Universal Description, Discovery, and Integration or UDDI. UDDI is an industry effort started in September of 2000 by Ariba, IBM, Microsoft, and 33 other companies. Today, UDDI has over 200 community members.

This chapter describes UDDI, the final piece of the Web Service puzzle, in greater detail. It explains how UDDI links together consumers of Web services with providers and how it works. We also learn who is backing the UDDI effort and what UDDI means to the future of Web services. We learn how UDDI works and what it means with respect to the technology of Web services.

UDDI Structure

UDDI is a platform-independent framework for describing services, businesses, and integrating business services. While the UDDI project is not part of a regular standards body like the W3C or the IETF, the structure of UDDI is based on Web service standards, which means that UDDI registries are theoretically accessible through the same means as all other Web services. In short, UDDI is a directory for Web services, and it is a Web service. Currently IBM, Microsoft, SAP, and NTT Telecom host public versions of the UDDI directory, which are kept in sync via a form of replication. URLs for registry sites as well as the latest version of the UDDI specification can be found at `http://uddi.org/`. Like a typical yellow pages directory, UDDI provides an indexed database of businesses searchable by the type of business.

Finding Web services with UDDI

Each of the four public UDDI Registries (IBM, Microsoft, SAP, and NTT) has its own interface and UI to access its registry via the Web. You typically search using business taxonomy such as the North American Industry Classification System (NAICS) or the Standard Industrial Classification (SIC). You could also search by business name or geographical location. Regardless of the interface provided, the UI is notoriously hard to navigate for Web developers that are used to more user-friendly HTML search sites. However, like WSDL, the main users of the UDDI registries are intended to be Web services rather than developers. As a testament and/or a response to this, Microsoft, IBM, and a few smaller players have released UDDI SDKs, which make developing Web Service front-ends to UDDI registries more accessible to anything on the other end of the SDK, be it human or machine. Microsoft SDKs can be downloaded at `http://uddi.microsoft.com/`, and the IBM UDDI4J can be downloaded as part of the IBM Web Services toolkit from `http://alphaworks.ibm.com/tech/webservicestoolkit`.

These tools, and a few others, can also be used to set up private UDDI servers for use within an organization or via VPN, for groups that want to have the full benefits of a complete set of Web Services technologies, but don't want to share their Web Services with the world on one of the public sites.

Going back to our example of office supplies, a company could search UDDI for NAICS code 422120, which corresponds to providers of office supplies and paper goods. This search would return a list of such companies that are registered with UDDI. At this stage of Web service adoption, it is not uncommon to find no Web services for categories you search in UDDI. This does not mean, however, that no Web services exist for that category of business. It only means that none is registered using UDDI. In searching, the consumer will need to know which of the office supplies vendors exposes Web services that are compatible with the systems used within the company. For example, if our company supports a specific purchase order process that uses SOAP-based Web services for acquiring office supplies it would need to know which vendors have a Web service that is compatible.

This brings us to the taxonomic conventions of UDDI. There are a number of different types used in the UDDI model to identify a service or collection of services. These five types are shown in Figure 26-1.

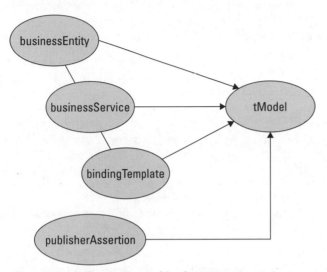

Figure 26-1: The types used in the UDDI taxonomy

publisherAssertion

To understand how they work together, let's look at UDDI from the perspective of an organization that wants to publish its services in the UDDI registry. In this case, we will imagine a company that has many subdivisions within its organization. The recommended practice for a business of this type that wants to register in a UDDI registry is for each division to register as a separate businessEntity. For example Microsoft may have a separate businessEntity entry for the Windows OS, Office divisions, and gaming division. Thus, rather than provide a single businessEntity entry in the UDDI registry which attempts to describe all the services Microsoft provides, it makes more sense to have each division submit a separate businessEntity that the division can support and maintain. However, it would be advantageous if the relationship between the different services offered by Microsoft's different businessEntity entries could be made known in UDDI. This is done through what is known as a publisherAssertion structure, which allows businesses to publish relationships between businessEntities. To prevent one publisher from claiming a relationship to another that is not reciprocated, both publishers must publish identical assertions for the relationship to become known. The allowed relationships are peer-to-peer. A peer-to-peer relationship is one where the two businessEntity structures are related as peers, and a parent-child relationship is hierarchical. Next, let's look at the businessEntity.

businessEntity

A businessEntity is simply the provider of a service, a businessService. There is not a lot to the structure of a businessEntity. Primarily, it contains:

✦ Name of the provider

✦ Description of the businessEntity

✦ Contact information, such as name, phone, fax, e-mail, and so on

✦ Identifiers: Classifiers for the business using specifications like DUNS, NAICS, or SIC

As mentioned before, a businessEntity may not necessarily be a separate business or organization. There is nothing in the specification to prevent a large business (or small one for that matter) from having divisions register services with UDDI using separate businessEntity entries. A businessEntity is described using a well-formed XML document and is created by someone who represents the provider of the service. UDDI specifies a schema for structuring the information in the businessEntity entry. In short, the businessEntity describes who is providing a businessService.

businessService

This data structure is used to describe each offered service in business terms. You have to specify at least a name and one binding template. A single businessService may contain more than one binding template, but it must contain at least one. Listing 26-1 shows some of the XML content of a businessService entry.

Listing 26-1: A View of Some of the Elements in a businessService Entry

```
<businessService serviceKey="...">
   <name> SymbolService </name>
   <description>Description of the service here</description>
   <bindingTemplates>
        <bindingTemplate>
             <accessPoint
                 urlType="http">
                 http://mycompany.com/myservice
                  </accessPoint>
             <tModelInstanceDetails>
             <tModelInstanceInfo tModelKey="12345678"/>
             </tModelInstanceDetails>
        </bindingTemplate>
   </bindingTemplates>
</businessService>
```

As you can see here, the core of the businessService entry is the binding template. A binding templates structure serves as a container for one or more binding template structures. A binding template structure describes how to get access to a service. They contain what are known as access points, which are usually just URLs. Valid values for an accessPoint element are:

- ◆ mailto
- ◆ http
- ◆ https
- ◆ ftp
- ◆ fax
- ◆ phone
- ◆ other

Another attribute called a hostingRedirector can be used if the binding template refers to another one that has already been specified. In this case, the access point need not be specified a second time. Another element called tModelInstanceDetails holds information for a particular tModel, which is referenced by its key.

tModels

Each business registered with UDDI lists all its services and gives each of these services a type. This service type has a unique identifier (GUID-style number) and comes from a group of well-known service types that are registered with UDDI. These service types are called tModels (technology models). Let's recall that the two primary goals of UDDI are to:

- ◆ Make it possible to describe a Web service, and make that description meaningful for searches

- ◆ Provide a way to make these descriptions useful enough so consumers can interact with a service without needing to know its inner workings

This being so, we need a way to tag the service so others can easily know its behaviors, the standards with which it is compliant, and so forth. All of the other types we have seen up to this point (publisherAssertion and so on) relate to who owns, publishes, describes, and maintains the Web service. A tModel is concerned with the service itself. A tModel makes it possible to describe compliance with a specification, concept, standard, or a collectively shared design. The first goal is met by using tModel as a namespace or categorization, while the second goal is met by its usage as a tag that is technically recognizable.

Each tModel has a name, description, and the unique identifier. This unique identifier is a UUID and is called the tModelKey. For example, the tModelKey uuid:d819efe0-4471-11d6-9b35-000c0e00acdd identifies the tModel called uddi-org:http, which has the description "An HTTP or Web browser-based Web service." By having a pool of well-known service types, UDDI makes it possible to find out how to do electronic business with a company. This is the primary advantage UDDI has compared to other Web-based business directories.

As part of the registration process, registrants can use an existing tModel or they can create their own. It might make sense for an organization or a group of organizations to develop their own tModels to classify a service they all offer (competitively even), but that would make it easier for potential consumers of the service to find the group of vendors who offer a certain type of service. For example, package delivery companies (UPS, FedEx, Airborne Express, USPS, and so on) may decide to agree upon a mutual standard tModel for package tracking. This tModel would behave in the same way for all shippers, the same method names with the same parameters.

tModels store information that includes:

✦ The name of the model

✦ The publisher of the model

✦ The categories that describe the service type

✦ Pointers to related technical specifications, interface definitions, message formats, message protocols, security protocols, and other details that would help a potential consumer of the service be able to use it

Listing 26-2 shows an example of a tModel fully exposed. Notice how it uses the reference to a WSDL document as an identifier for what the service does (see Chapter 25 for more on WSDL).

Listing 26-2: An Example of a tModel

```
<tModel
authorizedName="..." operator="..."
tModelKey="UUID:12345678>
    <name>Our special service</name>
    <description xml:lan="en">
        WSDL description of our service
    </description>
    <overviewDoc>
        <description xml:lang="en">WSDL source document.
        </description>
        <overviewURL>
```

```
                http://mycompany/ourservice/service1.wsdl
        </overviewURL>
    </overviewDoc>
    <categoryBag>
            <keyedReference tModelKey="UUID:987654"
            keyName="uddi-org:types"   keyValue="wsdlSpec"/>
    </categoryBag>
</tModel>
```

Fortunately, there are already a host of categories defined as tModels within the UDDI world. If you visit a UDDI site such as http://uddi.microsoft.com, you will see that there are business classification code models for SIC (Standard Industrial Classification) and NAICS (North American Industry Classification System), in addition to other categorization standards.

Note More information on UDDI and links to public servers and tModels can be found at http://uddi.org/.

As of this writing, the current public servers include:

✦ `uddi.microsoft.com` – Microsoft's UDDI Business Registry Node

✦ `uddi.ibm.com` – IBM's UDDI Business Registry Node

✦ `uddi.sap.com` – SAP's UDDI Business Registry Node

✦ `www.ntt.com/uddi` – NTT Com's UDDI Business Registry Node

UDDI APIs

To ensure most platforms can access UDDI's services, the UDDI directory exposes a bunch of APIs in the form of a SOAP-based Web service. There are currently two main nodes that expose the UDDI Web service: http://uddi.microsoft.com/inquire and `http://www-3.ibm.com/services/uddi/inquiryapi`. The API is concerned with registering and discovering Web services.

Note You can download the API specification from the following link: http://www.uddi. org/pubs/ProgrammersAPI-V1.01-Open-20010327_2.pdf

The APIs are accessed only through SOAP messages with the appropriate body content. For example, to search for a company called XYZ Industries you would send the XML in the body of a SOAP message as shown in Listing 26-3.

Listing 26-3: **Finding a Business Using UDDI**

```
<find_business generic="1.0" xmlns="urn:uddi-org:api">
<categoryBag>
  <keyedReference tModelKey=
"uuid:70a80f61-77bc-4821-a5e2-2a406acc35dd"
keyName="Advertising" keyValue="7310" />
</categoryBag>
</find_business>
```

The SOAP response that comes back from UDDI contains all businesses that match your search criteria and the registered services for each business. This information comes back as an XML data structure, of course. These structures are called businessInfos. The UDDI APIs accept and return several data structures, and these are all spelled out in the documentation of the API. Remember that the UDDI API, as an API, is not concerned with it is actually accessed. Any vendor can create class libraries that call the API to interact with UDDI. Listing 26-4 shows how the response is received from the previous inquiry using the tModel in Listing 26-3. Notice how the request and the response are all in SOAP, the bedrock dependency of anything related to UDDI.

Listing 26-4: **The SOAP Response from a UDDI Request**

```
<?xml version="1.0" encoding="utf-8"?>
<soap:Envelope
 xmlns:soap="http://schemas.xmlsoap.org/soap/envelope/"
  xmlns:xsi="http://www.w3.org/2001/XMLSchema-instance"
  xmlns:xsd="http://www.w3.org/2001/XMLSchema">
  <soap:Body>
   <serviceList generic="1.0"
        operator="Microsoft Corporation"
        truncated="false" xmlns="urn:uddi-org:api">
  <serviceInfos>
        <serviceInfo serviceKey=
        "d5b180a0-4342-11d5-bd6c-002035229c64"
        businessKey="ba744ed0-3aaf-11d5-80dc-002035229c64">
        <name>XMethods Barnes and Noble Quote</name>
        </serviceInfo>
  </serviceInfos>
  </serviceList>
  </soap:Body>
</soap:Envelope>
```

Because the UDDI is really just a collection of SOAP calls through a Web service, we must use classes that wrap the Web service and provide calls. You can write your own classes to do so if you wish. While there may be some compelling reasons for doing so out there in the universe, chances are that the reasons are not ones you will stumble upon very easily. It is probably a better idea to use some that have already been created for you. Microsoft and IBM are the most prominent leaders in the UDDI realm, and both have provided SDKs to interact with UDDI via SOAP.

The Microsoft UDDI SDK

Microsoft has created classes that work directly with the UDDI APIs for sending/receiving SOAP messages. These classes are well documented and come with samples. You can download the Microsoft UDDI SDK from `http://msdn.microsoft.com/UDDI`. The links change every now and then, but you can poke around a little and find the SDK pretty easily. When you download the SDK, you will see that there are both COM-based and .NET-based components that let you search the UDDI registry as well as publish to it.

To show you how to use the UDDI SDK, let's take a look at the SDK sample. The main form of the sample is shown in Figure 26-2. Submitting the information in the search form will bring back a result from Microsoft's UDDI registry.

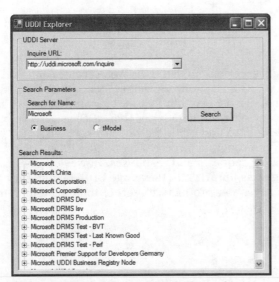

Figure 26-2: The main form of Microsoft's UDDI SDK sample with a search result

Now, let's see how the code works that makes the request in Listing 26-5. You will quickly notice how simple things are compared to the full SOAP requests we have seen elsewhere. Here, a class, FindBusiness, is used to go get businesses that match the search criteria. All of the plumbing and complexity is hidden.

Listing 26-5: **Searching Using the Microsoft UDDI Classes**

```
searchResults.BeginUpdate();
FindBusiness fb = new FindBusiness();
fb.Names.Add(name.Text ;
try
{
    //
    // Perform search
    //
    BusinessList bl = fb.Send();
    searchResults.Nodes.Clear();
    foreach(BusinessInfo bi in bl.BusinessInfos)
    {
        searchResults.Nodes.Add(new TreeNode(bi.Name));
    }
}
```

Summary

Leveraging UDDI means that businesses can publish their Web services and find other Web services that they need. UDDI is a nonproprietary standard that uses XML, SOAP, and HTTP to make the registry maintainable and accessible on the Web. In this chapter, we learned about the different data types that UDDI uses to let businesses register their Web services and to find other Web services. Whether for commercial or internal uses, you can program directly against the UDDI API. This would take place in the form of SOAP requests and responses. However, other companies are already providing nice class libraries that leverage UDDI behind the scenes and that let you focus on developer productivity rather than the plumbing of UDDI.

✦   ✦   ✦

Microsoft Web Services

◆ ◆ ◆ ◆

In This Chapter

The MS SOAP Toolkit

Building server-side and client-side SOAP applications

WSML

The Office XP Web Services Toolkit

◆ ◆ ◆ ◆

If you have read the other chapters in this book about Web services, then you have often seen Microsoft mentioned as one of the biggest champions of the Web services paradigm. The fact is that Microsoft has been promoting Web services and remote component-based interaction using independent standards from the very start. It is worth noting that some have expressed a measure of surprise that Microsoft has been so enthusiastic about a technology that is platform-agnostic and based on standards that Microsoft does not own or control the way it does COM or the way Sun controls Java APIs. Microsoft .NET technologies are a huge reason why Microsoft is so excited about Web services, a subject that is handled more specifically in Chapter 29.

This chapter will help readers understand Microsoft's technology toolkit for creating and consuming Web services using its COM-based technologies. Without question, Microsoft's primary focus for Web services development is with .NET. However, Microsoft recognizes that not all companies can or will migrate to .NET at the drop of a hat. Adoption cycles for some organizations can take years. On the other hand, organizations who have a large body of COM-based applications do not want the Web services train to pass them by. Therefore, there must be a non-.NET way for Windows applications to take advantage of Web services technologies.

The primary COM-based vehicle for Web services is contained in the MS SOAP Toolkit. This chapter will describe how Microsoft has implemented its strategy in technologies that do not fall directly within the .NET initiative. We will look at version 3.0 of the MS SOAP Toolkit, a COM-based collection of code and documentation for working with SOAP in COM-based applications. We will also explore the Office XP Web Services toolkit, a clever Addin that lets Office applications consume Web services in productivity applications, all using MS SOAP under the hood.

The Microsoft SOAP Toolkit

Most of the focus with respect to Web services in the Microsoft world is on .NET-related technologies. However, there are still myriad applications that are written in COM-based code, and most of these will be around for years to come. As exciting as the .NET initiative is, it is important that non-.NET Windows applications need to be able to connect to Web services. Recall that in order for an application to communicate using SOAP (the protocol that specifies how requests and responses are structured and passed between the client and the Web service) it must have the ability to understand XML and communicate over some transport protocol (normally HTTP). Because XML is used to package messages between the client and Web service, both parties in the relationship must package the messages in XML using a certain structure, and some mechanism must be able to both do the packaging and process packages that are received. The Microsoft SOAP Toolkit has these ingredients so that COM applications can both expose and consume Web services.

What's in the SDK

The MS SOAP Toolkit is an SDK you can download from the Microsoft Website as a free download. After downloading and installing, you will see four main directories. They are:

✦ **Binaries:** Contains the executables and other files that are used by some of the utilities for use with COM-based SOAP

✦ **Documentation:** Contains a pretty nice .chm file chock-full of overview and detailed information about how to program with the SDK

✦ **Inc:** Contains a single include file you can use if you are programming with the SDK in C++

✦ **Lib:** A C++ inline file containing definitions of inline functions, as well as template function definitions

As discussed in Chapter 24, SOAP is an XML-based standard for describing objects that are used to make calls and responses in Web Services over HTTP. In the end, SOAP is just the grammar for describing remote component calls. Fortunately, XML is syntactical language for such descriptions. When a client makes a call to a Web service, the request must be structured in a specific way. While an ambitious developer could create a custom component to assemble the request in the correct hierarchy with the correct XML syntax so that the call is intelligible to the remote component, it would be much more convenient to have one that everyone using the same development platform can share. MS SOAP is that ready-to-use library for packaging up SOAP requests and responses for COM-based applications. The MS SOAP Toolkit has everything that a COM developer needs to get up and running with Web services on Windows.

Not surprisingly, the MS SOAP 3.0 relies heavily on MSXML 4.0. Earlier releases of the Toolkit used earlier XML parser versions, but, if you do not have legacy applications that require previous MS SOAP versions, it is recommended that you uninstall the older version and go ahead with a clean installation of version 3.0. You must also have Microsoft Internet Explorer 5.01 or greater installed whether you are running MS SOAP on the client or server. From a server perspective, you need IIS 5.0 or greater if you are running Windows 2000, Windows XP, or Windows .NET Server. If you are still running Windows NT 4.0, you will need IIS 4.0 or greater. You will need IIS installed because (forgive the declaration of the obvious here, but it does perhaps merit emphasis) Web services are, after all, Web applications. Therefore, there must be some service to listen for Web requests and then send back the responses. From a client perspective, you need Microsoft(r) Windows(r) XP, Microsoft Windows 2000 SP1 or greater, Microsoft Windows NT(r) 4.0 SP6, Microsoft Windows 98, or Windows ME.

Overview of the MS SOAP component library

As one might expect, when writing client-side code with MS SOAP 3.0 things are much simpler than when writing server-side code. However, in either case the same library is in play. The MSSOAP30.DLL contains a primary set of components for sending and receiving SOAP messages. The classes defined therein include:

✦ SoapClient30: If you are ever going to do any client-side programming with MS SOAP 3.0, you will probably use this class more than any other. It is actually a fairly intelligible class with methods for initializing the SOAP request, sending it and then processing the response that is sent from the server.

✦ SoapServer30: As you might think, there is a server-side counterpart for the client-side one. SoapServer30 is that server-side class. It has methods for processing an incoming SOAP request and then returning a SOAP response.

✦ SoapReader30: While it is true that SOAP requests and responses are made in XML, if you are working with, say, an instance of SoapClient30, you are not working directly with an explicit instance of the DOM when working with the SOAP messages. If you want to go a level lower and work with the XML directly when reading SOAP messages, you can use the SoapReader30 class. This is a useful class when you are working with messages at a lower level for customization purposes.

✦ FileAttachment30: Lets you send a file as an attachment to a Web service.

✦ ByteArrayAttachment30: Lets you send a byte array as an attachment to a Web service.

✦ SteamAttachment30: Lets you read a stream and send it as an attachment to a Web service.

✦ StringAttachment30: Lets you send a simple string as an attachment to a Web service. You may wonder why to use this rather than sending a string as a parameter to a Web service method. The reason is that parameters to methods should really not be large data loads that will be used by the method itself. It is better to use method arguments to specify things that define *how* a method should execute, not large data payloads that contain *what* the method is going to process.

✦ SentAttachments30: This is a collection that contains the attachments being sent to the server.

✦ ReceivedAttachments30: This is the collection of attachments that the server-side code can pick up and unpack for processing.

✦ SoapSerializer30: This class lets you build your SOAP messages at a lower level rather than letting the built-in classes (like SoapClient30) do the work for you.

✦ HttpConnector30, SoapConnectorFactory30, SoapTypeMapperFactory: If you do not like the behavior of the built-in connector that binds your SOAP objects to HTTP, you can customize how MS SOAP creates, sends, receives, and processes your SOAP messages. If you are doing custom security or other advanced operations, these classes are particularly useful.

Server-Side Programming with MS SOAP

Recall that one of the main drivers behind Web services generally is to make a remote component accessible over HTTP so that applications can interact without needing to share their bits one with another. To the client, the remote component should still look and act like a local component. When you create the remote component, you are not obligated to do anything special to make it available via a Web service. Listing 27-1 shows the code for a simple component with a single method that accepts a key for quote and then returns the quote text from database. Notice how there is nothing Web service related in this code. It is just good old-fashioned COM code.

Listing 27-1: COM Code for a Component That Will Be Exposed as a Web Service

```
Public Function GetQuote(ByVal QuoteKey As String) As String
Dim CN As ADODB.Connection
Dim RS As ADODB.Recordset
Set CN = New ADODB.Connection
Set RS = New ADODB.Recordset
If Len(QuoteKey) > 0 Then
```

```
CN.ConnectionString = "Data Source=C:\quotes.mdb;" _
& "Provider=Microsoft.Jet.OLEDB.4.0;"
  CN.Open
  RS.Open "SELECT Quote FROM QuoteTable WHERE QuoteKey='" _
& QuoteKey & "'", CN, adModeRead
    If RS.State = adStateOpen Then
      GetQuote = RS.Fields(0).Value
    Else
      GetQuote = "Quote not found"
    End If
Else
  GetQuote = "No criteria provided"
End If
End Function
```

Once this component is compiled, it has all of the functionality it needs to be exposed on a Website as a Web service. Now, in order for a client to connect to the component remotely, there must be an intermediary to translate requests and responses as SOAP messages because there is no SOAP information in this custom component. The intermediary must also know which custom code DLL to load that will do the actual processing of the data contained in the SOAP request and produce response data that can be sent via SOAP to the client. That intermediation is what the MS SOAP Toolkit is all about. When you install the Toolkit, an ISAPI DLL is installed on the server that allows IIS to receive SOAP requests and then route the request to the appropriate processing code.

Let's take a step back and revisit the installation of the Toolkit for just a moment. When you complete the installation, there are some other files installed that we have not yet looked at. One of these files is the SOAPIS30.DLL. This is the handler that will receive requests that are routed from IIS. This DLL then is the ISAPI listener or handler for SOAP. There is a registry key that has settings you can adjust in order to modify the behavior of the ISAPI listener. This key is found at: HKEY_LOCAL_MACHINE\SOFTWARE\Microsoft\MSSOAP\30\SOAPISAP. Figure 27-1 shows how these keys look in the registry.

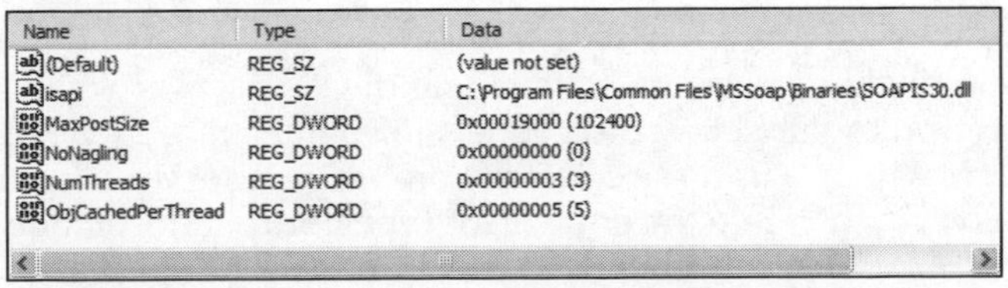

Name	Type	Data
(Default)	REG_SZ	(value not set)
isapi	REG_SZ	C:\Program Files\Common Files\MSSoap\Binaries\SOAPIS30.dll
MaxPostSize	REG_DWORD	0x00019000 (102400)
NoNagling	REG_DWORD	0x00000000 (0)
NumThreads	REG_DWORD	0x00000003 (3)
ObjCachedPerThread	REG_DWORD	0x00000005 (5)

Figure 27-1: Keys pertaining to the ISAPI handler for MS SOAP 3.0

The keys and their purpose are:

✦ Isapi: This value is the physical path for the ISAPI DLL used by IIS.

✦ MaxPostSize: This value is the maximum size of any SOAP message that the ISAPI handler can manage. The default is 100KB, and it is a good idea to keep it as low as your applications can accommodate so that hackers are not able to cause DOS attacks against your Web server.

✦ NoNagling: This value has to do with response times using TCP/IP, and its value should normally be 0.

✦ NumThreads: This value sets the maximum number of threads the ISAPI handler can manage. The default is for the value to be two times the number of CPUs plus one. If messages are stacking up, you can increase the number of threads, but keep in mind that this can impact other server resources.

✦ ObjCachedPerThread: Caching is a popular technique for improving performance in Web applications. This value sets the maximum number of files that can be cached for a single message thread. When a call is first received, the ISAPI handler caches the WSDL and WSML files for the SOAP service in question. As requests for other services are received, they are also cached. This value should be equal to the number of services you are running on your server via the MS SOAP Toolkit.

Now, just because you have installed the MS SOAP Toolkit does not mean that the ISAPI filter is automatically going to be invoked when a SOAP request comes in. There is actually one more step you need to take in order to tell the ISAPI listener which Web sites where it should be enabled. This is done using a special script that is also found in the Toolkit, SOAPVDIR.CMD. By running this command, you effectively map a virtual directory in IIS to the ISAPI handler. This makes it possible to thus link the SOAP requests and responses directly to the ISAPI listener without using ASP Web pages to field the request and hand it off to SOAP.

> **Note**
>
> In some situations, it is needful to be able to switch between version 3.0 of the handler and earlier versions. If this is so, you can indeed change which binary is used in the mapping between IIS and the SOAP requests/responses. The registry key HKEY_LOCAL_MACHINE\SOFTWARE\Microsoft\MSSOAP\30\SOAPISAP is where you can change this mapping.

Now that we have reviewed what pieces are installed on the Web server when MS SOAP is installed, let's return to our server-side code shown in Listing 27-1. This code is compiled in a DLL, which is in turn registered on the Web server. The first thing that needs to be done is to create the equivalent type library information for the component(s) in the DLL. This type library information is the WSDL file. Gratefully, the Toolkit has a tool for creating this WSDL for you. It is called the WSDL Generator and is executed by running wsdlgen3.exe. This executable is found in the MSSOAP\Binaries directory where you have installed the Toolkit and works only on Microsoft Windows(r) XP, Microsoft Windows(r) 2000, or Microsoft(r) Windows NT(r) 4.0. When you run the WSDL Generator, just click Next to get past the introductory screen and click Next again to bypass the Specify Configuration screen. This will bring you to a screen like the one shown in Figure 27-2.

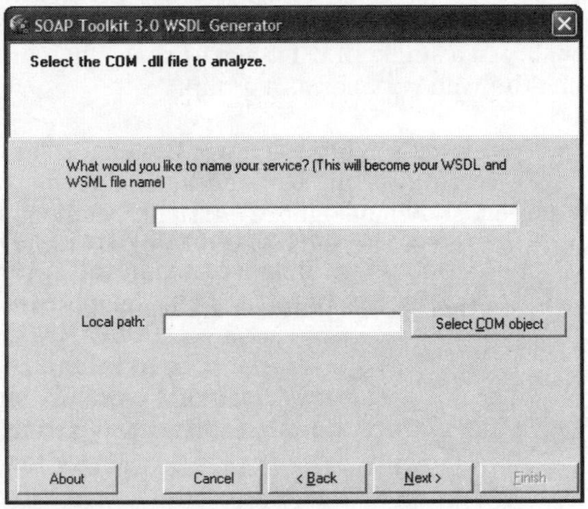

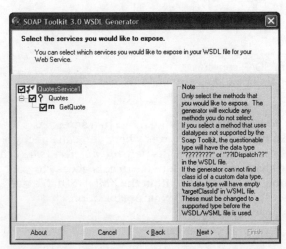

Figure 27-2: Specifying the source DLL for generating WSDL

Here you need to provide a name for the Web service. Keep in mind that the name you specify here will be the name for the WSDL and WSML files. What the WSML file means will be explained in a moment. After specifying this information, click Next, and you see the screen shown in Figure 27-3.

Figure 27-3: Exposing services and methods for a given component

Here you need to specify which service(s) will be exposed. If you check a service and one or more of its methods, these will be represented in the resulting WSDL and WSML files so that SOAP clients can make calls to them. Implicit in the design of the WSDL Generator tool is that you can have more than one Web service in a single component or in the components of a single DLL. It is a good idea to attempt to aggregate Web service functionality in a single DLL if it makes sense in your business and if you plan on maintaining the Web services as a group.

After you have told the WSDL Generator what methods you want to expose in the Web service, you need to map the SOAP requests and responses to a specific Web site. This is done in the following screen, shown in Figure 27-4. Here, you need to specify a valid Web site address on a machine where the MS SOAP Toolkit has been installed. It should go without saying that this is also the server where your DLL is installed. Make sure you also specify on this screen that you are using an ISAPI listener and not an ASP listener.

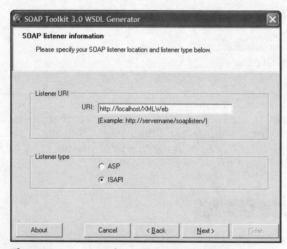

Figure 27-4: Mapping your custom SOAP service to a Web site that users or developers can address

With this information specified you can click Next and move to a screen as shown in Figure 27-5. Here you will see a number of text boxes where you can specify a namespace for use within your Web service. The URIs here *are not necessarily* the same as the URI for the Web site that users will reference to gain access to your Web service. These URIs are namespaces for use within the XML WSDL file and should correspond to namespaces you use within your organization.

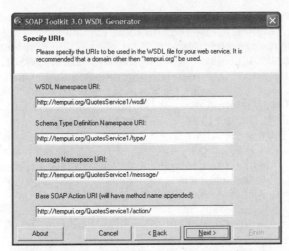

Figure 27-5: Specifying namespace URIs for your Web service

After setting your namespaces, you need to tell the WSDL Generator where to place your configuration files. This location does not have to be the same as where the Web site directory is stored, but it should be in a location where client applications can get access to it in some way. If do not want to make the WSDL file accessible directly to client applications from the server, you still need to get the WSDL file to client workstations in some way, a technique we will discuss in greater detail when we discuss building client applications that use MS SOAP. This is done via a screen as shown in Figure 27-6.

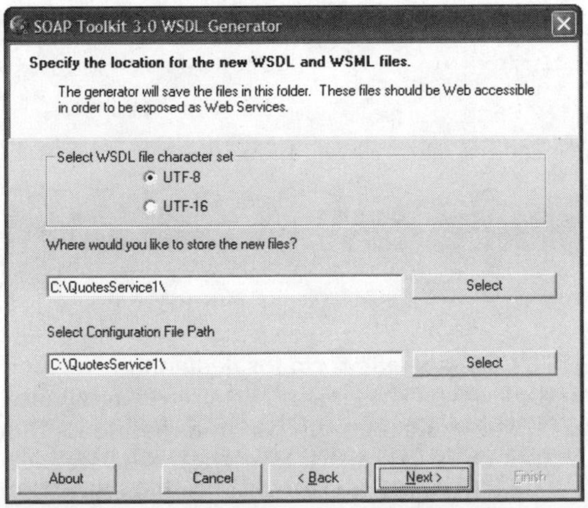

Figure 27-6: Specifying file locations for the output of the WSDL Generator

With these things done, you have done all that is needful to make a COM object available as a Web service. But, something else remains to be explained. You see, neither the WSDL nor the SOAP standard has any specifications that deal with mapping SOAP requests directly to COM objects. In other words, with just the WSDL file on the server, IIS will know that a given SOAP request should be handled by a Web site and passed to the appropriate ISAPI handler. On the other hand, the ISAPI DLL does not know that the request for a method really is targeting a method in a COM DLL. Hence, we need another file to do that job for us. That file is Web Services Meta Language (WSML) file on the server. WSML has nothing whatever to do with the Web services standards such as WSDL, SOAP, or UDDI. A WSML file contains information that maps the methods of service to specific methods in the COM object. The WSML file is responsible for acknowledging which COM object to load to make it possible for a SOAP request to be handled.

The WSML for the Web service created in this chapter is shown here in Listing 27-2.

Listing 27-2: **WSML for the QuotesService Web Service**

```
<?xml version='1.0' encoding='UTF-8' ?>
  <servicemapping name='QuotesService1'

xmlns:dime='http://schemas.xmlsoap.org/ws/2002/04/dime/wsdl/'>
  <service name='QuotesService1'>
    <using PROGID='QuoteService1.Quotes' cachable='0'
ID='QuotesObject' />
    <port name='QuotesSoapPort'>
      <operation name='GetQuote'>
        <execute uses='QuotesObject' method='GetQuote'
dispID='1610809344'>
          <parameter callIndex='-1' name='retval'
elementName='Result' />
          <parameter callIndex='1' name='QuoteKey'
elementName='QuoteKey' />
        </execute>
      </operation>
    </port>
  </service>
</servicemapping>
```

Notice in this file how the PROGID, a COM-specific term for designating a given component installed and registered on a Windows machine, is referenced here. The ports for the SOAP request are also listed here, and they are mapped to methods provided by the COM DLL itself. Parameters for the COM method are listed as well. So, as you can see the WSML file is vital for making COM components directly accessible through SOAP on the Web.

Client-Side Programming with MS SOAP

With the server-side pieces installed, it is now possible to access the Web service from a client application. Clients can be non-Windows clients, COM-based clients, ASP applications, .NET applications, and Windows forms applications of varying sorts. The field is quite large. Here, we will focus on building COM-based clients. First, we will make an extraordinarily simple client application, a console application.

To do this, we will create a simple VBScript file that will invoke the method of our Web service and report its results in a message box. The text of the VBScript file is shown in Listing 27-3.

Listing 27-3: **A Simple Console Application to Call an MS SOAP-Based Web Service**

```
Option Explicit

Dim soapClient3
set soapclient3 = CreateObject("MSSOAP.SoapClient30")
On Error Resume Next
Call SoapClient3.mssoapinit("QuotesService1.wsdl", _
  "QuotesService1", "QuotesSoapPort")
if err <> 0 then
  wscript.echo "initialization failed " + err.description
end if

wscript.echo  SoapClient3.GetQuote("HNEY-4TTL6B")
if err <> 0 then
  wscript.echo   err.description
  wscript.echo   "faultcode=" + SoapClient3.faultcode
  wscript.echo   "faultstring=" + SoapClient3.faultstring
  wscript.echo   "faultactor=" + SoapClient3.faultactor
  wscript.echo   "detail=" + SoapClient3.detail
end if
```

The key to this file is really where the SOAP client is initialized, the mssoapinit method call. This call requires that we pass the path to the WSDL file for the Web service. The second parameter is the name of the service. Recall that we specified this when we generated the WSDL file using the WSDL Generator tool. The last parameter passed is the name of the SOAP port we are going to call. A port is the target of a SOAP request, and this maps to a method in the component. See Chapter 24 for more on SOAP. After that, we use the instance of the SOAPClient30 object, here in a variable called SoapClient3, to call the method and retrieve a quote.

What is remarkable about this code is that it is so simple. The client is almost always on a remote workstation, which means that this code is making a method call to a remote server, and it is done in a way that both shields the complexity from the user or developer while also making it possible to modify the underlying pieces of the conversation if the need should arise.

Admittedly, this console application is neither very attractive nor is it realistic for a typical, true business solution. What we want to do now is make it possible to call this same service from a more sophisticated client. You can create a Windows application using Visual Basic 6 or the .NET Framework if you wish; the latter technique is dealt with in a different chapter. One possible client for the Web service is an office productivity application. You can create a Web service client using really any COM-enabled application, and pretty much any version of Microsoft Office or other applications like WordPerfect would also do. However, Microsoft Office XP has added a tool to make it even easier to create a Web service client for Microsoft Office.

Office XP Web Services Toolkit

The Office XP Web Services Toolkit (version 2.0 as of this writing) is a free download from Microsoft's Website. The main thrust of the toolkit is to install a special Addin in Office so that you can easily call Web services in your VBA code. There are other things that accompany the Addin such as whitepapers and some samples. Let's use the Web services toolkit in an Office application, in this case a VBA application in Microsoft Word. To get to the point of creating the VBA project, you need to open Word and go to Tools | Macro | Visual Basic Editor to open up the editor. Once in the editor, you can go to Tools | Web Service Reference to open up the dialog box shown in Figure 27-7.

The main purpose of this dialog box is to get a reference to a WSDL file. Based on the contents of that WSDL file, the toolkit will create a wrapper class for you that will expose the same methods as the actual Web service on the remote server. The wrapper class' methods will have the same signature as those on the remote service; they will just be accessible as if on a local DLL rather than a remote component.

If you know where the WSDL is located, you can begin referencing it in the dialog box by clicking the Web Service URL radio button and typing the URL to the WSDL in the text box provided. If you need to find a service, you can use the UDDI browser that is also part of the dialog box. For more information on UDDI and browsing UDDI directories, see Chapter 26.

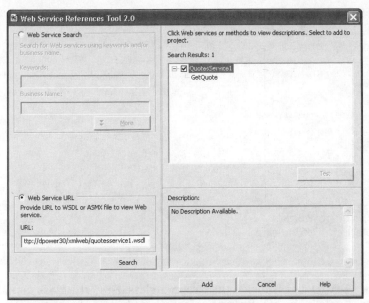

Figure 27-7: Creating a Web Services Reference using the Office XP
Web Services Toolkit 2.0

As you can see in Figure 27-7, we are referencing the Web service created earlier in this chapter. What is important to know here is that Microsoft Word application that is being used here is actually on a separate computer on the network. After referencing the WSDL file, you click on Search, and the toolkit will load the WSDL file, if it can find it. If a WSDL file cannot be found in the location your specify, then the dialog will inform you of that fact.

Notice how the QuotesService1 service is listed, and the GetQuote method is also shown. If the service had multiple methods, you would see those here. It is important to know that the Office XP Web Services Toolkit is not restricted to referencing Web services created using the MS SOAP Toolkit. The only MS SOAP dependency that exists here is that the SOAPClient30 class be defined on the client machine. That way the client machine can package up the requests to be sent to the Web service and parse responses that are returned. The client can access .NET or COM Web services in addition to ones not running on Windows at all.

After you have selected the Web service you want to use, just click Add to make it part of your project. This creates the wrapper class for you. Figure 27-8 shows how this class is located in the VBA project.

Figure 27-8: The resulting wrapper class in a VBA project after referencing a Web service

Let's take a quick peek at what is inside the wrapper class. First, the class contains some information that tells the SOAP client object where to go to make the call, as shown in Listing 27-4.

Listing 27-4: Declarations in the Wrapper Class for a Web Service

```
Private sc_QuotesService1 As SoapClient30
Private Const c_WSDL_URL As String = _
"http://dpower30/xmlweb/quotesservice1.wsdl"
Private Const c_SERVICE As String = "QuotesService1"
Private Const c_PORT As String = "QuotesSoapPort"
Private Const c_SERVICE_NAMESPACE As String = _
http://tempuri.org/QuotesService1/wsdl/
```

This code has some of the same bits of information we saw in our less-sophisticated example in Listing 27-3. In fact, upon close inspection of the class, you will find that there is little difference between what it contains and what is in the types of things spelled out in Listing 27-3. The essentials are nearly identical. However, the beauty of the wrapper class is that you can use it in your code as if it were just a locally installed component.

Here, in Figure 27-9, you see a simple user interface created to call the Web service and receive a response. The code behind it, in Listing 27-5, is extraordinarily simple. This is the benefit of the Web Services Toolkit. The complexity of calling and using the service is hidden, although if you wish to edit it you still can.

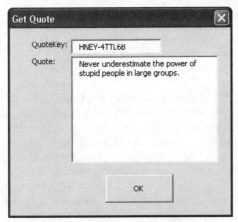

Figure 27-9: The Microsoft Office user interface for using a Web service

Listing 27-5: Code for Calling a Web Service within the Office Project

```
Private Sub cmdOK_Click()
  Dim qs As clsws_QuotesService1
  Set qs = New clsws_QuotesService1
  txtQuote.Text = qs.wsm_GetQuote(txtKey.Text)
End Sub
```

While the code needed to make SOAP calls through the MS SOAP client is not terribly difficult, the Office XP Web Services Toolkit does make it less of a developer-centric task than one that is approachable to even power-users.

Utilities in the MS SOAP Toolkit

Now that we have had a chance to really get into the MS SOAP SDK and create some sample applications, it is useful to take a broader look the utilities that are provided in the Toolkit. These include:

✦ SOAPVDIR.CMD

✦ wsdlgen3.dll

✦ MsSOAPT3.exe

We have already learned the purpose of SOAPVDIR.CMD, namely that it tells IIS which Web sites should be tied to the ISAPI listener. We also used the wsdlgen3.exe utility to create WSDL and WSML files for a custom Web service. The last utility is the Trace Utility. Have you ever wondered what kind of information gets sent along the wire when a SOAP call is made and when the response is given? If so, then the Trace Utility is for you. This tool makes it possible to see what information is passed along the wire. The Trace Utility does not show all of the TCP/IP protocol information, as this is better handled by lower level listeners. Rather, the Trace Utility is concerned specifically with SOAP messages.

Starting the utility is easy enough. Just double-click the executable or run it from the Start menu in Windows. However, you need to do a couple of things to make it possible for the utility to intercept SOAP traffic as it is sent to and from IIS. To do this, the utility must listen in on a specific TCP port. The client that wishes to use the Web service must then reference that port when sending requests to the Web service. The Trace Utility then passes along the message to the Web service on its original port number (usually 80) so that the Web service is none the wiser. The response is then routed back to the Trace Utility, which then in turns sends the information back to the client that made the original request. The client does not know that there is a listener involved, nor does the Web service. All the client knows is that instead of making requests to port 80, it will make them to a different port. To make that possible, you will need to modify the *client's copy* of the WSDL and add the special port number to a specific section in the WSDL file. This is done in the <port> element of the client-side WSDL. Listing 27-6 shows that section of the file with the subsequent modification.

Listing 27-6: Changing the Client-Side WSDL So That Messages Can Be Intercepted by the Trace Utility

```
<service name='QuotesService1' >
<port name='QuotesSoapPort'
binding='wsdlns:QuotesSoapBinding' >
<soap:address
```

```
location='http://localhost:8080/XMLWeb/QuotesService1.WSDL'/>
   </port>
 </service>
```

The only modification here is the addition of the ":8080" to the end of the server name. In a production scenario, the server name would normally not be here and would be instead replaced by a DNS name that hides the name of the actual host.

Now that the client-side WSDL is modified, we need to start up the Trace Utility and get it to intercept all requests made to the port we have added, 8080. Which port you choose is up to you, but it is probably not a good idea to use other well-known ports, like 21 or 443. Usually 8080 will work for you without any hassles.

With the Trace Utility running, go to the File | New | Formatted Trace menu, and you will see a dialog box like the one shown in Figure 27-10. This dialog box simply tells the Trace Utility which port to listen on and which port to which it should send traffic as it receives it.

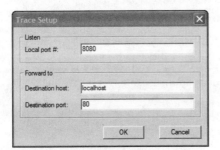

Figure 27-10: Enabling the Trace Utility to listen in on a specified port number

With these things enabled, running the same client application in VBScript produces results as shown in Figure 27-11. Here you can see the SOAP messages in their entirety. These, of course, are somewhat simple because the Web service is not terribly complex. As you add more information such as SOAP headers and security information to your Web service, your SOAP messages may be more verbose. In addition to seeing the XML representation of the messages, you can also look at the SOAP headers and look at the encoded representations of the messages.

The Trace Utility can be helpful in creating and troubleshooting Web services, and you should become familiar with its operations to save yourself time and agony as you create and deploy Web services.

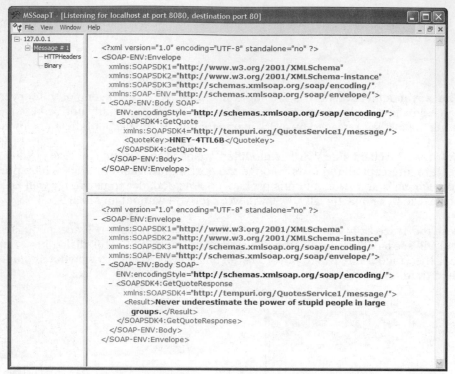

Figure 27-11: The results of a SOAP request and response using the Trace Utility

Summary

In this chapter, we have explored the features of the MS SOAP Toolkit SDK. While much of the interest in Web services is around Java and .NET, COM developers (there are millions of them) need not be left behind. In fact, in some respects, COM developers have helped fuel the interest in Web services all along, precisely the reason why the SOAP Toolkit is now on version 3.0. The toolkit contains utilities and other DLLs to make it possible for COM-based technologies to send and receive SOAP messages. One of the key features is the installation of an ISAPI handler on the target server so that IIS can receive SOAP messages and route them directly to COM DLLs that are exposed as Web services. Clients can use a set of client objects to connect to Web services and treat them as if there were local components. We also saw how to build client applications including using the Office XP Web Services Toolkit, a clever Addin that turns applications like Microsoft Excel into full Web service consumers. Finally, we saw how to use the Trace Utility to get a good look at the SOAP requests and responses passed to and from a Web service.

✦   ✦   ✦

J2EE Web Services

The Java 2 Platform, Enterprise Edition (J2EE), is a Java-based component model that simplifies enterprise Java Application development and deployment. The J2EE platform is accessible though J2EE application servers, such as IBM WebSphere Application Server, BEA WebLogic, Sun ONE, and Apache Tomcat. J2EE classes and methods manage infrastructures and provide supports for Java, XML, and Web service applications. The J2EE platform is also the foundation technology of Sun's Open Network Environment (ONE) platform and Web services strategy.

However, core J2EE classes, methods, and properties have absolutely nothing to do with XML or Web services. Fortunately for J2EE developers, J2EE classes do contain robust and flexible support for text, and Web services are based on XML, and XML is text (Web services are based on very complicated XML text , but it's still text). Web service code is based on manipulating this text, and converting the text to other platform formats.

There are several architectural options that can be used to efficiently develop and deploy Web services in J2EE. In this chapter we'll introduce an example of a basic J2EE Web Service architecture. We'll use the example to describe some of the advantages of working with Web services in J2EE. I'll also introduce you to vendor platforms that support the architecture. In Chapter 32 we'll discuss the details of the tools available for developing Web services.

Web Services: .NET or J2EE?

It's hard not to discuss Web service architecture without discussing both .NET and J2EE. Both platforms are big supporters of Web services. Often, both platforms are compared and contrasted as opposite Web service camps, but that's not the way that it has to be at an enterprise level. In fact, many organizations to which I have provided XML and Web service architectural services have plans to deploy both platforms. J2EE's multi-platform base makes it a natural choice for enterprise applications. Also, many vendors, such as SUN, IBM, and Oracle, provide robust interfaces to their relational data stores via J2EE/JDBC, XML and Web service interfaces. Microsoft and many other software vendors provide .NET interfaces to their enterprise products, and .NET's Web service client implementation provides a compelling platform for smart Web service clients.

Yeah, blah, blah, blah, Brian: Which one do I pick?

Of course, the enterprise-level scenario we've described doesn't help if you're planning to start a Web services project and have to start with...something. Usually, that something means picking a platform, at least as a starting point. How should you make that decision?

In most cases, the software and hardware products that a company has chosen to work with and the skill sets that the company has available for a project should determine a solution platform. Because Web services use industry-standard formats for communication, it's not imperative to stick with one platform or the other as the scope of a project or solution grows. But before you start a project, you usually must have to pick one. This is what makes Web service architecture interesting! The consolation is that Web service architecture can often accommodate imperfect platform decisions. For example, if you start a project with Oracle XML DB as a Web service data repository, then for some reason decide to switch the data to SQL server or DB2, the change from one RDBMS platform to another should not be difficult within a well-designed multi-tier Web service architecture. Before Web services, this change would probably require a rewrite of the client, the access method to the data, and the application server that accesses the data.

When selecting a Web services platform, what you already have to work with should be a big factor. Existing platforms and development tools, existing developer skill sets, and existing investment in software and hardware are important factors in determining future direction. Because Web services are supported by most major software vendors and development tools these days, the deciding factor often comes down to the OS platform that the Web service solution will run on. J2EE has an advantage in multi-platform applications, while .NET has a clear advantage in Windows server environments.

Don't overlook smart clients!

Windows has something that J2EE does not, and may never have — a smart Web services client. Smart clients are applications that function at the application or OS level of client hardware, and are easily integrated with other parts of the client hardware and software to provide rich, configurable functionality to the user. This functionality is usually automated and requires little or no custom development. Because they require no developer assistance, smart clients are often overlooked when designing and building Web service applications, in favor of server-based Web browser solutions. As Web service clients, Web browsersare great for basic display of data. However, one of the key features of Web services is the ability to access data over the Web from any client, not just a Web browser. This means that you can add Web services to a column of a spreadsheet or integrate Web services into a calendar application on your desktop or a smart wireless phone. The smart client can be easily integrated with other applications at the client level, making it easy to build robust, customizable client applications that access data via Web services. For example, a Web browser is handy for booking a flight online. However, once you book a flight, how do you get the flight data into your calendar or your PDA? This is usually a cut and paste procedure, or the task of a third-party tool that can read the flight data and knows how to insert the data in your client application. But what if you could just add an airline's or hotel's reservation system directly into your calendar? You could select dates, make reservations, and store itinerary data from your calendar as if the airline's reservation system was part of your calendar application. This is the promise of Web service smart clients.

.NET and MS Office have already added very impressive Web service client capabilities into many Windows client applications. This functionality increases with each new version of Windows and Office. Another potential Web service client competitor is Lotus Notes, which integrates e-mail, calendaring, applications, an integrated application development environment, and much more into their very impressive Notes client application. At the moment, Notes has an advantage over other smart clients in terms of client application security and multi-platform server support, but MS Office and .NET applications have the advantage of providing robust and easy client access to Web services.

About portals

J2EE's answer to smart clients is the portal. Applications that use J2EE Web services commonly use a Web browser as the client, which accesses data from a server. The server is usually a mid-tier J2EE server, which has access to other servers to retrieve and process data. This model usually referred to as a "thin client" architecture. I question the thin part, as modern browsers are actually quite complex clients — but in this case thin can describe the workload, not just the footprint of the client. In thin client architecture, the client, usually a Web browser does little or no work. Almost all of the processing is done on a middle-tier J2EE application server. The browser's job is to send requests to a J2EE server, and wait for an HTML page response. The J2EE server usually sends requests to one or more other servers for data and then processes the HTML page that is sent back to the browser.

A portal provides a common interface to multiple applications. The portal acts as a central point of contact for various applications that serve data on multiple platforms, and is usually customizable by the user. User configuration information is usually stored on a centralized portal server, so that the user can interact with their customized environment on any machine that can access the portal server. Portals are currently a very popular segment of J2EE development, because they are well-suited to a multi-tier J2EE application architecture.

Having a large number of users connect to a centralized portal server presents scalability issues that multi-tier J2EE architectures are designed to address. .NET does have portal capability integrated as part of its framework as well, but the jury is still out when it comes to enterprise-level Web service scalability on a Windows-only platform.

Web services can be an important part of J2EE portal architectures. They act as the glue that holds together the communication infrastructure between the tiers. Instead of having to adapt data formats and platform protocols to communicate with each other, Web-service-enabled data providers can connect to each other via the Web service "lingua franca" of SOAP. Portals and Web services extend the functionality of the thin-client model by providing more interactivity between a thin client and a J2EE application server. Instead of a smart client that interacts with server data, the portal aggregates and processes data, and serves the data to a thin Web services client. Portal servers take on the role of the smart client in this scenario.

Portal servers have two advantages over a smart client in Web service architectures. The first advantage is that the portal is always on. In the case of a smart client such as a PDA, smart wireless phone, or laptop, there are times when processing will be limited because the client is not accessible. The second advantage is that user configuration is stored on a centralized server. Theoretically, this means that any client that can access the portal server is automatically configured to a user's centrally stored settings. These advantages have to be weighed, however, with the rich and flexible display and application integration options that smart clients offer. I predict that as Web services evolve, "thin" Web service clients will start to look more and more like smart Web service clients, as features are added to process data at the client level. This has happened with Web browsers and HTTP servers, and I expect the same evolution for Web service clients and servers. Even today, portals and smart clients can interact. There's no law stating that Web service portals can only serve HTML pages to browser clients. Portals can also send and receive SOAP to interact with a smart Web service client.

J2EE Web Service Architecture

While it is true that there is an exception to every rule, exceptions tend to be more plentiful in the fast-evolving Web services world. That's why we tend to use words like "usually" and commonly" a lot when describing Web service architectures. With that warning in mind, let's run through the basic building blocks of a J2EE Web services architecture.

Multi-tier J2EE Web service client architectures start with a thin client, which is usually a browser, but could be any hardware or software device. Other common software clients are another Web service, a proxy class in VB, Java, C++, or any other language, or a smart client that generates SOAP envelopes.

 Note   Instead of clients and servers, W3C documentation refers to service requestors and service providers. This is to account for the fact that Web services can have many layers, and that in some cases a "client" may be another Web service on another server.

Requestors connect to a server that processes requests. Requests and responses between the requestor and the provider are usually, over HTTP. W3C-standard calls and responses can be sent and received using SMTP as well, but this is not very common.

The messages that are sent between the requestor and the provider are contained in SOAP envelopes. The SOAP envelope can contain anything, but usually contains XML. There are two basic ways that SOAP envelope contents can be formatted, remote procedure call (RPC) and anything else. The most common method is RPC. In SOAP envelopes, the XML contents of the envelope follow a basic call and response protocol between the requestor and the provider. The requestor makes a call and waits for a response. The provider receives the call and makes a response. If the SOAP envelope is not formatted as RPC, the call-and-response mechanism, if there is any, has to be described as part of the envelope contents.

 Cross-Reference   SOAP is covered in more detail in Chapters 23 and 24.

A Web Service Requestor sees a Web Service provider as a single entity. However, a single Web service provider is usually made up of multiple layers.

A *portal* is an optional first layer for J2EE Web services. The portal can be part of a J2EE application server environment, or a separate portal server. Portals act as a smart client proxy to manage information and tasks on behalf of a user. In a J2EE Web service architecture, the portal interacts with the J2EE application server to process Web services. (For more information on portals, and how they can be useful for Web Service architectures, see the "About portals" section earlier in this chapter.)

If a portal server is not implemented, the first layer in a J2EE Web service is a *J2EE application server*, such as IBM's WebSphere Application Server, BEA WebLogic, Sun ONE server, or Apache Tomcat.

If SOAP envelope contents are formatted as RPC, the J2EE application server uses an *RPC Router* and a *deployment descriptor* to process the functionality associated with the Web service. Deployment descriptors are used to make the link between Web service requests and responses and an application. Deployment descriptors are XML documents that are stored on the J2EE application server. The RPC router uses these deployment descriptors to find classes and methods associated with the Web service. The J2EE application server controls the calls and responses to other entities that make up the Web service. Processing could include calling another Web service, calling a Java class, or retrieving data from a data repository such as a RDBMS. When the appropriate responses have been received, the J2EE application server builds a SOAP response envelope and sends it back to the requestor. Figure 28-1 shows a typical J2EE application server architecture.

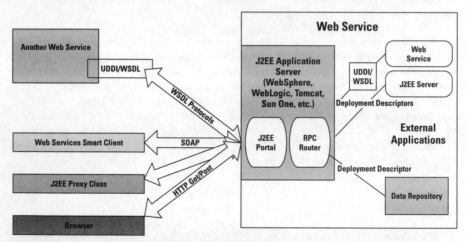

Figure 28-1: A typical J2EE Web services architecture

Now that you have an overview of what a J2EE Web service looks like, let's drill down a little deeper into the workings of a J2EE application server. Specifically, let's look at how associated applications make up a Web service. Once again, I'll start with a browser as a Web service requestor.

A Web service requestor can optionally access a UDDI server entry. J2EE UDDI functionality is usually implemented using IBM's UDDI4J or Sun's JAXR. The UDDI entry points to the latest version of a WDSL file. If the requestor already has an instance of the WSDL file located, they can skip this step.

Tip JAXR includes a registry server as part of the implementation classes.

The WSDL document contains information about a Web service. J2EE proxy classes can be used as a requestor interface. Proxy classes are designed to read the WSDL file at a predefined location on a J2EE server. WSDL files are registered on the J2EE application server. A well-written proxy class is designed to adapt calls and responses to the Web service according to WSDL values.

Cross-Reference WSDL is covered in more detail in Chapters 23 and 25.

When a Web service requestor makes a call to a Web service provider using a SOAP envelope formatted as RPC, the request is routed to a transport-independent SOAP RPC router. The RPC Router is usually based on the `org.apache.soap.server.RPCRouter` class, which is a member of the Apache AXIS packages. The RPC Router listens for HTTP POSTs that are sent to a URL on the J2EE application server. SOAP envelopes are retrieved from the POST. The RPC Router builds an RPC call object from the SOAP envelope contents, and checks the validity of the object and makes the call. If the call requires a response, the RPC Router waits for a response, and generates a SOAP response envelope from the response object.

Note Creating a SOAP envelope from a call or response object is known as *marshaling* a SOAP envelope. Breaking down a SOAP call into another object is called *unmarshaling* the SOAP object.

The unmarshaled RPC call is directed to its destination by a deployment descriptor. Deployment descriptors are XML documents that reside on the J2EE application server, and describe a SOAP action. SOAP actions are mapped to applications. Those applications can be a simple class on the J2EE server, another Web service, a RDBMS query, or virtually anything else that can accept an RPC call.

Tip The Apache AXIS packages contain classes that accept a Java class as input and generate a WSDL document. AXIS can also generate a client proxy class for the source J2EE class. Proxy classes can act as a client-side interface between Java applications, servlets, or applets. AXIS can also generate a deployment descriptor at the same time it generates the WSDL and the proxy class.

Figure 28-2 shows the structure of a Typical J2EE application server that is configured for Web services, with all of the components we've described in this section of the chapter.

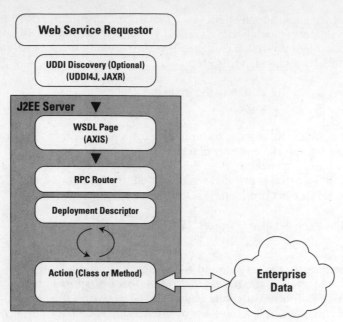

Figure 28-2: Structure of a typical J2EE Application Server, configured for Web services

Software Support for J2EE Web Services

J2EE Web services are built on a platform of Web service standards. They are also built on a set of components that adhere to those standards. Multi-tier J2EE Web services start with a thin client, usually a Web browser. In between the browser and the data that is being accessed, there are one or more tiers that provide data formatting and processing. Software for developing and deploying multi-tier J2EE Web services is based on java developer community effort. Most of these efforts center on projects at the Apache Software Foundation. Most J2EE Web service software providers use the latest version of the Apache software foundation's AXIS as the core of their offerings. AXIS stands for "Apache eXtensible Interaction System," and is a J2EE reference implementation of the latest W3C recommendations for SOAP and WSDL. AXIS code can be implemented on the client side as proxy classes and on the server side as routers and implementation classes. We'll get into the architecture in more detail later in this chapter. For now it's just important to know that AXIS code is used in most J2EE implementations where SOAP and WSDL functionality is needed.

Apache Offerings

The Apache Software Foundation is a non-profit consortium that provides organizational, legal, and financial support for Apache open-source software projects, all of which can be seen at `http://www.apache.org/`. The goal of all of the Apache Web service projects is to provide high-quality standards-based XML solutions that are developed in an open and cooperative fashion. Apache project participants are in a unique position to provide feedback to W3C Web service working groups regarding implementation issues, based on real-life implementation attempts. All implementation code is available in Java. Server code is based on J2EE. Some projects produce other code in other languages as well. For a full list of Apache projects, go to `http://apache.org/`.

Apache AXIS

Apache Software Foundation code is weaved in to most commercial and non-commercial J2EE development tools for handling XML and Web services. For example, IBM and Sun both have features built in to their J2EE development UIs that generate a WSDL file from a Java class, and vice versa. These tools are based on AXIS code that has been integrated into the product. AXIS also provides RPC Router functionality and classes to handle SOAP envelopes on J2Ee servers and in developer UI test environments.

Web Services Invocation Framework (WSIF)

The Web Services Invocation Framework (WSIF) is a Java API for invoking Web services without directly accessing a SOAP API, such as AXIS. It provides the same kind of functionality that JAXP does for Web parsing. A WSIF interface can be used on any WDSL-compatible Web service, regardless of the original SOAP or WSDL version or implementation. Additional information can be found at `http://ws.apache.org/wsif`.

Web Services Inspection Language (WSIL)

The Web Services Inspection Language is a standardized way to find out about published WSDL without a USDDI server implementation. WSIL also provides rules for how inspection-related information can be revealed by a site. WS-Inspection documents point to WSDL and other forms of Web service descriptors. The WSIL specification can be reviewed at `http://cvs.apache.org/viewcvs.cgi/*checkout*/xml-axis-wsil/java/docs/wsinspection.html`.

XML security

Apache has implemented Java reference implementations of the XML-Signature Syntax and Processing Recommendation, and the XML Encryption Syntax and Processing. By the time this book is in print, they probably will have finished the XML Key Management recommendation implementation in Java as well.

 We cover Web service security in more detail in Chapter 37.

Jakarta Tomcat

Tomcat is the official J2EE Reference Implementation for Java Servlet and JavaServer Pages technologies. Tomcat is a J2EE application server that also supports SOAP and WSDL implementations via AXIS classes. This includes an RPC Router, which is based on the AXIS `rpcrouter` class. Additional information about Tomcat can be found at `http://jakarta.apache.org/tomcat/index.html`.

IBM Offerings

Aside from integrating Apache and other Web service tools as part of the WebSphere Studio Application Developer, IBM also provides the WebSphere Application Server (WAS). WAS is an integral part of J2EE Web Service architectures on IBM platforms. AlphaWorks is also an important place for learning about and using cutting-edge technologies.

WebSphere Application Server

IBM's WebSphere Application Server (WAS) is IBM's offering in the J2EE application server marketplace. WAS provides the glue that holds a J2EE Web Service architecture together. Support for multi-platforms, including IBM mainframe hardware, ensures scalability. More information can be found at `http://www.ibm.com/websphere`.

WebSphere Portal Server

As we mentioned earlier in this chapter, portals are the J2EE version of a Web Service smart client. IBM WebSphere Portal is a platform more than it is an application or server. It seamlessly integrates with WebSphere Application Server, which seamlessly integrates with just about anything else — :you just have to write most of the seams yourself. The WebSphere Portal Collaboration Center integrates IBM's Lotus Domino for collaborative applications. Features include integrated instant messaging, team workspaces and online meetings. More information can be found at `http://www.ibm.com/websphere`.

IBM AlphaWorks

IBM AlphaWorks (http://alphaworks.ibm.com) is a very important resource for anyone who has to code XML or Web Service applications in J2EE. For those unfamiliar with the site, it contains a wealth of free tools and utilities that can be downloaded and integrated into a Web services developer's arsenal. Many of the tools adhere to recent or developing W3C recommendations, and are a great complement for J2EE Web service infrastructures. A good example is the XML Security Suite, which adds W3C-defined security features such as digital signature, encryption, and access control to Web service and XML applications.

 Cross-Reference I discuss AlphaWorks tools offerings in more detail in Chapter 32.

Eclipse Tools for J2EE Web Service Developers

The eclipse.org Website (http://www.eclipse.org) is the center of the Eclipse consortium. Eclipse is an open source, freely distributable platform for developer tool integration. In essence, it provides a "lowest common denominator" for developers to integrate functionality into a development UI. IBM provided most of the code for the startup, and since then other large players have joined in at the board level, including Borland, MERANT, QNX Software Systems, Rational Software, Red Hat, SuSE, and TogetherSoft. Several other very large players have also joined as non-board members, including Sybase, Fujitsu, Hitachi, Oracle, SAP, and the Object Management Group (OMG).

The Eclipse Modeling Framework

The Eclipse Modeling Framework (EMF) is a framework for generating applications based on class models. EMF uses Java and XML to generate Java code from application models. The intention is to provide the same sort of functionality that is found in other, more expensive application architecture and modeling tools. In addition to a Java code generator, EMF saves objects as XML documents that can be transformed and adapted for use with other tools and applications. In addition, an updated model can regenerate Java code, and updated Java code can be used to update a model.

Here's a listing of the EMF framework components:

✦ The EMF framework core includes a set of tools for describing models using metadata. The metadata starts with an instance of an object, then describes all of the features of that object, including properties, methods, and so on. The framework core is implemented as a plug-in to the Eclipse platform UI.

✦ The EMF.Edit component contains reusable classes that developers can use to build EMF model editors. Classes include support for class content, labels and source code. Also included is support for display of the classes in the Eclipse platform UI.

✦ The EMF.Codegen component generates J2EE code from an EMF model. Classes include support for a developer UI for specifying generation options and calling generators. Code can be generated for EMF Models, implementation classes for editing and display of the model in the Eclipse Platform UI, and editors that manage the editing and display of the model in the Eclipse Platform UI.

BEA Offerings

BEA sells their very popular WebLogic J2EE application server and an integrated development environment as a bundle. BEA also sells a high-performance JVM for Windows client machines, called JRockit. More information on BEA offerings can be found at `http://www.bea.com`.

Sun Offerings

Sun owns the Sun ONE Studio Developer, which is the biggest competitor to IBM's WebSphere Studio Application Developer. Sun also offers the Sun ONE Server, which competes with IBM's WebSphere Application Server (WAS, and BEA's WebLogic Server.

Like IBM, Sun also provides a huge amount of J2EE and Web service resources for free download from Sun's Java site. In addition, free XML tutorials, articles, and sample code are available from the Sun Developer Services Website.

Sun ONE Application Server

The Sun ONE Application Server is a J2EE application server that is integrated with the Sun ONE application developer Studio and the Sun Web Services Developer Pack. More information on the Sun ONE application server and related offerings can be found at `http://wwws.sun.com/software/products/appsrvr/home_appsrvr.html`.

The Sun Java Web Services Developer Pack

The Java Web Service Developer Pack (WSDP) is downloadable from Sun at `http://java.sun.com/webservices/webservicespack.html`. The current version of the WSDP is compatible with JDK 1.3.1 and higher. The WSDP APIs include the following:

✦ **JAXP (Java API for XML Processing)** supports processing of XML documents, including WSDL documents, SOAP envelopes, and deployment descriptors.

✦ **JAXB (Java Architecture for XML Binding)** automates mapping between XML documents and Java objects, making elements and attributes classes, properties and methods.

✦ **JAXM (Java API for XML Messaging)** provides an Interface for SOAP messages, including SOAP with attachments.

✦ **JSTL (Java Server Pages Standard Tag Library)** consists of four custom Java Server Page (JSP) tag libraries called the core, XML, I18N & Formatting, and database access libraries.

✦ **JAX-RPC (Java API for XML-Based RPC)** provides an Interface for XML messages using an RPC transport, including, but not limited to, SOAP calls over RPC to Web services.

✦ **JAXR (Java API for XML Registries)** provides an interface for XML registries, supporting UDDI and OASIS/U.N./CEFACT ebXML Registry and Repository standards, among others.

✦ **The Java WSDP Registry Server** implements Version 2 of the UDDI (Universal Description, Discovery and Integration) specification. It provides a registry that is compatible with JAXR (Java API for XML Registries).

✦ **SAAJ (SOAP with Attachments API for Java)** provides support for producing, sending, and receiving SOAP messages with attachments.

Summary

In this chapter we compared the .NET Web services that you were introduced to in Chapter 27 with J2EE architectures, and compared the features of each Web service platforms. We also introduced you to a basic J2EE Web service architecture and some of the ways that the architecture can be implemented. By now you should have a pretty good understanding of the way a J2EE Web service architecture is structured and how it can be created in the real world using vendor tools that are available today:

✦ The structure of .NET and J2EE Web service infrastructures

✦ J2EE Web service architecture

✦ How Web service calls and response are made in J2EE

✦ How a J2EE Application server handles Web services

✦ How an RPC Router works

✦ An introduction to deployment descriptors

✦ Tools available to build your J2EE Web service infrastructure

✦ IBM, BEA, Sun, and Apache offerings

The next couple of chapters will highlight .NET Web Service examples. After that, we'll describe the tools that developers can use to build Web services, and give you a lot more detail on the offerings available from major Web service vendors. In Chapters 35, 36, and 37, we'll show some advanced examples of Web services in action.

✦   ✦   ✦

Microsoft.NET and Web Services

Part VI covers the techniques and tools for building Web services for MS .NET. These include using ASP.NET for creating and deploying .NET Web services, accessing .NET Web services from Web applications, and building a Windows-based .NET Web services Client application using Visual Studio.Net and Visual Basic.NET.

Creating and Deploying .NET Web Services

Without question one of the most compelling technologies for building Web services is Microsoft's .NET Framework. The .NET Framework comes with all of the building blocks for Web services built right in. Essentially, any server with the Framework and IIS installed is ready to provide Web services. Furthermore, .NET carefully balances the need for making Web services easier to create, deploy, and maintain with the requirement that developers still be able to go under the hood and do more advanced techniques.

In this chapter, we will see how to build Web services using the .NET Framework. We will look at the APIs provided in the Framework that make Web services possible. We will also inventory what is needed to deploy a Web service into a production scenario, and how Web services can be further customized. Most importantly, we will see how XML is used throughout the .NET Framework support for Web services, which classes use XML, how the configuration files use XML, and how other Framework XML classes can be used when creating Web services.

This chapter does not deal with creating .NET client applications for consuming Web services. This is dealt with in Chapter 31. However, we will take advantage of a couple of client applications, both in .NET and in COM, to show how the Web services created here work.

Introduction

The .NET Framework comes with a large number of APIs, and some of them deal directly with the operations of Web services. Fortunately, the level to which you want to learn these classes is really up to you. In other words, if you want to get going with Web Services in .NET, you are not obligated to have a mastery of every building block that undergirds the .NET Web Services architecture. On the other hand, if you want to do more and more advanced things, the complete blueprint of these building blocks is open to you. You can inherit and extend the underlying classes and use them to accomplish rather specific needs.

Brief overview of .NET

Before diving into the .NET Web Services classes, it is useful to understand the general architecture of .NET and how the .NET Framework works. This overview is intended to be brief as our focus remains on Web Services more directly. If you wish to more fully grasp the .NET Framework, you can go to Microsoft's Website dedicated to .NET as well as a number of excellent other Websites that are dedicated to the understanding and promotion of .NET.

Websites include:

✦ `http://msdn.microsoft.com/net`

✦ `http://www.gotdotnet.com`

✦ `http://www.asp.net`

✦ `http://www.dotnet247.com`

Perhaps the most succinct definition of .NET is this: .NET is an entirely distinct (read not COM-based) runtime that is designed to run on operating systems in the Windows family. There is no overstating that this runtime is unique and is not based on the legacy of runtimes that have been part of the Windows development platform up to this point. This new runtime is not just a reworking of previous runtimes with some enhancements. Instead, it is a runtime that is new from the ground up, while it also benefits from lessons learned in other runtimes (even those that are not Windows-based). The .NET runtime manages all code execution, code and user security, memory management, the type system, JIT compilation, exception handling, and so much more. What is especially notable about this runtime is that *all* of these things that the runtime does are the same irrespective of which language is used. For example, instead of a string type being different in Visual Basic .NET, C#, or J#, they all use the same underlying type and use the same name. Additionally, the API used to create and manage Windows forms is the same no matter which language is used.

What this means is that the .NET runtime is not tied to any specific language. In fact, the runtime does not really understand the development languages you would use to create applications. It understands a single language called Microsoft Intermediate Language or MSIL. This language is an assembler-style language, and, although you can program directly in this language, it would not be terribly fun to do so, as Figure 29-1 shows.

```
Product::Ship : valuetype [mscorlib]System.DateTime()

.method public newslot strict virtual instance valuetype [mscorlib]System.DateTime
        Ship() cil managed
{
  // Code size       23 (0x17)
  .maxstack  1
  .locals init ([0] valuetype [mscorlib]System.DateTime Ship)
  IL_0000:  nop
  IL_0001:  ldarg.0
  IL_0002:  ldfld      class Projects.Product/ShippedEventHandler Projects.Product::ShippedEvent
  IL_0007:  brfalse.s  IL_0015
  IL_0009:  ldarg.0
  IL_000a:  ldfld      class Projects.Product/ShippedEventHandler Projects.Product::ShippedEvent
  IL_000f:  callvirt   instance void Projects.Product/ShippedEventHandler::Invoke()
  IL_0014:  nop
  IL_0015:  ldloc.0
  IL_0016:  ret
} // end of method Product::Ship
```

Figure 29-1: A look at the common language that is understood by the .NET runtime

As you can see, while the language is intelligible, it would be difficult to create killer applications in short order using this language. What this means is that to get your application into MSIL, you need to pass your project files through a language compiler. So, you can use Visual Studio .NET or a simple text editor if you wish to create your project files. Then, you use a language compiler to turn your project files into a compiled executable. That executable has the MSIL embedded directly within itself. The .NET runtime then looks at the executable, pulls out the instructions it needs in the common language and then compiles the code into native code that can be scheduled on the processor of the machine where the code is running. This is why the .NET runtime is called the Common Language Runtime or CLR.

The .NET Framework has two main components: the CLR and the .NET Framework class library. The CLR is the foundation of the .NET Framework. It manages code at execution time, providing core services such as memory management, thread management, and remote component invocation, while enforcing strict safety and accuracy of the code. Code that targets the CLR is known as managed code, while code that does not target the Runtime is known as unmanaged code.

The .NET Framework also includes an extensive and comprehensive, object-oriented, hierarchically organized collection of reusable classes that will help you develop applications ranging from traditional command-line or Graphical User

Interface (GUI) applications to applications based on the latest innovations provided by ASP.NET and Web services. For example, to create a Windows form and work with controls on that form one would use classes contained in `System.Windows.Forms`. Again, all of these things are independent of the development language you choose to use. So, if you want to write a Web Service using VB.NET syntax, you can. Or you can use a more C-based syntax by using C# (pronounced C-sharp). In the end, your development language choice has more to do with the syntax with which you are comfortable than anything else. As you may expect, newsgroups are filled with debates about the merits of .NET-compliant languages. Read these as you wish, but perhaps your time is probably better spent learning the language-independent classes defined in the .NET Framework and how to leverage the CLR. Figure 29-2 shows generally how the languages use the .NET Framework classes to do things like create forms, Web Services, access data, use XML, and do other things that are managed by the CLR. It also shows how Visual Studio .NET can be used to create applications that target the .NET Framework.

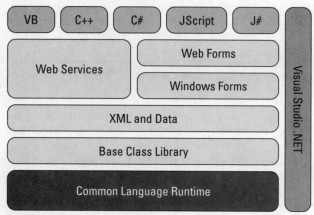

Figure 29-2: Developer-oriented languages target .NET Framework classes to do programming tasks that run inside the CLR.

In this chapter, we will use Visual Studio.NET exclusively to create Web Services. In subsequent chapters, we will also use Visual Studio.NET to create client-side applications that can consume Web Services. If you are unsure about how Web Services work, you should make sure you look at Chapters 23 through 26 that deal with the general concept of Web Services and how they work. Here, we will assume you are already familiar with these concepts, and we can focus uniquely on how to build them targeting using .NET technologies.

Web Services Class and Attributes

The main class that makes Web Services possible in .NET is `System.Web.Services.WebService`. The name is sensible and simple enough, and, to be truthful, you will not find that this class has a lot of special properties and methods. This class is really just a generic one that you will inherit and thereby get hooks into the SOAP plumbing and other things that make Web Services possible. As you can see, the `WebService` class is found in the `System.Web.Services` namespace, and there are other classes there that let you take .NET Web Services from the simple to the advanced level. There are many classes, and each of these has many members, too many to cover in this chapter. Thus, we will focus on the things that will let you get up and running with Web Services while also going beyond a simple "Hello World" Web Service.

First, let's look at the classes that help you instance and define your own Web Service class. They include:

✦ `WebService`

✦ `WebServiceAttribute`

✦ `WebServiceBindingAttribute`

✦ `WebMethodAttribute`

Let's take a moment to understand what these classes do. First, the `WebService` class is what the .NET Framework will create to represent your "object" when the Web Service runs. You give your custom class a name and make it inherit from this `WebService` class so that it becomes something the runtime can render in a specific way. Listing 29-1 shows all of the code you need to get your Web Service going using this class. The `System.Web.Services.WebService` class, which defines the optional base class for XML Web services, provides direct access to common ASP.NET objects, such as those for application and session state. By default, XML Web services created in managed code using Visual Studio inherit from this class. While it is possible to produce a custom class that does not inherit from the `WebService` class yet still fields Web Service requests, it requires more coding to do so, and you must use ASP.NET `System.Web.HttpContext.Current` property in your class to pull it off. In some advanced situations, this may be the way to go, but for the most part, just inherit from the `WebService` class to make your class SOAP-enabled.

Listing 29-1: Basic Code Using the WebService Class to Create a Custom Web Service

```
Imports System.Web.Services

<System.Web.Services.WebService(Namespace := _
"http://tempuri.org/GetQuote/QuoteService")> _
Public Class QuoteService
    Inherits System.Web.Services.WebService
    Public Sub New()
      MyBase.New()
    End Sub
    <WebMethod()> Public Function QuoteFinder( _
ByVal Key As String) As String
        Return("Quote will go here eventually.")
    End Function
End Class
```

The coding in Listing 29-1 alone is enough to create a simple, functional Web Service. Before we get ahead of ourselves, let's take a moment to understand how this code would suddenly become a service that a remote user could access via SOAP. First, .NET in and of itself cannot respond to HTTP requests over TCP/IP. In other words, just putting the .NET Framework on a server and creating a Web Service makes it available. The .NET runtime works closely with Windows and IIS to field SOAP requests and send back SOAP responses. So, this class, as such, only does part of the work of fielding the request and processing it before sending a response. Windows and IIS are involved all along the way to route the user's request to the .NET application that in turn runs this Web Service.

That said, we should take note of a few other things in this simple code. First, you notice that there are attributes in the code (offset with < and > tags) that add special behaviors. These attributes are there to tell the .NET runtime more about what the Web Service does and how it is supposed to function.

One of these attributes is the WebServiceAttribute and is shown in our code as:

```
<System.Web.Services.WebService(Namespace :=
"http://tempuri.org/GetQuote/QuoteService")>
```

This attribute lets you specify a namespace for the Web Service. The Namespace allows you to organize your Web Service in a hierarchical Namespace so that it makes more sense in your organization. In addition to the Namespace you can specify a description of your Web Service in this attribute so that external consumers can learn more about what it does.

The second attribute we see here is the `WebMethod` attribute. This attribute has several properties that let you further define the behavior of your Web Service. For example, you can provide additional SOAP Header information in this attribute in order to pass along special information with method calls, typically information that you do not want to include as part of the method parameters themselves. For example, when you call the `QuoteFinder` method in the Web Service in Listing 29-1, you pass along a key value that the code will use to find the quote. It makes sense to specify the key value as part of the method. On the other hand, what about credentials? It would not make as much sense to provide credentials or other glob-ally used information in this parameter. Passing this information as part of SOAP Header in the `WebMethod` attribute would make a lot more sense. It contains sev-eral properties for configuring the behavior of the XML Web service. Here, we change the `WebMethod` attribute so that the method provides a description of itself to a consumer:

```
<WebMethod(Description:= _
"Accesses Quotes database to retrive a quote")>
```

The only one of the four classes mentioned earlier we are not using in our sample is the `WebServiceBindingAttribute` class. We are not using it because we are using the default bindings in our Web Service. A binding is defined in Web Services Description Language (WSDL), and it defines the operations of the Web Service. Our method, `GetQuote`, is a single method located in a specific binding. In some cases it might be useful to further define a binding, thus adding attributes to it. For exam-ple, you may want to create a custom Web service proxy class that gives clients applications options for when and how they access the service, rather than just using the default options (which is good for most uses).

To summarize up to this point, we have looked at the four basic classes you will need to use in order to get a .NET Web Service up and running. The two principal classes are the `WebService` and `WebMethod` classes. Using them gives you direct access to the SOAP capabilities of the .NET Framework and its ability to team up with IIS to make your application accessible over the Web.

Visual Studio .NET and Language Support

As mentioned previously, the .NET runtime is not tied to any specific development language such as VB.NET or C#. The CLR derives its name from the fact that it is a runtime that understands a single, common language: MSIL. That said, there are many languages you can use to create your Web Services in .NET. You can use the ones Microsoft supports (VB.NET, C#, J#, C++, JScript.NET), or you can use one of your own creation along with ones developed by third parties. The most likely case is that you will use a Microsoft-supported language. However, you can write the application entirely in a simple text editor if you wish. From there, you take your source files and pass them to a language compiler. For example, the language compiler for VB.NET files is vbc.exe. Thus, you point the compiler to your project and the compiler will in turn create an actual executable for you.

For the most part, you will use Visual Studio.NET to create your projects and add the necessary files for you. When debugging and developing you will use Visual Studio.NET to compile the application. However, there are still times to use the command-line compilers, as when you create scripts for an automated build process. In this case, the final executable is created without the help of the IDE. This process is described in greater detail in Chapter 30.

Let's create our QuoteService Web Service in Visual Studio.NET by opening the IDE and either using the Start Page or the File | New Project menu to begin our new project. When you do, you will see a dialog box as shown in Figure 29-3. You can choose the language that interests you, normally C# or Visual Basic.NET. You also designate where the Web Service will be created.

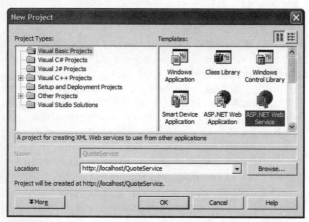

Figure 29-3: Choosing the project type in Visual Studio.NET

After specifying the basic information for your Web Service, Visual Studio.NET will create the Website and set up the necessary project files for you (see Figure 29-4).

Figure 29-4: The basic
project files of a Web Service

By default, Visual Studio.NET creates a service file for you called Service1.asmx,
and this contains a default Web Service class called Service1. You can just delete
the file and add your own with a Web Service name and file name that makes more
sense to your application. Or you can simply rename the default file and class
name. At this point, you are ready to add code to the Web Service class definition.
You can add methods using the Web Method attribute as already explained. What
you put in the Web Service method is completely up to you, and there is nearly no
limit to what a Web Service can do. You can access databases, make calls to other
Web Services, open XML files, transform XML, instantiate custom component
libraries, and work with security infrastructures. The choice is up to you.

XML Support for Web Services

Because this book is about XML, you may be wondering just what all this talk about
creating Web Services in .NET has to do with XML classes. Well, to begin with, client
applications that call Web Services package their requests in XML, and the Web
Service packages its responses in XML. All of this is explained in greater detail in
Chapters 23 through 26. These chapters contain descriptions of SOAP, WSDL, UDDI,
and how XML is used in each of these protocols to make Web Services possible.

Fortunately, all of the work that goes on to use XML with these protocols is done for
you by the .NET Framework itself. In other words, you are not responsible for
assembling SOAP messages in XML, because that is what the .NET Framework
classes are supposed to do. On the other hand, what about using XML in your Web
Service itself? That is entirely possible, and is in fact quite easy to do.

To illustrate this, we will take our QuoteService Web Service and use the
System.XML.XmlDocument class in the .NET Framework to load a list of the
quotes in an XML file. Then we will locate a quote that corresponds to a key value
that is passed to the Web Service method. Finally, the Web Service will return the
quote that is found by the Web Service.

Listing 29-2 shows the code that is used to locate a quote by the quote's key value. Here, we are using the System.XML Namespace of the .NET Framework. This Namespace contains the classes that deal with parsing, transforming, navigating, reading, and writing XML content within the Framework. The XML Framework in .NET provides a comprehensive and integrated set of classes, so that you can work with XML documents and data.

The XML classes in the .NET Framework can be categorized in the following way:

✦ Parsing, editing, and writing XML using the XmlReader, XmlWriter, and the XmlDocument classes

✦ Querying using the XPath classes

✦ Transforming using the XslTransform classes

✦ Editing schema definitions using the XslSchema classes

The XmlDocument class implements the W3C Document Object Model (DOM) Level 1 Core and the DOM Level 2 Core. So, it is used for loading, parsing, navigating, and saving XML content. This is the class we use in our Web Service to load the XML data and find the target quote.

Listing 29-2: **Locating a Quote in an XML Document Using an XPath Expression**

```
<WebMethod()> Public Function QuoteFinder( _
    ByVal Key As String) As String
  Dim oDoc As New Xml.XmlDocument
  oDoc.Load("http://localhost/QuoteService/Quote.xml")
  Dim oNode As Xml.XmlNode
  oNode = oDoc.SelectSingleNode( _
      "dataroot/QuoteTable[QuoteKey='" & Key & "']")
  oNode = oNode.ChildNodes(2)
  Return (oNode.InnerText)
End Function
```

In this function, a simple XPath expression is used to locate the node that contains the desired quote. This is done by using the SelectSingleNode method from the instance of the XmlDocument object. This method accepts a query string in the form of an XPath expression and returns the first node, if any, that matches the query definition. The "dataroot/QuoteTable" portion at the beginning of the XPath expression tells the query processor to find any node called "QuoteTable" beneath the root node of the XML hierarchy. It further tells the query processor to look for a "QuoteTable" node that has a sub node calls "QuoteKey" whose text value is equal to the contents of a variable. A sample of the XML is shown in Figure 29-5.

```
<?xml version="1.0" encoding="UTF-8" ?>
- <dataroot xmlns:od="urn:schemas-microsoft-com:officedata"
    xmlns:xsi="http://www.w3.org/2001/XMLSchema-instance"
    xsi:noNamespaceSchemaLocation="Quote.xsd">
  - <QuoteTable>
      <Date>03/30/1998</Date>
      <Source>Tammy Vanoss</Source>
      <Quote>Each day I try to enjoy something from each of the four food groups: the bonbon
        group, the salty-snack grou</Quote>
      <QuoteKey>HNEY-4TTL6G</QuoteKey>
    </QuoteTable>
```

Figure 29-5: XML content in the Quotes.XML file

Calling the Web Service returns a value in well-formed XML document. That is shown in Listing 29-3.

Listing 29-3: XML Output from a Call to the QuoteService Web Service

```
<?xml version="1.0" encoding="utf-8" ?>
 <string xmlns="http://tempuri.org/QuoteService/Service1">
 Very funny Scotty, now beam down my clothes.
 </string>
```

If you are wondering how to build a client application to call this Web Service, that is dealt with specifically in Chapter 31. Here we are using Internet Explorer to make direct calls to the Web Service. What this example does show is how you can leverage XML within your Web Service. There are so many other ways that the XML classes of the .NET Framework can be used, and the other chapters in this book should give you plenty of ideas on what you can do.

Summary

In this chapter, we have taken a look at building Web Services using the .NET Framework and Visual Studio.NET. The .NET Framework classes, like `WebService`, make it extraordinarily easy to get hooks into the world of sending and receiving SOAP messages. Designing your Web Service using Visual Studio.NET is a particularly wise choice in that the IDE takes care of setting up all of the pieces you need for a Web Service. However, it does not do so at the expense of flexibility and power. If you are not pleased with the basic set up of a Web Service, you can use the classes in the Framework to customize your Web Service as you need.

✦   ✦   ✦

Accessing .NET Web Services

CHAPTER

30

✦   ✦   ✦   ✦

In This Chapter

Authentication and authorization

IIS integration with .NET Web Services

Windows security

Working with Web Service assemblies

Moving from legacy code to .NET Web Services

✦   ✦   ✦   ✦

Creating Web Services is deceptively easy. Furthermore, the Microsoft Visual Studio .NET tools make creating a Web Service surprisingly simple. The MS SOAP Toolkit, even though it is based on COM technologies, also simplifies Web Service creation quite a bit. However, there are more things to think about before rolling out your first production Web Services.

In this chapter, we take a step back and look at some of the issues that encompass more than the simple client-server relationship itself. We will look at security with .NET Web Services. We will also explore how to deploy these services and make them highly available. We will look at some of the things you should think about as you consider upgrading an existing application to use .NET Web Services.

Web Services Security

In one sense, Web Services are really just another Web application. A Web Service class instance runs on a Web server that receives the request, detects that it is for a Web Service, and passes it along to the right processing engine. However, one should attempt to control what code can run on the server, and one should also be able to constrain which users can gain access and what they can do.

The .NET Framework works closely with IIS to restrict access to what is available on the Web server. Microsoft ASP.NET architecture and IIS do the following:

   ✦ Authenticate code to verify whether it should be granted access to server resources

   ✦ Authenticate user credentials

✦ Grant users access to resources

✦ Serve up resources as allowed by granted permissions

Given the tight integration between .NET and IIS, it is important to understand a little bit more about how they work together to provide a secure runtime environment. ASP.NET is an ISAPI extension loaded by IIS, and it ultimately receives SOAP messages that are passed along from the SOAP client to the Web server. Before a Web Service can entertain any messages, the request must first pass through the security in IIS. All IIS modes can be used here. They include:

✦ Basic

✦ Certificates

✦ Digest

✦ NTLM

✦ Kerberos

✦ Anonymous

Microsoft's product documentation is filled with information about these authentication mechanisms. Additionally, you can configure a site to use Microsoft Passport for authentication, client certificates, or a simple form-based mechanism.

IIS controls the request to the Web server resources by looking at the credentials being offered up by the client and comparing them to some privileged source. That source can be a custom database, the Windows Active Directory, or some other custom store. If the credentials can be verified, then the request is passed along to the Website and the appropriate ISAPI application, in this case ASP.NET. That is when the Web Service actually kicks in, and the runtime can use the identity of the code and the user to verify whether the desired permissions can be granted.

One of the most important files you can use as part of your .NET Web Service configuration is the Web.Config file. This file is located at the root of the Web Service application, but one can also include other Web.Config files in subsequent directories that are located in the Web Service application site. Each Web.Config file controls settings for the directory in which it is found and for any directories contained therein, unless there is a Web.Config file in a child directory. In the Web.Config file, you can specify authentication and authorization information. First, let's look at the authentication information in Listing 30-1. These settings would prevent any user who is not authenticated as having a valid Windows account from accessing the site.

Listing 30-1: Integrating the Windows Security Infrastructure into the Authentication of a Web Service

```
<authentication mode="Windows">
</authentication>
```

Using Integrated Windows authentication is a compelling choice, among the possible ones already listed. The reason why is because a user need not supply special credentials to access the Web Service. If the user has logged onto the Windows-based workstation, things are simple enough. No further authentication will be requested when IIS fields the request. Again, other authentication mechanisms like forms-based authentication could be used with Web applications, but these require a user to provide extra credentials, something that is not really possible with a Web Service.

Once a user is authenticated, code can load and methods can be requested. Sometimes, it is necessary for a user's identity to be preserved within the code that will run in the Web Service. For example, if the user is calling the Web Service to access a database, it might be a very good idea to have the Web Service method use the user's identity when making the database call. In this kind of scenario, unless we make a couple of special modifications, the database call would be made using the identity of the account that the Web Service is running under, in this case the identity that IIS uses `IUSR_[MACHINENAME]`.

To make the Web Service use the user's identity, we need to change the Web.Config file for the Web Service so that it knows to impersonate the user when doing its processing. Table 30-1 shows different Web.Config settings and what they mean to the final identity used by the Web Service.

**Table 30-1
Web.Config Settings**

Web.Config Setting	Context	Effective Identity
`<identity impersonate="true"/>` `<authentication mode="Windows" />`	WindowsIdentity Thread	Domain\UserName Domain\UserName
`<identity impersonate="false"/>` `<authentication mode="Windows" />`	WindowsIdentity Thread	MACHINE\ASPNET Domain\UserName

In this table you can see that there are two different contexts listed. They are `WindowsIdentity` and `Thread` (or `Thread Identity`). These are two of the different contexts that apply within your code. If you decided to look at the user identity in your code by using the `WindowsIdentity` class, and the settings were configured as described here, then you would find the effective identity value shown in the table. If you chose to access the identity under which a thread is running, you would find that its effective identity would be as shown. You can use Windows security then to restrict what users can do and what files they can access.

While using Integrated Windows authentication is a great way to simplify the administration on your site, it is sometimes useful to configure some authorization using the Web.Config file itself. The settings in Listing 30-2 would allow only users who are in the Administrator role to access the files on the site at this level. All other users would be denied.

Listing 30-2: **Specifying Authorization in a Website Using a Web.Config file in a Web Service Site**

```
<authorization>
  <allow roles="Administrator" />
  <deny users="*" />
</authorization>
```

In a Web.Config file, authorization is controlled in an `<authorization>` tag, with accompanying `<allow>` and `<deny>` elements. For example, the following authorization configuration in Listing 30-3 allows some user, Bob, as well as Administrators to access the Web application, but denies everyone else.

Listing 30-3: **Customizing Authorization Information for a .NET Web Service**

```
<authorization>
  <allow users="Bob" />
  <allow roles="Administrators" />
  <deny users="*" />
</authorization>
```

The asterisk (*) wildcard in use here is used to denote all users. Optionally, a question mark (?) could be used to denote all non-authenticated users.

Deploying .NET Web Services

Once you have developed your Web Service, you need to deploy it. There are a few different ways to deploy your Web Services, and which one you elect to use will depend on what your Web Service does and what kind of environment will host it. First, let's deal with the simplest deployment mechanism: Copy/Paste. Yes, that's right. Finally, because of the advent of the .NET Framework, one is no longer required to mess around with the Windows registry when deploying completed components. When you compile a release version of your Web Service, you will find that there is a resulting DLL in the application's bin directory. This DLL is what contains the MSIL for your Web Service along with other metadata. This DLL is essential in deployment, and so is the .asmx file that Web Service clients will address when making SOAP requests. These two things, the DLL and .asmx files, are the two principal requirements for getting your .NET Web Service to run on a server. But you should include your Web.Config file and a few others as shown in Figure 30-1. These are the bare minimum files that you should copy to the production server.

Figure 30-1: Files and directory needed for a release version of a .NET Web Service

Just copying the files is not enough, however. You need to create an IIS Website or Virtual Directory whose main directory has the contents shown in Figure 30-1. Only then is the application accessible through IIS. Other than that, there is little else to do to make the application accessible over the Web. Obviously, you will want to configure security and make other modifications as needed.

If your .NET Web Service has dependencies that are not purely .NET, such as using COM components or special files such as XML files, you will want to copy them and deploy them according to their needs. COM DLLs will need to be registered (the Windows registry is the only way) just the way COM requires. You can do all of this manually, or you can create a setup project in Visual Studio.NET. The beginning of this process is shown in Figure 30-2 where a setup project is created for a custom Web Service.

You should consult MSDN documentation for the complete instructions in completing this process. After you create the setup project, you will have a Microsoft Installer file that you can launch to create the Website and install the project with any dependencies.

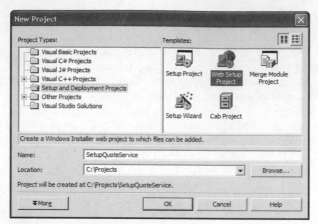

Figure 30-2: Creating a setup project for a .NET Web Service using Visual Studio.NET

The final technique that we'll mention for creating a production version of a Web Service is to use the NMAKE.exe utility to create project output. NMAKE is a 32-bit tool that builds projects based on commands contained in a description file. You can create special Makefiles to tell NMAKE how it is supposed to create your final project output. The contents of these files amount to scripts that let you customize the final project output so that file and directory locations are fully customizable. Using NMAKE is great for automated processes that require you to compile Web Services automatically and then deploy them on a production server without user intervention.

Upgrading Existing Applications

There is no doubt that Web Services are an exciting technology. Much of the computing industry is now turning its attention to how Web Services could influence how new technologies emerge and how legacy technologies can benefit from this promising technology. As you consider Web Services in your organization, you have to weigh your options.

First, know that the performance of Web Services is not necessarily going to be as good as that to which you may be accustomed in your existing application framework. If you are in a tightly coupled environment rather than a remote one, the difference will probably be more dramatic. If you are already in a distributed environment, the difference may not be as noticeable. Remember that Web Services are really just Web applications in a different form. You are using remote calls over HTTP to execute application functionality.

Second, recognize that security concerns are different for Web Services than for non-Web applications. In a tightly coupled scenario, security is also not the same as for a Web application such as those that host a Web Service. A Web Service is a remote application where the security on the client is not necessarily the same as on the server. Using Integrated Windows authentication and impersonation can make it easier to leverage a user's credentials on the server automatically.

Third, remember that Web Services are stateless. In a tightly coupled environment, a component creates an instance of another component and can access its state at any time. In a Web Service, a client application is really only using an instance of a proxy class that makes calls to the remote server for the client. State can actually be retained in a Web Service by passing a cookie in the response headers to the XML Web service client. This cookie would uniquely identify the session for the client and allow the client to identify the session for that XML Web service client. In this way, the client could later access the state of the state of the existing session. This is an advanced technique and requires a more deft use of the .NET Framework APIs.

Summary

In this chapter, we have taken a look at some of the broader issues you need to consider as you develop and deploy your Web Services. This is exciting technology, but there is more to the process than just adding methods to a Web Service class and then running the project. You need to consider security, deployment, and how client applications will approach the application. You also need to prevent your Web Service from being compromised or used in a way that you did not anticipate or approve.

✦   ✦   ✦

Building a .NET Web Services Client

In previous chapters dealing with Microsoft and Web
Services, we have focused almost entirely on building the
server-side pieces of the distributed application. We have also
explored the various protocols, like SOAP, WSDL, and UDDI,
that make remote Web Service invocation possible. Now,
we need to turn our attention to the client-side part of the
application.

Web Service client applications can take many different forms.
They can be Windows Forms applications, Web applications,
custom components in a class library, a control, a Windows
service, or even another Web Service. There is no way to adequately cover all of these techniques in one chapter. And, the
truth of the matter is that, in great measure, the access
method would be very similar in all cases. The main difference is that the Web Service is simply being called from a different container, but the way it is called is largely the same.

In this chapter, we will build a couple of client applications to
call a Web Service. Along the way we will explore some of the
techniques and application operations needed to get a client
application off the ground.

Introduction

The advent of Web Services has caused quite a stir in the
development community because of what it promises: the
possibility of allowing client applications to invoke remote
components in a standard way, independent of platform differences. No remote code is installed on the client application to

invoke such services. Thus, there must be a mechanism in the runtime environment that makes it possible to invoke calls to the remote service in a way that is similar to the way a typical client invokes local application functionality. Figure 31-1 shows the relationship between concepts endemic to any application and how these are provided by the runtime environment where the application is invoked.

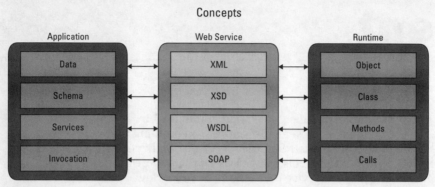

Figure 31-1: Application concepts and how they are provided in Web Services and the runtime environment

To explain it further, let's look at the general application concepts (the first column in Figure 31-1). When a client application uses external application functionality such as a locally installed component there are certain things that must occur or must be known. First, the client consumer must have a way to invoke methods in the server component. It must also know what methods and behaviors are offered by the server component. Also, the request to the server component's functionality must be packaged up in a standard way. Finally, the message sent to the server component must contain data that the server component can process so a response can be returned describing the result of the operation.

In Web Services (the second column in Figure 31-1), the same concepts exist, and they are expressed using specific protocols. The client application communicates with the remote service and invokes its operations using SOAP. This is the protocol that both parties use to send request and response messages. The client application knows about the methods and behaviors of the Web Service via the XML description of the Web Service in the WSDL file. The messages passed back and forth between the client and server applications are structured using XML according to a specific schema, and finally, the actual data in the messages is in a structured XML document.

In the runtime environment, it is best if the client application does not need to directly contain all of the code to use SOAP, WSDL, XSD, and XML. In other words, the developer would never get many client applications out the door if it were always necessary to write the routines to structure the messages in SOAP format and so forth. It would make more sense if the runtime environment provided class that abstracted these operations so that a developer can focus on the actual methods and how to use them, just they way one would with a locally installed component.

The .NET Framework provides those very types of classes so that the actual code in a client application to invoke remote methods does not reveal whether the calls are remote or local. In Chapter 29, a Web Service is created to acquire quotes from a Web Service. In this chapter, we will begin by creating a client application to call the existing method of that service as well as a new method. Then, we will tear apart the client-side code and application structure to see how it works.

Browser-Based Client

Thin-client applications are still growing in popularity, and their future is perhaps going to increase more rapidly as the proliferation of mobile devices continues. More and more mobile devices are flooding the market, and they are becoming more affordable. That being so, it is important to create applications that can serve both workstation users and those who may be using a variety of devices.

The Microsoft .NET Framework includes the ability to create Web applications using its ASP.NET architecture. We are going to create a browser-based application that will work both on a regular PC workstation as well as on a PocketPC. We will then see it work in both environments. The application is a simple Web page that displays an image. Each time the page refreshes, the same image appears, but its underlying link is to a different URL. The URL when accessed will return a new quote from our QuoteService Web Service created in Chapter 29. While the application is not terribly unusual, how it is developed is quite uncommon, and it will help you see how to use XML, Web Services, ASP.NET, and the mobile device extensions of the .NET Framework to build applications.

First, let's look at the main page of the Web application. To begin, we create a new application in Visual Studio.NET, but instead of choosing a typical ASP.NET application, we choose an ASP.NET Mobile Application as shown in Figure 31-2.

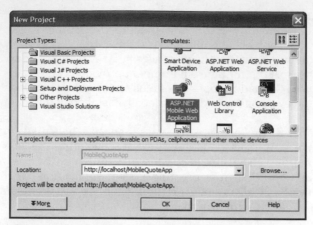

Figure 31-2: Creating an ASP.NET application for a mobile device

The Web Forms used by ASP.NET Mobile Applications are fundamentally a little different than those created for Web browsers used on a typical computer. The class used for this form is `System.Web.UI.MobileControls.Form`, a definite indication that something is different about this form. The blank form, shown in Figure 31-3, also looks a little different than we have come to expect in a blank Web page. You notice that this form is sized.

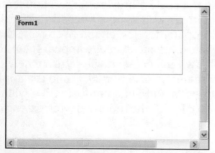

Figure 31-3: A generic ASP.NET form specifically designed to work with mobile devices

To make things more interesting, we are going to add a Server Control to the form, in this case the AdRotator control. This control accesses an XML that contains information that the control will display or that will control its behavior. To add the control, we go to the Mobile Web Forms tab of the IDE's toolbox and drag the AdRotator control to the form. The result is shown in Figure 31-4.

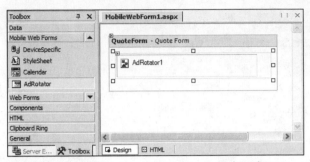

Figure 31-4: Adding the AdRotator control to the target form

Now, we need to modify the settings for the control a little so that it knows where to look for the XML file that will control its behavior. That is done in the HTML View of the form in the IDE. Listing 31-1 shows that we have added a setting called AdvertisementFile along with the reference to an XML file. This file is used by the control so that it knows what URL links to provide on the target Web page. It also will contain URLs to images that will be displayed on the Web page.

Listing 31-1: Adding the AdvertisementFile Setting to the AdRotator Control So It Can Access an XML File That Will Control Its Behavior

```
<body
Xmlns:mobile="http://schemas.microsoft.com/Mobile/WebForm">
    <mobile:Form id="QuoteForm" runat="server" title="Quote
Form">
        <mobile:AdRotator id="AdRotator1" runat="server"
        AdvertisementFile="Quotes.xml"></mobile:AdRotator>
        </mobile:Form>
</body>
```

The XML file is an important part of the way the AdRotator control works. Listing 31-2 shows the contents of that file. Each "Ad" element contains an element for the URL of an image that will be shown, what URL will be accessed, the alternate text that shows as the user hovers over the image, a category name, and impressions or a numeric value that indicates the likelihood of how often the ad is displayed.

Listing 31-2: The Contents of the Quotes.XML File Used by the AdRotator Control

```xml
<?xml version="1.0" encoding="utf-8" ?>
<Advertisements>
  <Ad>
        <ImageUrl>Quotes.gif</ImageUrl>
        <NavigateUrl>
        http://localhost/ASPQuoteApp/WebForm1.aspx?ID=HNEY-
4TTL7U
        </NavigateUrl>
        <AlternateText>Get Quote</AlternateText>
        <Keyword>Quote</Keyword>
        <Impressions>80</Impressions>
  </Ad>
  <Ad>
        <ImageUrl>Quotes.gif</ImageUrl>
        <NavigateUrl>
        http://localhost/ASPQuoteApp/WebForm1.aspx?ID=HNEY-
5BGJ8R
        </NavigateUrl>
        <AlternateText>Get Quote</AlternateText>
        <Keyword>Quote</Keyword>
        <Impressions>80</Impressions>
  </Ad>
  <Ad>
        <ImageUrl>Quotes.gif</ImageUrl>
        <NavigateUrl>
        http://localhost/ASPQuoteApp/WebForm1.aspx?ID=HNEY-
5BAG9H
        </NavigateUrl>
        <AlternateText>Get Quote</AlternateText>
        <Keyword>Quote</Keyword>
        <Impressions>80</Impressions>
  </Ad>
</Advertisements>
```

Now, this file can be stored directly on the server, or it can be dynamically retrieved. The AdvertisementFile property value is simply the path, either relative or absolute, to the XML file. In our sample, we are going to download the contents of the file as the page loads. The contents of the file will be retrieved from a Web Service, then loaded into an instance of the XmlDocument class in .NET. The Web Service, in our example, will be the QuoteService that we created in Chapter 29, but we are going to add a new method to the class, a GetQuotesXML method. This method will load the contents of a local XML file and return a string containing the XML contents of the file. While it is true that we could return the XML document itself, we return a string in order to demonstrate a couple extra methods and properties of the XmlDocument class.

In a more elaborate scenario, we would access a database to retrieve the quotes as XML. Then we could transform the XML use the XSL capabilities of the .NET Framework classes and create XML data that match the structure needed by the AdRotator control. However, in our case, we will simply return the contents of the pre-rendered XML, already in the condition that the AdRotator control can use. The code for the new Web Service method is shown in Listing 31-3.

Listing 31-3: Web Service Code for Returning the Contents of an XML File That Are Needed by the AdRotator Control in a Client Web Application

```
<WebMethod()> Public Function GetQuotesXML() As String
   Dim oDoc As New Xml.XmlDocument
   oDoc.Load(Server.MapPath("QuotesForAdRotator.xml"))
   Dim s As String = oDoc.InnerXml
   Return (s)
End Function
```

To acquire this file, our client Web application will call the method from an instance of the QuoteService Web Service locally. It will do so in its `Page_Load` event, and the code to do so is shown in Listing 31-4.

Listing 31-4: Client-Side Code to Call the Web Service and Retrieve the File

```
If Page.IsPostBack Then
   Dim oDoc As New System.Xml.XmlDocument
   Dim s As String
   Dim oSVC As New FileGetter.QuoteService
   s = oSVC.GetQuotesXML() '
   oDoc.LoadXml(s)
   oDoc.Save(Server.MapPath("Quotes.XML"))
End If
```

Before this code can work, we need to create a Web reference to the QuoteService Web Service in the client application. This is done by right-clicking on the Web References folder in the Solution Explorer window (as shown in Figure 31-5). This brings up a dialog box where you can tell the IDE where to look for the WSDL for the target Web Service.

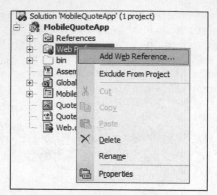

Figure 31-5: Adding a Web reference
in the Visual Studio.NET IDE

The dialog box shown in Figure 31-6 displays an address bar where you type the
URL to the WSDL file as well as the name of the service as you will use it in your
client application. As you can see in Listing 31-4, we use the name FileGetter for the
name of this local class.

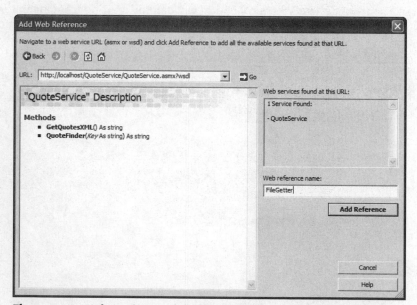

Figure 31-6: Referencing a valid WSDL file when setting up a reference
to a Web Service

After you add the reference to the Web Service, Visual Studio.NET will add some files to your project. Figure 31-7 shows the highlighted area of these added files in the Solution Explorer window.

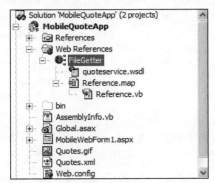

Figure 31-7: Newly added files for a reference to a Web Service

You can see that the WSDL file that we referenced in the dialog box was copied and saved locally. Also, a new class was added, contained in the Reference.vb file. This file contains a proxy class with the name that was specified in the Web Reference dialog box, in this case "FileGetter." This class is the one that is actually instantiated in the Page_Load event code shown in Listing 31-4. This local class instance will then handle sending SOAP requests to the Web Service as well as receiving responses.

At this point, the client application is ready to use the Web Service. However, there is one more thing to do. Take another look at Listing 31-2, and carefully note the NavigateUrl elements in the XML file. They refer to a Web page we have not created yet. In fact, the Web page referenced in the XML file is actually an ASP.NET page that will make a call to the same QuoteService Web Service. However, it will call a different method, the method created as part of an earlier chapter. The Web page calls the QuoteFinder method which accepts a key, then searches an XML file to return a specific quote based on that key. The entire code for the target Web page is shown in Listing 31-5.

Listing 31-5: **Code in a Page Load Event for a Web Page That Calls a Web Service Using a Key Value That Is Received as a QueryString Parameter**

```
Dim oSVC As New QuoteService.QuoteService
Dim s As String
s = oSVC.QuoteFinder(Request.QueryString("ID").ToString)
Response.Write("<SPAN>" & s & "</SPAN>")
```

The Web page passes the necessary key value to the Web Service. However, it acquires this key value from a QueryString object that is passed to the ASP.NET Web page. The page calls the service, receives a response, and then posts that response in a simple <SPAN> tag.

Now that all of the pieces are in place, let's confirm that it all works. Again, we could have created much simpler code to acquire the same functional result in our final application. But the goal of these code samples here is to demonstrate the capabilities of the underlying classes in a real software design. That said, the final Web page is shown in Figure 31-8.

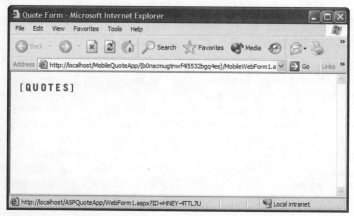

Figure 31-8: The final Web page shown using the AdRotator control

This Web page is displayed in Internet Explorer on a typical PC. The source HTML, if perused, would reveal that there is nothing unusual about this display. You can see that the URL for the link is shown in the bottom of the Web browser's window. This is the URL loaded by the AdRotator control as it found it in the local XML file that was downloaded from the Web Service.

Now we want to see this same page on a mobile device, in this case a PocketPC. Figure 31-9 shows the same page in Internet Explorer on a PocketPC.

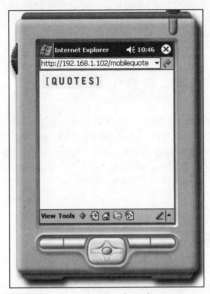

Figure 31-9: The final Web page shown in the Web browser of a PocketPC

The page functions the same way, and when the image is clicked, the URL for the quote is accessed from an ASP.NET Web page and returned in the browser, as shown in Figure 31-10.

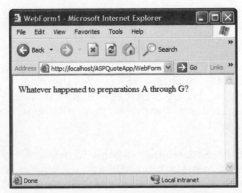

Figure 31-10: The results after clicking on the image provided by the AdRotator control

In this sample, we have seen how to fully integrate Web Services to do different tasks. We have created two clients for the Web Service methods. One is an ASP.NET Web page that targets mobile controls, and the other is an ASP.NET Web page that displays results after calling a Web Service. While the final output is not terribly dazzling, a lot of the features of .NET are demonstrated here, including using the Mobile Forms in ASP.NET.

Windows-Based Client (PocketPC)

To truly show the variety of Web Service clients you can create, there is perhaps no better way than to create a Windows Forms client that runs on the PocketPC. The difference between this sample and the previous one is that this sample runs, not in the Web browser, but in an actual executable on the device itself. To begin, we need to create a new type of application. This time, in Visual Studio.NET, we will create a Smart Device Application, as shown in Figure 31-11.

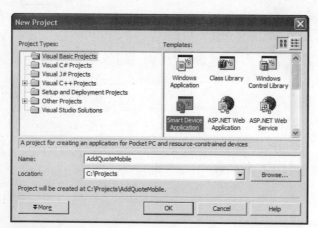

Figure 31-11: Creating a Smart Device Application in Visual Studio.NET

When you create this kind of application, Visual Studio.NET targets the .NET Compact Framework, a subset of the overall Framework that works on mobile devices. After specifying the location and name of the project, you will be presented with a dialog like the one shown in Figure 31-12.

This dialog box lets you tell Visual Studio whether you are going to use an actual PocketPC or the emulator that comes with Visual Studio.NET. In our example, we will target the emulator, even though an actual hardware device is also installed.

After specifying this information, the development environment will set up and create the project files for you.

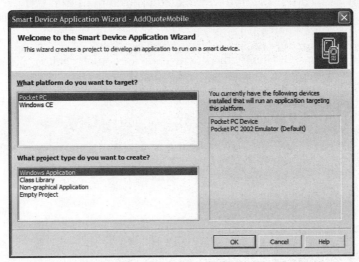

Figure 31-12: Specifying the target device for the application

At this point, you create an application in much the same way as you would any normal Windows Forms application. You add controls to the form, reference external libraries and so forth. Our form is for adding new quotes, and it looks like the one shown in Figure 31-13. This form has textboxes that will receive the user's input.

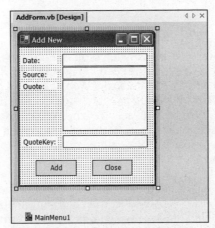

Figure 31-13: PocketPC form for adding new quotes to the database

Behind the scenes, this form is going to collect the user's input and make a call to a .NET Web Service that receives the input and returns a Boolean result. The method we call is a new one added to the QuoteService Web Service created earlier. It accepts four parameters, all represented by the textboxes on our form. To reference the Web Service in a mobile application, you follow the exact same steps as shown previously for referencing a Web Service. The process is identical. Fortunately, the .NET Compact Framework has built-in support that makes a PocketPC application a potential SOAP client. The code for actually calling the Web Service in our PocketPC application is shown in Listing 31-6.

Listing 31-6: Calling a Web Service from a Windows Forms Application on a PocketPC

```
Dim oSVC As New AddQuoteService.QuoteService
Dim bln As Boolean = _
oSVC.AddQuote(txtDate.Text, _
txtSource.Text, txtQuote.Text, _
txtQuoteKey.Text)
If bln = True Then
  MessageBox.Show("Quote added", "Result", _
  MessageBoxButtons.OK, MessageBoxIcon.None, _
  MessageBoxDefaultButton.Button1)
Else
  MessageBox.Show("Error in adding quote", "Result", _
  MessageBoxButtons.OK, MessageBoxIcon.Exclamation, _
  MessageBoxDefaultButton.Button1)
End If
Me.Close()
Me.Dispose()
```

Running the application produces an executable that is installed on the mobile device. That application, when launched, shows a form as seen in Figure 31-14. The form is ready to accept user input and then submit the data to a Web service. As should seem clear by now, the Web service is remote and accepts the data via SOAP calls over HTTP. Once the data are submitted to the Web service, the Web service code processes the message and completes its operations, in this case adding a quote to a database. Then, it sends a response back to the calling application so that the result of the operations can be known.

Submitting the data on the form shows a result as seen in Figure 31-15. When the calling application receives a response from the Web service, the client application can take whatever actions seem useful. Here, a simple message box is posted that tells the user that the quote was added to the database.

Figure 31-14: The Windows Forms application running on a PocketPC

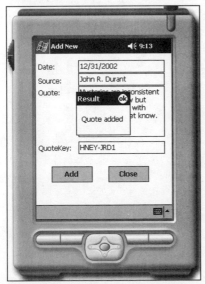

Figure 31-15: Results of submitting data to a Web Service using a PocketPC client

Summary

In this chapter, we have seen that we can create a variety of Web Service clients for different devices using the .NET Framework. We saw that we can create a browser-based client where the Web pages call code on the server to access a Web Service. We also saw that this type of Web application can be designed to work on a mobile device. Along the way, we explored using a control that is designed to work on a mobile device in the Web browser.

Taking a more advanced step, we approached Web Service clients in a rather unique fashion. We built a client application that runs as a Windows Forms executable. However, we again targeted a mobile device for the application. Using the .NET Compact Framework and the built-in classes that let us target smart devices, we built a Web Services client that runs on a PocketPC and submits new quotes to a Web Service. Much simpler clients could be developed, but many of the techniques would remain the same.

✦   ✦   ✦

Web Services and J2EE

Part VII illustrates techniques and tools for building Web services using J2EE. Examples are illustrated using open-source Web service Tools for J2EE from IBM, Apache, Sun, and others. We specifically illustrate Web service development with the Sun Java Web services Developer Pack, which includes all of the tools in the Sun Java XML Pack, plus a Java Server Pages Standard Tag Library (JSTL), the Java WSDP Registry Server, a Web Application Deployment Tool, the Ant Build Tool and the Apache Tomcat container. We also provide examples of working with the Apache SOAP toolkit, and the IBM Web services Toolkit. We finish this part of the book with examples for deploying J2EE Web services and techniques for accessing J2EE Web services.

Web Service Tools for J2EE: IBM, Apache, Sun, and Others

In Chapter 28, we covered the architecture of a J2EE Web service. In this chapter, we'll show you some of the tools that can help you build that architecture. When we introduced XML tools for J2EE developers in Chapter 14, we mentioned that core J2EE classes, methods, and properties have absolutely nothing to do with XML or Web services. Fortunately for J2EE developers, J2EE classes do contain robust and flexible support for text, and Web services are based on XML, and XML is text. Web services can be very complicated XML and XML can be very complicated text, but the base object is still text.

Fortunately for today's developers, Java development environments have evolved into rock-solid code tools that generate J2EE code, compile it, and let you test it on the J2EE application server of your choice. Tools for developing Web services have evolved as well. Today there are several excellent J2EE code libraries available for free that support Web service functions such as building SOAP envelopes and generating J2EE client proxy classes from WSDL files. You can also generate WSDL from Java classes, as we'll show you in Chapter 35. Most libraries even ship with the source code if you need to customize them for a particular application. In this chapter we'll review developer tool offerings from IBM, Eclipse, Sun, and Apache. There are literally hundreds of other offerings that come and go over the years, but these providers offer consistency and reliability in their offerings, which are pretty good things if you want to base your applications on them.

Tools for Building J2EE Web Services

As we mentioned when we introduced a basic J2EE Web service architecture in Chapter 28, most J2EE Web service software providers use the latest version of the Apache software foundation's AXIS as the core of their offerings. AXIS stands for "Apache eXtensible Interaction System," and is a reference implementation of the latest W3C recommendations for SOAP and WSDL. AXIS code can be implemented on the client side as proxy classes and on the client side as routers and implementation classes. We'll get into the architecture in more details later in this chapter. For now it's just important to know that AXIS code is used in most J2EE implementations where SOAP and WSDL functionality is needed.

Apache Offerings

The Apache Software Foundation is a non-profit consortium that provides organizational, legal, and financial support for Apache open-source software projects, all of which can be seen at `http://www.apache.org/`. These are the same people who bring you reference implementations of W3C Recommendations. Other prominent projects include Xerces for DOM parsing, and Xalan for XSLT processing. Apache project participants provide feedback to the W3C Web Service working groups regarding implementation issues, based on real-life implementation attempts. For a full list of Apache Web Service and XML projects, go to `http://xml.apache.org/`.

Apache Software Foundation code is weaved in to most commercial and non-commercial J2EE development tools for handling XML and Web services. For example, IBM and Sun both have features built in to their development tools that generate a WSDL file from a Java class, and vice versa. These tools are based on AXIS code that has been integrated into IBM and Sun's products.

AXIS: The Apache implementation of the W3C SOAP Recommendation

IBM donated the SOAP4J code library to the Apache XML project, where it became the Apache SOAP project, with a full implementation of the W3C SOAP 1.1 Recommendation. The latest implementation of the Apache SOAP project has been renamed AXIS, just to keep us on our toes. Axis stands for "Apache eXtensible Interaction System" but is still based the W3C SOAP Recommendation, with the equally inscrutable acronym of "Simple Object Access Protocol." AXIS supports all of the W3C SOAP 1.1 Recommendation, and most of the SOAP 1.2 Working Draft. It also contains tools for building and reading WSDL files from J2EE classes, and vice versa.

The latest version of AXIS source code and binaries, including complete documentation, can also be downloaded from the AXIS project site, at `http://ws.apache.org/axis`. AXIS includes an implementation of a single-thread Web service RPC router and server environment, which can be run from a command line without a J2EE server. The Simple Axis Server is a great tool for testing Web service code that uses AXIS as for SOAP and WDSL processing. The AXIS project has plans to implement a standardized SOAP server environment based on AXIS code, but for now this single-thread implementation is a useful developer testing environment.

Cross-Reference   SOAP is covered in more detail in Chapters 23 and 24. Apache AXIS code examples can be found in Chapter 34.

Xindice: A native XML database

Apache Xindice (pronounced zeen-dee-chay) is a database implemented in XML to store XML data. The idea is that XML data that is already in XML format doesn't need to be converted to another format. But it probably does need to be transformed to another XML structure, or parsed into a destination format. Because Web services transport data in SOAP envelopes, which are XML, the Xindice server could theoretically server as a Web service data store for SOAP. The Xindice query language is XPath. The XML:DB (`http://www.xmldb.org/xapi/`) API is used for record updates and for Java development. This enables other applications and languages to access Xindice via XML-RPC. Sun's JAXR Registry server for UDDI uses Xindice a repository for UDDI registries and Tmodels.

Web Services Invocation Framework (WSIF)

The Web Services Invocation Framework (WSIF) is a Java API for invoking Web services without directly accessing a SOAP API, such as AXIS. WSIF provides the same kind of functionality that JAXP does for Web parsing. A WSIF interface can be used on any WDSL-compatible Web service, regardless of the SOAP or WSDL version or implementation that the service was originally created under. For example, moving from Apache SOAP classes to Apache AXIS classes does not require any changes to application code if the WSIF interface is employed. The WSIF implementation code can be found at `http://ws.apache.org/wsif`. WSIF implementation code is also integrated into some application development tools, such as IBM's WebSphere application developer and Web Services Toolkit.

Web Services Inspection Language (WSIL)

The Web Services Inspection Language is a standardized way to find out about published WSDL without a USDDI server implementation. WSIL also provides rules for how inspection-related information can be revealed by a site. WS-Inspection documents point to WSDL and other forms of Web service descriptors. WSIL4J is the J2EE reference implementation of the WSIL. It can be used to locate and process WS-Inspection documents. The reference code downloads and additional information can be found at `http://ws.apache.org/wsif`.

XML Security

Apache has implemented Java reference implementations of the XML-Signature Syntax and Processing Recommendation, and the XML Encryption Syntax and Processing. By the time this book is in print, they probably will have finished the XML Key Management recommendation implementation in Java as well. The Java and C++ code downloads for XML security implementations can be found at `http://xml.apache.org/security/download.html`.

Note   If you're using JDK 1.4 or higher, check the FAQ associated with the download files for instructions on setting up a compatible version of Xalan.

Jakarta Tomcat

Tomcat is the official J2EE Reference Implementation for Java Servlet and Java Server Page technology. The Tomcat J2EE application server also supports SOAP and WSDL implementations via AXIS classes. This includes an RPC Router, which is based on the AXIS `rpcrouter` class. Tomcat can be run on a server or on a development workstation as a test server. Tomcat is integrated into Sun ONE developer studio, and is automatically invoked for servlet or JSP testing and debugging. You can download Tomcat from `http://jakarta.apache.org/tomcat/index.html`.

IBM Offerings

IBM sells one of the most prominent J2EE development tools, WebSphere Studio Application Developer. IBM also provides a lot of J2EE software for free download from the AlphaWorks Website. In addition to this, Free XML tutorials, articles and sample code are available from the IBM DeveloperWorks XML Zone.

WebSphere Studio Application Developer and Workbench

IBM's J2EE developer environment is based on the Eclipse platform, and is called WebSphere Studio. WebSphere Studio is actually the name that is used to describe several "product configurations" of the base tool. The last time that I checked the WebSphere Studio Website, there were nine configurations listed, all with similar-sounding and confusing names, but all starting with the WebSphere Studio prefix. However, there are really only two configuration options that Web Service developers need to focus on: WebSphere Studio Application Developer or WebSphere Studio Workbench.

The first choice is *WebSphere Studio Application Developer (WSAD),* which a rich J2EE developer UI combined with tools and wizards to simplify Web Service development tasks. Aside from J2EE, WSAD also supports JavaScript, Dynamic HTML, and Cascading Style Sheets. It also provides visual layout tools to create dynamic Websites with Java servlet or Java Server Pages (JSPs). WSAD also includes a built-in Web services development environment with support for AXIS, including SOAP envelope design and WSDL and WSDD document construction, among other features. WSAD also supports Rational ClearCase LT for software configuration management. IBM has also published a very good series of free online tutorials that cover building Web service applications using WebSphere Studio application developer, which can be found at `http://www7b.software.ibm.com/wsdd/techjournal/0111_lau/lau.html.` IBM offers a 60-day trial version of WSAD, which can be downloaded at the IBM DeveloperWorks WebSphere Studio Zone at `http://www7b.software.ibm.com/wsdd/zones/studio/.`

If WebSphere Studio Application Developer is simply too expensive and/or you take pride in coding your J2EE applications by hand, the second choice is *WebSphere Studio Workbench.* IBM has added several plug-ins to the base Eclipse Workbench platform and re-branded it as WebSphere Studio Workbench, which they offer as a free download at `http://www-3.ibm.com/software/ad/workbench.` (A free registration is required to download the software.) WebSphere Studio Workbench provides an efficient, if basic, developer UI for J2EE applications. The plug-in architecture of Eclipse-based products makes the platform easy to upgrade with customized tools and interfaces. Based on this architecture, it's possible to assemble a reasonable facsimile of WebSphere Studio Application Developer by downloading code libraries from Apache and SUN and free plug-ins from the Eclipse site. This approach, however, will take time and patience, and will never be as seamless as the WebSphere Studio Application Developer. But if you're a build-it-yourself developer on a tight budget, WebSphere Studio Workbench may be the way for you to go.

IBM AlphaWorks

IBM AlphaWorks (`http://alphaworks.ibm.com`) is a very important resource for anyone who has to code XML or Web service applications in J2EE. For those unfamiliar with the site, it contains a wealth of free tools and utilities that can be downloaded and integrated into a Web services developer's arsenal. The AlphaWorks site also helps to dispel the notion of free tools as something in which you get what you pay for, or more specifically, don't get what you don't pay for. My experience to date with the AlphaWorks tools is that they work well in most cases, and the only thing missing from comparative paid products are documentation, which is often compensated for with working examples. I've listed some of my favorites below, but there are many more, organized into XML and Web service subsections.

XML Security Suite

XML Security Suite adds W3C-defined security features such as digital signature, encryption, and access control to Web service and XML applications. Security has always been a challenge for Web service developers, because Web services are transporting text over standard protocols that don't support advanced security features by themselves. The XML Security Suite includes support for the W3C *XML-Signature Syntax and Processing* and *XML Encryption Syntax and Processing* Recommendations. There is also support for XML Access Control functionality, partly supported by the W3C *Canonical XML Version 1.0* Working Draft. The free XML Security Suite download includes a .jar file containing supporting classes and a number of examples of the XML Security Suite code in use. A good introductory article can be found at the IBM DevleoperWorks XML Zone at `http://www-106.ibm.com/developerworks/security/library/x-xmlsecuritysuite/?dwzone=security`.

The Emerging Technologies Toolkit (ETTK)

The ETTK is a grab-bag of new technologies rolled into J2EE code for developing and executing autonomic and grid-related technologies. The ETTK also includes Web service support for these technologies via an Apache AIXIS SOAP engine, and the Globus Toolkit grid infrastructure. The ETTK is the latest evolution of the very popular IBM Web Services Toolkit (WSTK). Most of the more stable code has been siphoned off as core components of IBM's WebSphere application developer (WSAD). The rest ended up in the ETTK along with additional related implementation code from IBM development and research lab projects. The ETTK supports Windows and Linux. More information is available at `http://www.alphaworks.ibm.com/tech/ettk`.

Eclipse Tools

The eclipse.org Website (`http://www.eclipse.org`) is the center of the Eclipse consortium. Eclipse is an open source, freely distributable platform for tool integration. In essence, it provides a "lowest common denominator" for developers to integrate functionality into a development UI. IBM provided most of the code for the startup, and since then other large players have joined in at the board level, including Borland, MERANT, QNX Software Systems, Rational Software, Red Hat, SuSE, and TogetherSoft. Several other very large players have also joined as non-board members, including Sybase, Fujitsu, Hitachi, Oracle, SAP, and the Object Management Group (OMG).

Eclipse projects are broken down into three groups:

✦ **The Eclipse Project** is the original open-source software development project that is developing open-source developer UI platform.

✦ **The Eclipse Tools Project** was developed to provide services and support to tools developers who want to integrate their tools into the Eclipse platform.

✦ **The Eclipse Technology Project** provides support for Eclipse project research, incubators, and education. Research projects explore programming languages, tools, and development environments applicable to the Eclipse project. Incubators implement new capabilities on the Eclipse platform and may or may not be based on research. Education projects develop educational materials, teaching aids, and courseware.

Sun Offerings

Sun owns the Sun ONE Studio and Sun ONE J2EE application server, which is the biggest competitor to IBM's WebSphere Studio Application Developer and WebSphere J2EE Application Server. Like IBM, Sun also provides a huge amount of J2EE and Web service resources for free download from Sun's Java site. In addition, Free XML tutorials, articles, and sample code are available from the Sun Developer Services Website.

Sun ONE Studio

Sun's open-source, free distribution offering is based on the former Forte Tools for Java. As with the IBM WebSphere Studio offerings, the plug-in architecture of Sun ONE-based products makes the platform easy to customize to a developer's tastes. Also like the IBM offering, Sun's developer tools offer a robust but expensive option and a simple but free option. The Free Sun ONE Community Edition is the base platform for the very uncheap Sun ONE Enterprise edition. Like WebSphere Studio Workbench, Sun ONE Community Edition has some very good, if basic, features that can be updated for dedicated do-it-yourself types. All Sun One products are based on the open-source but sun-controlled NetBeans platform. Both flavors of Sun ONE studio can be downloaded from `http://www.sun.com/software/sundev`.

The Sun Java Web Services Developer Pack

The Java Web Service Developer Pack (WSDP) is downloadable from Sun at `http://java.sun.com/webservices/webservicespack.html`. The current version of the WSDP is compatible with JDK 1.3.1 and higher. Outlined below are the WSDP APIs and their associated benefits.

JAXP (Java API for XML Processing)

The Java API for XML Processing (JAXP) supports processing of XML documents, including WSDL documents, SOAP envelopes, and deployment descriptors. JAXP supports DOM 1, 2, and some of DOM 3, SAX 1 and 2, and XSLT. JAXP enables applications to change the processor that is used to parse and transform XML documents without changing the underlying source code for the application that is doing the parsing or transformation. JAXP also supports the W3C XML Schema 1.0 Recommendation and an XSLT compiler (XSLTC).

JAXP is covered in more detail in Chapter 17.

JAXB (Java Architecture for XML Binding)

JAXB automates mapping between XML documents and Java objects, making elements and attributes classes, properties and methods by marshaling and unmarshaling them in a customized XML document.

JAXB is covered in more detail in Chapter 17.

JAXM (Java API for XML Messaging)

JAXM provides an Interface for SOAP messages, including SOAP with attachments. Because JAXM is based on XML, the messaging format can be changed to other message standards that support XML formats.

JAXM is covered in more detail in Chapter 33.

JSTL (Java Server Pages Standard Tag Library)

JSTL consists of four custom Java Server Page (JSP) tag libraries called the core, XML, I18N & Formatting, and database access libraries. All are based on the JSP 1.2 API. The core JSP library supports basic HTM page generation features. The XML library contains support for XML functionality, such as transformations and parsing. The database access library contains support for database access functions, and the I18N & Formatting library contains functionality for internationalization and formatting of Web pages.

JSTL is covered in more detail in Chapter 17.

JAX-RPC (Java API for XML-Based RPC)

JAX-RPC provides an interface for XML messages using an RPC transport, including, but not limited to, SOAP calls over RPC to Web services.

JAX-RPC is covered in more detail in Chapter 33.

JAXR (Java API for XML Registries)

JAXR provides an interface for XML registries, supporting UDDI and OASIS/U.N./ CEFACT ebXML Registry and Repository standards, among others.

JAXR is covered in more detail in Chapter 33.

Java WSDP Registry Server

The Java WSDP Registry Server implements Version 2 of the UDDI (Universal Description, Discovery and Integration) specification. It provides a registry that is compatible with JAXR (Java API for XML Registries). The Java WSDP Registry Server can be used as a standalone UDDI server and also as a testing tool for JAXR applications.

The Java WSDP Registry Server is covered in more detail in Chapter 33.

SAAJ (SOAP with Attachments API for Java)

SAAJ provides support for producing, sending and receiving SOAP messages with attachments. Sun's SAAJ library provides an interface to the features and capabilities described in the W3C SOAP 1.1 attachment note, which have not changed much in their current form. The current W3C specification is the W3C SOAP 1.2 Attachment Feature, currently in the Working Draft stage of the W3C Recommendation process. The W3C SOAP 1.2 Attachment Feature Working Draft states that a SOAP message may include attachments directly the W3C SOAP body structure. The SOAP body and header may contain only XML content. Non-XML data must be contained in an attachment under the SOAP body. This provides facilities for providing binary information and non-XML data in a SOAP envelope.

SOAP and SOAP attachments are covered in more detail in Chapters 23 and 24. SAAJ is covered in more detail in Chapter 33.

And Others . . .

Most of the tools that we've shown here, and many others, are available for download on the Web. A good place to start your search for products appropriate to your needs is `http://www.xmlsoftware.com`. In subsequent chapters, we'll show examples of the Xerces and Xalan libraries, the IBM XML Toolkit, and the Sun Web Services Developer Pack.

Summary

In this chapter, you were introduced to Web service tools for J2EE developers:

✦ The Apache XML Project - AXIS code for SOAP development

✦ Other apache offerings

✦ IBM products

✦ IBM AlphaWorks offerings

✦ XML Security Suite

✦ The Emerging Technologies Toolkit (ETTK)

✦ Eclipse offerings

✦ Sun products

✦ The Sun Web Service Developer Pack (WSDP)

In the next few chapters, we'll be putting many of these tools to use in practical examples. In Chapter 35 we'll use WebSphere application developer and integrated components from the IBM Web Services Developer Kit to build a basic Web service application. After that we'll show you how to integrate Web services with popular RDBMS products and how to secure your Web service applications.

✦   ✦   ✦

Web Services with the Sun Java Web Services Developer Pack

Sun's Java Web Services Developer Pack (JWSDP) represents a compilation of Web Service specifications and reference implementations. It holds all the fundamental pieces a developer would need to support the consumption, development, and deployment of a Web Service. In reality, the JWSDP is made up of a whole spectrum of tools, some of which aren't targeted specifically at Web Service development. In Chapter 17, we looked at the whole range of XML processing tools (JAXB, JAXP, and so on) that are part of the JWSDP. Here, we will focus our attention exclusively on those elements of the JWSDP that are related to Web Service development.

This chapter will explore the Java API for XML Messaging (JAXM), which provides developers with standard API for developing message-based solutions that use Web Services and SOAP as their messaging infrastructure. As part of covering JAXM, we'll also briefly touch on Soap with Attachments API for Java (SAAJ). SAAJ presents developers and vendors with a standard API for assembling the SOAP messages that are at the heart of all Web Service interactions.

We'll also cover the Java API for XML-based RPC (JAX-RPC). This specification provides developers with a powerful, standard framework for consuming and developing Web Services. Later, in Chapter 34, we'll examine Apache's Axis, which represents a complete implementation of the JAX-RPC specification.

Finally, no discussion of Web Services would be complete without taking a peek at registries. We'll explore the Java API for XML Registries (JAXR), a specification that offers developers a single, standard interface for interacting with various registry technologies.

JWSDP Overview

The JWSDP includes two APIs, JAXM and JAX-RPC, which are focused directly on developing and consuming Web Services. JAXM is intended to address message-based solutions, while JAX-RPC introduces the RPC programming model to the Web Services protocol. Neither of these two APIs is trying to break new conceptual ground. Programmers of distributed systems have been leveraging these fundamental technologies for years. JAXM and JAX-RPC simply take these established paradigms and make them available on the Web Services infrastructure. Certainly, being based on the Web Service standards enables some new modes of interoperability. However, the mechanics of programming with these APIs still closely conform to mold created by their messaging and RPC predecessors. The result is a simplified, standardized set of APIs that enable programmers to apply well-understood, proven programming techniques to the world of Web Services.

In addition to providing standards for messaging and RPC, the JWSDP also provides a standard API for interacting with registries. This specification, JAXR, calls out an API for interacting with existing registry implementations without having to be familiar with the specifics of the given registry. This area of the JWSDP is extremely valuable, since it's likely there will always be multiple competing registry technologies, each with its own interface and idiosyncrasies.

The biggest upside of these Web Service APIs is that they insulate developers from the continually changing world of Web Service protocols and standards. Each of these APIs makes a distinct effort to remain detached from the specifics of any particular Web Service implementation. While the APIs defined in the JWSDP try to maximize flexibility, they also define strict compatibility requirements in an effort to guarantee that each implementation will offer a standardized set of functionality that developers can rely upon.

The API Puzzle

At times, the JWSDP can start to taste a bit like alphabet soup. The bundling of all of these different specifications into one kit, while convenient for distribution and setup, can make it difficult to determine how and when a developer should apply each API. The problem is, depending on the requirements of your solution, you may find yourself leveraging any number of these APIs to build your solution. Since we're really focusing exclusively on Web Services for this chapter, our view will be constrained to just those APIs that play a direct role in the Web Service development model. This mostly limits the scope of our chapter to JAXM, JAX-RPC, and

JAXR. We'll also touch on SAAJ as part of our JAXM discussion (since that's where it's most relevant to developing Web Services). The diagram shown in Figure 33-1 illustrates the intended role for each Java Web Service APIs.

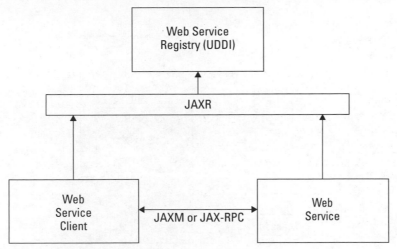

Figure 33-1: Web Service APIs

As you can see, the JAXM and JAX-RPC APIs are targeted at providing an infrastructure that facilitates building, deploying, and consuming Web Services. JAXR, on the other hand, supports a separate set of client and service-related features. Each Web service you create can use JAXR to register itself in a given registry. For clients, they will use JAXR to look up the list of services that have been published in a registry.

Java API for XML Messaging (JAXM)

Messaging is a concept that's been around for some time. Vendors have historically offered a number of proprietary solutions based, in some cases, on proprietary transports mechanisms. It was only natural for someone to come along and offer up a solution that married a messaging framework to the Web Services paradigm. JAXM is just that, an API that provides all the traditional elements of a messaging API built upon the messaging protocol (SOAP) defined by the Web Service community. The result is a clean, simple API that will be easily assimilated by any Java programmer familiar with message-based programming. The beauty is, in leveraging SOAP as the message construct, JAXM delivers a message-based solution that allows your messages to be sent or received by any service that complies with Web Service standards. This platform neutral level of messaging interoperability opens the world of messaging to a realm of new possibilities.

The JAXM model is a very simple conceptual model (shown in Figure 33-2). JAXM Clients (sometimes referred to as applications) create connections, construct messages, and send messages. These clients may, optionally, send their messages to a message provider that assumes responsibility for any special manipulation of the message, including routing it to one or more receivers. JAXM servers or services receive messages from JAXM clients. In the sections that follow, we'll discuss each of these areas of the JAXM framework.

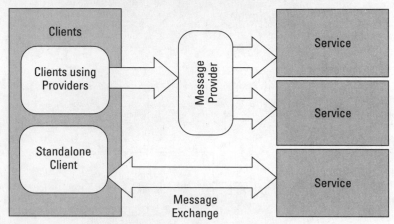

Figure 33-2: Conceptual JAXM view

The JAXM provider model

If you're going to dig into the JAXM architecture, it actually makes the most sense to start in the middle, at the message provider layer. This layer is the most fundamental building block of the JAXM architecture, enabling much of the architecture's depth and flexibility. Message providers are the traffic cops in the message exchange lifecycle. They intercept messages as they pass from client to service, inserting additional information into messages, persisting them, routing them, and adding whatever additional functionality a vendor might choose to include in their provider implementation. In fact, if you are evaluating JAXM implementations, you're going to want to focus your effort on evaluating the robustness and flexibility of each vendor's message provider. Through these message providers, vendors will introduce all the higher end bits of functionality you would expect to find bundled with any commercial grade messaging middleware. Specifically, you should find most vendors offering options that will improve the reliability of your message delivery. In most instances, vendors will allow undeliverable messages to be persisted until they can be successfully delivered. JAXM message providers may also offer some ability to route messages to other message providers.

The truth is, there is no specific set of functionality that is universally included by a provider. Fortunately, while each vendor's implementation might vary, the JAXM architecture hides all these variations from the developer. From the JAXM consumers prospective, all providers are created equal. In fact, the API remains the same for all providers, allowing developers to be freed from the details of how their message is processed.

Message providers also require a servlet container to function. By using a servlet container in conjunction with a message provider, JAXM is able to decouple requests from responses. This opens the door for one-way messaging, where a client can send a request without immediately receiving a response from the server.

JAXM clients

JAXM clients are responsible for constructing and sending valid SOAP messages to recipients. JAXM supports two basic types of clients, each with its own behavior. These two models are described following.

Standalone clients

The "standalone" client, the simplest of the two client models, is typically used in rare situations where a client requires more of a real-time, request-response model. This mode of messaging is achieved by bypassing the message provider layer entirely. Without the provider in the loop, a standalone client must create a synchronous, point-to-point connection where it sends messages directly to a single Web Service. All standalone client messages must be sent synchronously, where the client will send a message and block until a response is received.

Clients using providers

While the standalone client is the most conceptually simple model, it is also the least flexible. This is why, in most cases, developers will choose to employ clients that use a message provider. In this client model, which creates and maintains a connection to a provider, the client can send messages both synchronously and asynchronously. It also offers the option of acting as both a client and a server, where it can receive messages from other clients.

SOAP messages and SAAJ

Each message that is exchanged between a client and a service is exchanged using SOAP, the cross-platform standard that is the backbone of Web Service interactions. JAXM leverages the SAAJ (SOAP with Attachment API for Java) specification, which provides a standardized API for constructing, validating, and reading SOAP messages. This API, like JAXM and JAX-RPC, strives to abstract developers away from the details of SOAP, providing them with simple, intuitive Java interfaces for interacting with SOAP messages. In addition to supporting the standard SOAP components (envelope, header, body, and so on), SAAJ provides support for adding optional attachments to a message. The shape of a SOAP message with attachment is shown in Figure 33-3.

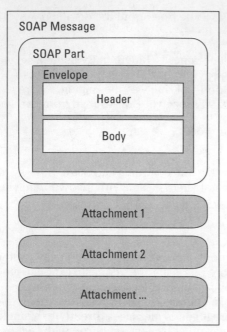

Figure 33-3: SOAP message with attachments

Messages that are exchanged between client and server can be exchanged in synchronous and asynchronous modes. In reality, there are a few variations on these two modes. The complete list of message exchange modes is as follows:

✦ **Asynchronous Inquire:** A message is sent and a response must be received (not immediately, but at some point in the future)

✦ **Asynchronous Update with Acknowledgement:** A message is sent and a specific acknowledgement must be received

✦ **Synchronous Update:** A message is sent and the sender blocks until a response is received

✦ **Synchronous Inquiry:** This is the same as Synchronous Update; however, the response is only needed to unblock the client

✦ **Fire and Forget:** A message is sent and no response is expected or received

Connections

All messages that are exchanged via JAXM are sent and received via connections. A connection simply represents any link between a client (a sender) and its corresponding service (a receiver). Based on the type of client you are developing, you may choose to connect directly to a service or you may connect to a message provider, which will route your message to its ultimate destination.

Each connection is created using the typical factory pattern. For example, if you wanted to create a direct connection to a service, referred to as a point-to-point connection, you would simply invoke the static `SOAPConnectionFactory.newInstance()` method, which would return a `SOAPConnection` object. You could then use that connection for all of your synchronous interactions with the service. For asynchronous messaging, you would create a `ProviderConnection` by invoking the `ProviderConnectionFactory.newInstance()` method. The interfaces for both of these models are very straightforward.

JAXM package structure

When JAXM was initially introduced, all of it classes and interfaces were contained in the `javax.xml.messaging` package. This made perfect sense until JAXM inherited its dependency on SAAJ. Since SAAJ really offers a set of API that can (and do) exist outside the JAXM domain, it no longer made sense to package it alongside JAXM. So, to clarify this point and eliminate some unnatural coupling, the elements of SAAJ were broken out of the JAXM package and made part of the `javax.xml.soap` package. JAXM still retains its dependency on the `javax.xml.soap` package (as it should), but `javax.xml.soap` has no dependency on `javax.xml.messaging`. This move also freed up the SOAP APIs so it could be more cleanly referenced by other APIs, most notably the JAX-RPC API. The items shown in Table 33-1 represent some of the key classes and interfaces that appear in these two packages.

Table 33-1 Axis Package Contents	
javax.xml.messaging	*javax.xml.soap*
ProviderConnectionFactory	SOAPConnectionFactory
ProviderConnection	SOAPConnection
ProviderMetaData	SOAPEnvelope
ReqRespListener	SOAPHeader
OneWayListener	SOAPBody
EndPoint	AttachmentPart
JAXMException	SOAPFault

Profiles

Out of the box, JAXM supports the SOAP 1.1 and SOAP with attachments specifications. However, the JAXM architecture also allows the SOAP model to be extended to support additional protocols via profiles. These profiles call out additional messaging specifications, which allow messages to conform to any number of new protocol requirements. So, messages received with a given profile will contain specific header attributes that are part of the agreed upon protocol for that profile's specification. Each profile will be accompanied by an API that will support the processing and manipulation of these custom header attributes. In the case of JAXM, APIs are included for both ebXML and SOAP-RP profiles.

As Web Services gain wider acceptance, we may also see the introduction of new, more industry-specific profiles. JAXM's ability to support these profiles so seamlessly will put it in a good position to accommodate these continually evolving specifications.

JAXM versus JMS

At this point, you may be wondering where JAXM fits into the grand messaging scheme with JMS. It's true that at some abstract level all of these technologies represent alternative approaches to messaging. They all seek to provide a reliable framework for routing and receiving messages. However, even though they share this higher-level objective, they are still different enough in their execution that they shouldn't be seen as being interchangeable.

JMS and JavaMail implementations typically rely on some incarnation of Messaging Oriented Middleware (MOM) or mail infrastructure to transport and manage their messages. This is still a perfectly valid model for some problem domains. In fact, it may be the preferred solution in more controlled development environments (where both the sending and receiving technology is more under your control).

JAXM is not making any attempt to be a superset of all these message solutions. Instead, it is focused specifically on being a Web-centric messaging solution, embracing the Web Service vision of SOAP flowing freely across a multitude of applications and programming environments. Certainly, given the level of standardization being achieved with the SOAP protocol, JAXM will have clear advantages in terms of its ability to interoperate with a broad range of technologies.

The JAXM technology does offer a few options that are not available with JMS. In general, JAXM is viewed as a lighter-weight solution than JMS. Its support for synchronous, point-to-point connections is also not available to JMS developers. These features, although marginally important, are worth mentioning.

Building a client

Now that we've covered the fundamental concepts behind JAXM, let's put them to work by building some sample clients. Fortunately, with JAXM (and most messaging APIs), there are very few gory details buried within the API. In fact, as we move through this example, it should become evident that the JAXM learning curve is fairly minimal. The steps involved in building our examples, and most JAXM clients, will typically follow the same basic pattern.

- ✦ Create a connection from one of JAXM's connection factories
- ✦ Construct a message
- ✦ Populate the content of the message
- ✦ Add attachments (if you have any) to the message
- ✦ Send the message
- ✦ Receive a response
- ✦ Extract the content from the received message

Building a standalone client

Standalone clients are the simplest to build, so let's start there. As we mentioned before, a standalone client does not use a message provider and is constrained to synchronous communications. In this example, we'll just send a simple message directly to a service and receive a response. The first step involved in building our client is to acquire a connection to the service from a connection factory. The code to get our connection is shown in Listing 33-1.

Listing 33-1: **Getting a Connection**

```
SOAPConnectionFactory connFactory = SOAPConnectionFactory.newInstance();
SOAPConnection conn = connFactory.createConnection();
```

Whew, that was hard. Our connection object is ready, now we need to construct the message we want to send to the service. As we saw earlier in our discussion of JAXM packages, the `javax.xml.soap` contains all the classes and interfaces we'll need to build a SOAP message that we can exchange with a service. In our example, we'll send messages to the Cosmic Astrology service, which will take some simple demographic data points and return a horoscope. The message will be constructed with the code shown in Listing 33-2.

Listing 33-2: **Constructing a Message**

```
// get the SOAP elements
MessageFactory msgFactory = MessageFactory.newInstance();
SOAPMessage msg = msgFactory.createMessage();
SOAPPart soapPart = msg.getSOAPPart();
SOAPEnvelope envelope = soapPart.getEnvelope();
SOAPHeader header = envelope.getHeader();
SOAPBody body = envelope.getBody();
header.detachNode();

// create a name for our service entry point
Name methodName =
    envelope.createName("GetHoroscope", "ASTRO", "http://www.astro.com");
SOAPBodyElement getHoroscope = body.addBodyElement(methodName);

// add parameter birth date
Name dobParamName = envelope.createName("DateOfBirth");
SOAPElement dobParam = getHoroscope.addChildElement(dobParamName);
dobParam.addTextNode("05/03/1964");

// add parameter for favorite color
Name colorParamName = envelope.createName("FavoriteColor");
SOAPElement colorParam = getHoroscope.addChildElement(colorParamName);
colorParam.addTextNode("Purple");
```

This code starts out by getting a message from the `MessageFactory`. We can then use this message to pull out all the separate elements of the SOAP message (`SOAPEnvelope`, `SOAPHeader`, and `SOAPBody`), which will then be used to assemble our service call. In this particular example, we won't need to have any header information and, since header information is optional in SOAP message, we'll use the `detach()` method on `SOAPHeader` to remove the header portion of our message.

Next, we need to create a `Name` object that represents the entry point for the operation (`GetHoroscope`) we want to call on our service. This is achieved by creating a `Name` object with the method name (`GetHoroscope`), namespace (`ASTRO`), and URI (`http://www.astro.com`). Our constructed `Name` is then added as a body element to the message body.

To round out our message, we need only add the parameters that will be passed with our call. In this sample, we'll pass `DateOfBirth` and `FavoriteColor` parameters to our service. Again, we'll construct these parameters as `Name` instances before adding each one as a child element to the `getHoroscope` body element that we have already created.

Now, when JAXM sends this message, it will transform it into a valid SOAP message with each of the data elements we added mapped to the appropriate part of the message. In this example, the SOAP message shown in Listing 33-3 would be produced.

Listing 33-3: **The SOAP Message**

```
<SOAP-ENV:Envelope
 xmlns:SOAP-ENV="http://schemas.xmlsoap.org/soap/envelope/"
  <SOAP-ENV:Body>
    <ASTRO:GetHoroscope xmlns:ASTRO="http://www.astro.com">
      <DateOfBirth>05/03/1964</DateOfBirth>
      <FavoriteColor>Purple</FavoriteColor>
    </ASTRO:GetHoroscope>
  </SOAP-ENV:Body>
</SOAP-ENV:Envelope>
```

There's only one thing left for us to do — send the message and get our response. This achieved by constructing an EndPoint and invoking the call() on our connection. Once the call is completed, a SOAPResponse will be returned with your horoscope. The code for making this call is shown in Listing 33-4.

Listing 33-4: **Making the Call**

```
SOAPMessage response = conn.call(msg, endPoint);
conn.close();
System.out.println("Received reply");
SOAPPart soapRespPart = response.getSOAPPart();
SOAPEnvelope soapRespEnv = soapRespPart.getEnvelope();
SOAPBody soapRespBody = soapRespEnv.getBody();
Iterator it = soapRespBody.getChildElements();
SOAPBodyElement bodyElement = (SOAPBodyElement)it.next();
String horoscope = bodyElement.getValue();
System.out.println("Horoscope returned: " + horoscope);
```

Alas, we have our horoscope. Now, to get the text of our horoscope, we extract the SOAPBodyElement from response and display its value. As a matter of housekeeping, we also close the connection to free up the resource.

Clients with message providers

Building a client that uses a message provider follows much of this same logic as our standalone client, but it requires a few extra pieces of information to handle messages. Let's look at some the nuances that differentiate the clients that leverage message providers.

When clients wish to use a message provider, they have two options for acquiring their connection. They can use the `ProviderConnectionFactory.newInstance()` mechanism, which will return the default provider. The other approach would be to use the Java Naming and Directory Interface (JNDI) to look up a provider based on its name. The following code provides an example of how this would be executed.

```
Context jndiContext = new InitialContext();
ProviderConnectionFactory provFactory =
  (ProviderConnectionFactory)jndiContext.lookup("RegisteredProvider1");
ProviderConnection provConn = provFactory.createConnection();
```

JAXM also provides a number of different options for constructing messages that will be routed through a message provider. With a message provider, we may choose to use a message format that conforms to one of the available message profiles (remember, profiles let us include data in the SOAP header that allows a message to comply with a given message specification). If we're planning on using a message that uses one of these profiles, we'll need to get a special message factory type for that profile. This factory is acquired as follows:

```
MessageFactory ebXMLFactory = provConn.createMessageFactory("ebxml");
EbXMLMessageImpl ebXMLMessage = (EbXMLMessageImpl)ebxmlFactory.createMessage();
```

In this example, we created a message factory that references the `ebXML` profile and then uses this factory to create a message. You'll notice that the value returned from our `createMessage()` call must be cast to an instance of an `EbXMLMessageImpl`. Now, with the instance of an `EbXMLMessageImpl`, we can use this classes' type-safe interface to set the `ebXML` compliant header values. Each provider connection actually maintains a list of all the profiles it supports as part of its metadata. The following line of code will return an array of strings that represent the collection of profiles that are supported for the `provConn` connection instance:

```
String[] profiles = provConn.getMetaData().getSupportedProfiles();
```

Naturally, each profile comes with its own set of requirements that will influence how you'll go about populating your message. It's outside the scope of this book to explore the message requirements for each of these profiles.

That last step is to send the message, which is also slightly different for clients that use message providers. Instead of using the `call()` method, the `Provider`

Connection uses send() to initiate the message exchange. The send() message takes a single parameter, the populated message. You'll notice that with send() we were not required to include an endpoint. With message providers, the endpoints are actually included as part of the deployed configuration for that message provider, allowing the provider to assume reponsibility for assigning the ultimate destination for your message. It's also important to note that the send() method does not require a response. Once the method is called, control is immediately returned to the caller.

Handling a SOAPFault

In the JAXM world, error conditions cannot be raised as exceptions. The only data that passes between sender and receiver is SOAP messages. So, instead of employing your usual handy try/catch block, you'll need to peek into SOAP reponses to see if they include a SOAPFault object. This object defines a standard "exception-like" interface for setting and retrieving information about a given error condition. The following snippet of code demonstrates the detection and display of a SOAPFault condition:

```
SOAPMessage response = conn.call(messsage, endPointURL);
SOAPBody respBody = response.getSOPAPart().getEnvelope().getBody();
if (respBody.hasFault() == true) {
    SOAPFault fault = respBody.getFault();
    System.err.println("Fault Code: " + fault.getFaultCode() +
                    "Fault Text: " + fault.getFaultString());
}
```

The SOAP 1.1 specification actually calls out each of the attributes of the SOAPFault and how they must be populated. If you plan on throwing your own SOAPFault objects, you'll want to look more closely at this area of the specification.

The Provider Admin tool

The JWSDP includes a utility that is used to manage your message provider configurations. This Web-based application includes tools for adding and editing endpoints, configuring log file options, message retry intervals, and so on. Once you've got Tomcat up and running, you can access this tool by selecting the "Provider Administration" link on the http://localhost:8080/index.html page.

Java API for XML-Based RPC (JAX-RPC)

In the preceding discussion of JAXM, our emphasis was on broadcasting and receiving SOAP messages. In fact, it should be clear by now that JAXM and SOAP are heavily intertwined. Nearly every line of JAXM code you will write will require some awareness of the SOAP API. In stark contrast, the JAX-RPC API has the expressed goal of completely isolating developers from SOAP. How a message is delivered and how its results are returned should be of little concern to the JAX-RPC developer. Each JAX-RPC implementation should be measured, to some extent at least, on how well it executes on this vision. Ideally, building or consuming a Web Service with JAX-RPC should be as simple as it would be with any other traditional distributed model.

Part of what makes the JAX-RPC learning curve so minimal is the fact that much of its approach borrows directly from the existing RMI and RPC models. Developers who have experience with these technologies should find the transition to JAX-RPC especially smooth. If we allow some room for over-simplification, in fact, it would probably be safe to think of JAX-RPC as RMI that swaps out the RMI transport layer and plugs in standard HTTP and SOAP 1.1 compliant message exchange.

If we look at the diagram shown in Figure 33-4, we'll see that JAX-RPC clients leverage generated stubs that then pass off controls to a JAX-RPC run-time layer that takes on the responsibility for dealing with all the serialization and SOAP message formatting that's needed to send our call to a Web Service. On the service side, as you might expect, the JAX-RPC plumbing listens for incoming service calls, de-serializes the SOAP messages into Java types, and ends up calling a method on our service.

Now, even though the JAX-RPC API isn't exactly revolutionary, what it enables for developers is still significant. With JAX-RPC, developers will be able to build and consume Web Services relatively easily. And, with SOAP as its underlying protocol, it opens up a whole new level of interoperability. With a few simple steps, our clients can reach out across the Web and interact with a broad range of services developed with any number of different Web Service compliant tools and technologies. We can also build and deploy our Java classes as Web Services with very little extra plumbing added to our every day Java classes.

All this talk of the simplicity of JAX-RPC might lead one to overlook its power. Even though JAX-RPC implementations limit ramp-up time, they also offer a fairly rich set of more advanced features. The specification calls out mechanisms for mapping user-defined types, custom message handler chains, embedding documents in your messages, and so on. The type-mapping system should be of particular interest, since you're likely to need to exchange additional data types in your service interfaces. We'll touch on some of these more advanced topics in the sections that follow.

 Cross-Reference This section provides a general overview of the JAX-RPC specification and the reference implementation included with the JWSDP. Chapter 34, Apache Axis, provides a detailed look at a more complete implementation of this specification.

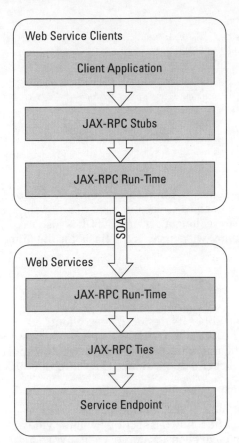

Figure 33-4: JAX-RPC overview

WSDL at work

As you begin to work with any JAX-RPC implementation, you're likely to find that WSDL (Web Services Description Language) is going to represent the logical starting point for developing any client or service. WSDL is a standardized markup language that is used to express the interface contract that is published by any Web Service. It defines the set of valid operations that are exposed for a given service as well as any parameters that are included in the signature of these operations.

JAX-RPC takes advantage of this standardized service specification, using it as the source for generating client and service Java classes that correspond to a service's interface (see Figure 33-5).

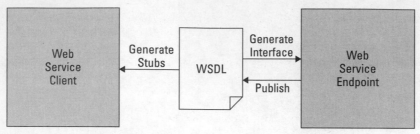

Figure 33-5: Leveraging WSDL

From the client side, this is especially useful. If we have access to the WSDL for a service, it contains all the information we need to construct a set of stubs that give us a much cleaner, more type-safe mode for calling a service. WSDL is also used to assist in the generation of the interfaces that will serve as the basis for the implementation of your service.

Developing clients

The JAX-RPC specification is very specific about its desire to keep clients as platform/protocol neutral as possible. The JAX-RPC client API, in fact, shields developers from any awareness of service implementation technologies and transport protocols. This approach allows JAX-RPC clients to maximize their interoperability and general flexibility.

The JAX-RPC API calls out three different models for developing Web Service clients, each with its own pros and cons. The following sections will provide an overview of each of these client types. In each client example, we'll invoke a `getPrediction()` method on a `MagicEightBall` service, which will yield a randomized prediction string.

Dynamic Invocation Interface (DII)

DII clients are the most truly "dynamic" of the client options. DII clients require developers to fully assemble all the elements of a `Call` before invoking any operation on a service. Certainly, if you're looking for maximum run-time flexibility, this would be your preferred model. However, if you're at all interested in type-safety and some degree of ongoing synchronization with your evolving service specification, you may want to try one of the other client offerings. Listing 33-5 provides an example of a DII client.

Listing 33-5: **A DII Client**

```
Public class EightBallDIIClient {
    public static void main(String[] args) {
        try {
            svcFactory = ServiceFactory.newInstance();
            Service service =
                svcFactory.createService(new QName(eightBallSvcQName));
            QName predictionPort = new QName(eightBallPortQName);
            Call call = service.createCall(predictionPort);
            call.setTargetEndpointAddress(endpointAddress);

            call.setProperty(Call.SOAPACTION_USE_PROPERTY,
                             new Boolean(true));
            call.setProperty(Call.SOAPACTION_URI_PROPERTY, "");
            call.setProperty(ENCODING_STYLE_PROPERTY, URI_ENCODING);

            call.addParameter("String_1", QNAME_TYPE_STRING,
                             ParameterMode.IN);
            call.setReturnType(QNAME_TYPE_STRING);

            call.setOperationName(
                new QName(BODY_NAMESPACE_VALUE, "getPrediction"));
            Object[] inParams = new Object[] {"Does this work?"};
            String prediction = (String)call.invoke(inParams);
            System.out.println(prediction);
        } catch (Exception ex) {
            ex.printStackTrace();
        }
    }
}
```

Now that's a lot of work for one call. We're basically using the property interface of the `Call` object to construct the entire signature of our method call. It should be clear that this model is highly sensitive. The slightest change in your WSDL and you'll be in here tweaking these options to conform to the new interface. That doesn't mean you should never use DII. There may be scenarios where this level of control is exactly what you're looking for.

Generated Stubs

If your service interface is fairly stable or you are in a controlled environment, you're probably going to prefer the Generated Stubs client model. Clients using this model use a set of generated "Stub" classes that were generated directly from your service's WSDL. These classes provide a more readable, more type-safe mode of interaction with your service. Listing 33-6 provides an example of a stub-based client.

Listing 33-6: **Generated Stubs Client**

```
public class EightBallStubClient {
    public static void main(String[] args) {
        try {
            EightBallProvider_Stub eightBallStub =
                (EightBallProvider_Stub)
                    (new EightBallService_Impl().getEightBallProviderPort());
            eightBallStub._setProperty(Stub.ENDPOINT_ADDRESS_PROPERTY,
                eightBallAddress);
            String prediction =
                eightBallStub.getPrediction("Does this work?");
            Sytem.out.println(prediction);
        } catch (Exception ex) {
            ex.printStackTrace();
        }
    }
}
```

Dynamic Proxy

The Dynamic Proxy client is somewhat of a hybrid of the DII and Generated Stub models. It does not require the client to fully assemble the `Call` object with all the pain-staking detail that was required with DII. However, it does not have a static, pre-generated stub to use either. Instead, it acquires the signature of the service call at run-time and constructs a proxy that can then be used to call the service. So, this approach allows us to remain fully dynamic, but eliminates much of the extra work that went into building our DII client. Listing 33-7 provides a simple example of a Dynamic Proxy client accessing our `MagicEightBall` service.

Listing 33-7: **A Dynamic Proxy Client**

```
public class EightballDynamicProxyClient {
    public static void main(String[] args) {
        try {
            URL serviceUrl = new URL(UrlString);
            ServiceFactory svcFactory = ServiceFactory.newInstance();
            QName svcQName = new QName(nameSpaceURI, serviceName);
            Service eightBallSvc =
                svcFactory.createService(serviceUrl, svcQName);
            predictQName = new QName(nameSpaceUri, portName)
            EightBallProvider eightBallProv =
                (EightBallProvider)eightBallSvc.getPort(predictQName,
                    EightBallProvider.class);
            String prediction =
```

```
        eightBallProv.getPrediction("Does this work?");
        System.out.println(prediction);
    } catch (Exception ex) {
        ex.printStackTrace();
    }
  }
}
```

As you can see, we passed the `ServiceFactory` a set of parameters (our service URL and service name) and it returned our dynamically referenced service. After that, we requested a reference to the `getPrediction()` port and executed our method.

Developing services (endpoints)

Defining a new Web Service, if we stick strictly to the JAX-RPC terminology, is all about exposing a "service endpoint" definition. Each endpoint represents a visible method exposed in our service implementation. In our client examples, however, you'll notice that each of our service methods was referred to as a "port," which is the terminology used within the WSDL specification. For the purposes of our discussion, you should view ports and endpoints as being synonymous.

So, how do we go about implementing one of these service endpoints? Well, the first thing we need is an interface that defines the signature of our service. This interface, which must extend Java's `Remote` interface, will contain all of the endpoints that we want to expose. Let's look at the interface for simple `MagicEight BallService` we referenced in our earlier client examples:

```
import java.rmi.Remote;
import java.rmi.RemoteException;
public interface MagicEightBallProvider extend Remote {
    public String getPrediction(String question) throws RemoteException;
}
```

This interface exposes a single endpoint with its `getPrediction()` method. You'll notice that our method also throws a `RemoteException`, which is a requirement for every endpoint you implement with JAX-RPC. Now, with our interface in place, all that remains is to provide an implementation of this class that contains the code for our `getPrediction()` endpoint. The following is an example of how this class would be constructed:

```
import java.xml.rpc.server.ServiceLifecycle;

public class MagicEightBallService implements MagicEightBallProvider,
ServiceLifecycle {
```

```
public String getPrediction(String question) throws RemoteException {
    try {
        //
        // TODO: insert your implementation here
        //
    } catch(Exception e) {
        throw new RemoteException("failed getting prediction");
    }
}
}
```

After you've finished this step, your service is ready to go. To make it available to clients, it must be deployed into a container that supports the JAX-RPC run-time (Tomcat, for example). JAX-RPC imposes no limitation on the server container that can host your service. However, the current examples tend to leverage servlet-based containers. The `wsdeploy` tool (discussed later in this chapter) discusses deployment of your service.

Mapping data types

Every call that is processed by a service must be able to be described within the context of the WSDL specification. That means every data type that participates in a service call must, at some point in the process, be transformed into a valid WSDL data type. In the past, this mapping could represent a sticky subject. The continually evolving protocols and the variations in Web Service tools meant you were at the mercy of dealing with a moving target. The JAX-RPC specification attempts to overcome this issue, explicitly defining the mapping between Java and WSDL data types. For example, JAX-RPC includes default WSDL mappings for all of the primitive Java data types, arrays, and standard classes (`String`, `BigInteger`, `BigDecimal`, `Calendar`, and `Date`).

While these mapped types may cover the majority of what you choose to include in your service interface, you'll inevitably find yourself in situations where you want to pass additional types across the wire. JAX-RPC addresses this need, providing developers with a "pluggable" type mapping framework for serializing and de-serializing additional data types (including user-defined and collection data types). This framework uses serializers to map a Java type representation to an XML representation. It also includes de-serializers to handle this transformation in the other direction.

The JAX-RPC specification also introduces the idea of a Type Mapping Registry. This registry serves as an encoding configuration manager, allowing developers to define alternate encoding schemes for different system configurations. At the time of encoding, the JAX-RPC implementation would call the Type Registry, requesting a serializer or deserializer for a given Java and XML type mapping. The resulting serializer would then be used to process the mapping.

Even though this custom type mapping system is quite powerful, using it could come at a cost. First, JAX-RPC vendors may provide varying levels of support for custom type mapping. Additionally, using anything other the standard WSDL types in your interface is going to impact the interoperability of your interface. So, while there are certainly scenarios (especially in controlled environments) where using custom type mapping would make sense, proceed with caution.

Message handlers

The JAX-RPC specification recognizes the need to allow developers to extend the message handling model. This advanced functionality permits incoming messages to be intercepted and manipulated, allowing for the introduction of message encryption and decryption, logging, and so on. Handlers can also be combined into "handler chains" where a configuration will define a pipeline of handlers that are linked together to serve a specific purpose. This message handling framework brings an additional level of power and flexibility to the JAX-RPC architecture.

Using wscompile and wsdeploy

The JAX-RPC reference implementation provides two tools, `wscompile` and `wsdeploy`, that are used in building and deploying your Web service solutions. The `wscompile` utility is used for a variety of purposes, including generating client stubs, server ties, serializers, and WSDL. This functionality is essential to simplifying the development of Web Service clients and services. The other half of this tandem, `wsdeploy`, covers the deployment of your Web Service. Before you can use `wsdeploy`, you must package your service into a WAR file containing your service RMI interface and implementation files, along with a `jaxrpc-ri.xml` that describes the configuration parameters of your service. This WAR file is fed into `wsdeploy`, which invokes `wscompile` behind the scenes to generate the fully processed, ready-to-use WAR file.

The JAX-RPC specification doesn't actually dictate strict requirements for these tools. In fact, when we look at Apache's Axis in Chapter 34, we'll find that it has its own twist on how to address this area of functionality.

Java API for XML Registries (JAXR)

So, with all this talk of Web Services one wonders how, in the vast world of the Internet, we are supposed to know what services are available and what features are offered by each of these services? We need some universal way to hunt, both internally and externally, for available services and examine their attributes. That's where registries and JAXR come into play.

A registry is often seen as being the virtual "yellow pages" for Web Services, providing a centralized location where vendors may publish and discover services. To date, there are two major players in the continually evolving registry space: UDDI (Universal, Description, Discovery, and Integration) and ebXML. These two registry schemes are by far the most popular and most heavily used.

The existence of two competing standards, in some respect, is what created the need for JAXR. With two standards already in place, both with their own feature set, it became important for developers to have an API that kept them from being so tightly coupled to the UDDI or ebXML implementations. Developers really want to be able to use a registry without concern for whose particular scheme they might be leveraging behind the scenes. The JAXR API was designed and architected to address this specific goal. It has the lofty goal of providing developers with a standard API that is a superset of the functionality offered by both UDDI and ebXML. Its flexible architecture supports both of these standards and, in doing so, puts in place a framework that will evolve with these standards and others that may be introduced in the future.

Capability profiles

JAXR's challenge of being a true union of the exiting registries required some quick thinking. UDDI and ebXML both include their own unique sets of functionality. To address this problem in a generic fashion, JAXR introduced the concept of Capability Profiles. These profiles are use to determine the level of functionality that's available for a given instance of a registry. A profile is arrived at by assigning a capability level to every method exposed in the JAXR API. The combined view of all of these levels represents a JAXR provider's profile in that it defines the set of operations that are valid for that provider.

Every profile is classified with a certain level of compliance. JAXR defines two specific levels. At level 0, a profile is said to support all the basic, business-focused registry functionality. In general, most registry providers should fully support level 0. At level 1 compliance, a registry would be expected to support a set of more advanced, more generic registry operations. Naturally, if a registry supports level 1, it automatically must support level 0.

JAXR architecture

The JAXR architecture is fairly straightforward, following the same familiar "provider" model that is so pervasive in many of the JWSDP APIs. It should be noted that, while registries are often thought of as Web-centric tools, the JAXR API supports clients of all types (applications, browsers, and so on).

The diagram shown in Figure 33-6 illustrates how the JAXR API sits on top of each of the registry providers. The API is a simple abstraction layer that also incorporates the Capability Profile functionality described earlier. The real bulk of the functionality is found in each provider, which assumes responsibility for invoking each operation on the native registries.

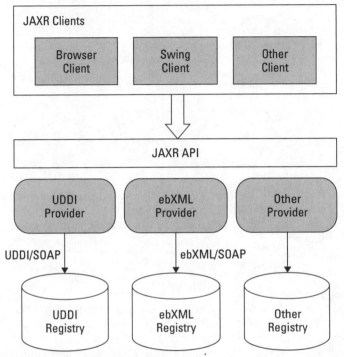

Figure 33-6: JAXR architecture

Every provider must implement the APIs from the `javax.xml.registry` and `javax.xml.registry.infomodel` packages. The later of these two is where registry objects are actually transformed from their native representation into the JAXR information model. Developers will need to acclimate themselves to this new model and how it represents each native registry type. If you're familiar with the ebXML model, the transitions shouldn't be that difficult since many of the ebXML model elements map very directly to their JAXR counterparts.

A few registry scenarios

There is a multitude of operations and uses for JAXR that could vary widely based on the needs of your specific application. For the purposes of this JAXR overview, we won't try to enumerate every possible usage for JAXR. Instead, we'll cover a few of the more common scenarios to give you a taste of what the API has to offer.

Getting a connection

Before you can start interacting with a registry, you'll need to get a connection. The JAXR API uses a property-based approach to acquiring a "configured" connection. The following code provides a simple example of opening a JAXR connection:

```
Properties props = new Properties();
props.setProperty("javax.xml.registry.queryManagerURL",
    "http://uddi.ibm.com/testregistry/inquiryapi");
props.setProperty("javax.xml.registry.lifeCycleManagerURL",
    "https://uddi.ibm.com/testregistry/protect/publishapi");
props.setProperty("com.sun.xml.registry.http.proxyHost",
    "myhost.mydomain");
props.setProperty("com.sun.xml.registry.http.proxyPort",
    "8080");
ConnectionFactory connFactory = ConnectionFactory.newInstance();
connFactory.setProperties(props);
Connection conn = connFactory.createConnection();
```

The only real work associated with getting a connection is determining which properties you might need to set. This example represents the most basic set of options. You should consult the JAXR specification to determine which options you might need to set for your solution.

Registry queries

JAXR includes a class, `BusinessQueryManager`, which provides developers with a series of methods that are used to search a registry for organizations and their published services. Specifically, this class will allow clients to access most of the key elements of the information model, including the `Organization`, `Service`, `ClassificationScheme`, and `Concept` objects. You'll find that most calls to the `BusinessQueryManager` return a `BulkResponse` object, which is a general-purpose response object that is, essentially, a collection wrapper class that can return a list of items. It also includes a collection of any exceptions that may have occurred during the execution of the called method. The following snippet of code demonstrates the API calls needed to retrieve a list of `Organizations` sorted by their names.

```
RegistryService rs = conn.getRegistryService();
BusinessQueryManager qm = rs.getBusinessQueryManager();
Collection findQualifiers = new ArrayList();
findQualifiers.add(FindQualifier.SORT_BY_NAME_DESC);
Collection letters = new ArrayList();
letters.add(firstLetterString);
BulkResponse response = qm.findOrganizations(findQualifiers,
        letters, null, null, null, null);
Collection organizations = response.getCollection();
```

In this example, we get an instance of the `RegistryService` from our connection which is then used to get an instance of the `BusinessQueryManager`. We're now ready to build and execute our query.

Our query construction begins by building a list of `FindQualifiers` we want to use, adding the constants that represent the type of search we want to perform. In this case, we want a list of organizations sorted by name, so we add the `SORT_BY_NAME_DESC` qualifier. Next, we need to create a collection of letters that represent the first letter of the organization names we want to find. All that remains now is to invoke the `findOrganizations()` method on the `BusinessQueryManager`. We can then get the collection of matching organizations from the returned `BulkResponse` object.

If this approach to finding an `Organization` is too broad, JAXR provides another interface that can help you perform a more qualified query. Instead of building a list of names we want to search for, we can build a list of `Classification` objects that represent criteria for the type of organization we want to find. We can then pass this list as another parameter to the `findOrganizations()` method. In all other respects, the process follows the same basic flow. As you can imagine, you can also mix-and-match these options to perform even more specialized searches.

Services and ServiceBindings for organizations

After you've acquired a list organizations via the query mechanism, you can then use the `Organization` object's interface to determine what `Services` and `ServiceBindings` are supported by that `Organization`. The following code illustrates how this would be achieved:

```
Organization org = (Organization)iter.next();
Collection services = org.getServices();
Iterator iter = services.iterator();
while (iter.hasNext()) {
    Service service = (Service)iter.next();
    Collection serviceBindings = service.getServiceBindings();
    Iterator bindIter = serviceBindings.iterator();
    while (bindIter.hasNext()) {
        ServiceBinding sb = (ServiceBinding)bindIter.next();
    }
}
```

Publishing an organization

Of course, for any of the JAXR query operations to work, an organization must first publish itself in a registry. This process is very much like any traditional database operation, requiring developers to populate data structures and submit them to the registry to be persisted. An organizaiton will need to provide basic demographic information (name, phone, and so on) along with classifcation data that will help clients who are searching for organizations that match specific service criteria.

The following snippet of code illustrates some of the basic steps that are required to publish an orgranization:

```
RegistryService rs = conn.getRegistryService();
BusinessLifeCycleManager lm = rs.getBusinessLifeCycleManager();
BusinessQueryManager qm = rs.getBusinessQueryManager();
Organization astroOrg = lm.createOrganization("Cosmic Astrology");
astroOrg.setDescription("Horoscopes for all ocasions!");
Collection phoneNums = new ArrayList();
phoneNums.add("555-1212");
astroOrg.setTelephoneNumbers(phoneNums);
Collection orgList = new ArrayList();
orgList.add(astroOrg);
lm.saveOrganizations(orgList);
```

This is a simplified example. You'll want to look at the JAXR information model for the `Organization` and all of its related objects that are used to hold the profile of your organization. Each organization is added to a list, which is then persisted to the registry via a call to the `saveOrganizations()` method.

Summary

In this chapter, we touched on all the APIs in the JWSDP that are focused on consuming, building, and deploying Web Services. The goal here was to provide an overview of the role each of these APIs play in the bigger Web Services pictures. Along the way, we covered the following topics:

✦ Using the JAXM messaging and SAAJ APIs to send message between Web Services

✦ Building Web Service clients and services (endpoints) using the JAX-RPC API

✦ Leveraging the JAXR API to locate services and examine their published services

Each of these new Web Service APIs provide developers with a rich set of Web Service technologies. And, in most cases, they have been able to keep the learning curve relatively manageable. The APIs also seem to remain true to the Web Service vision of maximizing the opportunity for interoperability.

✦   ✦   ✦

Apache Axis

If you're going to develop Web Services with Java, you're
definitely going to want to take a look at leveraging
Apache's Axis. Axis is a generalized SOAP message-handling
system that is focused on providing developers with a rich set
of tools and infrastructure for developing and consuming Web
Services. This open-source tool contains all the basic elements a developer would need to rapidly consume, build,
deploy, and host a Web Service. As we will see, Axis strikes a
nice balance between power and complexity, allowing developers to quickly build Web Services with a relatively short
learning curve while still allowing more advanced customization of message processing, type mapping, and so on.

In this chapter, we'll cover the fundamentals of the Axis architecture, taking an in-depth look at how the Axis engine processes requests and responses. The chapter will examine
some of the goals of the architecture and how these goals
influenced the solution that was ultimately implemented. It
will also discuss each of the deployment models that are supported by Axis. Specifically, the chapter will look into how
developers can customize their Web Service configuration via
deployment descriptors.

Additionally, this chapter will cover some of the tools that are
provided with Axis. It will provide an overview of how the
Java2WSDL and WSDL2Java tools can be used to generate the
client and Web Service implementation files. We'll drill down
into the contents of these generated files and explain how
they are processed by the Axis engine. Additionally, the chapter will look at the TCPMON utility and discuss how it can be
used to monitor the flow of messages to and from your Web
Service.

The Axis Evolution

Apache Axis represents the most recent offering of what was
originally known as SOAP4J, which was introduced by IBM.
After being donated by IBM and becoming part of Apache

Software Foundation's open-source effort in late 2000, SOAP4J became Apache SOAP and underwent a number of revisions, finally achieving a wide level of acceptance with release of Apache SOAP 2.2. Over time, however, it became clear that this version's rigid architecture was not prepared to take on the rapid evolving world of Web Services development. Acknowledging this reality, the Apache Software Foundation set out to define a next generation version of Apache SOAP that could overcome its performance issues and position it as a more general-purpose, more flexible message processing solution, a solution that was no longer so exclusively linked to the SOAP specification. Naturally, this broader vision for the product meant that the Apache SOAP name would no longer adequately capture the true flavor of the product. Thus, the new Apache eXtensible Interaction System, Axis, was introduced. Now, the reality is, while Axis is a completely new implementation that opens the door to support alternative transport protocols and message specifications, its initial focus is still primarily on HTTP and SOAP. The key point here is that the Axis architecture has been structured to allow for the future introduction of new protocols, messaging specifications, and providers. So, under this new modular architecture, Axis expects to be able to easily embrace any new specification that might eventually gain acceptance with the development community.

Axis is certainly still getting its footing and is working toward reaching a point of real stability. That said, the version 1.1 release (which this chapter is based on) represents a very complete, ready-to-use implementation. The Axis 1.1 release, in fact, surpasses Apache SOAP 2.2 in performance, function, and interoperability. The following represents some of the key elements of the new Axis architecture.

Performance enhancements

Performance was one of the most limiting factors of the Apache SOAP implementation. A key contributor to these performance problems was the system's XML processor, which used the DOM (Document Object Model) for processing the XML stream. This problem was addressed by making the switch to SAX (Simple API for XML Parsing), which reduced memory consumption and offered generally faster parsing of the message stream. This switch alone allows Axis to deliver significantly better performance.

Flexibility and extensibility

Axis was built from the ground up to be a "pluggable" architecture. This design creates an opportunity for developers and third-party integrators to provide their own plug-in components for logging, system management, internationalization, and so on. By standardizing on a "pluggable API" for the key system components, Axis has made it much easier for vendors to achieve a significantly tighter, more seamless integration of the Axis technology into their platforms.

Supporting the SOAP specification

In the current Axis release, the system fully supports the SOAP 1.1 specification and offers partial support for the SOAP 1.2 specification. For example, the 1.1 release of Axis does not support envelope versioning or namespaces from the SOAP 1.2 specification. Full support for the 1.2 specification, however, does appear to be a high-priority item for the Axis team.

Improved interoperability

One of the goals of the Axis implementation was to provide a higher degree of interoperability with other SOAP implementations. This goal is at least partially realized in the 1.1 release of the product. The introduction of support for untyped parameters certainly opens the door for Axis to more easily interoperate with implementations from other vendors. The architecture's modular approach to "providers" also allows the framework to interoperate additional technologies (COM, EJB, and so on).

Transport independence

The Axis implementation goes out of its way to abstract itself away from any awareness of a given transport protocol. While developers are still likely to use it primarily with HTTP, the underlying design actually allows for supporting alternative protocols (SMTP, message-oriented-middleware, and so on).

JAX-RPC and SAAJ compliance

In the prior chapter, we talked about JAX-RPC and SAAJ, which are part of the Java Web Services Development Kit. The Axis implementation aims to fully support both of these specifications. In fact, in its current form, Axis purports to be 100 percent JAX-RPC and SAAJ compliant. It is assumed that Axis will always remain tightly bound to these specifications.

WSDL support

Axis provides support for version 1.1 of the WSDL (Web Service Description Language) specification. With WSDL support developers are able to leverage and easily generate stubs for accessing remote services. Additionally, the WSDL support allows Axis to interrogate a deployed service and view its configuration.

Architecture Overview

The Axis architecture, in its simplest form, represents a generalized framework for processing messages. As such, the role of the Axis engine serves a very simple purpose. It must accept incoming SOAP messages from a given transport, validate and de-serialize that message, route that message to the appropriate service, then construct and serialize a SOAP response for the client. Axis took this basic message processing model and partitioned it into a series of well-defined layers that maximize the opportunity for developers to modify and direct messages as they flow through the system. This modular approach is also at the heart of what allows Axis to evolve and support the introduction of new transports, message protocols, and so on.

To better understand each of the distinct steps in the lifecycle of a message, let's look into the details of how the Axis engine processes each incoming server message (see Figure 34-1). As a message arrives at the Axis server, it is initially processed by the Transport Listener, which assumes responsibility for creating a valid Message object and placing that message into a Message Context. This Message Context will hold both the request and response messages, along with any additional properties that are associated with these messages. Message Context properties are examined by the Axis engine as it moves the data through each message processing layer, and, in many cases, these properties will end up directly influencing how messages flow through the system.

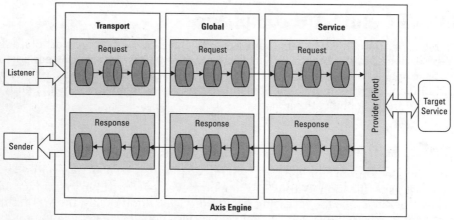

Figure 34-1: Processing server messages

Ultimately, the message context will arrive at a provider, which will invoke an operation on the target service. This stage, where the request reaches the provider and begins the transition to processing the response, is referred to as the "pivot." Any results that are returned from the service are then handed back to the provider and placed into the response portion of the Message Context (services are not required to return a response). The response is then sent back out through each of the pipeline processors (in the reverse order of the incoming request). Each step along the response path also provides the opportunity for the engine to modify or interact with the contents of the response.

The client implementation, as expected, processes messages in the reverse order of the server example. The client message processing model employs all the same mechanisms that are part of the server-side implementation, including both request and response message paths. The client begins by invoking the service handler before optionally handing off control to the global request chain, and, finally, control is passed to the transport handler. A Transport Sender performs the last step in the client process, transforming the message into a valid SOAP message. If the call from the client returns any results, they will be passed back through the response message path where it too can be processed by the same series of handlers.

Message handlers and message chains

Each message that is encountered by Axis is processed by a Message Handler. These handlers represent the smallest unit of processing that can be applied to a message. They are then linked together to address a given message's processing objective. The resulting "pipeline" of linked handlers is referred to as a Handler Chain. This mechanism is very much modeled after the Chain of Responsibility design pattern, where a collection of objects is assembled into a chain. Each object in that chain may handle a message or just forward the message along to the next handler in the chain.

The Axis architecture supports three specific types, each representing different stages in the message processing flow. In any one Handler Chain, there may be a transport, global, and service handler that represents a path for processing a specific service call. Each of these handler types can be applied to the request or response stream in the Axis engine. The following is an explanation of each of these individual handler types:

✦ Transport Handlers: These handlers, as their name implies, are responsible for performing transport specific operations on requests and responses. Each individual transport (HTTP, SMTP, etc.) has a corresponding transport handler that provides the basic message formatting according to the requirements of that transport's specification.

✦ Global Handlers: A global handler does not play any specific role in terms of processing messages. It exists primarily to allow developers an opportunity to introduce any general-purpose message handling. While the transport handler that is invoked will vary based on the transport that is being used, global handlers are always invoked for every message that is handled by the Axis engine.

✦ Service Handlers: Service handlers are directed at processing incoming messages and routing the actual implementation of an operation on a Web Service. As part of processing a message, each service handler constructs request and response chains that are responsible for processing the target Web Service operation.

Message Chains are configured and deployed as part of the Axis configuration file. Developers may build their own custom message handlers, assemble them into chains, and deploy them. Once a chain has been deployed and is "live," the Axis engine does not allow for any dynamic modification addition of new handlers to that chain. This ability to build and easily deploy specialized handlers represents one of the clear architectural strengths of the Axis engine.

Subsystem overview

The Axis architecture is conceptually divided into a distinct set of subsystems. The goal here, as it is with any architecture, is to isolate and compartmentalize each logical area of the implementation. Ideally, this will prevent any one subsystem from being too tightly coupled to another. The diagram shown in Figure 34-2 represents all the subsystems that are employed by the Axis engine. The following sections provide a brief explanation of the role each of the subsystems plays in the Axis implementation.

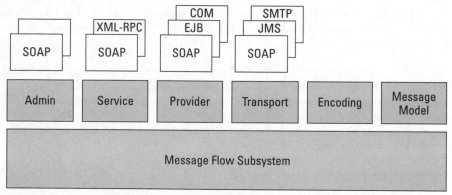

Figure 34-2: Axis subsystems

Message flow subsystem

As you might expect, the Message Flow subsystem is at the heart of Axis architecture. It is responsible for providing all the system's basic message-handling infrastructure. Specifically, it includes all the Message Handlers, Message Chains, and fault processing employed by the engine.

Administration subsystem

The Administration subsystem supports the administration and configuration of the Axis engine. It is this system that assumes responsibility for instantiating each message-handling pipeline based on the descriptions provided in the configuration file. Global configuration options are also loaded and set by this subsystem. This configuration can be loaded dynamically or it can be brought in from a WSDD (Web Service Deployment Descriptor). Both of these configuration mechanisms are covered later in this chapter.

Provider subsystem

Within the Axis architecture, a provider represents the point at which a message will be turned into an actual call to a Web Service. The Provider subsystem is responsible for providing a generic, technology-independent solution for achieving this task. The abstraction of this layer allows Axis to support a variety of technologies at the provider level. The configuration of each service simply specifies a provider type (RPC, EJB, and so on), and this parameter will determine how to process the message and invoke the service. The flexibility of this mechanism, where providers can be introduced in such isolation, means Axis will be able to support current and future mechanisms for accessing a given service implementation.

Transport subsystem

The Transport subsystem is responsible for providing the framework for processing any and all transport protocols. This is actually a byproduct of complying with the JAX-RPC specification, which requires implementers to abstract their solutions away from reliance on any specific transport protocol. Architecturally, Axis has achieved this. However, as it stands, the current release only supports the HTTP protocol.

Encoding subsystem

As data moves through the system, it must be able to translate Java data types into generic XML data types and vice versa. This transformation, which is typically referred to as "serialization" and "de-serialization," is managed by the Encoding subsystem. The Axis engine uses the JAX-RPC mapping model as the basis for its type-mapping implementation.

Message model subsystem

The Message Model subsystem has the responsibility of parsing the stream and constructing valid SOAP messages, which consist of an envelope, a header, and a body. This particular area, which leverages the SAX parser, has been optimized to limit memory consumption and parse the stream as efficiently as it can.

Type mappings

Every time a method is invoked on a Web Service from Java, the Axis engine must transform the signature of that native Java call into a valid SOAP message. A big part of this translation involves the mapping of each of the incoming Java data types to a standard SOAP representation of that type. The Axis implementation supports all the mappings that are called out in the JAX-RPC specification.

You should pay special attention to type mappings, since each type that is referenced in your service interface becomes part of your contract with the outside world. Clients of your service, which may use one of many available programming languages, will need to conform to this contract. The more basic types you select, the better chance you have of achieving interoperability. Table 34-1 illustrates the mapping between the fundamental WSDL data types and their corresponding Java data type.

Table 34-1
Axis Type Mappings

WSDL Type	Java Type
xsd:base64Binary	byte[]
xsd:Boolean	boolean
xsd:byte	byte
xsd:dateTime	java.util.Calendar
xsd:decimal	java.math.BigDecimal
xsd:double	double
xsd:float	float
xsd:hexBinary	byte[]
xsd:int	int
xsd:integer	java.math.BigInteger
xsd:long	long
xsd:Qname	java.xml.namespace.QName
xsd:short	short
xsd:string	java.lang.String

In looking at this table, it's clear that, for the most part, WSDL data types have a fairly clean mapping to Java data types. However, it's important to note that a user-defined Java object may not have any direct mapping to a WSDL data type. While a user-defined Java object may provide its own serialization, this serialization can only be brokered in environments where both client and server are written in Java. In order for Axis to be able to handle user-defined types, these types must be registered with the Axis serializer. This is achieved by implementing your class using the JavaBean pattern and registering it with the Axis BeanSerializer.

To make matters simpler for Java developers, Axis does provide a serializer for many of the common Java collection classes. You can take advantage of these serializers; however, you should be aware of the fact that using these types will impact your interoperability with other implementations. The SOAP specification does not currently cover complex object types.

 Note   The SOAP and JAX-RPC specifications do not allow for remote references being passed between client and server.

Installing and Running Axis

The installation process for Axis is relatively straightforward. Before you can get under way with the install process, though, you'll need to make sure that you have an application server installed. For the purposes of our discussion here, we'll assume that you are going to be using Axis with the Jakarta Tomcat server (version 4.1.x). Axis will actually work with other servers, as long as they support version 2.2 or higher of the servlet API.

Axis distribution files

Once you've gotten your application server setup squared away, you'll need to download the distribution archive from the Apache Axis Website. Within this archive you'll find the following items:

✦ A series of JAR files that represent the Axis implementation, most significant of which is `axis.jar`. Accompanying the JAR are `jaxrpc.jar` and `saaj.jar`, which are used to reference the APIs from these two specifications. There are also JAR files included to support logging (`commons-logging.jar` and `log4j-core.jar`).

✦ WSDL tools, WSDL2Java and Java2WSDL, that are used for processing and generating WSDL (`wsdl4j.jar`).

✦ HTML documentation covering the Axis APIs.

✦ A collection of sample programs that demonstrate some simple scenarios for building and deploying Web services.

Copying WEBAPPS and LIB files

Before you can fire up Apache Axis, you'll still need to move a few files into the appropriate Tomcat directories. Within the Axis distribution package, you'll find a WEBAPPS\AXIS directory, which contains Axis configuration files, samples, and JARs. This Axis directory needs to be copied to the WEBAPPS directory of your Tomcat installation.

The last piece in the puzzle is to copy a few JARs to the Tomcat COMMOM\LIB directory. First, you'll need a JAXP 1.1 compliant parser (Axis recommends using Xerces). Download this parser and its corresponding JARs and place them in Tomcat's COMMON\LIB directory. Then we need to move one of the Axis JARs, jaxrpc.jar, to this same COMMON\LIB directory. This file contains classes that are part of the java.* and javax.* packages, which violates a Tomcat constraint that prohibits the loading of any class from these packages if they are deployed in the WEBINF\LIB directory.

Starting the server

All the pieces are now in place. Simply bring up the Tomcat server and go to the Axis start page in your browser. Assuming you're running the browser on the same computer as the server, you can access this page via http://localhost/axis/. If you've successfully started the server, a screen similar to the one shown in Figure 34-3 will be displayed.

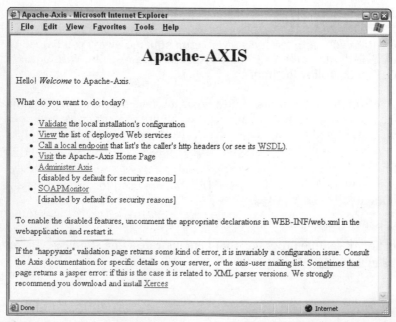

Figure 34-3: Axis start page

The Axis start page provides a very simple set of operations that will allow you to evaluate the basic state of your Axis installation. The most significant option offered on this page, at least at this initial stage, is the "Validate" option, which, when selected, will validate the state of your Axis installation. Upon selecting this link, you'll be presented with the Happiness Page. It should be similar to the one shown in Figure 34-4.

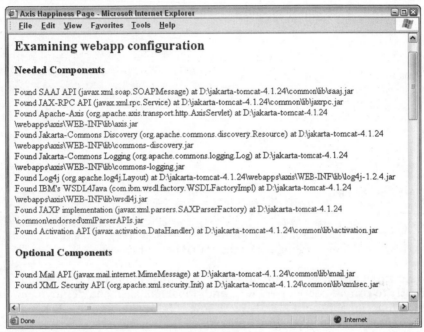

Figure 34-4: Validating your Axis installation

You should inspect the contents of the validation screen carefully. It will highlight any issues that might exist with your installation, including situations where required and optional JARs cannot be located, among other things. You may want to consider incorporating this validation mechanism into your automated testing environment, where it can continually validate the state of your Axis server.

Back on the start page, there are a few other options worth mentioning. The "View" option is used to interrogate the Axis server and return a list of services that are deployed on the server. With each service listed, there will also be a corresponding WSDL link that will allow you to access and review the WSDL for that service. The screen shown in Figure 34-5 provides an example of the service list view.

Figure 34-5: Service list

There's also a "Call a local endpoint" option on the start page. This option will make a call to the Axis Server to get a list of the HTTP headers for the caller.

One would expect that, as Axis matures, this administration area will be enhanced significantly to provide developers with additional management, deployment, and inspection functionality. As it stands right now, this startup page really offers a fairly minimal set of administration options.

Building and Consuming a Simple Web Service

While it's nice to understand all the underpinnings of the technology that's at play in the engine, it's also comforting to know that the Axis implementation has done an excellent job hiding most of these details from your day-to-day existence. The truth is, if you're just after getting a basic Web Service up –and running, then Axis is the tool for you. In fact, for Java developers familiar with RMI development, this transition should be especially smooth, since the Axis (JAX-RPC) implementation borrows heavily from the RMI model.

To demonstrate the simplicity of the Axis technology, let's go ahead a build ourselves a basic Web Service and make ourselves a client to consume that service.

Setting up your environment

Before you can begin to develop with Axis, you'll need to set up your CLASSPATH. Axis requires the following items to be added to your CLASSPATH:

```
<axis directory>\lib\axis.jar
<axis directory>\lib\jaxrpc.jar
<axis directory>\lib\saaj.jar
<axis directory>\lib\common-logging.jar
<axis directory>\lib\common-discovery.jar
<axis directory>\lib\wsdl4j.jar
<your Xerces path>xerces.jar (or another JAXP 1.1 compliant parser)
```

Creating a service

For our example, we'll build a `MagicEightBall` service, which takes a question and returns a random answer. The code for our service, shown in Listing 34-1, doesn't look any different than any other Java class you might write. In fact, if your service's interface were to limit its interface to simple data types, its implementation and deployment would remain fairly simple. The complexity of developing and deploying your service will typically vary based on the complexity of the types that it references.

Listing 34-1: **MagicEightBall Web Service**

```java
import java.util.Random;
import java.util.Date;

public class MagicEightBallService {
    private static String[] predictions = {"Possibly",
                                    "It could happen",
                                    "Unlikely",
                                    "Try again later",
                                    "The prospects seem good",
                                    "Definitely not",
                                    "It's a definite maybe",
                                    "Odds are favorable"};

    private static Random randGenerator =
            new Random((new Date()).getTime());

    public String getPrediction(String question) {
        int rndIdx = randGenerator.nextInt(predictions.length);
        return predictions[rndIdx];
    }
}
```

This service implementation contains a random list of responses and exposes a single service operation, getPrediction(). Each time the service is called, it gets a random index into the list of responses and returns a string containing the response. The only step left to make this class available as a service is to deploy it using one of the deployment techniques described later in this chapter.

Building the client

Oddly, developing the client for your Web Service actually requires more explaining. First, developers have a choice of developing dynamic or static clients. These two models take very different approaches to how they interact with the server. The following section explains these two client types.

Dynamic invocation

Dynamic clients follow a late-bound model, in which the clients use a general purpose interface to locate services and construct method calls (Listing 34–2). This generality comes at a cost of complexity and readability, though.

Listing 34-2: **TestDynamicClient.java**

```
import org.apache.axis.AxisFault;
import org.apache.axis.client.Call;
import org.apache.axis.client.Service;
import org.apache.axis.encoding.XMLType;
import org.apache.axis.utils.Options;

import javax.xml.namespace.QName;
import javax.xml.rpc.ParameterMode;
import java.net.URL;

public class TestDynamicClient {

    public String getAnswer(String question) {
        String answer = "Failure";
        try {
            URL server_url = new
                URL("http://localhost:8080/axis/MagicEightBallService.jws");
            Service service = new Service();
            Call call = (Call)service.createCall();
            call.setTargetEndpointAddress(server_url);
            call.setOperationName(new QName("", "getPrediction"));
            call.addParameter("question",
                            XMLType.XSD_STRING,
                            ParameterMode.IN);
            call.setReturnType(XMLType.XSD_STRING);
```

```
            Object ret = call.invoke(new Object[]{question});
            answer = (String)ret;
        } catch(Exception e) {
            e.printStackTrace();
        }

        return answer;
    }

    public static void main(String args[]) {
        try {
            TestDynamicClient client = new TestDynamicClient();
            String response = client.getAnswer("Do dynamic clients work?");
            System.out.println(response);
        } catch(Exception e) {
            e.printStackTrace();
        }
    }
};
```

This client acquires a `Call` object using the URL of our Web Service, configures the operation, and invokes it. It should be clear there's almost no type-safety in this client model, which makes it fragile. The slightest mistake in a parameter type, operation name, or return type and your client will be very unhappy.

Static invocation

Thankfully, Axis offers an alternative to the dynamic model. The static model, the preferred client model, represents a more intuitive, type-safe approach to developing your Web Service clients. The static model uses generated stubs that wrap up all the details of connecting to and invoking operations on your service. These stubs are created with the WSDL2Java tool described later in this chapter. The client for the static model is shown in Listing 34-3.

Listing 34-3: **TestStaticClient.java**

```
import MagicEightBall.*;

public class TestStaticClient {
    public static void main(String args[]) {
        try {
            MagicEightBallServiceServiceLocator svcLocator =
                            new MagicEightBallServiceServiceLocator();
            MagicEightBallService svc =
                            svcLocator.getMagicEightBallService();
```

Continued

Listing 34-3 *(continued)*

```
        String response = svc.getPrediction("Do static clients work?");
        System.out.println(response);
    } catch (Exception e) {
        System.out.println("failure" + e);
    }
  }
}
```

Deployment

Once you've gotten your Web Service built, the last thing you need to do to make it available to the world is to deploy it. Axis provides a few different models for deploying your service, each with its own pros and cons. The next two sections explore these models.

Dynamic deployment (JWS)

Dynamic deployment, which is sometimes referred to as Java Web Service (JWS) deployment, is one of the nicest features of the Axis implementation. It provides developers with a very simple approach to deploying an existing Java class as a service.

So, let's say you've just completed development of your new service (we'll call it `SampleService` for the purpose of this explanation), which is implemented in the file `SampleService.java`. In order to make this service available to clients, you need only perform the following two steps:

✦ Copy your `SampleService.java` file to Tomcat's `WEB-INF\axis` directory.

✦ Rename your SampleService.java file to SampleService.jws.

That's it. Your service is now officially online and accessible. Clients may invoke the operations on your service by accessing the following URL similar to the following (this will change based on your server name, port, and so on):

```
http://localhost:8080/axis/SampleService.jws
```

Once the service is online, we can also view the WSDL for the service by appending a WSDL parameter to the URL as follows:

```
http://localhost:8080/axis/SampleService.jws?WSDL
```

In many respects, this model is very much like the JSP model, where the extension on the file name triggers the server to perform special processing of that file. With Axis, when a client accesses a JWS service that has been deployed in the Axis context, the system will call the `AxisServlet`. This servlet will then assume responsibility for locating the file, compiling it, and transforming the incoming SOAP message into a valid Java invocation on the service.

Of course, this simplified deployment scheme comes at a cost. First, this model should really be constrained to fairly simple services. You really wouldn't want Axis attempting to compile complex services. Also, there are some limitations to what Axis developers can do with a dynamically deployed service. Here's a list of some of the constraints that are applied to a JWS deployment:

✦ **Security:** Services cannot support any level of authentication if they are deployed with the JWS model.

✦ **Type Mapping:** Dynamically deployed services do not allow developers to define custom type mappings. These services can only reference basic data types in their interface. So, if you want to pass around any of your own custom data types, this model is certainly not for you.

✦ **Method Visibility:** JWS deployments do not provide any mechanism for controlling which methods of your service are exposed to clients.

✦ **Custom Handlers:** Because JWS deployments cannot be configured by the server, they cannot make use of any of the Axis custom message-handling framework.

Given this set of limitations, it's clear that the JWS model is really targeted at small, simple services. The idea of deploying your native Java files and compiling them on the fly simply isn't practical for services of any real size or complexity.

WSDD deployment

If you think about it, what the JWS model achieves is quite impressive. The ability to take a plain Java file and have it transformed into a Web Service with such ease represents a significant accomplishment. Eventually, though, you're going to get to a point where you're going to want more control over how your service is deployed, how it maps types, and how messages are processed. That's where the WSDD (Web Service Deployment Descriptor) deployment comes in. With WSDD we overcome all those limitations that we encountered with the JWS model, opening the door to all the power and flexibility offered by the Axis implementation.

Working with WSDD files to configure your service can be a little time-consuming when you're ramping up on all the configuration options. Specifically, you'll need to learn to work through all the idiosyncrasies associated with type mapping. There's plenty of opportunity to introduce small problems in your WSDD file that aren't handled all that gracefully by the Axis WSDD deployment tools. That said, once you have worked though most of the common scenarios, this problem tends to fade to the background.

So, let's build a sample service that we can deploy using the WSDD model and see how the configuration file influences the shape of our service. In our example, we'll create a loan amortization service that will take the basic loan parameters and return an amortization schedule with a simple list of each payment and the balance remaining after that payment. For the purpose of our sample, we'll keep this very simple. Listing 34-4 is a listing of our `AmortizationManager` service.

Listing 34-4: **AmortizationManager Service**

```
package myservices.amortization;

public class AmortizationManager {
    public ScheduleItem[] getSchedule(double loanAmount,
                                      double interestRate,
                                      int duration) {
        ScheduleItem[] paymentList = new ScheduleItem[duration];
        int paymentNumber = 1;
        double totalLoan = loanAmount + (loanAmount / interestRate);
        double balance = totalLoan;
        double monthlyPayment = 0;

        while(balance > 0) {
            monthlyPayment = totalLoan / duration;
            if (balance < monthlyPayment) {
                monthlyPayment = balance;
                balance = 0;
            } else {
                balance -= monthlyPayment;
            }
            paymentList[paymentNumber-1] =
                    new ScheduleItem(paymentNumber, monthlyPayment, balance);
            paymentNumber++;
        }

        return paymentList;
    }
}
```

From our listing, you can see that our service supports one operation, `getSchedule()`, which returns an array of `ScheduleItem` objects. It's this return type, the array of `ScheduleItems`, that will force us to define a mapping in our

WSDD file that describes how Axis should map this data type during serialization and de-serialization. The `ScheduleItem` class is defined as shown in Listing 34-5.

Listing 34-5: **The ScheduleItem Class**

```
package myservices.amortization;

public class ScheduleItem implements java.io.Serializable {
    int paymentNumber = 0;
    double paymentAmount = 0;
    double balanceRemaining = 0;

    public ScheduleItem() {}

    public ScheduleItem(int paymentNumber,
                        double paymentAmount,
                        double balanceRemaining) {
        this.paymentNumber = paymentNumber;
        this.paymentAmount = paymentAmount;
        this.balanceRemaining = balanceRemaining;
    }

    public int getPaymentNumber() {
        return this.paymentNumber;
    }

    public double getPaymentAmount() {
        return this.paymentAmount;
    }

    public double getBalanceRemaining() {
        return this.balanceRemaining;
    }

    public void setPaymentNumber(int paymentNumber) {
        this.paymentNumber = paymentNumber;
    }

    public void getPaymentAmount(double paymentAmount) {
        this.paymentAmount = paymentAmount;
    }

    public void getBalanceRemaining(double balanceRemaining) {
        this.balanceRemaining = balanceRemaining;
    }
}
```

This class is a simple bean implementation that wraps up each of the data elements that are associated with a given payment. It conforms to the bean model and implements the serializable interface, allowing it to be handled by the bean serializer provided by Axis. In many instances, you'll package your own objects (that need to pass to and from the service) using this same approach.

Now we have our service implementation ready to go, but we need to put together the WSDD file that will be used to deploy the service. WSDD files are simply XML files that have a specific grammar for describing the configuration of your service. The configuration for our service is shown in Listing 34-6.

Listing 34-6: AmortizationManager.wsdd

```
<deployment name="test" xmlns="http://xml.apache.org/axis/wsdd/"
          xmlns:java="http://xml.apache.org/axis/wsdd/providers/java"
          xmlns:xsd="http://www.w3.org/2000/10/XMLSchema"
          xmlns:xsi="http://www.w3.org/2000/10/XMLSchema-instance">

   <service name="AmortizationService" provider="java:RPC">
       <parameter name="className" value="AmortizationManager" />
       <parameter name="allowedMethods" value="getSchedule" />
       <parameter name="scope" value="Application" />

       <beanMapping qname="ns1:ScheduleItem"
        xmlns:ns1="urn:AmortizationScheduleType"

        languageSpecificType="java:myservices.amortization.ScheduleItem"/>

       <typeMapping qname="ns1:ArrayOfScheduleItem"
         xmlns:ns1="urn:AmortizationScheduleType"
         type="java:myservices.amortization.ScheduleItem[]"
         serializer="org.apache.axis.encoding.ser.ArraySerializerFactory"
      deserializer="org.apache.axis.encoding.ser.ArrayDeserializerFactory"
         encodingStyle="http://schemas.xmlsoap.org/soap/encoding/" />
   </service>
</deployment>
```

Our WSDD file is broken into a few key sections. The first portion of the file calls out some global settings for our service, including its name, provider type, exposed methods, and scope. Scoping is of particular interest, since it determines when new instances of the service will be created. Axis supports three scoping options: request, session, and application. The request scope will cause Axis to create a new instance of the service for every request that is received. With session scoping, Axis will produce a single instance that will be used throughout the life of a client's session. Finally, selecting an application scope means there will only be a single instance of the service for all clients. Which scope you choose depends entirely upon the state requirements of your service.

The next two sections of the WSDD file are required to describe our `ScheduleItem[]` data type, which is returned by our service. First, we must describe the `ScheduleItem` class itself, so we can tell Axis how it is serialized. We achieve this by specifying the `BeanMapping` section of the WSDD, which will employ the bean interface to access and serialize/de-serialize the object's contents. The `BeanMapping` tag in the WSDD is basically a specialization of the `TypeMapping` tag that uses the `BeanSerializer` in place of the usual serializers. With the `BeanMapping` set up, all that remains is to set up the `TypeMapping` settings to describe the array of `ScheduleItems`.

Deploying with AdminClient

The final step in WSDD deployment is to register our WSDD service configuration with the Axis server. Axis provides a command-line administration utility, `AdminClient`, which will take our WSDD file and deploy its service configuration data to the global Axis configuration file. So, to deploy our Amortization sample to the Axis server, we would invoke the `AdminClient` as follows:

```
javac org.apache.axis.utils.client.AdminClient AmortizationManager.wsdd
```

After successfully completing this step, you should be able to peek into the Axis configuration file and see that your service's configuration options have been inserted into the file. Ideally, this would be the last step, but we still have one more key task to complete before we can say the deployment is done. We need to copy our actual compiled file(s) to the Axis classes directory. In our example, we would have two class files (`myservice\amortization\*.class`) that would need to be copied to the `<Tomcat dir>\axis\webapps\WEB-INF\axis\classes` directory.

At last, we're done. Well, kind of. Tomcat won't immediately load and publish the existence of our new service. The server must be stopped and restarted before our service will be available to clients. Once you've restarted the server, you'll be able to bring up the Axis administration page and view the list of deployed services, which will include our `AmortizationService`.

Remote administration

Via the WSDD, Axis allows each service to enable and disable support for remote administration. This is achieved by adding another parameter setting to your WSDD file.

```
<paramater name="enableRemoteAdmin" value="true">
```

Adding this option now means that administration options can be invoked from machines other than the server where the service is deployed. Naturally, there are certain security issues that are associated with opening your service up to remote administration. Typically, this option is left disabled and, in fact, if this parameter is not included with your configuration, remote administration will automatically be disabled.

WSDL Tools

WSDL (Web Service Description Language) is a technology-independent XML markup specification that is used to express the characteristics of your Web Service. As such, a WSDL file can be used by both client and service developers in the creation of code that will comply with a service's interface specification. Given the information that can be expressed in a WSDL file, it's only nature that Axis would leverage this information to help simplify the Web Service development cycle. The Java2WSDL and WSDL2Java utilities provided with Axis are both targeted at just this purpose. These two utilities work in concert, allowing developers to easily move back and forth between WSDL and Java.

WSDL2Java

WSDL2Java is a very useful tool that will take an incoming WSDL file and generate Java classes that are derived directly from signature of the operations and data types expressed in that file. In a simple scenario, this transformation is relatively straightforward. Essentially, the WSDL2Java tool generates Java classes for each of the data types along with a binding `impl` class that has methods for each of the operations on the service. Let's look at an example of WSDL for a simple Order service where we have one operation on the service, `getOrder()`, that looks up an Order by its ID and returns it in an Order object. Let's look at some snippets from the WSDL file for our service, as shown in Listing 34-7.

Listing 34-7: Order Service WSDL

```
...
<!-- type defs -->
<xsd:complexType name="order">
  <xsd:all>
    <xsd:element name="orderId" type="xsd:int"/>
    <xsd:element name="description" type="xsd:string"/>
  </xsd:all>
</xsd:complexType>

<!-- message declns -->
<message name="GetOrderRequest">
  <part name="orderId" type="xsd:int"/>
```

```
</message>

<message name="GetOrderResponse">
  <part name="order" type="typens:order"/>
</message>

<!-- port type declns -->
<portType name="OrderManager">
  <operation name="getOrder">
    <input message="tns:GetOrderRequest"/>
    <output message="tns:GetOrderResponse"/>
  </operation>
</portType>
```

Now, to generate the Java for this WSDL, we will invoke the WSDL2Java utility, passing in our WSDL file. The generated code will appear as shown in Listing 34-8.

Listing 34-8: **Order Service Generated Java**

```java
package orderGrabber2;
public class Order implements java.io.serializable {
    private int orderId;
    private java.lang.String description;

    public Order() {...}
    public int getOrderId() {...}
    public void setOrderId(int orderId) {...}
    public java.lang.String getDescription() {...}
    public void setDescription(java.lang.String description) {...}
}
...
public class OrderManagerSOAPBindingStub extends org.apache.axis.client.Stub
implements OrderGrabber2.OrderManager {
    ...
    ...

    public OrderGrabber2.Order getOrder(int orderId) throws
java.rmi.RemoteException {
        if (super.cachedEndpoint == null) {
            throw new org.apache.axis.NoEndPointException();
        }
        org.apache.axis.client.Call _call = createCall();
        _call.setOperation(_operations[0]);
        _call.setUseSOAPAction(true);
        _call.setSOAPActionURI("");
        _call.setSOAPVersion(org.apache.axis.soap.SOAPConstants.SOAP11_CONSTANTS);
```

Continued

Listing 34-8 *(continued)*

```
        _call.setOperationName(new javax.xml.namespace.QName("urn:
OrderGrabber2", "getOrder"));

        setRequestHeaders(_call);
        setAttachments(_call);
        java.lang.Object _resp = _call.invoke(new java.lang.Object[] {new
java.lang.Integer(orderId)});

        if (_resp instanceof java.rmi.RemoteException) {
            throw (java.rmi.RemoteException)_resp;
        }
        else {
            getResponseHeaders(_call);
            extractAttachments(_call);
            try {
                return (OrderGrabber2.Order) _resp;
            } catch (java.lang.Exception _exception) {
                return (OrderGrabber2.Order) org.apache.axis.utils.JavaUtils.
convert(_resp, OrderGrabber2.Order.class);
            }
        }
    }
}
```

Out of this process we received a series of files. However, in Listing 34-8, we focus on two key classes that are of particular interest. The first class, `Order`, is a bean compliant objects that wrappers all the data elements of our Order. It will be serialized and returned with each call to the `getOrder()` operation on the `OrderManager` service. While WSDL2Java generated a bean in this sample, the tool does not always yield a bean. The other class you see here is our binding object, which has a method that corresponds to the one operation supported by our service. WSDL2Java took care of filling this method in with all the details that are required to call our service.

While this translation was pretty simple, there are plenty of examples where a valid WSDL file cannot be turned directly into Java. For example, if one of the elements in your WSDL had a name that conflicted with a Java keyword, this would cause the generated Java to be invalid. To get around this problem, the WSDL2Java can reference metadata with mappings that will be used to resolve these translation issues.

So, how do we use this generated code? Listing 34-9 shows a simple client example that would use the generated classes to interact with our service.

Listing 34-9: **Using the Generated Classes**

```
public class TestOrderService {
    public static void main(String args[]) {
        try {
            OrderProcessingServiceLocator svcLocator =
                    new OrderProcessingServiceLocator();
            OrderManager orderMgr = svcLocator.getOrderManager();
            Order order = orderMgr.getOrder(123);
        } catch (Exception e) {
            System.out.println("failure" + e);
        }
    }
}
```

This class uses the `OrderProcessingServiceLocator`, which provides a method to retrieve an instance of the `OrderManager` class. Once we are able to retrieve this service reference, we can begin to make calls on the service that correspond to each of the operations appearing in the WSDL specification. The result is a very intuitive, very natural mode of interaction with your service. In reality, the WSDL2Java generated classes are so simple that you barely know you're working with a remote service.

Additional generation options

In this example, we focused our attention on generating a set of client-side classes to simplify the implementation of our client. However, WSDL2Java actually offers a series of options that can be selected to generate additional classes for use on server side. In fact, you should look over all the options to see what additional WSDL2Java features you might want to leverage.

Java2WSDL

Java2WSDL, as you might suspect, allows developers to generate a WSDL file from any existing Java class or interface. The WSDL generated by Java2WSDL contains all the appropriate WSDL types, messages, portType, bindings, and services descriptions that are required to conform with the SOAP specification. There are two primary uses for the resulting WSDL file. You could use it to publish the specifications of your interface to external consumers of your service. Or, you could use the WSDL as input into WSDL2Java to generate client stubs (as we did in our example above) that would simplify your client development.

Monitor SOAP Message with TCPMON

Debugging your Web Service can be challenging, especially since each message handled by Axis undergoes so much transformation. To assist in this area, Axis comes packaged with a utility, TCPMON, that can be used to monitor each SOAP request and response in its raw form.

There's actually nothing specific to Axis in the TCPMON tool. It is implemented as a simple proxy that sits between the client and the Axis server. TCPMON receives each request, extracts the request contest, then forwards the request along to the Axis server. When a response is generated, the response is intercepted by TCPMON where its contents are also extracted before forwarding the response to the client.

As you can see, this solution allows us to intercept and record the contents of every request and response exchanged between the client and Axis server. So, as you're debugging your Web Service, you'll be able to inspect each of your SOAP messages to see if they contain what you expect them to contain.

TCPMON setup

Before we can start sniffing messages, we need to bring up the TCPMON utility and add a monitor. TCPMON is started as follows:

```
java org.apache.axis.utils.tcpmon
```

This will bring up the TCPMON screen (shown in Figure 34-6), where we can add monitors for each server we want to monitor. For each monitor we add we need to specify the port that TCPMON is going to be running on, the IP address of the Axis server, and the port the Axis server is running on. If we just provide this basic information and press the Add button, TCPMON will add another tab to our screen configured with the supplied parameters.

Monitoring messages

Now, with the monitor added, you must use the monitor port number to access your Web Service. This will redirect each of your messages to TCPMON, which will then forward the request to the Axis port that was provided when you set up the monitor. As each of these messages is processed, they are added to the list of messages near the top of the monitor tab. Now, just select any message in this list and the request and response will be displayed in the bottom portion of the screen (as show in Figure 34-7).

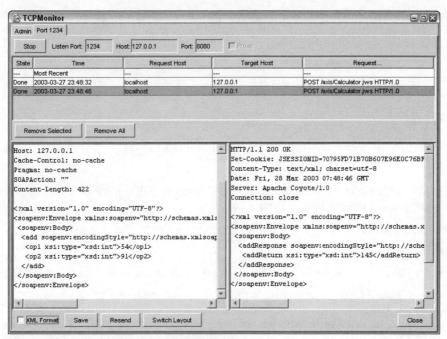

Figure 34-6: The TCPMON Admin screen

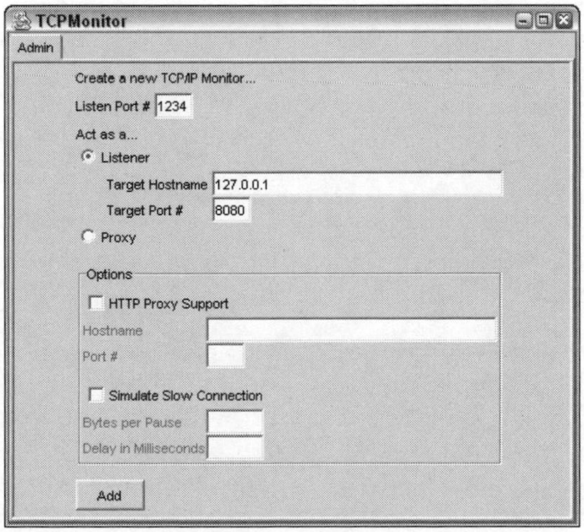

Figure 34-7: TCPMON messages

There are a few other options supported within the monitor tab, the most significant being the ability to resend a message directly from TCPMON. TCPMON will also allow you to add multiple monitors, where each monitor might represent the message activity of a given Axis server.

Summary

This chapter provided a glimpse into the functionality that is offered by Apache's Axis. The chapter covered the following topics:

✦ An overview of the Axis architecture, examining all the major subsystems that are part of the Axis implementation

✦ An example of a simple Web Service

✦ The JWS and WSDD deployment models

✦ The use of WSDL tools to simplify the development of Web Service clients

✦ Using the TCPMON utility to monitor message exchanges

As you begin to work with Axis, you're likely to find yourself digging into even more advanced topics that are outside the scope of this book. You should be able to see, however, that Axis is also relatively easy to get started with, allowing developers to ease their way into the subtle details that will likely influence how they build, deploy, and consume Web Services.

✦   ✦   ✦

Accessing Web Services from Java Applications

After the last few chapters, you should have a good idea of what a good J2EE Web service architecture should look like (Chapter 28). You should also be familiar with the tools that are used to build J2EE Web service applications using Apache AXIS (Chapter 34). In Chapter 21 we showed you how to convert a J2EE application into a multi-tier J2EE application. That application used servlets to serve MS SQL data to a J2EE client application. The connection between the client application and the servlet was made possible by an `ObjectInputStream` on the client side communicating with an `ObjectOutputStream` from the servlet.

In this chapter we've rewritten the servlet code that we developed for Chapter 21. It's a common task for a developer these days to upgrade a servlet-based application to a Web service application. By showing you how to adapt the code from Chapter 21, you get to see how to set up a Web service, and also how to convert servlets to Web services.

Instead of a servlet-to-J2EE client connection this time, we use Apache AXIS on the client side to create a SOAP envelope that is sent to the server. On the "server" (really just my workstation), we're using the Apache AXIS Simple Server, which is a very handy tool for developing and testing Web services.

When NOT to Use J2EE Web Services

In this chapter my example will show you how to serve Web services through a third-party application server such as WebSphere or Tomcat. On the client side we use a Java application as an example.

There is a lot of recent hype surrounding Web services. Quite often we see Web services oversold in boardrooms and in the press as the cure for all IT problems. However, despite the fact that Web services are a great solution for many problems, there are times when the application overhead of dealing with Web services is not worth the potential benefits. It's important to note that we don't show you how to serve Web services directly to a Web browser client. The reason for this is that Web service architectures are best suited to a multi-tier application environment that serves data to either a smart client or a portal. If you plan to just serve a SOAP envelope to a browser, and have the SOAP parsed and transformed directly to HTML, then Web service architecture is probably not the right choice. SOAP envelopes can be bulky and bandwidth-intensive to transport. Also, extracting data from a SOAP envelope and transforming it to HTML involves a lot of processor overhead. In this situation, we would either send the data from a servlet to the screen as HTML, or send a lightweight XML document format to a client or portal processor to be transformed.

Example: A Three-Tier System Combining Java Applications, Web Services, and Relational Data

In this section we'll convert the multi-tier J2EE servlet application that we created in Chapter 21 into a Web services application. The first Tier is the J2EE application, which provides the user interface. The next tier is made up of four J2EE Web services, which handle requests for data from the J2EE client application and retrieve data from the third-tier, which is the MS SQL Server and its associated databases. The connection between the Web services and SQL Server data is handled by JDBC.

Separating the user interface from the data access processes

The Java Application, called XMLPBWSApp.java, is based on the Swing UI classes and the AWT event classes. To the user, the application looks the same as the application in Chapter 21, but this time instead of running all the Java code on the client and accessing SQL Server data over the network or via servlets, the J2EE application makes calls to Web services on a J2EE server. This means that the J2EE client does not have to have access to .jar files for JDBC or servlets. This also means that the application handles client-side functionality only, and does not have to handle intensive data processing functions, such as generating XML documents from JDBC result sets. This division of processing makes each side of the application perform better than single-tier solution, and the addition of Web services adds another layer of flexibility in the application.

Prerequisites for Developing J2EE Web Services

Because you're developing Web services on a J2EE server for this example, there is a little work to be done in setting up the application. Before you get into application development, let's review some of the prerequisites for making this application run.

Downloading and installing AXIS

The first thing you need to do for this example is to install the latest implementation of the Apache SOAP toolkit, which has been renamed AXIS to keep us on our toes. Axis stands for Apache eXtensible Interaction System but is still based on the W3C SOAP Recommendation, with the equally inscrutable acronym of "Simple Object Access Protocol." The entire library can be downloaded from http://xml.apache.org as a .zip or .tar file and installed on the file system.

If you're running a J2EE application server, the axis subdirectory should be moved to the WEB-INF or WebApps directory, depending on the server. After that the server usually needs to be restarted.

Tip

If you want to test the application developed in this chapter without running an application server, the latest version of AXIS comes with a client-side server tool that can be used for testing Web services on a server or a development workstation. We'll show you how to use this in a later section of this chapter.

Once AXIS is downloaded and installed, edits are needed on the system CLASSPATH for the AXIS RPC router to function correctly. Please refer to the AXIS installation instructions for the latest details.

Deploying Web service class, WSDL, and WSDD files

The example in this chapter uses four Web services:

- ✦ **XMLPBWSServletGetAuthorList** gets a list of unique quote authors for display in the J2EE Application.

- ✦ **XMLPBWSServletGetSingleAuthorList** gets a list of quotes for a single author.

- ✦ **XMLPBWSServletBuildElementXML** returns a quotation in element-based XML format.

- ✦ **XMLPBWSServletBuildAttributeXML** returns a quotation in attribute-based XML format.

Each Web service is associated with a Web Service Description Language (WSDL) file and a Web Service Deployment Descriptor (WSDD) file. Each associated file has the same name as the Web service class file. We'll cover what each of these file types does later in the chapter. For now, you just need to know enough about them to set them up.

All the Web services in this example and associated files can be downloaded from the XMLProgrammingBible.com Website, in the Downloads section.

Running Web services on a J2EE application server

After downloading all related Web Service files from the XMLProgrammingBible.com Website, copy the Class files and the Web Service Deployment Descriptor (WSDD) files to the AXIS\class directory on the J2EE server or the Development workstation. In a J2EE server environment, the WSDD Files can be locate elsewhere if your organization has rules against loading WSDD files in the class directory.

After copying the files, consult the J2EE application server's documentation for instructions on deploying Web services and editing the WSDD files with any required server-specific variables.

Running the Web services without a J2EE server

The latest version of AXIS contains an implementation of a simple Web services RPC router and server environment, called the Simple Server. The Simple Server can be run from a command line without installing a J2EE server, so it's easy to set up and maintain on most computers. The server is single threaded, which makes it great for testing, but not appropriate for a production environment.

Run the AXIS simple SOAP server

Once AXIS is downloaded, installed, and configured, open a command window and type the following command at the prompt:

```
java org.apache.axis.transport.http.SimpleAxisServer -p 8080
```

You should get a message that says:

```
- SimpleAxisServer starting up on port 8080.
```

This indicates that the server has started. There is no confirmation message; this is the last message that runs in the DOS Prompt widow.

 Note The prompt window needs to be kept open for the Simple AXIS Server to run.

Deploying the Web services to the AXIS simple SOAP server

After loading the AXIS Simple SOAP Server, the Java class files need to be deployed and registered on the server. The WSDD files handle the details of setting this up on a J2EE application server or the AXIS simple server. If you're using a J2EE server, refer to that server's documentation for Web service deployment instructions. If you're using the AXIS simple server, open a second command window and go to the AXIS/Class directory where the Java class and WSDD files should be located. Type the following four commands:

```
java org.apache.axis.client.AdminClient
deployXMLPBWSServletGetAuthorList.wsdd
```

```
java org.apache.axis.client.AdminClient
deployXMLPBWSServletGetSingleAuthorList.wsdd
```

```
java org.apache.axis.client.AdminClient
deployXMLPBWSServletBuildElementXML.wsdd
```

```
java org.apache.axis.client.AdminClient
deployXMLPBWSServletBuildAttributeXML.wsdd
```

We'll discus the contents of the WSDD files a bit later, for now you just need to know that these commands load the Java class files into the server and establish rules for running and accessing the Web services.

Testing the server status and deployment

To test the server implementation and ensure that the Web services are deployed, open a Web browser window and type the following URL, substituting the IP address if necessary:

```
http://127.0.0.1:8080/axis
```

You should get a basic HTML Web page that looks like this:

```
Content-Type: text/html; charset=utf-8 Content-Length: 977
And now... Some Services
AdminService (wsdl)
AdminService
XMLPBWSServletBuildAttributeXML (wsdl)
GetSingleQuoteAttribute
XMLPBWSServletBuildElementXML (wsdl)
GetSingleQuoteElement
XMLPBWSServletGetAuthorList (wsdl)
GetAuthorList
XMLPBWSServletGetSingleAuthorList (wsdl)
GetSingleAuthorList
Version (wsdl)
getVersion
```

This page confirms that the Web services have been deployed. There are two system Web services at the top and bottom of the page, and the rest of the service listed are your Web service classes that were deployed by your prompt commands. Each service is followed by a single method name for each class, which is registered on the server by the WSDD file.

Tip

If there is an error on this screen, or not all of the classes and methods are installed, the first place to check is the AXIS CLASSPATH settings. If the CLASSPATH is set up okay, then check the location of the class and WSDD files.

Installing the XMLPBWSApp J2EE application

The XMLPBWSApp.class file should be installed in a directory of a workstation that is accessible to the Java JDK.

On
The
Web

The XMLPBWSApp application and all of the Web service files can be downloaded from the XMLProgrammingBible.com Website, in the Downloads section.

Installing the WSDL files

The WSDL files should be loaded on the same J2EE server as the Java class files. They don't have anything to do with the functionality of the Web service, but the WSDL files should be located in the HTML directory of the J2EE application server in a production environment. If any UDDI entries refer to the Web service, the discovery URL for the WSDL file should be published in the UDDI entry or other references to the Service, such as an entry at Xmethods.com.

Running the Web service client

Once the application is downloaded and all of the installation steps have been completed, run the application by typing "java XMLPBWSApp" from a command prompt or the Windows "Run" menu option. The application will appear on the screen in its own Java window.

Developing Web Services

As we've mentioned a few times in this chapter, the Quote XML Generator – Web Service Edition application is an adaptation of the servlet-based multi-tier application in Chapter 21. In this section we'll take you "under the hood" of one of the four Web services to show you how the Java class file, the J2EE, and the WSDL files all work together to create a Web service.

Inside the XMLPBWSServletGetAuthorList Web service

The code in Listing 35-1 shows a Web service that returns a unique listing of quote authors from a MS SQL Server database via JDBC. The class starts by making a JDBC connection to the MS SQL server XMLProgrammingBible database. Next, an MS SQL Server JDBC driver instance is created. A connection is defined to the SQL Server instance. In this case, we're running the SQL Server instance and the J2EE application on the same machine, so the IP address is the home IP address of the machine - 127.0.0.1. The JDBC user and password for the database are set up in the connection string. Because the XMLProgrammingBible database is specified in the connection string, we don't need to explicitly name the database in my SQL server query.

A JDBC result set object is created, which is the result of the query string passed to the SQL server. An array is built from the result set with the buildArray class, which we'll show you in the next listing. Once the result set is processed, the connection and the result set are dropped. The contents of the author list object are created by the array and passed to the application window.

The SQL command, select AuthorName from Authors, selects all of the values in the AuthorName column of the Authors table. The buildArray class that is used by the GetAuthorList and GetSingleAuthorList classes to build an array from an SQL Server JDBC result set. An ArrayList is created, which is an implementation of the List interface. The most important feature of ArrayLists for the purposes of this code is that they are automatically resizable, via the `add()` method.

 Note   We have explicitly specified `java.util.List` because the `java.awt` package also has a List interface.

The JDBC specification contains a `.toArray()` method for result sets, which would be great for this purpose. However, not all JDBC drivers implement a complete set of methods for JDBC classes. The code in the `buildArray` class can be used when the `toArray()` method is not supported, as is the case with the MS SQL Server JDBC driver, or when you want all JDBC result set array output to be the same regardless of driver-specific formatting.

An SQL Server result set is passed from the calling object and an `ArrayList` is defined called `arrayResults`. The code loops through the result set and retrieves the current result set row value as a string. SQL Server result set values returned by the SQL Server JDBC driver sometimes contain leading and trailing blanks, so the trim() method is sued to trim spaces off the string as it is created. The string is added to the `arrayResults` object using the `ArrayList.add()` method. Next, a string array called `sarray` is created, and the value of the `ArrayList` is passed to the string array using the `ArrayList.toArray()` method.

The `buildArray` class creates a string array from the JDBC result set, which is passed to the J2EE application that called the Web service via a SOAP envelope.

Listing 35-1: The XMLPBWSServletGetAuthorList Web Service Code

```
import java.util.*;
import java.io.*;
import java.sql.*;

public class XMLPBWSServletGetAuthorList {


    public String [] GetAuthorList() {
        String authorList [] = null;
        String sql = "select AuthorName from Authors";

        try {

            Class.forName("com.microsoft.jdbc.sqlserver.SQLServerDriver");
            Connection conn =  DriverManager.getConnection
            ("jdbc:microsoft:sqlserver://127.0.0.1:1433;
            User=jdbcUser;Password=jdbcUser;
            DatabaseName=XMLProgrammingBible");
```

```
        Statement s = conn.createStatement();
        ResultSet rs = s.executeQuery(sql);

        authorList = buildArray(rs);

        rs.close();
        conn.close();
    }catch(Exception e) {
        e.printStackTrace();
    }

    return authorList ;

}

String[] buildArray(ResultSet rs) {
    java.util.List arrayResults = new ArrayList();
    try {
        int rownumber= 0;
        String rowvalue = new String();
        while(rs.next()) {
            rownumber++;
            rowvalue = rs.getString(rownumber++);
            arrayResults.add(rowvalue.trim());
        }
    }catch(Exception e) {}
    String[] sarray = (String[]) arrayResults.toArray(new
    String[arrayResults.size()]);
    return sarray;
}

}
```

Next, we'll show you how the WSDL and WSDD files work together with the Java class to make a Web service.

The XMLPBWSServletGetAuthorList WSDL and WSDD files

Each Web service in the Quote XML Generator – Web Service Edition application has two files associated with it — :a Web Services Description Language (WSDL) file and a Web Service Deployment Descriptor (WSDD) file. We'll explain the files associated with the XMLPBWSServletGetAuthorList class as a guide for all four Web services. Each WSDL and WSDD file is virtually the same as its counterparts, except for the names of the classes, the names of the methods, and the data types returned. Listing 35-2 shows the WSDD file associated with the XMLPBWSServletGetAuthorList Web service.

Deployment descriptors are well-formed XML documents that control Web service deployment, security, and administration. The deployment descriptor declares the name of the Web service and two XML namespaces. Next, the Service data-binding format is defined as Java remote procedure calls (RPC). The RPC router on the server parses incoming SOAP RPC requests and extracts data from a SOAP envelope. Responses from the Web service are wrapped in a response SOAP envelope by the same RPC router.

Next, the service's class name is defined as XMLPBWSServletGetAuthorList. Access to all methods contained in the Web service is permitted by the wildcard character (*) in the allowedMethods parameter.

Listing 35-2: The XMLPBWSServletGetAuthorList WSDD File

```
<deployment
    xmlns="http://xml.apache.org/axis/wsdd/"
    xmlns:java="http://xml.apache.org/axis/wsdd/providers/java">
  <!-- Services from XMLPBWSServletGetAuthorListService WSDL service -->
  <service name="XMLPBWSServletGetAuthorList" provider="java:RPC">
      <parameter name="wsdlTargetNamespace"
       value="http://www.xmlprogrammingbible.com/wsdl/default/"/>
      <parameter name="wsdlServiceElement"
       value="XMLPBWSServletGetAuthorListService"/>
      <parameter name="wsdlServicePort"
       value="XMLPBWSServletGetAuthorList"/>
      <parameter name="className"
       value="com.xmlprogrammingbible.www.
       XMLPBWSServletGetAuthorListSoapBindingSkeleton"/>
      <parameter name="wsdlPortType" value="XMLPBWSServletGetAuthorList"/>
      <parameter name="allowedMethods" value="*"/>
      <typeMapping xmlns:ns=
       "http://www.xmlprogrammingbible.com/wsdl/default/"
       qname="ns:ArrayOf_soapenc_string"
       type="java:java.lang.String[]"
       serializer="org.apache.axis.encoding.ser.ArraySerializerFactory"
       deserializer="org.apache.axis.encoding.ser.
       ArrayDeserializerFactory"
       encodingStyle="http://schemas.xmlsoap.org/soap/encoding/"
      />
  </service>
</deployment>
```

The deployment descriptor describes a Web service from a J2EE server point of view. A WSDL file describes the same Web service from a client point of view. As mentioned in Chapter 25, reading a WSDL file can be a daunting task, but it's best to keep in mind that if everything goes well, humans should rarely have to read a WSDL file themselves. WSDL files are a way of defining a Web service interface programmatically to another Web service, smart client, or portal. Listing 35-3 shows the WSDL interface for the XMLPBWSServletGetAuthorList Web service.

The WSDL file declares several XML namespaces, which are used to define WSDL structure and SOAP data types. Next, data types are defined as parts of call and response messages. The messages become part of ports, which become part of operations. The Web service is defined as one or more operation. Last, the endpoint address for the Web service is specified in the location attribute of the wsdlsoap:address element.

Listing 35-3: **The XMLPBWSServletGetAuthorList WSDL File**

```
<wsdl:definitions xmlns="http://schemas.xmlsoap.org/wsdl/"
xmlns:apachesoap="http://xml.apache.org/xml-soap"
xmlns:impl="http://www.xmlprogrammingbible.com/wsdl/default/-impl"
xmlns:intf="http://www.xmlprogrammingbible.com/wsdl/default/"
xmlns:soapenc="http://schemas.xmlsoap.org/soap/encoding/"
xmlns:wsdl="http://schemas.xmlsoap.org/wsdl/"
xmlns:wsdlsoap="http://schemas.xmlsoap.org/wsdl/soap/"
xmlns:xsd="http://www.w3.org/2001/XMLSchema"
targetNamespace="http://www.xmlprogrammingbible.com/wsdl/default/">
  <wsdl:types>
    <schema targetNamespace="http://www.xmlprogrammingbible.com
    /wsdl/default/" xmlns="http://www.w3.org/2001/XMLSchema">
      <import namespace="http://schemas.xmlsoap.org
      /soap/encoding/"/>
      <complexType name="ArrayOf_soapenc_string">
        <complexContent>
          <restriction base="soapenc:Array">
            <attribute ref= "soapenc:arrayType"
            wsdl:arrayType="soapenc:string[]"/>
          </restriction>
        </complexContent>
      </complexType>
      <element name="ArrayOf_soapenc_string" nillable="true"
      type="intf:ArrayOf_soapenc_string"/>
    </schema>
  </wsdl:types>
  <wsdl:message name="GetAuthorListResponse">
    <wsdl:part name="return" type="intf:ArrayOf_soapenc_string"/>
  </wsdl:message>
  <wsdl:message name="GetAuthorListRequest">

  </wsdl:message>
  <wsdl:portType name="XMLPBWSServletGetAuthorList">
```

Continued

Listing 35-3 *(continued)*

```
  <wsdl:operation name="GetAuthorList">
    <wsdl:input name="GetAuthorListRequest"
     message="intf:GetAuthorListRequest"/>
    <wsdl:output name="GetAuthorListResponse"
     message="intf:GetAuthorListResponse"/>
  </wsdl:operation>
</wsdl:portType>
<wsdl:binding name="XMLPBWSServletGetAuthorListSoapBinding"
 type="intf:XMLPBWSServletGetAuthorList">
  <wsdlsoap:binding style="rpc"
   transport="http://schemas.xmlsoap.org/soap/http"/>
  <wsdl:operation name="GetAuthorList">
    <wsdlsoap:operation/>
    <wsdl:input>
      <wsdlsoap:body use="encoded"
       encodingStyle="http://schemas.xmlsoap.org/soap/encoding/"
       namespace="http://www.xmlprogrammingbible.com/wsdl/default/"/>
    </wsdl:input>
    <wsdl:output>
      <wsdlsoap:body use="encoded"
       encodingStyle="http://schemas.xmlsoap.org/soap/encoding/"
       namespace="http://www.xmlprogrammingbible.com/wsdl/default/"/>
    </wsdl:output>
  </wsdl:operation>
</wsdl:binding>
<wsdl:service name="XMLPBWSServletGetAuthorListService">
  <wsdl:port name="XMLPBWSServletGetAuthorList"
   binding="intf:XMLPBWSServletGetAuthorListSoapBinding">
    <wsdlsoap:address location="http://127.0.0.1/
     XMLPBWSServletGetAuthorList"/>
  </wsdl:port>
</wsdl:service>
</wsdl:definitions>
```

Putting the WSDD, Class, WSDL, and SOAP together

So far this may look like much more work than the application and servlet examples
in Chapter 21. Keep in mind that each interface plays an important role in dividing
the labor of each component of the application. This separation of functionality
also adds flexibility to the application. For example, the deployment descriptor can
be used to redirect calls to another Java class file or another platform entirely without having to change the name, location, or functionality of the Web service.

As we mentioned earlier, the Web service WSDL file is not important for the day-to-day functionality of the Web service. However, the WSDL file is very useful for specifying the format for SOAP call and response related to the Web service. Many Web service clients can read the WSDL file for a Web service and dynamically adapt the calling agent interface to the serving agent.

Listing 35-4 shows a sample SOAP envelope contents that is generated by the XMLPBWSServletGetAuthorList WSDL file. The Method name in the SOAP call maps directly to the incoming message in the WSDL file. The GetAuthorList method call maps to the WSDL GetAuthorList operation.

Listing 35-4: A Sample XMLPBWSServletGetAuthorList SOAP Call

```
<SOAP-ENV:Envelope xmlns:SOAP-ENV="http://schemas.xmlsoap.org/
soap/envelope/" xmlns:SOAP-ENC="http://schemas.xmlsoap.org/soap/
encoding/" xmlns:xsi="http://www.w3.org/2001/XMLSchema-instance"
xmlns:xsd="http://www.w3.org/2001/XMLSchema">
  <SOAP-ENV:Body>
    <m:GetAuthorList
    xmlns:m="http://www.xmlprogrammingbible.com
    /wsdl/default/" SOAP-
    ENV:encodingStyle="http://schemas.xmlsoap.org/
    soap/encoding/"/>
  </SOAP-ENV:Body>
</SOAP-ENV:Envelope>
```

The XMLPBWSServletGetSingleAuthorList Web service

The XMLPBWSServletGetSingleAuthorList Web service is called when a user clicks on a quote author in the J2EE client application. The CategoryName parameter is passed to the Web service in the SOAP request envelope. This triggers a JDBC query on the Authors and Quotations tables in the XMLProgrammingBible database. The buildArray class builds an array from the JDBC result set.

The Web service returns an array of quotes for the author back to the J2EE client application in a SOAP response envelope. The RPC router on the server converts the string array to an XML-based SOAP string array format. Listing 35-5 shows the XMLPBWSServletGetSingleAuthorList code.

Listing 35-5: **The XMLPBWSServletGetSingleAuthorList Web Service Code**

```
import java.util.*;
import java.io.*;
import java.sql.*;

public class XMLPBWSServletGetSingleAuthorList {

    public String [] GetSingleAuthorList(String CategoryName) {
        String singleauthorList [] = null;
        String sql = "SELECT dbo.Quotations.Quotation FROM dbo.Quotations
        INNER JOIN dbo.Authors ON dbo.Quotations.AuthorID
         = dbo.Authors.AuthorID INNER JOIN dbo.Sources ON
        dbo.Quotations.SourceID = dbo.Sources.SourceID WHERE
        (dbo.Authors.AuthorName = '"+CategoryName+"')";
        String fromrow="1";
        String torow="50";
        String threshold="50";

        try {

            Class.forName("com.microsoft.jdbc.sqlserver.SQLServerDriver");
            Connection conn =
            DriverManager.getConnection("jdbc:microsoft:sqlserver:
            //127.0.0.1:1433;User=jdbcUser;Password=jdbcUser;
            DatabaseName=XMLProgrammingBible");
            Statement s = conn.createStatement();
            ResultSet rs = s.executeQuery(sql);
            singleauthorList = buildArray(rs);

            rs.close();
            conn.close();
        }catch(Exception e) {
            e.printStackTrace();
        }

        return singleauthorList ;

    }

    String[] buildArray(ResultSet rs) {
        java.util.List arrayResults = new ArrayList();
        try {
            int rownumber= 0;
            String rowvalue = new String();
            while(rs.next()) {
```

```
                    rownumber++;
                    rowvalue = rs.getString(rownumber++);
                    arrayResults.add(rowvalue.trim());
            }
        }catch(Exception e) {}
        String[] sarray = (String[]) arrayResults.toArray(new
        String[arrayResults.size()]);
        return sarray;
    }

}
```

The XMLPBWSServletBuildElementXML Web service

The code in Listing 35-6 is called when a quote is selected by a user and the output option is set to `"Element XML (Table=Root, Field Name=Element)"`. A string containing the quote formatted as an XML document is passed from the `GetSingleQuoteElement` class back to the Web service as a string. Previous examples returned arrays of strings representing quote authors or a list of quotes for a single author.

The `buildElementXML` class generates custom element-based XML document for the SQL Server output. The first thing the `buildElementXML` class does is create a new `StringBuffer` in which to store the XML document. An XML document declaration is sent to the `StringBuffer`, along with a root element, called `resultset`. Next, an element called `sql` is created, which contains the SQL Server query that was used to generate the result set. The code also retrieves the JDBC result set metadata into the XML document. This information can be used by applications to parse the XML values by data type and column name. We also use the metadata column name to name the elements that represent columns in the XML document.

Rows of data are returned as children of a `records` element. Because the result of a query is always a single row, a single `record` element contains the column values. Column values are stored in text data, and column names are represented as element names. The `entityRefs` and `StringReplace` classes work together to convert illegal XML characters in the text data (&, ', >, <, and ") into legal entity reference values.

The `buildElementXML` class retrieves the XML document from the `StringBuffer` and returns the XML document to the calling object as a string. The XML output string is passed back to the RPC Router on the server, which passes the result back to the Java application inside a SOAP response envelope.

Listing 35-6: The XMLPBWSServletBuildElementXML Web Service Code

```java
import java.sql.*;
import java.util.*;
import java.io.*;

public class XMLPBWSServletBuildElementXML {

    public String GetSingleQuoteElement(String PassedQuote) {
        String XMLDoc=null;

        String sql = "SELECT dbo.Quotations.Quotation,
        dbo.Authors.AuthorName, dbo.Sources.[Source Name]
        FROM dbo.Quotations INNER JOIN dbo.Authors ON
        dbo.Quotations.AuthorID = dbo.Authors.AuthorID
        INNER JOIN dbo.Sources ON dbo.Quotations.SourceID =
        dbo.Sources.SourceID WHERE (dbo.Quotations.Quotation =
        '"+PassedQuote+"')";
        String fromrow="1";
        String torow="50";
        String threshold="50";

        try {

            Class.forName("com.microsoft.jdbc.sqlserver.SQLServerDriver");
            Connection conn =
            DriverManager.getConnection("jdbc:microsoft:sqlserver:
            //127.0.0.1:1433;User=jdbcUser;Password=jdbcUser;
            DatabaseName=XMLProgrammingBible");
            Statement s = conn.createStatement();
            ResultSet rs = s.executeQuery(sql);
            XMLDoc = buildElementXML(rs, sql);

            rs.close();
            conn.close();
        } catch(Exception e) {
            e.printStackTrace();
        }

        return XMLDoc ;

    }


    String buildElementXML(ResultSet rs, String sql) {
        StringBuffer strResults = new StringBuffer("<?xml version=\"1.0\"
        encoding=\"UTF-8\"?>\r\n<resultset>\r\n");
        try {
            strResults.append("<sql>" + sql +" </sql>\r\n");
            ResultSetMetaData rsMetadata = rs.getMetaData();
```

```java
        int intFields = rsMetadata.getColumnCount();
        strResults.append("<metadata>\r\n");
        for(int h =1; h <= intFields; h++) {
            strResults.append("<field name=\"" +
            rsMetadata.getColumnName(h) + "\" datatype=\"" +
            rsMetadata.getColumnTypeName(h) + "\"/>\r\n");
        }
        strResults.append("</metadata>\r\n<records>\r\n");

        int rownumber= 0;
        while(rs.next()) {
            rownumber++;
            strResults.append("<record
            rownumber=\""+rownumber+"\">\r\n");
            for(int i =1; i <= intFields; i++) {
                strResults.append("<" + rsMetadata.getColumnName(i) +
                ">" + entityRefs(rs.getString(i).trim()) +
                "</"+rsMetadata.getColumnName(i) +">\r\n");

            }
            strResults.append("</record>\r\n");
        }
    }catch(Exception e) {}
    strResults.append("</records>\r\n</resultset>");
    System.out.println(strResults.toString());
    return strResults.toString();
}

String entityRefs(String XMLString) {
    String[] before = {"&","\'",">","<","\""};
    String[] after = {"&amp;","&apos;","&gt;","&lt;","&quot;"};
    if(XMLString!=null) {
        for(int i=0;i<before.length;i++) {
            XMLString = stringReplace(XMLString, before[i], after[i]);
        }
    }else {XMLString="";}
    return XMLString;
}

String stringReplace(String stringtofix, String textstring, String
xmlstring) {
    int position = stringtofix.indexOf(textstring);
    while (position > -1) {
        stringtofix = stringtofix.substring(0,position) + xmlstring +
        stringtofix.substring(position+textstring.length());
        position = stringtofix.indexOf(textstring,position+
        xmlstring.length());
    }
    return stringtofix;
}


}
```

The XMLPBWSServletBuildAttributeXML Web service

The code in Listing 35-7 is called when a quote is selected by a user and the output option is set to `"Attribute XML (Table=Root, Field Name=Attribute)"`. The `buildAttributeXML` class is used to create a custom attribute-based XML document for the SQL Server output. It's very similar to the `buildElementXML` class, but this time the code produces row data as attributes of a single element, instead of multiple nested elements under a `records` element.

The first thing the `buildAttributeXML` class does is create a new `StringBuffer` in which to store the XML document. An XML document declaration is sent to the `StringBuffer`, along with a root element, called `resultset`. Next, an element called `sql` is created, which contains the SQL Server query that was used to generate the result set. Metadata is also retrieved into the XML document, which can be used by applications XML result values by data type and column name. We also use the metadata column name to name the elements that represent columns in the XML document.

Row data is returned as a child of the `records` element. Because the results contain a single row, a single `record` element contains all of the column values as attributes. Column values are stored in text data, and column names are represented as element names. The `entityRefs` class converts any illegal XML characters in the text data (&, ', >, <, and ") into legal entity references for those values.

The `buildAttributeXML` class retrieves the XML document from the `StringBuffer` and returns the XML document to the calling object as a string. The XML output string is passed back to the RPC Router on the server, which passes the result back to the Java application inside a SOAP response envelope.

Listing 35-7: The XMLPBWSServletBuildAttributeXML Web Service Code

```
import java.util.*;
import java.io.*;
import java.sql.*;

public class XMLPBWSServletBuildAttributeXML {

    public String GetSingleQuoteAttribute(String PassedQuote) {
        String XMLDoc=null;

        String sql = "SELECT dbo.Quotations.Quotation,
        dbo.Authors.AuthorName, dbo.Sources.[Source Name]
        FROM dbo.Quotations INNER JOIN dbo.Authors
        ON dbo.Quotations.AuthorID = dbo.Authors.AuthorID
        INNER JOIN dbo.Sources ON dbo.Quotations.SourceID =
        dbo.Sources.SourceID WHERE (dbo.Quotations.Quotation =
        '"+PassedQuote.trim()+"')";
        String fromrow="1";
```

```
        String torow="50";
        String threshold="50";

        try {

            Class.forName("com.microsoft.jdbc.sqlserver.SQLServerDriver");
            Connection conn =
            DriverManager.getConnection("jdbc:microsoft:sqlserver:
            //127.0.0.1:1433;User=jdbcUser;Password=jdbcUser;
            DatabaseName=XMLProgrammingBible");
            Statement s = conn.createStatement();
            ResultSet rs = s.executeQuery(sql);
            XMLDoc = buildAttributeXML(rs, sql);

            rs.close();
            conn.close();
        } catch(Exception e) {
            e.printStackTrace();
        }

        return XMLDoc ;

    }

    String buildAttributeXML(ResultSet rs, String sql) {
        StringBuffer strResults = new StringBuffer("<?xml version=\"1.0\"
        encoding=\"UTF-8\"?>\r\n<resultset>\r\n");
        try {
            strResults.append("<sql>" + sql +" </sql>\r\n");

            ResultSetMetaData rsMetadata = rs.getMetaData();
            int intFields = rsMetadata.getColumnCount();
            strResults.append("<metadata>\r\n");
            for(int h =1; h <= intFields; h++) {
                strResults.append("<field name=\"" +
                rsMetadata.getColumnName(h) + "\" datatype=\"" +
                rsMetadata.getColumnTypeName(h) + "\"/>\r\n");
            }
            strResults.append("</metadata>\r\n<records>\r\n");


            int rownumber= 0;

            while(rs.next()) {
                rownumber++;
                strResults.append("<record rownumber=\""+rownumber+"\"");
                for(int i =1; i <= intFields; i++) {
                    strResults.append(" "+rsMetadata.getColumnName(i) + " =
                    \"" + entityRefs(rs.getString(i).trim()) + "\"");
                }
                strResults.append("/>\r\n");
            }
```

Continued

Listing 35-7 *(continued)*

```
    }catch(Exception e) {}
    strResults.append("</records>\r\n</resultset>");
    System.out.println(strResults.toString());
    return strResults.toString();


}

String entityRefs(String XMLString) {
    String[] before = {"&","\'",">","<","\""};
    String[] after = {"&amp;","&apos;","&gt;","&lt;","&quot;"};
    if(XMLString!=null) {
        for(int i=0;i<before.length;i++) {
            XMLString = stringReplace(XMLString, before[i], after[i]);
        }
    }else {XMLString="";}
    return XMLString;
}

String stringReplace(String stringtofix, String textstring, String
xmlstring) {
    int position = stringtofix.indexOf(textstring);
    while (position > -1) {
        stringtofix = stringtofix.substring(0,position) + xmlstring +
        stringtofix.substring(position+textstring.length());
        position =
        stringtofix.indexOf(textstring,position+xmlstring.length());
    }
    return stringtofix;
}


}
```

Inside the XMLPBWSApp J2EE Client Application

The XMLPBWSApp J2EE client application is a fully functional Java Application that uses Swing Classes and AWT events to generate a UI. The J2EE client makes SOAP calls to Web services, which connect to relational data on MS SQL server using JDBC. The Web services manipulate the JDBC query result sets and return responses to the J2EE client application.

How the application works

When the application window is opened, a Web service is called that retrieves a list of unique quote authors. The Web service retrieves data from the Authors table of the XMLProgrammingBible database on SQL Server. The connection from the Web service to the SQL Server databases is made via JDBC. The application then draws the various Swing panels on the page and attaches AWT events to the panels. Users can scroll up and down the list of quote authors in the author List panel, and select a single author by clicking on it in the list.

Clicking on an author name triggers another call to another Web service. That Web service query to retrieve all the quotes attributed to the selected author. The quotes are displayed in the quote list panel on the top right of the screen.

When a user clicks on one of the quotes in the quote list panel, another J2EE Web service is called to generate XML document output for the selected quote and display it in the output panel in the lower half of the application window. In the middle of the screen is a combo box that can be used to select output format options. Table 35-1 lists the four options and what they produce:

Table 35-1 Quote Output Formatting Options	
Just the Quote	Generates plain quote text in the output window.
Element XML (Table=Root, Field Name=Element)	JDBC metadata and columns of a table represented as elements nested in a parent `record` element.
Attribute XML (Table=Element, Field Name=Attribute)	JDBC metadata and columns of a table represented as attributes in a `record` element.

Aside from being a good J2EE Web Services application prototype, the Quote XML Web Service application is also a good example of applying a user interface to SQL Server data. It's also a good prototype for any application that uses Web services, JDBC, and Java GUI classes. The application contains examples of accessing and displaying SQL Server data in several different ways, including strings, arrays, and XML documents.

About the example SQL Server data

In this chapter we're reusing tables from the XMLProgrammingBible SQL Server database. Setup instructions for the database can be found in Chapter 18.

Creating the Java Application User Interface

 We have broken down the source code into segments that relate to a specific topic, rather than showing the source code in its entirety on the pages. All of the examples contained in this chapter can be downloaded from the XML ProgrammingBible.com Website, in the Downloads section. Please see the Website for installation Instructions.

Defining public variables and the application window

Let's look under the hood of the Java Application by breaking down the Java Application source code into topical sections with detailed explanations of the code, starting with the introductory application setup in Listing 35-8.

The J2EE client application imports the `java.io` classes for writing to the screen, `javax.swing` classes to handle UI features and selected `java.awt` classes to manage action events. The `org.apache.axis` and `java.rmi` classes are used to create SOAP envelopes and make calls to Web services.

The beginning of the code sets up a `Jframe` window, which becomes the application window, and creates an instance of an `actionlistener` to watch for the window to be closed. When the window is closed, the application exits.

Listing 35-8: Defining the Public Variables and the Application Window

```
import javax.swing.*;
import javax.swing.event.*;
import java.util.*;
import java.awt.*;
import java.awt.event.*;
import java.io.*;
import java.net.*;
import org.apache.axis.*;
import org.apache.axis.client.*;
import java.rmi.*;
import org.apache.axis.encoding.*;
import org.apache.axis.utils.*;

public class XMLPBWSApp extends JPanel {
    JTextArea output;
    JList authorList;
    JList QuoteList;
    ListSelectionModel authorListSelectionModel;
    ListSelectionModel QuotelistSelectionModel;
```

```
public String[] listData;
JComboBox comboBox;

public static void main(String[] args) {
    JFrame frame = new JFrame("Quote XML Generator - Web Service
    Edition");
    frame.addWindowListener(new WindowAdapter() {
        public void windowClosing(WindowEvent e) {
            System.exit(0);
        }
    });

    frame.setContentPane(new XMLPBWSApp());
    frame.pack();
    frame.setVisible(true);
}
```

Setting objects in the window and implementing ActionListeners

Listing 35-9 shows the code that is used to define the main UI on top of the application window. The first task is to retrieve a unique list of quote authors from the SQL Server Authors table calling the `GetAuthorList()` class, which I will cover a bit later.

Once this is done, the `AuthorList` object is created, and an `AuthorList SelectionHandler` object is attached to the list. When users click on a quote author, the `AuthorListSelectionHandler` class is called to handle the action. Next, a `JscrollPane` called `SourcePane` is created for the list object, and the pane is placed in the top left of the application window.

The instantiation steps are repeated for the `QuoteList` object, which will be used to display quotes for a selected author on the top right of the application window. A `QuoteListSelectionHandler` object is attached to the quote list.

Next, a drop-down combo box containing the application output options is created, which will be located in the center of the application window, just below the author list and quote list panes. The hard-coded output options are defined and the default is set to the first object.

A `JtextArea` object is defined and placed in the bottom half of the application window. This is where the XML and text output is sent when a user selects a quote from the quote list.

The balance of the code in Listing 35-9 is Swing and AWT class housekeeping to create the details of the layout that the user interface needs.

Listing 35-9: **Setting Objects in the Window and Implementing ActionListeners**

```java
public XMLPBWSApp() {
super(new BorderLayout());


listData = GetAuthorList();
String[] WelcomeMessage={"Click on a Source in the Left Pane to
Retrieve Quotes"};

authorList = new JList(listData);

authorListSelectionModel = authorList.getSelectionModel();
authorListSelectionModel.addListSelectionListener(
new authorListSelectionHandler());
JScrollPane SourcePane = new JScrollPane(authorList);

QuoteList = new JList(WelcomeMessage);
QuotelistSelectionModel = QuoteList.getSelectionModel();
QuotelistSelectionModel.addListSelectionListener(
new QuoteListSelectionHandler());
JScrollPane QuotePane = new JScrollPane(QuoteList);

JPanel OutputSelectionPane = new JPanel();
String[] OutputFormats = { "Just the Quote", "Element XML
(Table=Root, Field Name=Element)",
"Attribute XML (Table=Element, Field Name=Attribute)"};

comboBox = new JComboBox(OutputFormats);
comboBox.setSelectedIndex(0);
OutputSelectionPane.add(new JLabel("Select an output Format:"));
OutputSelectionPane.add(comboBox);

output = new JTextArea(1, 10);
output.setEditable(false);
output.setLineWrap(true);
JScrollPane outputPane = new JScrollPane(output,
ScrollPaneConstants.VERTICAL_SCROLLBAR_ALWAYS,
ScrollPaneConstants.HORIZONTAL_SCROLLBAR_AS_NEEDED);

JSplitPane splitPane = new JSplitPane(JSplitPane.VERTICAL_SPLIT);
add(splitPane, BorderLayout.CENTER);

JPanel TopPanel = new JPanel();
TopPanel.setLayout(new BoxLayout(TopPanel, BoxLayout.X_AXIS));
JPanel SourceContainer = new JPanel(new GridLayout(1,1));
SourceContainer.setBorder(BorderFactory.createTitledBorder(
```

```
"Source List"));
SourceContainer.add(SourcePane);
SourcePane.setPreferredSize(new Dimension(300, 100));
JPanel QuoteContainer = new JPanel(new GridLayout(1,1));
QuoteContainer.setBorder(BorderFactory.createTitledBorder(
"Quote List"));
QuoteContainer.add(QuotePane);
QuotePane.setPreferredSize(new Dimension(300, 500));
TopPanel.setBorder(BorderFactory.createEmptyBorder(5,5,0,5));
TopPanel.add(SourceContainer);
TopPanel.add(QuoteContainer);

TopPanel.setMinimumSize(new Dimension(400, 50));
TopPanel.setPreferredSize(new Dimension(400, 300));
splitPane.add(TopPanel);

JPanel BottomPanel = new JPanel(new BorderLayout());
BottomPanel.add(OutputSelectionPane, BorderLayout.NORTH);
BottomPanel.add(outputPane, BorderLayout.CENTER);
BottomPanel.setMinimumSize(new Dimension(400, 50));
BottomPanel.setPreferredSize(new Dimension(800, 400));
splitPane.add(BottomPanel);
}
```

Listings 35-10 and 35-11 show the AWT Class `ActionListeners`, which facilitate the UI functionality in the application.

Defining the action for the Author list

Listing 35-10 shows the code that is called when a user clicks on a quote author. When the `ActionListener` detects that the user has selected a quote author, the `GetSingleAuthorList` class is called, which returns a single-column listing of quotes for that author. The quotes are displayed in the quote list object on the top right of the application window.

Listing 35-10: Defining the Action for the Author List

```
class authorListSelectionHandler implements ListSelectionListener {
    public void valueChanged(ListSelectionEvent se) {
        ListSelectionModel slsm = (ListSelectionModel)se.getSource();
        String [] s = GetSingleAuthorList(authorList.getSelectedValue()
        .toString());
        QuoteList.setListData(s);

    }
}
```

Defining the action for the Quote list

When a user selects a quote by clicking on a selection in the quote list, the code in Listing 35-11 is called. When the `ActionListener` detects that the user has selected a Quote, the `QuoteListSelectionHandler` checks the combo box to see which output format is selected by the user.

If `"Just the Quote"` is selected, the quote is sent to the output object as text. If the `"Element XML (Table=Root, Field Name=Element)"` option is chosen, the `GetSingleQuoteElement` class is called to generate Custom XML for the output, with SQL Server table column values formatted as elements in the XML document. If `"Attribute XML (Table=Element, Field Name=Attribute)"` is chosen, the `GetSingleQuoteAttribute` is called to generate result set table column values as attributes.

Listing 35-11: Defining the Actions for the Quote List

```
class QuoteListSelectionHandler implements ListSelectionListener {
    public void valueChanged(ListSelectionEvent qe) {
        ListSelectionModel qlsm = (ListSelectionModel)qe.getSource();
        String OutputFormatChoice = (String)comboBox.getSelectedItem();

        if (OutputFormatChoice.equals("Just the Quote")) {
            output.setText(QuoteList.getSelectedValue().toString());
        }

        else if (OutputFormatChoice.equals("Element XML (Table=Root,
        Field Name=Element)")) {
            output.setText(GetSingleQuoteElement
            (QuoteList.getSelectedValue().toString(
            ))); }
        else if (OutputFormatChoice.equals("Attribute XML
        (Table=Element, Field Name=Attribute)")) {
            output.setText(GetSingleQuoteAttribute
            (QuoteList.getSelectedValue().toString()));}
        else {
            output.setText(QuoteList.getSelectedValue().toString());
        }


    }
}
```

Retrieving a list of authors by calling a Web service

The code in Listing 35-12 returns a unique listing of quote authors by calling the `XMLPBWSServletGetAuthorList` Web service. A new instance of a SOAP call is created and assigned a Web service target endpoint of `http://127.0.0.1:8080/ axis/servlet/AxisServlet`. This endpoint accesses the AXIS Simple Server, which contains an RPC router. The RPC router parses the SOAP envelope and the HTTP POST Header, extracts a request object from the SOAP envelope, and routes the request to the appropriate Web service class. The routing of the request object is based on the current deployment descriptor configuration.

The `GetAuthorList` class in the `XMLPBWSServletGetAuthorList` Web service processes a JDBC query against the SQL server database and returns a result set. A new instance of a string array is created using standard SOAP encoding of data type `ArrayOf_xsd_string`. Converting data types from their native types to SOAP or other types of encoding is an integral part of Web services, and allows typed data to flow between platforms and operating systems by being serialized and de-serialized on sending and delivery of the SOAP envelope. The string array is passed back to the RPC router. The RPC router then wraps the response object in a SOAP response envelope and sends the response back to the J2EE client application. The string array result is extracted from the SOAP response envelope by the AXIS call object. The response is assigned to the `AuthorList` string array variable, which is passed back to the application for display in the UI.

Listing 35-12: Retrieving a List of Authors from the SQL Server Authors Table

```
public String [] GetAuthorList() {
      String AuthorList [] = null;

      try{
          Service   service = new Service();
          Call call = (Call) service.createCall();
          call.setTargetEndpointAddress( new
          java.net.URL("http://127.0.0.1:8080/axis/servlet/AxisServlet")
          );
          call.setOperationName( new
          javax.xml.namespace.QName("XMLPBWSServletGetAuthorList",
          "GetAuthorList") );
          call.setReturnType(new
          javax.xml.namespace.QName("http://www.xmlprogrammingbible.com/
          wsdl/default/", "ArrayOf_xsd_string"));
          AuthorList = (String [] ) call.invoke( new Object[] {});
      }

      catch(Exception e) {
          e.printStackTrace();
      }
      return AuthorList ;

   }
```

Retrieving a list of quotes from a selected author

When a user clicks on a quote author, the `ActionListener` for the author list object passes the author name as a string value to the `GetSingleAuthorList` Class, shown in Listing 35-13. This class uses the passed value, called `Category Name`, to retrieve all the quotes for an author using an SQL query passed to the server via JDBC.

The `GetSingleAuthorList` class is similar to the `GetAuthorList` class. `GetSingleAuthorList` in the `XMLPBWSServletGetSingleAuthorList` Web service passes a parameter value to a JDBC query against the SQL server database and returns a result set. A new instance of a string array is created using standard SOAP encoding of data type `ArrayOf_xsd_string`. The string array is passed back to the RPC router. The RPC router then wraps the response object in a SOAP response envelope and sends the response back to the J2EE client application. The string array result is extracted from the SOAP response envelope by the AXIS call object. The response is assigned to the `singleAuthorList` string array variable, which is passed back to the application for display in the UI. The contents of the quote list object are then created by the array and the quote list object is displayed in the upper-right panel of the application window.

Listing 35-13: **Retrieving Quotes for an Author**

```
public String [] GetSingleAuthorList(String CategoryName) {
    String singleAuthorList [] = null;

    try{
        Service  service = new Service();
        Call call = (Call) service.createCall();
        call.setTargetEndpointAddress( new
        java.net.URL("http://127.0.0.1:8080/axis/servlet/AxisServlet")
        );
        call.setOperationName( new
        javax.xml.namespace.QName("XMLPBWSServletGetSingleAuthorList",
        "GetSingleAuthorList") );
        call.addParameter( "CategoryName", XMLType.XSD_STRING,
        javax.xml.rpc.ParameterMode.IN );
        call.setReturnType(new
        javax.xml.namespace.QName("http://www.xmlprogrammingbible.com/
        wsdl/default/", "ArrayOf_xsd_string"));
        singleAuthorList = (String [] ) call.invoke( new Object[]
        {CategoryName});
    }

    catch(Exception e) {
        e.printStackTrace();
    }
```

```
        return singleAuthorList ;

}
```

Generating Custom XML Output

When a user clicks on a quote, a call is triggered to the `QuoteListSelection Handler`, which is outlined in Listing 35-11. This triggers one of three actions, depending on the output format chosen in the combo box. The first action is to send the plain text directly to the output object. The code in Listing 35-14 is called when a quote is selected in the quote list object and the `Element XML (Table=Root, Field Name=Element)` option is chosen from the output format combo box. The quote text is passed to the `GetSingleQuoteElement` class. This class calls a Web service to retrieve the quote from SQL Server and format the XML as an element-based XML document.

The `GetSingleQuoteElement` class in the `XMLPBWSServletBuildElementXML` Web service passes a parameter value containing a quotation to a JDBC query. The JDBC query returns a result set. A new instance of a string is created using standard SOAP encoding of data type `xsd_string`. The string is formatted as an element-based XML document and passed back to the RPC router. The RPC router then wraps the response object in a SOAP response envelope and sends the response back to the J2EE client application. The string result is extracted from the SOAP response envelope by the AXIS call object. The response is assigned to the `XMLDoc` string variable, which is passed back to the application for display in the UI. The contents of the string are displayed in the lower panel of the application.

Listing 35-14: **Retrieving Custom XML from a Web Service**

```
public String GetSingleQuoteElement(String PassedQuote) {
        String XMLDoc=null;

        try{
            Service  service = new Service();
            Call call = (Call) service.createCall();
            call.setTargetEndpointAddress( new
            java.net.URL("http://127.0.0.1:8080/axis/servlet/
            AxisServlet") );
            call.setOperationName( new
            javax.xml.namespace.QName("XMLPBWSServletBuildElementXML",
            "GetSingleQuoteElement") );
```

Continued

Listing 35-14 *(continued)*

```
        call.addParameter( "PassedQuote", XMLType.XSD_STRING,
        javax.xml.rpc.ParameterMode.IN );
        call.setReturnType(new
        javax.xml.namespace.QName("http://www.xmlprogrammingbible.com/
        wsdl/default/", "string"));
        XMLDoc = (String ) call.invoke( new Object[] {PassedQuote});
    }

    catch(Exception e) {
        e.printStackTrace();
    }


    return XMLDoc ;

}
```

Listing 35-15 shows a typical element-based XML document that is returned by the XMLPBWSServletBuildElementXML Web service.

Listing 35-15: Custom XML Output Generated by the XMLPBWSServletBuildElementXML Web Service

```
<?xml version="1.0" encoding="UTF-8"?>
<resultset>
  <sql>SELECT dbo.Quotations.Quotation, dbo.Authors.AuthorName,
  dbo.Sources.[Source Name] FROM dbo.Quotations INNER JOIN dbo.Authors ON
  dbo.Quotations.AuthorID = dbo.Authors.AuthorID INNER JOIN dbo.Sources ON
  dbo.Quotations.SourceID = dbo.Sources.SourceID WHERE
  (dbo.Quotations.Quotation = 'When the hurlyburlys done, When the battles
  lost and won.') </sql>
  <metadata>
    <field name="Quotation" datatype="char"/>
    <field name="AuthorName" datatype="char"/>
    <field name="Source Name" datatype="char"/>
  </metadata>
  <records>
    <record rownumber="1">
      <Quotation>When the hurlyburlys done, When the battles lost and
      won.</Quotation>
      <AuthorName>Shakespeare, William</AuthorName>
      <SourceName>Macbeth</SourceName>
    </record>
  </records>
</
```

The GetSingleQuoteAttribute class in the XMLPBWSServletBuild AtrtributeXML Web service also passes a parameter value containing a quotation to a JDBC query. The JDBC query returns a result set and a new instance of a string is created using standard SOAP encoding of data type xsd_string. The string is formatted as an attribute-based XML document and passed back to the RPC router. The RPC router then wraps the response object in a SOAP response envelope and sends the response back to the J2EE client application. The string result is extracted from the SOAP response envelope by the AXIS call object. The response is assigned to the XMLDoc string variable, which is passed back to the application for display in the UI. The contents of the string are displayed in the lower panel of the application. Listing 35-16 shows the code for the GetSingleQuoteAttribute class in the J2EE client application.

Listing 35-16: Custom XML Output Generated by the XMLPBWSServletBuildAttributeXML Web Service

```
public String GetSingleQuoteAttribute(String PassedQuote) {
      String XMLDoc=null;

      try{
          Service  service = new Service();
          Call call = (Call) service.createCall();
          call.setTargetEndpointAddress( new
          java.net.URL("http://127.0.0.1:8080/axis/servlet/AxisServlet")
           );
          call.setOperationName( new
          javax.xml.namespace.QName("XMLPBWSServletBuildAttributeXML",
          "GetSingleQuoteAttribute") );
          call.addParameter( "PassedQuote", XMLType.XSD_STRING,
          javax.xml.rpc.ParameterMode.IN );
          call.setReturnType(new
          javax.xml.namespace.QName("http://www.xmlprogrammingbible.com
          /wsdl/default/", "string"));
          XMLDoc = (String ) call.invoke( new Object[] {PassedQuote});
      }

      catch(Exception e) {
          e.printStackTrace();
      }


      return XMLDoc ;

  }
```

Listing 35-17 shows an example of an Attribute-based XML document created by the XMLPBWSServletBuildAttributeXML Web service.

Listing 35-17: Custom XML Output Generated by the GetSingleQuoteAttribute Class

```
<?xml version="1.0" encoding="UTF-8"?>
<resultset>
  <sql>SELECT dbo.Quotations.Quotation, dbo.Authors.AuthorName,
  dbo.Sources.[Source Name] FROM dbo.Quotations INNER JOIN dbo.Authors ON
  dbo.Quotations.AuthorID = dbo.Authors.AuthorID INNER JOIN dbo.Sources ON
  dbo.Quotations.SourceID = dbo.Sources.SourceID WHERE
  (dbo.Quotations.Quotation = 'When the hurlyburlys done, When the battles
  lost and won.') </sql>
  <metadata>
    <field name="Quotation" datatype="char"/>
    <field name="AuthorName" datatype="char"/>
    <field name="Source Name" datatype="char"/>
  </metadata>
  <records>
    <record rownumber="1" Quotation="When the hurlyburlys done, When the
     battles lost and won." AuthorName="Shakespeare, William"
     SourceName="Macbeth"/>
  </records>
</resultset>
```

Summary

In this chapter we've provided an example of a multi-tier J2EE Web Service application that works with XML documents and relational data. We showed you how to implement the server solution suing SXIS, WSDL, and WSDD documents. We also showed you how to create a J2EE client application to access Web service data.

  ✦ A multi-tier J2EE Web service application

  ✦ Using JDBC with Web service applications

  ✦ Controlling custom XML formats using Web services

  ✦ A Three-tier J2EE application combining Java applications, servlets, and JDBC

  ✦ Accessing Web services from a J2EE application

The next two chapters delve much deeper into Web service architectures. We'll cover XML and Web service transactions and how to handle Web service security and authentication, among other things.

✦   ✦   ✦

Advanced Web Services

Part VIII covers RDBMS support for Web services. We also delve into the developing standards associated with Web service security. Standards-based options for Web service encryption, signatures, and authentication are discussed in detail in Chapter 37.

Accessing Relational Data via Web Services

Relational database vendors have not ignored Web services. Most RDBMS vendors have added features to their database products that handle WSDL and SOAP. In most cases, the Web service features are an extension of XML features in the same product.

In this chapter we'll cover the ways that MS SQL Server, IBM DB2, and Oracle databases support Web services. We'll outline each vendor's methods for Web service support. We'll show examples of setting up a SQL Server Web service using IIS and SQLXML. We'll discuss implementation of Web services on Oracle9iAs Application Server. We'll also introduce you to DB2 Web service features, including the Web services Object Runtime Framework (WORF). WORF and Document Access Definition Extension (DADX) files. We'll finish off the chapter by showing you an example that uses a DB2 Web service in a multi-tier J2EE Web service environment.

MS SQL Server and Web services

MS SQL Server provides Web service support via SQLXML and the MS Internet Information Server (IIS) HTTP server. Before you can create Web services that access SQL Server data, IIS must be running on the same machine as the SQL Server instance. You also have to download and install SQLXML 3.0 or higher and set up a virtual HTTP server root that is enabled for SOAP. If you already are running a version of SQLXML that is older than version 3.0, you will have to download and install the latest version to support SOAP functionality. At the time that we are writing this chapter, the current version is SQLXML 3.0 SP1. You can download the latest version of SQLXML from `http://www.microsoft.com/sql/techinfo/xml/default.asp`.

Installing and configuring SQLXML

Once SQLXML is downloaded and installed, applications can make SOAP calls to SQL Server stored procedures and User-Defined Functions (UDFs). Microsoft Internet Information Server (IIS) provides the services that convert SOAP requests to stored procedure or UDF calls.

The IIS Virtual Directory Management for SQL Server utility can be accessed by selecting "Configure SQLXML Support in IIS" from the SQL Server start menu options. The utility creates an association between a virtual directory on the IIS server and SQL Server data. A URL containing the IIS server address, the virtual directory, and an SQL expression can be passed from a Web browser or an application over HTTP to the IIS server. The IIS server will route the request to the SQL server based on the virtual directory name. Security and port information that is preconfigured in the virtual directory connects the request to a database for execution. The help associated with the IIS configuration tool covers all of the setup details. We do, however, have a few additional tidbits that may be useful for the setup:

✦ TCPIP must be enabled via the network utility, and the port must be configured to port 1433.

✦ Windows and SQL server login support must be enabled (the default is "Windows Only").

✦ A version of SQLXML must be loaded and installed. For the examples in this chapter, SQLXML 3.0 SP1 should be installed. The examples may work with older SQLXML installations, but have not been tested with anything other than the most recent version.

Configuring IIS Virtual Directory Management Web Services

The current IIS configuration tool help is a little coy when defining settings for SQL Server Web services, so we've provided the following example to take you though the steps.

Open the IIS configuration tool by choosing the "Configure IIS Support" option from the SQLXML menu.

Create a new virtual directory under the default directory by right-clicking on the Default Website, and choosing New⇨Virtual Directory from the pop-up menu.

Under the general tab, choose a name for the new virtual directory. We name mine XMLPBWS (XML Programming Bible Web Services). Create a new folder with the path from the wwwroot directory:

```
C:\Inetpub\wwwroot\XMLPBWS
```

Note We always create new directory for Web services versus other SQLXML functions such as templates. This splits the security away from the regular SQL functions. It also makes it less confusing to find and maintain WSDL files, templates, etc.

Under the Security Tab, choose "Use Windows Integrated Authentication" if you're working on the same machine as the SQL Server instance (recommended). Otherwise, provide the connection info to the server.

Under the Data Source tab, choose the server name or (local). Select the default database for login. Define the database later in your UDF or stored procedure if you're not accessing the default database.

Under the settings tab, select Allow POST. Web service request envelopes are sent over HTTP as a POST.

Under the virtual names tab, create the name of the Web service. If you want to make it confusing, you can use something other than the name of the virtual directory. We use the same name (XMLPBWS). For the type, choose SOAP so that SOAP envelopes can be sent and received. Use the same path as specified for the virtual directory:

```
C:\Inetpub\wwwroot\XMLPBWS
```

Figure 36-1 shows the Virtual Names tab of the XMLPBWS Web service.

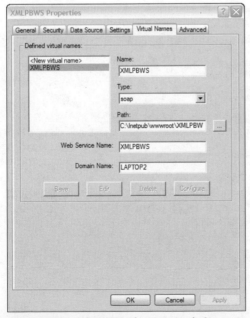

Figure 36-1: The Virtual Names tab for an SQL Server Web service

Now you have a Web service set up with a name of XMLPBWS, but the Web service doesn't actually do anything yet. Next, you have to add methods that the Web service will use. Web services refer to these methods as actions. To do this, select the XMLPBWS virtual name from the Virtual Names tab. Click on the "Configure" button on the lower-right side of the dialog box. Create a method name for the Web service, and link it to a stored procedure or a user-defined function. We use the same name for the stored procedure and the Web service to avoid confusion in the future. Set up the output formatting according to your needs (output formatting is covered in the help, and We will discuss it later in this chapter). Repeat this step for each method that should be part of the Web service.

Figure 36-2 shows the GetAuthorList method of the XMLPBWS Web service. This method namemaps to the GetAuthorList stored procedure in the XMLPBWS database.

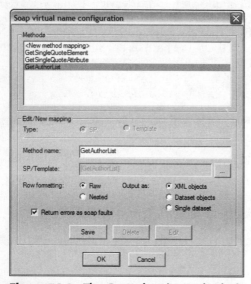

Figure 36-2: The GetAuthorList method of the XMLPBWS Web service

Below is the `GetAuthorList` stored procedure. As you can see here, `GetAuthor List` contains a very simple query that returns all of the column values from the Authors table.

```
CREATE PROCEDURE GetAuthorList AS select * from Authors
GO
```

Handling Microsoft Web service data in other platforms

So far we have created a Web service and added a method. When the XMLPBWS Web service is defined, a new, blank WSDL file is created. Each time a new Web service method is added using the "Configure" button of the Virtual Names tab, a new Web service operation is added into the WSDL file with the same name. The WSDL file is located in the virtual directory that you specified when you set up the Web service. Web service clients can now read the WSDL file and call the Web service using a SOAP envelope with no parameters. The body of the envelope looks like this:

```
<SOAP-ENV:Body>
    <m:GetAuthorList xmlns:m="http://LAPTOP2/XMLPBWS/XMLPBWS"/>
</SOAP-ENV:Body>
```

A Web service client calls the Web service using its URL. The element name contains the name of the method to use (GetAuthorList). The URL maps to the stored procedure using the methods defined in the virtual names tab. A W3C standard SOAP request envelope containing the above envelope body is sent to the Web service. A response envelope is returned. That's where things get tricky with MS Web services. Some readers may have heard about incompatibilities between MS SOAP envelopes and other kinds of SOAP envelopes. This is very true at the API level.

Most software platforms have developed a way of reading WSDL files and generating object code that can access Web services. Microsoft provides APIs for this functionality through the .NET framework and the MS SOAP toolkit. Java developers can use the Apache AXIS and the WSDL2Java class to generate Java objects from WSDL. Both APIs function well on Web services that restrict them selves to the W3C SOAP data types and W3C Schema data types. This includes simple data types by themselves, and complex data types that are derived from simple data types.

 Cross-Reference   For more information on the WSDL2Java class and its use, please refer to Chapter 34.

Microsoft has chosen to provide complex data type names on their return data that are incompatible with anything described in the W3C schema or SOAP recommendations. These data types are specifically named, but not specifically defined. Following is a sample response body of the SQLXML response that is generated by the GetAuthorList Web service. For this example, the GetAuthorList method has been configured to return "XML Objects" in the IIS configuration tool. The result is broken into two data types. The AuthorListResult is an SqlResult Stream, and the contents of the result stream is SqlXml. These are not W3C standard data types. The content in the result, however, does not consist of anything that could not be a W3C standard data type. Also, the content of a dynamic data type such as SqlXml cannot be specifically defined, because the contents differ for each Web service and method that uses this data type.

MS SOAP toolkit and .NET applications read and accept these data types without the user having to code custom data types into their Web service client applications. MS applications also fully support W3C Web services and standard data types. Developers can work with objects that are created, rather than having to hand-code object handlers that map to XML elements. However, the use of these data types means that other APIs, such as the Apache AXIS WDSL2Java class, cannot create objects based on these data types. Instead, a J2EE has to hand-code a class with methods that define and accept the SqlXml data type, and parse the data into something useful to Java.

```
<SOAP-ENV:Body>
    <tns:GetAuthorListResponse>
        <tns:GetAuthorListResult xsi:type="sqlresultstream:SqlResultStream">
            <sqlresultstream:SqlXml xsi:type="sqltypes:SqlXml"
             sqltypes:IsNested="false">
              <SqlXml>
                <row>
                    <AuthorID>1001</AuthorID>
                    <AuthorName>Shakespeare, William</AuthorName>
                </row>
                <row>
                    <AuthorID>1002</AuthorID>
                    <AuthorName>Joyce, James</AuthorName>
                </row>
              </SqlXml>
            </sqlresultstream:SqlXml>
            <sqlresultstream:SqlResultCode xsi:type="sqltypes:SqlResultCode"
             sqltypes:IsNested="false">0</sqlresultstream:SqlResultCode>
        </tns:GetAuthorListResult>
    </tns:GetAuthorListResponse>
</SOAP-ENV:Body>
```

By contrast, Oracle and DB2 Web services return W3C standard data types for row data. In DB2, you also have the option of just passing XML in the envelope body, without data type definitions. We'll show you an example of a DB2 Web service later in this chapter.

Note   Oracle's application server now has a set of classes that reads and manages MS Web service data types. This feature is implemented in the latest version of the Oracle 9i Application Server (Oracle9iAS).

The MS DataSet data type is even more complex, though it does contain some useful information. For this example, the GetAuthorList method has been configured to return "DataSet Objects" in the IIS configuration tool. The data that is returned in a DataSet is preceded by a W3C schema. The schema contains metadata describing the structure of the data and the W3C data types for each data element in the result envelope. This is similar to JDBC result sets, which provide optional metadata for results. The metadata can be used by the receiving application to analyze and manipulate the data in the result set. Unfortunately, the data is wrapped in a non-W3C standard `SqlRowSet` data type, which only MS .NET and SOAP toolkit applications can handle. MS and .NET Web services use the provided schema to create objects, therefore dynamically defining the previously indefinable `SqlRowSet` data type. If there were an option for omitting the `sqlResultStream` and `SqlRowSet` data types from the Web service definitions, other platforms could work with MS Web services in the same way. However, non-MS developers are once again left on their own to manually read the result envelope and develop handler classes to extract and parse the data from within the `SqlRowSet` data type.

```
<SOAP-ENV:Body>
    <tns:GetAuthorListResponse>
      <tns:GetAuthorListResult xsi:type="sqlresultstream:SqlResultStream">
        <sqlresultstream:SqlRowSet
         xmlns:sqlresultstream="http://schemas.microsoft.com/
        SQLServer/2001/12/SOAP/types/SqlResultStream"
         xmlns:xsi="http://www.w3.org/2001/XMLSchema-instance"
         xsi:type="sqltypes:SqlRowSet" sqltypes:IsNested="false">
         <xsd:schema id="Schema1"
           xmlns:xsd="http://www.w3.org/2001/XMLSchema"
           xmlns:msdata="urn:schemas-microsoft.com:xml-msdata">
            <xsd:element name="rowset" msdata:IsDataSet="true">
              <xsd:complexType>
                <xsd:choice maxOccurs="unbounded">
                  <xsd:element name="row">
                    <xsd:complexType>
                      <xsd:sequence>
                        <xsd:element name="AuthorID" minOccurs="0"
                          type="xsd:int"/>
                        <xsd:element name="AuthorName" minOccurs="0"
                          type="xsd:string"/>
                      </xsd:sequence>
                    </xsd:complexType>
                  </xsd:element>
                </xsd:choice>
              </xsd:complexType>
            </xsd:element>
          </xsd:schema>
          <diffgr:diffgram xmlns:msdata="urn:schemas-microsoft-com:xml-
            msdata" xmlns:diffgr="urn:schemas-microsoft-com:xml-diffgram-
            v1">
          <rowset>
            <row>
              <AuthorID>1001</AuthorID>
              <AuthorName>Shakespeare, William</AuthorName>
            </row>
            <row>
              <AuthorID>1002</AuthorID>
              <AuthorName>Joyce, James</AuthorName>
            </row>
```

```
            </rowset>
          </diffgr:diffgram>
        </sqlresultstream:SqlRowSet>
        <sqlresultstream:SqlResultCode xsi:type="sqltypes:SqlResultCode"
          sqltypes:IsNested="false">0</sqlresultstream:SqlResultCode>
      </tns:GetAuthorListResult>
    </tns:GetAuthorListResponse>
  </SOAP-ENV:Body>
```

As you can see from these examples, the current crop of MS Web service tools are great for consuming Web services, but not so great for providing universal multi-platform Web services. Consequently, many Web service providers are creating non-MS Web service providers, or routing the SOAP envelope though an application server, where the SOAP contents are parsed and reformatted.

MS tools are great for quickly creating smart Web service clients. We hope that someday they will be as good at providing smart Web services to any client application. In the meantime, other vendors are adapting in the name of cross-platform compatibility. The most recent release of Oracle's jDeveloper includes a feature called ".NET Web services interoperability," which handles dynamic MS data types such as SqlRowSet and SqlXml as part of J2EE applications.

Oracle and Web services

Oracle has implemented Web service provider functionality through the Oracle 9i Application server (Oracle9iAS). Oracle9i Web services rely on J2EE connections such as JDBC and JMS to make the connection between the Oracle database and the Oracle application server. The application server receives SOAP requests and translated the request into a database connection. When the database returns a response, the application server repackages the response as SOAP and sends it back to the calling agent.

Because the Oracle9iAS is a J2EE application server, you can use regular J2EE Web service packages such as Apache AXIS. However, most of Oracle's Web service and XML packages are based on (Java Community Process) JCP JSRs, but are developed in-house. Oracle9iAS also supports JAXB standards for binding WSDL to Java objects. Oracle also supports its own UDDI server that is compatible with IBM and MS UDDI browser applications.

The Oracle9iAS and the jDeveloper development tool add several customized facilities for Web services on top of the standard J2EE functionality. One unique feature is that Oracle9iAS applications can access .Net Web services that use MS dynamic data types. This provides the ability for J2EE Web service clients to handle regular SOAP and schema data types and MS dynamic data types at the object level like an MS Web service client.

Oracle can expose servlets, EJBs, and Java classes on the Oracle9iAS, and PL/SQL or Java stored procedures on the database server. It supports dynamic generation of these objects when they are registered as Web services. Web services are registered and described on an Oracle9iAS server via `config.xml` files.

The only Web service functionality that is not part of Oracle9iAs is consuming Web services from an Oracle application. For this, an optional SOAP client can be set up as part of an Oracle9i database server's JVM. The Database server can then run triggers or scheduled batch jobs that pull data in from external Web services into Oracle tables.

Oracle has also created a portal server called OmniPortlet. OmniPortlet features allow end-users to select and configure a customized portal page that supports dynamic Web service client generation along with other data delivery and display formats.

Most of the example DB2 multi-tier J2EE application that we show you later in this chapter could be easily adapted for the Oracle9iAs and Oracle databases. We'll point out the places where changes need to be made as we go though those examples.

DB2 and Web services

DB2 can act as a Web service consumer and provider with the addition of the Web services Object Runtime Framework (WORF). WORF uses a Document Access Definition Extension (DADX) file to define SQL queries. DADX files are XML documents that map SQL, stored procedure, and XML collection expressions to one or more Web service operations. SQL queries can use the `<query>` and `<update>` elements, and stored procedures can use the `<call>` element. XML collection expressions can use the `<retrieveXML>` and `<storeXML>` elements in conjunction with WORF .jar files to manipulate SQL results as XML collections.

If you use WebSphere Studio Application developer (WSAD), WORF tools for creating WSDL files, deployment descriptors. You can also generate DADX files from SQL queries in WSAD.

If you don't use WSAD, you have to hand-code the DADX files, but WSDL and deployment descriptor files can be generated via URLs and Java command-line calls.

The following example uses the DB2 JDBC driver and a DB2 Web service using WORF as part of a multi-tier J2EE Web service application.

Example: A Multi-Tier Web Service Using J2EE and DB2

In this section we'll adapt the multi-tier J2EE Web service application that we created in Chapter 33 to use a DB2 Web service. Instead of a JDBC call to DB2 that returns XML, we've set up a Web service that creates an XML. The XML file is passed from DB2 to a servlet via a SOAP envelope, rather than a JDBC result set.

Note

Readers who followed through the example in Chapter 35 will find much of this application repeats the same code. Instead of making you wade through all of the code again, we'll list the changes here, and you can probably skip over the rest.

You should read over the "Prerequisites for Developing J2EE and DB2 Web Services" section to familiarize yourself with the process of creating a DB2 Web service using WORF. We removed the two servlets that created Chapter 35's XML results and replaced them with a single servlet called `GetSingleQuoteDB2 Format`. This servlet makes a Web service call using AXIS and returns XML results that are formatted by DB2. In the remaining servlets, we replaced the SQL server JDBC connection string with a DB2 JDBC connection string, and edited the queries for DB2. In the client application, we removed references to the deleted JDBC servlets and added a reference to the new GetSingleQuoteDB2 servlet.

The first tier of the J2EE application provides the user interface to the data. The application connects to servlets on a J2EE application server. The middle tier is made up of two servlets that make JDBC connections to DB2 data and one Web service requestor that calls DB2 data via a Web service. The JDBC servlets connect to connect to a DB2 database that contains quote, source, and author information. The Web service servlet returns quotations from the database. This is a good illustration not only of when to use Web services, but also when not to use Web services. When the application makes a request to retrieve a list of authors or quotations for an author, a single column of data is returned that could potentially contain hundreds or thousands of values. Packaging requests that return a single but large column of data as a Web service would be inefficient from a bandwidth point of view, and performance would be poor because of SOAP envelope wrapping and unwrapping. Also, because the data does not require a hierarchical structure, XML is not really necessary for handling the result sets. For these reasons, it was easier and more efficient to go with a regular JDBC call. The other two actions in the application return a single row of data with three or four values in it. The end result is formatted as XML. Because of the relatively small result size and the hierarchical structure of the data that is returned, XML is a good format for delivery, and a Web service is a natural choice of delivery method.

Separating the user interface from the data access processes

The Java Application, called XMLPBWSMTApp.java, is based on the Swing UI classes and the AWT event classes. To the user, the application looks the same as the application in Chapters 21 and 35, but this time instead of running all the Java code on the client and accessing SQL Server data over the network or via servlets, the J2EE application makes calls to Web services on a J2EE server. This means that the J2EE client does not have to have access to .jar files for JDBC or servlets. This also means that the application handles client-side functionality only, and does not have to handle intensive data processing functions, such as generating XML documents from JDBC result sets. This division of processing makes each side of the application perform better that single-tier solution, and the addition of Web services adds another layer of flexibility in the application.

Prerequisites for Developing J2EE and DB2 Web Services

Because you're developing Web services on a J2EE server for this example, there is a little work to be done in setting up the application and the DB2 server. This section will take you through the setup and configuration for AXIS and DB2 Web services and the client application.

Downloading and installing the DB2 JDBC driver

The latest version of the JDBC driver is part of the DB2 UDB installation. The `db2jcc.jar` is located in the default Java directory of your DB2 installation. This is usually located on a Windows server at `C:\Program Files\ibm\SQLLIB\ java\ db2jcc.jar`. A reference to the file needs to be added to your system CLASSPATH. You can optionally add `sqlj.zip` to your system CLASSPATH if you intend to use SQLJ connectivity. The DB2 JDBC driver requires a minimum of JRE 1.3.1. Updates to the DB2 JDBC driver can be found in at `http://www-3.ibm. com/software/data/db2/udb`.

Tip   If you have more than one JDBC driver installed and referenced in your CLASS-PATH, you may have conflicts when referencing the `java.sql.*` package classes in your import statement. Most J2EE IDES have a way to specify a CLASSPATH for a project. If yours does not, you'll have to rearrange the JDBC driver references in your system CLASSPATH so the one that you need is in front of all of the others.

Downloading and installing WORF

The DB2 Web services Object Runtime Framework (WORF) comes as part of DB2 UDB 8.1 and higher and WebSphere Studio Application Developer 5 and up. DB2 version 7 and higher can also use WORF. The latest version can be downloaded from `http://www-3.ibm.com/software/data/db2/udb`. The file comes in a compressed format and contains a few samples, but no documentation to speak of. The best place for WORF documentation is the Document Access Definition Extension (DADX) specification, which can be found at `ftp://ftp.software.ibm.com/ps/products/db2extenders/software/xmlext/docs/v72wrk/webserv/dadxspec/dadx.html`.

Once the file is downloaded and decompressed, you need to reference worf.jar in your system CLASSPATH. See the readme file in the installation files for more details.

Creating and deploying a DADX file

The first thing to do for DB2 Web service enablement is create a DADX file. There are two ways to create a DADX file to work with your Web service. If you use WebSphere Studio Application Developer, you can use a wizard to create DADX files, based on SQL statements. Otherwise, you'll have to hand-code your DAD files. Below is an example of a DADX file that returns quotations from the XMLPB database. The operation name is defined as `GetDB2XML`. A parameter named `PassedQuote` is used to pass a string containing a quotation to the Web service. The query in the <query> element uses the passed parameter to create a query. The query returns the author name from the AUTHORS table, the source name from the SOURCES table, and the quotation from the QUOTATIONS table. The DADX is called `GetDB2XML.dadx`.

 For a complete listing of the DB2 tables and their columns and data types, please refer to Chapter 20.

```
<?xml version="1.0" encoding="UTF-8"?>
<DADX xmlns="http://schemas.ibm.com/db2/dxx/dadx"
xmlns:xsd="http://www.w3.org/1999/XMLSchema"
xmlns:wsdl="http://schemas.xmlsoap.org/wsdl/">
  <wsdl:documentation>XML Programming Bible example - Returns a DB2-
    formatted XML document</wsdl:documentation>
  <operation name="GetDB2XML">
  <dadx:parameter name="PassedQuote" type="xsd:string"/>
    <query>SELECT ALL Quotations.Quotation, Authors.AuthorName,
           Sources.SourceName FROM Quotations INNER JOIN Authors ON
           Quotations.AuthorID = Authors.AuthorID INNER JOIN Sources ON
           Quotations.SourceID = Sources.SourceID WHERE
           Quotations.Quotation = :PassedQuote;
    </query>
  </operation>
</DADX>
```

The DADX file is deployed on a J2EE application server in the CLASSES directory under the WEB-INF directory. For example, on Apache Tomcat the reference should be located in WEB-INF/classes/GetDB2XML.dadx.

To test the DADX-based Web service on a J2EE application server, type the following URL for the DADX file:

```
http://localhost:8080/XMLPB/GetDB2XML.dadx/TEST
```

You should get an automatically generated documentation and test page if the DADX file is deployed correctly.

Downloading and installing AXIS

The first thing you need to do for this example is to install the latest implementation of the Apache SOAP toolkit, which has been renamed AXIS to keep us on our toes. Axis stands for "Apache eXtensible Interaction System" but is still based on the W3C SOAP Recommendation, with the equally inscrutable acronym of "Simple Object Access Protocol." The entire library can be downloaded from http://xml.apache.org as a .zip or .tar file and installed on the file system.

If you're running a J2EE application server, the axis subdirectory should be moved to the WEB-INF or WebApps directory, depending on the server. After that the server usually needs to be restarted.

Tip   If you want to test the application developed in this chapter without running an application server, the latest version of AXIS comes with a client-side server tool that can be used for testing Web services on a server or a development workstation. We'll show you how to use this in a later section of this chapter.

Once AXIS is downloaded and installed, edits are needed on the system CLASSPATH for the AXIS RPC router to function correctly. Please refer to the AXIS installation instructions for the latest details.

Deploying Web service class, WSDL, and WSDD files

The example in this chapter uses two AXIS-based Web services and one DB2-based Web service. The XMLPBWSMTServletGetAuthorList gets a list of unique quote authors for display in the J2EE Application. The XMLPBWSMTServletGetSingle AuthorList gets a list of quotes for a single author. Each of the AXIS-based Web services listed here is associated with a WSDL (Web Service Description Language) file and a Web Service Deployment Descriptor (WSDD) file. Each file has the same name as the Web service class file. We'll cover what each of these file types does later in the chapter. The DB2 Web service does not use a deployment descriptor. The J2EE code reference points to the DADX file instead of the object in the AXIS server. The DADX file needs to be located as described in the previous section.

Running Web services on a J2EE application server

After downloading all related Web service files from the XMLProgrammingBible.com Website, copy the Class files and the Web Service Deployment Descriptor (WSDD) files to the AXIS\class directory on the J2EE server or the development workstation. After copying the files, consult the J2EE application server's documentation for instructions on deploying Web services and editing the WSDD files with any required server-specific variables.

Running the Web services without a J2EE server

The latest version of AXIS contains an implementation of a simple Web services RPC router and server environment, called the Simple Server. The Simple Server can be run from a command line without installing a J2EE server, so it's easy to set up and maintain on most computers. The server is single threaded, which makes it great for testing, but not appropriate for a production environment.

Run the AXIS Simple SOAP Server

Once AXIS is downloaded, installed, and configured, open a command window and type the following command at the prompt:

```
java org.apache.axis.transport.http.SimpleAxisServer -p 8080
```

You should get a message that says:

```
- SimpleAxisServer starting up on port 8080.
```

This indicates that the server has started. There is no confirmation message; this is the last message that runs in the DOS Prompt widow.

The prompt window needs to be kept open for the Simple AXIS Server to run.

Deploying the Web services to the AXIS Simple SOAP Server

After loading the AXIS Simple SOAP Server, the Java class files need to be deployed and registered on the server. The WSDD files handle the details of setting this up on a J2EE application server or the AXIS simple server. If you're using a J2EE server, refer to that server's documentation for Web service deployment instructions. If you're using the AXIS simple server, open a second command window and go to the AXIS/Class directory where the Java class and WSDD files should be located. Type the following four commands:

```
java org.apache.axis.client.AdminClient
deployXMLPBWSMTServletGetAuthorList.wsdd

java org.apache.axis.client.AdminClient
deployXMLPBWSMTServletGetSingleAuthorList.wsdd
```

We'll discuss the contents of the WSDD files a bit later, for now you just need to know that these commands load the Java class files into the server and establish rules for running and accessing the Web services.

Testing the server status and deployment

To test the server implementation and ensure that the Web services are deployed, open a Web browser window and type the following URL, substituting the IP address if necessary:

```
http://127.0.0.1:8080/axis
```

You should get a basic HTML Web page that looks like this:

```
Content-Type: text/html; charset=utf-8 Content-Length: 977
And now... Some Services
AdminService (wsdl)
AdminService
XMLPBWSMTServletGetAuthorList (wsdl)
GetAuthorList
XMLPBWSMTServletGetSingleAuthorList (wsdl)
GetSingleAuthorList
Version (wsdl)
getVersion
```

This page confirms that the Web services have been deployed. There are two system Web services at the top and bottom of the page, and the rest of the services listed are your Web service classes that were deployed by your prompt commands. Each service is followed by a single method name for each class, which is registered on the server by the WSDD file.

Tip   If there is an error on this screen, or not all of the classes and methods are installed, the first place to check is the AXIS CLASSPATH settings. If the CLASSPATH is set up OK, then check the location of the class and WSDD files.

Installing the XMLPBWSMTApp J2EE application

The XMLPBWSMTApp.class file should be installed in a directory of a workstation that is accessible to the Java JDK.

On The Web   The XMLPBWSMTApp application and all of the Web service files can be downloaded from the XMLProgrammingBible.com Website, in the Downloads section.

Installing the WSDL files

The WSDL files should be loaded on the same J2EE server as the Java class files. They don't have anything to do with the functionality of the Web service, but the WSDL files should be located in the HTML directory of the J2EE application server in a production environment. If any UDDI entries refer to the Web service, the discovery URL for the WSDL file should be published in the UDDI entry or other references to the service, such as an entry at Xmethods.com.

Running the Web service client

Once the application is downloaded and all of the installation steps have been completed, run the application by typing `java XMLPBWSMTApp` from a command prompt or the Windows "Run" menu option. The application will appear on the screen in its own Java window.

Developing Web Services

As we mentioned earlier in this chapter, The Quote Generator – DB2 Web Service Edition application is an adaptation of the multi-tier Web service application in Chapter 35. In this section we'll take you "under the hood" of one of the four Web services to show you how the Java class file, the J2EE and the WSDL files all work together to create a Web service.

Inside the XMLPBWSMTServletGetAuthorList Web service

The code in Listing 36-1 shows a Web service that returns a unique listing of quote authors from a DB2 database via JDBC. The class starts by making a JDBC connection to the DB2XMLPB database. Next, a DB2 JDBC driver instance is created. A connection is defined to the DB2 instance. In this case, we're running the DB2 instance and the J2EE application on the same machine, so the IP address is the home IP address of the machine - `127.0.0.1`. The JDBC `user` and `password` for the database are set up in the connection string. Because the `XMLPB` database is specified in the connection string, we don't need to explicitly name the database in our DB2 query.

A JDBC result set object is created, which is the result of the query string passed to the SQL server. An array is built from the result set with the buildArray class, which we'll show you in the next listing. Once the result set is processed, the connection and the result set are dropped. The contents of the author list object are created by the array and passed to the application window.

The SQL command, `select AuthorName from Authors`, selects all of the values in the `AuthorName` column of the Authors table. The buildArray class that is used by the GetAuthorList and GetSingleAuthorList classes to build an array from an DB2JDBC result set. An `ArrayList` is created, which is an implementation of the List interface. The most important feature of ArrayLists for the purposes of this code is that they are automatically resizable, via the `add()` method.

Note   We have explicitly specified `java.util.List` because the `java.awt` package also has a List interface.

The JDBC specification contains a `.toArray()` method for result sets, which would be great for this purpose. However, not all JDBC drivers implement a complete set of methods for JDBC classes. The code in the `buildArray` class can be used when the `toArray()` method is not supported, as is the case with the DB2JDBC driver, or when you want all JDBC result set array output to be the same regardless of driver-specific formatting.

A DB2result set is passed from the calling object and an `ArrayList` is defined called `arrayResults`. The code loops through the result set and retrieves the current result set row value as a string. DB2result set values returned by the DB2JDBC driver sometimes contain leading and trailing blanks, so the `trim()` method is sued to trim spaces off the string as it is created. The string is added to the `array Results` object using the `ArrayList.add()` method. Next, a string array called `sarray` is created, and the value of the `ArrayList` is passed to the string array using the `ArrayList.toArray()` method.

The `buildArray` class creates a string array from the JDBC result set, which is passed to the J2EE application that called the Web service via a SOAP envelope (Listing 36-1).

Listing 36-1: The XMLPBWSMTServletGetAuthorList Web Service Code

```
import java.util.*;
import java.io.*;
import java.sql.*;

public class XMLPBWSMTServletGetAuthorList {


    public String [] GetAuthorList() {
        String authorList [] = null;
        String sql = "select AuthorName from Authors";

        try {
```

Continued

Listing 36-1 *(continued)*

```
            Class.forName("com.ibm.db2.jcc.DB2Driver");
            Connection conn =  DriverManager.getConnection
            ("jdbc:db2://127.0.0.1:7778/XMLPB,
             User=jdbcUser,Password=jdbcUser");
            Statement s = conn.createStatement();
            ResultSet rs = s.executeQuery(sql);

            authorList = buildArray(rs);

            rs.close();
            conn.close();
        }catch(Exception e) {
            e.printStackTrace();
        }

    return authorList ;

}

String[] buildArray(ResultSet rs) {
    java.util.List arrayResults = new ArrayList();
    try {
        int rownumber= 0;
        String rowvalue = new String();
        while(rs.next()) {
            rownumber++;
            rowvalue = rs.getString(rownumber++);
            arrayResults.add(rowvalue.trim());
        }
    }catch(Exception e) {}
    String[] sarray = (String[]) arrayResults.toArray(new
    String[arrayResults.size()]);
    return sarray;
}

}
```

Next, we'll show you how the WSDL and WSDD files work together with the Java class to make a Web service.

The XMLPBWSMTServletGetAuthorList WSDL and WSDD files

Each Web service in the Quote XML Generator – Web Service Edition application has two files associated with it, a Web Services Description Language (WSDL) file and a Web Service Deployment Descriptor (WSDD) file. We'll explain the files associated with the XMLPBWSMTServletGetAuthorList class as a guide for all four Web services. Each WSDL and WSDD file is virtually the same as its counterparts, except for the names of the classes, the names of the methods, and the data types returned. Listing 36-2 shows the WSDD File associated with the XMLPBWSMT ServletGetAuthorList Web service.

Deployment descriptors are well-formed XML documents that control Web service deployment, security, and administration. The deployment descriptor declares the name of the Web service and two XML namespaces. Next, the Service data-binding format is defined as Java remote procedure calls (RPC). The RPC router on the server parses incoming SOAP RPC requests and extracts data from a SOAP envelope. Responses from the Web service are wrapped in a response SOAP envelope by the same RPC router.

Next, the service's class name is defined as XMLPBWSMTServletGetAuthorList, as shown in Listing 36-2. Access to all methods contained in the Web service is permitted by the wildcard character (*) in the allowedMethods parameter.

Listing 36-2: **The XMLPBWSMTServletGetAuthorList WSDD File**

```
<deployment
    xmlns="http://xml.apache.org/axis/wsdd/"
    xmlns:java="http://xml.apache.org/axis/wsdd/providers/java">
  <!-- Services from XMLPBWSMTServletGetAuthorListService WSDL service -->
  <service name="XMLPBWSMTServletGetAuthorList" provider="java:RPC">
      <parameter name="wsdlTargetNamespace"
       value="http://www.xmlprogrammingbible.com/wsdl/default/"/>
      <parameter name="wsdlServiceElement"
       value="XMLPBWSMTServletGetAuthorListService"/>
      <parameter name="wsdlServicePort"
       value="XMLPBWSMTServletGetAuthorList"/>
      <parameter name="className"
       value="com.xmlprogrammingbible.www.
       XMLPBWSMTServletGetAuthorListSoapBindingSkeleton"/>
      <parameter name="wsdlPortType" value="XMLPBWSMTServletGetAuthorList"/>
      <parameter name="allowedMethods" value="*"/>

      <typeMapping
        xmlns:ns="http://www.xmlprogrammingbible.com/wsdl/default/"
        qname="ns:ArrayOf_soapenc_string"
        type="java:java.lang.String[]"
        serializer="org.apache.axis.encoding.ser.ArraySerializerFactory"
        deserializer="org.apache.axis.encoding.ser.
        ArrayDeserializerFactory"
        encodingStyle="http://schemas.xmlsoap.org/soap/encoding/"
      />
  </service>
</deployment>
```

The deployment descriptor describes a Web service from a J2EE server point of view. A WSDL file describes the same Web service from a client point of view. As mentioned in Chapter 25, reading a WSDL file can be a daunting task, but it's best to keep in mind that if everything goes well, humans should rarely have to read a WSDL file themselves. WSDL files are a way of defining a Web service interface programmatically to another Web service, smart client, or portal. Listing 36-3 shows the WSDL interface for the `XMLPBWSMTServletGetAuthorList` Web service.

The WSDL file declares several XML namespaces, which are used to define WSDL structure and SOAP data types (Listing 36-3). Next, data types are defined as parts of call and response messages. The messages become part of ports, which become part of operations. The Web service is defined of one or more operation. Last, the endpoint address for the Web service is specified in the `location` attribute of the `wsdlsoap:address` element.

Listing 36-3: **The XMLPBWSMTServletGetAuthorList WSDL File**

```
<wsdl:definitions xmlns="http://schemas.xmlsoap.org/wsdl/"
xmlns:apachesoap="http://xml.apache.org/xml-soap"
xmlns:impl="http://www.xmlprogrammingbible.com/wsdl/default/-impl"
xmlns:intf="http://www.xmlprogrammingbible.com/wsdl/default/"
xmlns:soapenc="http://schemas.xmlsoap.org/soap/encoding/"
xmlns:wsdl="http://schemas.xmlsoap.org/wsdl/"
xmlns:wsdlsoap="http://schemas.xmlsoap.org/wsdl/soap/"
xmlns:xsd="http://www.w3.org/2001/XMLSchema"
targetNamespace="http://www.xmlprogrammingbible.com/wsdl/default/">
  <wsdl:types>
    <schema targetNamespace="http://www.xmlprogrammingbible.com
    /wsdl/default/" xmlns="http://www.w3.org/2001/XMLSchema">
      <import namespace="http://schemas.xmlsoap.org
      /soap/encoding/"/>
      <complexType name="ArrayOf_soapenc_string">
        <complexContent>
          <restriction base="soapenc:Array">
            <attribute ref= "soapenc:arrayType"
            wsdl:arrayType="soapenc:string[]"/>
          </restriction>
        </complexContent>
      </complexType>
      <element name="ArrayOf_soapenc_string" nillable="true"
       type="intf:ArrayOf_soapenc_string"/>
    </schema>
  </wsdl:types>
  <wsdl:message name="GetAuthorListResponse">
    <wsdl:part name="return" type="intf:ArrayOf_soapenc_string"/>
  </wsdl:message>
  <wsdl:message name="GetAuthorListRequest">
```

```
    </wsdl:message>
  <wsdl:portType name="XMLPBWSMTServletGetAuthorList">
    <wsdl:operation name="GetAuthorList">
      <wsdl:input name="GetAuthorListRequest"
       message="intf:GetAuthorListRequest"/>
      <wsdl:output name="GetAuthorListResponse"
       message="intf:GetAuthorListResponse"/>
    </wsdl:operation>
  </wsdl:portType>
  <wsdl:binding name="XMLPBWSMTServletGetAuthorListSoapBinding"
   type="intf:XMLPBWSMTServletGetAuthorList">
    <wsdlsoap:binding style="rpc"
     transport="http://schemas.xmlsoap.org/soap/http"/>
    <wsdl:operation name="GetAuthorList">
      <wsdlsoap:operation/>
      <wsdl:input>
        <wsdlsoap:body use="encoded"
         encodingStyle="http://schemas.xmlsoap.org/soap/encoding/"
         namespace="http://www.xmlprogrammingbible.com/wsdl/default/"/>
      </wsdl:input>
      <wsdl:output>
        <wsdlsoap:body use="encoded"
         encodingStyle="http://schemas.xmlsoap.org/soap/encoding/"
         namespace="http://www.xmlprogrammingbible.com/wsdl/default/"/>
      </wsdl:output>
    </wsdl:operation>
  </wsdl:binding>
  <wsdl:service name="XMLPBWSMTServletGetAuthorListService">
    <wsdl:port name="XMLPBWSMTServletGetAuthorList"
     binding="intf:XMLPBWSMTServletGetAuthorListSoapBinding">
      <wsdlsoap:address location="http://127.0.0.1/
       XMLPBWSMTServletGetAuthorList"/>
    </wsdl:port>
  </wsdl:service>
</wsdl:definitions>
```

Putting the WSDD, Class, WSDL, and SOAP together

Keep in mind that each interface plays an important role in dividing the labor of each component of the application. This separation of functionality also adds flexibility to the application. For example, the deployment descriptor can be used to redirect calls to another Java class file or another platform entirely without having to change the name, location, or functionality of the Web service.

As we mentioned earlier, the Web service WSDL file is not important for the day-to-day functionality of the Web service. However, the WSDL file is very useful for specifying the format for SOAP call and response related to the Web service. Many Web service clients can read the WSDL file for a Web service and dynamically adapt the calling agent interface to the serving agent.

Listing 36-4 shows a sample SOAP envelope contents that is generated by the `XMLPBWSMTServletGetAuthorList` WSDL file. The Method name in the SOAP call maps directly to the incoming message in the WSDL file. The `GetAuthorList` method call maps to the WSDL `GetAuthorList` operation.

Listing 36-4: A Sample XMLPBWSMTServletGetAuthorList SOAP Call

```
<SOAP-ENV:Envelope xmlns:SOAP-ENV="http://schemas.xmlsoap.org/
soap/envelope/" xmlns:SOAP-ENC="http://schemas.xmlsoap.org/soap/
encoding/" xmlns:xsi="http://www.w3.org/2001/XMLSchema-instance"
xmlns:xsd="http://www.w3.org/2001/XMLSchema">
  <SOAP-ENV:Body>
    <m:GetAuthorList
    xmlns:m="http://www.xmlprogrammingbible.com
    /wsdl/default/" SOAP-
    ENV:encodingStyle="http://schemas.xmlsoap.org/
    soap/encoding/"/>
  </SOAP-ENV:Body>
</SOAP-ENV:Envelope>
```

The XMLPBWSMTServletGetSingleAuthorList Web service

The `XMLPBWSMTServletGetSingleAuthorList` Web service is called when a user clicks on a quote author in the J2EE client application. The `CategoryName` parameter is passed to the Web service in the SOAP request envelope. This triggers a JDBC query on the `Authors` and `Quotations` tables in the `XMLPB` database. The `buildArray` class builds an array from the JDBC result set.

The Web service returns an array of quotes for the author back to the J2EE client application in a SOAP response envelope. The RPC router on the server converts the string array to an XML-based SOAP string array format. Listing 36-5 shows the `XMLPBWSMTServletGetSingleAuthorList` code.

Listing 36-5: The XMLPBWSMTServletGetSingleAuthorList Web Service Code

```
import java.util.*;
import java.io.*;
import java.sql.*;
```

```
public class XMLPBWSMTServletGetSingleAuthorList {

    public String [] GetSingleAuthorList(String CategoryName) {
        String singleauthorList [] = null;
        String sql = "SELECT Quotations.Quotation FROM Quotations INNER
        JOIN Authors ON Quotations.AuthorID = Authors.AuthorID INNER JOIN
        Sources ON Quotations.SourceID = Sources.SourceID WHERE
        (Authors.AuthorName = '"+CategoryName+"')";
        String fromrow="1";
        String torow="50";
        String threshold="50";

        try {

            Class.forName("com.ibm.db2.jcc.DB2Driver");
            Connection conn =  DriverManager.getConnection
            ("jdbc:db2://127.0.0.1:7778/XMLPB,
            User=jdbcUser,Password=jdbcUser");
            Statement s = conn.createStatement();
            ResultSet rs = s.executeQuery(sql);
            singleauthorList = buildArray(rs);

            rs.close();
            conn.close();
        }catch(Exception e) {
            e.printStackTrace();
        }

        return singleauthorList ;

    }

    String[] buildArray(ResultSet rs) {
        java.util.List arrayResults = new ArrayList();
        try {
            int rownumber= 0;
            String rowvalue = new String();
            while(rs.next()) {
                rownumber++;
                rowvalue = rs.getString(rownumber++);
                arrayResults.add(rowvalue.trim());
            }
        }catch(Exception e) {}
        String[] sarray = (String[]) arrayResults.toArray(new
        String[arrayResults.size()]);
        return sarray;
    }

}
```

The XMLPBMTWSServletDB2Format Web service

The code in Listing 36-6 is called when a quote is selected by a user and the output option is set to `"DB2 XML"`. A string containing the quote formatted as an XML document is passed from the `GetSingleQuoteDb2` class back to the Web service as a string. The code is nice and short in this class because AXIS and DB2 do most of the work in retrieving and formatting the XML.

Rows of data are returned as children of a `GetDB2XMLResult` element. The result of a query is always a single row. A single `GetDB2XMLRow` element contains the DB2 column values. Column values are stored in text data, and column names are represented as element names. These element names are based on the Web service operation name, `GetDB2XML` (Listing 36-6).

> **Listing 36-6: The XMLPBWSMTServletDB2Format Web Service Code**

```
import org.apache.axis.*;
import org.apache.axis.client.*;
import java.rmi.*;
import org.apache.axis.encoding.*;
import org.apache.axis.utils.*;

public class XMLPBMTWSServletDB2Format {

    public String GetSingleQuoteDB2(String PassedQuote) {
        String XMLDoc=null;

        try {

            Service  service = new Service();
            Call call = (Call) service.createCall();
            call.setTargetEndpointAddress( new
            java.net.URL("http://127.0.0.1:8080/
            XMLPB/GetDB2XML.dadx/GetDB2XML") );
            call.addParameter( "PassedQuote", XMLType.XSD_STRING,
            javax.xml.rpc.ParameterMode.IN );
            call.setReturnType(new javax.xml.namespace.QName
            ("http://www.xmlprogrammingbible.com/wsdl/default/",
            "string"));
            XMLDoc = (String ) call.invoke( new Object[] {PassedQuote});

        } catch(Exception e) {
            e.printStackTrace();
        }
```

```
        return XMLDoc ;

    }


}
```

Listing 36-7 shows the result of the GetDB2XML Operation.

Listing 36-7: The XML Returned as a Result of the GetDB2XML Operation

```
<?xml version="1.0" encoding="UTF-8"?>
<ns1:GetDB2XMLResponse xmlns:ns1="urn:/XMLPB/GetDB2XML.dadx"
xmlns:xsd="http://www.w3.org/1999/XMLSchema"
xmlns:xsi="http://www.w3.org/1999/XMLSchema-instance">
  <return>
    <xsd1:GetDB2XMLResult xmlns="http://127.0.0.1:8080/
    XMLPB/GetDB2XML.dadx/GetDB2XML/XSD"
    xmlns:xsd1="http://127.0.0.1:8080/XMLPB/
    GetDB2XML.dadx/GetDB2XML/XSD">
      <GetDB2XMLRow>
        <QUOTATION>When the hurlyburlys done, When the battles lost and
        won.</QUOTATION>
        <AUTHORNAME>Shakespeare, William</AUTHORNAME>
        <SOURCENAME>Macbeth</SOURCENAME>
      </GetDB2XMLRow>
    </xsd1:GetDB2XMLResult>
  </return>
</ns1:GetDB2XMLResponse>
```

Inside the XMLPBWSMTApp J2EE Client Application

The XMLPBWSMTApp J2EE client application is a fully functional Java Application that uses Swing Classes and AWT events to generate a UI. The J2EE client makes SOAP calls to Web services, which connect to relational data on DB2using JDBC. The Web services manipulate the JDBC query result sets and return responses to the J2EE client application.

How the application works

When the application window is opened, a Web service is called that retrieves a list of unique quote authors. The Web service retrieves data from the Authors table of the XMLPB database on DB2. The connection from the Web service to the DB2 databases is made via JDBC. The application then draws the various Swing panels on the page and attaches AWT events to the panels. Users can scroll up and down the list of quote authors in the author List panel, and select a single author by clicking on it in the list.

Clicking on an author name triggers another call to another Web service. That Web service query is to retrieve all the quotes attributed to the selected author. The quotes are displayed in the quote list panel on the top right of the screen.

When a user clicks on one of the quotes in the quote list panel, another J2EE Web service is called to generate XML document output for the selected quote and display it in the output panel in the lower half of the application window. In the middle of the screen is a combo box that can be used to select output format options. The options are *Just the Text*, which just returns the quote as text, or *DB2 XML*, which returns the XML output shown in Listing 36-7, which is generated by the XMLPBWSMTServletDB2Format Web service. Aside from being a good J2EE Web services application prototype, the Quote XML Web service application is also a good example of applying a user interface to DB2 data. It's also a good prototype from any application that uses Web services, JDBC, and Java GUI classes. The application contains examples of accessing and displaying DB2 data in several different ways, including strings, arrays, and XML documents.

About the example DB2 data

In this chapter we're reusing tables from the XMLPB SQL Server database. Setup instructions for the database can be found in Chapter 20.

Creating the Java Application User Interface

We have broken down the source code into segments that relate to a specific topic, rather than showing the source code in its entirety on the pages. All of the examples contained in this chapter can be downloaded from the XML ProgrammingBible.com Website, in the Downloads section. Please see the Website for installation Instructions.

Defining public variables and the application window

Let's look under the hood of the Java Application by breaking down the Java Application source code into topical sections with detailed explanations of the code, starting with the introductory application setup in Listing 36-8.

The J2EE client application imports the `java.io` classes for writing to the screen, `javax.swing` classes to handle UI features, and selected `java.awt` classes to manage action events. The `org.apache.axis` and `java.rmi` classes are used to create SOAP envelopes and make calls to Web services.

The beginning of the code sets up a `Jframe` window, which becomes the application window, and creates an instance of an `actionlistener` to watch for the window to be closed. When the window is closed, the application exits.

Listing 36-8: **Defining the Public Variables and the Application Window**

```
import javax.swing.*;
import javax.swing.event.*;
import java.util.*;
import java.awt.*;
import java.awt.event.*;
import java.io.*;
import java.net.*;
import org.apache.axis.*;
import org.apache.axis.client.*;
import java.rmi.*;
import org.apache.axis.encoding.*;
import org.apache.axis.utils.*;

public class XMLPBWSMTApp extends JPanel {
    JTextArea output;
    JList authorList;
    JList QuoteList;
    ListSelectionModel authorListSelectionModel;
    ListSelectionModel QuotelistSelectionModel;
    public String[] listData;
    JComboBox comboBox;

    public static void main(String[] args) {
        JFrame frame = new JFrame("Quote XML Generator - DB2 Web Service
        Edition");
        frame.addWindowListener(new WindowAdapter() {
            public void windowClosing(WindowEvent e) {
                System.exit(0);
            }
        });

        frame.setContentPane(new XMLPBWSMTApp());
        frame.pack();
        frame.setVisible(true);
    }
```

Setting objects in the window and implementing ActionListeners

Listing 36-9 shows the code that is used to define the main UI on top of the application Window. The first task is to retrieve a unique list of quote authors from the DB2 Authors table calling the `GetAuthorList()` class, which we will cover a bit later.

Once this is done, the `AuthorList` object is created, and an `AuthorList SelectionHandler` object is attached to the list. When users click on a quote author, the `AuthorListSelectionHandler` class is called to handle the action. Next, a `JscrollPane` called `SourcePane` is created for the list object, and the pane is placed in the top left of the application window.

The instantiation steps are repeated for the `QuoteList` object, which will be used to display quotes for a selected author on the top right of the application window. A `QuoteListSelectionHandler` object is attached to the quote list.

Next, a drop-down combo box containing the application output options is created, which will be located in the center of the Application window, just below the author list and quote list panes. The hard-coded output options are defined and the default is set to the first object.

A `JtextArea` object is defined and placed in the bottom half of the application window. This is where the XML and text output is sent when a user selects a quote from the quote list.

The balance of the code in Listing 36-9 is Swing and AWT class housekeeping to create the details of the layout that the user interface needs.

Listing 36-9: Setting Objects in the Window and Implementing ActionListeners

```
public XMLPBWSMTApp() {
super(new BorderLayout());


listData = GetAuthorList();
String[] WelcomeMessage={"Click on a Source in the Left Pane to
Retrieve Quotes"};

authorList = new JList(listData);

authorListSelectionModel = authorList.getSelectionModel();
authorListSelectionModel.addListSelectionListener(
new authorListSelectionHandler());
JScrollPane SourcePane = new JScrollPane(authorList);
```

```java
QuoteList = new JList(WelcomeMessage);
QuotelistSelectionModel = QuoteList.getSelectionModel();
QuotelistSelectionModel.addListSelectionListener(
new QuoteListSelectionHandler());
JScrollPane QuotePane = new JScrollPane(QuoteList);

JPanel OutputSelectionPane = new JPanel();
String[] OutputFormats = { "Just the Quote", " DB2 XML"};

comboBox = new JComboBox(OutputFormats);
comboBox.setSelectedIndex(0);
OutputSelectionPane.add(new JLabel("Select an output Format:"));
OutputSelectionPane.add(comboBox);

output = new JTextArea(1, 10);
output.setEditable(false);
output.setLineWrap(true);
JScrollPane outputPane = new JScrollPane(output,
ScrollPaneConstants.VERTICAL_SCROLLBAR_ALWAYS,
ScrollPaneConstants.HORIZONTAL_SCROLLBAR_AS_NEEDED);

JSplitPane splitPane = new JSplitPane(JSplitPane.VERTICAL_SPLIT);
add(splitPane, BorderLayout.CENTER);

JPanel TopPanel = new JPanel();
TopPanel.setLayout(new BoxLayout(TopPanel, BoxLayout.X_AXIS));
JPanel SourceContainer = new JPanel(new GridLayout(1,1));
SourceContainer.setBorder(BorderFactory.createTitledBorder(
"Source List"));
SourceContainer.add(SourcePane);
SourcePane.setPreferredSize(new Dimension(300, 100));
JPanel QuoteContainer = new JPanel(new GridLayout(1,1));
QuoteContainer.setBorder(BorderFactory.createTitledBorder(
"Quote List"));
QuoteContainer.add(QuotePane);
QuotePane.setPreferredSize(new Dimension(300, 500));
TopPanel.setBorder(BorderFactory.createEmptyBorder(5,5,0,5));
TopPanel.add(SourceContainer);
TopPanel.add(QuoteContainer);

TopPanel.setMinimumSize(new Dimension(400, 50));
TopPanel.setPreferredSize(new Dimension(400, 300));
splitPane.add(TopPanel);

JPanel BottomPanel = new JPanel(new BorderLayout());
BottomPanel.add(OutputSelectionPane, BorderLayout.NORTH);
BottomPanel.add(outputPane, BorderLayout.CENTER);
BottomPanel.setMinimumSize(new Dimension(400, 50));
BottomPanel.setPreferredSize(new Dimension(800, 400));
splitPane.add(BottomPanel);
}
```

Listing 36-10 and 36-11 show the AWT Class `ActionListeners`, which facilitate the UI functionality in the application.

Defining the action for the author list

Listing 36-10 shows the code that is called when a user clicks on a quote author. When the `ActionListener` detects that the user has selected a quote author, the `GetSingleAuthorList` class is called, which returns a single-column listing of quotes for that author. The quotes are displayed in the quote list object on the top right of the application window.

Listing 36-10: Defining the Action for the Author List

```
class authorListSelectionHandler implements ListSelectionListener {
    public void valueChanged(ListSelectionEvent se) {
        ListSelectionModel slsm = (ListSelectionModel)se.getSource();
        String [] s = GetSingleAuthorList(authorList.getSelectedValue()
        .toString());
        QuoteList.setListData(s);

    }
}
```

Defining the action for the quote list

When a user selects a quote by clicking on a selection in the quote list, the code in Listing 36-11 is called. When the `ActionListener` detects that the user has selected a Quote, the `QuoteListSelectionHandler` checks the combo box to see which output format is selected by the user.

If `"Just the Quote"` is selected, the quote is sent to the output object as text. If the `"DB2 XML"` option is chosen, the `GetSingleQuoteDB2` class is called to generate DB2-generated XML for the output, with DB2 table column values formatted as elements in the XML document.

Listing 36-11: Defining the Actions for the Quote List

```
class QuoteListSelectionHandler implements ListSelectionListener {
    public void valueChanged(ListSelectionEvent qe) {
        ListSelectionModel qlsm = (ListSelectionModel)qe.getSource();
```

```
String OutputFormatChoice = (String)comboBox.getSelectedItem();

if (OutputFormatChoice.equals("Just the Quote")) {
    output.setText(QuoteList.getSelectedValue().toString());
}
else if (OutputFormatChoice.equals("DB2 XML")) {
    output.setText(GetSingleQuoteDB2
    (QuoteList.getSelectedValue().toString(
    ))); }
else {
    output.setText(QuoteList.getSelectedValue().toString());
}


    }
}
```

Retrieving a list of authors by calling a Web service

The code in Listing 36-12 returns a unique listing of quote authors by calling the
`XMLPBWSMTServletGetAuthorList` Web service. A new instance of a SOAP call is
created and assigned a Web service target endpoint of `http://127.0.0.1:8080/
axis/servlet/AxisServlet`. This endpoint accesses the AXIS Simple Server,
which contains an RPC router. The RPC router parses the SOAP envelope and the
HTTP POST Header, extracts a request object from the SOAP envelope, and routes
the request to the appropriate Web service class. The routing of the request object
is based on the current deployment descriptor configuration.

The `GetAuthorList` class in the `XMLPBWSMTServletGetAuthorList` Web service processes a JDBC query against the DB2 database and returns a result set. A
new instance of a string array is created using standard SOAP encoding of data type
`ArrayOf_xsd_string`. Converting data types from their native types to SOAP or
other types of encoding is an integral part of Web services, and allows typed data
to flow between platforms and operating systems by being serialized and de-serialized on sending and delivery of the SOAP envelope. The string array is passed back
to the RPC router. The RPC router then wraps the response object in a SOAP
response envelope and sends the response back to the J2EE client application. The
string array result is extracted from the SOAP response envelope by the AXIS call
object. The response is assigned to the `AuthorList` string array variable, which is
passed back to the application for display in the UI.

> ### Listing 36-12: **Retrieving a List of Authors from the DB2 Authors Table**

```
public String [] GetAuthorList() {
      String AuthorList [] = null;

      try{
          Service   service = new Service();
          Call call = (Call) service.createCall();
          call.setTargetEndpointAddress( new
          java.net.URL("http://127.0.0.1:8080/axis/servlet/AxisServlet")
          );
          call.setOperationName( new
          javax.xml.namespace.QName("XMLPBWSMTServletGetAuthorList",
          "GetAuthorList") );
          call.setReturnType(new
          javax.xml.namespace.QName("http://www.xmlprogrammingbible.com/
          wsdl/default/", "ArrayOf_xsd_string"));
          AuthorList = (String [] ) call.invoke( new Object[] {});
      }

      catch(Exception e) {
          e.printStackTrace();
      }
      return AuthorList ;

}
```

Retrieving a list of quotes from a selected author

When a user clicks on a quote author, the `ActionListener` for the author list object passes the author name as a string value to the `GetSingleAuthorList` Class, shown in Listing 36-13. This class uses the passed value, called `Category Name`, to retrieve all the quotes for an author using an SQL query passed to the server via JDBC.

The `GetSingleAuthorList` class is similar to the `GetAuthorList` class. `GetSingleAuthorList` in the `XMLPBWSMTServletGetSingleAuthorList` Web service passes a parameter value to a JDBC query against the DB2 database and returns a result set. A new instance of a string array is created using standard SOAP encoding of data type `ArrayOf_xsd_string`. The string array is passed back to the RPC router. The RPC router then wraps the response object in a SOAP response envelope and sends the response back to the J2EE client application. The string array result is extracted from the SOAP response envelope by the AXIS call object.

The response is assigned to the `singleAuthorList` string array variable, which is passed back to the application for display in the UI. The contents of the quote list object are then created by the array and the quote list object is displayed in the upper-right panel of the application window.

Listing 36-13: Retrieving Quotes for an Author

```
public String [] GetSingleAuthorList(String CategoryName) {
    String singleAuthorList [] = null;

    try{
        Service  service = new Service();
        Call call = (Call) service.createCall();
        call.setTargetEndpointAddress( new
        java.net.URL("http://127.0.0.1:8080/axis/servlet/AxisServlet")
        );
        call.setOperationName( new javax.xml.namespace.QName
        ("XMLPBWSMTServletGetSingleAuthorList",
        "GetSingleAuthorList") );
        call.addParameter( "CategoryName", XMLType.XSD_STRING,
        javax.xml.rpc.ParameterMode.IN );
        call.setReturnType(new
        javax.xml.namespace.QName("http://www.xmlprogrammingbible.com/
        wsdl/default/", "ArrayOf_xsd_string"));
        singleAuthorList = (String [] ) call.invoke( new Object[]
        {CategoryName});
    }

    catch(Exception e) {
        e.printStackTrace();
    }

    return singleAuthorList ;

}
```

Generating DB2 XML Output

When a user clicks on a quote, a call is triggered to the `QuoteListSelection Handler`, which is outlined previously in Listing 36-11. This triggers one of three actions, depending on the output format chosen in the combo box. The first action is to send the plain text directly to the output object. The code in Listing 36-14 is called when a quote is selected in the quote list object and the DB2 XML option is chosen from the output format combo box. The quote text is passed to the `GetSingleQuoteDB2` class. This class calls a Web service to retrieve the quote from DB2 and format the XML as an element-based XML document.

The `GetSingleQuoteDB2` class in the `XMLPBWSMTServletDB2Format` Web service passes a parameter value containing a quotation to a second Web service. The Web service returns a result set based on a DB2 DADX document. A new instance of a string is created using standard SOAP encoding of data type `xsd_string`. The string is formatted as an element-based XML document and passed back to the RPC router. The RPC router then wraps the response object in a SOAP response envelope and sends the response back to the J2EE client application. The string result is extracted from the SOAP response envelope by the AXIS call object. The response is assigned to the `XMLDoc` string variable, which is passed back to the application for display in the UI. The contents of the string are displayed in the lower panel of the application.

Listing 36-14: **Retrieving DB2 XML from a Web Service**

```
public String GetSingleQuoteDB2(String PassedQuote) {
    String XMLDoc=null;

    try{
        Service  service = new Service();
        Call call = (Call) service.createCall();
        call.setTargetEndpointAddress( new
        java.net.URL("http://127.0.0.1:8080/axis/servlet/
        AxisServlet") );
        call.setOperationName( new
        javax.xml.namespace.QName("XMLPBWSMTServletDB2Format",
        "GetSingleQuoteDB2") );
        call.addParameter( "PassedQuote", XMLType.XSD_STRING,
        javax.xml.rpc.ParameterMode.IN );
        call.setReturnType(new
        javax.xml.namespace.QName("http://www.xmlprogrammingbible.com/
        wsdl/default/", "string"));
        XMLDoc = (String ) call.invoke( new Object[] {PassedQuote});
    }

    catch(Exception e) {
        e.printStackTrace();
    }


    return XMLDoc ;

}
```

Summary

In this chapter, we've outlined techniques for combining Web services with relational data. We reviewed Web service features in MS SQL Server, Oracle, and DB2. We also showed you how to retrieve XML data from a DB2 Web service in a multi-tier J2EE Web service application infrastructure:

✦ Options for RDBMS Web services

✦ Web services support in Oracle, DB2, and MS SQL Server

✦ Data compatibility issues with MS SQL Server Web services and other Web services

✦ Working with the DB2 Web Services Object Runtime Framework (WORF)

✦ An example of DB2 and J2EE Web services working together

In the next chapter, we'll wrap up the book by covering the brave, new, bleeding edge world of Web service authentication, security, and transactions.

✦   ✦   ✦

Authentication and Security for Web Services

Web services are often described as having "industry buy-in." In most cases, it's the software "industry" that has bought in to Web services. For other industries to "buy in" to Web services, they have to be secure and reliable. Several projects are under way to meet the needs of industry strength solutions. For Web services, this means security and authentication. There are several groups working together to form standards around Web service security.

Web services also need a way to interact with other Web services and applications as a single, seamless process. Efforts are being made to develop standards that manage groupings of Web services as a single transaction, with full commit and rollback functionality, among other features.

The individuals and groups that are organizing these projects come from many different backgrounds. The W3C, the WS-I, and OASIS all have their hands in one or more of these projects. Some standards are competing, and some are complementary. In this chapter, we sort through the options and help you define the current projects, the problem that a project is trying to solve, and where overlap between projects occurs.

The standards described in this chapter are evolving. We'll be updating this chapter on-line at `http://www.XMLProgrammingBIble.com` as things change, so check there for updates.

Secure, Reliable Web Service Requirements

Many Web services are completely open and available, acting as conduits between Web service consumers and unsecured data on a back-end system. Many more Web services require registration to be able to use their Web service. Web service providers that require registration and an identity check for consumers can use simple authentication, such as an unencrypted, pre-assigned ID. They can also use more sophisticated methods, such as ID and password combinations that are encrypted in transit using SSL, or some sort of certificate authority scheme such as X.509 certificates. Authentication can be taken another step further by using new XML security and authentication standards. Current standards are supported through libraries such as IBM's XML Security Suite and the Apache XML Security Library in Java. The Web Services Enhancements 1.0 for Microsoft .NET (WSE) provides similar capabilities for .NET applications.

Aside from basic authentication, there are times when systems need to pass authentication from one Web service to another, so that a Web service consumer does not need to re-authenticate with every new Web service that is needed to perform a task. In order to facilitate this, some sort of single sign-on feature is required that can pass authentication data from one service to another, and perhaps also to back-end systems that are accessed by Web services. This data should also be encrypted so that it is not intercepted and duplicated as it passes through a network.

Web services may also share data with other Web services without having access to their security and authentication data. In this case, data that is passed between systems, usually in the form of a token, has to be compatible with other types of security and authentication schemes. It also has to be compatible with other types of encryption, or at least be able to successfully translate authentication credentials from one format to another and back again.

On top of security and authentication issues, a group of Web services should be able to maintain user preferences and pass them to other Web services and applications. They also need to be able to communicate roles and procedures.

Web services also need to be able to record transactions in a way that all parties are satisfied with. In Europe, merchants once used "tally sticks" to manage negotiated agreements. A tally stick was a piece of a tree that was marked with notches that represented a number of goods for payment rendered. Once an agreement was made, the stick was marked and split in two. One half would go to the buyer, and the other half to the seller. When goods arrived at the buyer, tally sticks would be compared to ensure that an agreement was honored.

Today, a buyer that uses a vendor's Website does not have an independent way of tracking and verifying a purchase. On the Web, there is no "tally stick" — the vendor holds all the cards. When a buyer orders 100 widgets and agrees to a price, what proof does the buyer hold that this transaction will be fulfilled as agreed, other than the vendor's Website, which a buyer has no control over? In the past, this functionality was provided by mailed or faxed documents, but this approach slows down the frictionless transaction speed of the Web. Web services and new transaction standards provide the other part of the equation for many B2B transactions. Web services can track buyer and vendor records for a transaction on the buyer and seller's own systems, thus providing even more security than the traditional "tally stick" approach.

In a perfect world, Web service security, authentication, transaction tracking, and encryption tools would be designed to be compatible across all platforms, based on universally decreed standards. Of course, this is not a perfect world. Compatible tools and platforms have to be determined when designing a secure, reliable Web service platform, and when deciding how your Web services will interact with other Web services and applications. So what does the current crop of Web service security tools offer?

Current Web Service Standards for Security and Authentication

There are several recently defined Web service security standards that have either made it to specification (or in the case of the W3C, Recommendation) status, or are in the process of being completed. These are all, however, early-stage, version 1.0 specifications, and are most definitely subject to change and development in the marketplace. The current specifications are based on the three most popular security models: transport-layer security, Public Key Infrastructure (PKI), and the Kerberos model.

Transport-Layer Security

Without using the new security standards and toolkits, SOAP envelopes can be encrypted using Secure Sockets Layer (SSL). Web service consumers can be authenticated by a provider using pre-assigned IDs and/or passwords. The advantage of this approach is that existing transport-layer security features that ship with most Web browsers can be used. This is referred to as *transport-layer security*. However, SSL is only effective between two points, and cannot be interconnected between more than one Web service consumer and provider. For more than two points of contact, you need to make use of some of the new recommendations provided by the W3C and/or the specifications provided by OASIS.

Public key infrastructure (PKI)

PKI requires a central public key administrator (called a certificate authority) to issue certificates. These certificates contain public keys, which can be shared, and private keys, which cannot. When PKI authentication takes place, a shared public key token is compared with a private key token. If the two tokens are compatible, authentication is completed. The advantage in this approach is that the certificate authority has to issue a key, and the public and private parts of that key have to be physically present on the machines that are processing security and authentication. In transport-layer security, user IDs and passwords can be intercepted and reused for impersonation. With PKI, an impersonator would also have to acquire a user's private key. Most private keys are encrypted with a password, making this even more difficult.

Kerberos

Kerberos authentication takes the PKI model one step further by defining a central location where private and public key tokens are compared. The central location where authentication takes place is called a Key Distribution Center (KDC). The KDC performs authentication and passes authenticated and verified tokens to parties that require them. This approach reduces the possibility that a private or public key could be "spoofed" by another system by providing a central (theoretically), secure location for authentication.

W3C Recommendations

The W3C has developed two XML specifications for making Web services more secure: XML Signature and XML Encryption. As the titles indicate, these recommendations apply to any XML document, though they probably will find their most practical use as part of Web services, when applied to SOAP envelopes. Remember, SOAP is just XML, so security that applies to SOAP applies to any XML and vice versa.

XML Signature and XML Encryption

XML Signature is a W3C recommendation. This standard provides the ability to "sign" an XML document. This provides insurance that a document is derived from a trusted source, and that it has not been altered since it was sent from that source. Multiple signatures can be contained in a single XML document, and each signature can be assigned to one or more elements in the document. The capability for multiple signatures provides the "tally stick" verification facility described earlier in this chapter, between two or more entities. You can find more information about XML Signature at http://www.w3.org/Signature.

XML Encryption is another W3C recommendation. Like signatures, all or part of an XML document can be encrypted, and multiple encryption keys can be specified on a document. Encryption can be managed though standard public key algorithms such as X.509/PKIX, SPKI, or PGP. For more information about XML Encryption, refer to the W3C Recommendation page at `http://www.w3.org/Encryption/2001`.

The W3C has also published a note that is related to the XML signature recommendation. The XML Key Management Specification (XKMS) provides a way to distribute and register public keys that are used for signatures and encryption. There are two parts: the XML Key Information Service Specification (X-KISS) and the XML Key Registration Service Specification (X-KRSS). X-KISS manages private key information and authenticates between a key provider and a consumer. X-KRSS specifies a standard way to register and manage public key information. VeriSign and Entrust have developed XKMS toolkits in Java, and Microsoft provides an XKML toolkit for .NET as part of the Web Services Enhancements (WSE) for Microsoft .NET. For more information about XKMS, refer to the W3C Website for XKMS at `http://www.w3.org/2001/XKMS`.

OASIS Security and Authentication Specifications

Several new and advanced Web service specifications are in development from Microsoft, IBM, BEA Systems, RSA, SAP, and VeriSign, under the auspices of the Organization for the Advancement of Structured Information Standards (OASIS), a consortium of software and hardware companies and organizations. OASIS supports Technical Committees (TCs) that create and maintain OASIS specifications. Whenever possible, the OASIS TCs base their specifications on W3C Recommendations. The fruits of labor for OASIS XML TCs are usually specification documents backed up by one or more W3C schema. The schemas can be used to validate XML documents that have been created using the specification. The OASIS WS-Security, WS-License, and WS-Policy specifications are gathering industry support as they are developed. Other OASIS implementation projects such as Secure Assertion Markup Language (SAML) and XML Access Control Markup Language (XACML) specifications are also in development. Implementation of these specifications is intended to be included in most enterprise application frameworks, starting with IBM, BEA, and Microsoft.

WS-Security

WS-Security is an OASIS specification that uses SOAP extensions to provide encryption and security specifically to SOAP envelopes. Signature and encryption methods are based on the W3C XML signature and XML encryption recommendations.

WS-Security describes binary token encoding and attachment methods for standard security tokens, such as X.509 certificates and Kerberos tickets. This provides a good starting point for developers who want to create standardized SOAP envelope security based on the W3C XML signature and encryption recommendations. The SOAP encryption and security extensions provide a method to pass credentials between two or more Web services and other applications using W3C security standards. More information can be found at `http://msdn.microsoft.com/library/en-us/dnglobspec/html/wssecurspecindex.asp` or `http://www-106.ibm.com/developerworks/webservices/library/ws-secure`.

WS-Policy framework

WS-Policy is another OASIS specification that will describe how Web service providers can specify their requirements and capabilities. A *policy* is a generalized way of describing a set of characteristics about a Web service. For example, a Web service provider may create a security description using the preceding WS-security specification. They can communicate that specification as a WS-Policy document. The WS-Policy document would contain a description of the Web service's security policies using a related specification called Web Services Security Policy Language (WS-SecurityPolicy), which we describe in more detail later in this chapter.

> **Note** The WS-Policy specification does not describe how policies are discovered or attached to a Web service. It just describes how to format policies according to the WS-Policy specification.

WS-Policy can be used to describe Web service policies, including security policies, trust policies between two or more parties, privacy policies, and authentication policies. Many OASIS specifications contain a WS-Policy component, including WS-Security, WS-Trust, and WS-SecureConversation. More information about WS-Policy can be found at `http://msdn.microsoft.com/ws/2002/12/Policy` or `http://www-106.ibm.com/developerworks/library/ws-polfram`.

Web Services Policy Assertions Language (WS-PolicyAssertions)

WS-PolicyAssertions specifies metadata for WS-Policy. It provides an inventory of policies that are present for a Web service. Policy document references are defined using XPath, as a relative path from the WS-PolicyAssertions document for a Web service. More information can be found at `http://msdn.microsoft.com/ws/2002/12/PolicyAssertions` or `http://www-106.ibm.com/developerworks/library/ws-polas`.

Web Services Policy Attachment (WS-PolicyAttachment)

This describes the method for attaching policies to WSDL definitions, WSDL PortTypes, and UDDI entities. More information can be found at `http://msdn.microsoft.com/ws/2002/12/PolicyAttachment` or `http://www-106.ibm.com/developerworks/library/ws-polatt`.

Web Services Security Policy Language (WS-SecurityPolicy)

WS-SecurityPolicy is described as an "addendum" to WS-Security. It specifies the methods for providing policy assertions about a Web service's security implementation. This is because policy assertions were developed after WS-Security was defined. In the rest of the specifications listed following, the policy assertions are included in the specification documents. More information can be found at `http://msdn.microsoft.com/ws/2002/12/ws-security-policy` or `http://www-106.ibm.com/developerworks/library/ws-secpol`.

WS-Trust

WS-Trust describes a model for trust relationships. Trust relationships are terms that two or more parties have agreed upon. Trusts include identity and authentication. Trust can be established directly between two or more parties, or independently verified using a third party. Trust is established between Web services using security tokens. WS-Trust describes the methods for requesting and providing a token, including token keys and encryption requirements. This helps two Web services negotiate a connection based on standardized methods of identity verification. More information can be found at `http://msdn.microsoft.com/ws/2002/12/ws-trust` or `http://www-106.ibm.com/developerworks/library/ws-trust`.

WS-SecureConversation

WS-SecureConversation uses WS-Security and WS-Trust in SOAP envelopes to manage security beyond standard authentication encryption. This means that some parts of a Web service can be secure, while others are available to the public. For example, WS-Trust establishes identity for access to a provider's Web service, but does not dictate which actions are available to a specific requestor or class of requestors. WS-Security establishes available and valid encryption methods, but doesn't establish the data in Web services on which a specific encryption method should be used. A WS-SecureConversation implementation can be compared to a storefront Website, where most of the site is available for viewing, but purchasing items requires registration and encryption. Shoppers require no encryption and no identity verification. Purchasers require encryption to protect personal information, and authentication to establish the identity of the purchaser. Using WS-SecureConversation, developers can describe a token for a session, part of a session, or a one-time use token for a specific message. More information can be found at `http://msdn.microsoft.com/ws/2002/12/ws-secure-conversation` or `http://www-106.ibm.com/developerworks/library/ws-secon`.

Secure Assertion Markup Language (SAML)

Secure Assertion Markup Language (SAML) can be used for sign-on among non-adjacent Web services and applications. SAML is similar to the W3C XML Key Management Specification (XKMS). It provides a method for managing tokens in SOAP messages. SAML uses WS-Security standards for encryption and signatures, and ID made up of tags that define credential keys using elements.

You can find more information about WS-Security and SAML at `http://www.oasis-open.org/committees/tc_home.php?wg_abbrev=security`.

XML Access Control Markup Language (XACML)

XML Access Control Markup Language (XACML) is another OASIS group specification. XACML defines credentials in a standardized XML tag format. It can be used for authorization and for passing one or more authorization credentials from one Web service or system to another. More information is available at `http://www.oasis-open.org/committees/tc_home.php?wg_abbrev=xacml`. Sun has implemented a Java reference version of XACML, which can be downloaded from `http://sunxacml.sourceforge.net`.

Web Service Security and Authentication in Java

Sun has provided Java language reference implementations of several key W3C recommendation and OASIS specification features as part of Java Community Processes (JCPs). The output of JCPs are implemented as a result of a Java Service Request (JSR). JSRs provide a tracking number for the final product. Much of the code from the JSR implementations is in the Apache XML security library. IBM also provides reference implementation code for Java via the IBM XML Security suite.

Java community process initiatives for Web service security

Sun is providing several Web service security implementations as Java Service Request (JSR) implementations, which are part of the Java Community Process (JCP). The full list of XML JSRs, including Web service JSRs, can be found at http://www.jcp.org/en/jsr/tech?listBy=1&listByType=tech.

Cross-Reference For more information about the Java Community Process and JSRs, please refer to Chapter 17.

JSR number 104 defines an XML Trust Service API. A trust service provides a way of abstracting XML signatures by providing a token that compatible APIs can read, instead of re-authenticating from a source. This provides single sign-on capabilities and permits disparate security systems to act as a single unit. JSR 105 defines a standard API for XML digital signatures as defined by the W3C XML Signature Recommendation. JSR 106 defines a standard set of APIs for XML digital encryption services, also based on the W3C implementation of XML encryption. JSR 155 adds Secure Assertion Markup Language (SAML) assertions to Java, including credentials, authentication, sessions, and user preferences, profiles, and roles.

Apache XML Security

Apache has implemented Java reference implementations of the *XML-Signature Syntax and Processing* and the *XML Encryption Syntax and Processing* Recommendations. By the time this book is in print, they probably will have finished the XML Key Management recommendation implementation in Java as well. You can find the Java and C++ code downloads for XML security implementations at http://xml.apache.org/security/download.html.

Note If you're using JDK 1.4 or higher, check the FAQ associated with the download files for instructions on setting up a compatible version of Xalan.

IBM XML Security Suite

The IBM XML Security Suite Adds W3C-defined security features such as digital signature, encryption, and access control to Web service and XML applications. Security has always been a challenge for Web service developers, because Web services are transporting text over standard protocols that don't support advanced security features by themselves. The XML Security Suite includes support for the W3C *XML-Signature Syntax and Processing* and *XML Encryption Syntax and Processing* Recommendations. There is also support for XML Access Control functionality, partly supported by the W3C *Canonical XML Version 1.0* Working Draft. The free XML Security Suite download includes a .jar file containing supporting classes and a number of examples of the XML Security Suite code in use. A good introductory article can be found at the IBM DeveloperWorks XML Zone at `http://www-106.ibm.com/developerworks/security/library/x-xmlsecuritysuite/?dwzone=security`.

Web Service Security and Authentication in Microsoft .NET

All implementation of Web service security standards for the .NET platform is implemented in the Web Services Enhancements 1.0 for Microsoft .NET (WSE). Standards supported include digital signature and encryption, message routing, and SOAP attachments based on the OASIS WS-Security specification, with some extra Microsoft specifications called WS-Routing, WS-Attachments, and Direct Internet Message Encapsulation (DIME). WS-Routing describes a stateless, asynchronous method for SOAP message routing. The WS-Attachment specification describes Microsoft's way of attaching non-XML data to SOAP envelopes. DIME describes a way to include SOAP attachments and other non-XML data in XML documents, not just SOAP envelopes. The WCE is based on the Microsoft Global XML Architecture (GXA). GXA is a set of tools that provide protocols for Web services, applications, and the connections in between. You can find more information about the WSE and related standards as well as the WSE download files, at `http://msdn.microsoft.com/webservices/building/wse/default.aspx`.

Web Service Transactions: BPEL4WS and WSCI

Sorting through the current offerings and "standards" for Web service transactions can be a daunting task. In the middle of the confusion is the W3C WS-Choreography working group. WS-Choreography is actually a great name for unintended reasons; currently the WS-Choreography group is working hard to choreograph two groups that are trying to make their specification an accepted standard. On one side is the *Web Services Choreography Interface (WSCI)*, pronounced "whiskey," as in "You may want to have one after you hear about these competing standards." WSCI is a neat specification (sorry, had to say it), but has been put on the rocks (sorry again) by a competing standard, the *Business Process Execution Language for Web Services (BPEL4WS)*.

Web Services Choreography Interface (WSCI)

WSCI has the support of the W3C WS-Choreography working group, by virtue of the fact that it was first to submit its standard to the W3C. The proposed WSCI specification can be reviewed at `http://www.w3.org/TR/wsci`.

WSCI's goal is to describe how a grouping of Web services could work together. It does this by working with a WSDL document to specify how a Web service works with other Web services, and what WSCI-specified features are supported by the Web service. However, WSCI does not address *how* Web services are supposed to interact, just how to *describe* a Web service's interactive characteristics.

Sun Microsystems is the major supporter of WSCI. The Business Process Management Initiative (BPMI) actually submitted the standard to the W3C and is supporting ongoing development. Members of the BPMI WSCI specification development team include Commerce One, Fujitsu, IONA, Oracle, SAP, Sun Microsystems, and BEA. BPMI has also developed a competing standard to BPEL4WS, called the Business Process Modeling Language (BPML). BPML is a meta-language for the modeling of business processes, including the choreography of Web services.

You can find more information about BPMI, BPML, and WSCI at `http://www.bpmi.org`.

BPEL4WS

BPEL4WS is a business process and choreography specification created by IBM, Microsoft, and BEA, and supported by many other companies. Not to be outdone by the WSCI team, the BPEL4WS team has submitted their specification to the Organization for the Advancement of Structured Information Standards (OASIS). OASIS formed the Web Services Business Process Execution Language Technical Committee (WSBPEL TC) to develop the BPEL4WS specification. IBM, Microsoft BEA, and Sun Microsystems are the four most prominent players in the WSBPEL TC.

The BPEL4WS specification describes a workflow language that identifies Web services as part of a business process. Each Web service can be defined individually, and the order of execution and data that each Web service supports is described in BPEL4WS documents. BPEL4WS also defines how to send and receive XML messages, manage specific events, and trap errors and exceptions. For example, parts of a Web service grouping can be identified as critical, and if one of the Web services in the grouping fails, steps can be specified to roll back the process to a previous step. BPEL4WS is based on SOAP, WSDL, and XML Schema.

You can find more information about OASIS and BPEL4WS at `http://www.oasis-open.org/committees/tc_home.php?wg_abbrev=wsbpel`.

BPEL4WS, BPML, and WSCI working together

As you can see, there appear to be two competing standards for specifying how a Web service transaction will take place between more than one Web service consumer and provider. Both have their merits. BPEL4WS is backed by industry heavyweights in the OASIS group, and WSCI is supported by the group that brings us all of the other XML and Web service standards: the W3C. So how can this situation be resolved? Well, the actual outcome is anyone's guess, so in the meantime, here's the way we see things playing out.

One of the confusing things you may have noticed in the preceding specifications descriptions is that Sun Microsystems and BEA are members of the specification development groups for WSCI, BPML, and BPEL4WS. So far, there have been several APIs developed as reference implementations for BPEL4WS. Microsoft's Web Services Enhancements for Microsoft .NET (WSE), IBM's Business Process Execution Language for Web Services Java Run Time (BPWS4J), and BEA's WebLogic application server BPEL4WS implementation already support developers who want to code transactional Web service solutions. On the other hand, there are no reference implementations of WSCI to date. That is not to say that WSCI is unsupported. It contains most of the functionality needed to describe Web service interaction, but not the processes that make Web services interact.

The submission of the process-heavy BPEL4WS specification to OASIS, which supports business specifications related to technology, makes sense. The submission of the tag-based WSCI specification to the W3C, which supports technology specifications, not business specifications, also makes sense. We predict that a compromise is found between the process parts of BPML and BPEL4WS (which support much the same thing, but with different technical terms and approaches) in the next year or so, and a complementary single standard based on the best of WSCI and the best of BPEL4WS is published.

Tools for transactional Web services

In the meantime, as the standards gurus duke it out, until the final specification is in place, there are several tools you can use to develop transactional Web services now. Microsoft's Web Services Enhancements for Microsoft .NET (WSE) includes an implementation of BPEL4WS. IBM has developed the Business Process Execution Language for Web Services Java Run Time (BPWS4J) and has integrated BPEL4WS functionality into its WebSphere Application Server. BEA's WebLogic application server also supports BPEL4WS functionality and has integrated its transactional Web service functionality with Siebel System's Universal Application Network (UAN).

Microsoft's Web Services Enhancements for Microsoft .NET (WSE)

The latest version of Microsoft's Web Services Enhancements for Microsoft .NET (WSE) includes support for BPEL4WS specifications. For more information and downloads, go to http://msdn.microsoft.com/webservices/building/wse/default.aspx.

IBM's Business Process Execution Language for Web Services Java Run Time (BPWS4J)

Version 1.1 of IBM's Business Process Execution Language for Web Services Java Run Time (BPWS4J) includes a J2EE reference implementation of the BPEL4WS standard, documentation, and samples. BPWS4J also includes an eclipse plug-in and a BPEL4WS document validator. It can be downloaded for free from IBM AlphaWorks at `http://alphaworks.ibm.com/tech/bpws4j`. IBM has also bundled BPWS4J into the Emerging Technologies Toolkit (ETTK), which can be downloaded at `http://alphaworks.ibm.com/tech/webservicestoolkit`. IBM's WebSphere Studio Application Developer, including BPWS4J, is supported by the WebSphere Application Server via the WebSphere SDK for Web services (WSDK).

BEA WebLogic Workshop

BEA WebLogic Workshop also supports BPEL4WS. Applications developed with the BPEL4WS-supported features of Workshop run on Bea WebLogic servers and Siebel's Universal Application Network (UAN) via Web services.

Summary

In this chapter, we've covered some of the newer and developing parts of Web services technology. Security, authentication, and transactional management will provide the means to make Web services as secure and reliable as any other IT process.

✦ Web service security and authentication scenarios

✦ Web service security offerings from the W3C: XML Signature and XML Encryption

✦ Web service security offerings from OASIS: WS-Security, WS-Policy, and others.

✦ OASIS reference implementations, SAML, and XACML

✦ Web service security development tools for Java

✦ Web service security development tools for .NET

✦ Web service choreography: BPEL4WS, BPML, and WSCI

That's it for this chapter and the book. We hope you've found this book educational and occasionally entertaining. (In other words, we hope that my occasional jokes weren't *too* bad....) Please check the XML Programming Bible Website (`http://www.XMLProgrammingBible.com`) for book updates and more information.

✦　　✦　　✦

Index

Continued

Continued

Continued

Continued

element
    building, 552, 569–572, 580–583, 815, 830–831
    SQL Server query, containing in, 553
entity reference handling, 553–555, 557, 572, 815, 818
event handling, 544, 545–547
HTTP request handling using Servlet, 559–561, 566
JCP, relation to, 539
JDK, bundled with, 540
list, retrieving from table, 548–551
login, 541, 548–549, 850
metadata, working with, 553
ODBC, relation to, 540
Oracle connection, 507
query
    array, sending result to, 549–550, 566, 569,
        807–808, 813
    buffering result, 553, 557, 815, 818
    class, passing result to, 551–552, 555–556
    element, containing SQL Server query in, 553
    hard-coding, 548
    parameter, passing to, 828
    RPC Router, passing query result to, 815
    Servlet, displaying query result using, 569–575,
        829–832
    Servlet, retrieving query result using, 564–569
    space, trimming from result, 550, 851
    SQL Server, passing query to, 549, 550
    SQL Server query result, passing from calling
        object, 550
    URL, assigning to result, 566
screen, writing to, 544
Servlet, working with in
    HTTP request handling using Servlet,
        559–561, 566
    query result, displaying using Servlet, 569–575,
        829–832
    query result, retrieving using Servlet, 564–569
specification, 539
SQL Server
    connection, 548–549, 807, 821
    query, containing in element, 553
    query, passing to SQL Server, 549, 550
    query result, passing from calling object, 550
    support, 541
streaming
    input, 589
    output, 578, 580
TCPIP, configuring, 541
URL
    connection object, 589
    query result, assigning to, 566

user input, handling, 547–548, 551, 555, 823–825
user interface, creating, 543–551, 822–829
variable, defining public, 544, 822–823
window, managing, 544–547
X/Open SQL CLI, based on, 540
XSLT operation, 606–611
JDBCXMLtoDIV stylesheet, 617
jDeveloper utility, 842
JDK (Java Development Kit)
    javadoc API, 377, 378, 379
    JAXP compatibility, 365
    JDBC bundled with, 540
    WSDP compatibility, 363
Jframe window, 822, 861
JMS (Java Message Service), 754
JNDI (Java Naming and Directory Interface), 758
JscrollPane object, 545, 862
JSDK (Java Servlet Development Kit), 559
JSP (Java Server Page)
    buffering, 391
    CLASSPATH environment variable, 398
    container, 397
    context, 391, 396, 410, 416, 419
    declaration scripting element, 390
    described, 389
    directive, 390
    EL, 392, 393–397
    error handling, 416, 428
    expression, 390, 394
    factory object, 410, 419
    HTTP
        request/response handling, 391, 395–397
        session object, 391, 396
    import operation, 410, 412, 413–414
    initialization parameter
        java.util.map representation of, 396
        server instance, passing from, 395
    JSTL
        declaring JSP version in, 400, 402
        tag library, referencing, 399–400
    meta-language, as, 389
    object, implicit, 394–395, 397
    operators, 394
    Oracle support, 505
    parsing XML using JSTL and JSP
        class, importing, 418
        core library, defining, 417
        entity resolution, 405
        error handling, 428
        HTML table, defining, 417, 423
                                        Continued

Continued

Continued

Continued